•FOURTH REVISED EDITION•

HOME ORCHID GROWING

Rebecca Tyson Northen

SIMON & SCHUSTER

NEW YORK LONDON TORONTO SYDNEY TOKYO SINGAPORE

Simon & Schuster
Rockefeller Center
1230 Avenue of the Americas
New York, New York 10020

Copyright © 1990 by Prentice Hall Press

Originally published in 1950 by Van Nostrand
Reinhold Company, Inc.

Library of Congress Cataloging-in-Publication
Data

ISBN 0-671-76327-X

Designed by Nina D'Amario/Levavi & Levavi
Manufactured in the United States of America

5   7   9   10   8   6

CONTENTS

PREFACE   vii

CHAPTER 1 Orchids as a Hobby   1

CHAPTER 2 Basic Habits and Structure   9

CHAPTER 3 Care of Adult Cattleyas   19

CHAPTER 4 More on the Care of Adult Cattleyas   29

CHAPTER 5 Potting Mature Cattleyas   43

CHAPTER 6 Control of Flowering in Cattleyas   55

CHAPTER 7 Genetics and the Breeding of Hybrids   61

CHAPTER 8 Growing and Sowing Your Own Seed   85

CHAPTER 9 Seedlings from Flask to Bloom   105

CHAPTER 10 Divisions of the Orchidaceae   115

CHAPTER 11 Aerides Relatives—The Sarcanthinae Subtribe   119

CHAPTER 12 Angraecum Relatives—The Angraecinae Subtribe   139
Aerangis Relatives—The Aerangidinae Subtribe   139

CHAPTER 13 Cattleya Relatives—The Laeliinae Subtribe   145

CHAPTER 14 Cymbidium Relatives—The Cyrtopodiinae Subtribe   177

CHAPTER 15 Paphiopedilum Relatives—The Cypripedioideae Subfamily   195

CHAPTER 16 Dendrobium Relatives—The Dendrobiinae Subtribe   209

CHAPTER 17 Oncidium Relatives—The Oncidiinae Subtribe   221

CHAPTER 18 Catasetum Relatives—The Catasetinae Subtribe   249
Stanhopea Relatives—The Stanhopeinae Subtribe   249

CHAPTER 19 Collectors' Items—Bifrenariinae to Ornithocephalinae   269

CHAPTER 20 Collectors' Items—Pleurothallidinae to Zygopetalinae   289

CHAPTER 21 Problems, Diseases, and Pests   305

CHAPTER 22 Jungle Orchids   331

CHAPTER 23 Housing Your Orchids   345

APPENDIX: Orchid Literature   359

INDEX   369

PREFACE

IN THE FORTY YEARS SINCE THE first edition of this book was published, the lure of orchids has remained unchanged. In fact, the interest is spreading as more and more people discover the fascination of this, the largest family in the plant kingdom. The beauty and variety among the 30,000 species is the reason. No one can comprehend the workings of evolution that have produced the array of shapes, sizes, and colors they display, from minute to gigantic; from fantastic, often comical, to serene; from patterns of bold colors to delicate blends. Some flowers last for months on the plant and others, with few exceptions, stay fresh for weeks. The plants themselves are almost as varied as the flowers.

Amateurs can grow most orchids, some in a window, most in a greenhouse, and many outdoors in frostfree areas. Their culture is not difficult—in some ways it is easier than that of common house plants. As is true for any kind of plants, however, one must consider how they grow in nature and learn their basic needs. They grow all over the world, from Alaska to Tasmania, except in stark deserts and under permanent snow fields. Those native to cold climates are deciduous and have underground parts that survive over winter, and are not easy to cultivate in our gardens or greenhouses. The tropical and subtropical ones are easier to manage and they produce a glorious show all through the year. It is a lovely miracle that we can have, growing happily next to each other, orchids from parts of the world separated by thousands of miles.

It is the purpose of this book to introduce you to more than 650 of these marvelous plants, to help you choose kinds to grow, to explain their structure and function so that you can understand their workings, and to give instructions for their care. Then, when you have learned the fundamentals, to take you ahead to such special fields as pollination, seed germination and seedling care, cloning (micropropagation), genetics and hybridization, artificial light growing, and control of flowering time. Problems do occur with pests and diseases, and their possible solutions will be given.

Drawings and photographs illustrate cultural methods, special techniques, and construction and management of greenhouses and artificial light setups. A wealth of black-and-white photographs and a large section of color plates illustrate the orchids themselves.

This new edition has been thoroughly revised. Material no longer useful has been eliminated and new material introduced; the orchids have been updated taxonomically and the genera and species have been reorganized into better recognized associations.

Today's orchid growers have a special responsibility, although it is not new. Perhaps more than lovers of other plants, we have long been worried about the destruction of the tropical forests and its tragic effect on the environment and in loss of species. We must do everything we can to encourage preservation of what is left and restoration where possible. We must treasure and preserve the species by saving their natural habitats, propagating those in cultivation, and developing seed banks to save their genetic content for the future.

It is hoped that this book will bring pleasure for years, help the beginner to grow into an expert, and bring excitement and new ideas to those already knowledgeable.

Rebecca Tyson Northen
San Luis Obispo, California
1990

•1•

ORCHIDS AS A HOBBY

ORCHIDS ARE THE MOST FAScinatingly varied and beautiful of all flowers. There are now thought to be some 30,000 species, and there are many, probably thousands, still unknown. So different are they one from another that at first glance it is hard to believe they are related. Some are large and showy, others are almost microscopic; some have delicate coloring, others such bold colors and markings that one automatically compares them to tropical birds and animals; some are serenely simple in form, others

are incredibly modified and complicated. It is as if nature, having invented the basic orchid theme, has, like a musician, played every conceivable variation on that theme. In fact, nature's imagination has gone far beyond the capabilities of human imagination.

Once you have grown a plant or two, you will find yourself under their spell. Call it magic, or just plain curiosity, it is legendary among orchid growers that one cannot stop with but a few. Orchids are deeply satisfying plants. Even though the eventual reward is their flowers, there is joy in watching the new growths and roots, in seeing a plant that produced only one growth last year give rise to two this year with the promise of double the number of flowers. With the exception of a few whose flowers wink open, then close in a day or two, most plants produce flowers that last for weeks or months. The familiar corsage orchid, the *Cattleya,* stays fresh and perfect for two to six weeks, and *Phalaenopsis* can last from two to five months.

Growers who embark on the orchid adventure today are fortunate. They will not experience the trials and tribulations with which orchid growing was fraught in its early years or even the problems that faced those who began fifteen to twenty years ago. Plants are readily available and relatively inexpensive, growing methods are better understood, and materials and equipment are scaled to the needs of the small grower. There are still problems, as there are with all kinds of plants, but anyone who has grown flowers for a hobby will understand that plants are not machines, and that successful growing requires care in learning their needs, judgment in handling them, and a good deal of common sense. You may have read that orchids are as easy to grow as African violets. Well, they are, but you do not grow them like African violets. Nor do you grow an African violet like a cactus. Orchids come somewhere in between.

To understand the fortunate situation in which you will find yourself, you must know a little about the phenomenal history of orchids and orchid growing. In the late 1700s and early 1800s, many expeditions were sent to explore the tropics. The newly discovered plants intrigued the horticulturists of Europe, and botanical collectors eagerly searched out new forms and kinds. Among these were a wealth of orchids. The Europeans knew their native orchids but were overwhelmed by the tremendous quantity and variety of those being sent from the tropics. A kind of horticultural and scientific madness ensued, as more and more kinds were discovered. Much money went into the expeditions, and collectors suffered physical hardship, even risking their lives, in order to gain the prized plants. Competition was keen as the searchers scoured the lowlands, the river canyons, the jungles, and the high mountain areas. The collectors were quite jealous of their finds, and often kept locations secret, even falsifying their reports to throw other collectors off the track. Thus it was that sometimes the habitat of a certain kind of orchid was lost for years until later collectors rediscovered it.

The botanists whose job it was to study and classify the orchids had a monumental task, for orchids from the western hemisphere did not fit into the known genera. Orchids are peculiar in that kinds that look very different may actually belong to the same genus, and kinds that look alike are not always closely related. Botanists today are still trying to straighten out the relationships. Also, it often happened that the same species, perhaps found in different countries by different people, or coming into the hands of different taxonomists, was given several names. Since it is a basic nomenclatural rule that the first name given should be the one to be perpetuated, taxonomists are trying to determine the chronology of names for each species. Perpetuation of the original name assures proper credit to the person who first applied it.

The people who first tried to grow these plants were faced with many difficulties. They found that they could not just put these strange plants in pots in ordinary soil. Nor could they grow them from seed in the usual manner. Their problems were multiplied by the fact that orchids came from widely different climates and temperature conditions. Some were found by waterfalls and streams, constantly bathed in spray and mists, while some came from places boldly exposed to the drying sun. Some lived at low elevations where the temperatures were hot, others near the tops of mountains where the temperatures were cool day and night. Some perched on tree branches, and some grew on the ground in meadows and glades. Considering what we now know about the plants, it is a wonder any of them survived these early attempts to cultivate them. However, those growers who were successful fell into the same error as the early collectors, and jealously guarded their secrets. The wealthy people who could afford the traditional conservatory greenhouse did not do their own growing but hired trained growers to care for their orchids. The cloak of secrecy was kept drawn about orchid growing long into the twentieth century, except that the barrier was broken now and then by an occasional amateur willing to learn by trial and error. It was so generally believed that only the initiated could grow orchids that most novices gave up after a failure or two and others were afraid to try when there seemed so little chance that they would succeed.

Commercial orchid growing expanded tremendously between 1900 and 1920, and by this time the number of patient amateurs had also increased. The demand put a great pressure on the supplies of wild plants. Unless one could obtain divisions of plants already in cultivation, the usual way to obtain more was by importation. The reason behind this was that it was so difficult to grow orchids from seed. Although a seed capsule contains close to a million seed, and although growers had learned to make hybrid crosses, attempts to germinate the seed often resulted in complete failure or in the production of but a handful of seedlings. Ruthless stripping of the native plants, especially of cattleyas, threatened their extinction in certain areas, and brought about eventual embargoes on their exportation.

A revolution in orchid growing was brought about by a discovery made by Professor Lewis Knudson of Cornell University in 1922. He was experimenting with the germination of various kinds of seed, including that of orchids. He found that orchid seed germinated readily in a glass flask containing an agar jelly to which chemical nutrients and sugar had been added. This medium is much like that on which bacterial cultures are grown. Orchid seed is tiny, as fine as dust, and contains little or no food for the developing embryo. The availability of the nutrients and sugar enabled the embryo to develop and grow. Dr. Knudson's discovery meant that instead of fifteen or twenty seedlings, thousands could be grown from one capsule. It opened up a whole new world of possibilities to orchid lovers.

Out of pure exuberance, growers excitedly crossed any orchid with any other orchid to see what beautiful or bizarre results might be obtained. Growers sold millions of seedlings on the naive assumption that any cross would embody the best qualities of its parents. Then the truth began to emerge—that not all crosses were good, that often all of the seedlings, or a large portion of them, were actually inferior. Occasionally good things would emerge from some crosses, and many of these older hybrids proved invaluable as the basis for further hybridization. Although much time and effort was spent in raising plants that eventually had to be discarded, both by the growers and by the amateurs who bought them, much was learned.

Thoughtful growers began to slow down and study the problems more cautiously. They learned, for instance, that one fine flower when crossed with another equally fine might give good offspring, but that when crossed with a different flower might not. Some flowers seemed to have the ability to transmit their best qualities, while others did not. Perhaps most valuable of the information gained during the explosive years was that not only could related species be crossed quite freely, but even related genera. Hybridizers are still exploring the thrilling possibilities thus offered. We can't say that orchid breeding is fully worked out even now, but the chance of obtaining good plants from seedlings is far better now than it used to be. Now, in exploring the possibilities of new hybrids, growers make the untried crosses in full knowledge that they must wait for the results before judging their worth. And buyers who purchase these seedlings also know that they must wait to see what happens.

Hybrids do not always come true from seed. A plant can be divided, but the number of divisions increases only slowly. The rather recently developed methods of tissue culture allow great numbers of new plantlets to be obtained from one original plant. The term micropropagation has been invented to cover such methods. Single cells or groups of cells are obtained from undifferentiated tissue at stem tips, called meristematic tissue, and cultured to give rise to many tiny plantlets. Leaf tissue can also now be propagated using special techniques.

It once was possible for amateurs to go orchid hunting, and it was a joy to bring home collected plants. The endangered species convention now prohibits orchid collecting except for scientific purposes, and then only with permits from the government of the host country. The tropical forests are being destroyed at such an alarming rate that it would seem now sensible to allow orchids in threatened areas to be brought out to safety. However, nothing is simple when conflicting interests are involved—in this case those of the orchid lovers and conservationists on the one hand and the developers and exploiters on the other. Creation of national parks and preserves is being encouraged to save areas of forests and other types of

Figure 1–1 Cattleya gigas, *the largest and most showy of the species cattleyas, typical of the large, ruffled, corsage orchid.*

native vegetation for the plants and the animals that inhabit them. It is still possible to import plants from licensed dealers, especially nursery-grown plants.

And what are these orchids that have provoked such love and excitement for generations? They are the most highly specialized plants in their line of evolution, topping the lilies and irises. They grow wild all over the world, except in regions of perpetual snow and in parched deserts. You probably know *Calypso* and the moccasin flowers, most showy of our native North American orchids. However, the tropics offer species in the greatest profusion, and it is the tropical orchids sought for greenhouse collections that are the progenitors of our present hybrids.

Among the kinds most frequently seen and widely grown for corsages are *Cattleya*, whose showy flowers with their spectacular lips come in white and shades of lavender, pink, rose, yellow, bronze, and green (Figs. 1–1 and 1–2); *Cymbid-*

Figure 1–2 Cattleya *Bow Bells 'Serene', one of the first of the modern white hybrids.*

Figure 1–3 *These are all orchids.* CENTER: Phalaenopsis *Grace Palm. Clockwise from the* LEFT *side:* Pholidota imbricata, Oncidium ampliatum, Cycnoches aureum *(male flower),* Lycaste aromatica, *and* Psychopsis papilio.

ium, of more modest style, but with a wide range of colors; *Phalaenopsis,* whose round white or pink flowers are serenely beautiful, and which now come in shades of yellow and green as well, often barred and speckled; and *Paphiopedilum,* the waxy Asian ladyslipper, which can be delicately beautiful or boldly reptilian (Fig. 1–3). Others, to mention but a few that are also the delight of growers, are *Dendrobium, Epidendrum, Oncidium, Odontoglossum,* and *Vanda,* all of which give sprays of charming, brightly colored flowers in varied designs and sizes.

Most orchids live in the tropics, and in the greatest numbers inhabit the cloud forests, at elevations between 3,000 and 9,000 feet. Orchids are found above and below this belt, but they become fewer in number and variety as the mountain tops or sea level are approached. In these jungles, vegetation is dense and competition for light is almost vicious. Plants grow so thickly that the jungles are really forests upon forests. Giant ferns and other vegetation completely covers the ground. Plants that need more light than they can get on the ground contrive in some manner to reach up above the undergrowth. Vines grow up the tree trunks and form a tangled network among the branches. Some trees whose seedlings would die on the ground send their seed to germinate on branches of other trees; when the seedling develops it sends roots down into the ground and eventually smothers the tree that gave it support. Light- and air-loving orchids would have been pushed out of existence long ago if they had not evolved some way to live above the stifling mass of undergrowth.

The whole top of a forest is an aerial garden (Fig. 1–4). Orchids and some other plants have learned to cling to the trees. Sometimes the burden of plants grows so heavy that a thick branch may break under its weight. Plants that live on other plants are called "epiphytes," "epi" meaning above or on, and "phyte" meaning plant. The epiphytes obtain no nourishment from the plants on which they grow—they are not parasites. They merely grow where they can find a foothold and a collection of humus material, dead leaves and bugs. Epiphytic orchids may also be found growing on thatched roofs (often placed there by the natives), stone walls, fallen logs, or rocky cliffs.

The epiphytes have cleverly adapted their structure to their needs as air dwellers. Since they are cut off from a continuous supply of water, they must depend on catching rain and dew, and for this purpose their roots have a spongy coating that soaks up water. To withstand the period between rains, their stems and leaves are thickened, like the stem of a cactus, for the storage of water. When such a plant is grown in a flowerpot, the potting medium must be extremely porous to allow the roots plenty of air.

Many kinds of orchids may live on the same tree. Those that can resist drying most efficiently and which also require a lot of light live in the tops of the trees and on exposed branches. Those that cannot resist drying quite so well, or which do better when shaded somewhat more, may live lower down on the tree, and some miniature orchids often find protection among the roots and stems of a larger plant.

In addition to epiphytic orchids, there are other kinds that live on the ground and are not equipped to resist drying. They are found in more open forests, in meadows, or along the banks of streams where the break in vegetation allows light to reach them. These are called terrestrials. The ground in which they grow is always fluffy with humus, such as rotting wood or thick layers of dead leaves, so that even these, when grown in pots, must have an open, well-drained compost.

Most amateurs start a collection with a few cattleya plants, and add other kinds as they go along. Each kind has it own blooming season, so that even with a small collection it is possible to have a spread of flowers throughout the year (Figs. 1–5 and 1–6). We always suggest beginning with mature plants, either species or hybrids. In the first place it is hard to wait years for flowers, so we think it is fun to get something that will bloom soon. Also, the mature plants are better able to withstand changed conditions and are more likely to survive what mistakes you may make in learning to care for them. In growing a mature plant, you learn to know its habits, how it makes its growths and roots, how the flowers develop, etc. After you have served an apprenticeship in this way, you are ready to try some seedlings, perhaps a few very young ones, just out of the flask, or some two- or three-year-olds.

Tiny seedlings just out of the flask are delicate, and even though they are about a year old, they are so small that they are put twenty-five to thirty in a community pot or small flat. Their growth for the next year is slow, and some do not survive. They need to be shaded carefully and kept quite damp. During their third and fourth years they are moved from small single pots to increasingly larger ones, and become robust and more demanding of light.

Seedlings are priced according to their size: Very

Figure 1–4 *In the damp tropical forests epiphytes cover the trees.* UPPER: *A tree growing alongside a river in Peru is heavy with orchids, bromeliads, aroids, and ges-neriads. An agile Indian boy climbs where the author fears to go.* LOWER: *The tip of the smallest twig is an aerial garden.*

Figure 1–5 *The variety to be found among orchids is half of their charm. Gathered together here from this* varied collection are Cattleya, Odontoglossum, Vanda, and Miltonia. (COURTESY OF LORD AND BURNHAM.)

Figure 1–6 *Lovely cluster-type "cocktail" hybrids are being made with many small, waxy flowers to the stem.* LEFT: Cattleya Beverly Boswell (Celia X December Snow). RIGHT: Cattleya Claesiana (loddigesii 'Stanley' X intermedia var. alba).

young plants in flasks or community pots cost less than those in two- or three-inch pots, and these in turn are less expensive than ready-to-bloom ones. Plants in any one cross are not all of equal quality. The chance of obtaining choice ones is increased by buying several in the same cross. You can have a nice variety by acquiring seedlings from several different crosses for only a small outlay.

The suspense of waiting for a new hybrid, or any plant new to your collection, to bloom is beyond description. Day by day you watch the buds grow larger, until one day you see that the tip of the bud is opening. Within a few hours the sepals and petals swing out and the lips starts to unfurl. You can almost see the flower parts move. It takes about twenty-four hours for the flower to open, but it is somewhat limp during this stage, and the colors are pale. As another twenty-four to forty-eight hours pass, the color intensifies, the flower becomes firm, its parts stretch open to their fullest, and finally its peak of perfection is reached. Here is one of nature's most artful creations, and it is yours to enjoy for days or weeks, and will repeat itself for years to come.

·2·

BASIC HABITS AND STRUCTURE

THE CHARMING ARRAY OF shapes, sizes, and habits of just a few different kinds of orchid plants adds to the fun of orchid growing and keeps an amateur constantly adding new kinds to his collection. Also, it makes an orchid grower something of a marvel in the eyes of his friends.

In general, there are two basic growth habits, or patterns of growth, among orchids. Essentially, one type makes a new growth (or lead) each year from the base of the preceding growth, and this new growth produces flowers, makes its own set of roots, and in turn gives rise to another new growth the following season. Such a plant consists of several stems, or "pseudobulbs," arising from a creeping ground stem, or "rhizome." In the other type of growth pattern, there is but one main upright stem that grows taller each year, adding new leaves to the top but not making any new growth from its base. It has no rhizomes and forms no pseudobulbs. Flowering stems and aerial roots come from between the leaves, following each other in succession up the stem year after year. While the plant does not form new vegetative growth from its base, it may branch from buds in the axils of the leaves.

The names for these two growth habits are rather descriptive. The kind that makes new seasonal growths from a rhizome is called "sympodial" which freely translated means "feet together" (Fig. 2–1). The type that has but one main stem is called "monopodial," or "one-footed." There are far more sympodial than monopodial kinds, but each type contains some of our best-loved orchids, so you will undoubtedly have both types in your collection.

When you first glance at a cattleya plant, you will be struck by how stiff and strong it is. The heavy, thickened stems and the thick, hard leaves may remind you of a cactus plant. Actually, there are some similarities, because both are built to withstand periods of dryness. The cactus has been reduced to a water-storing stem (its spines are its "leaves"), because it must subsist through long periods of drought. In the cattleya and other orchids like it, the enlarged stem and thickened leaves are reservoirs for water and food. In addition, a heavy coating of wax protects the leaves. While in nature a cattleya has to withstand only short periods of drying between rains or baths of fog or dew, some other kinds live where there are definite seasons of dry weather. These orchids, including the cattleya, have the capacity to go for weeks without water.

The thickened stems of sympodial orchids are called pseudobulbs. Actually, the stem of the cattleya is not as bulbous as the stems of many other kinds, which are truly spherical or pear-shaped.

9

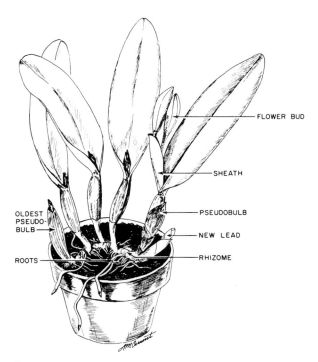

FLOWER BUD

SHEATH

OLDEST PSEUDO-BULB

PSEUDOBULB

NEW LEAD

ROOTS

RHIZOME

Figure 2–1 *Cattleya plant. Sympodial type of growth, with many stems arising from a creeping ground stem or rhizome. The new growth of the season, the "lead," comes from the base of the growth of the previous season.*

The term pseudobulb is used to distinguish these fat stems from true bulbs, because they are quite different in structure. A true bulb, a lily for instance, is made up of scalelike leaves. An orchid pseudobulb is purely a stem, actually a jointed stem.

In the cattleya the new growth, or "lead" as it is called, comes from a bud at the base of the growth made the preceding year. The bud swells, breaks through the dry covering scales, and elongates. It grows horizontally for an inch or so and then curves upward. The horizontal part becomes an extension of the rhizome or ground stem, and the upward-growing part produces the new pseudobulb, leaves, and eventually the flowers. The new growth is covered with tight, sheathing leaves that give it a criss-cross or braided look. When it is about three or four inches long, the true leaf emerges from the tip of the growth. Some cattleya species have a single leaf; others have two or three. As the growth continues the leaf expands, and within it you can see the "sheath," a thin, green envelope that grows from the top of the pseudobulb and encloses the flower buds during the early part of their formation. It takes five or six months

for the new growth to reach its full size, during which time it is soft and succulent. At the end of the growth period the pseudobulb becomes plump and the leaf also becomes thick and hard, a process called maturation or "hardening." Soon afterward, the thin sheathing leaves dry to white tissue. Good light and proper care contribute to a good, hard plant and to flowers of good substance.

Flower buds in cattleyas are "initiated," that is, the flower parts are formed microscopically at the tip of the pseudobulb, in some while the growth is developing, in others as the growth matures. But you may not be able to see the buds for some time. Some cattleyas flower as soon as the growth is formed, in which case the bud expansion follows right along as the growth approaches or reaches its full size. Others wait for several months before the flower buds start to grow. At any rate, when the buds begin development, they appear as little dark shadows at the bottom of the sheath, enlarging slowly at first, and then growing more rapidly until they push out through the tip of the sheath. The growth from base to tip of the sheath takes about six weeks, and another three weeks or so are required before the buds reach full size and are ready to open. The species normally flower once a year, each in its own season, but many hybrids make new growths and flower two or three times a year.

After flowering, the cycle starts over again when this growth gives rise to a set of roots and a new shoot. Thus one growth follows another. A pseudobulb does not flower again (there are exceptions among some other kinds of orchids). The pseudobulbs and leaves remain green for a number of years, sometimes as long as six to eight years. On a plant that makes but one growth a year, you can tell the age of the oldest pseudobulb by counting back from the youngest growth. Eventually the older leaves die and fall off, and finally the old pseudobulbs shrivel and die.

Each pseudobulb, with the portion of rhizome at its base, is essentially a plant in itself. Pseudobulbs divided singly from each other will give rise to new plants. But a plant started from a single pseudobulb is quite weak; its new growth is small, and it takes several years to attain flowering size again. Therefore, divisions are usually made of clumps of pseudobulbs, at least three, preferably four. There is a bud at each joint of the rhizome, but not all of the buds become active and develop into new growths. This is one of nature's safety factors. When a plant is divided, the removal of the growing end stimulates the development of one

Figure 2–2 *Vanda plant. Monopodial type of growth. A single, upright stem grows taller year after year, adding new leaves at its tip. Aerial roots come from the stem between the leaves, as do the flower stems.*

or more dormant buds on the older part, so that division results in two active halves.

Sometimes two buds will develop simultaneously from the base of a single lead, giving rise to two new pseudobulbs from one. Each of these in turn will produce a new growth, so that the plant becomes forked into two growing parts. Sometimes a bud farther back on an older pseudobulb will also start development, establishing still another line of growth. A plant with many leads is most desirable; it gives a greater number of flowers and yields many separate plants when divided. The habit of breaking extra leads is inherent in some plants, but is encouraged by good culture.

The roots of cattleyas and of all epiphytic orchids are covered, except for the green tip, with a white, spongy coating called "velamen," which probably has several functions—to soak up water, to protect the inner root tissues, and to cling to surfaces to give the plant support. As the roots start to grow from the rhizome the green tip appears; then as the root elongates the velamen develops behind the green tip. The roots grow along in an exploratory manner, some penetrating the growing medium, others gliding across it to go down over the side of the pot. They cling tightly to any surface they meet, and those that do not meet with anything solid simply hang out in the air. This is their habit in nature, where they cling to the tree bark or hang down from the branch. The roots usually remain unbranched the first year, but if the growing tip is injured after the root has reached a fair length, branch roots will develop behind the tip. Older roots send out new branches each year.

Sympodial orchids that you will come to know, in addition to cattleyas, are epidendrums, most of which have slender reedlike stems: oncidiums and odontoglossums, among which are kinds with rounded and kinds with tall pseudobulbs, often flattened to a knife edge; dendrobiums, some of which have thickened pseudobulbs while others have tall "canes"; and many that have no pseudobulbs at all, such as masdevallias and paphiopedilums. In all orchids, flowers come from within leaf axils, sometimes at the top of a pseudobulb, sometimes from leaves along the stem.

The stately vanda is a monopodial plant (Fig. 2–2). It has a single main stem and grows quite tall, adding several new leaves to its tip every year. The leaves grow close together, alternating on the right and left sides, to give a beautifully symmetrical plant. The flower stems also alternate sides, coming from the axils of the leaves on the upper part of the plant. The huge aerial roots make their appearance farther down, splitting the base of the leaves as they force their way out from the stem. Each new root comes somewhat above the one made previously. The vanda seems always to be making new leaves, but the roots occasionally undergo a period of dormancy. The tips cease growth and velamen covers the end. Then sometime later, the roots resume growth from the same tip. At the same time, branch roots grow along the length of the root.

The vanda shown in Figure 2–2 is of the strap-leaf type, with rather broad, flat leaves. There are also kinds whose leaves are cylindrical, pencil-shaped.

You will come to know several other lovely monopodials. Phalaenopsis, which grows slowly, adds but one or two broad, flat leaves a year. Its flower stems develop near the base of the plant, giving a graceful, arching spray. Aerides grows quite like a vanda and gives drooping sprays of the most delightful little flowers.

The monopodials listed above are all epiphytic, and can withstand some drying. Their leaves are thick, sometimes tough and leathery, and store some water. Perhaps the main stem and the large roots are also reservoirs.

FLOWER STRUCTURE AND POLLINATION

The orchid flower is built on a very simple pattern of three outer and three inner flower parts, albeit the often fanciful shapes these parts take make some flowers look quite complex (Fig. 2–3). The outermost flower parts are the three sepals, which can be identified as they enclose the rest of the flower in the bud. Within these are three petals, one of which has been so modified that its appearance is entirely different from the other two and is therefore called by its own name, the "lip" or "labellum." The lip is not only shaped differently from the other petals, but it is embellished with its own markings of color and is often fantastically decorated with crests, horns, tails, or other protuberances. The lip is usually the most striking part of the flower, but there are some kinds in which the sepals or the petals are more elaborate. You may come across the term "tepals" in your reading, a word used to refer to sepals and petals when they are similar in appearance.

The least conspicuous part of the flower is most diagnostic of an orchid, its hallmark. This is the

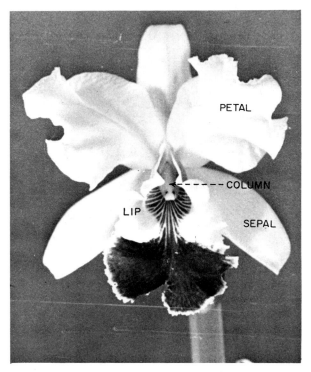

Figure 2–3 *Parts of the orchid flower, illustrated by a cattleya.*

Figure 2–4 A: *A cattleya column. At the very top is the anther cap, tipped up to show the fuzzy tails of the pollinia within. Below the anther, separated from it by the rostellum, is the stigma.*
B: *A bee that has visited a cattleya flower and bears on its back the four pollinia that became fastened to it as it crawled out from under the column.*
C: *The column of* Trichopilia suavis, *decorated with a fringed bonnet. The "beak" of the column is the viscid disc.*
D: *The column with the anther cap removed and the side sliced away to show the pollinia lying in the anther chamber. The pollinia are attached by a taillike band (caudicle, or stipe) to the viscid disc. The viscid disc will adhere to an insect touching it, and as the insect leaves it will bear the pollinia on its back.*

column, a fleshy structure that sits in the center and consists of the fused reproductive parts (Fig. 2–4). It adds charm to the flower, however, and if you take time to look at it you may decide that it is the most delightful part of all. Surely it is the most cleverly designed, both outwardly and from the point of view of function. It may be quite simply shaped, a white or pink or green cylinder, or it may look like a little figure, a doll, a bird, an insect, a face wearing goggles, or the neck of a swan. Often the column is decorated with wings, or a cap, or a fringed bonnet. At the tip of the column is the anther, bearing the pollen. Instead of being dusty, the pollen grains are molded by wax into hard pellets. The pellets, called "pollinia," lie in a cavity covered by a hinged cap, where they look like a pair of eyes. Just below the anther, separated from it by a partition, is the female receptive organ, the "stigma," a shiny depression filled with extremely sticky fluid. The column may be stubby and upright or may arch out over the base of the lip.

By offering nectar to a visiting insect, the lip lures it into an ambush, for the column poised over the lip is equipped with a tricky device to fasten its pollen to the insect (Fig. 2–5). The pollen-fastening mechanism is so designed that it applies the pollen to the insect as it *leaves* the flower, causing it to carry the pollen off and deposit it on the next flower it visits, ensuring cross-pollination. Some kinds of orchids are pollinated by only a single kind of insect. It is fun to discover this mechanism in the column of any orchid you may have. In the cattleya, the partition (rostellum) that separates the anther from the stigma bears a gland that secretes sticky fluid. The pollinia within the easily tipped-up anther cap have fuzzy tails (caudicles) that lie just under its edge. In search of nectar an insect, usually a bee, has to crawl underneath the column, between it and the lip. As it backs out, it presses against the gland on the rostellum, ruptures it, and becomes smeared with "glue." At the same time, its movement tips up the anther cap and the fuzzy tails of the pollinia are caught in the glue. It flies away with one or two, sometimes all four, of the pollinia attached to its back.

I am sure the South American bees that are accustomed to orchids think nothing of this, but the bees in this country are puzzled by the sudden burden they have acquired. Although we do not like to have bees in the greenhouse (because a pollinated flower quickly wilts and is therefore ruined), we have had a lot of fun watching an occasional bee that has happened to enter. The pollinia on its back are just like a load of suitcases, and they throw the bee off balance. Some are unable to fly, and spend their time helplessly crawling around over the plant. Others make attempts at wobbly flight. One may become well enough adjusted to visit another flower, whereupon, as it forces its way into the throat, the pollinia are caught in the viscid fluid of the stigma and are torn off the caudicles. The bee emerges from the second flower with the stubs of one set of caudicles, bearing on top of them the new set of pollinia it has just acquired.

Some kinds of orchids have even more ingenious methods. Instead of having a gland on the rostellum, the pollinia are themselves attached by a little strap to a disc that is viscid on its under surface and hangs down like a beak from the end of the column. Pollinia, strap, and viscid disc are together called the "pollinarium." As an insect enters the flower it does not touch the sticky side of the disc. But as it backs out, or flies up from the lip, it hits the viscid surface, which instantly becomes stuck to the insect. So, as it flies off, it pulls the attached pollinia out of the anther and bears them off on its back to another flower. Try this yourself, with a needle or the tip of a pencil. Touch the underside of the beak and you can pull out the attached pair of pollinia, golden globules as shiny and beautifully shaped as jewels.

The pollinia are usually in an upright position when they are withdrawn from a flower, but in many kinds the stalk goes through motions afterward to bring the pollinia into a better position for contacting the stigma of the next flower visited. In some kinds the stalk bends forward to point the pollinia straight ahead. In *Vanda* 'Miss Joaquim', the stalk does a triple turn—it bends forward, then backward, then forward again in an S curve, which results in shortening the stalk and at the same time presenting the pollinia in a higher position so that they will touch the arching stigma. In some other kinds the stalk bends forward and then the pollinia rise up at its tip. Much fun can be had in learning just what the pollinarium does in various species. The shapes of the pollinia, the viscid disc, and the strap (stipe) that joins them together are distinctive in each species, as also are the motions they go through when they are withdrawn. These characteristics are among the many that help to separate species.

Among orchids, some are pollinated by bees, wasps, flies, moths, butterflies, beetles, ants, spiders, or even birds. Many are quite selective and

Figure 2–5 *Steps in pollination, as it would be performed by an insect.*
A: A Vanda flower.
B: The column with flower parts removed. The swellings of the anther cap show the location of the pollinia within. Touch the underside of the "beak" and the viscid disc will stick to the needle.

C: The pollinarium attached to the needle.
D: Put the needle bearing the pollinarium into the stigmatic cavity.
E: Touch the pollinia to the sticky fluid of the stigma.
F: Pull out the needle. The pollinia will be left on the stigma, held so strongly by the sticky fluid that they are torn off the caudicle.

rely on just certain species, or only one species, to do the job. These are adapted in peculiar ways to their pollinators. Some (two species of *Trichoceros,* for example) imitate the female of the species of insect so that the male is lured into attempting to mate with the flowers, performing pollination in the process. Some have devious ways of forcing their servants to perform pollination. The catasetum has a trigger, which is actually a lever, that when touched causes the pollinarium to shoot out and stick to the bee with a fast-setting cement (Fig. 2–6). If you imitate a bee by touching the trigger with a pencil, you can actually feel the recoil of the flower when this happens, and you will have difficulty removing the pollinarium from the pencil, so tightly does it adhere.

Many species place the pollinia on a certain part of the anatomy of an insect, in a position where

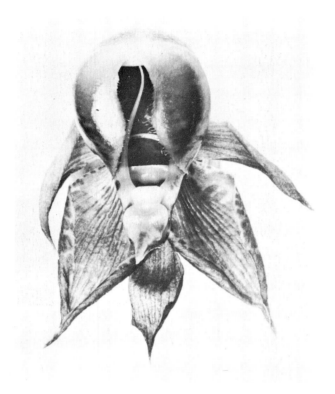

Figure 2–6 Catasetum macrocarpum. *When a visiting insect touches the whip-shaped trigger within the hood-like lip, the pollinia fly up and become attached to it by means of the viscid disc.*

they are sure to be brought into contact with the stigma of the next flower visited (Fig. 2–7). Some of our native orchids are pollinated by mosquitoes. Drs. Warren Stoutamire and Leonard Thien have confirmed the observations of others and are independently conducting detailed studies. A fascinating example they describe is the pollination of *Habenaria obtusata*, which they have observed in the field and in the laboratory, with mosquitoes caged with the flowers (Fig. 2–8). Oddly, it seems that only female mosquitoes are attracted to the flowers. The flower has a divided anther, each half with its own viscid disc standing on either side of the stigma. The lip bears a projection extending backward over the entrance to the nectary, so that the mosquito is forced to probe into the flower on one side or the other. As it retreats from the flower, its head comes in contact with a viscid disc, and it leaves with a pollinarium stuck to its eye—the left eye if it probed into the right side of the nectary, the right if it probed on the left side!

There are two orchids whose entire life cycle is spent underground. Of all the strange habits of orchids, it would seem that this would be most inef-

ficient and least likely to lead to survival. Yet they survive. One is *Rhizanthella gardneri* of western Australia, the other is *Cryptanthemis slateri* of eastern Australia, and they are both saprophytic. The only time they come to the surface is at the time of flowering, when the flower head barely breaks the ground under the litter covering the soil. They were first found accidentally when the ground was ploughed by farmers. Searchers failed to find additional specimens until just recently, when several locations have been "turned up." They produce a cluster of small, tubular flowers, perfect in every way. We wonder about them. Are they pollinated by small soil dwellers who crawl in and out of the flowers, and, if so, which species? How is the seed distributed? It cannot be wind-blown. Do ants do the job? Or are the flowers eaten by animals who drop the seed eventually? Someday naturalists will have the answers.

Figure 2–7 *Section through the ovary of a paphiopedilum flower, showing the rows of ovules. When fertilized, each ovule becomes a seed.*

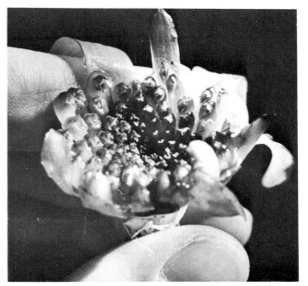

Figure 2–9 *The underground orchid* Rhizanthella gardneri. *The head of small flowers is produced and seed is formed entirely underground.* (Courtesy of Alex S. George.)

Figure 2–8 *A female* Aëdes *mosquito leaving a flower of* Habenaria obtusata *with a pollinarium attached to its right eye.* (Courtesy of Warren P. Stoutamire.)

TEMPERATURE GROUPS

When the many varied climates to which orchids are native are compared, it turns out that there are three basic temperature ranges into which most of the species can be fitted. Winter temperatures are kept somewhat cooler than summer temperatures, partly because we can control the winter temperatures and partly because when artificial heat is used moderate temperatures give healthier plants and better flowers. Night temperature is critical; in fact, some kinds of orchids will not flower if the night temperature runs above a certain limit and others do poorly if it goes below a definite point. The three temperature groups that have been established are therefore based on *winter night* temperatures. Winter day temperatures are kept about ten degrees higher. Summer temperatures, partic-

ularly where the days become very hot, offer special problems that will be dealt with later on.

The three temperature groups are: "cool," with nights held between 50° and 55°; "intermediate," with nights from 55° to 60°; and "warm," with nights from 60° to 65°. A different group of plants is grown in each temperature range, except that if the temperature runs a little warmer or a little cooler in some spots in a greenhouse it may be possible to add plants from another temperature range. In choosing an orchid it is of utmost importance to learn first its temperature requirements and be sure that you can give it the range it needs. It is to no avail to put a "warm" orchid in a "cool" greenhouse, or vice versa.

The cool greenhouse (50° to 55°) is used widely throughout this country for many kinds of plants; in fact, it is used for many of the florists' cut flower crops such as carnations, stock, snapdragons, and camellias. If you already grow some of these flowers, you can slip in a few cool orchids such as cymbidiums, some paphiopedilums, and others that come from cool climates or high elevations. It is the most economical of the three ranges, since heating costs are lower. However, many orchids that demand cool conditions in the winter also prefer cool summers, so that in general the cool types are better grown in the cooler part of the United

States. With special coolers and attention to keep environmental factors in balance, they may sometimes be grown in warmer climates.

The "intermediate" greenhouse (55° to 60°) accommodates by far the greatest number of kinds. It is often referred to as the "cattleya house" because it is the range in which cattleyas are usually grown. Along with the cattleyas you can grow epidendrums, laelias, oncidiums, dendrobiums, vandas, some kinds of miltonias, paphiopedilums, odontoglossums, and a tremendous array of odd and unusual kinds of orchids.

The "warm" greenhouse (60° to 65°) is used for kinds that do not do well with nights under 60°. These include phalaenopsis, some paphiopedilums, and others, in general kinds that come from lower, warmer climates.

You may ask why, since the upper range of the intermediate and the lower range of the warm greenhouse meet at 60°, should there be a distinction between the two: Why not grow everything at 60°? In running a greenhouse, it is almost impossible to keep the temperature at an exact point. There is always a fluctuation of a few degrees as the heat goes on or off. By keeping the air circulating we narrow the margin of fluctuation, but about five degrees of difference inevitably occurs. These five degrees can be critical for many kinds. If you run the temperature repeatedly below 60°, phalaenopsis and some others may not do their best. If you run it repeatedly above 60°, you automatically eliminate many kinds that you could otherwise grow. While some people grow cattleyas at 60° to 65°, problems often arise that are eliminated in the 55° to 60° range. In the intermediate range, we feel that cattleyas are stockier, flowering is more regular, and the flowers are of better substance and last longer. Since cattleyas do so well at 55° to 60°, and since using this night temperature range allows you to grow so many other kinds, there is a real reason for adhering to it, and for separating it from the warmer 60° to 65° range.

·3·

CARE OF
ADULT
CATTLEYAS

❧

SINCE CATTLEYAS ARE THE most widely grown of all orchids and since most growers start with them, the conditions that suit cattleyas and their method of culture have become a sort of base, or point of departure. For orchids that are to be treated exactly like cattleyas (as to light and water in addition to temperature), it is customary to say "handle like cattleyas," or "likes cattleya conditions." Then, for those that vary a bit one way or another from the needs of cattleya we say "cattleya conditions except a bit

more shade, or more frequent watering, etc." We shall therefore spend the longest time and give most space to cattleya culture. In this section you will find the basic rules for all orchid culture. When we take up other kinds, we will give their specific needs and tell you how to vary the basic rules for them.

Adult cattleyas include plants just matured from the seedling stage and propagations made from older plants. The matured seedlings show a succession of leaf sizes from the small leaves up to the larger flowering lead. A propagation is a division of a plant. It may be made from the lead end of a plant—the youngest growth plus the two or three pseudobulbs just behind it, in which case it should flower on its next new growth—or it may consist of the older half of the plant. If these older pseudobulbs (or backbulbs as they are sometimes called) are plump and still have their leaves, the first new growth they make may flower. But if the pseudobulbs are shriveled and have lost their leaves, the first new growth may be quite small, and it may require another two years before a flowering size growth is produced. It is therefore preferable, in buying mature plants, to get those in flowering condition, unless you know that the backbulbs are from very good plants and that it would be worth waiting the several years for them to flower again. The plant should be vigorous and healthy. If it is a propagation it should show evidence, by cut flower stems on each pseudobulb, of having flowered regularly.

You can buy species or hybrids. There are two groups of species. One, the "labiata" group, has the wide frilled petals and lip with which most people are familiar, and its pseudobulbs bear a single leaf. The other, the "bifoliate" group, has smaller, waxier flowers, some with a spade-shaped or fiddle-shaped lip and a remarkable array of colors and markings. The species are usually quite inexpensive and dependable, and many add exceptional interest to any collection. Hybrids are priced according to their quality. It is wise to buy inexpensive plants at first, and quite nice ones can be had for relatively little. Later on, when you are sure of your growing ability, you will want to have some of superior quality, which you may buy as higher priced mature plants or raise from seedlings that cost less. If you live near a professional orchid grower, you will benefit from picking out your plants in flower so that you know exactly what you are getting. However, this is possible for relatively few of us. Otherwise, send for catalogues of reputable dealers, and buy but a few plants at a time until you know with whom you like best to deal, and which growers furnish the best plants.

Cattleya flowers come in many sizes and a great range of colors. Orchid hybridizers for years were so intrigued by their ability to produce ever-larger flowers that giant flowers became the vogue, and small ones, unless they had exceptional coloring or some other unusual quality, were rather looked down upon. Truly, some of the nine- and ten-inch cattleyas are spectacular, and if their color and shape are good, they are very handsome. But many people had the feeling that grace and daintiness were lost in the giant size, and that the smaller flowers should be loved for their special appeal. Now the small flower has come into its own. More often crosses are being made using the delightful smaller species, which offer their waxy substance and unusual coloring along with more flowers to the stem. Their three- to four-inch flowers are often called "cocktail" orchids and are, along with the standard five- and six-inch flowers, most popular for corsages. There is a widespread trend toward miniature orchids, both species and hybrids. Little intergeneric hybrids in the cattleya group are being made with *Sophronitis, Epidendrum, Encyclia, Laelia, Broughtonia,* etc.

In judging the quality of cattleya flowers, regardless of the size, there are certain characteristics to look for. A strict point system is used in judging flowers for awards. The color must be pure and fresh. It may be dark or light, but never dull or muddy, and the color in the lip should be in harmony with, or make a pleasing contrast to, the rest of the flower. The flower should have an aristocratic, graceful bearing. Its parts should be generous according to its kind. (In some of the species the parts are normally slender.) In the large-flowered hybrids, we look primarily for broad, straight sepals and broad, flat, or gently curving petals that do not fold back on themselves, as well as a nicely ruffled lip that opens fully to show the markings in the throat. Good substance is important. The more turgid, waxy flowers are better looking, do not become floppy, and last longer. Fragrance is an added attraction. Most cattleyas have a delightful, delicate perfume, and in some the fragrance is so aromatic that it fills the house.

The plants may be shipped to you out of their pots. Many growers like to save shipping weight and packing difficulties by removing the plant from the pot and substituting a polyethylene bag. You should have some pots of various sizes on hand in which to put these when they arrive. Plants are also shipped "bare root." Since most of the potting material has been shaken off these, you will have to furnish them with fresh potting material. If you prefer to receive them in their pots, inform the dealer. Perhaps your first plants should arrive this way, to give you a chance to get used to them before you tackle a repotting job.

Years ago, practically all orchids in this country were grown in osmunda fiber, the roots of the osmunda fern. This fiber is tough and springy so that the roots get plenty of air, yet in the process of decay it furnishes all the nutrients the plants really need. It is somewhat difficult to learn to use it properly, and potting with it is a slow process requiring a strong arm. Also, it has become scarce and rather expensive with increased demand. A number of other potting materials have been tried, and it has been proved that orchids will accept a variety of materials if they have the basic qualities of giving the plants a firm foothold, of not breaking down rapidly, and of furnishing good drainage and aeration. Out of the experiments to find new materials came the discovery that the chopped bark of various trees, principally fir and Douglas fir, worked beautifully. Chopped bark has the advantage of being easier to use and less expensive than osmunda fiber. Growers in Hawaii introduced "hapuu," tree fern which is similar to, but tougher than, osmunda fiber, and this is now quite widely used. Lightweight aggregate, experimented with forty years ago, is being used again, as is volcanic rock or scoria. Slabs of cork oak bark and tree fern are useful for growing some orchids. Various prepared mixes are on the market, some especially useful for certain kinds of plants or certain climates. In the section on potting, Chapter 5, we will tell you how to handle the various materials and how to transfer plants from one to another.

TEMPERATURE, HUMIDITY, AND LIGHT

Plants do not keep accounts, of course, but if balance sheets were published for them, they would be quite similar to those you receive from the bank each month. If you spend more than you earn, you end up in debt. If you earn more than you spend, you have money left over for savings, and philosophically savings mean better living. The earning of plants is the food they make, and their spending is the food they use for energy. Their savings go into growth and flower production, with a reserve kept over toward launching the next season's growth.

During the day a plant carries on three activities: the making of food (sugar) for which light is necessary, the use of food (respiration, similar to our own use of food for energy), and growth. At night respiration and growth continue, drawing on the food made during the day.

Temperature regulates the rate of the plant's activities. Low temperature slows down the processes; rising temperature speeds them up, although not all at the same rate and not indefinitely. The reason behind what we call an optimal temperature range is that within this range the plant can carry on all of its life processes in a normal way, with no activity out of balance with the rest.

The ideal night temperature chosen for a particular kind of orchid is the temperature at which growth and respiration are in good balance so that the plant makes good growth without using too much of its food reserve. For cattleyas this is between 55° and 60 °. At lower temperatures growth is slowed down; at higher temperatures there is a tendency for respiration to exceed growth and for the plants to become depleted.

With abundant light, food making increases as the temperature rises, up to about 85°. The day temperature should ideally be about ten degrees higher than it is at night. In the winter and in cool weather, this is easy to maintain. Problems come with hot weather. The plant's activities remain in pretty good balance up to about 85°, but over this the equilibrium is upset. With higher temperatures there comes the danger of burning and finally death. Plants can tolerate 95° for a few hours, and 100° for shorter intervals, but when the temperature rises above this the situation rapidly becomes critical, for the lethal point is not far off.

There are ways to modify the greenhouse conditions with shading, ventilation, humidity, and air circulation, so that we can pretty well control the environment. We don't wait for extremes to arrive, we anticipate them, and we use the various means in coordination with each other throughout the year to give the plants a good balance of the various factors; a balance between day and night temperatures, between the amount of light and the day temperature, and between humidity and all the other factors.

TEMPERATURE. Winter for most of us means cold weather, but for some it is merely a cool season. In some regions winter brings dull skies, long periods when the sun shines but rarely; in others, winter is a season of bright sun. For these reasons no one set of rules can be made as to just what to do in what month. The basis must therefore be the needs of the plants themselves, and each grower must adjust his own conditions accordingly.

In the winter we can maintain what we consider the ideal temperature conditions for cattleyas, 55° to 60 ° at night, and days of 65° to 72° degrees. On a dark day, or during a spell of dull weather, it is good to let the days hover between 65° and 68°. With the lessened amount of light the plants cannot make as much food as when the sun is shining, and a higher day temperature would cause them to use the food as fast as it is made. On a sunny day, however, let the temperature run up to 70° or 72°. The sun helps to warm the greenhouse with a heat more natural than that produced artificially, and the good light allows the plants to make a generous amount of food. On these nice bright days, open the ventilators a crack to give the plants fresh air. We always try to maintain a buoyant atmosphere for orchids. The winter greenhouse tends to become a bit dank, and airing it out whenever you can gives the plants a lift and helps prevent disease. Always open the ventilators away from the direction of the wind.

Day and night, winter and summer, the air within the greenhouse should be kept in circulation. Circulation of the air keeps the temperature more uniform, preventing layering of hot and cold air or pockets of dead air. One method is to move the air from one end to the other under the benches and return it up and over the plants. In a small greenhouse a single fan may do the job, blowing the under-bench air against the opposite end of the greenhouse, where it rises against the wall and naturally flows back toward the end where the fan is located. In a larger greenhouse it may help to have a second fan placed at the opposite end, pointing up, to keep the air in circular motion. Another method uses fans placed at ground level to blow air toward the roof, or above the benches to pull it upward. Both systems move the cooler, damper air up from the ground. Nearly all makes of natural gas heaters come equipped with a fan. Often the fan runs only when the heat is on. The wiring should be changed to make the fan run constantly. If you have no fan in connection with the heating system, which would be the case with hot-water heat, one can be installed separately. Not only is moving air a means of keeping a uniform temperature, but it is an important aid in disease prevention. Moving air does not hurt the plants as long as it is of the proper temperature and moisture content. Hot dry air blowing on them is harmful, as is a current of cold air.

More suggestions on heating systems will be given in Chapter 23, but we should say here that *artificial gas should never be used within a greenhouse, nor should gas that has any amount of artificial gas mixed with it, for it is fatal to orchids.* Natural gas is safe to use, but even with this the heaters should be vented to carry out all fumes of combustion. These fumes contain constituents that are harmful to cattleyas, causing what is known as "sepal wilt," and injuring other kinds as well. Buds just ready to open are aged prematurely so that the buds may be blasted before opening or, if they open, the sepals are thin and tissuelike and the flower is ruined. Strong fumes can even injure the plants, aging them prematurely, so that they lose their older leaves before they normally should.

During an unusual cold spell it may not be possible to keep the greenhouse temperature quite up to normal. A few nights of 50° or 45° will not harm cattleyas, although it may retard their flowering somewhat. Some kinds that grow with cattleyas may possibly drop their buds. Plants should be kept from contact with the cold glass, else they may have some leaves frozen. In England during World War II, fuel rationing forced growers to run their greenhouses at low temperatures, and although growth and flowering were poor, they were nevertheless able to keep their valuable plants. Heat may be conserved by tacking up sheets of polyethylene film on the inside of the greenhouse or by double glazing.

Problems with the heating system, power failure, etc., can bring on emergency conditions. We have no data on the length of time cattleyas can stand freezing or near-freezing temperatures. We have had a number of near-fatal experiences ourselves, and have learned of others which have been worse. It is not as bad for the temperature to dip to freezing for half an hour and then rise again as it is for the temperature to stay at freezing for a longer period. During a short interval perhaps only some leaf tips and flowers may be frozen, but during a longer interval freezing may progress to the whole plant. We will give the treatment and handling of frozen plants in the section on ailments. Two aids against such emergencies are the installation of a temperature alarm, which rings a bell in the house to warn you of a dangerous drop (or rise) in temperature, and making provision for some form of auxiliary heat.

Spring brings such changeable weather that you have to watch the greenhouse rather carefully. The sun is traveling more nearly overhead, and the days are becoming warmer. On a bright, warm day the greenhouse can heat up in a short time. For a comparable example, consider how hot a closed car becomes when it is parked in the sun. Shading is an important means of controlling day temperature. We shall go further into shading under "light," but the relation between light and temperature and humidity and temperature makes it difficult to separate these three factors. As the days brighten, you can control midday heat for a while by opening the ventilators. The afternoon temperature drops quickly, so be sure to close them by midafternoon. Automatic ventilator controls can be bought and might be necessary for those who have to be away from home all day. Soon, shading must be installed, and perhaps be increased as hot weather arrives. (See Chapter 23.) The aim is to keep the day temperatures between 70° and 80° yet allow the plants enough light to get their season's growth off to a good start.

Summer brings the real problems in temperature control. We do not worry about summer nights. They will usually run somewhat higher than the winter nights, in fact, we simply have to accept what the outdoor night temperature brings. Cattleyas probably would prefer a summer night temperature not exceeding 65°, but nights may go to 70° at times. There is always a contrast between day and night temperatures in the summer. The cooler night air brings the plants relief from the hot days. During hot weather we like to keep the ventilators open both day and night. It takes some time for the greenhouse to cool off—everything is warm, the pots, the benches, etc. Open ventilators during the night bring about cooling earlier than would be the case if the greenhouse were closed up and keep it cool during the early morning.

When you can keep the summer day temperatures under 85° you are doing the plants a favor. As the leaves absorb light they become warmer than the surrounding air. If the greenhouse air goes to 100°, the leaves are even hotter and a further rise in air temperature will take them dangerously close to the burning point. Thick-leaved cattleyas and other kinds are more susceptible to burning than are some of the thinner-leaved kinds. Keep the fans running to circulate the cooler ground air, and step up the humidity to keep a current of moist air moving through and over the plants. Additional shading will be necessary, but try not to cut the light below the needs of the plants, about which more in a moment. Keep the ventilators open a few inches to let the heated air move out.

Evaporation of water into the air cools the air and the surfaces from which it is being evaporated. Air blown through a mist of water or a wet pad becomes cooled in the process. An evaporative system of one sort or another is a great help in cooling a greenhouse as well as in supplying humidity. A unit cooler such as those built for home use is satisfactory for a small greenhouse. Pads are incorporated in the walls of the unit and are kept wet by means of a circulating pump. Air is drawn through the wet pads by a blower which blows the damp cool air into the greenhouse (Fig. 3–1). For most efficient cooling, the unit should be placed so that it draws air from outdoors. Another cooling arrangement is a "pad and fan," which can be operated in two ways. The pad, with a circulating water system (see Chapter 23 for details), is set in the wall of the greenhouse at one end, and a fan is

Figure 3–1 *An evaporative cooling unit. Pads built into three sides are kept wet by means of a circulating pump and distributing tubes. A blower draws outside air in through the wet pads and forces it into the greenhouse.* (Courtesy of International Metal Products Div., McGraw-Edison Co.)

installed to draw air through it. The fan may be an exhaust fan placed in the wall at the opposite end of the greenhouse, which pulls air through the pad and through the greenhouse and exhausts it at the other end. Or the fan may be placed directly in front of the pad so that it pulls air through the pad and pushes it through the greenhouse. A ventilator must be open at the opposite end to allow air to move out. Such evaporative cooling systems are capable of lowering greenhouse temperatures by as much as fifteen degrees.

HUMIDITY. The older growers used to say that they could gauge humidity with "their noses." We like to be more specific, but you can sense when the atmosphere is right, or nearly so. When you walk into a greenhouse and it smells dry to you, when you can "smell the heat" as it were, chances are that the walks and ground are dry, and dry air will soon dessicate the plants if they are not quickly given some moisture. Or, if the air is stagnant and dense with moisture, oppressive to the point where you feel as if you must open the door for some relief, trouble of another kind is in store. But if, when you enter a greenhouse, you feel that you have opened the door on a spring morning, if the air is light and invigorating, moving as if in a gentle breeze, and you smell the gentle, damp, earthy fragrance of the plants, then you know that the atmosphere is right for orchids.

Warm air can hold much more water vapor than cool air, and relative humidity, expressed as a percentage, indicates the amount of water actually held by the air compared to the amount it could hold at a given temperature. For instance, at noon of a day when the temperature is 80°, the air may actually be holding only 35 percent of the water it could hold, so the relative humidity is expressed as 35 percent. But in the cooler evening, if the temperature drops to 50° without any change in the actual amount of water, the air is now saturated, and the relative humidity becomes 100 percent. It is the temperature that determines whether the air can hold more or less water. Warm air therefore tends to attract water, to draw it from surfaces and from plants. You have seen garden plants wilt on a hot day when the warm air is drawing water from them faster than they can replace it by root action. And you have seen these same plants become turgid again in the evening when the cooler air allows them to replace the lost water.

Plants lose water through pores, or stomata, and

it is through the stomata, also, that they take in carbon dioxide with which to make sugar (Fig. 3–2). They lose water to the air faster when the relative humidity is low than when it is high. The thick-leaved cattleyas do not wilt; but if the air is too dry for them over a period of time, they cannot replace it fast enough through the roots, and the plants become emaciated, the leaves become thinner, and the pseudobulbs shrivel. Flower stems may be weak, unable to hold the flowers up properly, and the flowers themselves may be of poor substance.

In the winter, with moderate greenhouse temperatures, a relative humidity of 40 to 60 percent creates a good moisture balance for the plants. It is helpful to have a humidity gauge in the greenhouse so that you can actually know what the relative humidity is at all times. If your climate is mild and naturally humid and artificial heat is needed only occasionally at night, you may not have to add much moisture to the greenhouse air. But in a dry climate or one where artificial heat is needed throughout the winter, the greenhouse air becomes very dry, and humidity must be added.

You can add moisture to the air by "damping down," wetting the walks and under-bench areas

with the hose. With a fan in operation the air picks up and circulates the moisture. Damping down is the old, standard method; but someone must be home to do it. Those who are away from home all day or who object to getting their shoes wet may prefer to add a humidifier of some sort. Various types with various capacities are manufactured. These may be controlled by an electric humidistat, which turns the humidifier on or off according to the setting. A simple system consists of a mist sprayer installed in front of a fan, so that the air blown by the fan picks up the moisture. We also damp down the floor on bright days when the sprayer does not furnish quite enough moisture. The number of mist sprayers could be increased, so that there are several at intervals under the benches. There is now an overhead mister that gives a very fine fog. It can be mounted high in the greenhouse and controlled by a timer, with the intervals adjusted to avoid excessive moisture. Overhead mist sprayers that put out a lot of water are dangerous to use because they keep the plants too wet.

Although the natural state of affairs is for the relative humidity to rise at night as the temperature drops, in the winter the air may become quite dry

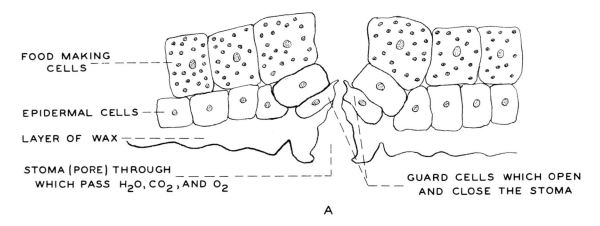

FOOD MAKING CELLS

EPIDERMAL CELLS

LAYER OF WAX

STOMA (PORE) THROUGH WHICH PASS H_2O, CO_2, AND O_2

GUARD CELLS WHICH OPEN AND CLOSE THE STOMA

A

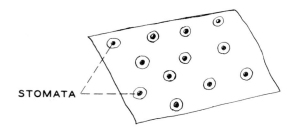

STOMATA

B

Figure 3–2 A: *A section of a cattleya leaf, showing the structure of a single stoma and the cells surrounding it. Note particularly the guard cells that regulate the opening and closing of the stoma, and the heavy layer of wax.*
B: *A microscopic view of the undersurface of a leaf showing how the stomata appear externally. In such a view one actually sees the pits in the waxy covering of the leaf.*

when the heat is running. A factor that contributes to this is condensation (or freezing) of moisture on the cold glass, taking it out of the air. When we were new at running a greenhouse, we did not realize that this was happening, and only learned it when plants began to show some dehydration. We then made it a practice to damp down the floor in the evening.

Hosing the plants with a sprayer, often called "syringing," is a practice that was once used rather freely, but is now used with caution, especially in the winter. The need for this practice has been reduced by the more general use of humidifiers. When a current of sufficiently moist air is kept moving through the greenhouse, it is ordinarily not necessary to mist the plants directly. There are circumstances when it is helpful, such as when it is necessary to protect plants from drying, and to help cool them when the sun is hot. The plants can absorb some water through their leaves, and water on the foliage also creates a saturated atmosphere for the plant, preventing excessive evaporation from the plant tissues. Syringing is therefore advised for newly potted plants until their root systems are again functioning, for hanging plants that dry out faster than benched ones, for seedlings, and for kinds that are more moisture demanding than cattleyas.

Any syringing, or watering, should be done early enough in the day to allow the plants to dry off before night. This does not mean that the air or the potting medium should become dry but simply that no water should be left standing on the plant parts. Fungal and bacterial spores can germinate only on wet surfaces. Water standing on the plants gives the spores a chance to germinate and infect the plants. Dry foliage and rhizomes resist infection. Often a spreading infection in a greenhouse has been traceable to too-frequent syringing. Crowding plants too close together on the bench also contributes to over-damp conditions. The air does not move as freely between the pots or through the plants as it does when they are well spaced. This is particularly important to watch in damp climates and where the winters are dull.

Signs of too much humidity or of stagnant, over-damp conditions are the appearance of brown watery spots on the leaves, little brown or pinkish spots on the flowers, and blackened sheaths. A local spot of infection can be quickly treated, but if spotting becomes general throughout the greenhouse, the first thing to do is lower the humidity, dry off the plants, and increase the circulation of air. Sometimes water that has condensed on the glass drips onto the plants below, keeping the foliage or the potting medium too wet. If you can't cure the drip, move the plants. Diseases and their treatment will be taken up in a later chapter. We mentioned earlier that a relative humidity of 40 to 60 percent is good in the winter. We rather like a fluctuating humidity; 60 percent at night and for most of the day, dropping to 40 percent sometime during the day. We feel that a brief period of lowered humidity—a short "drying off" time each day—contributes to the general health of the plants.

Although it is a challenge to do so, the humidity should be stepped up in hot weather, so that it reaches 70 percent some of the time if possible. With rising and falling temperatures and the need to have the ventilators open the humidity will fluctuate, but this is a healthy condition provided that the plants do not lose too much water during the heat of the day. Be sure that the current of air moving over the plants is moist enough to help them conserve water. Dry air in motion will only serve to hasten water loss. If your humidifier or evaporative cooler plus damping down does not supply enough moisture, a light, quick syringing by hand with a mist spray will help. This can be done several times a day in hot weather, provided you have the foliage dry by nightfall. In order to determine when the plants need misting, feel the leaves with your cheek. Your hands are usually cooler than your cheek, so the leaves may feel warm to your hand but cool to your cheek. When they feel hot, it is time to syringe them.

LIGHT. Good light is important at all times of the year. Gone are the days when cattleyas were grown with heavy shade. When it was discovered that cattleyas made more flowers with bright light, the pendulum swung all the way in the other direction to where "all the light short of burning" became the slogan. This is a little too close for comfort, and most of us prefer not to keep our plants under the constant threat of burning. Burned areas on the leaves and leaves in which chlorophyll has been destroyed cut down the efficiency of the plant. We strive to give them as much light as they need, anticipating from season to season what changes to make in the amount of shading, and keeping the light balanced with temperature and humidity.

The plants themselves show whether they are receiving the right amount of light. In good light the pseudobulbs are plump and hard, the leaves thick and firm, and the color is a medium to light green. Plants that give colored flowers may show red or purple pigment in the newly developing leads and often in the sheaths, and some leaves will retain a tinge of purple on their undersides. Plants that give pure white flowers do not show any of the purple pigment. Flowering is the final clue to light conditions; plants that flower well, giving flowers with strong stems and good substance, show that they have had enough light during the important period of growth and maturation, as well as during the time of flower bud development and the opening of the flowers.

Insufficient light leads to spindly growth that tends to be soft and succulent. The pseudobulbs do not round out well; the leaves may bend over at their juncture with the pseudobulbs; and the plant may fail to flower. Growths that produce no sheaths, or sheaths and no buds, are called "blind" growths. (Don't write off such growths entirely, though. Sometimes flower buds come without a sheath, and a blind growth occasionally flowers later on.)

Too much light causes the loss of chlorophyll, the leaves becoming yellow or bronze and dry looking. Extremely strong light can burn the foliage. A burn first appears as a scorched area that later becomes dry and brown. It can be distinguished from a diseased spot by the fact that the latter remains soft and spreads if not arrested by treatment. Burning is actually a heat effect, produced when strong light raises the leaf temperature to the killing point.

These various signals are used to determine how much light to allow the plants at each season. It is not possible to bring all of the plants to the same shade of green, or to have them all make pseudobulbs of the same dimensions. Under the same light conditions, among plants standing side-by-side on the bench, one may have bulldog proportions and another be slim and dainty, one a light shade of green and another somewhat darker, depending on inherited differences, yet all may be doing well and all may flower eagerly. Watch their flowering and their new growths. When you have made all the adjustments that seem necessary for the plants in general, let well enough alone. If any one plant fails to flower, or if its new growths are smaller than the previous ones, you can suspect that this one needs more light. (We shall see later that watering and potting are other things to check.) Some individual plants may be more light-demanding than their neighbors. Some of the hybrids between *Cattleya* and *Laelia (Laeliocattleya)* are in this category. Find a brighter spot for them, stand them on an inverted pot, or hang them above bench level where they will not be shaded by other plants.

It is helpful to have some measure of the amount of light to give cattleyas. It has been found that they need, and can take, between 2,000 and 4,000 foot-candles, or about 20 to 40 percent of full sun. The lower levels may have to be used in the summer when the heat of the sun, added to the warmer air temperatures, would make the greenhouse too hot. The level may even have to be reduced a bit more in some areas, but try not to go below 1,800 foot-candles. The higher level is possible in the winter when the sun is not as strong and the air is cooler. It is also possible to give more light in the summer when the air can be cooled by means of an evaporative cooler. Foot-candles can be measured by those photographic light meters that have an attachment with which foot-candles can be read directly, or a conversion table that translates the reading into foot-candles. If yours cannot be used, perhaps you can borrow one. Follow the directions carefully.

One method of shading a greenhouse is to apply a white shading compound to the glass itself. Such

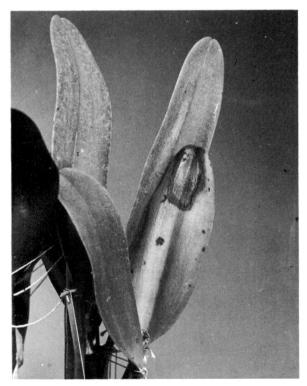

Figure 3–3 *Burned spot caused by too-intense light.*

compounds can be obtained from a greenhouse supply company. Mixed according to directions, it is sprayed or painted on the glass to the desired thickness. There are also types of fixed shading, such as louvered-aluminum or wooden-slat shading, that can be fastened by sections to the outside of the greenhouse. And there are roller blinds that can be raised and lowered according to the weather and various types of plastic or fiberglass netting. These are described more fully in Chapter 23.

In many regions in the winter, in order to give the plants enough light, the glass must be clear (unshaded), but in parts of the West it is necessary to keep some shading through the winter. As winter approaches, watch the plants carefully. Don't let them burn by allowing the shading to become too thin during October and November. Only you can tell, by watching the signals from your plants, whether to let the glass become clear or to keep some shading on all winter.

Toward the end of winter, as the days lengthen and the sun becomes stronger, keep an eye on the plants for the time when shading must be applied again. When you see leaves becoming yellow, it is time to put on some shading; since spring often bursts upon us without much warning, do it before the plants become burned.

Cattleyas do better if light is not increased too suddenly. Plants that have been grown "hard" (with good light) can take sudden changes better than soft plants. A few days or a week of dull weather will not soften plants enough to keep them from taking the usual clear weather that follows. However, six weeks to two months of continuous dark weather can make them susceptible to burning when the sun comes out, hence the warning to beware of the onset of bright spring weather following a dull winter. Cattleyas in nature do not have full sun. They are shaded by the moving foliage of the trees in which they grow, so that in our temperate zone, a zone of extremes, it seems logical to aim at some wise modification of outdoor light.

·4·

MORE ON THE CARE OF ADULT CATTLEYAS

❧

WATERING

ALTHOUGH IN NATURE CAT-
tleyas receive almost a daily rain or a
drenching fog, in cultivation they rarely need a
daily watering. On their native branches their roots
grow in a shallow substratum of mosses and lichens, perhaps an inch thick, or hang free in the
air. Some cling to almost bare bark. Hence they
are freely aerated at all times and are subjected to
alternate wet and dry periods. In pots they have
most of their roots confined to the potting medium, which dries out relatively slowly since it is

enclosed. The difference is comparable to that between the drying rate of a shirt hung on the line
and one left crumpled in the laundry basket. The
former dries in a few hours, the latter may stay
damp for days. The roots in the pot receive a good
wetting when the plant is watered and then for
some days can absorb all the water they need from
contact with the damp potting medium.

The various media used for potting have been
chosen purposely for their porous nature and
water-holding capacity. They allow free drainage
and excellent aeration, and at the same time hold
water while allowing the interstices to be filled with
air. With these media it is a temptation to water
more frequently than necessary; it is difficult to realize that it is actually possible to overwater them.
The secret is to be very observant, to check the
medium from day to day, and *not to water until
you are sure it is needed.* Beginners are usually
cautioned to "err on the dry side," because it is
much easier to step up the frequency of watering
if you haven't been watering quite enough than it
is to recondition a plant whose roots have become
rotten from too much water.

Osmunda fiber, tree fern, and mixes with a high
fibrous content, such as those made with bark,
redwood fiber, peat moss, and perlite, hold water
well from the start. If properly watered, they have
a clean feel and remain firm up to two years or
longer. Each watering should be thorough. Run
the hose over the surface of the pot until the water
runs copiously out of the bottom. It is not good
just to give the pot a dribble, for this does not soak
it uniformly or wet it through. After a thorough
watering, the medium should be allowed to become *almost* dry before watering again. Feel the
medium, press it with your fingers, or force your
fingers between it and the pot. If it is at all springy
and if your fingers feel cool from it, it still has
enough water for the plant. Try to judge a point
when it is *approaching dryness,* just before it
reaches the crisp state, to water again. If you let it
become bone dry it is difficult to get it thoroughly
wet again, and this means that you will have to
water it two or three times over at intervals of a
few minutes, or else soak the pot in a bucket of
water. When it is slightly damp it will readily take
up more water. Usually you can tell when it is
ready for water by the weight of the pot; when
nearly dry, it is light; when damp, it is heavier.

The bark, being in chunks, allows the water to
run through very quickly, so you must be careful,
again, to let the hose run in the pot long enough

29

to insure getting the bark wet clear through. Bark in small pieces, used for seedlings and plants with fine roots, and even the larger chunks of bark before they are well held by roots, are easy to wash out of the pot with a strong stream of water. Use a water breaker on the hose such as a "rose" or a Dramm "400" which breaks the water into gentle streams (Fig. 4–1). After a thorough watering, watch the bark from day to day, and *do not water again as long as it is damp.* The surface bark may dry out before the rest, so you will have to dig down a bit to see what is going on within the pot. New bark does not hold water well at first. It takes a while for bacterial action to get going and for the process of breakdown to set in. Fresh bark therefore is not very absorbent and it may be necessary to water it every day or two for several months. After this period you will notice quite a difference

in it; it stays damp much longer, and becomes a shade darker in color. When this stage is reached, it will not be necessary to water so often. Douglas fir bark takes longer to reach this point than white fir, as it is much harder and sheds water more readily. Some tree fern is softer and holds water well, other types are more wiry and dry more quickly.

Frequency of watering depends on many things, so it is not possible to give an absolute watering schedule. Small pots dry out faster than large ones; drying is more rapid in warm weather than in cool; and of course dry air causes more rapid drying than damp air. Plastic pots hold water longer than clay ones. The condition and size of the plant in the pot also has much to do with the drying rate. A plant with many growths and an extensive root system will use water more rapidly than one with

MIST SPRAYER

DRAMM "400" WATER BREAKER

ROSE

Figure 4–1 *Equipment for watering, mist spraying, and fertilizing.*

just a few pseudobulbs. Therefore a plant that has been in the pot for two or three years and is just about ready for division will use more water than one just becoming established after division. A big old plant that has a heavy aggregation of pseudobulbs and that is becoming root-bound is harder to water. It is necessary to run the hose around the rim of the pot and through the pseudobulbs for quite a time to be sure that enough soaks down in all parts to water it uniformly. To help in watering, it is a good idea to keep plants sorted as to size and condition. Plants in small pots that need frequent watering can be put together in one place, newly potted ones that need special care (see "potting") in another, and larger plants that should be watered less frequently in still another spot.

Seasonal differences in the frequency of watering are based on the actual use of water by the plant coupled with the effects of environmental conditions. Even though in nature cattleyas may not be subjected to appreciable changes in either moisture or temperature, they have periods when their outward activity pauses. In our greenhouses, they have periods of activity when new roots and new growths are developing or flowers are being produced, and periods when, so far as we can see, no activity is going on. A species or a hybrid that flowers as soon as its new growth is formed makes a set of roots and then shows no further activity for several months until eventually new growth starts again. Another will make and mature its new growth and then rest for several months before producing flowers. But the plants are not inactive during these periods of rest. Internal changes are going on which, when the time is ripe, will trigger the start of new vegetative growth or the production of flowers. During a period of rest the plant's processes may be slowed down, but it is still making and using food, and still needs water for the job. Just be sure that the medium is almost dry before watering, and all will be well. There are, however, some kinds that do need to be kept dry during dormancy. There are a few species, especially of laelias, that require less water than cattleyas when at rest. These and their hybrids with cattleyas may need to become thoroughly dry between waterings in the winter.

During the winter, because of cooler temperatures and shorter days, the plants do not use water as fast as in the summer. Also, the cooler temperatures retard the rate at which the potting medium dries. It may not be necessary to water large plants in a fibrous medium (pots of eight to ten inches or

so) more often than once every two weeks, and those not quite so large (five- to seven-inch pots) once every week or ten days. The barks usually have to be watered somewhat more often, especially the coarse grades; eight- to ten-inch pots every week or ten days, and five- to seven-inch every four to seven days.

It is well to take the chill off the water in the winter. Try to have a means of mixing some hot water with the cold to bring it to about 50° or 55°.

In the summer you will have to water more frequently, perhaps twice as often as in winter, depending on conditions, especially humidity, in your area. When it is necessary to syringe the plants with a mist spray, as during hot weather, be sure you do not actually water them at the same time.

When overwatered, osmunda and the fibrous mixes gradually become soggy and have a sticky feel, and the air spaces become filled with water. Eventually they deteriorate into soft mush. Not only does the absence of air hinder the efficiency of the roots, but it allows the accumulation of toxic substances and promotes the growth of harmful bacteria and algae. This combination of conditions causes the roots to die. A potful of continually wet, soggy medium is usually full of rotten roots. The growth of algae over the surface and on the pots themselves is an indication of too much moisture. Mosses often appear. While these are not harmful to the plants, they may conceal the condition of the fiber and form a hiding place for slugs and insects.

Many of the same problems are met when bark is overwatered, although the aeration is not so much interfered with until the bark begins to break down. It first becomes quite dark in color, almost black, and the pieces may have a slippery feel to them. A plant in overwatered bark does not do well; its roots may become stunted and its growths gradually lose their vigor. Badly decomposed bark becomes compacted into a hard mass in the bottom of the pot.

Since overwatering contributes to the death or lack of vigor of the root system, it naturally follows that the plant itself cannot grow well. Waterlogged roots can absorb neither water nor minerals for the use of the plant. The leaves become yellow, especially the older ones, and new growths fail to flower and are smaller than the previous ones. A plant that has been overwatered for a short time can be assisted toward recovery if the potting medium is allowed to become thoroughly dried out and to remain dry for several weeks. The plant must then be put on a schedule of less-frequent watering. One that has been overwatered for a long time and that shows decayed roots had better be repotted and watered infrequently until new roots form. This is the way all newly potted cattleyas are handled.

There is an additional reason to water thoroughly rather than in dribbles. Salts can accumulated in the medium and on the inner surface of the pots (in plastic pots to a lesser extent) and there can also be a build-up of toxic substances. Both can damage the roots. You can see the results when a healthy root turns brown at the tip on coming in contact with the pot. Flushing out the medium at each watering helps prevent this. If fertilizer is given at each watering (of which more later), the pots would be flushed with plain water at regular intervals. Some water contains an appreciable amount of dissolved minerals, so that even if you do not add fertilizer to it salts may accumulate. The addition of fertilizers, of course, adds that much more to the salt content, so flushing the pots between "feedings" is a good general practice.

QUALITY OF WATER

Most contemporary greenhouse growers, of orchids as well as other crops, are able to use their community water supply. Collecting rain water, which was once thought to be the best way to obtain water for orchids, is far too expensive and unreliable a method. Instances where the local water supply has not been suitable are few and far between, but they do exist. Visit other growers in your area. If the greenhousemen use the city water successfully, and if gardens and house plants do well with it, it will be all right for you to use it. *Do not use water that has been softened by the addition of sodium, used in most home water softeners.* The sodium replaces calcium and magnesium, two nutritional salts, and it in itself is toxic in the quantities that result. With too much sodium, plants start many growths that reach an inch or two in length and then cease to grow. Water softened by the ion-exchange method is safe, and a small portable unit is available for amateur growers.

Cattleyas like a slightly acid medium, about pH 6.2. This refers to the pH of the potting medium itself. Tap water may be more or less acid than this. Osmunda, tree fern, and the fibrous mixes are able to maintain their normal pH even though the water used upon them is of a different pH, provided the difference is not extreme. Bark does this also, to some extent. We say they are "self-conditioning." (Bark is fairly acid at first but becomes less so after being put in use.)

The numbers in the pH scale refer to the degree of acidity or alkalinity. The midpoint in the scale, pH 7, is neutral. Below pH 7, decreasing numbers refer to increasing acidity, and each number is ten times more acid than the preceding number. For example, pH 6 is moderately acid, pH 5 more acid, and pH 4 very much more acid, and so on. Above pH 7, the numbers refer to increasing alkalinity: pH 8 is moderately alkaline, pH 9 more alkaline (very alkaline as far as plants are concerned), and so on. Cattleyas have been grown successfully with water up to pH 8. However, water that is above pH 8 should probably be treated to bring it closer to neutral, not necessarily below pH 7.5. The pH can be measured with Hydrion paper, which reacts by turning different colors, or with other types of measuring devices. Many dealers have a variety to offer.

If your water is more alkaline than pH 8, you can rectify it rather easily by adding a little acid to it as you use it. We suggest doing it as you use it rather than attempting to keep a quantity acidified between waterings. Phosphoric acid is probably the best to use for this purpose, although acetic and hydrochloric acid are also good. It will not take much to do the job. You can use phosphoric acid full strength, but should obtain a one-tenth normal solution of hydrochloric or acetic rather than handle them full strength. First you must find out how much acid to add to your water. Measure a gallon of water in a clean container. Check its pH with Hydrion paper. For measuring the acid, you should have a graduated cylinder marked in cubic centimeters (cc). Let us say that you put 5 cc of acid in the cylinder. Pour a very small amount into the gallon of water, stir thoroughly, and test with Hydrion paper. If the acidity is not yet down to where you want it, add a little more, stir, and test again. Do this until the pH level you want is reached. (It is not necessary to take it below pH 7.5) Now write down the amount of acid it required to bring the one gallon of water to that level, and keep this information handy.

Perhaps the easiest method of acidification is to add a measured amount of acid to a bucket of water and then water the plants by means of a Hozon siphon or other proportioner. Hozon is a device that is screwed on between the faucet and the hose. It has a little side vent to which is attached a small tube that goes into a bucket of water. The force of water as it travels from the faucet through the hose draws the water out of the bucket and adds it to the main stream of water, at the rate of one part from the bucket to sixteen parts of hose water. The solution in the bucket is therefore used in a concentration sixteen times as strong as you want the final product to be. To acidify the water, measure the amount the bucket holds, and add sixteen times the amount of acid it would take to bring this quantity to the proper acidity. For instance, if it takes one cc of acid to acidify one gallon of water, add sixteen cc for each gallon in the bucket. Before watering the plants, check the pH of the water delivered by the hose. There is also a jar-siphon mixer, called Hydro-mix, that holds enough solution to treat twenty-five gallons of water. Therefore, you add to the jar enough acid to adjust twenty-five gallons of water. Other proportioners are available, some more expensive than others and some designed for large greenhouses. Always follow directions when using them.

Such proportioners require good water pressure to work properly. If you have low water pressure, you might have to resort to a gravity tank or a tank with a pump. The former is a tank installed above bench level, with a hose through which the water will run by gravity. Determine the amount it holds, add the right amount of acid to bring it to the desired pH, stir thoroughly, and check the pH as the water comes through the hose. Be sure to keep the tank clean, and if you do not mix the acid solution fresh each time, be sure to check the acidity frequently.

We should say here that if your water is far too acid, you can make it less acid by adding potassium hydroxide solution. The same method of measuring and testing with Hydrion paper is used, this time to bring the water up the pH scale from a lower level to something in the neighborhood of pH 6 or pH 6.2.

FERTILIZING

The Influence of the Media

OSMUNDA FIBER. Osmunda fiber gives the plants a balanced diet of minerals, and the plants will grow and flower without any added fertilizers. However, dilute applications of fertilizers will give them a boost and produce somewhat stockier growth and more and heavier flowers. You must be cautious about applying fertilizers to osmunda fiber, partly because only a slight supplement to the minerals already present is needed, and partly because overfeeding is a danger. Too much feeding leads to soft growths that do not harden up properly and also tends to discourage flowering. The fertilizer should be one in which nitrogen (N), phosphorus (P), and potassium (K) are in equal proportions, a so-called 10-10-10 or 20-20-20 formula. There are many brands put out especially for orchids. These are obtainable from orchid supply houses, but any of the complete water-soluble fertilizers on the market will do, provided that these three minerals are in equal proportions. A concentration of one-half teaspoon per gallon of water is as strong as you should use, and many growers feel that one-quarter teaspoon per gallon is sufficient. Use every third or fourth watering.

In order to put the extra minerals to use, plants in osmunda must be in active growth and have enough light to make sufficient amounts of carbohydrates to balance the minerals. Most cattleyas make their new growth during the spring and summer, some starting as early as January, maturing the growths by July, and others starting later and maturing the growths in the fall. They should be fertilized only during this period of activity, and be given no fertilizer during the balance of the year. Some hybrids inherit the growth habit of one or another of their species ancestors, and should be fertilized accordingly. However, some hybrids are continually in a state of growth or flowering, often making two or more sets of growths a year, and starting new growths before the previous ones have matured. Such types can make use of some fertilizer through the winter, although because of the short days (fewer daylight hours) the concentration should be reduced to half, or the applications spaced farther apart.

BARK. By analysis, the various barks differ somewhat in the amount of available minerals, and all are lower in nitrogen than is osmunda fiber. Bacteria that feed on the bark and bring about its breakdown (a normal process that releases minerals for plant use) may use almost all of the available nitrogen, leaving little for the plant. Because of this, additional nitrogen should be added to the bark by the use of a fertilizer of high nitrogen content, with a ratio of 30-10-10 or 30-10-20. There are several on the market. Fish emulsion has too high a nitrogen content (5-1-1) to be used regularly, but may occasionally be alternated with one of the others. Be prepared for the characteristic aroma associated with this product. Too much nitrogen produces succulent, lush growth at the expense of flowers. Slow-release fertilizers are best used on plants that are grown in a soillike medium, which some growers prefer for cymbidiums. In general, higher levels of fertilizers may be used when the plants are making vigorous growth and when light conditions are at their best. The concentration will be reduced when the plants are less active and when the days are shorter or the weather cloudy. As a starting point, we suggest that you try the 30-10-10 or the 30-10-20 ratio, giving it in a concentration of one-half teaspoon to a gallon of water at every other watering. This schedule may be kept up for plants in active growth during seasons of bright light. For plants that are resting, or during spells of dull weather, reduce the concentration to one-quarter teaspoon per gallon of water. To prevent the buildup of salts in the pots and in the medium, the pots should be flushed with plain water at frequent intervals. One way of accomplishing this is to water everything thoroughly before applying fertilizer.

Orchids are slow to respond, and cattleyas are not "heavy feeders." It is difficult to diagnose why plants may produce fewer flowers one year than another, and equally difficult to know just what brings about more flowers. Bumper crops may be as much due to a happier combination of environmental factors, such as fewer cloudy days, a cooler summer, etc., as due to what fertilizer you used or whether you gave it at every watering or at every other watering. If all this seems to leave some questions as to where you should start, remember that, fortunately, in general, orchids will grow and thrive with a variety of fertilizers.

If you have an inquiring turn of mind, you might try fertilizing half of your plants at every watering and the other half at every second watering, or set up some other trial program, and compare the results. If you fertilize at every watering, you must find some time to flush the pots with plain water. A possible method might be to give fertilizer as usual one week and the next time give plain water all around before applying the fertilizer.

TREE FERN. While it is necessary to learn by experience how often it must be watered, it is handled essentially the same as bark as to kind of fertilizer and frequency of application.

FIBROUS MIXES. There are many mixes on the market, some under brand names and some put out by individual dealers. Most of them consist of various proportions of fir bark, redwood bark (either in chips or shredded), peat moss, and perlite or a similar substance. Some have added slow-release fertilizers such as bone meal, hoof and horn, superphosphate, and ureaform nitrogen.

Those that do not have the added fertilizers may be treated like bark—given a complete fertilizer, such as 30-10-10 or 30-10-20 formula, one-half teaspoon per gallon at every other watering, with modifications in quantity according to the season or the activity of the plants.

Those that contain the fertilizers will not need fertilizer applied to them. If directions come with the product, follow them implicitly. If no directions are given, begin by trying a 30-10-10 formula at the rate of one-fourth teaspoon per gallon of water. Then increase as you see fit.

GRAVEL AND AGGREGATES. Essentially, gravel culture differs from bark culture only in that gravel is used instead of bark, and that the entire array of necessary minerals must be supplied rather than just a supplemental fertilizer. The chief disadvantage of gravel is that it is heavy. In areas of heavy rainfall, where plants remain out-of-doors much of the year, some growers find that the aggregates are useful because they do not break down.

Plants can be grown in gravel all the way from community pot size to flowering size. For the smallest plants a very fine size is used, between one-sixteenth and one-eighth-inch diameter. The size of the gravel is gradually increased as the plants become larger, until for mature plants a size of one-half to three-quarters inch is used. The gravel should be from a type of rock that does not readily leach minerals into solution. For example, limestone is to be avoided. Weathered gravel is preferable to crushed gravel. The manufactured lightweight aggregates such as Haydite, Idealite, Solite, Holite, etc., are excellent. They can be obtained from manufacturers directly or from construction companies. They should be rinsed thoroughly before use and possibly screened if they contain particles smaller than the size desired.

From the time plants are in three-inch pots, unless they have a good root system to hold them in place, they should be supported with one of the rigid stakes used in bark culture or should have the rhizomes fastened down by means of a wire extending from one side of the pot to the other.

Plants in small pots have to be watered more often than those in large pots, but most have to be watered more frequently than with other media.

Each grower must devise his own schedule by observation of his own plants. During the winter, three- and four-inch pots may have to be watered every other day, and in the summer every day. Larger pots may need water every four to six days in the winter, and every three days or so in the summer.

Some growers like to add fibrous material, such as chunks of sphagnum peat, to about 25% of the total quantity of aggregate. This is especially useful for plants that require rather constant moisture. It is reported, however, that Solite holds 30% of its weight in water, and does not need as frequent watering as some of the others. You should experiment a bit with it, or any of the above, before planting everything in them. With all, be sure to watch the response of the plants.

Scoria, or volcanic rock, does hold a fair amount of water due to the irregularities in its surface. Some say it holds even more than bark. Caution is advised.

Fertilizer should be a water-soluble, complete formula. Hyponex, Instant Vigoro, or a complete orchid fertilizer such as described for bark can be used. Or you can mix your own according to the formula given below. This formula was the one used in experimental work with orchids in gravel at Ohio State University.

The Ohio W. P. Solution
(to be used half-strength)

Name	Symbol	Amount
Potassium nitrate	KNO_3	2.63 gm.
Ammonium sulfate	$(NH_4)_2SO_4$	0.44 gm.
Magnesium sulfate	$MgSo_4 \cdot 7H_2O$	2.04 gm.
Monocalcium phosphate	$CaH_4(PO_4)_2 \cdot H_2O$	1.09 gm.
Calcium sulfate ..	$CaSO_4 \cdot 2H_2O$	4.86 gm.
Iron sulfate (ferrous sulfate)	$FeSO_4 \cdot 7H_2O$	0.5 gm.
Manganese sulfate	$MnSO_4$	Make a one percent solution and add 2.5 cc of this
Water	H_2O	1.0 gallon

In preparing this solution dissolve each salt completely in the gallon of water before adding the next salt. Manganese is added by first dissolving one gram of manganese sulfate in 99 cc of water, then 2.5 cc of this solution is used per gallon of nutrient solution. The pH ranges between 5.5 and 6.5 and should be checked before use.

Fertilizer can be given twice a week, or even at every watering, according to your judgment. Pots should be flushed with plain water after every few feedings. Once-a-week fertilizing is still probably best during the winter. A concentration of one-half teaspoon of fertilizer to a gallon of water would be best to start with, but you may wish to vary this experimentally.

The fertilizer can be applied by means of a Hozon attachment, or could be mixed in a tank and applied by a hose. It is best to mix it fresh each time, or at least not to let it stand in the tank for longer than two weeks. Chemical changes can take place in a mixture that is allowed to stand for a long time, and the pH can also change. The plants in gravel do not have a store of minerals from which to draw as they do in organic media, nor do they have the protection from changes in pH furnished by an organic medium.

One of the problems of gravel culture is the accumulation of salts, particularly in the pots. This problem can probably be ameliorated by the use of plastic pots. Plastic pots would also alleviate the rapid drying, making it easier to keep the plants well watered, especially in the smaller sizes. With both clay and plastic pots, however, care must be taken to flush with plain water very thoroughly every week or two.

A second problem with gravel culture is that the iron may become precipitated from the solution, causing chlorosis and abnormal growth. The use of chelated iron should prevent this (see below). It would be well to use a fertilizer containing an iron chelate, or to add a small amount to each batch of fertilizer as it is mixed—approximately five grams for each ten gallons of solution.

APPLICATION OF FERTILIZER. Proportioners make fertilizing easy. These are described above in the section dealing with acidifying water. In using the Hozon, you make the concentration sixteen times as strong as you wish the solution for the plants to be. For a strength of one-half teaspoon per gallon, this would be sixteen one-half teaspoons, or eight teaspoons, for each gallon the bucket holds. In the Hydromix jar you would put twenty-five times the amount of fertilizer needed for one gallon, since it holds enough solution to treat twenty-five gallons of water. For other types follow directions. If the water pressure in your area is low, you might have to use a tank for fertilizing, also described above.

Mineral Nutrition

Man cannot live by love alone. Nor can a plant live by air and water. Every living thing, both animal and plant, depends on certain minerals for the development of its body structure and the maintenance of the living substance within it, protoplasm. Even plants that hang on such a sterile perch as a telephone wire *(Tillandsia)* have a source of minerals to nourish them—dust settling on the wire and minerals dissolved in rainwater—small amounts, to be sure, but enough for these particular plants.

It used to be thought that orchids lived entirely on materials taken from the air. Observers overlooked the accumulation of humus material present in breaks in the bark of trees or crevices in weathered rock and in the mosses and lichens thereon, the fertilizing minerals dissolved out of bird droppings and washed down to the plants by rain, and the yearly collection of dead leaves among the bulbs of the plants themselves. Even rainwater is not pure, since rain droplets form on dust particles and take up more dust on their way earthward.

A ten-ounce plant consists of nine ounces of water and one ounce of sugars, starches, proteins, fats, waxes, and numerous other substances. This single ounce represents the other chemical substances accumulated by the plant during its lifetime plus the amount of food it has on hand at the moment of weighing. To find out what part of the dry weight of the plant is mineral, the dried plant is ignited and burned to remove carbon, hydrogen, oxygen, and nitrogen. The ash that remains is the total mineral content of the plant, and amounts to approximately 0.076 of an ounce for a ten-ounce plant. A fraction of a cent would buy the chemicals that make up the plant. The value of the living plant is based on the marvelous things its protoplasm, governed by its genes, can do with that minute quantity of nonliving substances.

The minerals, in the form of mineral salts, are absorbed by the roots from the medium in which they grow. The salts are released from the organic matter by slow decay and are dissolved by moisture in the soil. The salts in solution are then taken up by the roots and transported to every part of the plant, where they enter into various vital activities.

In addition to the minerals, the plant needs water and two things absorbed from the air, oxygen and carbon dioxide. Oxygen, necessary for respiration, is absorbed by the leaves and stems from the atmosphere and by the roots from air in the soil. Carbon dioxide is absorbed by the leaves (and other green parts of the plant) and combined with water taken up by the roots to form sugar, the food of the plant. This process is called photosynthesis because it is carried on only in the presence of light. The simple sugars are turned into complex sugars, starches, and cellulose; and various products formed from carbohydrates are combined with nitrogen, sulfur, and phosphorus to form proteins.

The major mineral elements, necessary in relatively large amounts, and their activities, follow:

Calcium is necessary for cell wall formation and for regulation of cell activities. If calcium is deficient the new growths are stunted and distorted.

Nitrogen, an essential ingredient of proteins and chlorophyll, is necessary for good vegetative growth. When nitrogen is deficient the plants are stunted and mature too early. Older leaves turn yellow and drop off. Too much nitrogen produces excessive vegetative growth and delayed flowering.

Sulfur is also an ingredient of proteins. Sulfur deficiency may stunt root growth.

Phosphorus, the third important mineral in protein formation, is a catalyst and regulator of vital activity. Sometimes called the "dynamite of living cells," phosphorus deficiency leads to stunting; the leaves, instead of turning yellow, become dark green.

Potassium, another important catalyst, regulates many activities. Deficiency results in dwarfing with the edges of the leaves frequently scorched and dead.

Magnesium is part of the chlorophyll molecule, and therefore necessary to the manufacture of food. With lack of magnesium the older leaves become yellow between the veins and the plant does not thrive.

Iron is a catalyst in many reactions, including the formation of chlorophyll. Iron is seldom deficient but is insoluble unless the soil is sufficiently acid. Deficiency of iron causes the younger leaves to become yellow.

Certain other minerals are also necessary, but in extremely minute amounts. Very little is known about their specific activities, and it is thought that they act as catalysts in vital chemical reactions. These minor elements are *boron, molybdenum, manganese, copper,* and *zinc.* They are seldom deficient, for the faint traces found in most soils and as impurities in most chemicals are enough to supply the needs of the plants. Manganese is the only one of the minor elements that at times needs to be added to nutrient solutions. In fact, in order to do research on the role of the trace elements, workers must first remove the minute amounts of boron, copper, manganese, molybdenum, and zinc contained in the chemicals they will use. They must also redistill water many times before it can be considered pure. They can then study the effects of the minor elements by using them one at a time in measured amounts. It is known that their complete absence causes poor growth, and it is also known that amounts in excess of the smallest quantities are toxic to plants.

We have been talking about the various elements necessary to plant nutrition, but plants can use these elements only in the form of inorganic salts. In nature some inorganic materials are dissolved out of the rock particles in the soil. Additional inorganic salts are released from the humus material in the soil by bacteria and fungi that feed upon it. The same events take place in the potting materials used for orchids. The "breakdown" of organic materials such as osmunda, tree fern fiber, bark, leaf mold, etc., requires the activities of soil bacteria and fungi. We augment the store of chemical salts available to the plant when we apply additional amounts in the form of fertilizers and nutrient solutions. Inorganic salts occur as a variety of compounds, and choices may be made among them. We cannot list all the possibilities, but will give some of the more generally used compounds. Nitrogen may be furnished as nitrate salts or as ammonium salts, for example as ammonium nitrate, ammonium sulfate, potassium nitrate or calcium nitrate. It is generally agreed that plants need nitrogen in both the ammonium form (NH_4) and nitrate form (NO_3), but there is no agreement as to which form should be in greater quantity. Potassium may be furnished as potassium sulfate, potassium nitrate, or potassium chloride; calcium as monocalcium phosphate, calcium nitrate, calcium chloride; phosphorus is furnished in phosphate salts such as calcium phosphate or monopotassium phosphate; iron as ferrous sulfate; magnesium as magnesium sulfate; manganese as manganese sulfate; and sulfur as the sulfate salts just mentioned.

In order for a plant to thrive, it must have a balanced "diet" of the essential minerals. It needs larger quantities of some than of others. And in order to make use of the nutrients, it must have the proper conditions of light, water, and temperature. Curiously, a plant can starve in the midst of plenty if for some reason it is unable to take up the minerals it needs. Overwatering with the resultant inhibition of root function can produce a mineral lack for the plants. Underwatering, not as dangerous as overwatering, can deprive the plant of sufficient materials for growth. Excessive accumulation of salts in the potting medium can prevent the roots from absorbing both water and minerals. Insufficient light can prevent the plant's using the available minerals through failure to make the necessary amount of sugars, the building blocks for more complicated carbohydrates which, in turn, are combined with minerals from the soil to form proteins, enzymes, etc.

An important contribution to plant nutrition has been made by the introduction of chelates. In a culture solution, or (less likely) in a potting medium, the iron may combine with other ions such as the phosphate ion (PO_4) to form an insoluble compound. This removes the iron from solution and makes it unavailable to the plant. Chlorosis (yellowing) of the leaves will follow, with resultant poor growth. Other metals such as copper, zinc, etc., may be similarly precipitated from solution, although probably iron is the most important one to consider. A chelate is an organic substance that has a chemical attraction for certain elements and holds them loosely in solution, making them continually available for plant use. The chelate thus prevents precipitation of the particular element. Called the versene compounds, they have quite a complicated structure exemplified by one, called for short EDTA, which is ethylenediaminetetraacetic acid. It is possible to add this to a culture solution or to a fertilizer solution, but it is probably easier and better to obtain one that has already been combined with iron, such as the product called "Sequestrene." Some manufacturers of orchid fertilizers are including chelates in their prepared products. When used thus, the chelated iron may be substituted for iron sulfate or whatever other iron compound would have been included, or it may be used in addition to it.

The formulation of fertilizers is an experimental endeavor, and here the matter is complicated by the fact that the materials on which the fertilizers will be used vary so much from each other. The barks of different species of trees contain different amounts of nitrogen, phosphorus, potassium, etc.: Osmunda fiber collected in different regions varies quite strikingly in content. Any one of these materials may vary in the rapidity with which it releases its minerals under different conditions of watering, temperature, and atmospheric moisture. It is to be expected that fertilizers made up according to the experiences of one grower or another will also vary. There are also organic fertilizers, such as fish emulsion, favored by some. After trying several on your own plants, you yourself may come to have a preference for a certain one. This is good. It shows that all is *en rapport* between you and your plants. Such experiences among growers everywhere show that orchids can get along on quite varied diets, provided they are given the basic essentials.

CARE OF FLOWERING PLANTS

Flowering cattleyas are treated in the same way as those not in flower. They are watered on the same schedule and are allowed the good light that brings the flowers to their fullest color and firmest substance. Perhaps in hot weather they might be given a bit more shade after they are fully open to help them last. Once the flowers mature, that is, after they have been open three or four days, the plant can be brought into the house to be enjoyed, and can be placed on a table or the mantel or wherever it can be shown off, for the flowers do not need light in order to keep well. If you bring a plant into the house before the flowers are open, keep it in a bright (but not too hot) window until they are fully open.

We used to try to move flowering plants in the greenhouse to an area set aside for them so as to avoid getting water or insecticides on them. Moving plants, especially large ones, is a chore often involving shifting several others to make room for one. Sometimes new growths are damaged, or buds broken off in the process. We have learned that water does not hurt the flowers provided they can dry off quickly. Some prepared fertilizers have a coloring material added (so that you can know whether the proportioner is working properly); as this dries it will leave a deposit on the flowers, as will insecticides. Try to avoid splashing the flowers during watering, and avoid spraying them. But if

some do become wet with these materials, rinse them off with a fine spray of plain water before the materials have a chance to dry. Dust carried in by the wind may also be washed off.

It takes five to eight weeks for the buds to grow up to the tip of the sheath, depending on the individual plant. The length of time from the moment the buds break the tip of the sheath until they are open also varies. Some develop very quickly, requiring about a week, but most take two weeks or more. The flowers are not ready to cut until they have reached their fullest color and substance, at least two full days, sometimes four days, after the flowers open. Cattleya buds will not open in water, nor will flowers mature if they are cut too soon. They remain limp and green and soon wilt. After you have lived with your plants for a while, you come to know when the flowers have reached their prime, and how long it takes them. If you intend to use them for decoration or for corsages, or to sell them, it is important to avoid the disappointment of not having them last. Cymbidiums and a few other orchids will open the last few buds in water on spikes that already have most of the flowers open, but they may not reach full size or substance.

Cut flowers keep a long time in water, in a narrow-necked vase so that the flower parts are not submerged. Their life can be lengthened by putting them in a cool place at night, or in a refrigerator at not less than 45°. To keep a corsage, lay it on a little shredded wax paper in a polyethylene bag, close the bag tightly, and put it in the refrigerator. We learned some time ago that carnations can be kept for six to eight weeks after cutting when wrapped in polyethylene film and stored in a refrigerator or in a cool place, so we have tried this with orchids a few times. Usually some can be kept for longer than they would last on the plants, and can thus be saved for special occasions. Not all flowers will keep equally well. Those of heavy substance last better than thin ones, but the keeping qualities are sometimes a matter of individuality. They should be cut while in their prime, not during the first few days after opening, but not past the middle of their normal life. A fading flower or two can shorten the life of others stored with them. The flower stems are put in tubes, and they are then laid on shredded wax paper in a shallow box. The box is wrapped tightly in polyethylene film and stored at 45°. Among those we have tried, phalaenopsis kept particularly well, but some cattleyas kept for two weeks longer than they would have otherwise.

All cutting instruments must be sterilized between plants, when cutting flowers, potting, or trimming, to prevent spreading disease from plant to plant, particularly virus disease. Virus may be present even though no symptoms show, so it should never be assumed that a plant is free from it. Flaming is one way to sterilize instruments. An alcohol lamp is easy to use and to carry around with you in the greenhouse. In a stationary potting area, a Bunsen burner or a blowtorch can be used. When flaming, be sure to hold the blade in the flame long enough to heat the entire surface thoroughly. Blades and stakes may also be sterilized by first washing in hot soapy water and then heating for half an hour in the oven at 350°. An easier and satisfactory method for sterilizing tools is by the use of trisodium phosphate (TSP). This is a material used in painting to clean walls, etc., and is available from paint stores. Make a saturated solution in a widemouthed jar and stand shears and cutting tools in it. It will keep them bright and shiny and will not dull them. A saturated solution is made by putting enough in the jar so that there is always some undissolved material in the bottom. Rinse the tools after each use before putting them back in the jar. Follow precautions on the box. Moderate contact with the hands is not harmful, but it is best to rinse them frequently. Renew the solution when it becomes discolored. Razor blades can be soaked in a separate little jar.

Wash your hands frequently and thoroughly. Don't go from plant to plant, as I have seen some do, pinching off an old flower here and an old stem there. Fingers and fingernails can carry virus just as well as a knife can.

As plants come into bloom, watch to see that the buds are not cramped in the sheath or prevented from coming out through its top. Sometimes a sheath becomes dry before flowering time, or is too long in proportion to the length of the flower stems, or is too tough for the buds to force open. Except for those with a double sheath, you can see the buds by holding the plant against the light. If the stems become bent back on themselves, cut off the top of the sheath or open it with your fingers; otherwise the stems will become distorted and the flowers may not grow fully out of the sheath before they are ready to open. Watch to see that a sheath is not growing up under an adjacent leaf which would cause the buds to be injured or bent. You can slip one leaf behind another to allow room for the flowers, or tie back leaves that are in the way. If the group of flowers on a stem is too heavy for the stem, the stem may bend with their weight, in which case it should be staked so that the flowers will be held upright. Occasionally a flower has difficulty in opening; its parts may be very tightly clasped together. Let it alone for a couple of days to see whether it can open by itself, but if it doesn't you can ease the petals apart or unfold the rim of the lip with your fingers, or perhaps accomplish this by blowing into the flower.

The keeping quality of the flower partly is due to a protective covering of wax, but this is also an individual characteristic. In general, those of heavy substance last the longest, but some not particularly heavy can last for weeks. Good culture, of course, contributes to this.

As the flowers fade they should be cut. When the last flower on a stem is removed, the stem and sheath should be cut off close to their base. Dying flowers in the greenhouse are something of a hazard. They give off ethylene gas, which can cause sepal wilt in flowers just ready to open. Two or three fading flowers will not produce enough to harm others, but a large number of them may do so. Also, old flowers are susceptible to spotting by the botrytis fungus; and once this fungus is on the increase in the greenhouse, fresh flowers may become infected. Whenever such spots make an appearance, remove the flower at once. (See Chapter 21 for diseases that show up in flowers.)

Thrips, red spiders, and aphids are enemies. Thrips chew the surface tissues, leaving little silvery or brown scars. Red spiders and aphids puncture the tissues, leaving small wounds surrounded by a transparent halo. Insects also spread disease. The control for these is given in the chapter on pests. "Honey" is secreted at the tips of the sepals and also at their juncture with the stem. This is a pleasant, sweet-tasting substance. When the flowers are growing close together, sometimes a bit of this becomes smeared on an adjacent flower part and a transparent streak results. Wash it off with a touch of water and the streak will disappear.

Keep a record on the label of each plant as to the flowering time, the number and quality of the flowers, and how long they last. When your greenhouse becomes crowded, you will wish to dispose of some plants in favor of better ones, or plants that flower at a different time of the year. Don't discard a plant on the basis of its first flowering, unless the flowers are exceedingly poor on a well-grown plant. If they are nicely shaped, but small or poorly colored, see if better culture won't bring them along to be larger or brighter. A plant that consistently gives poor flowers is, of course, not worth keeping, nor is one that refuses to flower in spite of good culture. Sometimes a recalcitrant plant can be encouraged to flower by giving it better light, or a slightly warmer or cooler night temperature. It is worth a bit of experimenting to find out. However, often we find ourselves giving our best locations and our most earnest care to a plant that performs poorly, when it would be better to discard it in favor of a more rewarding plant. The value of keeping records is proved when you have an opportunity to trade plants with a friend, or to sell some, or when you wish to make room for new plants by culling out poor ones.

GENERAL SUGGESTIONS

When an orchid plant is making new leads, help it to maintain a nice upright position by staking the leads as they develop. Some leads will assume a good position by themselves, but others may lean out too far. Newly developing growths are quite soft and easy to break, so be gentle. You can't do much until a lead is about half grown, and then you can begin to train it. Place a steel stake in the center of the pot or use a clip-on stake. Usually one stake is sufficient for a medium-size plant. Using soft string, make a turn around the stake, then bring the string out and around the lead and back to the stake to be tied. You can snug in a young lead by placing the string fairly close to its base, where it is strong, to bring the main curve closer to the plant. When this lead is more fully grown, replace the string with another placed at the juncture between the pseudobulb and leaf. Never constrict a stem by looping the string around it; always tie the leads with a "sling" of string. A plant with many leads becomes a challenge to keep staked. Don't try to pull all the leads in close to the stake; just give them a good position and leave room between them for flower buds to emerge without crowding.

Keep the pots free from weeds. Oxalis is a particular pest, because it shoots its seed as the pods become ripe, thus insuring a new crop as soon as you have pulled one out. It is best to get oxalis plants out while they are tiny. The barks are free from weed seeds, and osmunda can be treated before being put into use. Hand-weeding is safe, of course.

As the sheathing leaves that surround the pseudobulbs become dry and start to fall away from the stem, they may be removed. They come off more completely when they are wet. Do not peel the still-green ones from the young pseudobulbs. When you have finished weeding, cutting old flowers, etc., gather up all trash and remove it from the greenhouse.

Physan-20 is an aid in keeping a clean greenhouse. Its general use is as a disinfectant and algae control in swimming pools and evaporative coolers. In a greenhouse it may be used to wash the benches, glass, and walks to free them from the unsightly algae that grow wherever it is constantly damp and which cut down the light through the glass. One ounce per eight gallons of water, or one teaspoon to one gallon, is sufficient for the job.

Whenever you are in the greenhouse, working or just looking, you may discover something that needs attention—crowded flower buds, a new lead that needs tying, a few weeds to be removed, bugs on some flower buds, a light burn, or a disease spot. Don't forget to look over the plants in the back row; they sometimes become neglected. A regular program of spraying for insects should be established as a preventive measure to keep insect populations under control. Keep a little hand sprayer ready between regular sprayings, in case you find a few aphids, red spiders, or other pests on flower buds (Fig. 4–2). And if you find a plant with a few suspicious spots, treat it with a little fungicide right away. See Chapter 21 for disease and pest control.

Two frequent pests are slugs and snails. The former are easier to control than the latter, but both are killed by preparations containing metaldehyde. Do not use an arsenic preparation on orchids. Chewed leaves and flowers, as well as root tips, are evidence of slugs, and you often see a slug lying along a stem or a newly developing lead. Regular treatment with a "slugicide" will keep them under control. More difficult to control are very small, hard-shelled, flat-coiled snails, the largest of which reach about three-sixteenths of an inch. They remain in the potting medium for the most part, wreaking destruction on the new root tips; occasionally they will be seen on the rhizome or the developing young growths. When you see new root tips badly chewed off, and do not find slugs, you can suspect that snails are present. It doesn't take many to keep the new root tips whittled off as fast as they form. The metaldehyde preparations should be used repeatedly, as pellets, meal, or powder, or formulated into crystals, sprinkled over the surface of the medium. The treatment should be repeated every few weeks, and then at intervals of three or four months. Where a bad infestation is found, we

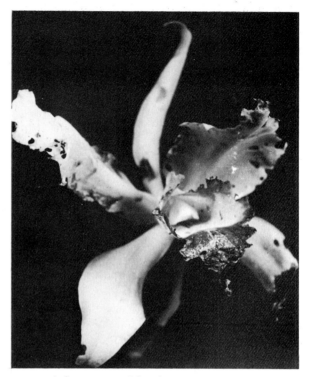

Figure 4–2 *LEFT: Closeup of flower damaged by red spiders.*

RIGHT: A flower ruined by slugs.

remove the plant from the pot, take off all the potting medium, pick off all the snails we can find, wash the bare roots with the hose, and dust the roots and the base of the plant thoroughly with metaldehyde powder before putting it in fresh medium. Other chemicals for snail control are given in Chapter 21.

Occasionally a plant is found whose roots just simply stop growing. Perhaps the plant was overwatered unwittingly at some time, possibly by drip from the roof, or salts may have been allowed to accumulate. Remove the plant from the pot to ascertain the cause. Perhaps the bark is moldy. Various kinds of mold can invade the medium, a slippery-feeling slime mold, a granular, dry-looking mold, or a cobwebby kind. The latter two can interfere with the water-holding capacity of the medium. Not all harm the plants, but where you find mold and root injury or lack of growth together, it is best to put the plant in fresh medium. Many growers feel that the addition of one-third part redwood bark helps hold down the development of mold.

As you go along the bench watering the plants, glance back from plant to plant to see whether the water drains rapidly through the pot. Once in a while, fine material becomes washed out of the bark into the bottom and clogs up the drainage hole. With your fingers or a screwdriver, push up the crock over the hole to let the water run out. Then flush out the pot thoroughly to remove the material that was clogging the drainage. If this doesn't remedy the situation, remove the plant from the pot to see what was causing the trouble.

Sometimes a grower is disappointed in the flowering of a plant which he bought while in bloom, and from which he expected a duplication of the flowers he saw. Changed conditions can alter the quality of flowers. A plant that gave brightly colored flowers under good light may give paler ones with less sun. An unusually hot summer, or a dull chilly fall can cause poorer blooming than usual. You will find this so from year to year with your own plants, so if it happens to one you have recently bought, see whether improved conditions won't remedy the situation.

·5·

POTTING MATURE CATTLEYAS

❧

MOST POTTING WILL BE DONE in the spring, since this is the time when most plants start their growth. Those that make new roots as early as January and February can be potted then, and those that do not start new growth until May or June can be potted at that time. Plants make their best growth during spring and summer, and it is well to put them in fresh medium in time to take advantage of the good growing weather. Individual plants that start new growth at some other time of the year may have to

be potted accordingly. We do not like to shift a plant that has finished its active growth phase and is going into a rest period. Disturbing it at such a time will force it to sit for months without an active root system.

MATERIALS

As described in the previous chapter, various media can be used for orchid growing. The oldest, osmunda fiber, has never been excelled but is in short supply, is expensive, and requires much time and effort. It is still preferred for certain uses. Sometimes a plant that is "touchy" in bark will do well in osmunda. Also, it is useful for growing plants on driftwood, where a pad of osmunda can be wired onto a base for establishing the plant, or in a basket. It is good to have some on hand.

The barks are satisfactory and are far easier to work with. They can be used straight, or incorporated in various mixes. Plain bark comes in various grades or sizes of pieces: 0 to ¼ inch, ¼ inch, ¼ to ½ inch, ½ to ¾ inch, and chunks up to 1½ inch for special purposes. The smaller sizes are used for seedlings and small species, the larger for larger plants. The size you choose depends on your personal likes and on the conditions under which you grow your plants—the medium sizes for dry climates, for instance, and the larger for damp climates and for outdoor growing where there is high humidity and much rain.

There are several different kinds of bark. At present fir bark is most widely used. This is composed largely of white fir (*Abies concolor*) with some red fir (*Abies magnifica*) occasionally mixed with it. These come from California and are essentially alike as to characteristics. Douglas fir (*Pseudotsuga menziesii*, also known as *P. taxifolia*) comes from the Pacific Northwest. It is hard and very solid and at first more resistant to water, but eventually cannot be told from the others. Redwood bark, which is much softer and shreds easily, is often mixed with fir bark (one part redwood to three parts fir). Some growers feel that it lessens the growth of mold or fungus. It is seldom used alone.

Various mixes using bark as a base are on the market, or you can make your own. Descriptions of mixes preferred by one grower or another appear frequently in the orchid publications, and many commercial growers package their own for sale. When used for the kinds of plants specified and following directions they give good results.

In buying bark and bark mixes, be sure to get carefully prepared material. The barks used should have been screened and heat-treated to eliminate snails.

Tree fern, or "hapuu" as it is called in Hawaii, comes from many countries. It can be bought as slabs and logs on which plants can be grown directly, or made into "pots," figurines, and balls. It also comes shredded or chopped, to be used in pots just as bark is used, in grades determined by the length of the fibers. Tree fern from different areas varies sometimes in quality, some being quite hard and wiry, some softer and more pliable. The latter holds water better. The type you choose depends on personal preference, and it may take a bit of experimenting to find out which you like best. Tree fern can be mixed with bark.

Perlite, a white volcanic tuff, is often mixed with either bark or tree fern for its water- and air-holding capacity. As the mix begins to break down, perlite helps keep it open.

Inert media such as lightweight aggregates, pumice, and scoria have found favor with some growers. These should probably be given a balanced fertilizer. Any can be mixed with bark if you care to try doing it. In fact the use of these media as well as others being promoted should be on an experimental basis. Other media are coconut fiber and chopped cork bark. My own experience with the latter is that it breaks down after a year or so into a fine, claylike mass. Perhaps using charcoal or perlite with it would help prevent this.

SPHAGNUM MOSS AND THE FUNGUS DISEASE SPOROTRICHOSIS. This is a chronic infection caused by the organism *Sporothrix schenkii,* a fungus present worldwide in soil, on plants, in decaying timbers, hay, and, among other things, on ordinary sphagnum moss. It enters the body through an ordinary cut, usually on the hand, and spreads along the lymph vessels, along which its course can be traced. It produces hard nodules under the skin, which may or may not be painful, but which eventually ulcerate and drain and may persist for a long time. It can also spread throughout the body, even to the lungs; when thus widespread it is difficult to cure. The early stages can be treated with potassium iodide, under a doctor's care, of course. And, of course, a doctor should be consulted at the first sign of infection. It is advised that rubber gloves be worn when handling sphagnum, or that it not be used at all. Only an

occasional orchid grower becomes infected, but it is not uncommon among rose growers who, one would imagine, have thorn-caused wounds.

Information about New Zealand sphagnum is incomplete at present, but it is possible that it harbors other infective agents, and caution is advised.

Both kinds of sphagnum are convenient for lining baskets for hanging plants. The baskets can then be filled with bark or tree fern. New Zealand moss is good for growing seedlings and small plants. Its use may be tricky, however, and it is best to get a lesson from a grower who is successful with it.

NEED FOR REPOTTING

A plant needs to be repotted (1) when it has outgrown its pot and (2) when the potting material is no longer in good condition. The first is easier to judge, but the second is more important from the point of view of the immediate health of the plant.

OUTGROWN POT. As a plant adds successive leads these come closer to the edge of the pot. Soon the leads will grow out over the edge, and the new roots will travel down the outside to wind around the pot or go along the bench. It does no harm for one lead to extend beyond the edge, provided it maintains a nice upright position or can be tied up straight. In fact, if the potting material is in good condition, it does no actual harm to the plant if two successive leads grow out of the pot. Roots hanging in midair seem to remain healthy, but they are subject to injury when the plant is moved, and if they cling to the bench they will, of course, have to be broken off eventually. A plant should not be allowed to grow for too long a period in this manner, for subsequent leads will grow downward, flower stems will stick out horizontally, and the shape of the flowers may be impaired. It must be confessed that almost all growers have a few plants that do not get repotted when they should be. Especially is this true with plants in osmunda, with which potting is a time-consuming job. Once the plants are in bark, moving them on is easier, although even so, when one has many plants and little time, or when family emergencies prevent attending to the plants at the right time, some are inevitably skipped. As long as the medium is good, and care is given to watering and fertilizing, the plants will survive in good condition.

CONDITION OF THE MEDIUM. Potting media will remain in good condition for varying lengths of time, depending on how the plants are watered and on the relative humidity of the environment. They break down more rapidly when they are watered to excess or kept in a very humid atmosphere. Two years may be as long as most will be good under these conditions. When moderately watered, or in a dry climate, or in a greenhouse where the relative humidity is kept only moderately high, they may last for three years. Thus plants can be left longer in the same medium under these conditions, provided they are doing well and still fit their pots.

How can you tell when the medium is not in good condition? Osmunda fiber becomes soft and spongy to the touch, and if you take a plant out of the pot you will find that the fibers have disintegrated into a soft mush. In such a pot you often find good roots only in the upper half or third of the pot where they are able to get more air and remain somewhat drier than in the wet mush toward the bottom. Or you may find no good roots at all. The same situation exists when other media have broken down. The lower half will have disintegrated more thoroughly than the upper half, and the broken-down material will have compacted into a solid mass. Here again, you may find good roots only in the upper part. In order to find out how the potting medium holds up for you, check a plant or two after a year and a half. If the medium is deteriorating, you will know that you have been keeping it too wet and should therefore

cut down on the frequency of watering. Possibly, also, you have been keeping the relative humidity too high.

Seedling-grade bark breaks down faster than the coarser grades, of course.

TIME TO REPOT

BEST TIME. The best time, in fact, the ideal time, to repot a plant is just before it starts the new roots of the season, or just as these roots begin to show. The new roots come from the base of the recently matured lead. Their first sign is little swellings underneath the curved basal section (rhizome) of the lead. The bright green root tips then push out through the brown covering of the rhizome. The root tips are very tender and are easily broken. By the time they have reached a length of half an inch it is difficult to repot a plant without injuring them. When a root tip is broken, the root ceases to grow from that point. Older roots will form branch roots behind the tip if the tip is broken, but the very new ones may simply stop growing for the season. At the time the new roots make their appearance, the older roots undergo a wave of activity that causes them to branch, and you can then see new root tips all through the medium. There is a real advantage in potting a plant just when this activity starts so as to let the new roots and branch roots grow into fresh medium (Fig. 5–1).

Figure 5–1 LEFT: *New roots too long to be handled without damage. Better to pot just as roots are starting or else wait until they are five or six inches long and capable of branching.*

RIGHT: *Plant that was potted just as new roots were starting, allowing them to grow immediately into fresh medium.*

NEXT-BEST TIME TO REPOT. If the new roots develop before you can take care of a plant, wait until they have grown to a length of five or six inches rather than risk breaking them. They are then old enough to form branch roots themselves. The older roots are still actively branching and if any of them are injured in the potting process they will form additional branches. Potting a plant at this time interrupts its growth for a few weeks, necessitating a period of recovery, and is therefore not as ideal a time as that given above. But it does offer a second chance to take care of plants you miss when the roots are first starting. Some species and hybrids habitually form new roots just when the flower buds are developing in the sheath. To prevent any setback to the flowers, such plants can be handled at this "next-best" time.

A hybrid that flowers two or more times a year will probably start growth cycles at various times of the year. Some may start a new set of growths before the last have flowered. Try to repot such plants during the spring or summer, catching them when they are forming a new set of roots.

PROBLEM PLANTS. An occasional plant may show signs of deterioration while its neighbors are in perfectly good health. If there is no disease involved (see Chapter 21), the cause is almost certain to be root loss, for which two possible reasons are over-watering and snail damage. More and more we have found the latter to be the cause of what seemed a mysterious cessation of root activity, with the roots still alive but blunted and crooked. The snails may have done their work and moved on to another plant, so that none, or perhaps only one or two, can be found. Since the roots are already inactive, whether from over-watering or damage by snails, and since you have the plant out of the pot, you might as well put it in fresh medium. This is particularly easy when the plant is in bark or a mix. Often a plant will make a remarkable recovery. Sections of roots that are still alive sometimes respond quite quickly with branch roots. An interesting phenomenon takes place when a plant with absolutely no roots starts a new lead. Ordinarily roots are formed only by a mature lead, but when no roots are present to support the young developing lead, it will often start its own set when it is still very small, barely an inch or two in length. The first new growths from plants that have been badly set back because of root loss may not be large enough to flower. But at least you will have rescued them from a bad situation and put them on the road to recovery.

TOOLS AND POTTING AREA

A sharp, long-bladed knife, scissors, pruning shears, and a metal potting stick are about the only tools needed. *All of these should be sterilized between plants as described earlier.*

Used pots should be washed, and then soaked in 10 percent Clorox (one part Clorox to nine of water) for at least ten minutes, and then be rinsed in several changes of water until no odor of chlorine remains. Clay pots will hold chlorine longer and should therefore be rinsed more than plastic ones, and left to air out for several days. Rinse them again just before use.

A plant to be potted must not come in contact with debris from other plants. A good method is to cover the potting area with paper. When you finish with a plant gather up all the debris in the paper and put it in a trash can, spreading fresh paper for the next one.

HOW AND WHEN TO DIVIDE PLANTS

Each pseudobulb with its individual basal part, that is, its section of rhizome, is potentially an individual plant. It makes its own set of roots, and gives rise to new leads from buds at the joints of the rhizome. If a plant is cut up into individual pseudobulbs, however, the new growths from them will be small, almost like those of young seedlings, and some may not grow. It may take several years for a one-bulb division to become a flowering plant. A new growth, if it is to be of flowering size, requires the support of several pseudobulbs behind it. For this reason, divisions are made in groups of connected pseudobulbs, three or four in a clump if possible.

Not all of the buds along the joints of the rhizome will develop into leads. Many remain dormant throughout the life of the plant, a sort of safety factor. The buds most likely to grow into new leads are the two located at the juncture of the pseudobulb with the rhizome, one on each side (Fig. 5–2). Sometimes a plant activates only one bud at a time from the base of each recently matured lead. This we call a one-lead plant. It grows along in a straight line, its pseudobulbs marching across the surface of the potting medium in single file. Sometimes, a plant will break two buds, causing a fork in its growth line, each of which then continues to give a new lead each year—a two-lead

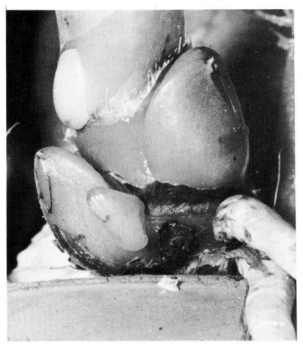

Figure 5–2 *Nature's safety factor. The base of a lead is shown. Covering tissues have been removed to show the buds, one at each joint. Usually one or two buds become activated and will develop into leads. Here two have enlarged and are growing. The small buds remain dormant, possibly to develop later or when the plant is divided. If the leads should suffer a catastrophe, one or the other of the dormant buds will become active. Note, also, roots growing from the base of the lead.*

plant (Fig. 5–3). If one of the forks breaks two buds concurrently, the plant will then have three growing ends. Some individuals grow so lustily that they break two buds from almost every pseudo-bulb, and quickly develop into plants with six, eight, or ten or more leads.

The decision whether to divide a plant depends partly on its habit, and partly on its size. A plant that consistently gives but one lead a year should definitely be divided when it has made enough pseudobulbs to give two strong divisions. This would be when seven or eight pseudobulbs had been formed, allowing for a lead division of four pseudobulbs and a backbulb division of three or four. Removing the growing end will stimulate one of the dormant buds on the back part to develop, so that you will have two plants. The lead division should flower on its next growth; the backbulb division, being not quite so vigorous, may take two years to flower.

Some growers like to anticipate the division of a one-lead plant by encouraging a bud on the back

part to break and develop into a good growth ahead of time. This can be done by notching the rhizome (cutting it halfway through) between about the third and fourth pseudobulb. Do this some time before new growth starts at the front end, so that hopefully the two will begin at the same time. Thus both will be in the same stage for repotting.

Interestingly enough, an occasional plant retains the habit of giving but one lead a year from the time it is a seedling until it is divided. The stimulus of division may cause two or three buds to break simultaneously on one or the other half, so that from that time onward that division becomes a plant with several leads (Fig. 5–4).

A plant with two or more leads may not require a pot any larger than a one-lead plant, and for the same amount of space will give you double or treble the number of flowers. So if you have a plant with several leads, and it is compact and growing in an orderly fashion, it would probably pay not to divide it. Such a plant can be moved along into a larger pot, perhaps removing only the backbulbs, and may become a very fine specimen. It is more thrilling to have a huge plant covered with flowers than to have several small ones with a few flowers each. Eventually, a plant becomes too large to handle conveniently, and then will have to be divided. You will have the choice of breaking it up into a number of smaller plants and waiting while some of these regain specimen size or of making two or three large divisions.

The accompanying diagrams (Fig. 5–5), give some types and suggestions. A shows a one-lead plant that should be divided. B shows a plant with two leads that also should be divided. The plant is

Figure 5–3 *Two leads developing from buds situated as in Figure 5–2.*

growing in two definite lines, but each line has produced only one lead since the original break that caused it to fork. Dividing it may stimulate it to make more leads at a time. Each growth line can be separated at the point where it forked from the original part of the plant. The group of back-bulbs can be potted if they are still plump and have some leaves, or be discarded if they are no longer vigorous. You will probably want to keep them if the plant is valuable, and in time they will make a third flowering plant.

C shows a two-lead plant from which the back-bulbs can be removed. Make the cut just behind the pseudobulb that gave rise to the two leads, so that they remain connected. The backbulbs are probably more vigorous in this plant than they are in A and B because they are younger. D shows a three-lead plant that should be divided in the same manner as the two-lead plant just described, keeping the three leads together and removing the backbulbs.

E shows a plant that has branched and re-branched, offering an opportunity either to keep it as a unit, removing just the backbulbs, or of making two or three divisions. The dotted lines show where it might be cut to make three plants, the solid line where it should be cut to make two divisions. F shows a similar plant that has made even more leads, each growing end making two leads a

Figure 5–4 A: *A plant that is growing in two distinct lines. Each half has two or more leads. This plant should be divided in the center, and probably each half kept intact.*
B: *A plant with several leads on the front half. Divisions should consist of the front half, to be carried on intact, and a back half, which will probably give several new growths.*
C: *A compact plant with five leads in a seven-inch pot. Such plants give many flowers in little space.*

Figure 5–5 RIGHT: *Diagrams showing how to divide plants. In each one the oldest pseudobulb is shown as solid black.*

A. ONE-LEAD PLANT. DIVIDE AT LINE.

B. TWO-LEAD PLANT. DIVIDE AT LINES, MAKING TWO FRONT SECTIONS.

C. TWO LEADS KEEP TOGETHER AS ONE SECTION.

D. THREE LEADS KEEP TOGETHER AS ONE SECTION.

E. PLANT THAT CAN BE KEPT AS UNIT, REMOVING ONLY BACK BULBS, OR BE DIVIDED INTO TWO OR THREE PARTS.

F. PLANT THAT SHOULD BE KEPT AS A UNIT.

year. This plant surely should be kept as a unit as long as possible, for it is a beautifully symmetrical specimen.

Diagrams cannot possibly include all of the shapes your plants can take. Some will make all of their growth forward, producing a plant heavy with leads on one side of the pot and practically nothing on the other side. Then there are those whose many leads cross over each other or force each other up in the air, offering a real challenge when it comes to dividing them. Each plant has to be dealt with according to its own needs. You can make a neater plant in some cases by removing one or two crowded leads with their connected pseudobulbs, leaving the rest of the plant intact. Also, a plant may send one lead over the edge, keeping the others neatly within the pot. The overhanging section can be clipped off and potted separately, leaving the rest of the plant undisturbed for another year or so. Its removal will stimulate into growth a bud behind the cut, so that a new lead will develop at that point on the old plant.

POTTING IN BARK AND MIXES

Choose a pot that will accommodate about two years' growth. For a plant that makes one lead a year, or one set of leads, judge the size needed by the distance between the pseudobulbs, estimating how much larger the plant will be with two years' growth added. For a plant that makes two or more sets of growths a year, the pot will have to be relatively larger. Ordinarily, a plant of four pseudobulbs that makes one growth a year will require a six-inch pot. A two- or three-lead plant that makes two or three growths a year should go into a seven- or eight-inch pot. Growers are cautioned not to put a small plant in a large pot because the medium stays wet longer in the center where the roots of the small plant are concentrated. Also, putting a plant in a larger pot than it needs is purely a waste of material and space. You must therefore judge the size of the pots according to your own observations of how the plants do for you. If they outgrow their pots before the two years are up, next time use a larger size.

We like to dampen the medium before using it. It seems to make it easier to settle it in the pot and around the roots. Some growers use bark dry, just as it comes from the bag, so you may take your choice.

To remove a plant for repotting, first soak it in a bucket of water or water it thoroughly to loosen the roots that cling to the pot. It can then usually be knocked out of the pot quite easily. With your fingers, work the roots clinging to the outside loose, then turn the pot upside-down and, holding the plant with one hand, tap the rim on the bench. The plant should drop down into your hand. If it does not come out this way, run a knife around inside the pot to separate the roots that cling stubbornly to it. You may also have to do this with the roots on the outside.

Much of the old medium will fall away as you shake the plant a bit and gently move the roots apart. Run the hose through the roots to remove as much of the remaining material as will come free, but do not try to pull away those pieces that cling tenaciously to the roots. Look for evidence of slug and snail injury. Decayed roots should be cut back to healthy tissue, or removed entirely if completely rotted. The healthy roots need not be cut back if their shape and length will allow them to be put into the new pot without being broken. Roots that have grown on the surface can be left on the surface. Any that have grown outside of the pot, and which would be broken in repotting, should be trimmed back to a stub of three or four inches in length. Cut off any shrivelled pseudobulbs (backbulbs) by severing the rhizome.

Pull off the old tissuelike sheathing leaves that cover the pseudobulbs. Do not remove the coverings from the rhizome unless they are particularly dry and loose, lest you injure dormant buds. Leave the covering on the young pseudobulbs. As you clean off the old tissue, look for scale insects which have a habit of hiding under it. The young scale insect is free moving, and crawls around until it finds a sheltered spot, then it settles down, sticks its proboscis into the plant tissues, covers itself with a dome of hard material, and remains permanently. Eggs are laid under the shell, and, as the young hatch, they move out and find a new location. Clusters of scales with whitish or brownish shells may be found in protected places, along the grooves and joints of the pseudobulbs and at the juncture of leaf and pseudobulb. We do not see as much scale as we used to. In fact, it rarely occurs in greenhouses that are sprayed regularly with Malathion. But it can occur, especially on old plants that you may have acquired from neglected collections. If you find scale, scrub it off with a soft toothbrush dipped in an insecticide, and then dip the whole plant in the same solution. If you do not find scale, it is not necessary to scrub or dip the plant.

Decide whether to divide the plant, and how best to do it, and cut through the rhizome. Put a label on each division. If snail and slug damage is present, dust the roots with metaldehyde powder or dip them in a metaldehyde solution. You are now ready to pot (Fig. 5–6). Choose a pot of appropriate size and shape. The three-quarter height pot is excellent in the larger diameters.

Put a generous layer of drainage material in the bottom. This can be gravel, broken clay pot, or styrofoam "peanuts." With one hand hold the plant in the pot so that the rhizome comes about half an inch below the rim and the back end touches one side, giving room at the other end for new growths. With the other hand pour handfuls of the medium in around the roots, filling it among them with your fingers. When the pot is about two-thirds full, thump the pot on the bench or tap the sides of the pot sharply with a potting stick to settle the medium, still holding the plant in position with one hand. Then add more medium up to the rim, thump the pot again to settle it, and then with your fingers or the blunt end of a potting stick press it down firmly around the inside of the pot. The rhizome should lie in a trench on the surface, with the medium lapping up against its sides and the upper surface exposed.

If the plant does not have many roots to hold it in place, place a piece of stiff wire cut a little longer than the inside diameter of the pot across the rhizome and wedge its ends against the sides of the pot. Clip a stake to the side of the pot, or drive one into the center and tie the pseudobulbs to it.

POTTING IN OSMUNDA FIBER

When moving plants from osmunda fiber to other media, one has a choice of methods. Some growers like to leave a chunk of fiber under the front end of the plant to provide something to help anchor the plant and to leave the roots of the younger part somewhat undisturbed. Other growers, including myself, prefer to remove practically all of the osmunda fiber. It does not hurt to leave a few shreds clinging to roots here and there, if by so doing you can prevent breaking the roots, but a large chunk of fiber holds water longer than the surrounding medium and creates a "wet spot" in the pot. If the plants are repotted when new roots are just forming, or when the roots are actively

branching, the plants will become reestablished rapidly.

When moving a plant into fresh osmunda, remove the plant from the pot as described above and follow the steps in Figure 5–7. Remove the fiber from the core and from the back part. Study the plant to see whether to divide it, and where to make the cuts. Now ease apart the sections of the plant. Try to leave a firm chunk of fiber under each growing end, with as many roots intact as possible. Remove the rest of the old fiber from each part. Cut off any decayed roots, and cut back any healthy ones (except those in the solid ball) to a four-inch stub. Remove the old tissue from the pseudobulbs, and treat for scale or slug and snail injury if these are found.

Prepare the fresh osmunda fiber by soaking it in water, wringing it out thoroughly, and letting it drain until it is no longer dripping, just damp. With a hatchet, chop the pieces into chunks about three inches wide depending on the size of pot to be used. Fill a clay pot to about one quarter its depth with crock, and lay a piece of fiber over the crock.

Take the plant in your hand and place chunks of fiber under the rhizome and between the root stubs to form a good ball. Set the plant with its ball of fiber in the pot, pressing the back end of the plant tightly against the back of the pot. With one hand squeezing the ball of fiber against the pot, push in additional chunks at the front and sides, between the fiber that is already in place and the side of the pot. The chunks should be inserted vertically. Do not build up layers of fiber on top of each other, but instead add them as you would add books at the end of an already crowded bookshelf. Osmunda fiber requires pressure from the sides to hold it in place. When you have put as much fiber in the pot as you can push in with your hands, lay a chunk on its side on the rim of the pot and force it in with a potting stick, pushing one edge down into the pot to bring it vertically alongside the rest, and always maneuvering the potting stick down and toward the center of the pot. Do not let the rhizome of the plant hump up. If it does this, pull out one or two pieces of fiber, settle it down, and start again. The rhizome should lie in a groove on the surface of the fiber with its lower surface in the fiber and its upper surface exposed. Mature plants should be potted "hard," that is, the fiber should have about the consistency of sod. If you can push your fingers between the pot and the fiber easily, it is not hard enough. Add more fiber to tighten it up. Drive a steel stake into the center of the pot, and tie the plant to it.

Figure 5–6 *Potting in bark.*
A: *A one-lead plant that will be divided. Growth has reached edge of pot. New roots are just starting at base of lead.*
B: *Remove plant from pot. Cut through rhizome to make a "lead" division of four pseudobulbs.*
C: *The plant divided. Ease the sections apart. Trim back any roots broken in the process and cut off any dead roots. Shake off most of old bark.*
D: *Pot has been prepared with several pieces of crock in bottom and enough bark to hold plant at right level.*

Place plant in pot with older end against one side. Scoop bark into pot, thumping it at intervals to settle it.
E: *Fill pot, thump again, and press bark down around edges with thumbs for extra firming. Note that rhizome is in a trench on surface, with bark lying against sides and top part exposed. Level of bark is one-half inch below rim.*
F: *Attach stake to rim to give plant rigid support. (There are several types made to use with bark.)*
G: *Tie each pseudobulb to stake. Use a "sling" of string, making tie at stake.*

Figure 5–7 *Potting in osmunda fiber.*

A: *A two-lead plant to be divided.*

B: *After removing oldest few backbulbs, plant is divided where it forked into two leads.*

C: *The front divisions. Each must be trimmed up.*

D: *Prepare osmunda by chopping into chunks.*

E: *A division ready for potting. Roots have been trimmed back so that stubs remain in a solid ball of fiber.*

F: *Pot has been prepared by filling it one-fourth full of crock and adding enough fiber to hold plant at desired level. Set division in place, with older end at side of pot. Place a large notched chunk of fiber under the lead.*

G: *Press fiber back with your hands and insert additional pieces vertically, until no more can be put in by hand.*

H: *Work in more fiber with a potting stick. Place a chunk on edge of pot, catch it in middle with stick, and force stick down and toward center of pot. Continue until fiber is uniformly hard.*

I: *Stake and tie the plant.*

CARE AFTER POTTING

All roots bruised or broken in the potting process, even those not visibly damaged, are vulnerable to rot if they are kept wet. They heal nicely if they are allowed to dry out and remain dry for several weeks. For this reason we let the potting medium go without water until we see the new roots developing. The barks dry more quickly than osmunda fiber, but the latter, even though it is damp when used, will dry in a few days. During the period of root recovery it is necessary to protect the plants from water loss through the leaves and pseudobulbs. We give them a little extra shade and a light mist spray twice a day on bright days. Just swish the sprayer over the plants to dampen the pseudobulbs and leaves. A bit of the spray will also dampen the rhizome and the merest surface of the potting medium. This will encourage new roots to form. As the root tips become visible throughout the medium, give light waterings for a while, not enough to soak clear through, then as the roots develop further increase the depth of the watering. When the roots are growing vigorously, remove the extra shade and put the plants on a regular watering and fertilizing schedule.

SPECIAL NOTES

Sometimes shortly after it has first been wetted, osmunda fiber develops a little fuzzy white mold. This is not dangerous to the plants. It disappears as the fiber dries out and does not come back. We do not know what it is—nor does it always appear. Just ignore it.

A system that is beneficial to newly potted plants is foliar feeding—adding a fertilizer (one-half teaspoon per gallon) to the water with which you mist the foliage. The leaves will take up only a small amount of the chemicals but the plants will thus receive a little boost until their roots are again active.

Backbulbs can be encouraged to start new growth by being enclosed in a polyethylene bag. Put some damp medium in the bag, set the backbulbs in it, and close the bag tightly. In time a bud may start growth. When this new lead has roots starting, remove from the bag and pot as you would any division.

Sometimes a newly collected plant, or a division, or a side-shoot removed from a monopodal plant, is reluctant to make roots. A rooting hormone, such as the product *Rootone*, can stimulate roots to form. *Rootone F*, which contains a fungicide, is good. Mix a small amount of the powder with lanolin, obtainable from a drugstore, or vaseline, and smear it on the base of the plant or on a pseudobulb or stem near its base. The hormone will be absorbed and be translocated to the rooting area.

Many orchids can be grown on mounts of various kinds—cork oak bark, tree fern, hardwood branches—and cattleyas are also amenable to such culture. This will be described farther along.

·6·

CONTROL OF FLOWERING IN CATTLEYAS

❧

IN THEIR NATIVE HABITAT, CATtleyas enjoy more uniform daylengths and smaller seasonal temperature fluctuations than can be found outside of the tropics. Yet small changes in daylength and temperature are apparently critical for their flowering in their native jungles. These species exhibit their sensitivity to daylength and temperature in various ways when grown in a greenhouse. Our greater seasonal differences in daylength are imposed upon their inherent flowering habits, and the temperatures we maintain in our greenhouses may influence their response to daylength.

Important to the understanding of their flowering habits is a knowledge of when and under what conditions flower buds are "initiated" and what conditions bring about the subsequent growth of the flower buds. Initiation of flower buds means the laying down of the flower parts in microscopic size by the meristematic tissue at the tip of the pseudobulb. The buds are not visible in the sheath at this time, in fact, in some species several months elapse between the initiation of the buds and the time they can be seen growing in the sheath. Since our daylength is constantly changing from shorter to longer, or longer to shorter, each species has to find a specific daylength compatible with its inherent habit and the stage of development of its pseudobulbs for the initiation of flower buds. The daylength that prevails during the period after initiation, and the temperatures of the season or in the greenhouse, may or may not be conducive to their further development. Thus, after initiating their buds, some species can develop them immediately, while others must wait for several months after initiation for the proper set of conditions to occur that will cause these buds to resume growth. *With cattleyas (and other orchids as well) we must deal with two sets of conditions—one that causes initiation of buds and another that brings them into active growth.* Once the buds have been put into active growth so that they are elongating rapidly, they will continue to grow regardless of the length of the days.

The sensitivity to daylength of many garden and house plants, and control of their flowering by manipulation of daylength, has been known for many years. Plants such as chrysanthemum and aster initiate flower buds and develop them immediately following initiation. The conditions that bring about initiation also bring about flowering. Thus when we speak of daylength in connection with their flowering, we mean the daylength necessary for the whole process from bud formation to the opening of flowers. Some are "short-day" plants, which initiate buds and produce flowers when the days are less than thirteen hours long (some require days less than twelve hours, and a few respond on a fourteen-hour day); "long-day" plants, which initiate flower buds and produce flowers when the days are longer than thirteen or fourteen hours; and "day-neutral" plants, which flower regardless of the daylength. Chrysanthemums and asters are typical short-day plants. They can be brought into flower at any time of the year by controlling the length of day—by giving them long days by means of electric lights until it is desired to have them start the flowering process, then short days to bring about bud formation and blooming. Calceolaria and scabiosa are examples of long-day plants. Their flowering can be brought about in midwinter by giving them artificially lengthened days. Night temperature can alter the flowering of many kinds. For instance, foxglove does not flower when grown continually with night temperatures of 55° to 60°; it will flower only after a period of nights of 40° to 50°. Stocks flower during the winter at a night temperature of 50° but not at 60°. Temperature can even change the response of a plant to daylength. Poinsettia will flower with short days when grown at night temperatures of 63° to 64°, but it becomes a long-day plant with nights at 55°.

Comparison of a few *Cattleya* species on which work has been done will illustrate the role of both daylength and temperature on their bud initiation and flowering. The following table gives the normal dates of flower bud initiation at Ithaca, New York, as discovered by Gavino Rotor from microscopic studies of the tips of pseudobulbs. The plants were growing in normal seasonal daylengths and temperatures. These species and some other kinds of orchids were then grown experimentally under continuously short and continuously long days, at continuous night temperatures of 55° and 65°, and compared to groups grown normally. The short days were held at nine hours in length by covering the plants with black cloth when the normal daylength exceeded this, and long days were kept at sixteen hours by using artificial lighting.

Normal dates of bud initiation under greenhouse conditions in Ithaca, New York*

	1949	1950
Cattleya		
gaskelliana		March 1
C. labiata	June 25	June 25
C. percivaliana...	September 3	September 1
C. trianaei	September 3	September 15
C. mossiae	November 15	November 1

*Bulletin #885, Cornell University Agricultural Experiment Station, "Daylength and Temperature in Relation to Growth and Flowering of Orchids," Gavino B. Rotor, Jr.

When *C. gigas* (*C. warscewiczii*) (similar to *C. gaskelliana* in the table) is grown with a night temperature of 55° and normal daylength, it initiates its buds during the short days of late February and early March. The daylength of the following weeks is conducive to the further development of the buds, and they grow rapidly and come into flower before the pseudobulb is fully mature. The buds are thus initiated and begin development during the short days of spring. If, instead of 55° nights, *C. gigas* is grown continuously with nights of 65°, it will not flower. If the plants are grown with continuous sixteen-hour days and either 55° or 65° nights, they generally fail to flower. From the point of view of both flower bud initiation and triggering the buds into growth, *C. gigas* is a short-day plant. Even though it completes its flowering during the long days of June and July, the significant daylength is that which causes the buds to begin growing up in the sheath. Once the buds have started this growth they will continue regardless of the daylength.

C. trianaei normally initiates its flower buds in mid-September when the days are short and waits until the even shorter days of November to start the buds growing up in the sheath. Temperature is not critical in its case, for it will initiate and develop its flowers with either 55° or 65° nights. The daylength is critical, however, for flowering is entirely prevented by continuous days of sixteen hours at either night temperature. *C. trianaei* is, therefore, another short-day plant.

C. mossiae initiates its buds during the short days about November 1, at a night temperature of 55°, and waits through December and part of January to start the buds growing up in the sheath. Continuous long days entirely prevent flowering. In work done on *C. mossiae*, it appeared that this species would initiate some buds with 65° nights and short days, but the flowering was delayed and spread erratically over a number of months. Experience in growing *C. mossiae* has shown that its best and most reliable flowering comes when it has at least two months of short days with nights of 55° to initiate the buds and start them growing in the sheath. Here, therefore, is another short-day species.

C. labiata, under normal seasonal conditions, initiates flower buds during the longest days of the year, close to June 21. The long days and warm nights that usually prevail through the summer prevent these buds from going ahead and developing, and this species waits until the shorter days and cooler nights of fall to resume growth of the buds and bring them into bloom. Experiments with *C. labiata* turned up some remarkable interrelationships between temperature and daylength. When it was grown with continuous long days and nights of 65°, it was entirely prevented from blooming (although we would expect from the above information that flower buds had been initiated). Grown with continuous long days but with nights of 55°, some plants flowered, though not all. A night temperature of 55° is apparently capable of somewhat offsetting the influence of long days. Grown with continuous short days and 65° nights, about half the plants flowered; better flowering was obtained with short days and 55° nights. As a matter of interest, when we sort out this data, we find the following to be true: (1) as far as flower bud initiation is concerned, *C. labiata* is day-neutral, for it initiates buds with either long or short days, regardless of night temperature; (2) at night temperatures of 55° it is day-neutral for it can both initiate and develop flower buds at this temperature with either daylength; (3) with 65° nights it is a short-day plant as far as growth of the buds and blooming is concerned; (4) the only combination that entirely prevents the growth of the buds and therefore prevents flowering is long days plus 65° nights; (5) growth of the flower buds resulting in flowering requires either 55° nights, or short days, or both.

Not enough work has been done on other species of *Cattleya*. We can only speculate about the habits of those not actually studied. But if we were to speculate on the basis of what we know of those that have been described and from the flowering times of others, we might guess that the kinds that flower in winter, spring, and early summer are all short-day plants. Where fall flowering is concerned, we would not know whether the plants follow the habits of *C. labiata*, or whether they have a pattern of their own. There are many *Cattleya* species, some quite unfamiliar and little grown. We do not know what any of these would show under experimental conditions. So far, the only patterns discovered are "short day" and "day neutral."

Hybrids inherit their growth and flowering patterns from their ancestors. Some members of a cross may inherit the pattern of one of the species in their makeup, others that of a different species. There are hybrids, however, that make several growths a year, and flower whenever a growth matures. We had a cross in which a number of flowering patterns appeared. There are individual plants that always flower in the spring, others always in the fall, and still others always in the winter. There are some that flower regularly twice a year, both in the spring and in the fall. All of these we would call short-day plants. In this same cross there are some individuals that flower three or four times a year, and which, through a period of several years, have hit nearly every month in the year. We have not studied their actual bud initiation, but we feel it would be safe to say that these individuals are day neutral.

Control of flowering has been worked out very exactly for *C. labiata* and its hybrids. *C. labiata* contributes its habits of bud initiation and flower development to its progeny. The more labiata there is in a hybrid, or the more recently it has been introduced into the strain, the more exactly can its flowering be controlled. The flowering of these hybrids can be timed for any date desired. Flowering has been prevented experimentally for as long as two years and the plants then brought into flower. Hybridists have created crosses especially for the control of flowering and greater success will be had in using them. This does not mean that you should not try control on any labiata hybrids you may now have.

Essentially, the method of control is to give the plants long days and a night temperature of 65° to retard flowering until it is desired to have the buds start to grow up in the sheath (Fig. 6–1). Then, give them the short days that will bring about blooming (Fig. 6–2). It has been found that complete control is had by starting the long-day, 65°-night treatment in June. You might wonder why it must be begun so early, since these plants normally do not flower until fall. As a group, these hybrids flower from September through November. Without studying each plant individually, there is no way to know exactly when the flower buds start to grow up in the sheath. If exact control is desired, it is best to keep the night temperature at 65° by means of thermostatically controlled heating; otherwise, a cool spell of weather might trigger some plants into starting the flower buds up in the sheath, thus bringing them into bloom ahead of the date you wish. Also, since the days begin to shorten after June 21 and we do not know just what the critical daylength is for the start of the flower bud growth, after this date the days are held to sixteen hours by means of electric lights. It takes about two months, more or less (you would have to time this for your own plants), for the flower buds to grow up in the sheath and be ready to

Figure 6–1 *Arrangement of lights for long-day treatment.*

open, so the long days and 65° nights are continued until about two months before the crop of flowers is desired. Day temperature during the long-day treatment is run ten degrees higher, around 75°. Suppose you want to have the flowers for the Christmas holidays. The long-day treatment is continued until the middle of October, at which time the plants are allowed to experience the normally short days of the fall season. The night temperature can now be dropped to the usual 55° to 60° range, although the buds will come along a little faster if 65° nights are continued. If you wish to have the flowers for Easter, you continue the long-day treatment until approximately two months before Easter, and then give short days. However, if you want flowers for June, the time for starting short days is April 1. Because the days are becoming longer at this time, you will have to shorten the daylight hours by covering the plants with black cloth from five o'clock in the evening to eight o'clock in the morning.

For merely prolonging the daylight hours, the light intensity does not have to be high. The lights should be of the incandescent type. Forty- to sixty-watt bulbs, placed in reflectors two to three feet above the plants and at intervals of about eight feet, will be sufficient to withhold flowering. They are turned on at sundown and kept on long enough to give a total of sixteen hours of light. In a greenhouse where other plants are grown, you must be careful to enclose the group of plants being lighted so as not to affect the flowering of other things. During the period of high night temperatures and long days, the plants should be given regular applications of fertilizer, and they must have as good sunlight as possible during the day, short of burning. Watering should be watched carefully to conform to what the plants actually need, so that they become neither dehydrated nor too soft. For shortening the days artificially, it is necessary to build a framework over which black cloth can be drawn every night, and the cloth must be lightproof.

From the time the buds show in the sheath, the length of time to bloom can be somewhat regulated by temperature. If the night temperature is 50° or 55°, the flowers will take about two weeks

Figure 6–2 *Black cloth for short-day treatment. The cloth is arranged on a framework so that it can be pulled* *over the plants to cut out the light or drawn back to admit light.*

longer to develop than when it is held to 65°. If the night temperature is pushed to 70°, development time can be reduced by a week or two. This can be useful if for some reason you find that you are going to miss the date for which you have planned. If the buds are farther along than they should be at a certain time, you can hold them back a week or two by dropping the night temperature. We do not advocate a 70° night temperature for anything but an emergency, but if it is a matter of meeting a certain date or losing the income from a crop of flowers, it would be worth raising the night temperature to 70° for the short time necessary.

A number of growers are producing two sets of flowers a year from the labiata hybrids. They have found that by using higher light intensities to prolong the days, they can stimulate plant growth so much that the year's cycle can be telescoped into six months. They use 100- to 150-watt bulbs, spaced about six feet apart and two to three feet above the plants. They maintain nights at 65° and days at 80° to 85°. Extremely good air circulation

is necessary because of the heat from the lights. Careful attention must also be given to the humidity, watering, and fertilizing. The long-day treatment is given from June to the middle of October, and the naturally short days from then on will bring on the flowers for the Christmas holidays. As soon as the flowers are cut, or by the first of January, the plants are put under long days again. The long days and 65° nights speed up the growth that normally starts at this time of the year. About the first of April, the plants are given short days, and the flowers are ready to cut by June. As soon as this crop is cut, the long-day treatment is started again, the plants now start another new growth, and the flowers can again be timed for Christmas.

It is a problem for an amateur with one greenhouse and a mixed collection of orchids to do much about temperature control of flowering. Keeping a high night temperature for much of the fall and winter to control labiata hybrids prevents many other kinds from flowering. Many amateurs have experienced difficulty in preventing light leaks when giving the long-day treatment, and if enough light reaches other plants it may prevent the flowering of some of them. To attempt the control of more than one kind of cattleya presents additional problems. If you are giving labiata hybrids long days and 65° nights, and then must give mossiae hybrids short days and 55° nights, you can see how the troubles would multiply. About the only way an amateur can do much with controlling flowering is to have two greenhouses, one maintained at 55° and the other at 65° at night. In each greenhouse there can be lights installed and a framework for cloth. Groups of plants would then be moved from one situation to another as their schedule demanded. In the 55° house you could grow a few of the intermediate kinds of orchids, and in the 65° house perhaps a few of the warm kinds, so as to have more variety than just two or three types of cattleya hybrids.

We cannot give you much in the way of schedules for types other than the labiata hybrids. Most commercial growers have found it easier to handle just these, since they comprise a wonderful array of richly colored flowers and can be managed so exactly. But if you have a large number of plants that flower regularly in the winter or spring, you might use what has been given earlier in this section as a basis for some experiments. It seems to be difficult to do much about controlling the kinds that, like C. gigas, start their growth in the winter and bloom on this young growth in early summer. At best they can be speeded a bit into flowering by extending the normal daylength in gradual stages, starting after the buds are well up in the sheath. Midwinter-blooming kinds can (if they are amenable to the treatment) be brought into bloom early,

say for Christmas, by giving them short days starting in September. Timing of these must include a period for bud initiation, which means adding a few weeks to the usual two-month period. These midwinter-blooming kinds are usually prevented from flowering by long days, so to delay their flowering until spring means giving them long days until about three months before you want to have them in bloom. Kinds that make up their growth in the fall and do not flower until spring do not offer much chance of control. The short days of November and December do not normally trigger the flower buds into growth, yet many of them require this period of short days and 55° nights in order to bloom at all. Their flowering can be brought about a little earlier than usual, say for Easter rather than in June, by giving the plants long days and 65° nights *after* the buds are well up in the sheath.

Remember that kinds other than labiata hybrids have not been much worked with. We do not know just what influence the various species have on their hybrids. Hybrids of complicated ancestry may have six or a dozen species in their makeup, often more. The fact that a certain hybrid had C. mossiae in it does not mean that it will behave like C. mossiae. As a matter of fact, it may behave more like some other ancestor whose habits have not been studied. We do know that most of the *Cattleya* species and hybrids grow well and flower faithfully with the normal daylengths of the seasons and with a night temperature range of 55° to 60°. An amateur who has a mixed collection of cattleyas and others can have something in bloom most of the time by choosing plants for their natural flowering period.

·7·

GENETICS AND THE BREEDING OF HYBRIDS

IN 1852, ORCHIDS WERE STILL new to Europeans. People were busy just learning to know and grow them. The possibilities of hybridization were apparently unthought of until a surgeon saw how it could be done and suggested it to an orchid grower. The surgeon was Dr. Harris of Exeter, and the grower was Mr. J. Dominy, foreman of the firm of Veitch and Sons. In 1852, with Dr. Harris' help, Mr. Dominy performed the first hand pollination, and in 1856 the first hybrid orchid flowered—*Calanthe* Dominyi

(*Calanthe masuca* × *Calanthe furcata*). Mr. Dominy worked for twenty years, and produced about twenty-five hybrids. The first cattleya hybrid to be awarded was *C.* Brabantiae (*C. aclandiae* × *C. loddigesii*), given the silver Banksian medal by the Royal Horticultural Society in London in 1863. The first bigeneric hybrid was also made by Mr. Dominy in 1863, *Laeliocattleya* Exoniensis (*C. mossiae* × *Laelia crispa*).

The exciting note injected into orchid growing by Dr. Harris had a powerful reaction. The best of the newly produced hybrids created a sensation at exhibitions. Old orchid books are full of glowing accounts of the new marvels, and predict wonderful things to come. Mr. Dominy worked alone in the field for most of the twenty years, for it was not until 1871 that a hybrid was produced by someone else. No one at that time could have foreseen the future extent of hybridization. In 1890, 200 crosses were registered. Now there are thousands, and the number grows each year.

Most of the best hybrids have been made by experienced growers, but amateurs have had a hand in hybridization, too. Success on both sides was largely a matter of chance, and indeed still is. Curiosity, plus the desire to create something unusual, prompted nearly everyone to cross whatever orchids he had at hand, in the hope that he would achieve some striking result. Many of the crosses made between hybrids of doubtful quality have not been wise and have only cluttered the lists. Crosses between species have always been valuable for the tremendous amount of knowledge they have given us, and crosses between genera have contributed even more. All such crosses are the result of the burning curiosity possessed by human beings—the desire to see "what would happen if ———." The early growers tried all sorts of things. During the first fifty years of hybridization, from 1856 to 1906, crosses were made in many genera, including *Cattleya, Calanthe, Dendrobium, Aerides, Paphiopedilum, Cymbidium, Lycaste, Zygopetalum, Miltonia, Odontoglossum, Stanhopea, Vanda, Epidendrum, Laelia, Phaius*, and many others. At least fourteen bi- and tri-generic hybrids were created, including combinations between genera of the cattleya alliance, as well as such things as *Odontioda* and *Odontonia*. Considering the difficulties encountered when germinating seed, this is a phenomenal record, for the crosses numbered over 1,500. Of these some 750 were in *Paphiopedilum* alone, the most difficult of all genera.

The nature of orchids themselves, which are slow to mature and flower, necessitated the keeping of accurate records, lest the parentage of seedlings be forgotten. The great interest in hybrids led to the registration of crosses, not only to insure credit to the first person to think of a cross but also to keep the information on file. The fortunate result of these factors has been the development of an orchid genealogy as accurate and complete as any family history in existence.

It early became the custom to give a hybrid a name of its own. At first this was done to honor the creator of a hybrid or someone who had achieved fame in the orchid world. The system gives us a handy way to identify the complicated hybrids that exist today. It would be impossible to call an orchid by the names of a dozen or more ancestors. It is even awkward to give the immediate parentage of a plant every time we want to speak of it. For instance, how much more simple it is to say *Cattleya* Hardyana, than to say *Cattleya dowiana* var. *aurea* by *Cattleya gigas*. Nowadays growers are pressed to find names that have not already been used. Hybrids are named after the gods of ancient mythology, the letters of the Greek alphabet, presidents, generals, opera stars, the grower's own relatives and friends, or names fanciful or descriptive. In writing out the parentage, it is customary to give the pod or female parent first.

At first, the names of genera involved in the making of an intergeneric hybrid were simply combined, e. g. *Laeliocattleya, Brassolaeliocattleya,* and *Sophrolaeliocattleya.* Now, so many genera are being combined that to continue this would be dreadfully awkward. Rather, abbreviations of the genera are combined, e. g., *Odontocidium* (*Odontoglossum* × *Oncidium*), and *Miltassia* (*Miltonia* × *Brassia*). When three or more genera are combined, a person's name is used as the hybrid epithet, with -ara added to the end, e. g., *Degarmoara* (*Brassia* × *Miltonia* × *Odontoglossum*).

Once a name has been given to a cross, it stands for any repetition of that cross. For instance, *Cattleya* Fabia is *Cattleya dowiana* × *Cattleya labiata,* and every time those two species are mated the offspring must be called *Cattleya* Fabia. *Cattleya* Fabia × *Cattleya* Hardyana produced *Cattleya* Princess Royal, while the mating of the white forms produced *Cattleya* Princess Royal, alba. Knowing the name of any hybrid enables you to trace its ancestry back to the species involved in all the branches of its "family tree."

Sander's *Complete List of Orchid Hybrids* covers crosses up to 1946. Addenda are published at intervals to cover later years. Current lists of hybrids appear in the *American Orchid Society Bulletin* and the British *Orchid Review.* These lists are straightforward and simple. They include the name of the hybrid, the names of its parents, the date of registration and the name of the person who registered the cross. Early volumes consist of two tables. Table I enables you to look up a hybrid by its name and gives you its parentage. Table II lists under each species and hybrid the species and hybrids with which it has been crossed and the resulting hybrid names. These volumes are a monument to Mr. Fred K. Sander, of Sanders St. Albans Ltd., England, who devoted over fifty years of loving work to their compilation, all done without remuneration except for the gratitude of orchid growers all over the world.

The late David F. Sander continued the work up to 1960 and produced the ingenious one-table form, beginning with a set of two volumes containing hybrids from 1946 to 1960. Registration of hybrids and the issuing of further volumes are now conducted by the Royal Horticultural Society. Additional volumes are published at intervals. All are obtainable through the American Orchid Society, Inc., as are forms for registering hybrids. If you wish, you may write directly to the Registrar of Orchid Hybrids, The Royal Horticultural Society, Vincent Square, London, SW1P 2PE, England. There is a fee for registration.

Primary crosses, crosses between two species, are likely to yield plants that are intermediate between the parents, and more or less uniform (Fig. 7–1). But crosses between two hybrids are more complicated and show great variety among the offspring. A hybrid is made up of factors inherited from each of its parents and, when two hybrids are mated, these factors recombine in many ways. The offspring will show various combinations of the characteristics of the parent plants, as well as combinations reminiscent of many of the types found in their ancestry. The same thing happens when a hybrid is selfpollinated, for its inherited characteristics also recombine to give a number of different kinds of offspring.

During the earlier years of hybridization it seemed sufficient to know the names of the two species or hybrids crossed to make a certain hybrid. Through the years it has become obvious to orchid breeders that certain individual plants have been better parents than others, and that some have been more consistent in transmitting their characteristics to their offspring. Often it is not a question of superiority but rather of distinctive characteristics obtained from certain individuals. It has, therefore, become important to know exactly what individual plants have been used as parents. To mark an outstanding plant it is given a varietal name, a name added to the hybrid name and set in single quotes, for example *Cattleya* Bow Bells 'Serene'. Thus this plant is set apart from other members of the cross, and the varietal name is carried with it and all of its divisions, which together form a "clone." The use of a clonal or varietal name to mark a superior plant is not limited to hybrids. Outstanding individual plants of a species may be so marked. When a plant that has been given a clonal name is divided, this name is carried on in each division.

We have seen that once a name has been given to a cross, that name stands for any repetition of the cross. Here we must explain lest some difficulties in understanding lead to confusion. Let's say that a certain cross proves to be so successful that there is more demand for seedlings than there are seedlings available. The originator of the cross may *remake* the cross, using the *identical parents* again. Another grower, who has *divisions of these same parents,* may also *remake* the cross. However, a grower who has other plants from the same hybrid groups, different individuals from those used in the original cross, will not get the same results by crossing them. It is true that the resulting seedlings will have the same hybrid name, and if his plants are superior his cross may be better, but the offspring will exhibit quite a different array of characteristics (Fig. 7–2). Let's say that there is a hybrid named *Cattleya* Alpha which has progeny ranging in color from pink to green, and one named *Cattleya* Beta that ranges from pale lavender to dark

Figure 7–1 *Modification of characteristics of two species parents in their primary hybrid.* UPPER: Cattleya bicolor, *a bifoliate species that has slender sepals and petals and a lip without side lobes.*
CENTER: Cattleya dowiana, *a member of the labiata group, with broad petals and a broad lip with the sides rolled over the column.*
LOWER: Cattleya Iris, Cattleya bicolor X Cattleya dowiana. *The lip, though wider and more ruffled than in C.* bicolor, *is still not as wide as in C.* dowiana, *and is still somewhat tongue-shaped as in C.* bicolor. *The side lobes of the lip have been reduced to the merest trace at the very base of the lip.* (CATTLEYA DOWIANA, COURTESY OF H.A. DUNN AND H. GRIFFIN.)

Figure 7-2 *Two plants from the same seed pod, showing possible variation from good to poor in the same cross. Both have the same lip pattern, but one has inherited large size and fairly good shape, while the other has inherited small size and less pleasing shape.*

purple. A cross between a green Alpha and a pale Beta will be quite different from a cross between a pink Alpha and a dark purple Beta. Or let's say that in a cross which we shall call *Cattleya* Delta one individual occurs that is tetraploid, having double the normal number of chromosomes. Crosses in which this tetraploid Delta is used as a parent will be different from crosses in which other Deltas, diploid plants, function as parents. One can readily see the need for distinguishing individual plants used in hybridization.

It was at one time hoped that new hybrid lists might include the clonal name of parent plants. Although the American Orchid Society tried to work out some method, it has not proven feasible. There are often dozens of outstanding clones in a single cross, and registration of each hybrid made with each clone would, the authorities felt, cause awkward duplication and unnecessarily long lists. Technically, the cross would be the same no matter which clones were used; the hybrid name would of course be the same. It was felt that the registration lists were not the place for this information; rather, the hybridizer should be responsible for keeping the records, and that those who wished to buy offspring from certain clones should be able to obtain the information from him. Additional in-

formation regarding a clone should also be kept in its record, including its chromosome number, if available, its color, and the characteristics of its offspring.

The results of a cross cannot be known until a fair percentage of the seedlings flower. The fact that the parent plants are handsome does not necessarily mean that their offspring will be equally good. If the seedlings are good, however, the grower will be encouraged to use their parents again in other combinations. Proving the merit of parent plants is a long job, for they must be tried in a number of crosses, not just one. Failure in one cross may not mean that the same plants will fail when combined with other individuals. Again, the need for records and for identification of plants used as parents can be clearly seen. How frustrating it would be for a cross to turn out exceptionally well and then not know which plants produced this cross! Equally sad is a situation, which has often occurred, in which divisions of valuable plants have been lost because of the lack of proper labeling. In the field of hybridization it is not enough to guess or think that a certain plant is a division of a particularly famous one. If a grower is going to represent his seedlings as offspring of certain famous parents, he must know beyond all doubt that this is so. If a buyer is desirous of obtaining a division of a certain plant, he must be given the assurance that the plant he receives is in fact that plant.

How do such differences among individuals occur? How are characteristics carried from parent to offspring? How is it that a characteristic that occurs in one generation may not show up in the next, but may instead be exhibited in a later generation? It is the purpose of this chapter to show, by highly simplified examples, the basic workings of inheritance. These basic principles will not cover all of the complications that arise in the passing on of traits from one generation to another but will give a glimpse into the general methods by which this takes place. When you have read through the "ABCs" of inheritance in this chapter, you will be better able to understand things that you can see in your own plants, and you will appreciate the work of the cytogeneticists who are now studying inheritance in orchids. Compared to what is known of genetics of the fruit fly, we know as yet very little about the genetics of orchids. The problem is complicated by the thousands of kinds of orchids, by the fact that transmission of characters in different genera may be accomplished by different gene groups, and by the length of time from seed to flower.

The discussion of genetics in this chapter will be based on *Cattleya* and some of its intergeneric crosses with *Laelia, Sophronitis,* and *Brassavola.* Descriptions of the latter genera will be found in Chapter 13, along with other *Cattleya* relatives (the Laeliinae), along with such related genera as *Epidendrum, Diacrium,* etc.

GENETICS

The foundation of the individual in all species of living things, both plant and animal, lies in its genetic makeup. Every cell in a plant, whether of roots, leaves, or flowers, contains in its nucleus a set of microscopic structures called chromosomes. On each chromosome there are still smaller structures called genes, so tiny that they cannot be seen with the ordinary microscope. The genes (from genesis, the beginning) control every single characteristic of the individual. Try to list all the observable traits of an orchid plant, from the most obvious to the most minute, including such things as: pseudobulbs, tall or short, thick or thin; leaves,

long or short, wide or narrow; sheath, single or double; lip, bordered or plain, "eyes" present or absent, throat open or tubular; texture of flower; substance, waxy or thin, and so on. You would soon have quite a list. The internal structure of the plant, if you could discern it, should be added to your list, as should its growth and flowering habits and the keeping quality of the flowers. Every one of these items is controlled by genes, and it probably takes several thousand, working together in a most complicated way, to produce the plant under scrutiny.

Environment cannot be overlooked in the making of a plant. Without the necessary growing conditions, a plant cannot develop properly. But proper growing conditions only give the genes a chance to express themselves. A plant that gives poor flowers under the best of care will never give good ones. It does not have the genetic makeup for good flowers. Such characteristics as petals that fold back too far or misshapen flower parts, are genetic faults. (However, if a plant that has consistently produced good flowers suddenly gives defective ones, you might look for insect injury, disease, or some environmental cause. Freak flowers appear occasionally but seldom repeat themselves.)

Every species has its own standard number of chromosomes. In man there are forty-six. In the fruit fly there are eight. The garden pea, used by Mendel in the experiments which gave the world the fundamentals of genetics, has fourteen.

Chromosomes exist in pairs, but the members of each pair actually stand side by side only during reduction division (see below). The two members of each pair of chromosomes are identical in shape and size, but not necessarily in gene content. Genes also occur in pairs, one member of a pair on each of the matched chromosomes. Each pair of chromosomes is different from every other pair in the cell. Fig. 7–3 shows a cell that has two pair of chromosomes; these have been made black and white to distinguish the individual members of each pair. The shape and size of the chromosomes, as well as the total number, are standard for the species. Of the forty chromosomes in C. *trianaei,* there are twenty distinct kinds, two of each, and every cell in the plant, except the reproductive cells, contains the full complement.

Certain tissues of a flower are set aside for the formation of reproductive cells. In these tissues the cells divide in a special way, called reduction division. The chromosomes come together in pairs.

Figure 7–3 *A cell with two pair of chromosomes.*

Then the members of each pair of chromosomes separate, and travel to opposite ends or poles of the cell, which then divides in half to form two new cells. Fig. 7–4 shows this process. Each of the new cells now contains one member of each pair of chromosomes, or half of the original number. This is called the "haploid" number. The haploid cells later develop into sperm and egg cells, which in genetic terminology are called gametes. When fertilization takes place, see Fig. 7–5, and a sperm and egg come together, the full number of chromosomes, the "diploid" number, is again present. The new individual that develops from the fertilized egg thus receives half of its chromosomes from one parent, half from the other. The chromosomes never fuse, but remain separate and distinct from each other. Each chromosome carries with it its own gene content, and when it goes into the making of a new individual it takes its genes along with it to that new individual.

At times a chromosome can break, so that halves or smaller sections go drifting away or become attached to another chromosome. Once in a while two chromosomes will cross over and then separate at the crossing point so that opposite halves (or smaller sections) become attached to each other. Such complications cause aberrations in in-

heritance but are too complicated to be detailed in the simplified glimpse we are giving here.

The haploid number is referred to as "n" for brevity and convenience. The diploid number then becomes "2n." We shall later talk about triploids, "3n," and tetraploids, "4n," plants that have three and four times the haploid number of chromosomes, and even pentaploids, "5n." Plants with more than the 2n number of chromosomes are called "polyploids."

During the development of reproductive cells, it is pure chance which member of a pair of chromosomes will go into a resulting sperm or egg cell. We can think of the chromosomes as pairing with one to the right of the other, but just as often, the position is reversed. If the members of each pair are identical in gene content, it does not matter how they separate, for the resulting reproductive cells will be identical. But where the members of a pair differ from each other, if by only one gene, it makes a great deal of difference. Fig. 7–6 shows the possible combinations of genes in the reproductive cells arising from one that has two pair of unlike chromosomes. Where only one pair of unlike chromosomes is involved, there are two types

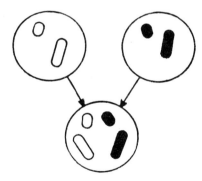

Figure 7–5 *Fertilization brings together a set of chromosomes from each parent.*

A   B

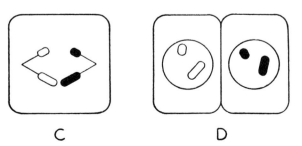

C   D

Figure 7–4 *Reduction division.* A: *The chromosomes pair.* B *and* C: *They separate.* D: *New cells are formed* *with half the original number.*

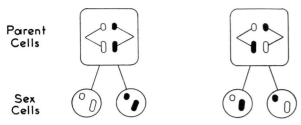

Figure 7–6 *Four types of sex cells arise from a cell having two pair of unlike chromosomes.*

of reproductive cells, or 2 to the first power, 2^1. Where two pair are concerned, there are four types, or 2^2, and where there are three pair of unlike chromosomes, there will be eight different types of reproductive cells, or 2^3. The figures become almost astronomical for cells that contain a large number of chromosomes. For instance, where there are 20 pair, if each member of every pair is unlike the other, the number of possible kinds of gametes is 2^{20}, or 1,048,576.

Such a figure gives some idea of the problems confronting geneticists who try to make a complete analysis of a plant or an animal. The genetic makeup of an individual cannot be known from its appearance. The only way to find out what genes it contains is to breed it and see what comes out in the offspring. This reveals why geneticists usually choose subjects with a short life cycle. In contrast to orchids, the fruit fly produces a new generation every few days, and wheat and corn in a matter of months. A planned study of orchid genetics, started now, would take several lifetimes to complete. We do have quite a body of facts, however, collected by careful observers, that show how certain factors in orchids behave, and their pattern follows the same general behavior seen in plants that have been studied in more detail.

Genes are of two general types, "dominant" and "recessive." Dominant genes have the power to induce the appearance of the characteristic they govern whenever they are present. Recessive genes can manifest themselves only in the absence of the dominant gene. In cattleyas, purple is dominant over yellow. A cross between *Cattleya gigas* (purple) and *Cattleya dowiana* (yellow) gives all purple offspring. In Fig. 7–7, the dominant gene for purple is indicated by P, and the recessive gene for yellow by y*. *Cattleya gigas*, the parent plant, has the pair of genes PP, and gives one to each reproductive cell. *Cattleya dowiana*, similarly, has the pair yy, so that each reproductive cell contains one y. Each individual among the offspring inherits a gene for purple, P, and a gene for yellow, y; and, since purple is dominant over yellow, the offspring have purple flowers. On the other hand, the yellow of *Laelia* is dominant over the purple of *Cattleya*,† so that a mating between *Laelia flava* and *Cattleya gigas* would give all yellow flowers. This is shown in Fig. 7–8 where Y now stands for dominant yellow and p for recessive purple.

There are cases where the dominant gene can manifest itself fully only when present in a double dose, that is, when two dominants are present for the same characteristic, instead of one dominant and one recessive. This seems to be true of flower size; see Fig. 7–9, where L stands for large size and s for small size. If a large cattleya, LL, is crossed

---

* The system of symbols used here has been devised for the sake of simplicity. It may well be that our single symbols may represent groups of genes.

---

† Species of Laelia that have been used to produce hybrids of various shades of yellow, orange, red-orange, and bronze, are *cinnabarina, flava, harpophylla, tenebrosa,* and *xanthina.*

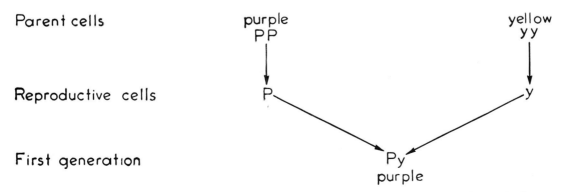

Parent cells   purple PP   yellow yy

Reproductive cells   P   y

First generation   Py purple

Figure 7–7 *A hypothetical cross between* C. gigas, *in which purple is dominant, and* C. dowiana, *in which yellow is recessive, produces all purple flowers in the offspring.*

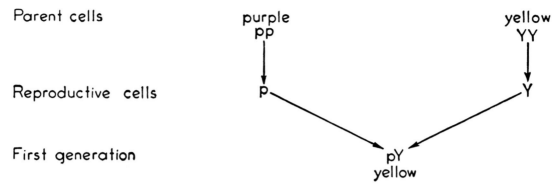

Figure 7–8 *A cross in which the purple of* C. gigas *is recessive to the yellow of* Laelia flava *will produce all* *yellow flowers in the offspring.*

with a small one, ss, each of the offspring will inherit one gene for large size and one for small, Ls. The size of the resulting flowers will be intermediate between the two parents. The gene for large size, when present in a single dose, is dominant to the extent that it can make the flowers of the new generation larger than the smaller parent, but it is not able to bring them up to the size of the larger parent. This is called "incomplete dominance."

When species of extremely different size are crossed, for example a large cattleya and a small epidendrum, the resulting flowers do not come all the way up to the midpoint, or average, between the two. For instance, a two-inch crossed with an eight-inch flower gives offspring of four inches across rather than the five-inch size one might expect. And a one-inch by a nine-inch gives a three-inch flower instead of a four and one half-inch one. Some years ago we reported an observation made on the number of flowers per spike in cymbidium primary hybrids, (see page 000) which showed that the number corresponds with the geometrical mean rather than the arithmetical mean or average. Dod-

son and Gillespie in their book *The Biology of the Orchids* state that the geometrical mean also operates in flower size. The geometrical mean is found by multiplying the two sizes and taking the square root of the result, whereas the arithmetical mean is found by adding them and dividing by two. For the examples above, $2 \times 8 = 16$, and square root of $16 = 4$; $1 \times 9 = 9$, and square root of $9 = 3$. When the sizes of the parents are closer to each other, e.g., six and eight inches, the size of the offspring comes closer to the arithmetical average, because this is also closer to the geometrical mean—geometrical mean, $6 \times 8 = 48$, square root of $48 =$ approximately 6.9; arithmetical mean, $6 + 8 = 14$, $\frac{14}{2} = 7$. Thus, one need be concerned only when the parents are of quite widely separated size. It does point out, however, some of the difficulties faced by a hybridizer who wishes to combine the characteristics of a large flower with those of a small one, as in creating a large red cattleya type by breeding with a small laelia or sophronitis (Fig. 7–9).

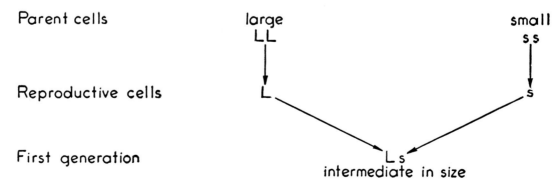

Figure 7–9 *Incomplete dominance. The incompletely dominant gene, L, for large size, when coupled with the* *recessive gene, s, for small size, gives offspring intermediate in size.*

Plants that have identical genes for any one character are said to be homozygous (pure) for that character. For instance, a plant that contains two genes for large size, LL, will give every one of its sperm and egg cells one of those genes, and when used as a parent, will transmit this gene to every individual among the offspring. The same is true of a plant that has identical recessive genes, such as one with two genes for small size, ss, which is said to be homozygous for this character.

A plant that contains unlike genes for any character is called heterozygous (impure, or mixed). If it is heterozygous for size, it means that it contains one dominant gene for large, and one recessive gene for small, Ls. The offspring of the two yellow-purple crosses described above are heterozygous for color, those of the cattleya cross being Py, and those of the laelia × cattleya, pY. When used as parents, heterozygous plants give half of their offspring the dominant gene and half the recessive.

The species tend to be homozygous. However, there are various types within a species, and these types pass their characteristics on to their progeny. There are, for example, good *Cattleya trianaei*, and poor ones. If the types are well-separated geographically, the chances are that the good and the poor are respectively homozygous. But if there has been interbreeding among them, they may be heterozygous. The only way to tell whether a flower is homozygous is to pollinate it with its own pollen (self-pollinate it). If all the offspring are identical to the parent, you may know that the parent is homozygous. But if the progeny differ markedly from each other in any way, you will know that the parent is a mixture. A plant that is homozygous for all of its good qualities can be used as a "stud" plant. One that proves to be heterozygous is not a "stud" plant. Self-pollination is not only valuable in "proving" an individual, but is a means of obtaining pure strains, strains that are homozygous and that will all breed "true."

There are many dominant characters among *Cattleya* and its relatives that can be detected in their hybrids. The bifoliate type of growth, with its slender, jointed stems and two or three leaves, is dominant over the thick pseudobulbs and single leaf of the labiata group. So, also, is the spade lip dominant over the labiate lip, and although in successive generations it may be broadened, it can often be identified by the notches that separate the middle lobe from the side lobes. The heavy substance of bifoliate flowers is transmitted to their hybrids. The characteristic veins in the lip of C.

dowiana and the mottling in the lip of C. *mossiae* both persist in their hybrids. C. *labiata* contributes its day-length sensitivity to its hybrids. The reed-stem epidendrums are dominant both for their growth habit and the character of their flowers. Of course, segregation of these dominant characters through successive generations will eventually cause them to appear only in a percentage of the hybrids.

Whether you intend to enter into a serious breeding program or just cross two orchids for the fun of it, it makes the work more interesting and insures a greater measure of success if you follow some plan based on genetic principles. If what you want is merely a large number of good flowers, perhaps to make your hobby profitable, you will be saved from making crosses that would produce a large number of poor flowers. Or if you want to obtain a unique combination of characteristics from two individuals, you will be spared much pain in knowing ahead of time that the type you want may be only one out of a wide assortment of types in the offspring.

It is interesting to go a little further into the inheritance of yellow in cattleyas. The purple *Cattleya gigas* crossed with the yellow *Cattleya dowiana aurea* gives a first generation (F_1 to geneticists) that is all purple, *Cattleya* Hardyana. Suppose *Cattleya* Hardyana is self-pollinated, and a second generation (F_2) of seedlings is raised. A person who did not know the inheritance of *Cattleya* Hardyana would be astonished to get some yellow flowers in this second generation. But those who knew its genetic makeup would have expected just that. Fig. 7–10 shows how this happens. *Cattleya* Hardyana is heterozygous. Its color genes are Py. In the formation of reproductive cells these genes segregate so that half of them contain P and half of them y. The second generation will recombine these genes in three ways, PP, Py, and yy. One-fourth of the plants will be homozygous purple, one-half of them will be heterozygous purple, and the remaining one-fourth will be homozygous yellow.

Again, someone who did not know genetics might think he could increase the "potency" of that homozygous yellow by crossing it back to the yellow *Cattleya dowiana aurea*. It is true that he would get all yellow flowers, but the yellow always remains a recessive gene. If he is looking for a plant to use for breeding yellows when crossed with purple, he will not get it this way. Fig. 7–11 shows why. The only way to get a yellow that will always

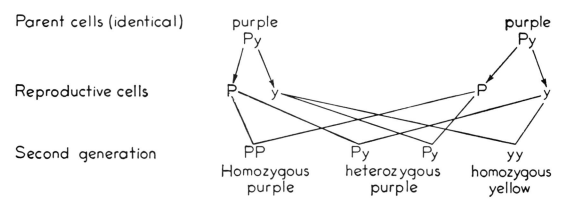

Figure 7–10 *the F₂ generation obtained by crossing members of the F₁ will be three-fourths purple and one-fourth yellow.*

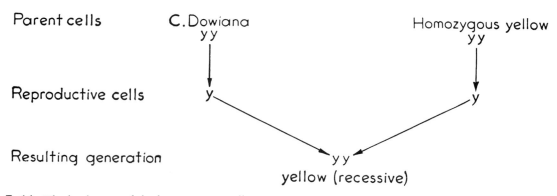

Figure 7–11 *The backcross of the homozygous yellow F₂ hybrid to* C. dowiana *simply produces another homozygous recessive yellow.*

be dominant over purple is to use a yellow laelia as a parent, as described below under laeliocattleyas.

In the last twenty years or so we have learned that it may make a great deal of difference which way a cross is made, that is, which bears the seed and which supplies the pollen. (In recording a cross, the female or "pod" parent is always given first.) Let's say we have plant A and plant B. If plant A receives pollen from B, the offspring will be different from those produced when B receives pollen from A. The reason is that the egg cell contains more genetic material than does the pollen. Some genes are contained in plastids, small structures in the cytoplasm (material outside the nucleus), and the egg cell has more plastids than does the pollen. Thus the egg contributes more genes, more inherited characteristics, than pollen can.

Laeliocattleyas

Laelia is used in crosses with *Cattleya* to lend bright coloring to the hybrids. *Laelia tenebrosa,* which is reddish brown with coppery suffusion and a darker lip, when crossed with *Cattleya* produces bronze flowers with a deep purple lip, in which the bronze ranges from yellow-bronze to purple-bronze. *L. purpurata* has perhaps been used more than any other in hybrids with *Cattleya,* partly because of the deep velvety purple of its lip, and partly because it is itself a large flower and the resulting hybrids are of good size from the beginning. Hybrids that have a small laelia parent have to be crossed again with a large cattleya to bring the size up to the desired dimensions.

In the discussion of yellow-purple crosses above you will remember that the yellow of *Laelia* is dominant over the purple of *Cattleya*. The great value of this type of cross is that it is possible to breed a stud plant that is homozygous for yellow (that carries the double dose) and in which the yellow is dominant. Such a stud plant should also be a yellow laeliocattleya that has the desirable cattleya shape. Two steps are necessary to achieve this.

Suppose we choose the all-yellow *Laelia flava* and cross it with any purple cattleya. Here we will be dealing with two characters, size and color. Fig. 7–12 shows the primary cross between these two, giving the first (F_1) generation. The cattleya is LLpp, where L represents the gene for large size, and p the gene for purple, which in this cross is recessive. *Laelia flava* is ssYY, where s stands for the gene for small size, and Y for yellow, which is dominant. The reproductive cells from the cattleya are all the same, Lp, and from *Laelia flava* similarly are sY. The offspring combining these genes are therefore identical, LsYp. They are of a size somewhere between the two parents, and all yellow, though the yellow is not quite as clear and pure as where the double dose of Y is present.

The plant we want to make in the next step is one that will be homozygous for both large size and yellow color, LLYY. Offhand, you might think that the way to get it would be to cross a member of the F_1 generation back to the laelia parent. The laelia parent gives only one type of reproductive cell, sY. The plant from the F_1 generation gives four types, LY, Lp, sY, and sp. Combine sY with each of these and you get LsYY, LsYp, ssYY, and ssYp. These come out in equal proportions as to the numbers of plants of each type. There are two types that are homozygous for yellow, LsYY and ssYY, but of these one is intermediate in size and the other is small. Nowhere can you find the plant

you want, the LLYY type. The back cross to the cattleya would not give it either, for here you would get Lp combined with the four types of germ cells from the F_1, and the results would be LLYp, LLpp, LsYp, and Lspp. Two would be homozygous for large size, but none for yellow. So we have to go at it another way, by mating members of the F_1 generation to get the F_2 generation in which the genes will be sorted out into the various possible combinations, and in which homozygous plants will occur. Incidentally, this is the real value of using the F_2 generation in any breeding program.

Look at the four types of reproductive cells that arise from a member of the F_1 generation, LY, Lp, sY, and sp. The homozygous large yellow plant we want would have to come from the fertilization of an LY egg cell by an LY sperm cell, and we can get this by self-pollinating a member of the F_1, or by mating one F_1 plant with another. Fig. 7–13 shows all the possible combinations, in checkerboard style. The four types of reproductive cells are written horizontally and vertically, and each line contains the combination of the genes at the left with each group on the top. The proportions of types in the second generation, F_2, are given in sixteenths. In the checkerboard the type LLYY occurs only once, so that this type will be one-sixteenth of the total number of offspring. (The large yellow plants in the offspring would have to be self-pollinated in order to discover which ones are the LLYY type.) Perhaps you will think it is hardly worth the trouble of making the cross to get only one out of sixteen. A plant breeder would consider it very worthwhile, for this LLYY plant when self-pollinated will give a whole generation of large yellow flowers, and when bred to any large cattleya will carry its dominant yellow to every

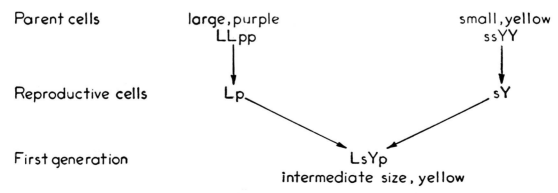

Parent cells   large, purple   small, yellow
    LLpp   ssYY

Reproductive cells   Lp   sY

First generation   LsYp
intermediate size, yellow

Figure 7–12 *The F_1 generation obtained by crossing a purple cattleya with yellow* L. flava *gives all yellow flowers, which are heterozygous for both size and color.*

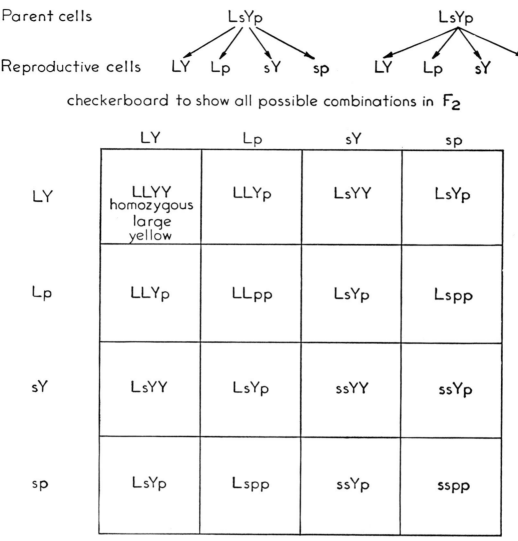

Figure 7–13 *The inheritance in the F₂ generation when members of the F₁ generation from Figure 7–12 are crossed.*

member of the offspring. Among the other types on the checkerboard, some will give good flowers of large and intermediate size, both yellow and purple, plants that will be an addition to your collection, though not useful in breeding.

Brassocattleyas

The naming of orchids has been a long and complicated business. Often, a modern taxonomist does not agree with the name used by a predecessor and finds some botanical difference that causes him to feel that a certain species belongs more ap-

propriately with a different group. Sometimes a new genus is set up for plants that do not quite fit the one in which they have been carried. Clearly, the names should be straightened out, for the record and for future generations of orchid lovers. But difficulties arise when the names of species used frequently in hybridization are changed after the hybrids have appeared in many lists.

"Brassocattleya" and *"Brassolaeliocattleya"* are terms long familiar. They represent a very particular concept of hybrids made with *Brassavola digbyana,* the species with the large fringed lip and lemony fragrance. Some years ago it was felt that this species and *B. glauca* fitted better with *Laelia*

and they were moved to that genus. We all tried to get used to calling them *Laelia digbyana* and *L. glauca,* and their hybrids, *Laeliocattleyas.* In 1918, Rudolf Schlechter created the genus *Rhyncholaelia* for these species because of botanical differences he found to be significant, among them the beak-shaped seed capsule. That was many years ago, of course, but the authorities of today have decided that that is where *digbyana* and *glauca* belong botanically. However, to avoid further confusion at this time, we are going to follow the advice of a leading taxonomist and keep the old name *Brassavola,* provided that everyone is well warned and will remember that it is synonymous with *Rhyncholaelia,* and may some day be changed to that.

Brassavola digbyana has long attracted hybridists, not only because the lip is fringed but because it is so huge and actually rolls around the column. In a primary cross with a member of the labiata group of *Cattleya* the sepals and petals are reduced toward the size of those of *digbyana,* but the lip is broadened and shaped more like that of *Digbyana,* with the fringe present though not as long. (See Fig. 7–14 for a picture illustrating this.) When *digbyana* is crossed with *Cattleya dowiana* the colors are diluted with green, which makes them very delicate and beautiful. Subtle coloring is also obtained when *digbyana* is crossed with a lavender cattleya—lovely tones of pink suffused with green for

example. The colors become stronger when first-generation hybrids are crossed with species or hybrids of darker tones, and some of the brilliant hybrids with large, full lip are among the handsomest of orchids. In a secondary cross, segregation of the genes causes both lip types to show up, so that there are some with the cattleya lip as well as some with the *digbyana* lip, some with fringe and some without it, or with the barest denticulation of the edge of the lip. The fragrance of the *digbyana* hybrids, reminiscent of citrus fruits, is another characteristic that frequently follows through a line of breeding.

It is interesting to note that a successful method for breeding yellows has been achieved through the use of *Laeliocattleya* Luminosa (*L. tenebrosa* × *C. dowiana*), a hybrid made in 1901, crossed with various hybrids containing yellow *Laelia* species and with some containing *digbyana,* such as *Brassocattleya digbyana* Mrs. J. Leemann.

Red Hybrids

Sophronitis coccinea, a gem of a flower in itself, has been made to contribute its redness to *Cattleya* and *Laeliocattleya* hybrids. The primary cross of *Sophronitis coccinea* with a cattleya necessarily gives quite small flowers, and even smaller and less well shaped with a laelia. But when either of these is recombined with a cattleya or laeliocattleya, larger flowers of various deep rosy or red-violet tones appear. It has been hoped that the clear red tones would, through self-pollination or further breeding, be combined with the desirable size, but this happens rather infrequently. It may be that the chromosomes from *Sophronitis* are so unlike those of *Cattleya* and *Laelia* that they fail to pair at reduction division and that many reproductive cells are therefore nonfunctional. This may account for the fact that the types of desired color and size are frequently lost from seedling progeny.

Potinara is the name given to the quadrigeneric cross *Brassosophrolaeliocattleya.* It can easily be imagined that a combination of all the desirable qualities of the four genera would be an outstandingly handsome thing. However, plants in which all the desired qualities show up occur in only a small proportion of the offspring, and the percentage of plants homozygous for all qualities even less often. A rather extensive breeding program would be necessary to achieve the ideal results. Many lovely combinations do occur in *Potinara* crosses, although relatively few have been made.

Figure 7–14 Brassocattleya *(or* Rhynchocattleya) Mrs. J. Leeman, *which shows the huge rolled lip and fringe of* Brassavola (Rhyncholaelia) digbyana.

The search for a way to breed large red hybrids has been given a new boost with the discovery of *Laelia milleri*. It is hoped that this species will not offer the genetic difficulties that have plagued hybridists using *Sophronitis*. Some encouraging results have already been achieved.

Blue Hybrids

Blue is the most elusive color in cattleya hybrids, and hybridizers will not be content until they achieve it. Thus far, few hybrids classed as blue have a clear blue color, being mostly a lavender-blue or having off-white sepals and petals with lavender-blue in the lip. Genetic study is under way and it is felt that progress is being made toward understanding how blue can be achieved.

White Cattleyas

Breeding white orchids has its own special problems genetically, as well as its own special appeal esthetically. The genetic problem has been pretty well worked out for cattleyas, so that you will not have the troubles experienced by some of the early growers. You will not have the sorrow of crossing two pure white flowers only to raise from them a batch of all purple offspring.

Before we discuss their genetics, we must first define what is a pure white orchid, odd though it may seem to have to define "white." From the point of view of its appearance, a pure white orchid is one in which there is not the slightest trace of purple pigment, either in the plant or in the flower. Plants that give purple flowers show purple pigmentation in the plant, in the new growths, sheaths, or leaves, even though their flowers may be extremely pale. Plants that give pure white flowers are all pure, bright green. Nor is there any trace of purple in the flowers. Green and yellow plastids are present, and the white flower may have yellow markings in the throat, but the rest of the flower must be a chaste paper-white, not tinged with color in any way.

The necessity for this definition arises from the carelessness of people who call any very pale flower white, even one that has the veins or the tips of the petals and sepals obviously tinged with color. These tinged whites are nothing but dilute color forms. It is not so significant when the tinged whites are sold by the florist for pure white, be-

cause the recipient of the corsage probably does not mind the slight tinting, may even prefer it that way. But a tinged white cannot be crossed with a pure white without giving colored offspring, at best a mixture of colored and white. Pure whites must be used if you want all pure white progeny. Or, if you are buying seedlings with the intention of having all pure white flowers, be sure that the parents are pure, and not "almost white" or "nearly white."

As if purposely to confuse the matter and make the breeding of whites more difficult than colored orchids, white cattleyas (and other genera, too) divide themselves into two groups genetically. It is simple when understood, but it puzzled early growers to find that combinations of the albino forms of some species gave all purple flowers, while different combinations of the same parents would give all white.

The mystery was solved by Charles C. Hurst, an English geneticist, who published his interpretation in *Experiments in Genetics* in 1925. He figured out the probably genetic makeup of white orchids from the way they behave in breeding. His deduction is briefly this. Manifestation of color in orchids depends on at least two types of genes working together. In order that a specific color may appear, there must be a gene, which Hurst calls R, to govern what color it is to be. And in order for that color to manifest itself, there must be another gene that allows color as such to be formed, which he calls C. In a colored orchid these two types are both present in their dominant form. However, if only the recessive form of the first type is present, no color may be made in the flower, even though the gene for color as such, C, is present. Or, if the situation is reversed and the plant contains only the recessive form of the second type, c, no color will show, even though the gene for specific color, R, is present. The two types of albinos are therefore, according to Hurst, ccRR and CCrr.

Any pure white when self-pollinated will give all white offspring, and any two of the same type when crossed will produce all white. You can see at a glance, however, that if ccRR and CCrr are crossed, the offspring will inherit c and R from its ccRR parent, and C and r from the CCrr parent, so that both types of genes will be present in the dominant form. The offspring will have the genetic makeup CcRr, and the resulting flowers will all be colored.

Hurst figured out to which of the groups, ccRR or CCrr, the various albino forms of the species belonged, according to the way they behaved when intercrossed. The *Cattleya* species from his list are given below, with the addition of other species that have shown their makeup by their behavior.

Any of the members of Group I when intercrossed will give all white offspring, and any of their hybrids may be crossed to produce all white. Similarly, any members of Group II and the hybrids derived from them will give all white offspring. But a member of Group I crossed with one from Group II will give colored offspring, as will a hybrid from Group I mated with one from Group II. An interesting example of crossing members from the two groups took place when the purple C. Enid resulted from C. *mossiae* var. *wageneri* × C. *gigas* 'Firmin Lambeau'.

Semi-Alba

Cattleyas and their hybrids which have pure white sepals and petals and a purple lip are called semi-albas or are designated W-C-L, white-colored-lip. We prefer the term semi-alba. Here we must emphasize that by pure white we mean the absolute absence of any color in the sepals and petals. Flowers that have a tinge of color in the sepals and petals, no matter how slight, would not come in the category of semi-alba, but instead would be considered colored flowers. There was for a while a tendency to call white with purple lip "alba," which was very confusing. Since the term alba means white, it should be used only for flowers that are all white. Semi-alba indicates half white, in other words, white sepals and petals and a colored lip.

The fact that a flower with pure white sepals and petals could have purple pigment in the lip indicated long ago that inheritance of lip color was separate from inheritance of color in the rest of the flower and was therefore governed by an independent set of genes. We saw, above, that a flower will be white if it has a double recessive in either the C or R category, that is, if its makeup is ccRR or CCrr no color at all will be formed. It would follow that for color to appear in the lip, there must be at least one dominant C and one dominant R present. How, then, would another set of genes operate to prevent this color from showing in the sepals and petals, but allow it to be expressed in the lip? G. A. L. Mehlquist proposed a solution, upheld by W. B. Storey and H. Kamemoto, based on studies of various crosses.

They postulate (and this is a clever piece of deduction and seems very logical) that a pair of genes

PP, or Pp, or pp* is present in all flowers, and which controls the distribution of coloring, whether the sepals and petals and lip shall all be colored or only the lip. (These genes have nothing to do with the yellow coloring in the lip of a flower.) When the genes C and R are both present in a flower, the gene P (whether present along with p or as PP) causes the color to appear in both sepals and petals and in the lip; but where the genes for color distribution are recessive, pp, color shows up only in the lip. White flowers, in which no color at all can be manufactured, due to the genetic constitution cc or rr, are obviously not influenced by the color distribution genes. White flowers can have PP, Pp, or pp.

Great confusion as to how to breed semi-albas has arisen from the fact that sometimes a cross between two semi-albas gives all semi-alba, sometimes both semi-alba and white, in the offspring. In crosses between two colored flowers, semi-alba and white sometimes occur among the colored flowers in the offspring. Two white flowers can give all colored progeny or a mixture of white and semi-alba, or even all semi-alba. The great difficulty in predicting what a cross will yield stems from the fact that you cannot know the exact genetic makeup of a flower by looking at it. Recessive genes are hidden when the plant is heterozygous, that is, when dominant genes are present to counteract their influence. Fortunately, hybridizers have been using for breeding only whites that have been proven to give all white progeny, and their descendants when crossed in the proper cc or rr group will give only whites. The danger of getting mixed progeny in a white cross would come from using whites of unknown heredity, such as whites that crop up in crosses between semi-albas or from colored parents. Let's look at the possible theoretical makeup of white, colored, and semi-alba flowers, and then see how these could react with each other.

White flowers can have the following genetic makeup: ccRRPP, ccRRPp, ccRRpp, CCrrPP, CCrrPp, CCrrpp, and to these we would have to add Ccrr and ccrR, each combined with PP, Pp, and pp. In other words, white flowers are always homozygous for either the cc or rr genes, and may have any combination of the color-distribution genes.

---

* By coincidence these workers chose the symbols P and p to represent color distribution, while I have used them to represent simply purple in the flower. In order to distinguish the two different sets they are given here in boldface type.

Possible colored types are CCRRPP, CCRRPp, CCRrPP, CcRrPp, CCRrPP, CCRrPp, CcRRPP, and CcRRPp. They must have at least one C, one R, and one P, but the other member of each pair may be dominant or recessive.

Possible semi-alba types are: CCRRpp, CcRrpp, CCRrpp, and CcRRpp. They must have at least one C and one R, and are always homozygous for the pp genes.

As you glance through the lineup of types, you can see that whenever you mate two flowers that could bring together a combination of C, R, and P in the offspring, you will get some colored flowers. Whenever you mate flowers that offer the possible combination of C, R, and pp, you will get some semi-albas. And when two flowers offer the combinations of cc or rr, regardless of the P or p genes, you will get some white.

Let's work out a few semi-alba crosses. These must be considered hypothetical crosses, because not all of them have actually been performed, or if performed have not been studied. First we will self-pollinate a homozygous semi-alba, or cross it with another homozygous semi-alba. This would have the genetic makeup CCRRpp. Only one type of sex cell could be produced, CRp, and the recombination of these would re-create the CCRRpp makeup. In other words, a homozygous semi-alba crossed with a homozygous semi-alba always gives semi-alba. Incidentally, if you wish to find out what a semi-alba contains in the way of genes, the best thing to do is self-pollinate it.

Next let's take a heterozygous semi-alba, CcRrpp, and self-pollinate it or cross it with one exactly like it. This is more complicated because four types of sex cells are produced, CRp, Crp, cRp, and crp. The following checkerboard shows this cross and the resulting types of offspring.

	CRp	Crp	cRp	crp
CRp	CCRRpp semi-alba	CCRrpp semi-alba	CcRRpp semi-alba	CcRrpp semi-alba
Crp	CCRrpp semi-alba	CCrrpp white	CcRrpp semi-alba	Ccrrpp white
cRp	CcRRpp semi-alba	CcRrpp semi-alba	ccRRpp white	ccRrpp white
crp	CcRrpp semi-alba	Ccrrpp white	ccRrpp white	ccrrpp white

Self-pollination of a semi-alba having genetic make-up CcRrpp. Ration of offspring = 9 semi-alba to 7 white.

A third possible cross would be between the CCRRpp and the CcRrpp semi-albas. Here the single type of sex cell from the first plant, CRp, would combine with the four types from the second, CRp, Crp, cRp and crp, to give offspring CCRRpp, CCRrpp, CcRRpp, and CcRrpp, all semi-albas.

The possible combinations among white types are almost too numerous to give, but let's try a few. As we said before, crosses between any of the ccRR types will give all white, regardless of the P or p content, as will crosses between any of the CCrr ones. But when we mate plants from opposite sides of the table many combinations might result. The color distribution genes now become significant because we are crossing plants that contain the dominant C with those that contain the dominant R. A ccRRpp white crossed with a CCrrpp white gives sex cells cRp from the first and Crp from the second, which combine to give CcRrpp offspring, all semi-albas. A ccRRPP white mated to a CCrrPP white would give sex cells cRP from one and CrP from the other, which would combine to form CcRrPP, all colored flowers in the offspring. A third cross might be between a ccRRPp white and a CCrrPp both heterozygous for Pp. The first would give sex cells cRP and cRp, and the second, sex cells CrP and Crp. Combined in the offspring these could give CcRrPP, CcRrPp, CcRrPp, and CcRrpp, a ratio of three colored flowers to one semi-alba.

It is not so easy for plant breeders to attain the desired results as for us to set up crosses on paper. They must come at it the other way, by making the crosses, raising large numbers of progeny and then, by studying the types and the ratios among them, figure out what the various contributions of the parent plants may have been. Geneticists who study these problems are often foiled by not having access to large enough populations of the progeny from certain crosses, or by not having complete records of crosses to study. They can be greatly assisted by growers, and will therefore be of greatest help to them in return, (1) if growers would call them in when a large population of seedling from one cross is in flower; (2) if growers would note the characteristics of the offspring as to size, color, whether the color is dilute or strong, pattern of color, blooming period, and other characteristics of each plant, and the number of plants among the various types; and (3) if growers would be willing to make certain critical crosses that would give the geneticists needed information. The ratio of one type to another in a generation of seedlings gives the geneticist a great deal of information, because it shows what the parents contain in the way of dominant and recessive genes.

POLYPLOIDS

A polyploid is a type of plant that has one or more extra sets of chromosomes. In a normal cattleya, the basic number of chromosomes is forty, and the reproductive cells (gametes) contain the haploid number, or twenty. We refer to this haploid number as "n," and to a plant that has two sets as a 2n, or diploid plant. Each haploid set represents the set of chromosomes inherited from one parent. A plant with three sets of chromosomes is a 3n, or triploid plant. One with four sets is a 4n, or tetraploid. Five sets makes a 5n, or pentaploid, and six sets a 6n, or hexaploid.

Polyploids occur occasionally in nature, usually arising from an abnormal genetic event. The first polyploids among orchids occurred in some such way, either in their native habitats or in the greenhouses of orchid growers. Only when the science of cytogenetics was developed, however, did growers know about polyploids as such.

If the chromosomes of a plant give it a happy combination of good qualities, the plant may be superior to other members of its group. If a plant has an extra set of the chromosomes that bear genes for the good qualities, it is likely to be quite superior. This is the case with the polyploids. Tetraploids, with four sets of chromosomes, are likely to be very large, heavy plants, with large flowers of heavy substance, broad parts, and wonderful keeping qualities. Triploids are also large and heavy, somewhat faster growing than tetraploids, and they often give more flowers. We must not give the impression that all polyploids are superior to all diploids. A diploid with all dominant genes for its good qualities may compare very favorably with the polyploids. The triploids have the disadvantage of being partially or completely sterile. This means that they may fail to make functional reproductive cells, or they may make but few, and are seldom successful as parents. If the triploid is exceptionally fine, or embodies qualities that are most unusual, the grower may be happy to have the few offspring he can obtain from it. Whereas diploids may produce 80 to 90 percent viable seed, triploids may give as little as 5 percent, and sometimes 0.5 percent viable seed. Pentaploids have

been rare, and have not always been of as good quality as triploids and tetraploids, although some are very fine. With the help of the geneticists we are learning much more about them and they may soon be more abundant.

Through the years, growers have selected the best individuals for hybridization, and the best often included some that were polyploid. Thus polyploids began to play their role in hybridization without anyone's having knowledge of their genetic makeup. Some of them became famous as extraordinary parents, such as the tetraploid *Cymbidium* Alexanderi 'Westonbirt' and *Cymbidium* Pauwelsii 'Compte d'Hemptinne,' the triploid *Paphiopedilum insigne* 'Harefield Hall,' and the hexaploid (6n) *Phalaenopsis amabilis* 'Elizabethae.' It is almost impossible to tell just when, and through what plants, polyploidy entered many of the lines of cattleya hybrids. Chromosome counts made upon named varieties of a number of species have turned up the fact that some are polyploid, for example a tetraploid *Cattleya labiata* 'alba,' the tetraploid *Cattleya trianaei* 'Llewellyn,' and the triploid *Cattleya mossiae* 'Mrs. Butterworth.' Undoubtedly other polyploid cattleyas have existed and been used as parents, both species and hybrids, but in the ensuing years their identity has been lost and they are not now available for study. Even now, crosses are being shown to be largely polyploid which had not been created with that intent, and often it is not known through what ancestors the polyploidy entered the line.

What brought about the occasional polyploid in nature and the first ones to occur in cultivation? The spontaneous appearance of triploids and tetraploids in an otherwise diploid population is felt to be caused largely by nonreduction in a few reproductive cells. It occasionally happens that in the formation of reproductive cells one or more may fail to go through reduction division, and these thus become functional gametes with the full or 2n complement of chromosomes. Fertilization of a 2n gamete by one that has the normal haploid number creates a 3n individual, a triploid plant. Fertilization of a 2n gamete by another 2n gamete creates a tetraploid or 4n individual. There are other possible ways in which polyploidy can be caused. One is the chance fertilization of one egg by two sperm. Another is that in the interval between pollination and the arrival of the pollen tubes in the ovary, a few egg cells may undergo division of the nuclear material without dividing into two separate cells, thus doubling their number of chromosomes. As soon as man got hold of polyploids he, of course, began creating more and more of them by breeding them.

It should be emphasized that only an actual count of the chromosomes, in material especially prepared for microscopic study, can show the chromosome number of a plant. The large size of a plant or its flowers cannot be taken as proof of its ploidy. Although a cross can be almost entirely polyploid, the discovery of a number of polyploids in a certain cross does not mean that all of the other members of the cross are also polyploids. In fact, it is often the case that 2n, 3n, 4n, and even occasionally 5n plants occur among the plants from the same seed capsule. Individuals whose chromosome number is ascertained should have this information recorded both in the grower's file and on the label that stays with the plant. If the plant turns out to be diploid when it was hoped that it might be a polyploid, the information is no less valuable, for fine diploids are very important in hybridization. Counting chromosomes is a time-consuming process, and can be done only by people who are trained or who have the background to train themselves to do it. Therefore it is not practical for a grower to have chromosome counts made on any and all plants. Plants that have proved valuable in breeding, or that have qualities that lead the grower to think they should be useful as parents, or plants that win awards or are interesting for some particular characteristic or behavior pattern are worth having counts made upon. Geneticists make numerous counts in species and in hybrid progeny in order to obtain information on how polyploidy occurs and is transmitted.

Much breeding at present is aimed toward the production of triploids, which, because they flower so profusely, are often preferred by amateurs and by the commercial cut-flower grower. Triploids are made by crossing a diploid by a tetraploid. Both diploids and tetraploids, having even sets of chromosomes, form abundant numbers of reproductive cells, and the combination of the haploid gametes from the diploid and the 2n gametes from the tetraploid give the 3n number that creates the triploids. Given an abundance of tetraploids, tremendous numbers of triploids in a wide variety of colors and types can be bred.

While the tetraploids themselves are very handsome plants, their value lies especially in the field of hybridization, for, at least up to now, they have not been available in large numbers. A rare tetraploid can show up in a 2n × 2n cross, but they occur more often in crosses involving one or more polyploid parent, in 3n × 2n or 3n × 4n crosses. A cross between two tetraploids regularly produces a tetraploid progeny, so that, now that growers have increasing numbers of tetraploids to work with, they can create more by mating them with each other. The chief lack of tetraploids is in certain color ranges, or in certain lines. Cymbidium growers, for example, are hopefully waiting for tetraploid greens to show up. Since tetraploids have a double dose of genetic material, their influence is quite strong in crosses where they are mated with diploids. Hence, once a tetraploid of a certain type or color occurs it can be used in crosses with diploids to produce triploids that come close to having the desired characteristics.

The more equally balanced in number and character the chromosomes in a plant are, the more regular the formation of reproductive cells is. Each chromosome must have a like chromosome to pair with at reduction division in order for the process to proceed in a regular fashion. The members of each pair are called homologous chromosomes, and are inherited, as you will remember, one from the male and one from the female parent. Pairing is less efficient when chromosomes are unlike, as is often the case when they are derived from species that are quite widely separated, and when odd numbers are present. Lack of pairing of the chromosomes gives rise to reproductive cells with odd numbers, and these cause the formation of aneuploid plants.

The term "aneuploid" is used to describe the condition of having a chromosome number over or under an exact multiple of the basic haploid or "n" number for the species. It is derived from the term "euploid" which means "true ploid." Euploid forms have exactly twice, or three times, or four or five times the n number. If *Cattleya* is used as an example, the euploid forms have exactly 40, 60, 80, or 100 chromosomes. Aneuploid means "not true ploid," and refers to plants that have something over or under 40, 60, 80, or 100 chromosomes. In plants that have two sets of unlike chromosomes, inherited from widely separated parent species, these chromosomes may not be able to pair at reduction division. Instead, they become assorted in odd ways, and, if functional sex cells are formed at all, they will probably contain odd numbers of chromosomes, such as 17 and 23, or 15 and 25, instead of the even 20 chromosomes each. Such sex cells will, when fertilized, give rise to aneuploid individuals, plants with chromosome numbers such as 37, 43, etc. The many failures to form functional sex cells accounts for the relative sterility of hybrids from quite unlike parents, as for example, *Cattleya* with *Schomburgkia*. (See Hybridization in Vanda in Chapter 11 for other examples.)

Aneuploids can also result from polyploid crosses. For example, in a triploid plant, which has three sets of chromosomes (60 in *Cattleya*) you might think that 30 of these would pair with the other 30. This is not what happens. A chromosome can pair only with its homologue. In a triploid there are three of each homologous type, instead of the usual two. Some chromosomes may form pairs, leaving the third homologue standing alone. Sometimes three will come together. As reduction division takes place, some of the pairs will separate normally. The unpaired chromosomes may drift to one pole or the other, but some may get stranded and, not arriving at either pole, fail to be included in the newly forming nuclei. The chromosomes that have come together by threes may separate so that two of them go to one pole and one to the other, or they may travel together so that one newly forming nucleus will receive all three while the other is left entirely without the genetic material they took with them. Some cells may be formed with only a few pairs and a few stragglers and thus have a very incomplete gene content. Most of such erratically formed cells cannot develop into functional sex cells, which accounts for the high degree of sterility in triploids. The same thing takes place in pentaploids.

A higher percentage of aneuploids occurs in some crosses than in others, showing that some plants are less regular in the formation of reproductive cells than others. Studies upon aneuploids show that those that have just one or two more or less than the euploid number can be quite normal. But plants whose chromosome numbers range far to one side or the other of a euploid number may suffer lack of vigor or be quite abnormal in some way. For example, if the euploid number is 60, plants with chromosome numbers of 58 or 59, or 61 or 62 may be quite normal, while those with numbers close to 50 or 70 may be abnormal. Whether the plants and their flowers appear normal, however, depends on the relative importance of the lost or added genetic material.

We mentioned earlier that occasionally gametes are formed without having their chromosome number reduced. The cells which are destined to form the sex cells go through the process retaining their full complement of chromosomes. It appears that some of the functional sex cells of triploids are of this nature. Crosses between triploids and diploids, and triploids and tetraploids seem to be more fruitful if the triploid is used as the female, or pod, parent. Diploids and tetraploids, having even sets of chromosomes, produce large numbers of functional reproductive cells, and when these types are used as the male, or pollen, parent, there is greater likelihood of obtaining some viable seed than if the triploid were used as the male parent. Although the fertility of triploids is notoriously low, *Cattleya* Bow Bells seems to be an exception. A number of triploid Bow Bells have been the parents of a long line of successful hybrids. We do not have all the data we could wish on these crosses, but it appears that successful matings have been made between triploid Bow Bells and diploid plants, as well as with triploid Bow Bells and tetraploids. Both tetraploids and pentaploids are among the progeny. The unusual fertility of these Bow Bells individuals seems to indicate that they are better able to form nonreduced gametes than many other triploids, and form them more freely. Since these Bow Bells crosses have appeared, some other crosses between triploids and tetraploids have been unexpectedly successful. It may well be that success depends on finding the more fertile of the triploids in any one group and then finding plants that will be compatible with them.

Pentaploids have been far fewer in number than tetraploids and triploids. Individual pentaploid plants have sprung from various polyploid crosses. In some cases these have not been as handsome or as vigorous as triploids and tetraploids, but this is not continuing to be true. Pentaploids can be formed by 3n × 4n matings, where the 3n parent contributes a nonreduced gamete and the 4n contributes a 2n gamete. A fairly high percentage of pentaploids occurs in crosses where *Cattleya* Bow Bells has been mated with a tetraploid.

Attempts to create pentaploids and to use them as parents have been frustrating. However, work that is being done now may point the way. Theodore Zuck reports that efforts to cross the pentaploid *Laeliocattleya* Rosa Kirsch with 2n and 3n plants failed, but that a fairly good number of seedlings was obtained when it was crossed with a tetraploid C. Titrianae. From among the seedlings, ten plants, counted at random, were all pentaploid. This would seem to have been brought about by fusion of 3n gametes from *Lc.* Rosa Kirsch with 2n gamete from C. Titrianae.

COLCHICINE

The chemical compound colchicine has been used by horticulturists for a good many years to create giant-size plants and flowers (tetraploids) and to make otherwise sterile hybrids capable of producing seed. Both results come from the same function of the chemical, which is to double the number of chromosomes. We often see tetraploids advertised in garden catalogs, for instance tetraploid snapdragons. The progenitors of most of these have been man-made tetraploids, formed by the use of colchicine.

In orchid genera where there is a lack of tetraploids in certain colors, for instance green in *Cymbidium,* it would be a great boon if desirable diploids could have their chromosomes doubled so that the resulting tetraploids could be used in breeding. Where hybrids are sterile, because of being triploids, or because they contain chromosomes from unlike parents, for example in *Schombocattleya,* semiterete *Vanda* hybrids, etc., or because of aneuploidy, they would become fertile if their chromosomes could be doubled. A number of workers have pioneered with colchicine, among them R. A. McLeod, Gavino Rotor, H. Y. Nakasone, H. Kamemoto, and Emma Menninger.

Colchicine upsets the normal process of cell division. Vegetative cells divide by a process different from that of reduction division. The process through which vegetative cells divide (as in the growing parts of plants) is called mitosis. In this process each chromosome duplicates itself so that each resulting cell receives the full complement of chromosomes. As a cell with 40 chromosomes divides, each newly forming cell receives a complete set of forty chromosomes.

The steps in mitosis are diagrammed briefly in Figure 7–15, using a cell with 4 chromosomes for the sake of simplicity. In this diagram, A shows a resting cell. In B, the chromosomes are shown after each one has duplicated itself. In C, the chromosomes are lined up in the center of the cell, with a protoplasmic strand attached to each. This arrangement of protoplasmic strands or fibers is called the "spindle." In D, the strands appear to pull the attached chromosomes to the poles of the cell, half of them to one pole, the other half to the other pole. In E, the chromosomes are reconstituted into two nuclei, and a cell wall grows between them, forming two separate cells.

The cell with 4 chromosomes has, for a brief interval, 8 chromosomes. In a cell with 40 chromosomes, at the time when these have duplicated themselves, the cell would momentarily contain 80. The peculiar action of colchicine is to interfere with the division process just at the point when the chromosomes have become duplicated. The cell is made to cease its activities and return to a resting condition, carrying the double number of chromosomes. When the effects of colchicine wear off, the cell begins the division process all over again. This time, the 80 chromosomes duplicate themselves so that there are 160. Half of these are drawn to each pole, so that the two new cells each receive 80 instead of the original 40. Thus the cells become tetraploid. The action of colchicine is shown in Figure 7–16.

The action of colchicine is not always perfectly regular. Sometimes an odd number of chromosomes is produced. Occasionally the doubling action is repeated, giving rise to cells that have four or eight times the normal chromosome number. Often not all cells are affected, so that the resulting plant may have some tetraploid parts mixed with normal parts. The ultimate aim is to produce plants

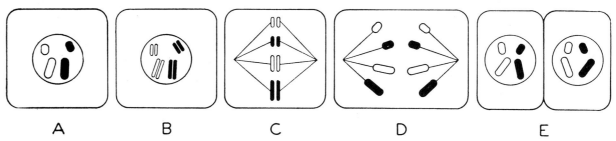

A   B   C   D   E

Figure 7–15 *Mitosis, the division of vegetative cells.*
A: *The resting cell.*
B: *Each chromosome duplicates itself.*
C: *The chromosome gather in a plane through the center of the cell.*

D: *Opposite duplicates of each chromosome are drawn to opposite poles.*
E: *The new cell wall comes between the newly separated sets of chromosomes, and two cells, each with a full complement of chromosomes, are formed.*

Figure 7–16 *The action of colchicine. Mitosis proceeds normally, A, B, and C, until colchicine is applied. Colchicine prevents migration of the chromosomes to the poles, C, and returns the cell to resting condition.*

D: *When mitosis resumes after the colchicine has worn off, the chromosomes duplicate themselves again.*
E: *The process goes to completion, F, G, and H, producing new cells with twice the chromosomes.*

that have tetraploid flowers, which will give reproductive cells bearing double the number of chromosomes.

Colchicine is poisonous to plants and to human beings. It must be used on plants in very weak dilutions, measured carefully. Too strong a concentration may kill the plants, yet the dose, to be effective, must be very near the lethal strength. Workers are cautioned not to let colchicine remain in contact with the skin, and particularly not to get it in the eyes. It should be kept away from children.

Mrs. Menninger reported her work in the *American Orchid Society Bulletin* for November 1963. She treated a cymbidium backbulb twice at a ten-day interval with a 0.3 percent solution of colchicine. Two years later a growth that developed from one of the eyes proved by root tip count to be tetraploid.

The work of Donald Wimber and Ann Van Cott is reported in the *Proceedings of the Fifth World Orchid Conference,* 1966, and further results by Wimber and Doris R. Wimber in the *American Orchid Society Bulletin,* July 1968. Seeds from diploid *Cymbidium* hybrids and a meristem culture from another diploid *Cymbidium* hybrid were treated. The seeds were first germinated in a liquid nutrient medium on a shaker until protocorms were

developed (four to six weeks). The meristem tissue was cultured in liquid medium on a shaker, then was cut up and put in fresh medium and returned to the shaker for two weeks. At this point sufficient 2.5 percent aqueous colchicine solution was injected into the flasks of both to make a concentration in the flasks of 0.05 percent, and the flasks were kept on the shaker for from ten days to three weeks. The protocorms from both flasks were then transferred to flasks of solid agar-nutrient medium. Five to six months later the plants were transferred to flats and from then on were grown under ordinary greenhouse conditions.

Approximately 40 percent of the treated seedlings and about 43 percent of the meristem plantlets proved to have become tetraploid. The rest had remained diploid except for a few chimaeras (plants in which there was some diploid, some tetraploid tissue). Ploidy determination was made by chromosome counts on root tip cells in some cases, and by measuring the stomata in others. (Wimber has done statistical studies on stomatal size in diploids and tetraploids and believes that they can be distinguished with fair certainty in this way.)*

---

* See Scott B. Wattrous and D. E. Wimber, "Artificial Induction of Polyploidy in *Paphiopedilum.*" *Lindleyana* 3(4): 177–183, 1988.

The later report (1968) on the flowering of the seedlings of one cross showed that in the tetraploids the flower parts were both broader and thicker, giving the flowers a fuller shape and heavier substance.

Wimber and Van Cott's treatment of protocorms was more fruitful than attempts of others to treat older seedlings, and had several advantages. For one thing, there was no problem of trying to avoid injury to roots, which is a factor with older seedlings, since colchicine can cause root damage. With such small masses of cells, not covered by layers of protective tissue, full penetration of colchicine was more likely.

Various techniques are being used for treating propagules made by means of meristem tissue culture. The protocormlike bodies are handled much like protocorms from seed germination. A great many genera have been worked on with varying results. In some cases the sterility barrier has been broken, allowing hybrids to be made that were otherwise impossible. Tetraploids have been created. The doubling of chromosomes in aneuploids has allowed interbreeding between plants that refused to form seed.

However, the fact that a plant is tetraploid does not guarantee that it will be a superior parent. If the diploid plant received an award before being converted, the award does not follow on to the tetraploid made from it. There should be some designation of the fact that a plant has been converted from one of a different ploidy.

It has been found that the guard cells of plants whose ploidy has been increased by colchicine treatment have been enlarged. Therefore a quick judgment as to whether the treatment was effective can be had by measuring the stomata (the opening around the guard cells). Their enlargement does not prove what kind of ploidy has been attained, however. Only actual chromosome counts can tell this (Fig. 7–17). (See footnote, page 81.)

DNA and RNA

The scientific inspiration of Dr. Watson and Dr. Crick in 1953 revealed the structure of DNA, deoxyribonucleic acid, the giant molecule that holds the coded information within each gene. This huge molecule, made up of thousands of chemical units, is in the form of a spiral ladder, which if magnified to a size we could climb would rival that in Jacob's dream and come close to reaching heaven. Its discoverers call it a double helix. The units can be described, purely schematically, as being "T" shaped, with the bar formed of a sugar (deoxyribose) linked to a phosphate, and the leg formed by one of four kinds of nitrogen bases, adenine, thymine, guanine, and cytosine. The units are called nucleotides, and the four kinds can be represented thus, using the initials D for deoxyribose, P for phosphate, A for adenine, T for thymine, G for guanine, and C for cytosine:

The nucleotides are manufactured by the nucleoplasm within the nucleus of the cell.

The D-P sections line up to make the sides of the ladder, while the A, T, G, C sections link across to make its rungs, A always joining with T, and G with C. A portion of the ladder would look something like this, flattened out from its spiral formation:

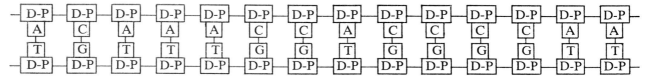

When cells divide and the chromosomes duplicate themselves, each DNA molecule also duplicates itself. It zips open up the center of the "ladder." Each A, T, G, C base attracts to itself its customary partner to form the other half of the DNA molecule, and thus two are formed identical to the original one. These are distributed equally to the new cells during mitosis.

And what does the DNA molecule do? It dictates the manufacture of a messenger to carry its information into the cytoplasm. The messenger is a ribonucleic acid molecule (RNA) a single-strand molecule slightly different chemically in having ribose sugar instead of deoxyribose, and uracil in place of thymine. RNA moves out of the nucleus into the cytoplasm, and there "tells" the cell to make a certain enzyme for a certain activity. Each DNA molecule (gene) therefore brings about the manufacture of its own RNA counterpart, which controls a certain function of the cell.

Figure 7–17 *Chromosomes in root tip cells of* Vanda. *From* LEFT *to* RIGHT: *a diploid, with 38 chromosomes; a triploid, with 57 chromosomes; a tetraploid, with 76* chromosomes; *a pentaploid, with 95 chromosomes.* (COURTESY OF H. KAMEMOTO.)

Considering that there are thousands of genes, each composed of a huge DNA molecule containing a thousand or more nucleotide units in a definite order, one must marvel at the exquisite precision with which cell division takes place. A "mistake" or a change in the succession of nucleotides would result in a new message being carried to the cell. Such a change in message would bring about altered activity, and therefore a change in the individual, or in other words, a mutation. Many of the "mistakes" never come to light because they result in failure or death of the organism. Many others, not lethal, have resulted in new forms; in orchids perhaps joined sepals, or longer stems, or a different lip pattern. Long accumulation of such changes has brought about new species. The myriad forms of life on earth today are the result of changes in the codes within the genes.

Many mysteries still remain to be understood. We do not know, for instance, where the impulse comes from to initiate cell division, to cause the unzipping of the DNA molecules and their reconstitution. Thus, while the discovery of DNA and RNA and the elucidation of their structure and function were great milestones in scientific understanding, we remain in awe of, and gratitude for, the orderly mechanisms of nature.

Group I, ccRR Whites	**Group II, CCrr Whites**
C. gaskelliana var. *alba* (H)	*C. eldorado* 'Alba' (H)
C. intermedia 'Alba' (H)	*C. harrisoniana* var. *alba* (H)
C. labiata 'Alba' (H)	*C. mendelii* 'Alba' (H)
C. labiata 'Harefield Hall' (M)	*C. percivaliana* 'Alba' (H)
C. loddigesii 'Alba' (C and D)	*C. schroederae* 'Alba'
C. loddigesii 'Stanley' (M)	*C. trianaei* 'Alba'* (C and D)
C. uddemanniana 'Alba' (C and D)	*C. warneri* 'Alba' (H)
C. mossiae var. *wageneri* (H)	*C. warscewiczii (gigas)* 'Firmin Lambeau'** (C and D)
C. Obrieniana 'Alba' (Nat. hybrid, *dolosa* X *loddigesii*) (M)	
C. skinneri 'Alba' (H)	
C. speciosissima 'Alba' (L and W)	
C. trianaei 'Alba'* (C and D)	
C. trianaei 'Broomhills' (M)	
C. trianaei 'Verdonck' (M)	
C. warneri 'Alba' (C and D)	

* *C. trianaei* 'Alba' seems to include both genetic types. Only breeding with other whites can prove to which group a particular plant belongs.
** Pure white *C. warscewiczii* are very rare. The 'Firmin Lambeau' by its behavior seems to fit in this group, but there is no data on other whites of this species.
(H) Hurst's original list.
(M) Added by Melquist.
(C and D) Added by Curtis and Duncan.
(L and W) Added by Lenz and Wimber?
The above expanded list from "Hybridization and Inheritance in Orchids," Lenz and Wimber, in *The Orchids*, edited by Withner.

·8·

GROWING AND SOWING YOUR OWN SEED

❧

O NE OF THE MAIN CARES OF nature, after assuring the nourishment and growth of a plant, is to insure its reproduction and the continuation of the species. Various ways have been devised for scattering the seed, for moving it away from the parent plant to more open ground.

The diversity of such mechanisms is a fascinating study in itself. There are plants that have ways of forcibly ejecting the seed from the pod or capsule, such as the Siberian pea and oxalis. Others offer fruits tender and tasty, brightly colored, which attract birds and animals that carry away their seed. The cockleburs make a nuisance of themselves by their method of forcing their seed upon whatever agent happens their way. The exquisite forms of wind-borne seed are well known for their delicate umbrellas and parachutes.

But not every seed that is produced finds conditions suited to its germination. Only those fortunate enough to land in just the right spot can grow to maturity. Hence plants in even the best of circumstances must produce more seed than will ever grow.

Epiphytic orchids face a special problem in seed dispersal. If only one seed from each capsule should germinate and survive to maturity the continuation of the species would be well assured, but the chances are slim that a seed will find some obscure crevice in the bark of a tree where it can germinate, or that it will have there the necessary conditions of air, light, moisture, and mineral nutrients. In order to guarantee success against overwhelming odds, each plant produces hundreds of thousands of seeds every year. A scientific count of the seed in a capsule of *Cycnoches chlorochilon* revealed that it contained 3,770,000.

The formation of so many seeds by rather small plants means that the seeds must be very tiny, which is true of all epiphytic orchid seeds. The seed of cattleyas is as fine as powder, and close to a million are formed in one capsule. Its small size allows it to be carried by the gentle air currents in the jungle that are not strong enough to lift heavy particles to great heights. As the seed capsule ripens and splits open, the drift of pale yellow powder is picked up by the moving air and dusted from branch to branch. Some of the seed is blown away by stronger winds that meet the upward air currents above the jungle. Much of the seed, of course, drifts down to the ground where it has no chance to grow.

Because of its small size, the seed contains little, if any, food to nourish the embryo during germination. It must find a ready supply where it falls. In a pocket of decaying vegetable matter, there will be available minerals and sugars released by the decomposing action of fungi and bacteria. And as will be seen in a moment, the presence of sugars is all-important to bring about the germination of the seed.

Even after successful germination, the seedling still faces hazards of destruction, overgrowth of fungi, burning by the sun if it has insufficient shade, or even desiccation if it does not receive frequent enough rain.

The first growers who tried to germinate orchid seed ran into problems that plagued them and their followers for three-quarters of a century. Various methods were tried to induce germination. The seed was sown on leaf mold, decaying bark, sphagnum moss, etc. More often than not, if the recalcitrant seed did germinate, much of it was killed by invading bacteria and fungi. When these attempts failed, growers set to work on the theory that germination might be induced by contact of the seed with some fungus found in association with parent orchid plants. The experiments that followed were intricate, and consisted of infecting the seed with isolated strains of fungi, called the symbiotic method. Enough success came from this work to carry the fungus method on for many years. But it was a technique that could be used only by experts, and even in their hands there was often destruction of the seed by the fungi.

It remained for Dr. Lewis Knudson of Cornell University, in 1922, to find a completely controlled, standardized, simple method for germinating orchid seed. He had done previous work that showed that sugars had a favorable influence on plant growth, which suggested to him that orchid seed might require the presence of sugar to germinate. He interpreted the success with fungi, not to its effect on the seed itself, but to digestion by the fungi of some of the carbohydrates and nitrogenous substances present in the growing medium. Sugars would be among the materials released in this process.

This proved to be true. Dr. Knudson found that the seed germinated readily without the presence of fungi when sown on an agar jelly to which had been added the necessary mineral nutrients plus sugar. Patiently he worked to find out what was the best sugar to use, and in what concentration. He also had to adjust the proportions of the mineral nutrients. The flasks containing the agar-nutrient mixture were sterilized, and the seed was disinfected to kill foreign organisms that might enter the flasks with it. The flasks were stoppered after being sown, and they were left untouched until the seedlings were well developed, some eight months to a year later. The flasks were perfect little glasshouses, protecting the tiny plants from insects and contamination, and providing them with a constantly moist atmosphere until they were well developed. This is called the asymbiotic method.

Dr. Knudson's method revolutionized orchid growing. He removed the guesswork, the confusion and the hazards, and gave growers a technique that was easy to use and certain of success. It is simple enough to measure out the ingredients for making the agar-nutrient jelly, and now it is even possible to buy the mixture all prepared except for the addition of water.

In the jungle, only an occasional seed of the tremendous numbers produced has a chance to germinate. Now, in the hands of man, nearly every seed may become a plant. Growers who once zealously guarded every hybrid seedling now hardly know what to do with the countless thousands they produce. This has put orchids on a par with other greenhouse crops and made orchid plants available to all.

Needless to say, Dr. Knudson's flask method has given a tremendous impetus to orchid growing, not only by increasing the numbers of plants grown commercially, but by making it possible for amateurs to grow their own.

POLLINATION

A simple maneuver with the forceps starts a seed capsule on its way in your greenhouse. The human hand can perform in an instant the function of pollination, which in nature requires the most elaborate preparation and clever groundwork. Few orchids are capable of self-pollination. In fact, most orchids are constructed so that self-pollination in nature is impossible. In the long struggle for survival, those orchids which were perpetuated by cross-fertilization were the more vigorous, and lived to maintain their kind.

The relationship between orchids and their pollinators is one of the marvels of nature. They are equipped with fascinatingly ingenious mechanisms by means of which insects are practically forced to carry the pollen from one flower to another. Each mechanism is so well designed as to be almost foolproof, but an individual orchid lives under a perpetual handicap. Its mechanism will work only if an insect of just the right size and shape enters the portals so attractively spread for its reception. A tiny orchid, just one-quarter inch in diameter, requires a very small insect, while another, whose nectar tube is in the form of a spur ten inches long, needs the services of a species of moth with a ten-inch proboscis. A flower may be visited by scores of insects, yet may wither and die before the kind comes along that can serve as bearer of its pollen. However, when the right one does visit the flower, the insect is not allowed to leave without carrying with it a parcel of pollen glued to its anatomy.

The pollen grains are fastened together in rather large waxy masses called pollinia, each of which contains enough pollen to fertilize another flower satisfactorily. Cleverly enough, in order to insure cross-pollination, orchids fasten the pollen masses to the insect as it leaves the flower.

Figure 8–1 shows in detail the reproductive parts of the cattleya. The column is shown from its underside in A, and cut in half lengthwise in B. The anther (a), the cap that covers the pollinia, is fastened by a tiny hinge (h) to the end of the column. Protruding slightly from under the anther are the

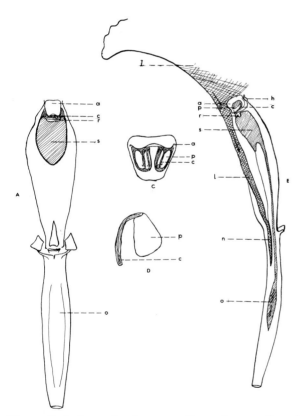

Figure 8–1 *Reproductive parts of a cattleya.* A: *the column from its underside, with the flower parts removed;* B: *a view of the column cut in half, wherein it is seen that what appears to be the stem of the flower is actually the ovary:*
(a) anther, (h) hinge that holds the anther in place, (p) pollinium, (r) rostellum, (s) stigma, (l) lip, (n) nectary, (o) ovary. C, *a view of the anther from its underside, showing the pollinia.* D, *a single pollinium with its caudicle.*

tips of the four caudicles (c) attached to the pollinia (p). The rostellum (r), the partition between the anther chambers and the stigma, has on its underside a gland that secretes a sticky fluid. The stigma, which is really two stigmas grown together through the processes of evolution, is indicated by (s). The lip (l) presses up close under the column, forming a narrow passageway down which an insect must travel to reach the nectary (n) at its base. Fig. 8–1C shows the pollinia as they are situated in the anther chambers, after the anther has been raised, and Fig. 8–1D shows a single pollinium with attached caudicle.

The flower is pollinated by any rather large bee. When the bee lights on the lip its weight depresses the lip somewhat, and it then passes down the tube to get nectar. As it backs out of the tube, it pushes against the rostellum (r), ruptures the gland, and becomes smeared with its sticky secretion. The force of the bee against the rostellum tips up the anther cap, touching off the spring. The anther flies back, rotating the pollinia so that the caudicles are exposed. As the bee backs farther out, the caudicles are caught in the sticky fluid on its back, and the pollinia are pulled out.

When the bee visits the next cattleya, the pollinia on its back are forced into the stigmatic cavity. The stigmatic fluid is so sticky that it grips the pollen masses and tears them from the caudicles. After its feast of nectar, the bee leaves the flower with only the stumps of the caudicles attached, but in the process it will take with it the pollinia from this flower (if they have not already been removed) and bestow them on the next one it visits. You can imitate this by using a cotton swab for a bee. Push it down between the column and the lip, and as you pull it out watch the pollinia come with it. Then push it back into the flower and watch the pollinia stick to the stigma.

The simple sleight of hand that human beings can substitute for the natural process is to remove the pollinia from one orchid and place them directly on the stigma of another. But there is a difference between your responsibility and that of the flower where pollination is concerned. The flower makes elaborate preparations to insure pollination and the production of a huge number of seeds, from which possibly only one or two seedling will grow. Your preparation consists of giving great care to the choice of parent plants so that the innumerable seeds you germinate will be worth your energy to raise.

A seedling blooming for the first time should not

be allowed to bear a seed capsule. The production of seed would take more food than it can afford and still be able to make good growth. A very large, heavy plant may carry two or three capsules at the same time or may bear capsules in successive years. If you wish to cross the same plant with two or three others, use a separate flower for each kind of pollen. Never put two kinds of pollen on one flower.

A flower must be allowed to reach its prime before it is pollinated, that is, it must have been open for several days. Remove its own pollinia before placing the pollen from the other plant on its stigma (Fig. 8–2). If you have a particularly handsome flower with nothing else at the moment to match it in quality, it is possible to keep its pollen for use in the future. (See below under storing seed and pollen.)

Figure 8–2 *Steps in pollination.*
A: *Remove the anther from the flower selected as the parent. Hold a clean piece of paper under the column and tip off the anther onto it.*
B: *The anther is separated from the column.*
C: *Nudge the pollinia out of the anther.*
D: *In order to pick up a pollinium, use a clean toothpick.*

Touch its tip to the sticky fluid of the stigma and then touch the caudicle of a pollinium. The pollinium will adhere to the drop of fluid.
E: *Place the pollinium on the stigma.*
F: *Pollination is completed, with two pollinia on the stigma.*

It is not necessary to use all four pollinia in the pollination of one flower. Actually, nature has provided enough pollen in one pollen mass to produce a capsule full of seed. The other three might be called a safety factor. However, it is customary to use two pollinia, one on the left lobe and one on the right lobe of the stigma.

To obtain the pollinia, hold a clean piece of paper under the tip of the column and gently tip up the anther cap with a clean toothpick or other pointed instrument. The anther chambers (actually the whole tip of the column) will come loose and fall onto the paper. Push the pollinia out of their chambers with the same instrument, being careful not to touch them with your fingers. An easy way to transfer a pollinium to the other flower is to touch the stigma with your instrument and then touch the pollen mass. The pollinium will stick to the viscid drop on the instrument. Pollination is performed simply by pressing the pollinia well into the stigmatic fluid, one on each side. Once covered by the sticky substance, they will not fall off.

The first reaction of the flower after pollination is to wilt, sometimes within a few hours, certainly after two days. After the flower parts have wilted they should be cut off at their base to prevent decay and possible infection of the column. The column is, of course, left intact during formation of the seed capsule.

DEVELOPMENT OF THE SEED CAPSULE

Within a week after pollination, the tip of the column becomes swollen and the pollinia seem to have been drawn deeply into the cavity. At about the same time, the ovary begins to enlarge. These reactions are merely the first responses to the presence of the pollen in the stigma. They are not a sign that fertilization of the eggs has taken place.

Each pollen grain, stimulated by the action of the stigmatic fluid, sends out a long slender tube. The pollen tubes grow down through the channel of the column, along the walls of the ovary, and eventually each tube penetrates an ovule. Figure 8–3A shows this process, and Figure 8–3B shows sprouted pollen grains. During the growth of the pollen tube, two sperm cells are formed within it, one of which unites with the egg nucleus in the ovule. (The other sperm cell unites with other nuclei in the ovule to form the endosperm, tissue used

as food by the developing embryo.) It takes sixty to ninety days for the pollen tubes to complete their growth and penetrate the ovules.

Every viable seed formed is the result of the penetration of an ovule by a pollen tube. Production of 500,000 seeds means that 500,000 pollen tubes were able to find their mark. How the 500,000th tube manages to find a still unfertilized ovule is something to puzzle over, let alone the millionth or three millionth. That many pollen tubes are not successful is attested by the fact that often the greatest concentration of viable seed is found near the top of the ovary.

Incompatibility between the pollen and the flower on which it is placed often occurs. Sometimes it shows up within a few days by the shriveling of the column. The same pollen used on another flower might, however, have effected a successful mating. Sometimes a capsule that seems to be progressing will turn yellow and drop off after two or three months. The ovules are immature at the time of pollination. Their maturation pro-

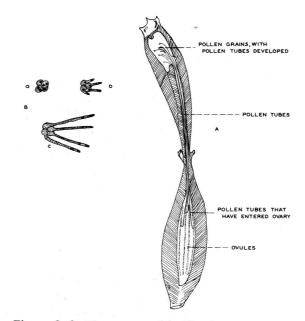

POLLEN GRAINS, WITH
POLLEN TUBES DEVELOPED

POLLEN TUBES

POLLEN TUBES THAT
HAVE ENTERED OVARY

OVULES

Figure 8–3 *The process of fertilization.*
A: *The column and ovary sixty days after pollination. The pollen tubes have grown from the pollen grains in the stigma down into the ovary, which by this time is definitely enlarged. During this sixty days the ovules have been maturing so that they are now ready to receive the sperm cells brought to them by the pollen tubes.*
B: *Pollen grains at various stages:*
a, as they originate, usually in groups of four; b, with tubes just starting; c, tubes elongating, and the nuclei carried along near their tips.

ceeds and the ovary enlarges while the pollen tubes are growing the necessary length. If for some reason the pollen tubes finally fail to effect fertilization, growth of the capsule ceases.

If the cross is compatible, the ovary enlarges steadily. During its development it becomes marked with three deep flutings, corresponding to the three faint linear depressions visible on the ovary before pollination. The capsule is completely hollow, containing three broad bands (placentae) to which the ovules are attached.

At six months the capsule is about the size of a lemon, and it does not enlarge much after this time. It ripens at about nine to ten months, occasionally later, and cracks open down the center of the flutings. The time to remove it is just when the cracks begin to show, before they have opened wide enough to allow the seed to spill out. To prevent losing any seed, it is a good idea to tie tissue paper over it a few weeks beforehand, and examine it from day to day. When the time comes for its removal, cut the stem that holds it to the pseudobulb, and place it in a clean glass jar to dry. Set the jar in a dry place, leaving it uncovered. Do not leave it in the greenhouse. If your climate is damp, the capsule should be wrapped lightly in tissue paper and dried in a desiccator containing calcium chloride. When it is dried and split completely open, the seed can be shaken out into a clean container. It is ready for sowing at this time, but excess seed should be stored properly.

STORING SEED AND POLLEN

A desiccator is a glass container having two chambers, one holding calcium chloride which absorbs water vapor and the other containing the stored material. They can be purchased, but are rather expensive. A makeshift one will do as well. Use a wide-mouthed jar, and put two tablespoons of calcium chloride in the bottom. Make a shelf, out of hardware cloth or screen, that will rest in the center and divide the jar into two compartments, separating the calcium chloride from the upper part. A layer of paper over the screen will afford additional protection, yet still allow free circulation of air. Put the material to be stored in the top section, and screw a vacuum sealing lid on tightly. While drying the capsule in the desiccator, let it remain at room temperature, as it will dry more rapidly this way than under refrigeration.

After the seed is removed from the capsule, it should be kept under refrigeration. Cut pieces of writing paper (not wax paper) about four inches square, and in the center of each write the names of the parent so that the label will be visible after the seed is wrapped. Then put a small amount of seed in each paper, and fold carefully, fastening the ends with a paper clip. Place the packages in the desiccator, screw on the lid, and put in the refrigerator.

Seed retains its viability for a long time when stored in this manner, sometimes as long as six years. The percentage of germination decreases gradually, however, so that it may give only twenty to forty percent after a long period.

Pollen does not remain viable for as long as seed, but may be kept for at least six months. Its viability is highest during the first few weeks. To store, place the pollinia in a glass tube, cork tightly, and dip the corked end in paraffin. Keep it in the refrigerator or at room temperature away from heat. Some advise the addition of a few granules of calcium chloride to the tube (in which case the pollinia must be wrapped in tissue paper to prevent contact with the calcium chloride), or the use of a small packet of silica gel. The pollinia may be dried in a desiccator for two days before placing in the glass tube.

Long-Term Seed Storage

The need to conserve the species has become more urgent with the destruction of tropical forests. The formation of seed banks offers a practical method for saving species now threatened with extinction as well as rare and valuable kinds that might be lost through carelessness. By freezing (cryogenics), seed can be preserved for many years, probably even for hundreds. It must first be desiccated because water allows crystals to form, with resultant disruption of the cell structure. After desiccation, it can be stored at temperatures ranging from -15° to -30°C (5° to -22°F).

CHECKING VIABILITY OF SEED AND POLLEN

Crosses between closely related species usually produce viable seed and pollen. Sterility is more likely to occur in complicated hybrids, particularly those derived from extremely dissimilar flowers. Testing the viability of seed and pollen is a simple matter, though in nine cases out of ten it is not necessary for amateurs to bother with it. Commercial growers and those who are carrying on serious breeding programs find it a necessary procedure.

To test the pollen, place a little of it on a flower that you do not wish to save, a "cull." Pollen tubes commence to grow within forty-eight hours and can be seen under a microscope. Remove some of the stigmatic fluid on a pin, mix it with a drop of water on a microscope slide, and cover with a cover glass. The sprouted pollen can be seen unstained, but if you wish to stain them add a drop of crystal violet solution to the water. Or, pollen may be tested in a 0.2-molar sucrose solution (about one teaspoon of sugar in thirteen teaspoons of water) with agar added, kept at 72°.

In any batch of seed there are some that do not contain embryos. To observe your own seed, mix a small amount with water and place on a slide under a cover glass. Count the seed with and without embryos and estimate the relative percentage of good seed; 80 to 90 percent is good. If no seeds have embryos, the lot must be discarded. You will have to use your own judgment as to whether to use seed that shows only a low percentage with embryos. Perhaps it will pay to try it for the sake of obtaining a few seedlings from a most unusual cross, or from one that rarely gives seed.

A further check of seed viability is to sow a flask or two and see how well it germinates. This necessitates waiting three or four weeks, or until the seed swells and turns green. It sometimes happens (though rarely) that seed that appears under the microscope to be good is actually not living. This check would be well worth your while for seed that has been stored an excessively long time or has not been kept under good conditions.

Seed may be differentially stained to make it easier to see the living embryos. Tetrazolium chloride, which colors living tissue red, and malachite green, which colors nonliving tissue green, are the two stains used. Dissolve 1 gram of tetrazolium, a yellow powder, in 100 ml of distilled water and store in a dark bottle. The pH must be 6–7. Soak the seed first in distilled water, and then add it to a vial of tetrazolium solution for 18–24 hours in complete darkness. After the seed turns red, wash it and put it in a watch glass (or any tiny glass dish) in a 0.01 percent solution of malachite green (1 ml to 1000 ml water), for 30–45 minutes. Then place some seed on a microscope slide in a drop of gly-

cerine, and study. The slide can be sealed and kept if you wish. The contrast between the red embryos and green seed coats is quite striking.

PREPARATION OF THE FLASKS

The agar-nutrient medium for growing flask seedlings can be bought ready mixed, so that beginners need not be awed by the list of chemicals involved. A number of companies offer prepared media, some for different kinds of orchids. Complete directions are given for all, requiring only the addition of distilled water and warming, and if followed carefully results should be perfect. The mixtures are adjusted to the correct pH, so that the beginner does not even have this to worry him.

If you wish to have the seed germinated for you, there are commercial growers who offer the service. It is a fine arrangement for those who wish to raise only a few seedlings each from their own crosses, or who do not have the time or place to care for flasks.

Usually, 500-cc Ehrlenmeyer flasks are used, but wide-mouthed clear glass bottles are frequently preferred (Fig. 8–4). The latter may have bakelite screw caps or be fitted with rubber stoppers. They must be able to take sterilization and be large enough to give several square inches of surface of agar. Large test tubes may also be used, although these will hold fewer seedlings. Everything should be washed thoroughly and be rinsed several times.

Rubber stoppers are much easier to handle than the conventional cotton plug. They should be boiled for fifteen minutes before use. The stopper should have a hole in the center, through which is put a piece of glass tubing bent over at the top, for ventilation of the bottle or flask. The bent-down end of the glass tubing is closed with cotton. This arrangement helps prevent the latent contamination of the flask, which is a nuisance with the cotton stoppers. Also, it is easier to sterilize the rubber stopper and neck of the flask at the time of seed sowing or transplanting.

When the agar-nutrient mixture has been prepared, it is ready to be poured into the flasks or bottles. These may be slanted, if you wish, or kept in an upright position. If you prefer them slanted, build a rack beforehand to hold them in the desired position. Many prefer the "slants" as they afford a somewhat larger surface area, and their horizontal position helps to prevent the entrance of mold spores when the flask is opened for sow-

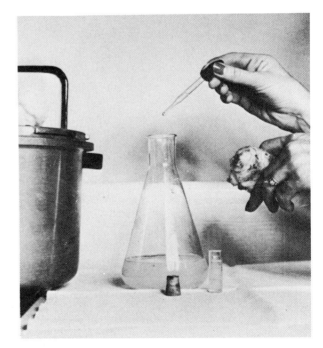

Figure 8–4 *Preparing flasks and sowing seed.*

UPPER LEFT: *Add measured amount of prepared agar-nutrient mixture to one liter of distilled water in double boiler. Heat until thoroughly dissolved.*

LOWER LEFT: *Pour the melted agar-nutrient mixture into flasks, using a long-stemmed funnel. The flasks are then stoppered and sterilized in a pressure cooker.*

UPPER RIGHT: *Disinfecting the seed. Calcium hypochlorite solution from the flask at the left is put in a small vial, to which is added a bit of seed on the tip of a knife. The dropper to be used in the sowing process is put to soak at the same time in a cup containing calcium hy-*

pochlorite solution. The vial of seed will be shaken for twenty minutes.

LOWER RIGHT: *Flasks are taken one at a time from the pressure cooker in which they were sterilized and allowed to cool. Here we have used cotton stoppers, but it is recommended that rubber stoppers be used instead (screw caps for bottles). These last should be put in a dish of sterilizing solution while the seed is being sown. Place a few drops of the suspended seed in the flask and replace the stopper. Cover the stopper and neck of the flask with foil or film.*

ing. Use a long-stemmed funnel for pouring the agar, so that it will reach down into the flask and prevent splashing agar on the sides or, most important, on the neck. This is essential to prevent the sticking of the stopper and to avoid giving molds a place to grow. The agar should be about an inch and one-half deep.

The flasks or bottles should be stoppered before sterilization. Screw caps should be tightened firmly and then released one-quarter turn.

Laboratory workers will be able to sterilize the flasks in an autoclave, but home canning equipment, preferably a pressure cooker, does just as well. You must be sure that no water enters the flasks. In a pressure cooker, twenty minutes at fifteen pounds pressure is sufficient. After sterilization, remove the flasks while still hot, pour the water out of the cooker, and quickly put the flasks back in and cover with a clean cloth. This will allow them to cool without becoming contaminated. If possible, keep them thus protected until you are ready to use them. They are ready as soon as they are cool and the agar is jelled.

SOWING THE SEED

This process is so simple that the doing of it takes no longer than the telling. In fact, none of the procedures is difficult, and if the detailed descriptions make any part of them seem so, you have only to try it all, step by step, to realize that each is essentially easy. The second time you go through the process you will wonder that you could ever have thought it complicated.

Sowing the seed consists of two main steps: (1) disinfecting the seed by soaking it in an antiseptic solution, and (2) putting a little of the suspended seed in each flask. We shall give you several methods—take your choice. In each method cleanliness is an important factor. The air is filled with mold spores. You are going to have to open the sterile flasks briefly to insert the seed, and you must take every precaution against contamination of the flasks during this time (Fig. 8–5). Wait until the day's activities are over in the kitchen and the air has had time to settle before you begin your work. I like to spread damp dish towels on the work surface as a protection against dust, and the effect is better if they are wrung out of a 10 percent Clorox solution (one part Clorox to nine of water). Ingenious "kitchen sowers" often find ways to make a

temporary protected area or "tent" of plastic film, such as that which come on dry cleaning. With the towels wrung out of Clorox on the work surface, the tents can be erected and everything be put inside. The worker then slips his hands under the front flap of plastic and quickly performs the operations.

METHOD 1. Equipment you will need in addition to the prepared flasks includes a one-quarter-ounce vial with a cork, a new medicine dropper, a glass or china cup, a graduated cylinder that holds 100 cc, two empty bottles, filter paper, a glass funnel, an open flame (gas burner or alcohol lamp), a small bowl, and a paring knife.

The seed may harbor mold spores acquired during handling and must therefore be disinfected. A solution of calcium hypochlorite* is standard for this purpose. Buy a bottle of it at the drugstore and keep it tightly stoppered in the refrigerator. To make up the solution put 10 grams of the solid calcium hypochlorite in one bottle and add 140 cc of distilled water. Shake it thoroughly and let it stand for one hour, shaking it at intervals. Then filter off the clear solution into the other bottle. This must be used at once. (Any amount left over must be thrown away and fresh solution made up each time you prepare to sow flasks.)

Fill the little vial two-thirds with the calcium hypochlorite solution, and add a tiny bit of seed. The amount you can pick up on the tip of a paring knife will sow ten or a dozen flasks. (The knife, incidentally, should be sterilized by flaming and completely cooled before touching the seed.) Cork the vial tightly. The seed must be thoroughly wetted with the calcium hypochlorite solution, which means that it must be shaken vigorously and continuously for at least twenty minutes to break up the minute air bubbles that surround each seed.

While you are shaking the seed, put some of the remaining calcium hypochlorite solution in the cup and place the dropper in it to soak, being sure to fill the bulb as well as the glass tube. You might also check on the arrangement of your equipment. Everything should be close together: the flasks, still in their covered container, and the cup with the dropper. In the bowl put a solution of 10 percent Clorox for disinfecting the stopper while it is removed during sowing.

---

* Note that calcium hypochlorite is an entirely different chemical from the calcium chloride used in the desiccator. Calcium hypochlorite may be purchased as chlorinated lime.

Figure 8–5 *A bio-clean work area called a laminar flow cabinet for aseptic procedures. A. A unit suitable for work on a small scale. B. Sowing seed. C. Transplanting flasks.* (A, COURTESY OF GENERAL ACOUSTICS CORPORATION, 12248 SANTA MONICA BOULEVARD, LOS ANGELES, CALIFORNIA 90025. B AND C, COURTESY OF THE JOHN WALTERS FAMILY.)

When the seed has been disinfected, you are ready to sow the flasks. With *Cattleya* and some other kinds, the good seed sinks to the bottom and the chaff floats on top. This top portion may be poured off. The work will move more smoothly if you can have a helper at your first session, either to attend to the flasks or to drop the seed into them, but you can manage alone if you must. The following operations must be performed quickly so that the flask will be open to the air for as short a time as possible.

Take one flask at a time from the covered container and remove the stopper or screw cap. Place this in the bowl of Clorox.

Seed that has sunk to the bottom of the vial or which in some cases has stuck to the sides, must be stirred up. This can be done by inserting the dropper into the fluid and forcing a few drops of air out of it. The bubbles will swirl the seed, and you can then take up a few drops of seed and fluid together to transfer to the flask. Put the dropper down the neck of the flask so that the drops will not run down the sides. Four drops is a good amount to put in each one, and if you move the dropper slightly in a circle you can put each drop in a different place on the agar. As soon as the seed

is dropped in, take the stopper from the bowl, drain off any excess Clorox so that none will enter the flask, and replace it on the flask.

When all of the flasks are sown, pick up each one and gently tilt it back and forth to spread the seed over the surface of the agar. The screw cap or stopper must be covered, preferably with foil fastened with tape. Be sure that all flasks are labeled and dated.

One or two of the flasks may have become contaminated at the time of sowing and they will show growth of molds on the agar within a few days. It is to be hoped that not all of them will be so affected. If you work very carefully you may be able to get rid of a spot of mold, provided you find it while it is still small. Swab the neck, rim and stopper with 10 percent Clorox. Sterilize a long-handled instrument. Working in an area prepared as for flask sowing, open the flask, reach in and cut out the spot with the surrounding agar, and gently lift it out. Be sure that you do not touch the sides of the flask in the operation, else the mold may thus be spread. Drop a few drops of a 1:2000 solution of 8-hydroxy quinoline benzoate or a 1:2000 solution of Natriphene on the area and re-stopper the flask. The more quickly this is done, the less chance there is for further contamination. If the seedlings are large enough to handle (or even if still protocorms) they may all be removed and be soaked in a 1% solution of Clorox, then put into fresh flasks.

METHOD 2. This method employs a hypodermic syringe to inject the seed into the flask. Instead of a bent glass tube in the rubber stopper, a short straight tube is used, with cotton placed in it as before. Put a few drops of 10 percent Clorox on the cotton. The seed in suspension is picked up with a sterile hypodermic (a large bore needle is necessary). The needle is then dipped in 10 percent Clorox, forced between the cotton and the glass of the tube, and the seed squirted into the flask. If the seed tends to stick to the needle, it can be alleviated by adding a bit of 10 percent warm agar solution to the vial containing the seed and disinfectant. The stopper should be covered with foil after the flasks are sowed.

METHOD 3. The actual process of sowing the flasks is the same as described in Method 1, but the danger of contamination is reduced by the use of a "sleeve box." This is a box constructed with a slanting hinged glass lid and holes in the front or ends through which you can put your hands. Some growers like to add sleeves made of cloth and fastened on the outside of the holes. These have elastic in the ends so that they fit well up over the forearm. Wipe or spray the inside surfaces of the box with 10 percent Clorox before use.

Place everything you need in the box before inserting your hands: sterilized flasks, sterilized dropper in cup of calcium hypochlorite solution, vial of disinfected seed, saucer of 10 percent Clorox for holding stoppers or lids, and squares of foil or polyethylene film for covering the flasks. You may wish to wear rubber gloves while working. It is not recommended that these be fastened to the ends of the sleeves, as the struggle to put them on often causes air to be sucked into the case with some force. After you have everything in readiness, put on the gloves, wash them in Clorox solution, insert your hands through the sleeves, and then wipe off the gloves with a cloth wrung out of Clorox solution placed in the box for this purpose.

Ready-made flasking "areas" are available. A plastic domelike case with holes for inserting the hands can be bought with or without racks for holding the flasks. Another and more expensive arrangement is a self-contained air-conditioned unit called a laminar flow cabinet. The unit keep sterile air moving through "absolute" filters, out through a shielded work space. In the air-conditioned area, where air is moving, dry seed cannot be exposed else it will be blown away.

CARE OF FLASKS

Cattleya seed germinates and grows best at temperatures between 70° and 75°. The temperature may rise a little in warm weather. Ideally the temperature should be 70° to 75° at night also, but if you cannot maintain this, let the night temperature drop to 65°. A fluctuation of more than 10 degrees either way is not good for the developing seedlings and will retard their growth. Flasks may be kept on a shaded shelf in the greenhouse or in a glass case with added humidity in the house. The latter is necessary to keep the flasks from drying in the drier atmosphere of the house. They need only 200 foot-candles of light. Flasks do very well under Gro-Lux lights, placed 12 inches under two 40-watt bulbs.

In extreme cases of drying, it is necessary to add a little sterile distilled water to the flask. This is a risky procedure, however, and unless done expertly may result in contamination. The screw cap or stopper and the rim and neck of the flask must be thoroughly swabbed with 10 percent Clorox before opening. Then lift the lid only high enough to admit the dropper (previously sterilized) and replace it quickly after the water is added. If you have used a stopper with a short straight tube, as in Method 2, put a few drops of 10 percent Clorox on the cotton and inject the sterile distilled water by means of a hypodermic syringe, inserting the needle between the glass and the cotton. Cover the stopper with fresh foil afterward.

During the development of the seedlings, disturb the flasks as little as possible. Jostling the flasks sometimes allows mold spores that have settled on the neck or the stopper to drop into the agar and cause contamination.

DEVELOPMENT OF THE SEEDLINGS

About ten days or two weeks after the seed is sown it begins to swell. Within six weeks the seed turns green, showing the development of chlorophyll. Figure 8–6 shows the stages of development of the seedling. The embryo continues to increase in size until it is a little green spherule, about $1/16$ inch in diameter, shaped like a top, with a depression in its upper surface. Absorbing hairs soon cover the surface. Between two and three months after the seed was sown, the first leaf point makes its appearance in the middle of the depression, and the spherule becomes larger and somewhat flattened. This disclike structure is called the proto-

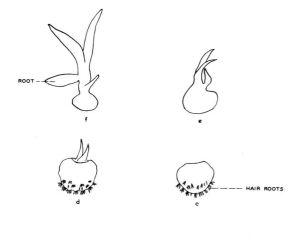

ROOT

f

e

d

c

HAIR ROOTS

a

b

Figure 8–6 *Development of cattleya seedlings.* A: *A seed with an embryo.* B: *A seed without an embryo.* C: *Protocorm developed; the embryo increases in size until it bursts the seed coat and then enlarges. Absorbing roots (small root hairs) develop on its surface.* D: *Protocorm, the first leaves developing (two to three months after sowing).* E: *Elongation of the stem, with more leaves appearing.* F: *Seedling at about four to six months, showing first root growing from the stem below the second leaf.*

corm. Soon a second and third leaf appear, the stem elongates, and the first root grows down. By the sixth month the seedling is well developed. During the following months the leaves grow larger, and additional roots may form. Nine to twelve months after sowing, the seedlings may be ready to transplant to community pots.

When the flasks are first sown, it is not possible to control the number of seeds per flask. Some will be very crowded, others not so heavily populated. There is always some difference in the growth rate among individual seedlings; some take hold and grow rapidly while others develop more slowly. Some never go past the protocorm stage. The differences are more marked in crowded flasks where competition for the nutrients allows the faster-growing ones to gain an advantage over the slower ones. After about six months, the growth rate in general slows down a little, due possibly to the accumulation of metabolic products in the agar as well as to depletion of the nutrients.

At the six-month stage, or earlier, even at late protocorm stage, commercial growers and many ambitious amateurs like to transplant the seedlings to fresh flasks. The seedlings receive quite a boost by being put into fresh medium. The commercial grower has a dual purpose, first to produce flasks with a uniform number of plants so that one customer will not receive 500 plants and the next only 50, and also to have plants of transplantable size ready for the market in a shorter time. Amateurs are motivated by the desire to have their seedlings come along as fast as possible, and also to have them as large as possible when the time comes to put them into community pots. Transplanting flasks is, however, a ticklish business, and the average grower need not feel at all compelled to undertake it. The process is described later on in this chapter.

KNUDSON'S FORMULA "C"

After you have grown seedlings with the prepared products, you may want to mix your own medium. You should start with a standard formula, and later, if you want to join the ranks of experimenters, you may want to try the addition of vitamins or other growth promoting substances to the medium. It should be said here that, up to now, research has produced no better formulas than those of Dr. Knudson. Therefore, Knudson's "C," is given as the standard.

Knudson's Formula "C"

Chemical	Symbol	Amount (grams)
Calcium nitrate ..	$Ca(NO_3)_2 \cdot 4H_2O$	1.00
Monobasic potassium phosphate	KH_2PO_4	0.25
Magnesium sulfate............	$MgSO_4 \cdot 7H_2O$	0.25
Ammonium sulfate............	$(NH_4)_2SO_4$	0.50
Sucrose.............	$C_{12}H_{22}O_{11}$	20.00
Ferrous sulfate ...	$FeSO_4 \cdot 7H_2O$	0.025
Manganese sulfate............	$MnSO_4 \cdot 4H_2O$	0.0075

These chemicals must be weighed with extreme care, using a fine balance. Any discrepancy in the proportions of the chemicals, even of the sugar, may be disastrous to the seedlings. If you do not have access to a fine balance, or are unaccustomed to its use, you had better ask your druggist to do the weighing for you. (Incidentally, he will also assist you with the name of a chemical supply house where you can buy the ingredients, or will sell them to you himself.)

Add the ingredients, one at a time, to one liter (1000 cc) of distilled water, and dissolve completely. Then add fifteen grams of plain agar, and warm in a double boiler until all of the agar is dissolved.

After the medium is thus prepared, and before sterilization, it is necessary to check the pH (which means hydrogen ion concentration). The pH scale is based on units from zero to fourteen, and indicates the degree of acidity or alkalinity of a solution; seven is neutral. Below seven the solution is acid, and the lower the number the more acid it is. Above seven it is alkaline. Cattleya seed (and that of most orchids) grows best in a solution that has a pH of 5.0–5.2. This degree of acidity is necessary to make the minerals available for the use of the seedlings. Too much acidity often kills the seed, and a too-alkaline condition impoverishes the seedlings by preventing the plants from obtaining the necessary minerals. Equipment to test pH can be bought from most supply houses; it ranges from the expensive electrode type to the cheaper color indicator papers. Full directions come with the equipment.

Checking the pH consists of removing a small amount of the agar-nutrient medium as soon as it is prepared (before sterilization), and testing it with whatever type of equipment you have. If it is found to be too alkaline, add a drop or two of 0.1 normal hydrochloric acid to the whole amount of medium, mix thoroughly, and then remove a small quantity again for checking. Continue until the pH reads between 5.0 and 5.2. If the medium as first mixed turns out to be too acid, add 0.1 normal potassium hydroxide solution, and proceed in the same manner.

USE OF WIRE LOOP FOR SOWING SEED

Experts prefer a fine wire loop instead of a dropper for sowing seed. The loop is a bit difficult for beginners to use, so the dropper has been suggested to simplify things at first. The loop has the advantage of picking up the seed with very little of the sterilizing solution clinging to it, and in an expert hand the seed may be spread evenly on the agar. It is particularly useful in handling seed that sticks to the sides of the vial—cymbidium seed, for instance.

The end of a fine platinum wire is made into a loop about three-sixteenths-inch in diameter, and attached by the other end to a long slender handle. When the loop is dipped into a suspension of orchid seed, it comes out with a thin film of fluid spread within the loop, holding a good number of seeds. For seed that floats, the loop is dipped only into the upper surface. Where the seed sinks, the sterilizing solution can be poured off first, leaving the collection of seed in the bottom of the vial.

The loop is sterilized by flaming, and completely cooled before touching the seed. To be sure that it is cool, you might dip it into another vial of the disinfecting solution you are using. To sow the seed, the loop is drawn lightly across the agar, not really touching the agar but merely the moisture that has exuded on its surface.

OTHER METHODS FOR DISINFECTING SEED

Calcium hypochlorite solution has long been the standard means of disinfecting seed. It is gentle yet efficient, and it does not harm the sensitive seed of vanda, phalaenopsis, and cymbidium. Cattleya seed can remain in it for several hours without harm, giving the beginner the advantage of extra time and allowing the seed to be kept over in case of an interruption during the seed-sowing process. Some growers like a three percent hydrogen peroxide solution as a disinfecting agent, and some prefer a solution made by adding one Clorazene tablet to two ounces of distilled water. With these last two time is saved by not having to make up the calcium hypochlorite solution, but the seed should be sown within an hour or two.

For seed that is not sensitive to a disinfecting agent, Clorox may be used, but always with extreme caution. The solution must be quite weak and the seed should not stand in it for very long. We recommend one part of Clorox to ninety-nine parts of water, although one of Clorox to fifty-four of water has been used. Shake the seed in the solution for exactly ten minutes, no longer, as after this length of time the percentage of germination may be reduced. As much as possible of the Clorox solution must then be removed and be replaced with sterile (boiled and cooled) distilled water. If the seed has sunk to the bottom of the vial, gently draw the Clorox solution off from above it with a sterilized dropper. If the seed is floating, insert the dropper below it and draw the solution into it. Replace with sterile distilled water and shake thoroughly. This may be enough rinsing for most seed, but the process can be repeated. Then sow the seed at once.

OTHER MEDIA FOR GERMINATING SEED

Research goes on to find new media for germination—media that will speed up the growth of seedlings and shorten the time they must be in flasks. So many things enter into such research that obtaining results that can be generally useful is a long, slow process. A substance that may stimulate the growth of one species may inhibit, or at least not benefit, the growth of another. A substance may be beneficial to some kinds in one concentration and to others in a different concentration. Thus it sometimes occurs that a report by one group of workers may seem to be in conflict with that of another, simply because seed from different individuals was used, or because of other differences in the work. It would take a tremendous amount of space to summarize what work has been done on various modifications of formulas and on the additives and substitutes that have been tried. For example, additions of substances from various plants, different sugars, numerous vitamins, and growth promoting chemicals have been used. Such work is discussed in a number of publications: Carl Withner in his chapter "Orchid physiology" in *The Orchids,* edited by him, 1959; Kunio Kano, *Studies on the Media for Orchid Seed Germination,* 1965; Joseph Arditti, "Factors affecting the germination of orchid seeds," *Botanical Review.* Vol. 33, No. 1, 1967; and "Appendix: Seed germination and seedling culture," in *Orchid Biology, Reviews and Perspectives, II,* edited by Joseph Arditti, 1982. The excellent bibliographies these include give references to other works.

However, from among the various plant substances tried in media, three have been found useful in germinating seed: coconut milk, tomato juice, and banana. Not all genera respond when tomato juice is used alone, but a mixture of coconut milk and tomato juice seems to be quite satisfactory for most genera. Coconut milk has been used in a great deal of work with seed germination; it and banana contain some substances that stimulate growth, but their exact nature has not yet been found.

The late Rev. Masao Yamada of Hawaii, who in the past published formulas using coconut milk and tomato juice, kindly gave me by letter a revised formula. He emphasized that best results are obtained with milk from green coconuts, in which the meat has just begun to harden. The milk at this stage is at its sweetest and is also in greatest quantity. Obviously, his formula will be most useful in areas where coconuts can be obtained at just the right stage of development.*

Coconut Milk Formula—M. Yamada

For one liter of medium:

250 cc	coconut milk
750 cc	distilled water
5 tsp	granulated table sugar
1 tsp	Peptone (powder, Difco Co.)
1/4 tsp	Gaviota Organic Orchid Fertilizer
3 tbls	Canned unsalted tomato puree (any standard brand)
15 to 20 gm.	Agar (Difco Co. plain agar)

* Other workers state that the ripeness of the coconut is not a factor in the effectiveness of the milk.

A tomato juice formula as reported by J. Meyer is very simple and may be useful for some things, although not for cattleyas, according to some workers.

Tomato Juice Formula—J. Meyer

250 cc	fresh, strained tomato juice
250 cc	distilled water
7.5 gm.	stick agar

Joseph Arditti outlined a method for transplant flasks *only,* using banana in the *American Orchid Society Bulletin,* Feb., 1968. His method has been modified according to information in *Orchid Biology II.*

Banana Formula—J. Arditti

1. Peel a sufficient number of greenish-yellow "Chiquita" brand bananas to obtain 150 grams (about 5 ounces) of fruit tissue.
2. Place tissues in a blender with one pint (distilled) water.
3. Homogenize for one minute.
4. Allow homogenate to stand in blender for 5 minutes.
5. Homogenize again for one minute.
6. Line a colander with a sheet of Whatman No. 1 filter paper, or a few pure white paper towels, or with four layers of cheesecloth, and filter the homogenate. Save the liquid. Freeze until used.
7. Collect the portion that has accumulated in the colander and freeze until used.
8. Add one third of the liquid to one pint of medium and make up total volume to one quart plus two ounces. Adjust the pH to 5.0–5.2.

The culture medium may be Knudson's "C" or the Vacin and Went medium given below.

Vacin and Went Culture Medium

Tricalcium phosphate....................	0.20 gm.
Potassium nitrate	0.525 gm.
Monopotassium acid phosphate	0.25 gm.
Magnesium sulfate	0.25 gm.
Ammonium sulfate	0.50 gm.
Ferric tartrate.............................	0.028 gm.
Manganese sulfate	0.0075 gm.
Sucrose	20.0 gm.
Agar..	16.00 gm.
Water..	1,000 ml.
Adjust pH to 5–5.2.	

To this may be added 25 percent by volume of coconut water, or if banana is used, follow Arditti's directions.

Note: Donald Nail finds that banana can foam badly, and suggests using three drops of Dow Corning DC200 or other dimethyl silicone to the medium before sterilizing.

If you wish to try a new medium, or to experiment on your own, it is advisable to have on hand a large quantity of seed from one capsule. You can then germinate some on a standard medium such as Knudson's "C," or the Difco or Hill prepared media, for comparison as well as safety. Don't risk precious seed of which you have only a small amount on a medium with which you are not familiar.

The addition of a small amount of finely granulated pure vegetable charcoal to any medium appears to enhance growth.

GERMINATING GREEN SEED: EMBRYO CULTURE

Cattleya seed is easy to disinfect and germinates readily. Some kinds, however, are sensitive to disinfecting solutions and others are reluctant to germinate. Research has been carried on with a view to finding some stage in the development of the seed when it may be removed from an unripe pod and will germinate when thus planted green.

Experiments have shown that the immature seed can be germinated soon after fertilization has taken place, which varies in length of time from species to species, being, for instance, between sixty and ninety days for *Cattleya* and seventy and 130 days for *Epidendrum.* Since the exact time can be known only through study of each species or hybrid, it might be best to wait for several months after pollination, or until half the time usually required for the ripening of the pod is achieved (Table 1, page 103).

Sowing seed from the green capsule can be helpful in many ways. This is commonly called "green podding." The seed within the unopened pod is absolutely clean and sterile, free from any contaminating organisms. If the capsule is harvested before it begins to split and is thoroughly washed with a disinfecting agent, the seed can be removed under sterile conditions and be sown without having to be treated with a disinfectant. This eliminates the danger of harming sensitive seed and also does away with one step in the usual procedure. Some kinds that are slow to germinate may do so more rapidly if sown before the seed coat is fully hardened. Although not all growers have difficulty with *Vanda, Phalaenopsis,* and *Cymbidium,* some definitely do, and these find that sowing the seed green gives them a better percentage of germination in these genera. *Paphiopedilum* is a problem unto itself. Poor germination is caused largely by the genetic makeup of the plants, but often apparently viable seed fails to germinate. It is thought that in *Paphiopedilum,* as in many other kinds of plants, the seed coat contains an agent that inhibits germination. Sowing the seed before the seed coat is fully developed has given better germination in some instances.

The flasks are prepared in the usual way and are kept covered until time to use them. In a pressure cooker or an autoclave sterilize the following, wrapped in a small towel: a pair of forceps, a scalpel or other sharp stainless steel knife, and a small bowl. Prepare a sleeve box or laminar flow cabinet by spraying it inside with a 10-percent Clorox solution, and lay on its floor a towel soaked in 10-percent Clorox and wrung out. As you uncover the flasks, move them one at a time into the cabinet, wiping each with the Clorox towel to be sure they do not carry with them any contamination from the air. If the cabinet is not equipped with a Bunsen burner, place in it an alcohol lamp, first cleaned with 10-percent Clorox. Finally, place in it the sterilized package of tools.

Wash the capsule with 10-percent Clorox, scrubbing it all over gently with a toothbrush, wrap it in a piece of toweling with the 10-percent Clorox wrung out, and place it in the cabinet. Put on rubber gloves, wash them in 10-percent Clorox, and wipe them again within the cabinet. Clorox must not touch the seed. Open the sterile package. Use the forceps to handle the capsule. Hold the capsule by its "stem" and slit it on both sides with the scalpel. Lay the two halves in the bowl. Flame the neck of a flask, remove the cork and lay it aside. Gently scrape some of the seed into the flask, letting it drop in little piles onto the agar. Reflame the neck and the cork and stopper the flask. Repeat with succeeding flasks.

Embryo culture should never be done on a plant infected with a virus, as there is danger of carrying it over to the seedlings. A prospective plant should be tested for virus very carefully.

TRANSPLANTING FLASKS

Seedlings are given a great boost by being put in fresh medium during their development. The chief hazard in transplanting flasks is the danger of contamination. The flasks must be open for quite a while, and you must move an instrument in and out of them as you transfer groups of seedlings, thus multiplying the chances for mold spores to enter the flasks. The professional grower, whose first failures are but a dim memory, can turn out clean flasks day after day, but the amateur is lucky if he doesn't have some troubles. Amateurs, being what they are, however, usually persist until they are successful!

The stage at which seedlings are reflasked (replated is a term often used) is a matter of choice. They may be moved in late protocorm stage, when the first leaf point becomes visible and before roots have developed, or when the first root is still very short. It is easier to handle them then, and they may be simply scattered on the agar and will orient themselves as growth progresses. If one waits until the roots have grown long, the seedlings will be tangled together and separating them becomes a problem that involves time. The more quickly the operation can be done, the less likely the chances of contamination.

To prevent contamination at any stage seedlings may be removed to a 1:2000 solution of 8-quinoline benzoate or Natriphene, or to a 1 percent solution of Clorox, and from this to the new flasks. If you are transplanting older seedlings, this gives you an opportunity to sort them by size, to put larger ones together in one flask and smaller ones in another.

Flasks for transplanting are prepared in the same way, and with the same medium, as the original ones, again one-and-one-half inches deep. (See above, Arditti's banana medium for transplant flasks.) The work of transplanting must be done under cover, and the usual equipment is the laminar flow cabinet described above. The fresh flasks are placed in the prepared work space (sprayed with 10 percent Clorox, etc.). The flasks from which the seedlings are to be taken are thoroughly washed on the outside with 10 percent Clorox, including caps or stoppers and the area between rim and stopper. The instrument for moving the seedlings may be a wire loop on the end of a handle, or a long-handled spoon with a small bowl. It should be sterilized with 10 percent Clorox after it is placed in the case and must then be rinsed in sterile distilled water just before use.

Flame the neck and cork of the flask from which seedlings are to be removed and of the new flask as well. Open both and lay the corks aside. Gently dip out a group of seedlings, skimming them off the old agar, and place them in the new flask. Nudge them apart so as to space them more or less evenly. They will regain an upright position as their roots go into the new agar. Reflame neck and cork and restopper the flask. Repeat until you have what you need. Cover all necks with foil. Their growth can be accelerated by Gro-Lux lights, sixteen hours a day.

MERISTEM CULTURE OR MICROPROPAGATION OR CLONAL MULTIPLICATION

A method for propagating thousands of plants from a single individual has been developed using a bit of meristematic tissue, or, more recently other plant tissues. The former has given rise to the term *meristem culture* or *clonal multiplication*. A more general term, and one that covers various methods, is *micropropagation*. We shall use the old term *meristem culture* for simplicity. The procedures use much the same equipment and techniques as seed germination, and result in the appearance of protocorms, so it seems logical to include them here.

The work was pioneered by E. A. Ball and George Morel, and further developed by Donald Wimber, Michel Vacherot, Robert Scully, Jr., Lee Kuhn, and others. The nursery of Vacherot and Lecouffle was the first to carry on meristem culture commercially, experimenting with various genera. Some amateurs now do their own meristeming, and a number of laboratories offer meristeming service.

Meristem culture was undertaken originally by Morel and Martin on dahlia and potato as a means of ridding individual clones of virus. Morel then turned his attention to *Cymbidium*. The theory was that the undifferentiated cells of the growing stem tip (the meristem) are often free from virus that infects the rest of the plant. This is only because these cells increase so rapidly that they may stay a "step ahead" of the spreading virus. If this very small group of cells can be cut out without taking with it cells into which the virus has already pen-

etrated, new plants free from virus can be raised from it. If infected cells are included in the culture, the resulting plants will still bear the virus.

Meristem culture is easier with cymbidiums, from which only a very tiny piece of the meristematic tissue need be taken. On the other hand, some leaf tissue has to be included with cattleya meristematic tissue, and this allows virus to be carried over into the resulting plantlets if the mother plant is infected. So much virus has been spread in this manner, and from microprogation of infected plants of other genera, that it seems best now not to attempt to free plants from virus and not to buy plantlets made from infected plants.

This technique is best used for the rapid propagation of outstanding species or hybrids which could otherwise be increased only slowly by division, and to obtain large numbers of meristem divisions from plants that are beautiful but sterile. A number of genera have been successfully meristemed: *Cymbidium*, *Cattleya* and its intergeneric hybrids, *Dendrobium*, *Miltonia*, *Oncidium*, *Odontoglossum*, *Odontonia*, *Phaius*, *Calanthe*, *Zygopetalum*, and others. The process is complicated, so only a brief outline will be given, that you may have a general idea of it. If you wish to try it yourself, consult the literature. The appendix of *Orchid Biology, Reviews and Perspectives*, I, 1977, Joseph Arditti, editor, contains an exhaustive manual.

A cube of tissue about $^1/_{16}$ inch on the side is removed from the very tip of young vegetative shoots, those which are just starting into growth and have reached a length of an inch or an inch and a half. The tissue from the tip of the shoot and the tips of buds in the leaf axils along the shoot is used. The cube of tissue is removed under sterile conditions with aid of a dissecting microscope. Each bit of tissue is placed in a vial or a small flask of liquid medium such as the Vacin and Went medium just described, without the addition of agar. Scully added 25 percent by volume of coconut milk for *Cattleya*. The containers are then placed in a rotary shaker, which agitates them at a predetermined rate. The motion keeps the fluid constantly oxygenated and bathes the pieces of tissue uniformly (Fig. 8–7).

Within a few weeks, each cube of tissue develops into a mass of tissue (callus) that gives rise to protocormlike bodies. These can be separated and will develop into plants when cultured on a solid medium. The main mass of callus can be divided and

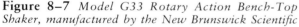

Figure 8–7 *Model G33 Rotary Action Bench-Top Shaker, manufactured by the New Brunswick Scientific* Co., Inc., 1130 Somerset St., New Brunswick, New Jersey 08903.

redivided with the same results. Thus, from one original bit of meristem tissue, great numbers of new plants can be obtained.

Most of the new plantlets actually duplicate the mother plant, but mutations can and do occur, so that here and there in the batch there will be plants with different attributes. Many of them may be perfectly acceptable, but some may be of poor quality. Occasionally a superior one will arise. It is best not to prolong the multiplication process too long, or an undesirable number of mutations may accumulate.

Meristem plants cannot bear the awards the mother plant may have won, but they do have to bear the hybrid name, and of course if of a species, that name.

Meristem culture, or micropropagation, holds promise in quite a different field from merely replicating plants already in cultivation. Rare or endangered species can also be multiplied and thus saved from extinction. It is even possible to raise plants in this manner for reintroducing into the wilds. A beautiful example is the recent propagation performed at the Eric E. Young Micropropagation Center at the Marie Selby Botanical Gardens. There Lee Kuhn propagated an *Epidendrum ilense,* one of only three or four plants originally found. Enough plants were raised to send fifty back to their native Ecuador, distribute some to botanical gardens, and sell some to private growers.

At present, research is going on toward finding how to utilize other tissues such as leaf tips and roots for micropropagation. Enough success has

Figure 8–8 TOP: *A mass of protocormlike bodies developed from a single meristem of* Cattleya. *These may be separated and transferred intact to solid medium where each will form a plant. The mass of callus may be divided and returned to liquid medium where it will form more protocormlike bodies.* BOTTOM: *Young plants four months after sectioning has stopped.* (COURTESY OF THE CYMBIDIUM SOCIETY NEWS AND GEORGE MOREL.)

TABLE 1
Time interval between pollination and harvesting of capsule for embryo culture*

Name	No. days	Name	No. days
Aerides species and hybrids	150–180	*Oncidium altissimum*	110–140
Ansellia species and hybrids	120–150	*O. bahamense*	65–70
Ascocentrum	110–180	*O. baueri*	110–140
Brassocattleya	130–180	*O. carthagenense*	180–240
Brassolaeliocattleya	130–180	*O. cebolleta (longifolium)*	110–130
Broughtonia	60–75	*O. flexuosum*	110–140
Cattleya bifoliate group	110–150	*O. jonesianum*	110–130
Cattleya unifoliate group	120–150	*O. krameranum (Psychopsis)*	90–120
Chysis	140–180	*O. lanceanum*	180–240
Cirrhopetalum	140–180	*O. limminghei (Psychopsisella)*	90–120
Cymbidium	280–360	*O. lucayanum*	65–70
Dendrobium devonianum	160–250	*O. luridum*	100–180
D. lituifolium	150–180	*O. maculatum*	110–140
D. nobile and hybrids	150–180	*O. microchilum*	130–170
D. phalaenopsis and hybrids	120–140	*O. papilio (Psychopsis)*	90–120
D. stratiotes and hybrids	150–200	*O. pulchellum*	65–70
D. superbiens and hybrids	150–200	*O. retemeyerianum*	180–240
D. superbum and hybrids	160–250	*O. sphacelatum*	110–140
Doritaenopsis	90	*O. splendidum*	130–170
Doritis pulcherrima	65–70	*O. stipitatum*	110–130
Encyclia	130–180	*O. teres*	110–130
Epidendrum	100–120	*O. tetrapetalum*	65–70
Laelia anceps	120–150	*O. urophyllum*	65–70
L. cinnabarina	110–120	*O. variegatum*	65–70
L. flava	110–120	*Paphiopedilum*	240–300
L. harpophylla	110–120	*Phaius*	120–150
L. perrinii	120–160	*Phalaenopsis* species and hybrids	110–120
L. purpurata	120–180	*Renanthera*	150–180
L. rubescens	120–150	*Rhyncholaelia*	120–180
L. xanthina	120–180	*Rodriguezia*	110–130
Laeliocattleya hybrids	120–180	*Sophrocattleya*	110–150
Maxillaria	120–180	*Sophronitis*	75–100
Miltonia	120–140	*Vanda* species and hybrids	150–195

been achieved to make the future very exciting. There is a possibility of preserving meristematic tissue by deep freezing, another step in conserving rare or useful plants for the future.

*Modified from Joseph Arditti (Ed.). *Orchid Biology: Reviews and Perspectives II.* 1982. Cornell University Press, Ithaca, New York. Used with permission from the publisher.

·9·

SEEDLINGS FROM FLASK TO BLOOM

☙

EVEN IF YOU DO NOT INDULGE in growing your own seed and sowing flasks, you will at some time or other want to obtain some flask seedlings, certainly some community pot seedlings. Flasks can be bought for between twenty-five and thirty dollars, and are usually transplanted flasks. That is, the seedlings have been moved from the flasks in which they were germinated into fresh flasks, and are of fairly uniform size and close to an estimated number. The price is low per plant, something like twenty-

five cents each. The seedlings are usually ready to go into communities as soon as you receive them.

Community pots may be bought, either freshly established from the flasks or with the seedlings ready to be moved on. Prices vary according to the number of plants per pot and their size. However, seedlings of community pot size are often sold individually, ranging from seventy-five cents to a dollar and one-half each. They are ready for individual pots. They are removed from the community pots or flats in which they are grown and are shipped in little polyethylene bags. The grower with limited space or a desire for greater variety can thus obtain a few each of many different crosses. Meristem plantlets are obtainable in the same way and are handled just like seedlings.

Seedlings of larger sizes are also obtainable, on up to flowering age.

When you buy seedlings, you make your choice from a list that gives the names of the parents, and usually a description of their size, coloring, and flowering season. The grower often adds helpful information as to what he expects from the cross, based on how the parents have behaved in previous crosses. Occasionally, crosses are offered that are repetitions of previous crosses, which have proved successful and for which there is still demand. If you know the history of the cross, and if the repeat is done with the original parents, it will undoubtedly be a good value. However, when repeats are not done with the original parents, you have to be wary. Such a cross is bound to be different from the original—it may be better or it may be worse. If you know the hybridist and his work, and if he has selected parents superior to the original ones for a definite purpose, you might like to try some of the seedlings on an experimental basis.

FLASK TO COMMUNITY POT

The flasks are packed carefully in boxes and sent by air. Sometimes they arrive in perfectly undisturbed condition, depending on the care with which they are handled and the distance they travel. Occasionally the soft jelly is jumbled and the little plants are clustered in tangled masses, which does not seem to harm them. If the flasks arrive in the latter condition, it is necessary to transplant them at once, but undisturbed flasks may be kept for a time.

If you have not seen flask seedlings before, nothing I can say will prepare you for their sheer beauty, the delicacy of their little shiny green leaves, and their tiny translucent roots. The plants are so small and fragile that you will handle them with tender awe, wondering that it has taken a year for them to grow to this size (Fig. 9–1). In transplanted flasks the plants will be quite uniform. In nontransplanted flasks there will be a few larger seedlings, perhaps an inch and a quarter from tip to tip, with several leaves and three or four roots, some with leaves and roots a quarter of an inch long, and some with leaves and roots just starting to form. Also, in nontransplanted flasks, you will see some that are no farther than the protocorm stage (see Fig. 8–6), the little round green ball stage that precedes leaf formation.

These little seedlings, when removed from the flasks, will be put into "communities," either pots holding about fifty or flats holding around a hundred plants. The communities not only save space and facilitate handling a large number of seedlings, but they can be kept more uniformly moist, thus providing better growing conditions than small individual pots afford. They will remain in communities about a year.

Before removing the seedlings from the flask, prepare the pots or flats, whichever you decide to use. The former should be the shallow type called bulb pans, three inches or, preferably, five inches in diameter. Flats may be made at home using strips of wood two inches wide for the sides and hardware cloth for the bottom, making them about six by eight inches large.

Of course, osmunda may be used for communities, and it is good in many ways. As the roots grow into it there is little danger of washing the plants out of the pots, and they need not be watered very frequently. However, removing the seedlings from the fiber after their roots have become intermingled causes many roots to be broken. We are going to suggest that you use fine bark plus one-fifth part perlite or a seedling mix or New Zealand sphagnum moss.

Some growers like a mixture of three parts bark screenings, mixed with one part sand. Another mix is one part one-quarter-inch bark, one part finely screened peat moss, and one part sand. Another mix is eight parts screened peat moss, two parts sand, and one part granulated charcoal. Growers in areas where fresh sphagnum moss is obtainable, as in the Pacific Northwest, can use it to advantage in the seedling mix. A fine grade of chopped tree fern is good, either plain or mixed with seedling grade bark. Whatever the composition of the mix-

Figure 9–1 *A flask of seedlings ready for community pots.* (COURTESY OF ROD McLELLAN CO.)

ture, it should be fluffy or open, and should not pack hard in the pots. It should be easy to keep the mixture damp.

Pots should have one-third of their depth filled with drainage material; flats should have a layer of fine gravel laid over the screen. They are then filled with potting medium to within one-half inch of their rim.

Now remove the seedlings from the flask. Open the flask and pour into it one-half cup of water that is about room temperature. Swirl the flask, and pour out the water and the seedlings that have come loose from the agar into a shallow bowl. Repeat a time or two. If some of the seedlings are deeply embedded in the agar, reach into the flask with a dinner knife and cut out the section of agar containing them, or use an old-fashioned buttonhook. Occasionally the flask has to be broken in order to remove the plants. Wrap it in an old towel or newspaper and strike it with a hammer. Then separate the glass fragments from plants. Let the plants remain in the water until all of the agar is dissolved from their roots. You can tease away stubborn bits if necessary.

The seedlings are then put in a fungicide solution, such as 1:2000 solution of 8-quinoline benzoate or Natriphene. They will remain in this until you pot them. Set out three shallow bowls and put some of the fungicide solution into each. Then sort the seedlings as to size, putting the largest into one bowl, the average size into the next, and the smallest ones and those that have not gone beyond the protocorm stage in the last. Sorting them at this time will facilitate potting, because it is wise to put plants of about equal size together. Also, it saves the eye strain that results from looking through the whole batch each time for another seedling of the size you want at that moment.

I like to use small forceps to pick up the seedlings and put them in the pot. An old pair from someone's high school biology dissecting kit is good. Bend the tips a little so that they come together with just enough space between them to lift a seedling but not to pinch it.

Make a trough and set a row of plantlets in it, pushing the medium against the roots, repeating until the pot is full. (Fig. 9–2). The seedlings should be set so that the level of the potting material comes just at the juncture of roots and stem. Some little plants will have nice straight short roots that are easily put in the hole. Others may have long curled roots that defy being set in place. Don't

Figure 9–2 *Transplanting flask seedlings into a flat. Set the seedlings in a row and press the medium up against them, repeating until all are planted.*

worry if the tips of the roots protrude above the surface. They will continue growth, and the plant will make new ones that will go into the medium. Just be sure that the plant itself is firmly in place. Place the seedlings about a half inch apart, allowing perhaps a little more space between very large ones.

Prepare a dilute fertilizer solution, one-quarter teaspoon of any complete orchid fertilizer to a gallon, and give each pot or flat a mist spray with this as soon as you finish potting it. You might like to add a bit of Superthrive or Best Grow to the fertilizer to speed growth. Follow directions; it takes only a drop or two to a gallon of water. Use this at every watering, for all stages of seedling growth. Label each community with the name of the cross and the date.

After you have potted all of the large and average size seedlings, you are faced with the problem of what to do with the smallest ones and those that are still protocorms. If the flask yielded a generous number of seedlings, you may by now have all that you can take care of, and you may not wish to keep the less well developed ones. But if the flask was sparsely populated, or if the cross is a particularly valuable or intriguing one, you should save every plant. The leftovers may take longer to reach flowering size, but on the other hand, if their small size was the result of crowding in the flask, they will make a spurt of growth when they are transplanted. Early in my growing experience, after potting a tremendous number of seedlings, I ran out of pots, yet I didn't want to discard the least seedling. So I put clean sand in a glass pie plate, wet it with nutrient solution comparable to "Ohio W.P." and set the little plants in it, even the protocorms. I covered it with a pane of glass and set it on the living room table. As the months went by I sprayed the plants with nutrient solution whenever the sand appeared to be drying. Each day I propped open the glass lid for a little while for ventilation. A large percentage of the seedlings grew very nicely. About half of the protocorms died, but to my surprise the rest developed good little leaves and roots. Although these were way behind their sisters out of the flask, they eventually matured into flowering plants.

A better method for handling these smallest seedlings is to put them in a community pot in bark screenings dampened with fertilizer solution, and then put the whole pot in a polyethylene bag and close the top with a rubber band. In place of the pot a glass jar can be used, filled two-thirds of its depth with bark screenings dampened with fertilizer solution, and then covered with polyethylene film fastened by a rubber band (Fig. 9–3). Such pots or jars may be kept along with regular communities in a seedling box. Protocorms may be put in flasks if you can prepare them.

Community seedlings need a constantly damp environment, which is most easily furnished by a box or case (Fig. 9–4). One can be made from a fruit lug or any wooden box about eight inches deep. The lid can be covered with polyethylene film or be made of glass. If you have a great many community pots you can keep them on a bench with board sides covered by a hinged sash.

A night temperature of 60° is necessary to keep the seedlings growing well, and they can be grown at this night temperature until maturity. They will grow a little faster if you can give them a night temperature of 65°. Perhaps a heating cable in an enclosure will do the job.

Community seedlings should be started with about the same amount of light they had in the flasks, about 200 foot-candles. Strong light will bleach the leaves and stunt their growth. Shade can be furnished by laying two thicknesses of cheesecloth over the lid of the box, or the boxes can be kept in an area curtained by cheesecloth. After about two months, gradually increase the light so that by the latter part of the year they are receiving 500 foot-candles. Growth can be accelerated by giving extra hours of light, up to a sixteen-hour day.

It is important to keep the seedlings growing vig-

Figure 9–3 *Glass jars containing seedling mix (with sand added if desired) make good growing cases for seedlings just out of the flask. The jar at the right has newly transplanted seedlings, the one on the left, older ones. This method is especially useful for the smallest, least-well-developed seedlings from a flask.* (COURTESY OF A.J. PILLICHODY.)

Figure 9–4 *Community pots and flats need a damp atmosphere. A wooden box with a glass lid makes a good growing case for them.*

orously, and for this reason they should not be allowed to dry out. Spraying with a fine mist once a day may be all the watering necessary. The spray will wet the box and the pots and so help maintain a humid atmosphere. But watch the potting material closely, checking down into the pots from time to time. It must be kept soft and moist, and water should be given in the pots when needed. Young seedlings require more water than mature plants, yet they must not be allowed to remain sopping wet. It doesn't take a very strong stream of water to wash the little plants out of the pots. For watering, either let the mist sprayer run long enough to wet the medium thoroughly, or use a very gentle water breaker. Once a week add fertilizer to the water, one-quarter teaspoon to the gallon at first, and then increase the strength to one-half teaspoon per gallon.

Although the seedlings require a humid atmosphere, they will benefit from some ventilation. Moisture will condense in drops on the lid during the night. During the warm part of the day, prop the lid open a few inches to let this excess moisture dry off. Then close the lid. Ventilation will discourage the development of fungus infections. If the box stays too wet even with ventilation, drill a few holes in opposite sides to allow a little air movement, or leave the lid open for longer periods. Pots enclosed by film do not have to be opened in this way, for the film excludes fungus spores. However, spores that were present when the film cover was put on can germinate, so watch them carefully.

Damping-off can occur even though the potting medium and seedlings were disinfected originally. Use an occasional preventive spray of a recommended fungicide. If you notice any seedlings turning brown and watery, remove the whole container from the box and drench it thoroughly with the fungicide.

Slugs and snails are vicious enemies. One slug can mow down a pot full of seedlings in short order. Slugs are easier to control than snails, however, and they are easier to see. Poisons containing metaldehyde are used to control both, but you should not wait until you see them. Dust the communities with a powder form, or spray them with a liquid containing metaldehyde every month or six weeks.

Some seedlings may make exceptional growth during the first six months of their stay in communities. Even though you may be tempted to put them in individual pots at this time, it would be best to separate them and replant them in communities, with more space per plant, continuing their care as before.

SMALL INDIVIDUAL POTS

After spending a year in communities, most of the seedlings should be ready for individual pots. They will now be fat little plants, with thick, waxy leaves (Fig. 9–5). Some will have outstripped the rest, so that while the average plant may be an inch and one-half tall, with leaves one-half-inch wide, others may be taller or broader. As always, a few will lag behind the rest, and these slower ones can well go back into communities for another few months.

You may now switch to osmunda fiber if you prefer it for your plants in general (Fig. 9–6). Little seedlings are not difficult to pot in osmunda, as are larger plants, and the fiber holds them firmly in the pot.

For osmunda we generally choose two sizes of pots, one-and-three-quarter inch for the average plants, two-inch for the largest ones. For bark we put the average plants in two-inch pots and the largest ones in two and one-half inch ones. Bark may be a seedlings grade of perhaps one-eighth to one-quarter-inch size, or you may continue with the zero to one-quarter-inch grade. A mixture of bark and tree fern or New Zealand moss may also

Figure 9–5 *A flat of husky seedlings ready to be moved* *into individual pots.* (COURTESY OF ROD MCLELLAN CO.)

be used. Osmunda fiber should be the soft brown kind, sometimes called "golden." Pots should have two or three pieces of crock in the bottom. One ingenious grower uses styrofoam coffee cups with holes punched in their sides, as pots.

Chunks of osmunda fiber should be thoroughly wetted and allowed to drain, and then cut into various-size pieces. Take a seedling in your hand and lay a small chunk of fiber on each side of the roots, forming a cube-shaped sandwich. The circumference of the cube should be about twice that of the pot. Then, squeezing the sandwich together firmly, push it into the pot. If the amount of fiber was correctly estimated, it should completely fill the pot and be quite firm in consistency, not as hard as for adult plants, but not open or loose either. If you underestimated the amount of fiber to give the desired result, work in a little more, pressing it between the sides of the pot and the fiber already in place. The plant should be situated with the level of the fiber just above the root crown.

To prepare bark or any of the mixes dampen

them first, then drain off the water. Hold a seedling in the pot so that its root crown comes just below the level of the pot rim, and pour the medium in around it, wiggling it in among the roots with your fingers. When the pot is full, thump the pot firmly on the bench a few times to settle the medium, and add more if needed. Then gently press it down all around the inside edges of the pot with your fingers. Do not force it in too roughly, else you may break the roots. A piece of stiff wire, cut just longer than the diameter of the pot, can be used to hold the plant in place. Press it across the rhizome, wedging it into the pot.

To use New Zealand sphagnum, fold some around the roots and push the whole bundle into the pot. Do not make it too tight. You will soon learn how much to use to make it just firm yet loose enough for good drainage.

Put a label in each pot. This should be a routine part of the potting process, not only because it is more interesting to know what each plant is, but because a plant without a label is technically an "unknown" for the rest of its life. You may think

Figure 9–6 *Transplanting from community pot to individual pot in osmunda fiber.* UPPER LEFT: *A community pot of seedlings removed from the pot.* UPPER RIGHT: *Seedlings separated from the fiber. Note difference in rate of development.* LOWER LEFT: *Place a chunk of fiber on each side of the roots. Judge amount necessary to fill tightly the pot into which the seedling is going.* LOWER RIGHT: *The potted seedling. If fiber is not firm, press the ball toward the center and add a few more pieces of fiber.*

you can remember that this group is cross such-and-such, and that that group is cross so-and-so. But pretty soon the plants will all look alike to you. Groups may be shoved together to make room for additional plants, and soon their identity is lost.

The newly potted seedlings should be shaded for the first few weeks to receive about 500 foot-candles of light. During this time, which is a recovery period, they should be misted lightly several times a day in bright weather to reduce loss of water until their roots are again active. Night temperature can be 60°, but, as with communities, they will grow a little faster with nights of 65°. They benefit from somewhat higher humidity than needed by adult plants, and although they should not be kept in as close an atmosphere as the communities, some means of giving them a humid atmosphere should be devised. A covered bench, suggested above for accommodating a large number of community pots, can be used for seedlings newly put in individual pots. The cover of the bench should be propped open for a fair part of each day. Another method is to fasten polyethylene film to a frame built around the seedlings. After the recovery period, the light should be gradually increased until they are receiving 1,000 foot-candles.

As with younger seedlings, plants of this age should not be allowed to become dry. Water them often enough to keep the medium damp. For bark, this will mean a daily watering until the bark begins to hold water efficiently. Then perhaps they will need watering only every other day or in cool weather every third day. Osmunda fiber will not need to be watered as frequently. Use a water breaker for either medium, as the full force of the hose can not only wash the plants out of the pots, but can tip over the pots themselves.

Plants in bark and mixes should be given fertilizer every other watering. One-half teaspoon of fertilizer to a gallon of water is a good concentration. Plants in osmunda fiber should not be fertilized until they are making active new roots, and then they may be fed every other week with the same strength used for plants in bark. For osmunda fiber use a 10-10-10 fertilizer and for bark 30-10-10.

THREE- AND FOUR-INCH POTS

After the first eight months in the individual pots, the plants will be sure to show quite a striking difference in size. They are then between two and one-half and three years old. A few will be large enough to go into four-inch pots, while most will require only three-inch. Seedlings appreciate being shifted to fresh medium, so that even those that have not made much progress should be repotted at this time.

It is a simple matter to remove a seedling from any of the mixes. Tap it out, give it a few gentle shakes and separate the roots a bit to loosen the bark and allow most of it to fall away. It is not necessary to remove bits that cling tightly to the roots. This is a good time to check for evidence of snails. If any are found, or if the roots look as if they have had bites taken out of them, dust the roots with a metaldehyde powder or dip them in a metaldehyde solution. Examine the roots and trim away any that are rotted. Roots that have grown over the side of the pot may be put inside of the new one if they will conform to the space. Otherwise trim them back to a two-inch stub. All of the roots, including the cut stubs, will send out branch roots in a short time.

Place the plant in its new pot, prepared with drainage material, and fill in with fresh, dampened medium. This time bark may be a little coarser, perhaps the one-quarter- to one-half-inch size. But in a dry climate it may be well to continue with the seedling grade for another year, or to use some tree fern mixed with the bark. To hold the rhizome down in the pot at the proper level, use a piece of wire described above.

If osmunda fiber is to be used, prepare the fiber and the pots as before. It is not necessary to remove the fiber from around the plant; many growers just transfer it intact. We like to loosen the ball a little by pulling away some sections of fiber that do not have roots in them. We then fit a few pieces around the old ball, set it in the new pot, and fill in with chunks of fiber that can be worked in with a potting stick. The fiber should be quite firm, but not hard.

Plants of this age should be staked as the next growth will double the present height of the plant. Stakes especially made for use with bark can be obtained from orchid supply companies, and these are a great help. They come in a number of designs, but all hold firmly to the rim of the pot, giving a rigid support for the plant. A straight steel stake can be used for osmunda, driven into the center of the pot beside the plant. Gently tie the tallest growth to the stake.

Seedlings in three- and four-inch pots can be placed on the open bench. Starting with 1,000 foot-candles of light, gradually increase the light so that by the end of the year they are receiving 2,000 foot-candles. Since they now occupy a larger area, it may be difficult to continue the 65° night temperature for them. They will do very nicely with the 55° to 60° nights usually maintained in the cattleya house. If you have a way of maintaining a 60° to 65° night temperature, they will grow a little faster, however. After this, their fourth year, the vigorous ones are going to be treated in the same way as adult plants, and should be gradually worked up to adult conditions. Keep them growing steadily. Do not let them dry out, and give them a mist spray on bright days. Continue the same vigil against slugs, snails and insects, and include the seedlings in the general greenhouse treatment for these pests. As before, give fertilizer to the plants in bark at every other watering, and to those in osmunda every other week.

FOUR- AND FIVE-INCH POTS

All the plants that have outgrown the three- and four-inch pots are shifted on to the next size, the threes into fours, and the fours into fives. Some will have developed two or three leads, an indication of vigor that is most welcome. Do not divide them. These are the specimen plants of the future. If they are large enough to justify it, move them into six-inch pots. If one of these plants with many leads turns out to be of fine quality, and if it carries on its eagerness to multiply its leads, some day you will have many wonderful plants from this one seedling.

Heretofore we have not had to consider any particular growth phase in repotting seedlings. But from now on it is best to pot them just as a new set of roots begins to form. Those in osmunda should be potted hard, as for adult plants. When they have resumed active growth, put them alongside the mature plants in your greenhouse and care for them in every way as you do the older plants.

FIRST FLOWERING

It would be quite difficult to choose any one seedling stage as the most exciting. Their development in the flask is beautiful to watch. Their year in communities, which sees them transformed from fragile little things into husky youngsters, is a joy. Their further development in individual pots is most rewarding, for you can see that they are beginning to grow up. An array of healthy, perky, bright green seedlings is a sight almost as lovely as an array of flowers, and an achievement to be proud of. But it is really thrilling as they approach maturity and you know that flowering is not far off. A few may flower at the age of four years, many at the age of five years, while some will take longer. The average age of flowering used to be seven years, but better cultural methods have shortened the time and we do not have to wait so long nowadays for their first blooms.

There are always some laggards in any group of seedlings. Some may still be only large enough for three-inch pots when the rest have moved on to fours and fives. The rate of development is not necessarily related to the quality of the flowers they will eventually produce. Some of the slow ones may give just as good flowers as the faster-growing ones, a few even better.

The most vigorous of the plants are usually the first to flower. Others may produce sheaths but no flowers, showing at least that they are nearly ready

to bloom. The first flowers may or may not show what a plant is capable of doing. A big stocky plant should give good flowers its first time, with more than one to the stem. But many give only one flower, and often the first effort is smaller and not so well colored or of as heavy substance as subsequent flowers will be. The second flowering is a better test of the capabilities of a plant. Don't write off a plant that performs poorly the first time. We can't say that it will necessarily do better the next time, but at least give it a chance to do so. Sometimes the second flowering is an incredible improvement.

You can get some idea of the value of the cross from the flowering of the first group of seedlings. If it is uniformly good, it indicates that the rest will also be good. If only one or two of a fair number have good flowers, you may have a cross in which the percentage of good plants will be low, but perhaps the good ones will by themselves make up for the trouble of raising the cross.

ACCELERATING THE GROWTH OF SEEDLINGS

Most seedlings make their best growth during the long days and warmer nights of summer. Their growth is speeded up somewhat during the winter by giving them a night temperature of 65°, as suggested earlier in this chapter. Growth can be speeded up even more by giving them a sixteen-hour day by means of artificial lighting and for this Gro-Lux lights are sufficient, or a combination of Gro-Lux with cool white fluorescent, two tubes per 25-inch-wide bench. It is not too difficult a matter to give additional light to a few community pots. The light is turned on at sundown and turned off when it has brought the total daylength to sixteen hours. Care must be taken not to let the light reach other plants in the greenhouse whose flowering schedule might be altered by it (see Chapter 6). Long days may be started while the seedlings are in the flask and continued until the plants approach flowering size. Each phase of their growth should thus be shortened by a few months, bringing them into flower perhaps a year or a year and a half earlier than normal. Perhaps, however, you can manage lights only while the plants are in flasks and communities, finding it difficult to light the greater area they will occupy when they go into individual pots. Giving them long days for just their first year or two will give you an advantage in the ultimate time it takes them to reach flowering size.

Herbert Hager worked out a schedule which brings 10 percent of a batch of cattleya seedlings into flower in two and a half years from seed. About 80 percent of the batch will flower at three years, and the remaining few will flower a year or so later. His program involves stepping up the night temperature, increasing the daylight intensity by faster jumps, and giving them a sixteen-hour day all year round. It is truly a forcing program, but its advantage is that you can very soon learn whether a cross is a valuable one or whether it should be culled. Mr. Hager warned that in order to make use of the higher night temperature along with the sixteen-hour days, the plants must have a great deal of natural sunshine and that it is therefore wise to try his program only in areas where this is possible.

Here is his schedule. The night temperature maintained through all stages of growth is 68° to 70°. Daylength of sixteen hours is produced in winter and summer by the use of 100-watt incandescent bulbs in reflectors placed two feet above the plants and five to six feet apart. The day temperature for plants in flasks should be between 80° and 85°, and the relative humidity should be between 50 and 70 percent. Natural light intensity is started at 200 foot-candles and is gradually increased to 400 foot-candles after germination. Plants are left in flasks from four to six months.

For plants in flats, the day temperature should be between 80° and 90° and the relative humidity from 50 to 70 percent. The natural light intensity is started at 400 foot-candles and is increased to a maximum of 600 foot-candles. Plants are left in the flats for about six months.

The plants are then put in one-and-one-half-inch pots for a year. During this time the temperature and relative humidity are the same as they are for the flats, but the light intensity is increased up to 1,500 foot-candles. The seedlings are then moved into three-inch pots. The day temperature is kept between 80° and 90°, and the relative humidity usually between 50 and 70 percent although it may sometimes reach 80 percent. The intensity of natural light is gradually increased from 1,500 to 4,000 foot-candles. The first 10 percent will flower at two-and-one-half years; about 80 percent will flower when they are three years old.

TRIACONTANOL

Triacontanol, abbreviated TRIA, is a growth stimulant serendipitously discovered in alfalfa. It enhances the growth of many plants, shortening the period to maturity in some, but it does not always shorten it in orchids. Plants with more leads and more flowers do result many times.

TRIA is difficult stuff to handle, particularly to put into solution, and it does not work unless thoroughly dissolved. We will not go into the various procedures, because it is available from several laboratories ready for use. William Collier has given me a great deal of information on this material, which can be bought from his company, Wm. R. Collier Orchids, 8677 Limonite, Riverside, California 92509. Other sources will be given at the end of this section.

To use TRIA, add 0.1 or even 0.01 mg/liter to the flasking and replating medium. (Stronger solutions are harmful, but even weaker ones may be effective.) Flasks should be given only 6 hours of light a day, and thrive if kept cool. For seedlings out of the flask, spray the foliage with the same dilution once a week. Of course, they must have regular applications of orchid fertilizer. For older plants, 1.0 mg/l of TRIA is mixed with the fertilizer and applied regularly. It is not, however, as effective in increasing growth as with young seedlings.

In addition to Collier's, formulations of TRIA can be ordered from: Alfa-Gro, Inc., 30 Cross Street, Suffield, Connecticut 06078; Analabs, North Haven, Connecticut 06473; Biochemical Research Corporation, 1008 Steeples Court, Falls Church, Virginia 22046.

OTHER KINDS OF ORCHIDS

All of the techniques described in this chapter may be used for any kind of orchid. In some kinds the capsule takes a longer or shorter time to mature than in *Cattleya,* and the length of time for the various stages—flask, community pot, etc.— may be different. Some kinds reach flowering size earlier. But essentially the same methods are used for handling the seed, sowing the flasks, transplanting to community pots, and carrying the plants on to flowering size.

·10·

DIVISIONS OF THE ORCHIDACEAE

❧

WHEN NATURE DREW THE designs for the orchid family, she combined and recombined the basic flower pattern in every conceivable way and decorated her handiwork with all of the colors at her command. She created forms of beauty so serene, so pure, as to be almost sublime. She created other forms rich and showy, almost sensual. And then she turned or twisted, reduced or enlarged, shortened or lengthened each floral part to make thousands of new forms, lurid or beautiful, giant or pigmy, satanic or humorous. If a mathematician or a statistician were to try to compete with her, he would find that he could put together no combinations that did not already have a counterpart in her work.

Man has been at work for more than a hundred years, naming and classifying the myriad orchids that have so far been discovered. Yet many are still hidden in jungle wilds or remote places, and each passing year brings to light some form new to his knowledge. It is characteristic of human beings that they must put a name to everything. And it is characteristic of scientists that the name must be so definite, so specific, that there can be no possible confusion of one object with another.

When a new orchid is found, even after it has bloomed and its major characteristics have been observed, it takes patient hours of dissection and study to determine with what group of orchids it belongs. Perhaps it does not fit with any established genus or tribe, and a new category must be made for it. Often the experts do not agree. One may feel that some slight difference is significant enough to warrant the creation of a new genus. Others may insist that it is only a variation of a kind already classified. An explorer in one country may have found the same thing that another person in another country discovered, and each may have been named, but by different people and with different appellations. Sometimes many years elapse between discoveries. When you look up an orchid in any technical book you will often find a list of names that have been given it and then abandoned in favor of a more authentic one. It is the policy of taxonomists to go back, if possible, to the first name published but at the same time to place the orchid in the most logical category according to nomenclatural rules.

The orchid family, Orchidaceae, is divided into several categories: first, subfamilies, and within them, tribes. The tribes are divided into subtribes, and these in turn into genera (sing. genus). Since the larger categories are complicated, and since not all taxonomists agree on their boundaries, we shall begin with subtribes, the divisions with which amateurs have to deal.

Each subtribe includes kinds that have certain basic structures in common, different from the characteristics that place others in different subtribes. Within the subtribes are the next-smaller divisions, the genera, in which the plants are even more closely related. Some subtribes are small, an

115

occasional one having only one genus, while some consist of a great many genera. Last in line are the species (sing., also species). The name of a subtribe is taken from one of its members, and is formed by dropping the Latin ending and adding -inae, for example, Laeliinae, Oncidiinae, and Catasetinae.

A subtribe can be likened to cards in a deck, which belong together because of the design on their backs. The deck is divided into suits, each with its own pattern, as diamonds, spades, etc., and a suit can represent a genus. Any individual card can represent a species, for in that deck there is no other like it.

The method of giving an orchid two names, or a binomial name, for example *Cattleya labiata,* allows it to be recognized as distinct from any other orchid. *Cattleya,* the genus name, always comes first, and is capitalized. The species name comes second and begins with a small letter, *labiata.* Both are italicized. (We must add that some taxonomists still adhere to an older custom of capitalizing a species epithet made from a proper noun. This custom is giving way to the rule of a small letter for a species.) Genus and species names should agree in gender, although this has not always been carried out. Sometimes the gender of a plant is arbitrarily set. When writing scientifically, the abbreviation of the name of the person who described the species is added, for example, *Cattleya labiata Lindl.* (the abbreviation for Lindley.) This not only gives credit to the author of the species, but points out which designation is meant, in case there are synonyms.

Hybrid names are capitalized and are not italicized, but the generic name is retained in italics, for example, *Brassolaeliocattleya (Blc)* Frank Fordyce. In some literature you will see an × in front of the hybrid name, for example, *Cattleya* × Helen Holguin. The × stands for grex, which means a group and refers to the offspring of a given cross. We are not using this symbol.

Not quite so easy to follow is another ruling, recently adopted in practice, that generic names are italicized only when the fact of their being genera is emphasized. We might, for instance, write, "He has many kinds of orchids—cattleyas, oncidiums, cymbidiums." But if we were to write specifically of the genus, we might put it this way "In *Cattleya* there are four pollinia."

A species often has a number of botanical variations distinct enough to merit an additional descriptive or varietal name. For instance, *Cattleya dowiana* has a yellow form designated *Cattleya dowiana,* variety *aurea, Dendrobium fimbriatum* has a form with a spot of deep purple on the lip called *Dendrobium fimbriatum,* variety *oculatum.* These botanical varieties (which might also be considered subspecies) occur in nature, usually in some numbers and often in separate geographical locations. The word variety may be abbreviated var., or v.

A grower who owns a particularly fine individual plant, whether species or hybrid, may designate it by a varietal or clonal name of its own. This name is added to the full name of the plant and is set off in single quotes. A famous example is *Cymbidium* Jungfrau 'Dos Pueblos'. Suppose you own a particularly beautiful *Cattleya trianaei,* of richer color or heavier substance than other members of the species, and you wish to mark this plant to separate it from the others. You could call it *Cattleya trianaei* 'Supreme' or *Cattleya trianaei* 'Aristocrat', or 'Jones', or anything else you wished. When you divide this plant you would put this name on each division, and when you again divide the divisions the name would still follow, so that you would keep track of each and every division made from the original plant. The original plant and all of its divisions are called a "clone." The importance of identifying with certainty the divisions of a valuable plant is obvious. The members of a clone have an additional value in experimental work, because results are more decisive when the plants used are identical in every way. An individual plant designated by its own varietal or clonal name is considered a horticultural variety, as opposed to a botanical variety.

Most orchid subtribes are so prolific that it would take a lifetime to collect a single specimen of all of the species included in just one, to say nothing of the varieties of each species. Should you start on such a project, you might run into difficulties. Some tribes are spread over a geographical area that includes all sorts of climatic conditions so that its members may not be suited to the conditions of a single greenhouse. In any subtribe, of course, there are some members more desirable for cultivation than others. Unless you have the urge to own every species, you will select those that have a special appeal for you. You may choose a plant for its graceful habit, its showy flowers, its intriguing shape, unusual coloring, delightful fragrance, or even for its size, for example, a dwarf plant whose minuteness is a charm in itself.

Botanists are interested in all kinds of plants, however insignificant they may seem to most people. Because of this, species that are of no value as cut flowers, or that are not widely known, are often called "botanicals." Many of the botanicals are every bit as lovely as those with which we have better acquaintance, and these are now finding a place alongside their more popular relatives. In fact, many amateurs find their chief interest in the species.

Genera are known which have as many as 2,000 species. For others only one or two are known, and the rest run somewhere between these extremes. Obviously nothing less than an encyclopedia could describe all the species. Instead of presenting them to you as disconnected genera, each will be introduced along with other members of its subtribe. Many lovely kinds exist in the less well known genera. To learn to know them in relation to their more famous relatives is to increase one's understanding. In most genera, we can give only a sampling of species.

Not only are the genera in a subtribe related structurally, they are also related genetically, and most will interbreed. Some intergeneric crosses are more fruitful than others, and so also are some species more easily interbred. Sometimes achieving a hybrid between two species that are reluctant to give offspring opens the way for further breeding, leading ofttimes to quite remarkable things.

Hybrid names are made in two ways. Where only two species are involved the name is usually a convenient combination of them, for example *Epicattleya (Epidendrum × Cattleya),* and we fondly call them Epicats. Where more than two are involved the combinations can become quite awkward, although many are used, as in *Brassolaeliocattleya (Brassavola × Laelia × Cattleya).* These we often reduce to initials as Blc. Such quadrigeneric hybrids are otherwise given the name of a person, usually someone outstanding in the orchid field, for example *Kirchara (Epidendrum × Sophronitis × Laelia × Cattleya).*

Taxonomic changes have been made in both genera and species. It is difficult to know, at times, which name to continue to use, the new one or the old one, in the registration of hybrids. The International Orchid Commission hands down decisions in these matters. Sometimes they readily accept a change, depending on how much confusion would result if the lists were to be altered. An example was the change from *Cypripedium* to *Paphiopedilum,* which affected only the one genus. More often than not, the name used over the years is the one they approve for purely horticultural use, emphasizing meanwhile that the correct botanical name should be used scientifically. It is a bit difficult for amateurs who like to keep up with the times to reconcile themselves to this, but it must be followed if one wishes to register hybrids.

Two works will greatly aid the orchid grower in keeping hybrid names straight and in identifying the parentage of labeled plants. One is *Natural and Artificial Hybrid Generic Names of Orchids.* 1966. Botanical Museum Leaflets, Harvard University Press, Vol. 21, No. 6, and its Supplement I, 1969. The other is *Handbook of Orchid Nomenclature and Registration.* This is published periodically by the International Orchid Commission on Classification, Nomenclature, and Registration. It is available through the American Orchid Society, Inc. For information on registering a hybrid, write to The Royal Horticultural Society, Vincent Square, London, SW1P 2PE, England.

·11·

AERIDES RELATIVES

The Sarcanthinae Subtribe

THERE ARE MORE THAN eighty genera in this subtribe, which includes some of the loveliest orchids known— *Phalaenopsis,* whose arching sprays of sweetly rounded, long-lasting flowers are sublime among orchids; *Vanda,* whose stately plants bear sprays of rounded, colorful flowers; and *Aerides,* which has dense clusters of fragrant flowers of waxy or crystalline texture. Many of the others are equally attractive, some large, some small. Those given here comprise a group of the better-known genera, along with some of special interest.

The growth habit is monopodial, illustrated by Figure 2–2. They do not have a rhizome, but instead have a single upright stem and grow by adding new leaves at the top and new roots from between the leaves along the stem. Flower stems come from the axils of the leaves. They are epiphytic, but do not withstand drying as well as kinds equipped with pseudobulbs. Their fleshy leaves, heavy stems, and large roots do store some water, however.

The genera range natively from the Philippine Islands through the Asiatic tropics and into Australia and Africa, although each genus inhabits its own particular area in this vast range. For the most part, they live in climates that are warm and humid, some being subjected to heavy rains the year round, others to more moderate amounts of precipitation. They are found growing mostly on trees, occasionally on rocks.

PHALAENOPSIS

The "moth orchid" (Greek, *phaluna* meaning moth, *-opsis* meaning resembling) receives its name from its similarity to some tropical moths. There are about fifty species, not all of which are well known in cultivation. Some which are quite rare are now proving their worth in hybridization. The beautiful flowers would be worth growing even if they lasted only a few days, but many last for from two to five months, and bloom succession keeps them in flower for much longer, making them all the more desirable. They are not light demanding, a fact which, together with their preference for 65° nights, makes them easy to grow in the house (Fig. 11–1).

The foliage is attractive. The long, broad curving leaves may be shiny or leathery, plain green or mottled with grayish green, often purple underneath. They are from four to fifteen inches long, so that a mature plant can cover a fairly broad area. The plants increase in height only slowly, and add but one or two new leaves a year. Mature plants retain an average of five or six leaves, although a few individuals may retain more. The robust, often flattened roots appear from the stem between mature leaves and grow down into the pot or outside of it to wander to some length. The flower spikes come from the axils of the lowermost leaves, often from the region where leaves have

Figure 11–1 *A house of* Phalaenopsis, *where breathtaking beauty abounds for months on end.* (COURTESY OF JONES AND SCULLY, INC.)

fallen, and therefore from the older portion of the plant.

The flowers divide themselves structurally into two groups. The first group, called Euphalaenopsis, is characterized by appendages on the lip and by petals much broader than the sepals. The second group, Stauroglottis, has petals similar to the sepals, and a lip without appendages. In both groups the variously shaped lip is united with an extension of the basal part of the column, called the column "foot."

In general, the growing season, the period during which new leaves and roots are produced, is from spring through fall, with the flower spikes appearing from late summer into winter. Some individuals are quite orderly in this matter, but a large percentage vary, particularly among the hybrids, so that flower spikes may be started at almost any time of the year without regard to the state of growth of the plant.

The flower spike is tall and arching in most species, usually unbranched in the white species, branched in some others. Some plants develop all of the buds on a spike at about the same time so that the whole spray is open at once. Others open the basal flowers first, while the tip of the spike continues to form more buds. Plants with the latter habit can remain in flower for the better part of a year, since individual flowers keep for several months and new ones open to replace those that fade. Do not cut off a spike until you are sure it has ceased to form new buds. There is sometimes an interval between fading of the first flowers and development of succeeding ones. In many of the species and hybrids, if the flower stem is cut just below the node that produced the first flower, a branch stem may come from one of the lower nodes, giving a second spray of flowers. Such branch stems may not bear as many flowers as the original spike and sometimes the flowers are smaller. But this is not always true, for we have had excellent secondary spikes of twenty flowers. When a plant is grown under less than ideal conditions it may not form new flower spikes when an old one is making a branch, so the grower must decide from experience whether to remove a spike entirely or leave it to form a secondary one.

Culture

POTTING. *Phalaenopsis* plants require rather small containers in proportion to their size and in general need be repotted infrequently. A plant should never be allowed to become run down, however. They usually do well in plain bark, medium or coarse, depending on the size of the plants. A preferred mix among many Florida growers is one-third each of shredded redwood chips, tree fern, and fir bark. Various other media used successfully are: osmunda mixed with tree fern; plain tree fern; plain bark; chunks of charcoal; and some of the proprietary mixes.

A plant should be repotted when the medium is no longer good, or when the plant has lost a good many lower leaves and roots, leaving the active part of the plant standing above the medium on a naked stem. Repotting should be done when new roots are developing, preferably when flowering is finished.

To repot, remove the plant and clean off the old medium. With your fingers break off the old inactive stub of the stem below the ring of living roots. Cut back the lower roots to a length that will fit in the new pot. These stubs will branch, giving new roots that will go directly into the medium, providing a firm foothold for the plant. Allow the upper roots to maintain their natural length, whether in or out of the pot. Osmunda fiber need not be packed as hard as for cattleyas, but it should be firm. Bark, or chunks of charcoal, should be of very coarse grade (large-size pieces), and potting is done as directed for cattleyas. The plant should be centered in the pot, and in any medium the basal part should be placed an inch or so down into the potting material.

Many growers place the plants on racks which

Phalaenopsis Orchid World 'Bonnie Vasquez' AM/AOS, Gold/11th WOC (COURTESY ZUMA CANYON ORCHIDS.)

Doritaenopsis Zuma White Puff 'Taupo', HCC/AOS (COURTESY ZUMA CANYON ORCHIDS)

Phalaenopsis Gallant Beau 'George Vasquez', HCC/AOS (COURTESY ZUMA CANYON ORCHIDS)

Vanda cristata

Euanthe sanderiana

Trichoglottis brachiata

Dyakia hendersoniana

Neofinettia falcata

Angraecum leonis

Cyrtorchis arcuata var. Whytei

Cattleya mossiae

Blc Wm. Stewart 'Magic', *Gold/HSU* (COURTESY STEWART ORCHIDS)

Cattleya aclandiae

Cattleya brabantiae

Cattleya bicolor 'Green Magic' (COURTESY STEWART ORCHIDS)

Cattleya walkeriana 'Perfect Charm' (COURTESY STEWART ORCHIDS)

Cattleya intermedia

Encyclia vitellina

Encyclia mariae

Epidendrum ilense

Barkeria lindleyana

Laelia flava

Laelia anceps, subsp oaxaqueña 'Nittany Frost'

Laelia furfuracea

Laelia harpophylla

LC Tiny Treasure (C. Porcia X L. lucasiana)
(Courtesy Stewart Orchids)

Laelia milleri 'Tom Northen'

Rhyncholaelia digbyana

Sophronitis wittigiana

Broughtonia sanguinea

Caularthron bicornuta

Cymbidium eburneum

Cymbidium pumilum

Cymbidium Jungle Jewels 'Nile Green' (Courtesy Stewart Orchids)

Grammangis ellisii

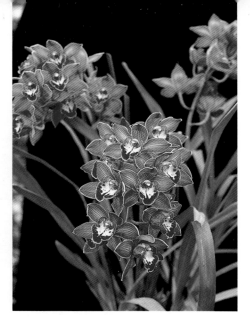

Cymbidium Khyber Pass 'Strawberry Pink' (Courtesy Stewart Orchids)

Grammatophyllum scriptum

Galeandra batemannianum

Paphiopedilum armeniacum

Paphiopedilum malipoense

Paphiopedilum urbanianum

Paphiopedilum barbigerum with Paph.

Phragmipedium caricinum

Paphiopedilum fairrianum

Paphiopedilum liemianum

are tilted to prevent collection of water in the leaf crown, but they may also be grown upright on benches. Delightful hanging containers and mounts made of tree fern are used in areas where sufficiently high humidity can be maintained. On the latter the plant is fastened with string or wire until the roots take hold, and these are particularly attractive for kinds that make young plantlets from flowering stems, which can then be trained to root at intervals around the mount, covering it eventually with a solid mass of plants.

After potting, water sparingly until new roots are well formed. Keep the atmosphere humid (60 to 70 percent relative humidity) and spray the plants with a fine mist once or twice a day. Since *Phalaenopsis* is not grown in strong light, additional shade after potting is not always necessary, but if the leaves become limp in spite of mistings the light should be reduced to about 500 foot-candles till the plants recover.

TEMPERATURE. These plants from the hot, humid tropics of Asia must be kept gently warm. The night temperature should not go below 60°, as temperatures below this cause growth to be poor and flower buds to drop. Actually, the plants do better with temperatures somewhat above 60° at night, preferably closer to 65°. Day temperature should be ten degrees higher in the winter, but can go higher in the summer with the usual precautions about excessive heat. If spikes do not form readily in the fall, give the plants a few weeks of cool temperatures, perhaps around 55° or even 50°.

WATER. The plants should be watered frequently enough to prevent the medium from ever becoming bone dry, but they do not like to be kept sopping wet. Watering needs to be more frequent in dry climates than in damp ones, and of course, more frequent when plants are in bark than in osmunda fiber. The atmosphere should be kept humid, by damping down and spraying the benches between the plants if humidity is not a great problem in your area or by means of humidifying equipment in dry climates. The plants welcome light mist sprays on bright days, but they must dry off by night. The growth tends to be succulent and is particularly liable to damage if kept wet. During the winter, watch for drip from the roof and move any plants that might catch the water.

FEEDING. *Phalaenopsis* benefits from applications of fertilizers. In osmunda, a 10-10-10 formula given every two or three weeks at a concentration of one-half teaspoonful to a gallon of water is about right. With bark a 30-10-10 formula should be used, unless some other means is devised for giving the higher nitrogen needed. Watch the plants carefully and adjust the frequency and concentration to their needs.

LIGHT. Strong light makes small, hard plants that do not do well. *Phalaenopsis* does best in less than half the light intensity allowed cattleyas. During the summer they should be given between 500 and 1,000 foot-candles. Toward fall increase the light gradually to encourage flowering and toughen the plants somewhat, and by winter let them have about 1,500 to 2,000 foot-candles.

VENTILATION AND AIR MOVEMENT. In a greenhouse, air movement is absolutely necessary. The moving air should be damp, and this means that unless the climate provides high humidity some means of adding water to the moving air should be provided. Whenever possible open the ventilators, at least a crack, but do not let cold air blow on the plants. Ventilation and air movement help keep the plants healthy at all times but are particularly important to prevent spotting of flowers by the *Botrytis* fungus.

PHALAENOPSIS MITE. The most vicious enemies of *Phalaenopsis,* and of many other genera, are the false spider mites. The species *Tenuipalpus pacificus* is called the phalaenopsis mite because of its affinity for this genus, but it also attacks other orchids. There are also very similar species of the genus *Brevipalpus* that resemble it in appearance and activity and which also attack *Phalaenopsis* and other genera. These false spider mites wreak devastating damage to the leaves, causing first irregularly shaped yellow flecks or spots that become pitted or sunken, then necrotic, remaining white or gray or turning brown, and causing early death of the leaves. The damage looks much like some fungus or virus diseases (Fig. 11–2). The mites themselves are invisible to the naked eye, which makes them such cunning enemies. They can just barely be seen with a ten-power lens. They are best seen with a low-power binocular microscope. Figure 21–15 in the section on pests shows a greatly enlarged photograph of *Tenuipalpus pacificus.* Once you have seen this mite and its relatives, or their empty skins, you will not mistake them for the common two-spotted mite or "red spi-

Figure 11-2 A: *Phalaenopsis leaf injured by phalaenopsis mite,* Tenuipalpus pacificus, *one of the false spider mites. Note grayish or whitish scars.* B: *Closeup of same* *leaf to show sunken and pitted areas.* (PHOTOS BY TOM NORTHEN.)

der." Often each little injured spot on a leaf is occupied by one or more mites, and others may be found hiding along the leaf veins and in the leaf axils. They can usually be found on either leaf surface, and the damage they do involves both surfaces. They spin no webs. The mites are orange or reddish, and their oval eggs are of the same color, laid either free on the leaf or under a deposit of scabby-looking material. Not all miticides will kill false spider mites—a few will get both them and the two-spotted mites. Pentac is effective for both kinds. Two sprayings should be given seven days apart, and then repeated in two weeks. An occasional preventive spray should then be included as part of the regular spray program. The best defense is to examine leaves with any suspicious yellow, brown or gray pits or spots, and take action if false spider mites are found.

PROPAGATION. *Phalaenopsis* does not lend itself as well to vegetative propagation as some other kinds. When side shoots develop on the plants, they can be removed after they have started their own roots. Sometimes young plantlets form from nodes on the flower spike. If a plant that you are

repotting is fairly tall and has a good array of roots, you can divide it to leave a basal stump with a few living roots. Often a young plant will develop at the top of the old part. When growing rapidly it can be removed. Any young plantlets such as those described should be potted and then pot and all should be enclosed in a polyethylene bag to give a damp atmosphere. When such plants are growing vigorously, they can be cared for like seedlings of a comparable size. Very rarely is a plantlet developed on a root.

A method to encourage the formation of plantlets from buds on the basal part of flowering stems has been achieved by Robert M. Scully, Jr. The stem is cut in sections bearing one bud to each, and these are then grown in a seed-germinating medium with banana or coconut milk added.

A clean, healthy stem is selected, cleaned thoroughly with 10 percent Clorox or 100 percent ethyl alcohol. The bracts covering the buds are then removed, scraping off the basal part where the bract is attached with care not to injure the bud. Sections are then cut leaving one-half inch above and one and one-fourth inch below the bud. The cuttings are then soaked in 10 percent Clorox for 15–

20 minutes, swirling them at intervals to make the soaking more thorough. Test tubes or vials with screw caps with an inch or so of medium are used, one for each cutting. These must be prepared in advance, and the transfer of the cuttings is done under sterile conditions, as for seed sowing. The cuttings are removed from the Clorox solution and drained on a sterile surface. A slice from the bottom of each stem (the long end) is taken off to give a fresh surface, and the stem is inserted into the medium in the test tube. The mouth of the tube or vial is flamed and quickly stoppered. The cuttings are, of course, placed so that the bud points upward. The cultures are grown with 150 foot-candles of light, sixteen hours a day, or can be grown with constant light. The buds start to grow quite rapidly, making little plants ready for potting in four to five months, sometimes longer. Some cuttings may fail along the way, but a fair percentage survive. If contamination occurs, the cutting may be removed, resterilized, and put in fresh medium. Sometimes a dark pigment diffuses out of the stem into the medium; this does not seem to be harmful. The young plantlets are grown in the same manner as seedlings.

A hormone preparation called Keiki Grow has been developed to stimulate plantlets to form at bud axils on the flowering stems. It is a cytokinin, or growth stimulant, benzyladenine. It comes as a paste, to be applied to a dormant bud after removing the covering bracts. Sometimes roots do not develop on the plantlet. Another product, Keiki Root, has been developed for this problem. When roots are well started, the plantlet can be potted as for a seedling. Keiki products are available through: Plant Hormones, P.O. Box 354, McMaster University, Hamilton, Ontario, L8S 1C0, Canada.

GROWING PHALAENOPSIS FROM SEED. Pollination is carried out by hand as for other genera. The seed capsules mature quickly, about five to six months after pollination. When it matures it dries and splits open quite suddenly, so that it should be covered in advance to prevent loss of seed. The seed loses its viability rather soon after it ripens, and though it may be stored in a refrigerator for a while, it should be used before very long. Also, it is more sensitive to disinfecting agents than seed from other orchids. Calcium hypochlorite is the safest to use, and the seed should be sown rapidly so that it does not remain in the solution any longer than absolutely necessary. If you are very speedy, you can use a solution made by dissolving one clorazene tablet in two ounces of water.

The best method is to use embryo or "green pod" culture. Remove the capsule at least a month before it would normally ripen; four to four-and-a-half months from pollination is generally accepted as the best time. Proceed according to the directions given in Chapter 8.

The seedlings grow rapidly and are ready to move out of the flask in six months or so. They may be transferred to flats or to five-inch community pots. They should be kept covered with glass to give them a warm, close atmosphere. When they are ready for individual pots, use the three-inch size. They reach flowering size in about three years, sometimes even less.

The Species: Group I, Euphalaenopsis

The lip in this group bears a pair of appendages, either antennalike cirri or slender horns. The petals are broader than the sepals and are contracted at their base into a slender "claw."

Phalaenopsis amabilis. This is one of the most popular of the genus, and, with its several varieties, is the basis for most of the modern white hybrids. It is the species on which the genus was founded. The leaves are plain green, six to twelve inches long. The tall arching flower stems carry many flowers, each three to five inches in diameter. The pure white sepals and petals are set off by a lip that is tinted with yellow and spotted and streaked with red, and that bears two wavy cirri that fold back from the outer end. Secondary sprays will develop if the stem is cut just below the node that produced the first flower. The plant—which occurs in Java, Borneo, Ambon, New Guinea, and Queensland—flowers in the fall and early winter. A form with large, well-shaped flowers is var. *rimestadiana,* and one that is pink or deep rose is var. *sanderiana.* Two famous plants which formed the background for the breeding line that led to our present day hybrids were the polyploid (6n) *P. amabilis* 'Elizabethae' (*amabilis* × *amabilis* var. *rimestadiana*) and *P.* Gilles Gratiot (*amabilis* var. *rimestadiana* × *aphrodite*). From this line came *P.* Doris, Chieftain, and Winged Victory. With the advent of the tetraploid Doris, new possibilities arose, as this hybrid proved to have far better keeping quality than others. *P.* Doris has contributed this quality to subsequent hybrids such as Grace Palm, Juanita, Dos Pueblos, Vallemar, etc. Recrossing of selected individuals, plus back-crossing to plants used previously, has led to a group of hybrids that are very much alike genetically and that exhibit near uniformity of perfection.

P. aphrodite. White flowers, sometimes flushed with pink, similar to *amabilis* but smaller, and borne in a drooping raceme. The lip is tinted pink and yellow and has two fine, twisted cirri. The leaves are brownish green, ribbed down the center, and about a foot long. Occurs in Java and the Philippines. Flowers in the spring and summer.

P. schilleriana. Marvelous drooping flower sprays, branched and carrying as many as a hundred flowers in tones of rosy lilac, make this a favorite species. The plants have long leaves, mottled with grayish white, and purple underneath. The roots are flat and rough. The flowers are about three inches across. The rosy tone of the petals and sepals pales toward the edges. The lip is of the same color, dotted with red. Instead of cirri, it has a pair of divergent horns at its tip. It occurs in the Philippines and flowers in the spring. This species is much used in hybridization, in order to combine its branched, heavily flowered inflorescence with the heavier substance and larger size of the white hybrids.

P. stuartiana. This charming species has small, oddly colored flowers. The leaves are mottled when young, grayish green with purple undersides when mature. The sepals are white, the lateral ones pale yellow on the inner half and speckled with red at the base. The petals are white, lightly dotted with purple at the base. The golden-yellow lip is margined with white, spotted with purple, and has a pair of horns at its tip. The flowers have especially good keeping qualities and are borne on generously branching sprays. This species occurs in the Philippines and flowers in the winter. It is also used in hybridization.

P. intermedia. A natural hybrid between *aphrodite* and *equestris (rosea),* which has been repeated in cultivation. The leaves are generally green above, purple underneath. The flower stem is sometimes branched and bears flowers two inches in diameter. The sepals and petals are white, the petals speckled with rose at the base. The lip has violet side lobes dotted with crimson, and a deep crimson middle lobe bearing a pair of short horns at its apex. It occurs in the Philippines and flowers from March to October.

The Species: Group II, Stauroglottis

The lip of this group is without appendages, and the petals are more nearly the size of the sepals. The plants are in general smaller than those in Group I, and the flowers, though also smaller, are usually brightly colored, often strikingly barred or spotted. The species in this group have been less widely grown than those in Group I, but now that the ultimate in white hybrids has been reached, hybridists have turned to this group, and to the pink species in Group I, for the variety they promise in the creation of new hybrids.

P. amboinensis. From the island of Ambon, west of New Guinea. It is pale yellow with concentric crossbars of cinnamon brown. The sepals are broad, the petals somewhat less so, and the lip is a broad diamond shape. The two- to three-inch flowers are borne throughout the year on a sometimes branched stem six to nine inches in length. The markings do not show up, or come through only slightly, in hybrids made with white or pink species. Very interesting color and marking combinations are present in hybrids made with species with similar characteristics.

P. cochlearis. A newly discovered species, it is yellow-green with two faint brown bars at the tip of the sepals and petals, and has a pretty lip, decorated with crimson on the white side lobes, with the deeper yellow midlobe having radiating lines of red-brown. The flowering stem reaches more than a foot in length. It is native to Borneo and blooms in the spring.

P. cornu-cervi. Yellow-green one- and one-fourth-inch flowers barred with brown and having a white lip are produced freely on a stem whose shape resembles that of a stag horn. The species is deciduous natively, but apparently requires no rest period in a greenhouse. It occurs in Burma and Java and flowers throughout the year (Fig. 11–3).

P. decumbens. See *Kingidium decumbens.*

P. equestris. This is the correct name for the species so familiarly known as *P. rosea.* The plant has small leaves, plain green with a pronounced notch at the tip. It produces several flower spikes a year and the flowers open over a period of months, keeping the plant in flower nearly all year long. The one-inch flowers have rosy purple sepals and petals bordered with white. The side lobes of the lip are pink, while the midlobe is brown at the base and bright rose-purple at the end. The crest can be yellow or white. It occurs in the Philippines and is used in hybridization. Its offspring have good substance and shape, and often appear with candy stripes or pink lips. It flowers throughout the year.

P. fimbriata. This is another new introduction, and promises green coloring among its hybrids. The flowers are about one to one-and-one-half inches in diameter, with sepals and petals of light lime to apple green, with a few amethyst spots near the tips of the lateral sepals. The lip is medium to dark amethyst, fringed in white and with a "toothbrush" of hairs on the upper side of the midlobe. It is a native of Java and blooms in the spring.

P. gigantea. This species is so named for its huge plant size, rather than flower size. In nature the leaves reach several feet in length, but in cultivation do not seem to grow so large. The flower spike can be from six to fifteen inches in length and is closely packed with fleshy, two-inch flowers. The very round flowers have a white ground and are spotted with brown or purple-brown. The lip is red-purple. The plants are rare in nature, but have been raised from seed. Mature plants require a coolish spot, with considerable shade. They cannot be kept too wet but like a very humid atmosphere. They are best mounted in a hanging position, and should be misted early in the day in bright weather. The species is native to a narrow region on the island of Borneo. Blooms in spring and summer.

P. hieroglyphica. This is much like *P. lueddemanniana* in general shape, though a bit larger, and in fact has been considered a variety of that species. It is now considered a distinct species. It is cream colored with distinctly hieroglyphiclike markings in cinnamon-brown. It comes from the Philippines and flowers in late summer.

P. lindenii. The pretty one- and one-half-inch flowers of this species are pink with an overlay of fine dotted lines of pale purple. The three-lobed lip is unusually large, and the oval midlobe is striped with purple. Its hybrid offspring often inherit its lip characteristics and have striped sepals and petals. The generously long flower spike produces many flowers over a long period. It is native to the Philippines, and flowers from March to August.

P. lowii. The plants of this species are not so vigorous as some, and the flowers are small, one-and-one-half to two inches in diameter. They make up for their size by their lovely coloring. The sepals and petals are white, flushed with amethyst toward the base. The middle lobe of the lip is deep violet-purple. The sprays may carry as many as twenty flowers. The species is deciduous in its native environment, Borneo and Burma. It flowers in the summer and requires a drier atmosphere than some.

P. lueddemanniana. This remarkable species has over thirty color forms. A number are rosy purple and of glistening waxy texture, some almost solid color, others striped sparsely or profusely with white.

The plants are rather small. Several flower spikes come at once, and elongate as they branch, continuing for several years. A burst of two-inch blossoms occurs at intervals as one, two, or three spikes are produced from each node on each stem. The sepals are broader than the petals, and the lip is narrow with a sharp, raised crest down the center bearing a few bristly hairs. It occurs in the Philippines and flowers throughout the year. Plantlets form frequently on old flower stems. An odd characteristic is that after pollination the flowers turn green and remain fleshy while the seed ripens.

P. maculata. This species is interesting because of its bright red lip. The flowers are less than three-fourths inch in diameter, creamy white with red-brown markings. It is native to Sarawak, Borneo, and flowers in summer.

P. mannii. This species gave the first break in the creation of yellow hybrids, and recently a number of successful yellows have been made. It is a small flower with slender sepals and petals, yellow, heavily overlaid with brown markings, and an anchor-shaped lip, white with some purple markings at its base. With most of the species in this

Figure 11–3 Phalaenopsis cornu-cervi. (COURTESY OF J. A. FOWLIE.)

group their potentialities as parents were not known until they were bred, often giving surprising results. This was true of *P. mannii* with which Lewis Vaughn did pioneering work in breeding yellows. The species is native to Assam, India. It has leaves six to twelve inches long, green, spotted with purple, and a flower spike that is branched and bears ten to fifteen flowers, fragrant and long lasting. It flowers spring and summer.

P. mariae. Resembling *lueddemanniana,* this species has yellow flowers that are marked with four transverse bars. The flowers are one and one-half inches across, and the lip is rose-purple with white margins, without bristles. It occurs in the Philippines, and is summer flowering.

P. micholitzii. Another species that resembles *lueddemanniana.* This one has white or yellow flowers that are not barred. It occurs in the Philippines (Fig. 11–4).

P. pulchra. This is as beautiful as its name indicates, a solid magenta on the front, silvery white on the back. Much like *P. lueddemanniana* in shape and size, it is another that was once considered a variety of that species. It is from the Philippines and flowers in late summer and fall.

P. sumatrana. A medium size plant with two-inch flowers that are quite heavy in substance. They are cream-white, barred with red-brown, about two inches in diameter. The lip has erect side lobes with orange spots on the inside, and a long midlobe that is white with purple lines on each side of the dense tuft of hairs down the center. It is native to Sumatra, Borneo, and the Malay Peninsula, and flowers in the spring.

P. violacea. This lovely species has two quite definite forms. One from Borneo is pale green or greenish white with a purple lip and a purple suffusion at the base of the dorsal sepal and petals, over the back of the column, and on the inside basal half of the lateral sepals. The lateral sepals converge toward the lip. The form from Malaya is more or less uniformly rose purple, with widespreading lateral sepals. There are forms of the Malayan type that are paler, as well as an albino variety. Plants of the Malayan type are somewhat smaller than those of the Borneo type, having leaves from six to nine inches in length and flowers of two inches, while those from Borneo run to twelve inches in leaf length and three inches in flower size. Also, the Borneo form is a reluctant breeder, while many hybrids result from the Malayan one. It flowers summer and fall.

PARAPHALAENOPSIS

The genus *Paraphalaenopsis* was created for three species which are separate from *Phalaenopsis.* They have terete leaves and are all native to western Borneo.

Paraphalaenopsis denevei. This species has leaves about two and a half feet long which may be upright or pendulous, usually the latter. Several flowers of two-inch diameter are produced on an erect stem from spring to summer. They are very attractive and long lasting. The petals and sepals are flat with wavy edges, light greenish-yellow to dark yellow-brown. The lip is three lobed with a narrow, blunt, tongue-shaped midlobe, and the tips of all lobes are red or red-violet. The crest of the midlobe is striped with transverse red lines. It is spring-blooming.

P. laycockii. Much like the former, but with larger flowers that are white suffused with pinkish lavender. The three-lobed lip has erect, twisted side lobes spotted with brown on the inside, and a midlobe that is lavender at the tip shading to brown, striped at the base. It is summer flowering.

Figure 11–4 Phalaenopsis micholitzii. (COURTESY OF J. A. FOWLIE.)

P. serpentilingua. The name is descriptive of the midlobe of the lip, which is long and narrow and forked at the tip. The flowers have quite wavy, moderately broad petals and sepals, which are white with a faint tint of pink. The lip is yellow with stripes of red transversing the midlobe, brown tips to the tall, upward-spreading side lobes, and spots on the tall, fleshy, double-pointed crest. It flowers in spring.

DORITIS

The single species of this genus was originally named *Doritis pulcherrima,* but was later placed in the genus *Phalaenopsis* as both *P. pulcherrima* and *P. esmeralda.* Although it breeds freely with *Phalaenopsis,* certain differences cause it now to be accepted by its original name.

Doritis pulcherrima. The plant grows tall, with many pairs of close-ranked, tough, stiff, six-inch-long leaves, and produces young vegetative growths from its base. The three-foot flower stem is branched and gives rise to twenty or so flowers on each branch, opening in succession over a long period. The delightful little flowers are one inch in diameter and of a pale rose-purple varying to darker shades. The side lobes of the lip range from purple to orange to brownish red, while the midlobe is purple and pointed in shape. Two cirri are situated behind a crest at the base of the midlobe. It spreads natively over an area of Southeast Asia and the Malay Peninsula, and flowers in fall and winter. The variety *buyssoniana* has larger, more richly colored flowers, with more flatly spreading parts, and is a tetraploid.

KINGIDIUM

A genus of several species, only one of which is well known, *Kingidium decumbens.* This was once known as *Phalaenopsis decumbens,* and also *P. amethystina,* and later as *Kingiella decumbens.*

Kingidium decumbens. Rather a small plant, with narrow, five-inch leaves that are quite thin in substance. The eight-inch flower stem holds many little flowers barely more than half an inch in diameter. The sepals and petals are white, the former purple-spotted toward the base; the lip is purple. It flowers more than once a year. It spreads natively through Southeast Asia into Malaysia and the Philippines.

VANDA

This genus of sun-loving, robust plants has won the hearts of orchid growers everywhere. The flowers are beautifully shaped and exhibit a wondrous blending of colors. They are of excellent substance, keep well, and are adaptable to many uses. According to the habit of the species, from three to eighty blooms may occur on one stem. Their name is the Sanskrit word, *vanda,* which was applied in ancient India to the vanda of Bengal and related orchids.

The fifty or more species grow natively through a variety of climates in tropical Asia. If the native habitat of each kind had to be reproduced in cultivation, it would make their culture quite difficult. Fortunately, vandas are most adaptable. They can be grown in either an intermediate or a warm greenhouse, with the possible exception of *Vanda coerulea* which prefers cooler nights. Even this species can be grown in a cool spot in a cattleya house.

The majority of the species have strap-shaped leaves, a few have cylindrical leaves, called the "terete" species, and a few come in between and are called "semiterete." Each group breeds freely within itself. However, hybrids between leaf types can usually be carried no farther than the primary cross, for they are almost entirely sterile. The low degree of fertility in the intertype groups and the few exceptions to this are discussed later.

Large, fleshy roots are produced from the stem between the leaves, which may grow into the pots, but which are likely to grow straight out into the air or into the pots of neighboring plants. The flower sprays arise from the axils of the leaves on the newly matured part of the plant. (See Fig. 2–2.) The flower stems alternate from side to side of the plants, each one being produced from the axil of the next higher leaf. One, two, or sometimes three sprays appear at once, or they may come in succession through the year.

The sepals and petals are usually similar in size, though in some the lateral sepals are larger. They are narrowed toward the base, rounded toward the apex, and usually flat and spreading. The lip is attached to the short foot of the column and is spurred at its base, with the side lobes fleshy and erect, the middle lobe spreading (Fig. 11–5). Colors include white, yellow, rose, purple, blue, and brown, often fantastically combined or fused in single flowers.

Culture

POTTING. Vandas require a large amount of growing medium and much nourishment. Osmunda fiber and tree fern have long been used, but bark is quite satisfactory for them. In fact, since bark allows the grower to keep up with the rapid growth of young plants, and since all ages do well in it, it is rapidly becoming the preferred medium in this country. The pots should have good drainage. Potting young seedlings simply requires that they be moved on into larger pots as they outgrow the smaller ones. After a plant has matured and flowered, it need be repotted only when the medium breaks down or the pot is no longer adequate. One could never use pots large enough to contain all the roots, so the aim is to furnish a size in proportion to the plant and its need for water and fertilizer.

Vandas increase rapidly in height. Some will

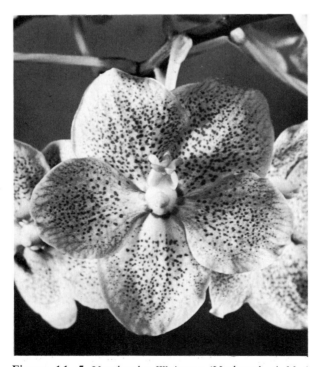

Figure 11–5 Vandanthe Waipuna 'Hodama', *A.M./A.O.S., A.M./H.O.S.* (Vandanthe Ellen Noa X Vandanthe Rothschildiana). (Courtesy of W. Kirch.)

grow to six or seven feet. This is not always an advantage. A large, heavy plant will produce more flowers for a while, but when it begins to lose the basal leaves and becomes straggly, flowering is sometimes reduced and the plant is no longer neat and handsome. Rather than allow them to become so tall, it is better to cut off the top half and pot it in fresh material. New hybrids tend to be more compact and height is less of a problem with them.

To divide a plant, make a cut through the stem so as to leave a goodly number of roots on both halves, and a number of leaves on the older part. Choose a time when new roots are growing and old roots are branching. Wet the roots thoroughly to make them more flexible; it may then be possible to wind them around in the new pot without injury. If they break, cut them off at the break and put the stubs in the medium. Roots that grow too high upon the stem to go into the pot are left as they are. Center the plant so that the base of the stem is two inches or so in the medium. Fill in with bark (or osmunda or tree fern). Stake the plant so that it will not wobble. Repot the good section of the old part. Given a damp atmosphere, new growth may break from a dormant bud along the stem. If the roots of the old part remain good, the new growth can be allowed to continue to grow upon it. However, most growers prefer to remove the new plantlet when it has made roots of its own. It will take such a plantlet several years to reach flowering size. Incidentally, any plantlets that develop along the stem of a plant may be removed in like manner.

Air layering may encourage a new root to start if none is present where you wish to divide the plant. Cut a notch in the stem just under a leaf, place a ball of damp sphagnum moss around the cut and the stem, wrap this in polyethylene film, and tie securely. When a new root has formed, the upper section bearing it can be removed and potted.

WATER. Vandas require abundant water during their growing season, with somewhat less during the winter, though not to the point of dryness. They can withstand drying far better than phalaenopsis, however. After potting, water sparingly until the roots take hold again. Roots that have been disturbed by potting will rot if they are kept wet, whereas they will start branch roots if they are kept on the dry side. Although vandas can take a drier atmosphere than phalaenopsis, they appreciate a humidity of 40 to 50 percent. In a very damp atmosphere, the plants will be larger and less tough than in a drier environment, although they will grow and flower well with a lower daytime humidity. A mist spray on bright days is beneficial, both to furnish humidity and give water to the aerial roots. Where an evaporative cooler or a humidifier is used, misting is not necessary.

TEMPERATURE. Vandas will do well with a night temperature of from 55° to 65°. This means they can be grown well either with cattleyas or with warmer-growing kinds. They can withstand an accidental cold spell very well, such as that produced when trouble arises with the heating system, although they should, of course, not be allowed freezing temperatures. While they are not as susceptible to burning as some, they should be protected from excessive daytime heat.

LIGHT. The terete-leaved species require stronger light than the strap-leaved ones, and in warm areas are grown outdoors in full sun. The strap-leaved kinds and hybrids between these and the teretes will adapt themselves to about the same amount of light as cattleyas. Not all of them do well where winters are dull however, but selected kinds, chosen for their adaptability, may. If you live where the sun shines year-round, you can grow almost any kind of vanda. If you have long spells of dull weather, buy vandas from growers who have chosen kinds for that type of climate. Give them the brightest spot in either the cattleya house or the warm greenhouse.

VENTILATION AND AIR MOVEMENT. Just as moving air and ventilation help to keep other orchids healthy, so do they benefit vandas.

FEEDING. Vandas are heavy feeders. In osmunda fiber and tree fern they may be given a complete fertilizer every two weeks. In bark they should be fed at every watering, with a fertilizer of high nitrogen content.

TRAINING ROOTS. If you have but few plants, you can control their habit of sending their heavy roots in all directions. Roots that have extended to some distance from the plant can be brought back toward the pot and finally trained to go into the medium. Newly growing roots can also be trained into the pot. Wet the root thoroughly to make it flexible, and then tie a sling of string around the root and the plant stem. Pull it in the direction you wish it to go until it resists the pull. Let it alone for a few days, and then every now and then, tighten the string. Finally, it will be in a position for you to maneuver the tip into the potting medium. Growers with many plants will probably not have time to do this; so when they water or use fertilizer solution, they should wet the aerial roots as well.

VANDAS FROM SEED. Vandas may be readily grown from seed, using the methods recommended for *Phalaenopsis*. The wide variety represented in the genus gives an opportunity for a wealth of hybrids. Intergeneric crosses with other members of this subtribe add to the possibilities. Growers in Hawaii and in the Orient have led the way with tremendous numbers of hybrids, fascinating in their combination of colors and shapes. The interest is spreading to other parts of the world.

The Species

Of the large number of species, fewer than half are well known. Some that are rather rare are now is being used in hybridization. The outstanding species are popular with amateurs, as are the many hybrids.

Vanda amesiana. This is a smaller plant than some, with semiterete leaves. It bears sprays of fragrant flowers which range from white to rose-purple on foot-long stems. It occurs in Burma and Thailand at elevations of 5,000 feet and flowers in midwinter.

V. coerulea. This is the famous blue vanda, much loved for its own sake as well as for its contributions to hybrids. It varies from clear cobalt to both paler and deeper shades of blue. Its dense sprays carry ten to twenty flowers that are each three to four inches across. The sepals and petals are nearly equal and overlap each other, giving the effect of a round, flat, compact flower. The little lip is three lobed, the front lobe a rich blue. The flowers last about a month when kept cool. This strap-leaf species occurs under sunny, cool conditions at high elevations in northern India, Thailand, and Burma. It flowers at any time from fall through winter and spring and it can be grown either in a cool spot in a cattleya house where it can have plenty of light or with cool orchids. *V. coerulea* crossed with *Euanthe sanderiana* produced one of the best known of all hybrids, the large, flat, blue *Vandanthe* Rothschildiana.

V. concolor. Rather rare in collections, this strap-leaf species is a tetraploid which has been used somewhat in hybridization. Its yellow-brown flowers are borne about seven to ten to a stem. The plant occurs in China and flowers in the summer.

V. cristata. Smaller than many, it has six-inch, leathery leaves, and an erect, short flower stem with half a dozen blossoms. A two-inch green form comes from an elevation of 4,000 feet, while a smaller, yellower one lives lower down. The elongated lip, which has divergent horns at the tip, is striped with red in both. Sepals and petals are narrow, the latter held forward and a bit downward. The flowers are waxy, fragrant, and long lasting. Flowering season is spring to summer. Occurs in Nepal, Bhutan, and Sikkim.

V. dearei. The fragrant, long-lasting flowers are creamy white with a yellow lip, qualities that endear them to growers although the species is not as striking as some. The cross *Vanda dearei* × *Euanthe sanderiana* produced *Vandanthe* Ellen Noa, one of the outstanding strap-leaf hybrids. *V. dearei,* a strap-leaf species, occurs in Borneo and Java and flowers in the summer.

V. hookeriana. See *Papilionanthe hookeriana.*

V. kimballiana. See *Holcoglossum kimballiana.*

V. lamellata. A dwarf strap-leaf species with slender recurved leaves. It bears many-flowered stems of light yellow blooms stained with brown and measure about two inches across. There is a more brightly colored variety, var. *boxallii* that is more commonly grown and is used in hybridization. It occurs in the Philippines and flowers in the winter.

V. luzonica. This striking species has two-inch flowers borne in generous numbers on sprays up to fifteen inches long. They are white with crimson markings and a bright red lip. The plant is rather short, growing about two feet high, with strap-shaped leaves fifteen inches long. It occurs in the Philippines and flowers in the spring. This species has been used a great deal in hybridization and contributes its coloring to its progeny.

V. merrillii. Although it was discovered only fairly recently, this species is already becoming popular. Its small creamy flowers are stained with red to red-brown and have a shiny, waxy texture. The lip has side lobes of white with purple dots, and a fiddle-shaped midlobe streaked and stained with red. It is a strap-leaf species that occurs in the Philippines and flowers spring and summer.

V. sanderiana. The name of this famous species has been changed to *Euanthe sanderiana.* (See below.)

V. spathulata. A tetraploid with tall spikes of golden yellow flowers, this tall plant has strap-shaped leaves that are only three inches long. Both leaves and flower stalks are spotted with red. The flowers are small, only an inch or so across, and have a lip of darker yellow marked with red-brown. It is a native of India and Sri Lanka and is being used in hybridization. It blooms in autumn.

V. sumatrana. Although not commonly grown, this species is being used in hybridization. It is similar to *dearei* in general aspect, with shiny, greenish brown flowers. The plant occurs in Sumatra and flowers in the winter.

V. teres. See *Papilionanthe teres.*

V. tessellata. This is the correct name for the species better known as *roxburghii.* It is the species upon which the genus was founded in 1820 by Dr. Brown, who adopted the name given it in Bengal, "vanda," as the name of the genus. It is a medium-size plant with strap-shaped leaves and a spike of six to eight greenish yellow flowers. The wavy sepals and petals are white on the back, and reticulated with olive brown on the front. The long middle lobe of the lip is violet. This native of Bengal flowers from May to August. It has been used in hybridization. Varietal forms range in color from pink through yellow.

V. tricolor. A well-known species, this has thick, waxy or leathery flowers, heavily spotted with bright red-brown on a yellow ground. The flowers are white to cream-colored on the back. The middle lobe of the lip is lyre shaped, rich purple, and decorated with elevated lines. The flowers are fragrant and long lasting. The variety *suavis,* sometimes treated as a distinct species, has sepals and petals of white, spotted and barred with reddish purple. The front lobe of the lip is pale rosy purple, the side lobes deep purple. Both are tall, strong plants with strap-shaped leaves. They are native to Java and bloom year-round.

EUANTHE

The single species in this genus has so long been known as *Vanda sanderiana* that it is going to be difficult to become accustomed to changing its name and the names of the many hybrids that have come from it.

Euanthe sanderiana. This is one of the most beautiful orchids known. Because of its beauty, size, and shape it has been used frequently in hybridization. It is a magnificent broad, flat flower, with rounded parts. The lateral sepals are especially large and are the most striking feature of the flower. The coloring is a fusion of hues. The dorsal sepals and the petals shade from white to rose. The lateral sepals are yellow-green suffused with reddish brown and marked with a network of brown. The little lip is dull crimson, with a squarish middle lobe and side lobes that form a little cup under the tip of the column. The color variations in this species are quite remarkable, some tending to purple, others to red. There is a greenish form lacking purple. It is a strap-leaf species, occurs in the Philippines, and flowers in the fall. *E. sanderiana* contributes its broad, flat, rounded shape to its hybrids, one reason why it is so frequently used (Fig. 11–6). Its hybrids are likely to have the reticulation (network) of deeper color

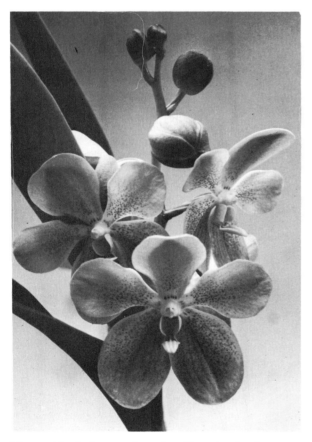

Figure 11–6 Opsisanthe Juliet (Euanthe Sanderiana X Vandopsis gigantea). (COURTESY OF WM. KIRCH.)

which is one of its charms. In *Vandanthe* Rothschildiana this is a deep blue. The influence of its shape is clearly seen in two of its hybrids—*Vandanthe* Nellie Morley and *Vandanthe* Ellen Noa.

HOLCOGLOSSUM

The species below, and *Vanda rupestris,* have been moved to this genus.

H. kimballiana previously *Vanda kimballiana.* A semiterete species requiring cool conditions. The plants are slender and rarely grow taller than fifteen inches. The lovely flowers are pure white except for the lip, the middle lobe of which is deep rose, marked with deeper veins; the side lobes are yellow. The base of the lip forms a spur about an inch long. The plant grows on the faces of cliffs, exposed to the sun, in the high altitudes of Burma, and it flowers in late summer to fall.

VANDOPSIS

Vandopsis, a genus whose name means "like Vanda," resembles *Vanda* except that the lip has no spur. The plants are very robust and heavy. The members of the genus are frequently crossed with *Vanda.*

Vandopsis gigantea. Heavy, pendulous plants produce flower stems ten to fifteen inches long with flowers three inches across. The flowers are golden-yellow, blotched with cinnamon, and have a white lip. The species occurs in Burma, and flowers in the spring.

V. lissochiloides. This is the most familiar of the species and is sometimes mistakenly called *V. batemannii.* The flower stem bears a dozen or more three-inch flowers that are yellowish, spotted with purple on the upper surface, and reddish purple underneath. The flowers are somewhat coarse in texture and last a long time. It occurs in the Philippines and flowers from spring through summer.

Hybridization in Vanda

Hybridization in *Vanda* is beset by special problems that arise from mixed hybrids made between species of different leaf types. Hybrids within each leaf type group are, with rare exceptions, entirely fertile, except that any triploids produced are by their nature quite sterile. Intergroup hybrids can be made by crossing a terete species with a strap-leaf species, or by crossing a terete hybrid with a strap-leaf hybrid, but most of the resulting hybrids are almost entirely sterile.

The basic haploid chromosome number in Vanda is 19 and (except for the tetraploid species) the species all have a diploid number of 38. In the intergroup hybrids, the 19 chromosomes from the terete species will not pair at reduction division with the 19 chromosomes from the strap-leaf species, and hence, because the distribution of chromosomes is very erratic, sterility results. Production of any viable seed by such hybrids is usually the result of nonreduced gametes. The situation is most unfortunate because the semiterete hybrids are very lovely, and one can imagine the wondrous hybrids that would result if they could be used freely as parents. When two striking exceptions to the sterility of the semiterete hybrids occurred in Hawaii, W. B. Storey and H. Kamemoto, by dint of a great deal of work with the microscope, worked out a fascinating genetic detective story (Fig. 11–7).

Vandanthe.* Mevr. L. Velthuis (*V*. Miss Joaquim × *Euanthe sanderiana*) is a semiterete diploid hybrid and would be expected to be quite sterile (Fig. 11–8). One individual plant of *Vandanthe* Mevr. L. Velthuis crossed with *V. coerulea* gave a small hybrid progeny, *Vandanthe* Nora Potter. Nora Potter immediately became famous, in the first place because they are very handsome; in the second place, because it was most unusual for a hybrid such as Mevr. L. Velthuis to be a successful parent; and in the third place because

the Nora Potters were discovered to be pentaploid. The question of how two diploid parents could give rise to a pentaploid progeny was worked out by W. B. Storey from a study of the formation of sex cells in Mevr. L. Velthuis. He discovered that it produced giant 4n gametes, sex cells that contained 76 chromosomes. These, united with the 19 chromosomes from *V. coerulea,* gave the 95 chromosomes of the pentaploid Nora Potter.

V. Emma van Deventer is a semiterete hybrid between *teres* and *V. tricolor.* Since the parents were diploid, it was assumed that the offspring Emma van Deventer were also diploid. Several plants of Emma van Deventer, owned by different people, were crossed with plants of *E. sanderiana.* At best a few seedlings might have been expected, but in each case seed formation was abundant and thousands of vigorous seedlings were raised. The unusual fertility was astonishing. The cross, *Vandanthe* Nellie Morley, proved to be triploid in each of the progeny, and all were quite uniform. It was thought that the triploidy had resulted from nonreduced 2n gametes from Emma van Deventer. Another cross between Emma van Deventer and *sanderiana* produced a pentaploid progeny, and this inspired H. Kamemoto to investigate the parents of both types of offspring. He found that the pentaploid progeny was produced in the same manner as the pentaploid progeny from Mevr. L. Velthuis; in this case a diploid Emma van Deventer had given rise to giant 4n gametes. Chromosome counts on the Emma van Deventers that had given the triploid offspring proved them to be, not diploid as had been thought, but tetraploids. The discovery of their tetraploid nature explained their

* For convenience we shall call this hybrid *Vandanthe* instead of a combination of *Papilionanthe* and *Euanthe* (which might come out to be *Papilionanthe* anyway).

Figure 11–7 *Variation in the formation of reproductive cells in* Vanda, *which leads to differences in ploidy.* LEFT: *A quartet of normally reduced haploid cells, containing 19 chromosomes.* CENTER: *A pair of nonreduced diploid cells, containing 38 chromosomes.* RIGHT: *A giant tetraploid cell with 76 chromosomes, formed by doubling of the diploid number.* (COURTESY OF H. KAMEMOTO.)

Figure 11–8 Vandanthe Mevr. L. Velthuis, *a diploid semiterete hybrid, whose genetics is described in these pages.* (Courtesy of Jones and Scully, Inc.)

unusual fertility, for tetraploids form reproductive cells with ease. The 2n gametes that had given rise to their triploid offspring were then known to be normally reduced (from the 4n cells of the parents) rather than to have been nonreduced gametes of a 2n parent.

Tetraploids of the type of Emma van Deventer are called "amphidiploids," for they contain the full diploid number of chromosomes from two unlike parents. The significance of this is that whereas the plant would be sterile, or nearly sterile, with 19 chromosomes from the terete parent and 19 from the strap-leaf parent, it has been made fertile by the doubling of these chromosomes. Each set of 19 terete chromosomes now has another set to pair with, and the 19 chromosomes from the strap-leaf parent also have a set to pair with. It is not known how this amphidiploidy, usually a rare event, occurred in several plants from the same seed pod.

The ability of some additional semiterete hybrids to give progeny in the two ways just described is testified by the recent findings of both triploid and pentaploid progenies. Thus the sterility barrier is being broken by the ability of individual plants to produce nonreduced gametes and occasionally to double their own chromosome number. Hybrids which give but very few viable seed may still be most useful if their polyploid offspring can in turn be used as parents. There are still large numbers of semiterete hybrids that appear to be completely sterile. If they could be made

to double their chromosomes, they, too, would become fertile. Here is a way in which colchicine might be useful (see Chapter 8), if a proper technique could be worked out.

We should not leave the subject of hybridization without mentioning the delightful small-flowered crosses being made. They combine *Vanda* and *Aerides* with *Rhynchostylis, Saccolabium, Ascocentrum,* and others to give plants of smaller dimensions that have clusters of flowers the size of a dime or a quarter, in a range of rainbow colors. Much more suitable to small greenhouses, these are jewels in themselves and sparkle alongside their larger and more stately relatives.

PAPILIONANTHE

Among several species taxonomically removed from *Vanda* are: *Papilionanthe hookeriana* and *P. teres.*

Papilionanthe hookeriana. A tall, terete-leaf species, its cylindrical leaves are channeled on the upper surface and pointed. Each stem bears five or six flowers which are about two-and-one-half inches across. The sepals are white flushed with purple, the petals, which are larger and wavy, are white flushed and spotted with purple. The side lobes of the lip are amethyst with pale lines, the middle lobe, which is broad and spreading, is white stained with deep purple. This species is very common in Malaya and also occurs in Borneo and Sumatra. It should best be grown outdoors in bright sun. The flowers appear in the fall. The plant has contributed its huge lip to the hybrid *P.* Miss Joaquim, which is grown in fields in Hawaii and imported into this country in large quantities.

P. teres. This very lovely species has played a great role in introducing vandas to this country. Its flowers are large, with broad wavy parts. The petals and sepals are similar in size; the sepals are white tinged with rose and the petals are a rich deep rose. The lip has large, yellow side lobes that fold over the column, and a triangular outer lobe that is rose, veined and spotted with yellow, spreading at its outer end and split in the center. The plant occurs in Burma and flowers from May to September. The hybrid *P.* Miss Joaquim, *hookeriana* × *teres*, was the first hybrid to be widely distributed. *P. teres* is a terete-leaved species which is very popularly grown, although it may be too light-demanding for parts of this country (Fig. 11–9).

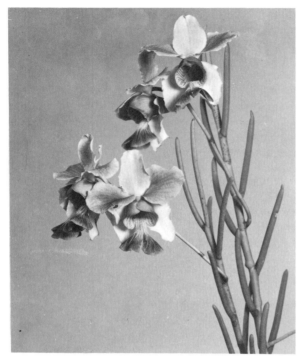

Figure 11–9 Papilionanthe teres. (Courtesy of the late Harry Dunn.)

AERIDES

Aerides, the type genus of the subtribe, is very much like *Vanda* in plant characters and cultural requirements. It offers drooping sprays of delicately beautiful flowers.

Aerides fieldingii. The nickname of this species is "fox brush" orchid, and although the flower spray is a fat cylinder about the size of a foxtail, the name in no way does justice to the flowers. About a hundred (or more) dainty, one-inch flowers are borne on the stem, each a bit of perfection that has to be looked at closely. They are saucer shaped, with an open pointed lip, solid pink in color, or with a bit of white at the edges. They have a sparkling crystalline texture, and a dainty perfume. The plant occurs in Sikkim and Assam, and flowers in the spring and summer (Fig. 11–10).

A. odoratum. This is the species upon which the genus was founded. The rather tall plants produce sprays of 15 to 20 waxy, exquisitely fragrant flowers. They are whitish, tinged with purple, and have short, rounded petals and sepals tipped with purple. The slipper-shaped lip is pinched laterally, its

tip curved up like the toe of a Persian slipper and green in color. It occurs in the Philippines and Vietnam and flowers in summer and early fall.

var. *lawrencea.* Once considered a separate species, this is now held to be a variety of *odoratum*. The flowers are not as large, nor quite as fragrant and are greenish white, tipped with amethyst. It flowers in late summer and early fall and is found in the Philippines.

var. *quinquevulnerum.* The most common of the genus, and perhaps the prettiest. The white flowers are tipped with bright amethyst purple, which gave it its name: "five wounds." There is also a dainty sprinkling of purple dots overall. The tip of the lip

Figure 11–10 Aerides fieldingii.

is greenish. This one is also from the Philippines, and it flowers in late summer (Fig. 11–11).

RENANTHERA

Renanthera is a genus similar to *Vanda,* grown for its brightly colored flowers, which, though small, are produced in great numbers and make a striking display. Subtle variations of yellow marked with red, and red with orange, are the general colors of the species. The purpose of crossing this genus with *Vanda* and other members of this group is to introduce its brilliant red and orange tones as well as its free-flowering habit and perky forms. The resulting hybrids have a wide variety of fanciful shapes which gives them a fascination all their own. *Renanthera* has four pollinia (in contrast to the two in *Vanda, Phalaenopsis, Aerides,* and *Angraecum*), and the lip is movable. The plants are

Figure 11–11 Aerides odoratum *var.* quinquevulnerum.

slender, with short fleshy leaves, and some reach such great height that they are almost too tall for the average greenhouse. They need exceptionally good light.

Renanthera coccinea. This species grows six to ten feet high. The branched flower stem comes from an upper leaf axil, and bears a hundred or more flowers two inches wide and four inches long. The very slender petals and dorsal sepal are bright red marked with yellow. The lateral sepals are longer and wider, and are clear red. The tiny yellow lip is tipped with red. A native of Vietnam, it flowers in the fall.

R. imschootiana. Similar to *coccinea,* but growing only about two feet tall, this species produces a wealth of flowers on a freely branching stem two feet long. The dorsal sepal and petals are short and slender, standing up above the broad lateral sepals and giving the flower the look of a butterfly. The dorsal sepal is dull yellow, the petals the same but dotted with red, and the lateral sepals are cinnabar red on the upper surface, dull yellow beneath. The species is a native of Assam; it flowers in the spring.

R. lowii. See *Dimorphorchis lowii.*

R. matutina. This smaller species from Java has flowers of bright yellow shaded with crimson. It flowers from autumn to midwinter.

R. monachica. The short leaves of this species are one-half inch thick and dark bluish green. The flower stem bears twenty-five or more flowers, one to one-and-one-half inches in diameter. They are bright orange with deep red spots. This native of the Philippines flowers in early spring.

R. storiei. Called the "fire orchid" in the Philippines, this species is quite similar to *coccinea.* The dorsal sepal and petals are brick-red; the lower sepals are brilliant crimson marked with lighter tones. The lip is crimson with yellow bars and a white center. The flowers last for two months. This is perhaps the most widely used species in hybridization. It flowers in the fall.

TRICHOGLOTTIS

Trichoglottis, best known for two exceptionally lovely members, has about thirty-five species ranging from the Philippines and other islands to the Malay Peninsula and the countries of Southeast Asia. The plants have rather heavy stems clothed with short, oval leaves, and some can reach five feet in height. The flowers are very long lasting.

T. brachiata has round, dark wine-red, velvety flowers, two inches across, which come singly from the upper leaf axils. The broad, oval sepals and petals have a narrow border of yellow. The midlobe of the five-lobed fuzzy lip is in the form of a cross. The lip coloring, yellow and white with wine markings, accents the dark, rich flower. The species occurs in the Philippines in Mindanao, Luzon, and other islands, and its fragrant flowers are produced over several months.

T. philippinensis is similar to *T. brachiata;* in fact the latter is sometimes given as a variety of the former. It is a taller plant with flowers a bit smaller, less rich, but nevertheless very attractive. They tend to greenish yellow with brown mottling. It covers the same geographical range as *brachiata.*

ARACHNIS

Arachnis is a genus also used in hybridization with *Vanda.* Its name means "spiderlike." The genus was at one time designated as *Arachnanthe,* and later was included in *Renanthera* by some authorities. Some of the species are now retained in *Renanthera.* *Arachnis* is characterized by four pollinia and by having the lip hinged to the base of the column and readily movable. The genus likes light, as much as or more than *Vanda.*

Arachnis flos-aeris. Native to the Philippines, these plants grow eight to ten feet tall and produce short flower stems with about ten three- to four-inch flowers. They are yellow barred with purple-brown and have a musky scent. The flowers appear from July to March.

A. moschifera. These striking cream or yellow-green flowers are spotted and barred with deep red or purple. They have the texture of enamel. The stems are slender and climbing. The flowering time is variable.

ASCOCENTRUM

Ascocentrum is a genus of charming *Vanda*-like plants that has sprays of brightly colored flowers ranging from orange to red. They are delightful for their own qualities, but they are also especially valuable in hybridization with *Vanda* to create ascodendas, plants of modest size that compete for

attention with their larger parents. They need bright light, freely moving air, and intermediate temperatures.

A. curvifolium grows some six inches tall and has half-inch flowers ranging from purple to red and orange. A native of the Himalayas, it flowers in the spring.

A. hendersonianum. See *Dyakia,* below.

A. miniatum is one of the most popular, only about four inches tall, but with a dense spike of orange flowers that reaches above the plant. The bright orange-to-red blossoms are nearly an inch wide, and the dark red anther cap punctuates their center. From the Himalayas to the Malay Peninsula, Java, and Borneo, it flowers almost any time of the year.

DYAKIA

Dyakia hendersonianum is a tiny charmer, three inches tall, with a spike of bright pink flowers. It really has no lip at all. The white tongue that hangs down from below the column is actually a spur, whose entrance is clearly visible. It is from Borneo and flowers in the spring.

RHYNCHOSTYLIS

Rhynchostylis. This is another genus that produces dense spikes of small flowers (Fig. 11–12). They are sometimes called "foxtail orchids." The roundish flowers have a slender lip that curves up from a saclike base, and a backward-jutting spur. Hybrids are made with its members and others of this subtribe.

R. coelestis. Its whitish flowers are marked with blue. The eight-inch plant gives many sprays of the fragrant, waxy blossoms in late summer and fall. It comes from Thailand.

R. gigantea derives its name from the large leathery leaves rather than from height. They are one foot long and two-and-one-quarter inches wide. The fifteen-inch spikes are densely packed with fragrant one-inch flowers that are white, spotted with magenta, and have a magenta lip. It flowers in fall and winter and comes from Thailand, Burma, and Laos.

R. retusa grows to two feet in height, and has two-foot, pendent flower spikes, very densely

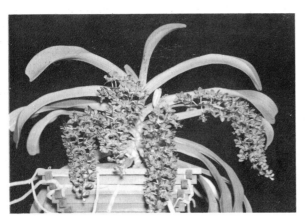

Figure 11–12 Rhynchostylis densiflora 'Ratana', *C.B.M./A.O.S., an exceptionally fine example of the delight offered by many of the less-well-known members of the Aerides tribe.* (COURTESY OF JONES AND SCULLY, INC.)

packed with three-quarter-inch flowers that are waxy, fragrant, white, and spotted with amethyst-purple. It inhabits southeast Asia and Thailand, and grows from India to the Philippines. It flowers in spring and summer.

SARCOCHILUS

Sarcochilus includes some of Australia's most charming and best-loved natives. The genus also spreads through the Malay Archipelago through the Pacific islands. The four given here are all from New South Wales and Queensland. They have small, round flowers, sepals and petals alike, and a small, fleshy, hinged, cup-shaped lip.

S. ceciliae, called "fairy bells." It is about five inches tall (often less) with small, coarse, slender, tufted leaves. The round, half-inch flowers are bell shaped, pink, with a velvety lip. It is cool growing.

S. falcatus, nicknamed "the orange blossom orchid." It is but a few inches tall but can grow into a plant with many growths that forms a perfect ball. Its leaves are sickle-shaped. The flowers are about an inch across, pure white except for orange dots at the base of the tepals, and a yellowish lip. It blooms in the spring and also likes cool temperatures.

S. fitzgeraldii has a more-open flower, and more-intense markings of red at the base of the tepals. It tends to ramble rather than to make a ball of compact growths. It is also spring flowering and cool growing.

S. hartmannii is very much like the two preceding species, not as boldly marked, with flowers a little smaller but produced in great quantities. The hybrid between this and *S. fitzgeraldii* combines all their good qualities. It prefers similar growing conditions.

NEOFINETIA

Neofinetia is a genus of but one species, a lovely miniature, *N. falcata.* It grows to about two and one-half inches tall and branches freely. The little white flowers are very fragrant at night. They have slender sepals and petals, a triangular lip, and a long curved spur. Three to seven flowers are borne on short inflorescences. It is native to Japan and Korea. It blooms in spring and summer.

DIMORPHORCHIS

This genus of two unusual species was once included in *Vanda.* The name derives from the appearance of two different flower forms on the same spike.

D. lowii grows to seven feet tall and has spikes of up to twelve feet. The two or three basal flowers are yellow, dotted with red, three inches across. The oval dorsal sepal stands straight up while the lateral ones curl backward. The oval petals also curl backward, and the tiny saclike lip juts forward to a point. The other flowers on the spike are cream, mottled with red, in places almost solid red. The parts are quite curly and wavy. It is from Borneo and flowers in early winter.

D. rohaniana also has yellow basal flowers dotted with red, but its sepals and petals are not curled. The other flowers have more-slender parts which are quite wavy, and are densely mottled with red. It is from Borneo and flowers in the fall.

GASTROCHILUS

This is a genus of about fifteen species of small *Vanda*-like plants, many of which have in the past been included in *Saccolabium.* As the name implies, they have a stomachlike or pouch-shaped lip. Sepals and petals form a fan.

G. bellinus is a miniature plant, barely two inches tall. It has a spike of four to seven waxy, one and one-half-inch fragrant flowers. They are greenish yellow, spotted with purple. The lip is white, spotted with red, while the interior of the pouch is yellow and has a tuft of hairs on each side. It comes from Burma and Thailand and flowers in late winter and spring.

G. bigibbus is equally small, and has smaller flowers, but its spike holds ten to twenty of them. They are golden yellow, fragrant, and waxy, with a fringed edge to the lip. From Burma, it flowers in the autumn.

G. dasypogon is probably the best known. It is also a small plant, and its flowers come in nestled at the base of the plant. They are yellow with a white lip that has some red spots on the side lobes, yellow spots on the outer part, and a short, dense fringe to the outer edge. It ranges from the Himalayas to Thailand, and flowers in the autumn.

HARAELLA

This is a genus of miniature, *Vanda*-like plants with charming flowers. There are few species, perhaps only two.

Haraëlla odorata. This bears four or five pair of leaves less than three inches long. The short flower stem holds several flowers in succession, with usually two open at once. The flowers are greenish yellow with small sepals and petals and a large lip. The latter is fiddle-shaped, fringed, with a large purple patch in the center that sometimes has a buglike shape. It occurs in Taiwan and flowers several times a year under intermediate conditions.

INTERGENERIC HYBRIDS IN SARCANTHINAE

Intergeneric hybrids in this subtribe are numerous, and more will undoubtedly appear as time goes on. The combining names given to the bigeneric hybrids do not as readily show their origin as do those of the Cattleya relatives, although some ingenuity was used in creating them. Some of them are as follows: *Aeridopsis = Aerides × Phalaenopsis; Aeridovanda = Aerides × Vanda; Arachnopsis = Arachnis × Phalaenopsis; Aranda = Arachnis × Vanda; Aranthera = Arachnis × Renanthera; Ascocenda = Ascocentrum × Vanda; Luisanda = Luisia × Vanda; Opsisanda = Vandopsis × Vanda; Renantanda = Renanthera × Vanda; Renanthopsis = Renanthera × Phalaenopsis; Renanopsis = Renanthera × Vandopsis; Sarcothera = Sarcochilus × Renanthera; Trichovanda = Trichoglottis × Vanda; Vandaenopsis = Phalaenopsis × Vanda; Vandanthe = Euanthe × Vanda.*

For additional intergeneric hybrid names, including a multitude of tri and quadrigeneric hybrids, consult Garay and Sweet, *Natural and Artificial Hybrid Generic Names of Orchids,* and the *Handbook on Orchid Nomenclature and Registration,* 1969.

·12·

ANGRAECUM RELATIVES

The Angraecinae Subtribe

AERANGIS RELATIVES

The Aerangidinae Subtribe

Native to tropical Africa, Madagascar, and the Seychelle Islands. There are numerous species. The plants are similar to *Vanda,* and they may be grown with cattleyas. However, the night temperature should not go below 55°. The lip typically produces a long spur at its base.

Angraecum dasycarpum. An enchanting miniature, whose little white flowers are star shaped with a rather long, tonguelike lip, apparently without a spur. The short plant stems bear alternate very fleshy, broadly oval leaves. It blooms in the fall.

A. distichum is a completely charming miniature with small, short, curved leaves tightly clasping the sinuous stems to give a braided affect. Tiny white flowers appear at intervals along the stem. A plant with many growths is extremely decorative. It is native to tropical eastern Africa, and flowers at any time of the year (Fig. 12–1).

A eburneum. A scoop-shaped, shiny white lip, and slender green sepals and petals make this species from the Comoro and Seychelle Islands most attractive. The spur is but three inches long. The large, heavy plants branch freely and the young plantlets can be removed. Flowering stems come several at a time and hold fifteen or more blooms, delightfully fragrant. The flowering time is winter (Fig. 12–2).

A. eichlerianum. A tall, climbing plant that reaches five feet in height. It has leaves four to five inches long, and usually produces one flower opposite each leaf base. The flowers are fragrant and

ANGRAECINAE

THERE ARE MORE THAN FIFteen genera in this subtribe: The ones given here are best known. The glistening, waxy flowers are fragrant, especially at night, and are moth-pollinated.

Figure 12–1 Angraecum distichum.

139

long lasting, three inches in diameter, with pointed oval sepals and petals and a lip shaped like a funnel or a candle snuffer. There is a short spur, curved in the middle. The sepals and petals are green to yellow-green, and the lip white with an emerald-green patch in the throat. Flowering time is summer and it is native to western Africa.

A. giryamae. This is the largest of the genus, and is so like *A. eburneum* that it may be but a variety of that species. It blooms in winter.

A. infundibulare. A rather dainty climbing plant, with oval leaves and thin roots at each node. It is

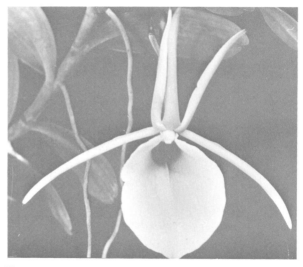

Figure 12–3 Angraecum infundibulare. (COURTESY OF BENJAMIN C. BERLINER.)

Figure 12–2 Angraecum eburneum, *one of the most widely grown of the genus.* (COURTESY OF JONES AND SCULLY, INC.)

ANGRAECUM RELATIVES—THE ANGRAECINAE SUBTRIBE

similar to *A. eichlerianum* but produces tremendous flowers. The sepals and petals are brownish green, quite slender, while the huge lip is rounded, trowel-shaped, and white shaded to yellow-green and then to deep green in the throat. The short, tapering, yellowish spur is five inches long. It flowers from fall to winter, and is native to western Africa (Fig. 12–3).

A. leonis is a decorative and unusual plant. Its leaves are "equitant," that is, they are folded vertically, and they curve down at their tips. Flower stems, which are also flattened, come from the base of the plant, holding two or three beautiful white flowers with long spurs. The flowers are three to four inches across and marvelously fragrant. From Grande Comore, it flowers in the winter.

A. magdalenae is a lovely species with four-inch, waxy, white flowers of glistening texture that last

four weeks or more. Petals and sepals are broad and pointed, and the broad lip comes to a sharp point. The plant is semiterrestrial and likes a cymbidiumlike medium. It also likes cooler temperatures than most others, good light, and moderate watering. The plant can reach a foot in height, and makes many keikis from the base. From Malagasy, it flowers in the summer.

A. scottianum. This species has terete leaves, deeply grooved on the upper surface, three to four inches long. The plant grows to between one and two feet in height. The flowers are held upside down, one to three to an inflorescence, and are very fragrant and waxy, about two inches in diameter. The parts are slender and whitish yellow, and the broad concave lip is white with a reddish brown four-inch spur. Native to the Comoro Islands, it flowers in the fall.

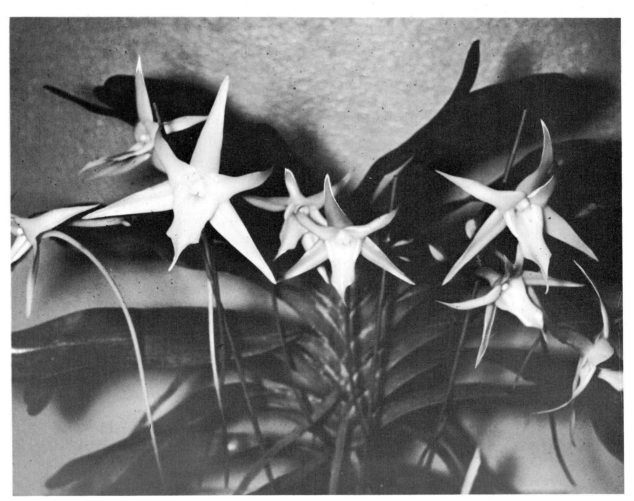

Figure 12–4 Angraecum sesquipedale, *the lovely "star of Bethlehem orchid."*   (COURTESY OF JONES AND SCULLY, INC.)

A. sesquipedale. Waxy white, five-inch star-shaped flowers with spurs ten inches long are produced on generous sprays and create a handsome species. The long spur and the close association of orchids with specific insects caused Darwin to predict that there must be a moth with a proboscis long enough to obtain the nectar from the base of the spur and so perform the act of pollinating this species. Later, the sphinx moth of Madagascar, home of *sesquipedale,* was thought to be the elusive species in question, but according to Dodson its role has not been verified. A Christmas flowering season has given *sesquipedale* its nickname of "star of Bethlehem orchid." It blooms in winter (Fig. 12–4).

A. superbum. Another species from Madagascar, this is similar to *eburneum* and may be a variety of it. It has a spur even longer than that of *sesquipedale.* The flowers are three inches across, are very fragrant, and appear in January to February.

AERANTHES

Aeranthes has spectacular, handsome, waxy green flowers. The sepals and petals form a five-pointed star, with broad bases and slender, pointed tips. The rather square lip is large, with the side lobes molded into two portions and the midlobe fleshy and tonguelike. There is a short spur at the base of the column foot. The plants are similar to *Angraecum,* and the flowers are borne on long wiry stems, occasionally singly but more often two or more together or in succession. These natives to Madagascar may be grown in the same manner as *Angraecum,* and flower from summer into winter.

A. arachnites has three-inch flowers of lime green. The white lip has a green midlobe. The flowers are borne on upright stems about as tall as the leaves.

A. ramosus is delightful and unusual. The wiry flowering stems can be several feet long, so thin that it is difficult to see how nourishment gets through. They are much branched, and buds come one after another at the tips. The flowers are pure green, from one and one-half to three inches across, depending on the variety, and are delightfully humorous in shape. They look almost like little leprechauns bouncing at the end of wires. From Malagasy, it flowers over a long period in spring or autumn.

DENDROPHYLAX

There are leafless orchids on all continents, plants that through evolution have lost their leaves and whose roots have taken over the job of photosynthesis. They have a short stem, covered with brown bracts, from which both roots and flowers arise. This genus and the one which follows are American representatives of the subtribe that includes *Angraecum* and *Aeranthes.*

Dendrophylax fawcettii has delightfully fragrant white flowers, one or two to a stem, emerging from a mass of rather large, straggly roots. The blossoms have a large, divided, white lip that hangs down from a fan of greenish petals and sepals. A five-inch spur curves down from the base of the lip. Native to Grand Cayman Island, it flowers in the summer.

D. funalis is similar to the above but has a rounder lip and a shorter spur. It is native to Jamaica and flowers in early fall.

POLYRADICION

This native of Florida has been called *Polyrrhyza* until just recently. There are few species, one of which is quite famous. All are leafless.

Polyradicion lindenii is called the "white frog orchid" or the "ghost orchid." The blossom hangs at the end of a long, thin stem that is quite invisible in the shaded forest. The flower is white, with sepals and petals that form a star, down from which hangs the extraordinary frog-shaped lip. A long spur hangs behind. Native to southern Florida and Cuba, it flowers from winter into summer.

AERANGIDINAE

The more than thirty genera in this subtribe include many charming species. Mostly white, with tints of pink or salmon or green, and mostly fragrant, they should be welcome in any greenhouse.

AERANGIS

Most of the graceful flowers of this genus resemble birds in flight, with their sepals and petals curved slightly backward and the lip held forward. The spurs arching from each blossom add to the airy appearance.

A. brachycarpa grows at fairly high elevations in central and eastern Africa, in damp shady places, and therefore needs cooler temperatures than most. The one-and-one-half-inch flowers are white, with slender, pointed parts and a long, salmon-colored spur. There are five to twelve flowers rather widely spaced on the pendent spray. Plants are from six to twelve inches tall, the leaves dotted with black on the undersides. It flowers in the fall.

A. citrata is a miniature plant, four to five inches tall, and gives a beautiful, dense spike of flowers with more rounded parts than many others. They are white to cream, and all face forward on the ten-inch inflorescence. It is from Malagasy and flowers in the spring.

A. friesiorum has two-inch, white flowers whose pointed parts are often tipped with pink. Plants can reach eight inches in height and have rather coarse-textured leaves, broader at the tip than at the base. Flower stems are pendent, with some ten to twelve blossoms, decorated with eight-inch spurs. It occurs in Kenya and flowers almost any time of the year.

A. rhodosticta (syn. *A. luteo-alba* var. *rhodosticta*) is a lovely miniature, a dainty plant with slender, shiny, green leaves four to five inches long that hang down in a fan from a mount. The spike grows horizontally and holds a dozen or more flat, cream or white one-inch blossoms, all facing upward on the stem. They have oval parts and a red anther cap that punctuates the flowers neatly. It occurs from the Cameroons to Kenya and flowers spring and fall. It needs to be shady and damp.

A. somalensis is an unusual plant. Its thick, gray-green leaves have a raised network on their surface. The edges are wavy and the color is often tinged with red. The plant itself is small. The flowering stems are pendent and hold ten or a dozen widely spaced flowers that are white, tinged with green or pink, and have pinkish spurs. It comes from semiarid areas in eastern Africa.

CALYPTROCHILUM

There are several species in this genus, an interesting one of which will be described here.

C. christyanum has a stem that can be either climbing or pendulous, with thick, rough, short, alternate leaves. A short inflorescence comes from a leaf axil and holds three to seven or eight white, very waxy blossoms. They are most peculiar in shape. The petals and sepals form a tulip-shaped upper part, while the scoop-shaped lip juts out below. The base of the lip extends directly backward in the form of a funnel-shaped spur, at the end of which a little bulb hangs down at a right angle, filled with nectar. It is an odd development, which would seem to hinder rather than aid pollination. The species comes from central Africa to Liberia and south to Malawi, and flowers in spring and summer.

CYRTORCHIS

The several species of this genus are widespread across central Africa to Zambia and Malawi.

C. arcuata var. *variabilis* is the smaller of two forms of this species. The plant resembles a strap-leaf vanda. The flowers, eight to fifteen on a spray, are pure white and fragrant, the bases of the sepals and petals forming a loosely closed tube, while the outer portions of the slender, pointed parts, together with the pointed lip, form an open star about one-and-one-quarter inches across. The spur is two inches long. Flowers in spring and summer.

var. *whytei* is the larger, handsomer of the two. Its flowers are two inches across, the spur more than three inches. It is deliciously fragrant at night, slightly so during the day. It occurs in West Africa, southern Tanzania and Malawi, and flowers spring to fall.

C. praetermissa is a charming miniature form, a wonderful contrast to var. *whytei.*

MYSTACIDIUM

Several miniature and dwarf species belong to this genus. Their hallmark is a little moustache projecting from under the column—actually the two-pronged rostellum.

M. capense is the best known of the species. It has several three-inch leaves from a short stem, and pendulous inflorescences that hold some ten pure white flowers each. Even the anther cap is white. The blossoms are one-and-one-half inches across, the spur about two inches long, pale green. From southern Africa, it flowers almost any time of the year.

TRIDACTYLE

Among the very interesting African orchids is *Tridactyle*, especially the species *tridactylites*, which grows natively from the Congo to southern Africa. The plant resembles a delicate vanda, with slender stems, narrow leaves, bilobed at the tip, and thick roots. The tiny and very complicated flowers are borne on short spikes where the leaf joins the stem. The half-inch flowers are somewhat star-shaped, brownish green. The lip is the complex part; it is spurred, with the entrance to the spur showing on its face as a pit. The midlobe is divided into a broad center point and two side branches, which are again divided at their tips into little fingerlike processes. The plant grows readily, climbing over a piece of driftwood or a tree fern slab, and flowers in the spring (Fig. 12–5).

Figure 12–5 Tridactyle tridactylites *has short, feathery sprays of dainty little spurred flowers.*

·13·

CATTLEYA RELATIVES

The Laeliinae Subtribe

CATTLEYA

CATTLEYAS AND THEIR HY-brids are probably the best-known orchids in the world. The relatives with which cattleyas are most frequently crossed are also well known, and many are very handsome. This subtribe includes not only these outstanding ones, but many others as well, for a total of some forty-four genera. As usual, we can give only a sampling of them.

Many wonderful things have been discovered by accident, and it was an accident that introduced the first cattleya plants to European botanists. The story goes that in 1818 a Mr. Swainson was collecting mosses and lichens in Brazil, and gathered some heavy, thick-leaved plants to tie around some of his collections for shipment to England. When this material arrived, William Cattley, an eminent horticulturist, realized that the odd plants were something unusual and rescued them from oblivion. The first of these plants bloomed in 1824, and was studied by Dr. Lindley, a renowned botanist, who found it to be of a genus entirely new to science. Lindley described the plant and gave the new genus the name *Cattleya,* after its happy possessor. The founding specimen he named *Cattleya labiata autumnalis,* because of its beautiful lip and its habit of flowering in the autumn (Fig. 13–1).

For many years these were the only *Cattleya labiata* in Europe, for no one could rediscover its native habitat. It seems odd that this was so, for many other cattleyas were discovered in the following decades, *Cattleya mossiae* in 1838, *Cattleya gigas* in 1848 or '49, *Cattleya trianaei* in 1856, and so on. No great numbers were imported and many plants did not survive the long voyage. The cattleyas were highly prized by horticulturists and brought high prices from wealthy collectors, but their future in the commercial market was not realized until 1891. In that year tremendous numbers of *Cattleya labiata* were found, and their purchase by two different companies, one English and one Belgian, caused quite a stir in orchid circles. There ensued a heated argument as to whether these were indeed the true *Cattleya labiata autumnalis,* each company hoping that it alone held the prize. Finally it was established that all of them were the real *labiata.* Possession of so many of the same species caused the price to drop from about $20 to about $1 per plant.

That was the beginning of the great demand for cattleyas for the commercial market. Improved steamship travel sent a stream of collectors to South America. They sent back hundreds of thousands of cattleya plants to importers in their various countries. These were sold at auction to commercial growers, horticulturists, and amateur growers.

As the kinds of cattleya were discovered one after another, in great profusion, and were classified by the botanists of the time, many were found to be so similar to *C. labiata* as to be considered varieties of that species rather than as separate spe-

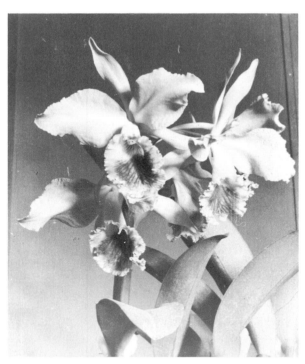

Figure 13–1 Cattleya labiata, *the species upon which the genus was founded, has played many important roles in orchid culture.*

twenty to a stem. The lip is small, often pointed, and may be kidney shaped or fiddle shaped, having a break between the side and midlobes referred to as a "spade" lip. They exhibit a fantastic array of colors and markings—yellow, green, yellow-green, brownish green, brown, orange, red-orange, white, bluish white, and tones of pink and pink-magenta that are often very brilliant. Many are spotted with brown or purple. The lip is often in complete contrast to the rest of the flower; for instance, *C. bicolor* is brownish green with a bright pink lip. With the interest now shown toward smaller flowers, these little species offer their individual charms both to the collector and to the hybridist. In crossing them with the larger labiata types, growers combine the characteristics of many smaller flowers to the stem, distinctive coloring, unusual shapes, heavy substance, and fuller, rounder form of the labiata type.

Except for a few which retain their popularity, the species of the labiata group are found less often now in amateur collections than in former years, when they once formed the bulk of cattleyas available to amateur and commercial growers. The more luxurious hybrids, with their wider range of colors, have almost entirely supplanted them. However, good specimens of species have a real value. The very best of them are almost unobtainable because they are retained by the hybridists and by collectors who prize them, and who often return to them in breeding programs. The value of the species to the amateur lies in their dependability for flowering times, and in the interest they have as the types that have gone into the making of the hybrids. Even though one may love his hybrids, he will know them better if he is familiar with some of their progenitors. If you have a good plant of any of the species, keep it.

The species of the bifoliate group, on the other hand, are becoming rapidly better known, and amateurs are eagerly adding them to their collections. This is a reflection of the widespread interest in the odd and unusual kinds of orchids. It also shows that the present-day amateur has come of age—he does not feel that he must have just the huge and the showy, although they have great attraction, but that he places value on the particular qualities each kind, large or small, has to offer. As a matter of fact, a single plant with many bright little flowers creates just as much of a show as one that gives larger flowers, and a tiny, dwarf plant holds it own by sheer contrast.

cies. These varieties of *C. labiata* are the ones with which the public early became entranced because of their large, showy flowers, and they have occupied the center of attention ever since. For convenience and brevity, it has become customary to treat them as separate species, but *C. mossiae* was named *C. labiata* var. *mossiae*, *C. trianaei* was named *C. labiata* var. *trianaei*, and so on for the rest of this group, *dowiana, eldorado, gaskelliana, lawrenceana, lueddemanniana, mendelii, percivaliana, rex, schroederae, warneri, warscewiczii* (called *gigas* more commonly). These and two other species, *luteola* and *maxima*, which are similar, are together referred to as the "labiata" group. They all bear one single leaf per pseudobulb, and for this reason they are sometimes also called the "unifoliate" group.

The other group of cattleyas is called the "bifoliate" group because its stems bear two, sometimes three, leaves. They are distinctive and delightful, quite different from the labiata type, and are rapidly coming into their own both from the point of view of popularity and for use in hybridization. Their flowers are usually smaller, with more-slender parts, but many are very waxy and some produce their flowers in clusters of from five to

I should like to translate for you a bit from a

1907 book, *Les Cattleya* by Léon Duval, a French orchid grower. "It is no more just to establish comparisons or classes of beauty among certain cattleya than it would be to compare certain works of art; let us leave to beautiful plants their own special qualities, which command our admiration for these same qualities, and not establish a royalty among the cattleya. . . ."

CATTLEYA—THE SPECIES

The cattleyas are all epiphytic, that is, growing naturally on trees and rocks. Their stems vary in height from two inches to three feet; in some they are club shaped and in others canelike. They have from one to three thick, hard leaves, borne at the top of the stem, and the stem is clothed with thin sheathing leaves that dry after the first season. The flower parts are free and spreading, the sepals similar, the petals broader than the sepals. The lip usually has three parts—two side lobes that fold up around the column and a middle lobe that is spreading. In some the side lobes are quite distinct from the middle lobe and are often more fleshy, especially among members of the bifoliate group. In others the side lobes are continuous with the middle lobe, as in the labiata group. The column is plain, not decorated with wings, and bears four pollinia, two in each of the two sacs in the anther. Most of the species are delightfully fragrant.

The Labiata Group

Cattleya dowiana. This variety of *labiata* is a beautiful nankeen yellow with a large purple lip veined with gold. It has contributed its yellow color to many hybrids. The flowers are between six and seven inches across; from two to six occur on a stem. It was discovered in Costa Rica in 1848 by a Polish gardener, Joseph Warscewicz. However, the specimens that he sent to Europe arrived in poor condition, and it was not until 1864 that good specimens were obtained by Mr. Arce and purchased by Messrs. Veitch and Sons, English horticulturists, who flowered it for the first time. The species was named for Captain Dow, whose ship carried many an orchid hunter and many a cargo of orchid plants. It is the most celebrated of Costa Rican orchids but is quite rare now, having been nearly cleared out by collectors.

C. dowiana var. *aurea.* This form occurs in Colombia, entirely separated from the *C. dowiana* of Costa Rica. The flowers are a deeper yellow and the lip is more copiously marked with gold. It is a large plant, similar in every way to *dowiana.* Its period of vegetative growth is from May to September, and flowering follows immediately in September and October. It rests during the winter. It is used a great deal in hybridization. Both flower in late summer and fall.

C. eldorado. Pale rosy-lilac with slender petals. The lip of this flower is the same color but marked with a central orange blotch surrounded by white and purple. It is a variety of *labiata,* not well known, discovered in Brazil in 1866. It flowers in late summer and fall.

C. gaskelliana. These large, fragrant, handsome flowers are six to seven inches across. The sepals and petals are usually purple-violet, suffused with white, occasionally marked with a median band of white. The lip is generous in proportions, and the tube is the same color as the petals. The front lobe of the lip is deep violet with a pale border, the throat streaked with yellow and marked on each side by a spot of yellowish white. French growers used to call this species *"Cattleya chou"* (Cattleya cabbage) because it is so easy to grow. It is a variety of *labiata* and is still quite popularly grown by amateurs. Vegetative growth starts in about April and flowering follows immediately, from July to September, after which is rests during the winter. The species occurs in Venezuela and Brazil, where it grows on rocks at elevations from five hundred to three thousand feet. It was introduced into England from Venezuela in 1884 or '85 and was named for a Mr. Gaskell of Woolton. There is a white variety, *alba,* and one that has white petals and sepals with the front lobe of the lip crimson.

C. gigas. This species should be correctly called *warscewiczii,* but the name *gigas* is commonly used and will be found in lists and catalogues. It was discovered in 1848 or '49 in Colombia by the same man who found *dowiana.* This is the largest-flowered of all the cattleyas: the blooms are seven to nine inches in diameter and most showy. The petals and sepals are rosy-lilac, and the huge, rich red-violet lip is marked with two brilliant yellow eyes. The edge of the lip is ruffled and has a pale border. *C. gigas* is demanding in its cultural needs. New growth starts in January or February, occasionally a bit later. Flower buds push up before the growth is mature, to open in June, July, or early

August. New roots form right after flowering, and this is the time to repot. These roots have to carry the plant on through fall and winter and the next spring's flowering. A curious habit is to make a second growth in the summer which does not flower. Some growers try to prevent this by withholding water after flowering, but are not always successful and may put the plant off cycle. In my opinion, it is a mistake to refuse water during the period of root growth, food making and storing, and maturation. If a second growth starts, better let it mature because the next flowering growth must come from it. Then give a decided rest, watering only sparsely from October until new growth starts. The swelling of the eyes will be the plant's own signal of renewed activity and the need for regular watering. It likes a bright airy place, except that when the flowers are open a bit of shade helps keep them fresh longer. The white variety, 'Firmin Lambeau', is very valuable (Fig. 13–2).

C. iricolor. This rare species was named by Reichenbach f. in 1874. It was drawn by John Day for his scrapbook in 1884, and then not seen again until rediscovered in Ecuador by Padre Andreetti in 1962. It is creamy yellow with very slender sepals and petals, the latter curving down at the middle. The lip is paler, most interestingly marked. Its rounded outer lobe has a saddle of magenta stripes that converge toward the center where they are replaced by a saddle of bright yellow. Flowers in the spring.

C. jenmanii. This rather rare species has been recently brought out of oblivion. It was discovered apparently about the turn of the century, and was named in 1906. It looks like a rosier *C. labiata* in many ways. Its petals narrow a bit more toward the tip. The lip has rather a long tube that flares into a ruffled outer lobe. The latter has a broad triangular patch of deep rose on its outer portion, with paler color on the part that curves into the tube. Yellow-orange veins mark the crest and throat. Five-and-one-half-inch flowers, four at a time, are held on a rather short spike. Its natural habitat is Venezuela and Guyana, and it is possibly winter or spring flowering.

C. labiata. These beautifully proportioned flowers, of wonderful texture, are a rich, vibrant rose, almost luminous in quality. The dainty lip is modest in size, with the throat more open than tubelike. The front lobe of the lip is ruffled, deep red-violet with darker lines which run through two orange spots into the yellow throat. The flowers keep a long time. The flowering time of *labiata*

and its hybrids can be controlled by manipulation of day length and temperature. See Chapter 6. *C. labiata* starts its growth in March or April, and flowers without pause in the fall, from October through November. The flower buds are produced in a double sheath, one sheath within the other. The period of rest is from the end of flowering to the start of new growth in late winter. Among the many color variations are a white form, var. *alba,* and one which has white petals and sepals with a crimson lip, var. *cooksoniae.* This native of Brazil was discovered in 1818.

C. lawrenceana. A small-flowered species, not well known, has reddish brown pseudobulbs. The flowers are four to five inches across with five to eight in a cluster. The petals are rather slender, and the lip small and tubelike. The color varies from pale rosy purple to white, and the front lobe of the lip is purple with a maroon blotch. The species occurs in Venezuela and British Guiana, where it was discovered about 1882. It grows actively during the summer and remains through the winter with the sheaths formed, to flower in the spring.

C. lueddemanniana, also called *speciosissima.* This species closely resembles *labiata.* The flowers are rose-purple, suffused with white, the front lobe of the lip is amethyst-purple, and lines of this color extend into the throat between two yellow blotches. It is one of the few whose handling is rather tricky. The clue to its culture is probably that it grows natively under such a variety of conditions that the plants show more individual differences than are found in most species. It grows actively from spring to fall, and can flower at any time from April to September. Its period of lessened activity is November to February. The species occurs in Venezuela, where it was discovered in 1850. It was named by Professor Reichenbach for Mr. Lueddeman, for many years his chief gardener and a well-known horticulturist. There is a white form, var. *alba.*

C. luteola. These charming little yellow flowers are only two inches across with petals about the same width as the sepals, and a small tubular lip that is yellow or whitish, often streaked with purple, or with rose in the throat. The pseudobulbs are two to three inches tall and leaves three to four inches long. The species occurs in Brazil, where it was discovered in 1853. It flowers in early winter. It is the parent of many miniature hybrids.

C. maxima. The flowers, though large and nicely colored, have slender parts and lack compactness. Sepals and petals are lilac or pale rose, the front

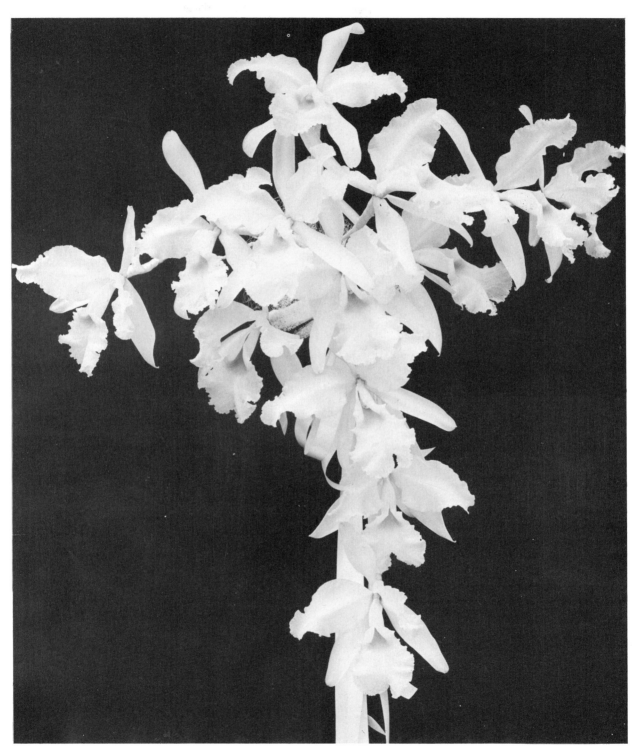

Figure 13–2 *A wedding bouquet made with flowers of*
Cattleya gigas 'Firmin Lambeau', *a rare white variety of*
this species. (Courtesy of B.O. Bracey and Co.)

lobe of the lip is ruffled, pale rose or a deeper shade, with a central stripe of yellow from which radiate darker lines, and a pale border. The plant is not grown much now, though it was once very popular. It occurs in Ecuador, Peru, and Colombia and flowers in the fall.

C. mendelii. One of the most distinct of the labiata group, this species has large, delicately colored flowers, seven to eight inches across. The sepals and petals are whitish or pale rose, and the lip is generous in size with the outer lobe very much ruffled and marked with a clean-cut patch of purple. The throat is yellow, more or less streaked with crimson. It is easy to grow, and much loved by amateurs. Its native habitat is Colombia, where it was discovered in 1870, and named for Samuel Mendel, an English orchid lover. In habit it is similar to *mossiae* (below). The species grows from June through September, and waits through the winter after the sheaths are formed to bloom in April and May.

Cattleya mossiae. Once called the Easter orchid, this beautiful species rivals *gigas* in richness of coloring. Its spring flowering season gave it great value for Easter and Mother's Day. It is rosy-lilac in color, with wide, beautifully ruffled petals. The lip is as wide as or wider than the petals, the broad front lobe frilled, mottled with violet-purple, with a pale border. The throat is yellow, striped with purple. It was discovered in 1836 in Venezuela, where it grows in large quantities, and flowered for the first time in the collection of a Mr. Moss, after whose wife it was named. It was collected so ruthlessly that it was threatened with extinction, and the Venezuelan government had to place a temporary embargo on its export to give it a chance to reproduce. There is wide variation in this species, including some that are thin and poorly shaped, but a good specimen is very pretty. There are many magnificent named varieties, of which the best known are var. *wageneri,* white with a yellow spot on the lip, and var. *reineckiana,* white with purple lip. The species grows during the summer and early fall, and waits through the winter with its sheaths formed to flower in April and May. Some individuals flower as late as August.

C. percivaliana. This is one of the smaller flowered of the labiata group, but a lovely orchid. The richly colored flowers are four to five inches across, varying from light to deep rose, and are nicely proportioned. The dainty, rather short lip has a pale, exquisitely frilled border surrounding a deep maroon center. The throat is orange, variegated with deep violet. It flowers at Christmas time. The species, which occurs in Venezuela, was introduced in 1882 to England by Sander. It is named after Mr. R. Percival, an English orchid grower. There is great variation in the species from good to poor quality. Growth may start in January, without any rest after flowering, or it may wait to begin new growth in April or May. Sheaths are formed by the end of the summer, but the flower buds wait until October to begin development and mature in December.

C. rex. These large, cream-white to pale yellow flowers are attractive but seldom grown. The lip is of good size, the throat yellow, veined with purple, the front lobe crimson, lightly veined, with a white, ruffled border. This rare species occurs in the Peruvian Andes. Growth starts in April, and the plants flower in the summer, after which they rest during the winter.

C. schroederae (also spelled *schröderae*). Lovely fragrant flowers are entirely pale rose, faintly suffused with white, except that the lip has yellow or deep rose in the throat. It was originally designated a variety of *trianaei,* and therefore belongs in the labiata group. However, it is much more ruffled than *trianaei* and has a later blooming season, rivaling *mossiae.* It is another of the handsome Colombian orchids, discovered in 1885 or '86, and named for Baroness Schroeder, wife of a famous orchid grower. The plant grows from May through September, and then, like *mossiae,* waits through the winter with the sheaths formed. The flower buds start to develop about the first of January, and open from March to May. The flowers mature more slowly than those of some other species and should not be cut until they have been open four or five days. There are many named varieties—a white form and several near-white ones.

C. trianaei. The flowers of this species are a little more plain, the petals and lip a little less ruffled than others of the labiata group, but they are still lovely, and a handsome specimen ranks with the best of the cattleyas. The sepals and petals are pale pinkish lavender. The lip is a little narrower than the petals, but sometimes equals their width. The front lobe is usually purple, but is often a brilliant crimson hardly rivaled among the cattleyas. The pale border of the lip varies in width, being fairly wide in some and hardly discernible in others. The throat is yellow, faintly streaked with deeper yellow. The average size of the flower is about six to seven inches. It is a species in which there is a great variation in coloring. *C. trianaei* is a native of Colombia, where it was discovered in 1856 by the celebrated traveler, J. Linden. The species was named for José Triana, a well-known botanist of Bogotá, who died in Paris. The blooming season extends from late December through March, with the largest number flowering in January. New growth starts a short time after flowering, in about March or April, and continues until August, at which time the sheaths are completely formed. The flower buds wait until October to begin developing. Among the varieties is a white form (Fig. 13–3).

C. *warneri.* A lovely member of the labiata group, this species is similar to *labiata,* but with larger flowers. The sepals and petals are rose-lilac, the front lobe of the lip is heavily ruffled and bright purple. The throat is yellow-orange, streaked with white or pale violet. Growth starts in February and the flowers develop as soon as the sheaths are formed, opening during May and June. Its period of lessened activity is during the winter. The species occurs in South Brazil where it was discovered

in 1859. There is a lovely white form, var. *alba,* that has a yellow throat.

The Bifoliate Group

Cattleya aclandiae. Greenish-yellow flowers are barred and spotted with chocolate-brown, with a bright rose-purple lip. The short fleshy side lobes curve up beside the column, and the spreading middle lobe is fleshy in the center and kidney shaped. The extremely broad rosy column is a decorative attribute of the flower. The plants are dwarf, the little two-inch stems spaced rather widely on the creeping rhizome. Each stem bears a pair of small rounded leaves. The four-inch flower is startlingly large for the size of the plant. The species, which was discovered in Brazil in 1839, blooms variably almost any time of the year. It was the parent, with C. *loddigesii,* of C. Brabantiae, the first cattleya hybrid to win an award. It was given the silver Banksian medal by the Royal Horticultural Society of England in 1863.

Figure 13–3 Cattleya trianaei.

C. amethystoglossa. Daintily colored, attractive flowers, three-and-one-half to five inches across, grow five to eight in a cluster. Sepals and petals are white suffused with rose-purple, and spotted with amethyst. The lip has small, white, erect side lobes, and a broad, rounded middle lobe that is violet-purple marked with radiating ridges of papillae. The plants are very tall, with pseudobulbs reaching three feet, and bearing two leaves, six to twelve inches long. The plant, discovered in Brazil in 1862, flowers in midsummer, with buds appearing before the leaves mature.

C. aurantiaca. A small, dainty plant with rather drooping racemes of little red-orange flowers, about one-half inch diameter. The flowers of some plants hold themselves partially closed and some have the peculiar habit of being self-pollinating. Popular in itself for its brilliant color, it is proving useful in making red hybrids, crossed with *Sophrolaeliocattleya* and *Laeliocattleya*. It is native to Guatemala and surrounding countries and it blooms in late winter and early spring.

C. bicolor. This remarkable flower is olive-green tinged with copperish brown, with a bright crimson tonguelike lip that has no side lobes and leaves the column completely exposed. The pseudobulbs are tall and jointed, one to three feet high, bearing two leaves, four to six inches long. This species has been used in hybridization with members of the labiata group. It was discovered in Brazil in 1837. It usually blooms in the fall, sometimes in the spring as well, giving four to six very waxy flowers to a stem.

C. bowringiana. A strong growing plant that sometimes produces as many as twenty flowers on a stem and is often used in hybridization with members of the labiata group. The canelike stem has a fat, bulbous swelling at its base. The flowers are small, less than three inches across, the sepals and petals rose-purple. The lip is similar to that of the labiata type, deep purple with white in the throat. It grows on rocks and rubble near streams in Belize, and needs a little more water than most cattleyas. The species grows during the spring and summer, flowers in October and November, and has a short midwinter rest. It was discovered in 1884.

C. citrina. See *Encyclia citrina.*

C. deckeri. See Natural Hybrids.

C. dolosa. This charming dwarf plant resembles *walkeriana,* of which it was once thought to be a variety. It is probably a natural hybrid between that species and *loddigesii.* The four-inch flowers are waxy, rose-magenta, with the front lobe of the lip amethyst-purple marked with yellow. The little side lobes of the lip are erect. The flowers are produced from the top in the pseudobulb. It is rather rare, occurs in Brazil, and blooms in June.

C. dormaniana. This lovely species was discovered in 1879 and named after Charles Dorman, who flowered it for the first time in 1880. One or two small flowers are formed from a sheath matured the previous season. They are about four inches across, bronzy-brown, with slender, pointed sepals and petals. The purple lip has long side lobes that completely hide the column; the inner edges meet and turn outward. The midlobe is dark purple, the side lobes lighter in color and strikingly veined with the darker shade. Occurs in Brazil and flowers in the fall.

C. elongata. A large, tough species that grows in Bahia, Brazil, on sparsely vegetated volcanic rock, where it endures almost desert conditions and full sun. Its roots grow into rock crevices where they find moisture and protection. Its canes are sturdy, one foot tall, and it bears a cluster of three-and-one-half-inch flowers at the top of a two-foot stem. The flowers are waxy, fragrant, and of a rich red color with a lighter purple lip. Sepals and petals are narrow, the latter charmingly waved. The lip has long side lobes that enfold the purple column and a generously spreading midlobe decorated with a triangle of yellow. It flowers in September.

C. forbesii. These pale yellow-green or tan-green flowers are three to four inches across, several to a stem. The somewhat tubular lip is colored most subtly; its side lobes are pale pink on the outside, striped with red on the inside, and the ruffled midlobe is bordered with white and has a deep yellow throat marked with wavy red lines on either side of a central yellow crest. The plant is dainty, with stems about the thickness of a pencil and eight to ten inches tall. It was discovered in South Brazil in 1823. It flowers in midsummer and rests during the winter (Fig. 13–4).

C. granulosa. This species and its variety *schofeldiana* (also treated now as a separate species) are very much alike. Some say that the latter is the kind seen most often. Both are yellow-green or brown-green, spotted with purple or crimson, sometimes quite densely, sometimes less so. The sepals and petals are about the same width, the latter wavy on the edges. The lip has a narrow isthmus and flares into a fan shape at the outer end and has white side lobes that are pink inside. The

Figure 13–4 Cattleya forbesii.

lip of *schofeldiana* is woody and very rough. A distinguishing feature is the shape of the lateral sepals, which in *schofeldiana* curve inward (are sickle shaped or falcate) while those of *granulosa* hang straight down. Both occur in Brazil and apparently flower from spring through fall (Fig. 13–5).

C. *guatemalensis*. See Natural Hybrids.

C. *guttata*. These beautiful yellow-green flowers are spotted with deep purple. The lip has long pink or white side lobes that enfold and almost completely conceal the column and a short, spreading middle lobe that is amethyst-purple marked with papillae. The pseudobulbs reach thirty inches in height, and bear two leaves, five to nine inches long. The flowers are three to four inches across, five to ten in a cluster. Discovered in southern Brazil in 1827, its flowering season is from November to January. The plant is frequently used in hybridization.

C. *harrisoniana* is very much like C. *loddigesii*. It is a rich dark rose, with slightly wavy petals, not much wider than the sepals. The edge of the lip is extremely ruffled, including the side lobes which turn out beside the tip of the column. From Brazil, it blossoms in summer and early fall (Fig. 13–6).

C. *intermedia*. Charming, delicately colored flowers make this a most desirable species. The four- to five-inch flowers vary from pale rose to milky white and are sometimes dotted with amethyst. The lip has smooth side lobes that enfold the column in a long tube, and the spreading middle lobe is ruffled and of a rich amethyst color. The slender pseudobulbs are about eighteen inches tall and bear two or three leaves. The flowers occur in a cluster of four to five. This is another of the spe-

Figure 13–5 Cattleya granulosa *var.* schofeldiana. (Courtesy of Jones and Scully, Inc.)

Figure 13–6 Cattleya harrisoniana, *typical of the bifoliate group, with its slender stems bearing two or three leaves.* (Courtesy of Rod McLellan Co.)

cies now being used in hybridization. It occurs in southern Brazil where it was discovered in 1824. The flowers appear through the summer. There is a white form (Fig. 13–7).

C. intermedia var. *aquinii.* This very rare form has petals that are broad, somewhat ruffled, and carry the coloring of the lip, having the tips deeply marked with rich amethyst. This characteristic is contributed to some of the hybrids made with *C. intermedia* var. *aquinii* as one parent, called "splash-petal," hybrids.

C. leopoldii. A Brazilian species much like *guttata,* and possibly only a variety of it, differing in the shorter, more squared side lobes of the lip which expose the end of the column, and in its flowering season, summer. The variety with pure white lip and green sepals and petals, long known as *guttata* 'alba', should be called *leopoldii* 'alba'.

C. loddigesii is paler in color than *C. harrisoniana* with petals a bit broader and lip not quite as finely ruffled. The edges of the side lobes, which turn outward, are quite plain, and the disc of the lip has several thick, heavy keels. It is from Brazil and flowers in summer and early fall, often also at other times of the year.

C. nobilior. This species produces its flowering growth from the base of the pseudobulb, as does *walkeriana,* which it resembles, and of which it is probably a variety. The purple-lilac flowers are very fragrant, three to four-and-one-half inches across, but only one or two grow on a stem. The lip is fleshy, the side lobes entirely enfolding the column; the middle lobe is broad and yellow. It occurs in Brazil and blooms in spring.

C. pachecoi. See Natural Hybrids.

C. schillerana. These rather large, striking flowers are four to five inches across, olive-green tinted with brown and spotted with black-purple. The side lobes of the lip are white externally, marked with purple inside, while the middle lobe is kidney shaped, crimson, with a white margin and streaks of white. It was discovered in Brazil in 1857, and flowers from June to September. A small plant, it somewhat resembles *aclandiae,* and is suspected of being a natural hybrid between that and *guttata.* It is rather rare.

C. skinneri. Called the "Flower of San Sebastian" in Costa Rica, where it is the national flower, this plant is used by the natives to decorate their altars and the roofs of their houses. It is also called "Guaria Morada" (purple native orchid). The flowers are three-and-one-half inches across, entirely rose-purple except for white in the throat. Five to ten grow on a stem. They have a sparkling, almost crystalline texture which gives them a radiant quality. They are not of heavy substance, but keep a long time. The lip is similar in character to the labiata type but somewhat more tubular. This is a popular species and widely grown. It occurs from Mexico to Guatemala, where it was discovered in 1836. The flowers appear in late winter or spring from a dry sheath. There is a pure white form. A variety called *patini* occurs in Venezuela and Colombia.

C. velutina. The tawny yellow flowers, spotted with maroon-purple, make this a striking species. The small side lobes of the lip are white, streaked with purple inside, and the middle lobe is white marked with a yellow spot and radiating purple lines at its base. It blooms in late summer and is fragrant. The plant is native to Brazil.

C. violacea. These very lovely, fragrant, bright rose-purple flowers of heavy substance are four to five inches across. The lip is fleshy, deep purple-violet, with triangular side lobes that enclose the column, and a rounded, ruffled front lobe marked with a patch of yellow streaked with purple. The plant occurs at rather low altitudes in the northern part of South America, where the temperature is quite hot. It can be adapted to the usual cattleya temperatures but needs a warm place in the green-

Figure 13–7 Cattleya intermedia. (COURTESY OF JONES AND SCULLY, INC.)

house and rather more water. The flowers appear through the summer. It was once known as *C. superba.*

C. walkeriana. A dwarf species whose stocky little pseudobulbs bear single leaves but whose flower characteristics put it in the bifoliate group. The flowers are among the most beautiful of all, with their perky shape, velvety texture, and sweet fragrance. They are three to five inches in diameter, rich rose-lilac, and hold themselves very flat. The side lobes of the lip flare open to form a collar for the enormous rose-colored column. The midlobe of the lip is triangular and spreads flat. The flowers may be produced from either the top or the base of the pseudobulb, most often, the latter. When the flowering stem comes from the base, it looks at first like a vegetative growth, but it remains slender and gives rise to a stem bearing flowers. From its base comes the next vegetative growth. The old flowering growths remain, looking like little aborted and leafless pseudobulbs, alternating along the rhizome with the regular pseudobulbs. This habit does not seem to carry over into its hybrids. It is a native of western Brazil, where there are definite wet and dry seasons. Discovered in 1839, it was brought to Europe for the first time in 1848. Its flowering season is irregular, extending from fall to spring, and its flowers last for six weeks. It requires much less water during its period of rest.

NATURAL HYBRIDS

The apparent ease with which the species within a genus will cross with each other, and even with the species of related genera, is one of the remarkable features of the orchids. Because this is true, it is to be expected that natural hybrids would occur in areas where related kinds grow together. That they do occur has led to some confusion in identification. Kinds which were at first thought to be species have later been found to be hybrids, and occasionally one that was thought to be a hybrid has been given the status of a species. Some of the natural crosses have been repeated in cultivation, thus proving their origin.

C. hardyana. Found in Colombia, this is a hybrid between *dowiana* var. *aurea* and *gigas.* The flowers are large, bright, rose-purple. The richly colored lip resembles the lip of *dowiana* var. *aurea* but has the two yellow eyes of *gigas.* This natural

hybrid has been repeated in cultivation. The man-made hybrid C. Hardyana is one of the best known of the older hybrids and has been used as a parent in a long line of subsequent hybrids.

C. deckeri, C. guatemalensis, and *C. pachecoi* are members of a hybrid swarm between *C. skinneri* and *C. aurantiaca,* although they have been called separate species at one time or another. They occur in Mexico and Guatemala.

C. victoria-reginae. This plant grows with *labiata* and *leopoldii,* and is probably a hybrid between the two. Its pseudobulbs are tall like those of the latter and bear one or two leaves. The flowers are attractive, intermediate between the two species in size, and have the three-lobed lip of the *leopoldii* parent, although the middle lobe is broadened by the influence of the *labiata* parent. The sepals are purple tinged with yellow, the petals purple; both are veined with red. This Brazilian plant, which was discovered in Pernambuco in 1891, is quite rare.

A few other natural hybrids have been found, and are sometimes described as species. They are rarely seen at present, and some may not be known in collections.

ENCYCLIA

This genus has been separated from the large conglomeration included in *Epidendrum,* as have a few other small genera. Essentially the basis for the separation is a distinctive difference in column structure between *Encyclia* and *Epidendrum,* as well as the fact that in *Epidendrum* the column is united with the lip for most of its length, while it is free or united for only a small distance in *Encyclia.* It happens that most of the species of *Encyclia* have pseudobulbs, while most of those in *Epidendrum* are reed stemmed, but this is not always true so it cannot be considered a means of differentiating between them.

Encyclias grow wild in tropical and subtropical forests from Florida to South America. Many are beautiful and showy, some delightfully fragrant. The first epiphytic orchid to flower in England was *Encyclia cochleata,* then called *Epidendrum cochleatum,* in 1787.

In general the species do well in a cattleya house, but some can be grown cooler. Many do well in hanging baskets or on mounts, placed where they receive the best light.

Encyclia alata. Its fragrance is one of the charms of this species. The two-inch flowers are variable in color, being yellow-green with purple at the base of the petals and sepals, and raised purple lines in the central part of the three-lobed lip. The pseudobulbs are pear shaped, about five inches tall, and bear two leaves that are long and slender and contracted almost to a tube at their base. It likes intermediate to warm conditions, and flowers from spring to fall. It occurs from Mexico to Nicaragua.

E. aromatica. Some may find the heavy fragrance of this species a bit overpowering. It has round, two-inch tall pseudobulbs with one or two leathery, often purplish, leaves. The panicle of flowers may reach three feet in length, and holds many long-lasting, one and one-half-inch flowers that are cream colored except for the three-lobed lip, which is veined with red-brown and sets off a reddish column. It flowers from summer to fall, and occurs from Mexico to Guatemala.

E. boothiana. A delightful, almost miniature species, whose small, flat, round pseudobulbs have earned it the nickname "little dollar" orchid. One to three slender upright leaves are borne from the pseudobulb and usually do not exceed three or four inches, although they can grow taller. The flower stem is erect, about twice the height of the leaves, and bears several bright, saucy, inch-wide flowers, yellow, spotted or barred with red. The strangely shaped little lip gives the impression of a pair of walrus tusks hanging under the column. It flowers in summer and fall, and occurs in south Florida, the Bahamas, Cuba, Mexico, and Belize.

E. boothii: See *Nidema boothii*

E. brassvolae. Flowers in tones of brown and green, with slender, long-pointed parts make this a striking species. The lip consists of a long claw (stalk) by which it is attached, and a pointed outer lobe. The plants are husky, with tall pseudobulbs. It flowers in late summer and fall, and occurs from Mexico south to Panama.

E. citrina. This attractive plant is a conversation piece in or out of bloom. It grows in a pendent manner, and should be put in a hanging basket or on a piece of driftwood. The egg-shaped pseudobulbs bear two or three silvery green leaves that have a "bloom" upon them. The flower buds appear from the growing lead and expand before the growth is mature. The lovely lemon-yellow flowers have a border of white around the frilled lip and are very waxy and spicily fragrant. In order to appreciate the beauty of the upside-down flowers, you must look up at them. Discovered in Mexico in the

17th century by the Jesuit, Hernandez, it was not until 1859 that any large numbers reached Europe. It flowers in late spring and early summer, and prefers a cool spot, which possibly can be furnished in an intermediate house (Fig. 13–8).

E. cordigera (syn. *atropurpurea*). This is one of the loveliest of the genus. The mahogany and green sepals and petals spread wide, the tip of each curving forward gracefully. The spreading lip is white with crimson stripes. Six to ten of these attractive, long-lasting flowers are borne on a long spray rising from the top of the short, oval pseudobulb. It grows from Mexico to Venezuela and flowers in late spring and early summer. A plant on a slab makes a magnificent display with its leads growing upward and a fan of flower spikes. The variety *randianum* (or *randii)* has the sepals and petals outlined in light green, and a white lip centered with a purple-rayed blotch. The variety *roseum* has a bright rose-colored lip that forms a pleasing contrast to the dark sepals and petals (Fig. 13–9).

E. ceratistes. This is a delightful species with apple-green flowers. Its slender sepals and petals are the same length, the latter a bit narrower at the base and slightly broader toward the tip. The side lobes of the lip are a darker green and lie along the column with their tips upturned. The lip is almost round, coming to a sharp point at its end with its

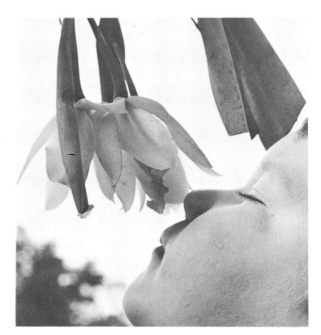

Figure 13–8 *The delightful fragrance of* Encyclia ci-trina *attracts a young orchid admirer.* (PHOTO BY TED DULLY, COURTESY OF H. PHILLIPS JESUP.)

Figure 13–9 Encyclia cordigera, *one of the most striking of the genus.* (COURTESY OF H. A. DUNN AND H. GRIFFIN.)

lateral edges slightly turned down, and is white with raised lines of red. The flowers are held on an airy spray that can be simple or branched. The plant is small, with onion-shaped pseudobulbs that bear three or four leaves. It is apparently widespread natively, from Mexico to Venezuela, and flowers in the summer.

E. chacoensis (syn. *ionophlebium*). This species is rather like *E. cochleata* in general shape, but greenish rather than creamy white, and with a fuzzy, squarish callus on the lip. It occurs from Mexico to Panama, and flowers in the winter and spring.

E. cochleata. The shape of these attractive, upside-down flowers suggests an octopus. The slender, yellow-green sepals and petals stream down from the shell-like, green- and purple-striped lip, which is almost black on the reverse side. The flower stem elongates through a period of five to seven months, producing a succession of flowers, with four or five open at a time. The slender, conical pseudobulbs are five to eight inches tall, bearing a pair of leaves. They may be found from Florida to Colombia. The variety *triandrum,* so called because it has three anthers, is native to Florida. The Costa Rican form is a much smaller plant and its flower stalk is shorter with smaller flowers spaced evenly along its length and with more open at a time. They bloom all year.

E. fragrans. The flowers of this species are spicily scented and pretty, similar in shape and size to *E. cochleata* but creamy white with a red peppermint-striped lip. Pseudobulbs are from four to five inches tall, bearing a short, single leaf. Since the flower stem is short, the cluster of blooms nestles close to the leaf. The plants occur from Guatemala through the West Indies to north Brazil and flower in late summer and early fall.

E. ghiesbreghtiana. Almost a miniature, rarely more than five inches tall, this species produces a flower huge for its size. The slender pseudobulbs hold a pair of narrow leaves that fold somewhat together. From within their bases comes a short flower stem that gives rise to one or two blooms. The sepals and petals are gold-green or yellow-green with dotted lines of brown, and are plain green on the back. The large squarish lip is white, with a few short purple veins at its base. The striking flower is about two and one-half inches long. It is a rare species in nature, coming from a restricted area of Mexico, but was raised from seed by the late John Lager, who distributed it. L. O. Williams in *Orchidaceae of Mexico* states that it is closely related to *E. mariae.* It blooms in summer.

E. hanburii is one of the prettiest of the genus, and its flowers last for several months. The conical pseudobulbs are some three inches tall and bear a pair of leaves eight to twelve inches long, thick and leathery. The inflorescence is upright and arched and carries twenty or more flowers. They are one-and-one-fourth inch across, with brown, oar-shaped sepals and petals that spread wide. The beautiful lip has a ruffled midlobe with sides turned down and wavy side lobes that stand up and forward. The entire lip is rosy lavender or may be white veined with lavender. It occurs in Mexico and flowers in spring.

E. mariae. A very lovely species, it has two-inch pseudobulbs and leaves only four inches long. The flower stalk is about eight inches tall and bears one to three large flowers. The petals and sepals are small, greenish-yellow, and the huge lip is spreading, with a deeply indented outer portion, white with green veins in the throat. It occurs in Mexico, and likes a cool spot in an intermediate house, and flowers in the summer.

E. mooreana. Compare this species with *E. ceratistes* to see how much they resemble one another but at the same time how different they are in aspect. The petals and sepals are more nearly the same in shape, and flare back from their bases. The side lobes of the lip are broader and are colored pink like the lip, rather than being a different color as in *ceratistes.* The midlobe of the lip is quite square, instead of being round, and has a notch where *ceratistes* has a point. The plant itself is larger and tougher, and the bloom spray is much longer, reaching four feet in length. It occurs in Costa Rica and Panama and flowers in late summer (Fig. 13–10).

E. nemorale. This is a very showy, fragrant species, with a wealth of two- to four-inch flowers, soft rose-red in color. The plant has large, fat pseudobulbs with foot-long slender leaves. The flowering stem can reach three feet in height, and produces many blooms that last a long time. It is native to Mexico where it grows at fairly high el-

Figure 13–10 *A:* Encyclia ceratistes. *B:* Encyclia mooreana.

evations, but it takes kindly to cattleya conditions, and it flowers in the summer.

E. oncidioides. The cause of much confusion, and with a long story behind it, this species is apparently rare even in its native Brazil. Robert Dressler had searched long among the various things called *E. oncidioides* without being convinced that any of them could be the plant originally described by Lindley in 1833. Finally he received some specimens from Brazil which gave masses of yellow flowers when they bloomed. Sweetly scented, they matched Lindley's description and also had the long, slender pseudobulbs he described. Another diagnostic feature mentioned by Lindley, but not possessed by those confused with it, were petals much broader than the sepals. Dressler spoke amusingly of the woes of the amateurs who had been trying to identify various species which always keyed out to *E. oncidioides* but which were not really that. Another that falls in this category is *E. gravidum,* or *E. oncidioides* var. *gravidum.* Flowering time is summer.

E. prismatocarpa. One of the most showy of the genus, this species has large, airy clusters of two-inch, boldly-marked flowers. They are waxy, pale yellow-green, spotted with purple-black. The sepals and petals are slender, and the spear-shaped lip is slender and pointed, pale purple with a yellow tip and a white border. It occurs in Central America and flowers in the summer. Some plants are quite tall, other specimens smaller, the conical pseudobulbs being from three to six inches in height and the leaves one foot long.

E. radiata. This species is similar to *E. cochleata* and *E. fragrans* in plant character and flower shape. The flower is more round than *E. fragrans* and heavier in substance, with the lip less pointed and the striping of a deeper shade. It occurs from Mexico to Venezuela and flowers variably (Fig. 13–11).

E. tampense. A native of Florida, this is an attractive, though not showy, orchid. The small greenish flowers are borne on a slender stem. The little lip is tinted with purple. This is the little orchid that for a while was rather widely sold by nonorchid dealers as the "butterfly orchid." It flowers any time of the year.

E. vespa. This distinctive species has chunky, waxy, boldly marked flowers that are held upside down on a stiff, erect spike. The plants can have rounded or elongated pseudobulbs, with conspicuous joints at the top where the second and third leaves are attached. The flower spike holds ten to

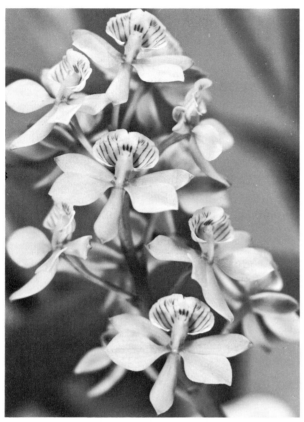

Figure 13–11 Encyclia radiata, *a waxy, creamy flower with candy-striped lip.* (COURTESY OF ROD MCLELLAN CO.)

twenty flowers, which are sweetly fragrant in spite of their somewhat reptilian coloring—greenish tan with red spots. The lip has no side lobes, and the midlobe is very short, with a fat, several-lobed crest and a flaring outer portion that looks like a mustache vertically striped with red. The species is widespread through tropical America: One of its native haunts is Machu Picchu, Peru. It likes to be grown cool, and flowers in the spring. It is also commonly known as *E. crassilabium.*

E. vitellina. The small plant, with pseudobulbs barely two inches tall, bears two slender leaves six to nine inches long. The eighteen-inch flower spike carries a dozen or more star-shaped, incredibly brilliant red-orange, one-and-one-half-inch flowers of velvety texture. Even the pedicels are red-orange and the beautiful winged ovary is striped with the same color. The pollinia bulge from the anther like two tiny red headlights, projecting over the small pointed yellow, red-tipped lip. The blossoms last for weeks on end. A variety *majus* is a heavier plant with larger flowers. Found in Mexico and Guate-

mala, it inhabits high elevations and likes a cool spot in a cattleya house. It flowers at any time, chiefly spring and summer.

EPIDENDRUM

This has been a catchall genus for a long time. Now groups of species are being separated from it because of structural differences. Most are being returned to their original genera. As now conceived, *Epidendrum* still has several hundred species, mostly with canelike growth and with the column attached to the lip for most of its length.

E. anceps. One of Florida's native species, this is also found all the way to Peru. It is not showy, except that the rather tall, vigorous plants are handsome, for its little flowers are only one-half-inch in diameter. They are greenish-tan with a green column, but are very waxy and prettily shaped. They occur in tight clusters at the tip of the canelike pseudobulb, and the same stem produces clusters in succession throughout the year, and year after year. It likes to be mounted on a driftwood log with osmunda fiber, but can also be grown in a pot.

E. boothii. See *Nidema boothii.*

E. ciliare. One of the best known, this fragrant species is loved for its easy-going habit. The plant looks like a cattleya and grows about a foot tall. The slender, graceful flowers are about five inches across and are borne in clusters of three to seven. The sepals and petals are yellow-green, set off by a dainty, three-lobed, white lip, with a needlelike midlobe and fringed side lobes. It grows abundantly in Mexico and flowers in the winter.

E. coriifolium. Of the sheerest pale green wax, the few flowers per stem are extremely beautiful. The stem that bears the flowers is zig-zag, and at each joint there is a huge bract that almost prevents the flower from opening. The lip is broad and spreading, very stiff. The sepals are narrow and the petals almost threadlike, so delicate that they often do not separate completely away from the sepals, and are often not noticed for that reason. The plant has flattened stems with a few spatula-shaped leaves on the upper section, quite rough and leathery. The species occurs from Mexico to Peru, and flowers in the fall and winter. There is also a form with almost-black flowers.

E. difforme (syn. *umbellatum*). A delightful small species, this one has slender stems and alternate pale green leaves. The waxy, fragrant, greenish white one-and-a-half-inch flowers are borne directly at the top of the stem in clusters of three to five. The sepals and petals are slender, while the lip is spreading and wavy at the edge. The plants occur from Mexico to Panama and flower in summer or early fall. There are slight variations in the flowers and the plant size from region to region.

E. endresii. (Syn. *Oerstedella endresii.* The genus *Oerstedella* can be easily recognized by what looks like a warty stem. Actually, it is the leaf bases that are warty.) This is a beautiful, dainty species, discovered long years ago and then "lost" until rediscovered recently by Clarence Horich in Costa Rica. The flowers are white, subtly touched with purple on the edges of the column and the center of the lip. They are about one inch in length, and are borne at the top of the delicate, reedlike stems, which are leafy from top to bottom. The plants are somewhat difficult to keep growing well, but are well worth the effort, as this little species will outshine many larger things around it. It is said to occur in Panama as well as Costa Rica, and blooms in the winter.

E. exasperatum. (Syn. *Oerstedella exasperata*) The charming flowers have brown petals and sepals, in front of which the little white lip hangs straight down. With its divided front lobe and split side lobes, it looks exactly like a child in a white snowsuit, with even the zipper flap outlined in purple, and with the column forming the head and face. The plants may retain a modest size in a greenhouse, but in nature they can grow several feet tall. The branching stems are slender, with alternate leaves their whole length, and the flowers appear in short sprays from their tops. The species flowers in the winter. It occurs in Costa Rica and Panama.

E. ibaguense. This is the preferred name for the species familiarly known as *E. radicans.* The plant is vinelike, having a tall, slender stem with rather widely spaced short leaves and long aerial roots. It should be trained to a support in the greenhouse. The tall and erect flower stem bears a dense cluster, actually a sphere-shaped head, of one-inch, brilliantly colored flowers, ranging from red to orange to yellow. Each flower is a little jewel, having waxy little sepals and petals and a fringed lip. *E. ibaguense* crossed with a number of other reed-type species has given an array of "reed-stem" hybrids. Selection has produced plants that are more compact and shorter than their parents, making them more suitable for small greenhouses. The

flowers run through all the tones on the yellow to red section of the color circle, including peach, pink, red violet, brick red, etc. The best known of the reed-stem hybrids is *Epidendrum* Obrienianum, *E. evectum* × *E. ibaguense,* registered in 1888. The latter is a little known species which is nevertheless useful in hybridization. *E. ibaguense* occurs throughout Central and South America, growing in open weedy soil in dense masses and flowering throughout the year. The reed-stem species are very dominant for plant character and flower size and shape, which may be due to the fact that some are tetraploid (Fig. 13–12).

E. ilense is a remarkable species found only a few years ago in Ecuador. Since few plants were found, it was micropropagated at the Marie Selby Botanical Gardens and fifty plants returned to its native habitat. It is a tall reed-stem type, but has the ability to continue to flower from all parts of old and new stems, new crops of buds coming from bracts behind the tip bud. The flowers come in clusters of from five to ten all year. They are white, with narrow green sepals and petals. The lip is broad and round but folds down as soon as it opens so that its fringed edges come together.

E. latilobium. The flowers of this species are

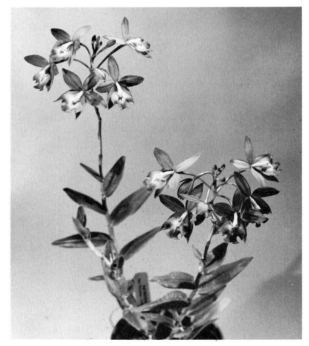

Figure 13–12 Epiphronitis *Veitchii, one of the earliest bigeneric crosses, made in 1890. It is* E. ibaguense (radicans) X Sophronitis grandiflora. (COURTESY OF ROD MCLELLAN CO.)

somewhat reminiscent of those of *coriifolium*, appearing to be made of translucent green wax, but they are larger and are borne in a fasciclelike cluster. The plants are quite different, as well. The side lobes of the lip are extremely broad, shaped like butterfly wings, and have wavy edges. The small midlobe is divided into two divergent parts. The sepals are very narrow, and the petals even narrower. The plant can be from a few inches to a foot tall, and has rounded leaves clasping the stem in funnellike manner. It occurs in Costa Rica and flowers any time from fall to spring.

E. laucheanum. Long chains of tiny flowers, extending from the tips of rather slender, few-leaved stems, make this species just as deserving of the nickname "necklace orchid" as *Dendrochilum*, to which the nickname is usually applied. The chains can be anywhere from a few inches to almost two feet in length, and the latter bear over a hundred little yellowish, fleshy flowers, all open at once. They are delicately fragrant, an additional charm. The stems may lose their leaves seasonally. The plants produce many new growths at a time, which gives many chains of flowers simultaneously. The species occurs through most of Central America and in Colombia and flowers in the winter.

E. lockhartoides. A delightful miniature resembling the genus *Lockhartia* in its braided appearance, this species is as decorative when not in flower as when blooming. Six to eight tiny green flowers are borne on a short stem, each barely exceeding its bract and folding back upon it. The plants occur in Costa Rica and Panama and flower in the fall. They like a bit more shade than others, and do well in an orchid case. They flower in spring.

E. (Nanodes) medusae. See *Neolehmannia medusae.*

E. mirabile. The lovely rosy lilac flowers of this species are more like a small cattleya than an epidendrum in general appearance, but the plant gives no doubt as to its identity. The climbing, sprawling canes branch and rebranch every which way, but since they are not too large they can be accommodated easily on a piece of log padded with osmunda fiber. The flowers are produced at the tip of the cane in clusters of three or so. They are about three inches in diameter and last for two or more weeks. The name *mirabile* probably stems from their beauty, but also perhaps from the fact that such attractive flowers could be produced by such an unlikely plant. The species is confined to a few places in one range of mountains in Costa Rica. It flowers in the fall and prefers a cool spot in a cattleya house. It has a lemony fragrance.

E. nocturnum. Spidery, white flowers grace rather tall canelike pseudobulbs. The flowers with their slender parts resemble those of several other species, among them *E. obesum* and *ciliare*. *E. nocturnum* is one of Florida's well-loved native species and spreads from there through Mexico and Central America, into South America, and through the West Indies. It is adaptable either to intermediate or warm conditions. Its evening fragrance is one of its charms. It is summer flowering.

E. obesum. The name hints that this species is fat, but it is a misnomer. The stem is about one-fourth-inch wide, and somewhat flattened, and the plant grows to fifteen to twenty-four inches tall. What deceives the viewer is that the bases of the leaves encircle the stem in a rather open, funnellike manner, giving the impression of a thick stem. The leaves themselves are almost spatulate, about four to five inches long and two-and-one-half inches wide in the middle. The flowers are of the spidery type, with very slender brown sepals and petals. The white lip is joined to the column, at the end of which its two side lobes flare out, and its needlelike midlobe hangs down. The species is native to Costa Rica and Panama. It blooms spring and fall.

E. paniculatum. Luxuriant panicles of tiny green and white flowers with a touch of pink make this a charming harbinger of spring. The tall canes may not grow higher than two to three feet in a greenhouse, but are said to reach six feet in nature. They are clothed with rather thin, prominently veined leaves, making them quite attractive plants. Each slender flower is about an inch long. The fleshy sepals are green, quite rough on the back, slender and sharply pointed. The petals are much more slender, threadlike in fact, each with a little oarlike tip. The white tip is roundish and bulges on its top surface, with the midlobe split into two divergent horns. Delicate red lines decorate the convex lip crest, which is furrowed in parallel channels. The species is widespread from Mexico to Brazil and Argentina. It blooms in April and May.

E. parkinsonianum. This peculiar and very beautiful species is widespread through Mexico and Central America. It grows in a pendent position, with the stout rhizome climbing upward and the long, flat, channeled leaves hanging down from short pseudobulbs. The two to three pure white six-inch flowers are held on short stems so that they are backed by the green of the foliage, giving the appearance of an arranged bouquet. The slender sepals and petals spread flat. The side lobes of the lip spread wide like a pair of wings; between them the needle point of the midlobe gives a sharp accent. The variety *falcatum* differs in having a less stout rhizome, pendent, thin pseudobulbs, and much more fleshy leaves. Also, the flowers are smaller and have more slender parts, and the petals and sepals are tinged with green and purple.

E. pfavii. A waist-high plant with each leafy cane topped by a cluster of eight or more large, bright rose-magenta flowers, it is a sight indeed. The flowers are bold, two inches or more long, with somewhat the shape of our native "shooting star," that is, with the sepals and petals bent backward along the ovary and the column and lip projected forward. They are fleshy and velvety. The lip is a lighter color with a white center, the side lobes bent down beside the midlobe, and the mid-lobe divided at its tip. It grows at the edge of cloud forests in Costa Rica and in cultivation it should not be allowed to dry out. It is summer-blooming.

E. porpax. See *Neolehmannia porpax.*

E. pseudepidendrum. This species is very similar to *E. pfavii* in general character and size, but is even more striking with its brilliant flowers, which have fluorescent green sepals and petals and a waxy bright orange lip. Its canes grow three or four feet high, and both old and new ones produce clusters of six to eight flowers each year. The flowers are almost three inches long, with their narrow petals and sepals bent backward. The broad, spreading, finely fringed orange lip is decorated with several yellow keels on the crest, and has no side lobes. The column is pink, adding another color note to the flower. The species is native to Costa Rica (and possibly Panama?), but was "lost" after its original discovery in 1871 until it was rediscovered by Costa Rica's well-known botanist Alexander Skutch in 1958. It flowers in the fall and makes a second set of flowers almost immediately.

E. pseudo-schumannianum. (Syn. *Oerstedella pseudo-schumanniana.*) This species is the Panamanian native previously mistaken for *E. schumannianum* (see right). Its flowers are blue-violet on the reverse. The sepals and petals are dusty yellow on the front, marked with brown spots. The longish lip is violet, shading to a paler tone at the tips of the lobes, and is not spotted. The side lobes are narrower than those of *E. schumannianum* and do not spread as sharply sideways. The midlobe is deeply divided. The slender pseudobulbs reach a height of about four feet. It flowers in the spring, with blooms of one-and-one-half inches.

E. pseudo-wallisii. (Syn. *Oerstedella pseudo-wallisii.*) This dainty spring-flowering Costa Rican species is less rare than *E. wallisii* of Panama and Colombia. The reedlike stems have six to eight leaves on their upper part. The leaf bases are speckled with fine red warts. Usually two clusters of four or so two-inch flowers come from the top leaf axils. The waxy, yellow, pointed-oval sepals and petals are spotted with red. The large wavy lip is white with red spots and has long down-pointing side lobes. The midlobe has a long central keel and two short side ones. The less divided lip of *E. wallisii* is decorated with purple lines. Both like intermediate conditions.

E. schlechterianum. See *Nanodes discolor.*

E. schumannianum. (Syn. *Oerstedella schumanniana.*) Long confused with a better-known plant from Panama, this species seems to be restricted to Costa Rica and to be the original one described by Schlechter. The flowers are of a bluish violet, their rounded sepals and petals spotted on the inner surface with red-violet. The lip has distinct, flat side lobes, widely separated from the midlobe, which spreads from a narrow central portion. It is colored like the rest of the flower but has fine dots down the center. The flowers are a bit over an inch in diameter, and occur on a tall stem. It is summer-blooming.

E. sophronitis. See *Kalopternix sophronitis.*

E. stamfordianum. This is a popular species, though it is a little hard to get started when shipped in from the wild. It produces its flower stalk from the base of the tall pseudobulb instead of the apex. The flowers are produced in generous numbers, and are fragrant. The sepals and petals are narrow, yellow spotted with red. The lip, which resembles a bird with its wings spread, is white to yellow. The plants grow from Mexico to Colombia and Venezuela, blooming in winter and spring.

DINEMA

This little species has been removed from *Epidendrum.*

D. polybulbon. This is a charming miniature that spreads quickly into a mat of tiny pseudobulbs about an inch tall, each with a pair of perky, slightly longer leaves. A single flower per pseudobulb is borne on a short stem that arises from a tiny sheath. The half-inch flowers are yellow, tinged with red, and have straight, spreading sepals and petals, with a broad, flaring white lip. The tip of the column is marked with bright purple. It flowers in winter and spring, and occurs natively from Mexico through Guatemala, Honduras, and Costa Rica, to Cuba and Jamaica.

KALOPTERNIX

A most unusual name for a most unusual species, removed from *Epidendrum*.

K. sophronitis. Surely one of the most unusual of all orchids, the bluish green leaves have a bloom upon them, an overlay of silver. They are oval and short, attached by twos to tiny unseen pseudobulbs. A plant with many growths therefore looks like a whorl or rosette of leaves. From within the leaves and nestled close down into them come very strange flowers. The name *sophronitis* does not describe them at all; *stapelioides* would be better, or something reminiscent of starfish. The sharply pointed, fleshy petals and sepals spread out like the arms of a starfish and are brownish green with dotted lines of red. The lip is broad at its base, purple and "juicy" looking, with a point that hangs down from its central edge. As the flowers age they become reddish, and if these are what Lindley saw as he described the species, he may be excused for the name he chose. The column is a very decorative part of the flower, short with broad wings that lie over the basal part of the lip. Each growth gives three or four flowers, open one or two at a time, through late winter and spring. The species is native to Peru and Ecuador and is cool growing (Fig. 13–13).

NANODES

This delightful species appears to have been the original *Nanodes,* although it has long been known as *Epidendrum schlechterianum.*

N. discolor. This little creeping plant is so stiff that it is almost impossible to bend a stem or leaf. The whole plant is waxy with very short leaves that clasp the stem in close-ranked order. The flowers open against the end leaves and are colored so much like the plant that they could go unnoticed. There is some variation in color and size; for instance, one from Costa Rica has light green leaves, the younger ones tinged with pink, and flowers of a pinky tan, and one from Panama, which is larger and heavier, is of an almost purple-green with flowers of green tinged with red. All are finely toothed on the edges of leaves and flower parts, and the latter are also papillose (covered with fine little waxy bumps). The species spreads all through Mexico and Central America, Brazil and Peru, Trinidad and Surinam. It flowers in the spring and also at other times.

NEOLEHMANNIA

Two well-known and much-loved species have been taken out of *Epidendrum* and placed in this genus.

N. medusae. José Strobel, Ecuador's well-known and lamented collector, found this species after it had not been seen in the wild for years. He described it as looking almost animallike among other plants on the branches. Indeed, it does have an animallike quality, perhaps like a marine creature with many swimmerettes. But it is a beautiful plant, one that does not need to bloom to draw attention in a greenhouse. The stems, which can be a foot long, hang downward, and are clothed with fleshy, three-inch, slender-oval, curving leaves that clasp the stem tightly with their bases. The three-inch flowers appear at the tip of the stem, barely extending beyond the last leaf. They are spectacular, with green petals and sepals stippled with red, and a huge, round, heart-shaped ruby red lip that is fantastically fringed and lacerated on its edge. It takes the new growths two years to mature. In the meantime, many young growths are developing, crowded close together. The flowers appear in the spring, two or three at a time, but sometimes singly. It occurs only in Ecuador, and likes a cool spot in the greenhouse, fairly shaded in the summer but somewhat brighter in the winter. It is best mounted on a log or grown in a hanging container. Do not let it dry out.

N. porpax. Tiny stems with five or six alternate succulent leaves grow from a creeping rhizome, branching and spreading to form a mat or to completely surround a mount. The incredibly waxy flowers look like so many beetles, carried singly on their short stems. They are an inch long, with narrow sepals and threadlike petals. The smooth red-brown lip is broad at the outer end, narrowing toward its base, and has a greenish border. It occurs from Mexico south to Peru and flowers from summer to fall.

A

B

C

D

E

F

Figure 13–13 *TOP:* Kalopternix sophronitis. *A: A single flower. B:* A plant with several flowers. *CENTER. C:* Encyclia prismatocarpa. *D:* Epidendrum mirabile. *BOTTOM. E:* Epidendrum Endresii. *F:* Epidendrum latilobium.

NIDEMA

Two species have been removed from *Epidendrum* and returned to their original genus *Nidema*. Their column curves up from the lip and has a tongue-shaped rostellum projecting from it.

N. boothii. This is about six inches tall, with small flattened pseudobulbs and single, slender leaves. The small, straw-colored flowers have slender pointed parts and a tongue-shaped lip that is hinged to the column foot. They are slightly fragrant and bloom fall to spring. The species occurs from Mexico to Suriname and Cuba.

N. ottonis is smaller and less attractive, and occurs from Costa Rica to northern South America and the West Indies.

BARKERIA

This genus of several delightful species was for a while included in *Epidendrum* but has now been moved out again. The plants are slender, with but a few slender, pointed leaves at the top. The flower spikes are also slender, and are tall and erect, with many, sometimes closely spaced, showy flowers. The leaves are deciduous and fall during the winter rest period at which time the plants must be kept quite dry. The species like intermediate temperatures. Those given here are a sampling of the many lovely species.

B. cyclotella (syn. *scandens*). This is a brilliant magenta with a yellow area at the base of the rectangular lip. The narrowly oval sepals spread flat, while the similar petals turn their face forward. Eight or ten one-and-one-half-inch flowers are held on a tall, upright stem. From south central Mexico, it flowers in midwinter.

Barkeria elegans. The sepals and petals are dark rose while the rectangular lip is white or near white with a large shield-shaped spot of crimson on the front half. The huge column is yellow spotted with purple. The flower is shaped much like that of *B. lindleyana.* It is native to Mexico and flowers in the fall.

B. lindleyana. This very lovely species has tall stems of two-inch flowers of a brilliant rose-lavender, almost cerise. The dorsal sepal bends forward, while the lateral ones flare back above the petals. The petals are turned over so that their dorsal surface is uppermost. They are oval,

pointed, and the sepals are keeled. The lip is large, rectangular, a bit wavy on the edges, with a paler central area and two raised crests down the middle. The plants vary a bit in color in their range from Mexico to Costa Rica. They flower in the fall.

B. spectabilis ranges from near white to lavender, and the flowers can be from two to three-and-one-half inches in diameter. The petals are turned forward, the sepals back. The elongated, oval lip is white in the center and has a dark patch on the end. The center of the three keels extends to the tip of the lip. The column is deep rose bordered with white. It occurs from Mexico to Honduras and flowers in summer.

LAELIA

Laelia is the most nearly like *Cattleya* in appearance, differing from it in structure by having eight pollinia, while the latter has four. Their similarity has given rise to some disagreement among botanists as to whether certain of them should be classed with *Cattleya* or *Laelia*. The special contribution of *Laelia* to hybrids is the brilliant coloring of some species, including yellow, coppery bronze, scarlet, and red-orange, as well as deep tones of violet. Their flower parts are slender, and with a few exceptions, the flowers are small. The object in hybridization is to combine the *Laelia* coloring with the better *Cattleya* shape.

The genus consists of about thirty species occurring in Mexico, Central America, and southern Brazil; none of the species is common to all these regions. They are found on rocks and trees, often at quite high altitudes. Their culture is the same as for cattleyas, with care to shift plants that do not thrive to warmer or cooler spots until the right conditions are found. Some may do well suspended from the roof of the greenhouse for maximum light. They need quite thorough drying between waterings, especially when not flowering or making active growth.

There is great variety among the species as to height of plants, shape of pseudobulbs, size, and other characteristics. They are often divided into different groups according to plant characters, and this scheme was followed in previous editions of this book. However, we feel there is little purpose in continuing the practice, so for greater convenience we now have put them in alphabetical order.

Figure 13–14 *TOP:* Epidendrum exasperatum. *A: The whole flower. B: Detail of the column. CENTER:* Epidendrum laucheanum. *C: Part of the chain of flowers. D: A single flower. BOTTOM:* Encyclia cochleata. *E: The column of the variety* triandra, *which has three anthers. F: The type form of the flower.*

The Species

L. albida. These small, fragrant flowers are two inches in diameter, pure white except for a yellow streak down the lip and crimson dots at its base. The lip has small, erect side lobes and a rounded middle lobe. The species occurs in Mexico and flowers through the fall and winter. It is popular in collections.

L. anceps. One of several species with large, showy flowers. The pseudobulbs are long and oval, about four or five inches tall, and are slightly compressed on two sides to form sharp ridges. They bear single leaves. The flower stems are tall and arching, occasionally reaching three feet in length, and each holds a group of three or so rosy-lavender flowers. A plant with many leads or a group of plants makes a beautiful show when in bloom. The flowers are four inches across, with slender, pointed sepals, petals slightly darker and almost twice as wide, and a brilliant three-lobed lip. The side lobes fold over the column, and are purple on the outside, yellow with red stripes within. The front lobe curves downward, and is deep red-purple with a wide yellow ridge down the center that divides into three parts as it passes out onto the crest. The flowers last a long time, two months or more on the plant, but do not keep well when cut. A native of Mexico, it flowers in midwinter. There are several white forms, one of which, *oaxaqueña*, is shown in Fig. C 22.

L. autumnalis. Similar to *L. anceps* in size and general shape, its pseudobulbs are somewhat conical, becoming furrowed with age, and bear two or three leaves. The sepals and petals are bright rose-purple. Side lobes of the lip are erect and partially enclose the column and are white or light rose on the outside. The midlobe has three raised ridges down the middle, the outer two white with purple dots, the inner one yellow. A native of Mexico, this species flowers in the fall. A fine variety goes by the name of *L. gouldiana* and is winter-blooming.

L. cinnabarina. Its charming flowers are bright red-orange, verging on red in some individuals, with slender sepals and petals that are flat and open. The lip has short, pointed side lobes, and a larger, ruffled midlobe. The pseudobulbs taper from a swollen base and are five to twelve inches tall, topped by a single foot-long leaf. The inflorescence is from one to two feet tall, and may hold from five to fifteen flowers. This has become very important in hybridizing. It is one of the rock-dwelling species native to Brazil and blooms in the summer.

L. crispa. A popular, summer-flowering species, its blossoms are large, fragrant, and white, except for yellow and purple in the lip. The petals and lip are attractively ruffled. Five or six flowers are produced per stem. The plants are large and cattleya-like, with pseudobulbs to seven inches tall, and a single leaf up to a foot long. The species is native to Brazil. It was crossed with *C. mossiae* in 1863 to form the first bi-generic hybrid, *Lc* Exoniensis (Fig. 13–15).

L. flava. Bright yellow two to two-and-one-half-inch flowers are borne in groups of four to eight on a stem a foot high. The lip has blunt side lobes and a ruffled midlobe with four elevated ridges down the center. The plant tends to be dainty, with slender pseudobulbs, about eight inches in height, tapering from a swollen base and bearing single, stiff, often purplish leaves. A rock-dwelling type, it occurs in Brazil and flowers in the fall. It plays a role in hybridization.

L. furfuracea is a delicately beautiful species that has four or five three-inch flowers to a twelve-inch stem. They are a soft rosy pink and of satiny texture, shaped somewhat like *L. autumnalis* but with broader parts. From Mexico, it flowers in midwinter.

L. harpophylla. A delightful species which has about ten brilliant scarlet-orange flowers on a short stem. It is quite similar to *L. cinnabarina.* The tubular lip has a ruffled edge. It is valuable in hybridization. It grows as an epiphyte although akin to the rock-living species. A native of Brazil, it flowers in February and March.

L. jongheana. These small plants are quite rare. They have pseudobulbs of two inches and solitary leaves up to six inches, and produce large flowers. The sepals and petals are light rose, the sepals slender and the petals twice their width. The remarkably beautiful rose lip is ruffled, chrome-yellow inside, with seven keels that end in wavy ridges. It is native to damp mountainous areas of Brazil, but where the light is bright.

L. lundii. A true miniature, with slender, almost terete stems and leaves, this species has beautiful little one-inch flowers. The petals and sepals are pale pink, while the much-ruffled, generous lip is marked with branched veins of cerise that converge into solid color in the center. The flowers come on the new growths soon after they make a start and open before the narrow, fleshy, channelled leaves begin to emerge. After flowering, the

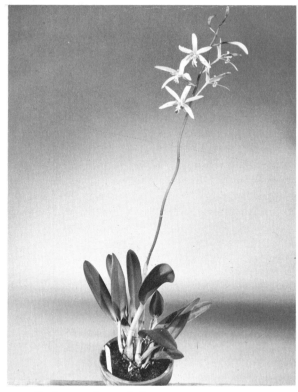

Figure 13–15 LEFT. Laelia crispa, *which has plant characters very much like* Cattleya. RIGHT. Laelia flava, *a small plant with a tall flower stem.* (COURTESY OF ROD MCLELLAN CO.)

Figure 13–16 Laelia lundii, *a miniature.*

growth proceeds to form leaves and pseudobulbs. Flowering time is midwinter. The species is native to Brazil (Fig. 13–16).

L. milleri. This is a new species, named in 1960 by Almiro Blumenschein, and it is causing great excitement for its brilliant red color and promising use in bringing red into crosses with *Cattleya*. It is one of the rock-dwelling species of Brazil. The pseudobulbs are rounded at the base and tapered at the top, three to four inches tall, with the single, narrow-oval, three- to four-inch leaf held at an angle. The flower spike is twelve to twenty inches high and bears four to ten star-shaped flowers, rather like those of *L. cinnabarina.* There seem to be two types of flowers, according to Carl Withner; one a larger flower with narrow sepals and petals and of red-orange color, and the other smaller, but with more rounded parts and blood-red in color. The latter is, of course, the more desirable. Flowering season is spring.

L. perrinii. This is one of the species quite close to *Cattleya* in plant characteristics and size of flower, which reaches five and a half inches. The dorsal sepal is erect but the lateral sepals curve toward each other. The petals are slightly broader than the sepals and their edges are wavy. The narrow, pointed lip holds its outer lobe reflexed. The flower is pale rose-purple, the lip deeper purple and streaked inside with yellow. Flowering time is winter. It is native to Brazil.

L. pumila. This pretty dwarf species has a fragrant flower almost as broad as the plant is tall. The moderately broad sepals, petals, and the tube of the lip are rose colored, while the outer lobe of the lip is bright red-violet with a tiny patch of white at the tip. The plant has little oval pseudobulbs and stiff, shiny, somewhat wrinkled leaves, and is about five inches tall. Flowering time is variable, mostly in the fall. It occurs in Brazil.

L. purpurata. The largest of the genus, it has flowers up to eight inches in diameter. The petals are white, suffused with light rose, and the handsome, bell-shaped lip is a rich velvety purple. The plant occurs in Brazil and flowers in the spring. It and its many varieties are used in hybridization more than any other *Laelia*.

L. rubescens. This is the "Flor de Jesús" of Guatemala, but it occurs all through Central America and Mexico, often dwelling on rocks. There are many color variations, from pink to dark lavender to white. A white form with a dark purple patch in the lip is somewhat reminiscent of a mariposa lily. The plant has round, flattened pseudobulbs that became quite wrinkled with age, and a single, narrow eight-inch leaf. The flowers are held on a tall stem, several in a cluster. They are two to three inches in diameter, with the petals broader than the sepals, and the lip three-lobed, the lateral lobes enfolding the column and the midlobe rounded. Flowers fall and winter.

L. sincorana is a lovely species that has been rediscovered recently. It is a small but striking plant, with perfectly round one- to one-and-one-half-inch pseudobulbs and stiff three- to four-inch leaves. The flowers are flat, and some tend to hold themselves horizontally rather than vertically. They are a rich rose-lavender, with a ruffled, dark purple lip. The blossoms dwarf the plant with their more than three-inch spread. The species is found in Brazil at high elevations, and flowers in winter or spring.

L. speciosa. Another almost dwarf plant with a large flower, it is one of Mexico's loveliest species. The plant has two-inch oval pseudobulbs, tightly covered with white, papery, sheathing leaves, and a single, stiff, five-inch leaf. The single flower is held on a short stem, and can reach six inches in diameter. It is of a pinkish lavender color, and has

good shape, with broad petals and a wide open ruffled lip. The lip is white inside with a long raised yellow crest from which radiate a few purple lines and has a broad lavender border. It blooms in the spring.

L. tenebrosa. Sometimes given as a variety of *L. grandis.* This species has flowers which are a little better shaped than many. They range from coppery-bronze to citron-yellow. The lip is trumpet-shaped, deep purple with a border of white, marked with darker veins. A very striking and unusual flower, it is the parent of many hybrids. The plant occurs in Brazil and flowers in the spring (Fig. 13–17).

L. xanthina. These are yellow flowers, somewhat variable in intensity, ranging from buff to yellow to yellow-green, three to five to a stem. The front lobe of the lip is white streaked with crimson. The flowers are somewhat leathery. This species occurs in Brazil and flowers in winter or spring.

RHYNCHOLAELIA

Two species formerly included in *Brassavola,* and for a while removed to *Laelia,* are now given the generic name *Rhyncholaelia.* Other species of *Brassavola* remain in that genus. The name *Brassavola* will continue in use horticulturally, however.

Figure 13–17 Laelia tenebrosa.

Rhyncholaelia digbyana. Slender pseudobulbs bear a single fleshy leaf. It is rather slow growing and not too floriferous. The greenish white flower, while waxy, has a remarkable satin sheen. The huge lip, often four inches across, is white or cream colored, its edges marvelously fringed. The lip remains wide where it folds up over the column, carrying the fringe around to meet at the top of the tube. The sepals and petals are slender and plain, tinted pale green with pinkish lavender. The flowers have a strong scent of citrus fruits. The species has eight pollinia, occurs in Honduras, and flowers in July and August. The plant needs especially good light and a warmish spot.

R. glauca. Rather short, slender pseudobulbs, somewhat compressed, bear a single leaf. The usually single flowers are fragrant, yellowish-green, with a large, spreading lip that is streaked with red in the throat. The plant occurs in Mexico and Guatemala and has eight pollinia. This species is used in hybridization as well as *digbyana* but with a view toward small, neat flowers.

BRASSAVOLA

Of the twenty or so species in this genus, some are little known, but many are grown widely for their individual charms and are crossed with other members of this subtribe. The plants have terete leaves, or leaves that are slender and so thick as to be almost terete, topping slender stemlike pseudobulbs. The flowers are basically similar, having very slender sepals and petals and a lip whose outer lobe spreads open from a slender tube. It occurs in Central and South America.

Brassavola cordata (syn. *subulifolia*). This plant has pale green sepals and petals, with a pointed heart-shaped lip that is white. The flowers occur three to six at a time on a stem shorter than the leaves. *B. cordata* is found in Jamaica and other islands of the West Indies. It flowers in summer and fall.

B. cucullata. This has very thin, pendent terete leaves from eight to eighteen inches long. The spidery flowers are greenish or straw colored and one to five will arise on an eight-inch stem. They have slender sepals and petals about four inches long, and a slender, arrow-shaped fringed lip. The species occurs from Mexico to northern South America and the West Indies. It flowers from summer into winter.

B. fragrans. As many as twelve of these fragrant flowers can occur on the stem. The sepals are yellowish-white, faintly spotted with purple, the petals are yellowish-white, and the white lip has a green spot at the base.

B. nodosa. These flowers are delightfully fragrant from evening to the middle of the night, earning the nickname "lady of the night." The sepals and petals are white or faintly greenish white. The front lobe of the lip is white, shaped like a long spade. Several flowers are borne on long, graceful stems. It is found from Mexico to Peru and the West Indies and flowers almost any time (Fig. 13–18).

SOPHRONITIS

This is a genus of some six species. They are miniature plants with brilliant flowers that bear eight pollinia. They are all from Brazil and like intermediate to cool temperatures and a damp atmosphere.

S. cernua has two forms, a yellow-orange one near sea level, and a red one from higher elevations. The one-inch pseudobulbs branch from a creeping rhizome and bear single, rounded, very thick leaves. The bright three-quarter inch flowers come in clusters of two to four on a short stem. They are star shaped, with oval, pointed sepals and petals and a scoop-shaped lip. The purple auricles of the column add a decorative touch. Flowers from fall to winter.

S. coccinea has slim, erect pseudobulbs some two inches tall, and narrow oval leaves up to three inches long with a purple midvein. The scarlet flowers are perfectly flat, with oval sepals and broadly rounded petals, the whole flower being about two-and-one-half inches across. The tubular, pointed lip is scarlet, with a yellow interior veined with red. This species has been widely used in hybridization with *Cattleya* and *Laelia* to create red or orange-red flowers, usually of smaller size than straight *Cattleya* hybrids. It flowers fall through winter (Fig. 13–19), and prefers cool temperatures.

S. brevipedunculata has smaller flowers on short peduncles (stems) that are deep, rosy-red. Flowers in the fall, with cool temperatures.

S. wittigiana has almost the smallest plant of the group but the largest flowers, two-and-one-half to three-and-one-half inches across, of rosy pink or

Figure 13–18 Brassavola nodosa 'Orchidglade'. *Nick-named "the lady of the night."*

(COURTESY OF JONES AND SCULLY, INC.)

rosy violet color. It was once called *rosea*. It flowers fall through winter, with cool temperatures.

SOPHRONITELLA

A single species makes up this genus, one often included in *Sophronitis* as *S. violacea*.

Sophronitella violacea. It has pseudobulbs one inch long and leaves of two to three inches. The tiny flowers are only an inch across and are bright rose in color. The species occurs in the Organ Mountains of Brazil and flowers in the winter.

BROUGHTONIA

Two lovely species of this genus occur in Jamaica. One, *Broughtonia sanguinea*, is coming into its own as parent of hybrids with *Cattleya*, made to obtain small red flowers.

B. sanguinea has beautiful, round, red flowers,

almost perfectly flat with an iridescent sheen. They are from one to one-and-one-half inches across, in clusters of four or five, on an arching fifteen-inch stem. The plants flower easily, often giving several inflorescences. The sepals are slender, the petals and larger lip broadly oval, and the lip is ruffled. There is a yellow form 'Carmen Gauntlett'. The plant requires good light and temperatures on the warm side. Flowers any time.

B. negrilensis. This species has flowers more like a cattleya, except that the lip is longer and the petals and sepals shorter than one finds in that genus. The lip has a very large midlobe veined with a darker pink than the flower and has some yellow hairs in the throat. It gives several blossoms at the end of a long stem and flowers in the winter.

SCHOMBURGKIA

There are about a dozen species in this genus, many of which harbor ants as symbionts. In fact, the pseudobulbs of some actually offer ants a

Figure 13–19 A: Sophronitis coccinea, *a delightful miniature. The plant is scarcely four inches, often only two inches tall.* (COURTESY OF ROD MCLELLAN CO.) B: *A fine form of this species.*

home, being hollow with a small opening at the base to allow them to enter.

S. lyonsii. This native of Cuba and Jamaica has two-inch white flowers spotted with purple, their petals and sepals very ruffled. They are borne in a cluster of ten to twenty at the end of a five-foot stem. The plant is smaller than *S. tibicinis* but quite similar. It flowers in late summer.

S. lueddemannii. The flowers of this species have long slender sepals and petals, very much twisted and ruffled. They are brown, against which the small purple lip, decorated with a yellow crest, forms a nice contrast. Many flowers are borne in a dense head atop a fairly tall stem. It occurs from Panama to northern South America, and flowers in the summer.

S. superbiens. Once included in *Laelia,* this is a large plant with pseudobulbs a foot high from which arise flower scapes five to six feet long. At the end of the scape is a huge cluster of ten to twenty six-inch flowers of a rich lilac-purple. The parts are slender, rounded at the tips, very much ruffled at the edges. The lip has yellow side lobes with purple stripes, and the midlobe is yellow with crimson margins and several toothed crests. It is native to Mexico, Guatemala, and Honduras, and has a variable blooming season.

S. thomsoniana. Much smaller than some, it has solid, fluted pseudobulbs six to eight inches tall. The flowers are borne on a three- to four-foot stem, and are a bit over two inches in size, creamy white or light yellow, with a purple lip. The sepals and petals are undulate. It is native to Cuba, Haiti, and the Cayman Islands, and flowers in the spring.

S. tibicinis. Huge, hollow, ant-infested pseudobulbs reach two feet in height and are three inches in diameter. The flowering stem can reach as much as twelve to fifteen feet, and holds a dense panicle of two- to three-inch flowers. Their color varies from purple to brownish-orange, and they have slender, twisted, wavy sepals and petals. The lip has rounded side lobes that enfold the column, and a small midlobe. It occurs from Mexico to Costa Rica and Cuba and flowers in the summer.

S. undulata. Waxy flowers, purple or brown-purple, with very ruffled sepals and petals are held in a dense head of twenty or more. The small, three-lobed lip of dark lavender exposes the nearly white column. The ridged pseudobulb stands on a long, slender stalk. The species is native to Colombia, Trinidad, Venezuela, and Panama, and flowers in early spring (Fig. 13–20).

CAULARTHRON

Two dainty and beautiful species of this genus are fairly well known. The name was changed some time ago from *Diacrium.*

Caularthron bicornutum is serenely lovely and is called the "Virgin orchid." The flowers are sparkling white; the oval, pointed sepals and petals are about the same size. The little bifurcated lip is faintly dotted with purple. The flowers are borne on an erect stem which produces up to twenty buds successively. The plant is rather tall, with horn-shaped pseudobulbs that are nine inches tall and have several leaves at their apex. The plant occurs

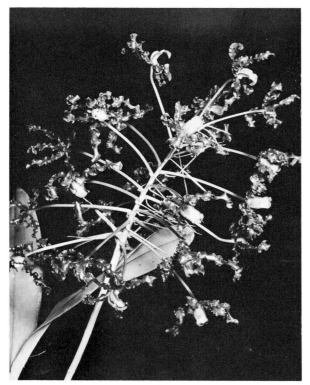

Figure 13–20 Schomburgkia undulata, *the ultimate in ruffles.* (COURTESY OF H.A. DUNN AND H. GRIFFIN.)

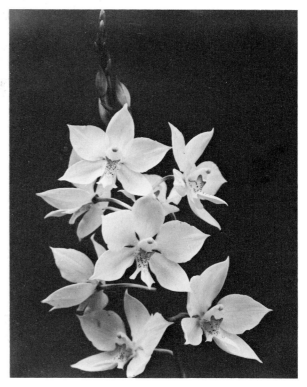

Figure 13–21 Caularthron bicornutum *a beautiful species.* (COURTESY OF H.F. LOOMIS.)

in northern South America, Trinidad, and Tobago, and is often found on sea cliffs, where it is bathed with salt spray. It flowers over a period of two months or more, usually during the summer (Fig. 13–21).

C. bilamellatum has smaller flowers and is not quite as robust a plant. Its flower stem can reach three feet in length. The blossoms are sometimes selfpollinating. It occurs from Guatemala south to Columbia and Venezuela and Trinidad, and blooms in the spring.

CATTLEYOPSIS

This genus is very much like *Broughtonia* except that it has eight pollinia, while *Broughtonia* has four, and its leaves are toothed on the edges.

C. lindenii is a small plant, three inches tall, with five-inch leaves. Its flower stem reaches three feet and bears twelve delicate, rose-colored flowers with a deeper rose lip. The lip is decorated with wavy lines of crimson, and has a yellow throat. It is from the Bahamas and Cuba and flowers from spring to fall.

C. ortgiesiana is smaller than *C. lindenii* but is longer flowering. The flowers open successively over a long period; they are brilliant magenta to pale rose with a lip marked with deeper color. It is found in the Bahamas and Cuba and flowers in late winter and spring.

LAELIOPSIS

The fact that this genus has eight pollinia differentiates it from *Cattleyopsis,* although the species are much like that genus.

L. domingensis is a bright rosy-pink, with a rather long tubular lip expanding at the outer end into a round, ruffled midlobe. From Haiti and the Dominican Republic, it flowers in late spring.

LEPTOTES

The few species in this genus are miniatures, with short, terete leaves.

L. bicolor has leaves about five inches long and two-inch flowers. The sepals and petals are narrow, white, and curve forward. The striking little lip is bright magenta, the column dark purple. It is said that its seed capsule contains vanilin and is used for flavoring in Brazil, where it occurs. It also occurs in Paraguay. It flowers in early spring.

L. unicolor is similar to *bicolor* except that it is solid rose color and is a smaller plant. It is from Brazil and usually flowers in winter.

ISOCHILUS

This genus may be only a distant cousin to the Laeliinae. The plants have tall, willowy stems with small, oval leaves spaced alternately for their entire length. Flowers come from the stem tips on short inflorescences.

I. aurantiacus. This was found only a few years ago. It is a delicate, feathery plant, with broom-straw-thin stems and narrow, thin leaves one to one-and-one-half inches long. The flowers are bright orange, waxy, one-half inch long, four or five to a short stem. They are tulip shaped, the parts almost closed at the tips. It is from Nicaragua and El Salvador and flowers almost any time, chiefly in late spring.

I. linearis is a larger plant with stems reaching twenty-four inches in height. They have heavier leaves about two inches long. The flowers are bright rose-purple, a little smaller than those of *I. aurantiacus.* It spreads widely from Mexico to Cuba and Argentina and flowers throughout the year.

I. major has flowers somewhat concealed by the upper leaves, which have a bit of the tint of the flowers. The blossoms are pale to deep rose-purple and appear throughout the year. It occurs from Mexico to Panama, and Jamaica.

HEXISEA

The plant habit of *Hexisea* is much like that of *Scaphyglottis* in that pseudobulbs form at the top of previous ones, and in *Hexisea* can form long chains. Flowers and roots come from the juncture between pseudobulbs.

H. bidentata has bright orange-red, one-inch, star-shaped flowers, with no side lobes to the lip,

which has a maroon spot in its center. There is a flap extending over each side of the stigma. The two-inch pseudobulbs are cylindrical, with deep grooves. It occurs from Costa Rica to Panama and flowers in the summer.

H. imbricata. This is very much like the preceding species but with broad, flattened pseudobulbs that are only slightly grooved, and heavier, somewhat larger flowers. These have a longer lip, more sharply bent, with a yellow spot in its center. It occurs from Mexico to Peru and flowers spring and fall.

SCAPHYGLOTTIS

Scaphyglottis has the habit of growing one pseudobulb on top of another, and of branching frequently when two are produced instead of one. Most species have pseudobulbs about two inches long, which, when built on top of each other, can make plants eight or ten inches tall. Others are quite tiny. The flowers are very small, somewhat like cattleyas in shape, produced in fascicles on short stems from the base of a pseudobulb, and translucent, ranging in color from greenish to pinkish. There are many species throughout Central and South America.

S. livida has pale, yellow-green flowers often tinged with pink or lavender. They are about one-quarter inch across, with a longish, downturned lip. It is found from Mexico to Honduras and it flowers in the winter.

S. prolifera (syn. *cuneata*). This is a pretty species, with branching pseudobulbs one to five inches tall that root at the nodes. The half-inch flowers are translucent, white, yellowish or greenish, veined with pink or blue, and of crystalline texture. The bold red-purple column is a striking note in the blossom. It is found in Central America, the West Indies, and northern South America and it flowers in winter and spring.

SOME INTERGENERIC CROSSES IN THE LAELIINAE

The bi- and trigeneric crosses between *Cattleya, Laelia, Brassavola,* and *Sophronitis* have already been described. In addition to these, many others have been made. *Diacattleya* and *Dialaelia* are crosses between *Diacrium* and *Cattleya* and *Laelia*, respectively. *Epicattleya, Epidiacrium, Epilaelia,* and *Epiphronitis* reveal their origin as crosses between *Epidendrum* and *Cattleya, Diacrium, Laelia,* and *Sophronitis. Leptolaelia* is the hybrid between *Leptotes* and *Laelia. Liaopsis* is the hybrid between *Laelia* and *Laeliopsis.* The ease with which the various genera may be crossed shows how closely related they are. An amateur might have a good bit of fun trying various combinations. The current interest in the smaller-flowered but distinctive hybrids made from the bifoliate cattleyas has spiked a renewed interest in the possibilities offered by epidendrums as parents, particularly the larger flowered kinds such as *E. cordigera, E. mariae,* etc.

For the names of the myriad other hybrid genera see the booklet on this subject by Garay and Sweet, 1966, and the *Handbook on Orchid Nomenclature and Registration,* 1985 (see the Appendix).

·14·

CYMBIDIUM RELATIVES:

The Cyrtopodiinae Subtribe

Cymbidiums are among the loveliest of orchids and the most useful. The familiar kinds have tall, arching sprays of waxy, delicately colored flowers that make a wonderful display in shades of yellow, green, rose, and white—plain or subtly blended. The plants themselves are attractive for their grassy foliage. The keeping quality of cymbidiums is unusual even among orchids, and the blooms last in perfection a minimum of six weeks and sometimes as long as three months.

The serene beauty of the flowers gives them a charm quite different from that of the showy, ruffled *Cattleya* or the curiously flagrant *Paphiopedilum*. Their oval, pointed sepals and petals are of nearly equal size and shape and are colored similarly. The dorsal sepal often bends slightly forward over the lip. The lip is fleshy, with side lobes that stand erect beside the column, and a front lobe that bends down in tonguelike fashion. It is from the somewhat boat-shaped lip that the genus gets its name *(Cymbid,* Greek for boat). The lip is usually marked with a pattern of spots and lines, bears one or more ridges, and is sometimes downy. The column is nearly erect, often flushed with color, and frequently speckled or lined with the same shade that marks the lip. The species bear from one to thirty blooms on a spike.

Most of the cymbidiums grown today are hybrids (Fig. 14–1). Until now these have been almost entirely the cool-growing types bred from the species with large showy flowers, which are found through high elevations in the Khasia Hills and the Himalayas. These hybrids flower most easily in areas where they have cool summer nights, nights below 60° and preferably around 55°. With ingenious handling, and especially with the help of cooling systems, some growers have been able to flower them where the nights are warmer. It has been found that the delightful miniature cymbidiums from China and Japan, along with a few small-flowered "pendulous" species, will do well in warmer areas. This, along with the current interest in smaller flowers, has opened a new field in breeding. Not only is there much variety and beauty in miniature hybrids, when these are crossed with the large-flowered kinds, the temperature tolerance of the resulting hybrids is broadened.

Cymbidiums are evergreen plants with abundant fleshy roots. The pseudobulbs vary with the species from robust spheres larger than your fist to a

CYMBIDIUMS ARE AS WELL known now as cattleyas used to be, and in fact rival them very closely as corsage orchids. They are also grown outdoors in mild climates and so have become a garden flower as well. The genus *Cymbidium* belongs to a group of definitely less well known genera, gathered into the subtribe Cyrtopodiinae. Many of the other genera are attractive, however, and some are becoming common in amateur collections.

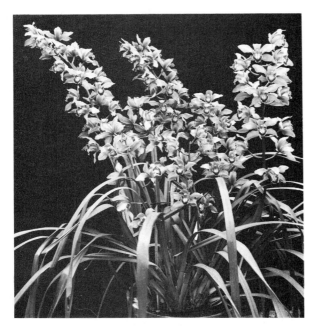

Figure 14–1 Cymbidium Peri 'Beefeater'. *A very floriferous hybrid.* (Courtesy of Armacost and Royston, Inc.)

pointed. The stems are clothed in sheathing leaves that remain tightly clasped during their early development. As the spike lengthens, the tip that encloses the buds is fatter than the rest of the stem. When the spike has reached about half of its ultimate length, the buds emerge from the last sheathing leaf. The section bearing the buds elongates, giving space between the buds, and the buds enlarge until finally they are ready to open. Usually the buds at the base open first and the rest follow in succession. If a stem is cut after several flowers are open and is kept in water in the house, the rest of the buds will open and attain really quite good color and substance, although the last few will probably not be up to the quality of the first. *Cymbidium* is one of the few orchids that will do this. It is therefore unusually useful in cut flower arrangements. However, if you want perfection in each flower, the spikes should be allowed to mature on the plant.

There are two types of growth and flowering habit. In one type, flower spikes are produced from the immature pseudobulb. In the other, the spikes

slender and barely apparent thickening of the stem. They are sheathed with the bases of the leaves. The leaves remain green for several years, and as they fall their dried bases remain attached to the pseudobulb. The plants are compact and cover a circular area. The leaves are slender, of leathery texture, not particularly fleshy, and vary in length from about a foot in the smaller species to sometimes three feet in the larger ones. The species differ somewhat in the number of leaves per pseudobulb, from nine to fifteen being usual. New growths arise from the base of mature pseudobulb.

In the large, standard types, flower spikes appear from June through October, according to the habit of the plant. Spikes that appear early may flower in the fall, while those that appear later may flower through the winter and spring. However, the development of the spikes and the time of opening of the flowers is not always conveniently associated. In some plants, spike development, enlargement of the buds, and opening of the flowers proceed in a swift, continuous sequence. In others, although the spikes appear at about the same time, the growth through fall and winter is slow, so that the buds are not ready to open until late spring.

The spike is at first similar in appearance to a vegetative growth, but by the time it is three or four inches long its character becomes apparent. The spikes are rounded and their tips are sharply

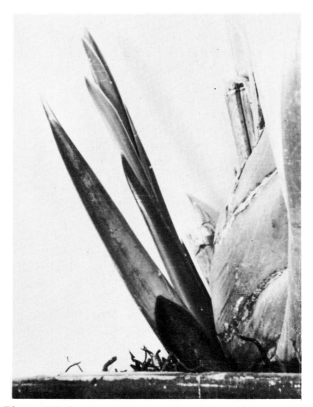

Figure 14–2 *Vegetative growth and flower spike coming from pseudobulb at nearly the same time. Note how tightly pointed the flower spike is.*

come from the fully mature bulb. In the first type, new growth starts in late winter or early spring. This growth is not completely mature when, in late summer or early fall, it gives rise to flower spikes. It continues to grow and mature while the flower spikes are developing. In the second type, new growths are started during the summer, making their appearance shortly before flower spikes arise from the same pseudobulb. These are sometimes so close in appearing that one cannot tell which are the vegetative growths and which the spikes. However, the flower spikes soon outstrip the vegetative growths, which develop slowly through fall and winter. In the spring they take on a new spurt and grow rapidly so that by midsummer they are fully mature and ready to start new vegetative growths. Soon thereafter the new flower spikes appear.

It is possible that some of the difficulties encountered in flowering cymbidiums with regularity are due to a mixing of these basic habits in the hybrids. Plants in both categories (those that flower on the immature bulb and those that flower on the mature bulb) must have reached just the right stage of development by late summer in order for flower spikes to be triggered into development. As the end of flowering approaches, push the plants into rapid vegetative growth: Step up fertilizing and watering, give all the sun you can, and let the night temperatures run about 55°.

Cymbidiums have become so important for commercial growers and the cut flower market as well as for amateurs that people all over the country are determined to grow them. There is great need for exact information as to what initiates cymbidium flowers. Research is being done, but is hampered by a number of things. Species cymbidiums are not too numerous in this country and when available are not obtainable in large numbers. Information gained from the study of species is basic and helps us understand the hybrids. But one cannot assume that because certain species behave in certain ways that other species will behave in the same way, or that hybrids containing them will do so. When research is done on hybrids, it is desirable that the plants studied should be identical, which means that they should be members of the same clone (divisions of the same original plant), and meristem culture helps here. The accumulation of measured information is slow, and we still have to go pretty much by what has been learned by general experience. Added to these problems is the fact that certain plants just won't

do what you expect of them. Certain of the modern hybrids, which by the flowering of the first seedlings look wonderful, may show themselves to be quite tricky, flowering just often enough to keep you hoping, or flowering for some people and not for others. Reluctant flowering may be caused by chromosomal aberrations, or it may be that certain individuals simply need a different combination of environmental factors.

Greenhouse Culture

TEMPERATURE. In general, we know that the standard cymbidiums flower with greater regularity in areas where the summer nights are cool, rarely up to or over 60°, close to 55° most of the time, and where they get good bright sun. They tolerate the higher daytime temperatures that go with bright sun, and although temperatures above 85° are not advantageous, with plenty of water and circulation of moist air they will tolerate temperatures as high as 95° to 100° for a short time. Cymbidiums do not burn as easily as the thicker-leaved kinds. It was at one time thought that perhaps what they needed was a wide difference between day and night temperatures rather than a specially cool night temperature. This has not proven out, however, for regardless of the day temperature and the spread between day and night temperatures, they actually flower better when the summer nights are close to 55°. Also, vegetative growth is better with cooler nights, the plants becoming more vigorous and the leaves tougher and stronger.

Flower spikes start forming during the summer and may appear on into the fall. Those spikes that appear last of all may have actually initiated buds earlier but have been slower in growing and therefore tardy in making their appearance. At any rate, the initiation of flower buds and the appearance of spikes in general seem to be brought about by the combination of low night temperatures and long bright days. Plants that fail to make spikes during this period rarely start spikes later on (in winter), undoubtedly inhibited by the short days of winter even though by then the night temperature is favorable for their formation.

If, during the summer (the period of long days) the plants can be furnished the necessary cool nights, flowering should take place. In a dry climate the temperature can be lowered a few degrees at night by means of an evaporative cooler. If the natural humidity in your area is such that an evaporative cooler would not reduce night temperature, we suggest instead using a refrigeration unit. Compact units of modest size are available for use in homes, motel units, etc., and one of these should reduce the night temperature in a small greenhouse. They are more expensive than evaporative coolers, and perhaps would run into too much money for a large greenhouse.

In order to allow the necessary bright light, less shading should be applied than to a cattleya house. The greenhouse temperatures therefore tend to go very high. Although the plants can take short periods of high temperature, they will do better if the temperature can be kept under 85° for the most part. This is possible with extremely free ventilation, all the ventilators open, and someone on hand to damp down the walks and benches and mist the plants several times a day. Far more efficient and easier on both grower and plants is an evaporative or refrigerative cooler, or a pad and fan arrangement, or mist nozzles with fans to move the air upward.

Growers in moderately warm areas have had some success with cymbidiums by putting them outdoors during the summer. The nights may be a few degrees cooler outdoors than in a greenhouse, and the freer air movement is a help. The plants are set on cinder or gravel beds or are placed on low stands in a lath house, under a roof of lath or plastic shading, or under a tall tree that will give some protection at noon. Be sure they get plenty of water and spray them for red spiders. They must be brought indoors before frost.

During fall and winter, temperature is less of a problem. The ideal night temperature is 50°, with a fluctuation to just one side or the other. Some growers confine the fluctuation between 50° and 55°, others prefer to keep it between 45° and 50°. Winter day temperatures are held close to 60° in dull weather and allowed to rise to 65° on bright days. Too-high temperature day or night can cause erratic opening of flowers or bud drop. This brings up a problem dealing with early flowering. The aim of many growers is to beat the season, with flowers as early in the fall as possible. However, spikes that come very early and have the flower buds out of the last sheathing leaf by September may drop their buds due to the high day temperatures still prevalent through that month. Such early-flowering plants should be kept as cool as possible.

LIGHT. During the summer, cymbidiums can take, and should have, a great deal of light, a minimum of 4,000 foot-candles, and up to 8,000 foot-candles where the temperature can be kept from going to dangerous extremes. If this cannot be furnished them in a greenhouse, even with methods to keep down the heat, it is better to move them outdoors. If any burning shows up, move them to where they will receive partial shade during the middle of the day, or provide a lath or plastic screen roof that will admit 70 to 80 percent of full sun.

During the winter, the plants must still have good light (clear glass except possibly in areas with extremely bright winter sun) in order to develop the flower buds. Those that have flowers in shades of pink and red will have richer coloring if they develop in bright light. Shade added after they are open helps them keep longer. However, those that have green or yellow flowers should be given shade from the time the buds emerge as these colors tend to fade in bright light. Remove the extra shade as soon as flowering is finished.

A brownish coloration develops along the center line of the back of sepals in most colored flowers in bright light. This is not usually deleterious, but in pale colors may spoil the purity. A strain of so-called nonstaining hybrids has been developed that lack the pigment to form this streaking. These yellows and greens remain pure in spite of the amount of light given, and the lip does not turn pink when the anther is disturbed or removed.

POTTING. Selection of a compost for cymbidiums is a matter of personal choice, the main requisite being that the compost hold water well and furnish free drainage. Types of compost used range from straight bark to various mixtures of materials. Composts may be one-third loam, one-third sand, and one-third bark; or sandy loam mixed with shredded redwood fiber (Palco Pete) and dried oak leaves; bark mixed with sand, peat moss, and oak leaves. Some of the mixes turn out to be largely of fibrous content, others are more soillike. Some growers package and sell their favorite cymbidium mix. To various mixes some like to add hoof and horn or bone meal for the slow release of phosphorus, and uramite for the release of nitrogen. A slow-release fertilizer may be added to the potting medium before use. One such is Osmocote, used according to directions.

Cymbidiums do not like to be disturbed too often, preferably not more often than every two or three years. Mature plants should therefore be given a pot large enough to accommodate a good many new growths. Often from one bulb two growths will come and from each of these two more the next year. The plants will do better and give more flowers if they are carried on into ten- or twelve-inch pots instead of being divided frequently. A plant needs repotting when its pseudobulbs become crowded against the edge of its container. This will usually happen before the medium has become unfit for growing. If a plant is not doing well, however, remove it from the pot and determine the cause, and then put it in fresh compost.

Plants should be repotted immediately after each one has finished flowering. This will mean that some will be ready in March or April (a few earlier) and some not until May or June. The former will not yet have started new roots, which is ideal, but the latter, even though root tips may be active, should be potted if they need it. Try to disturb the new roots as little as possible. Plants that did not flower should be included with the early group for repotting.

A plant that is not to be divided can be moved into a new pot with very little disturbance. Prepare the new pot with a fair amount of drainage material and add a layer of potting medium over the crock. Remove the plant from its pot, shake off the old compost, and trim off any dead roots. We usually do no root trimming other than this, unless some roots are so long that they would be broken in the potting process. There are growers who prefer to trim the roots back to a four-inch stub.

Set the plant in the pot so that the level of the new compost will come about half an inch above the rounded base of the pseudobulbs and half an inch below the rim of the pot. Pour in enough of the potting material, previously dampened, to fill the pot to half its depth. Work it in among the roots with your fingers and thump the pot on the bench to settle it. Then proceed to add compost and thump it in place until the pot is full. With your thumbs or a tamper, firm the surface around the inside edges of the pot.

In moving plants on into larger pots, it is well to remove any leafless backbulbs that are situated where they can be cut off without disturbing the green part of the plant. If the plant consists of a complete circle of green bulbs with a few backbulbs in the center, these had best be allowed to remain. When the plant has made its new growth toward one side, backbulbs can easily be removed from the other side. Sometimes when a large plant

has had the backbulbs removed from one side it leaves a long narrow green section that is awkward to pot. This had best be divided to make two or more plants of better shape.

Dividing a cymbidium is more of a challenge than dividing a cattleya (Fig. 14–3). The pseudobulbs grow so close together that often it is difficult to tell which one comes from which other one. The rhizome that connects them is rather short, and the bulbs must be pressed apart to reveal it. A one-lead division should consist of the lead bulb and at least the bulb behind it. However, since two leads so often come from each bulb, the smallest division it is wise to make often consists of two leads and the bulb from which they arose. From the point of view of flower production, it is better to keep together five or six bulbs. Smaller divisions often do not flower the first year.

After removing the plant from its pot, turn it around in your hands to study it. Press the bulbs apart a bit to see how the bulbs are connected, and

Figure 14–3 UPPER: *When dividing a cymbidium, press the pseudobulbs apart to determine the "lines" of growth.* LOWER: *Strip the old leaf bases away from the backbulbs. Insert base of pseudobulb in a sand-peat moss mix (or other mix), or use polyethylene bags as described in text.*

gently wiggle or twist a group here and there to see which ones are held together. This will help you plan where to make the divisions. The knife or pruning shears *should be sterilized between plants.* Each break or cut should be treated to prevent the entrance of fungi or bacteria. Swab it with a strong solution of fungicide or a slurry of Tersan. Dividing a plant of necessity causes many roots to be broken. Trim broken roots back to four-inch stubs. Then pot the divisions as described above.

Two diseases of cymbidiums often are not revealed until potting time. Since leafless pseudobulbs are sheathed with leaf bases, and since these bulbs often remain on the plant for some time, it is often not suspected that they may be internally rotted. However, if pseudobulbs lose their leaves too soon, resulting in a plant that has leaves only on the youngest bulbs, or if the bulbs are soft, infection may be present. Cut through the rhizome between the backbulbs. Infection is shown by brown, dark purple, or black tissue. Discard any bulbs that are infected. Continue to cut forward (sterilizing the knife between cuts) until clean white or cream-colored tissue is found. The infection spreads from bulb to bulb through the rhizome so that if it is found in the rhizome the chances are that it has already entered the next bulb. The bulbs become rotted inside, which kills the leaves. New growths from infected bulbs often show watery areas on the leaves, and, of course, the leaves soon die. A bacterial soft rot causes the brown to purple watery decay of the pseudobulb. A fungus, *Pythium ultimum,* produces the jet back color in the pseudobulb which soon shrivels and becomes "mummified." Plants from which infected areas have been removed should be soaked for twenty-four hours in 8-hydroxyquinolin benzoate, Natriphene, or some other fungicide, and then dried bare-root for ten days. If infection recurs after potting it is best to perform surgery again and re-treat, but if it persists the plant should be discarded (Fig. 14–4).

CARE OF NEWLY POTTED PLANTS. Growers differ on this subject. Some put the newly potted plant directly on a regular watering schedule, others prefer to water only lightly until new root growth is evident and then start heavier watering. Cut roots seem to heal better when kept on the dry side (the compost just damp), and the formation of branch roots is encouraged. A mist spray of the foliage on bright days helps to prevent water loss and makes up for lessened activity of the roots after potting. Whether the plants should be given extra shade during the recovery period depends on day temperatures. Those repotted early in the season may not need extra shade, while those repotted later may benefit from it for a few weeks.

STARTING BACKBULBS. Backbulbs may be started right away, or, as some prefer, they may be allowed to dry for ten days or so first. In the latter case, set the backbulbs from each plant in a separate paper bag with a label (a cardboard box will also serve) leaving them open to the air and in a dry place. They can be started in polyethylene bags in which a bit of damp potting medium has been placed. Set the bags on the bench between pots of plants, where they will be shaded by the foliage and kept in an upright position. If the bulbs fall over, the new growth will assume awkward angles. The bulbs may also be started in pots or flats in a mixture of fine bark and peat moss or either of these with sand. The new growths will start their own roots when they have reached a length of three inches or so. Those bulbs already in pots can be carried on in them, but those in polyethylene bags or flats should be potted as soon as roots reach a length of about an inch. New growths on backbulbs will come along faster if they are kept a little warmer for a while, with nights of about 58°. This can be accomplished by putting them in the cattleya house, for example. But if you do not have a warm spot for them, they will still make growth. A strong bulb should make a flowering growth the second or third year.

WATERING. Except for the period right after potting, cymbidiums should not be allowed to dry out. Depending on the medium you use, water frequently enough to keep the medium quite moist. In bright, hot weather, with the luxuriant foliage transpiring water rapidly, you may have to water every day. Large plants that fill the pot will use water more rapidly than newly potted ones. During the cool days of winter, watering will not need to be as frequent.

HUMIDITY AND VENTILATION. Cymbidiums need good ventilation and air movement. The relative humidity should be around 50 percent. If you do not have humidifying equipment, help the plants through the heat of the day by giving them a mist spray over the foliage and by damping down the ground. The relative humidity may be kept higher

Figure 14–4 *A black or purple discoloration of rhizome or pseudobulb indicates rot.* LEFT: *A healthy pseudobulb.* RIGHT: *A diseased one, cut in half to show internal tissues. Note the healthy, white buds at the base of the one at the left, and the blackened, killed buds on that at the right.*

during the growing season than when the plants are in flower. Flowers are susceptible to *Botrytis* spotting under too damp conditions, especially if air circulation is not good. Fresh air brought into the greenhouse, either by open ventilators or by fans, greatly helps to keep plants and flowers clean and healthy. Ventilators may be left open all night in summer.

FERTILIZING. There are almost as many systems of fertilizing cymbidiums as there are compost mixes. For plants growing in a mix containing a good bit of organic material, or in osmunda fiber, a 30-30-30 fertilizer used about every other water-

ing is sufficient. However, for plants grown in bark or a mix that is largely bark, a high-nitrogen fertilizer is necessary with every watering. When organic materials such as bone meal, leaf mold, etc., have been added, the materials that these release need not be duplicated in a chemical fertilizer applied with the watering. For instance, if uramite has been added to bark before potting, it is not necessary to use a high-nitrogen fertilizer; rather, a balanced fertilizer should then be used. A slow-release fertilizer such as Osmocote can be incorporated in the medium to begin with, and then renewed about every six months. This is best used with a soillike medium as it may sift through plain bark and be washed out the bottom of the pot. Quantities and frequencies are given with directions on the package.

Some growers use the same fertilizer throughout the year, but most like to schedule additional nitrogen in the spring to speed vegetative growth and a low-nitrogen–high-phosphorus fertilizer toward the end of summer to encourage flower spike formation. This can be accomplished in different ways. Ammonium nitrate can be added to a soluble fertilizer in the spring, one part to two of the latter, or dry fertilizer applied as described below. In August, superphosphate can be sprinkled on the potting medium and among the pseudobulbs (this is slow dissolving and gradually releases extra phosphorus through a long period), or one can buy a fertilizer lower in nitrogen.

A dry feeding program for plants grown in a soil mix is outlined as follows by Paul Gripp: May 15 and July 1, give blood meal, a handful sprinkled on a six-inch pot. August 1 and September 15, give a mixture of four parts blood meal, four parts single superphosphate, and one part potassium sulfate, also a handful to a six-inch pot. This regime is sufficient for the year as these are all slow-release substances. October 30, give a mixture of four parts blood meal, four parts single superphosphate, one part potassium sulfate, and one part dolomite lime. Apply a small handful over the surface of each twelve-inch pot, using proportionately less for smaller pots. He cautions that this is applicable only for plants in a soil or soillike mix. Plants in bark may be injured as the material would quickly filter down through it and burn the roots. On soil it remains on the surface, where the minerals are slowly released and carried to the roots by water.

Garden Culture

In regions where temperature does not fall below 26°, cymbidiums may be grown outdoors. Large trees will furnish noon shade with a little sunlight filtering through, or a lath house may be used in lieu of trees. The laths should run north and south so that the sun will cast moving shadows, and the space between laths adjusted according to the intensity of the sun in your area. Where day temperatures are moderate or where the sun is not too intense, the plants may be able to take full sun. When the thermometer shows signs of falling be-

low 26°, the plants should be covered for frost protection.

The plants may be grown in beds, with soil prepared in a ditch one foot deep and one foot wide. In the ditch, put a layer of leaf mold six inches deep and then a layer of horticultural peat to an equal depth. This is trampled down, and a layer of sandy soil added on top. Then, the compost is thoroughly mixed by turning it over two or three times with a shovel. Moisten the compost and wait a day or two before planting.

Remove the plants from their containers, and carefully loosen up the ball of fiber or compost. If it is possible to do so without injuring the roots spread them out about three inches below the surface, cover them with pure peat, and put some peat directly around the pseudobulbs. Then fill in with the compost. If the roots are too tightly tangled, set the loosened ball in the trench and fill the compost in around it. Water lightly until new growth starts, giving frequent syringings of the foliage. When the plants are established, they may be watered rather abundantly.

Cymbidiums are attractive grown among rocks along with other plants. Their location must be carefully prepared with sufficient compost.

Seedlings

Cymbidium seed is obtained by hand pollination and sown in flasks after the method described for cattleyas. It sticks to the sides of the tube of disinfecting solution but may be handled by keeping it agitated when a dropper is used or by picking it up with a platinum loop. The seed is somewhat slow to germinate, but the seedlings grow well.

When the seedlings are removed from the flasks, they may be put either into five-inch community pots, or, better, in flats. Pure osmunda fiber is satisfactory for their growth, as are the composts described earlier. The community pots should be kept in a covered box, or the flat covered with a pane of glass, to furnish them the close, damp atmosphere conducive to rapid growth. At this stage, they benefit from a night temperature of 58° to 60°. When the plants are three or four inches tall they may be moved from the community pot into three-inch pots. If those in flats still have room to grow, they may be left there for a while longer.

Seedlings may be shifted to larger pots as the need requires without disturbing the ball around the roots. They grow rapidly, and often flower at five years of age, though the naturally slower ones may take seven or eight years (Fig. 14–5).

Cymbidium seedlings are reasonably priced and are a good buy for the amateur. Since it takes backbulb propagations two or three years to reach flowering size, two- or three-year-old seedlings will actually flower about as soon. Unless you have a particular interest in obtaining propagations from certain plants, young seedlings will give the greatest satisfaction.

THE SPECIES

Of the sixty or more species of *Cymbidium*, only half have gained importance from a cultural point of view. Even these appear less and less in cultivation as their place is taken by the superior hybrids. In addition to the large-flowered species, there are a number with smaller flowers, some most generous in the numbers they produce, which may increase in importance and popularity because of their tolerance for warmer temperatures. Lastly, there are the charming miniature species, many of

Figure 14–5 *A seedling in a five-inch pot developing its first flower spike.*

which may also be grown under warmer conditions.

The Species: Large-Flowered, Mostly Cool-Growing

C. eburneum. This species seems to be rather hard to grow, and is now rarely cultivated. But it has had a great influence on hybrids, in fact it was one of the parents (with *C. lowianum*) of the first *Cymbidium* hybrid, made in 1889, the famous C. Eburneolowianum. The broad flower parts of *C. eburneum,* its round, flat, open shape, and delightful fragrance have come down through a long line of hybrids, largely through mating other species with the primary hybrid C. Eburneolowianum. Its fragrant flowers are rosy-white, or pure white, with a creamy lip, dotted with rose-purple and having a yellow ridge down the center. The flowers are three to four inches across, usually only one to a stem. The plant is rather weak-growing, with slender pseudobulbs and leaves one to two feet long. It grows in the Khasia Hills at elevations of 5,000–6,000 feet and flowers in late winter and early spring.

C. erythrostylum. So called because of its red column, this species has flowers that are white with a few rose-colored dots at the base of the petals and sepals. The creamy lip is heavily lined with red-violet. The petals are held forward, meeting at the top edges, and give the appearance of a hood over the lip. This hooded aspect is often inherited by hybrids that include this species. The early flowering habit of this species is one of the characteristics sought in its hybrids. The plant is small, with pseudobulbs one and a-half to two inches tall, and leaves ten to fifteen inches long. The arching flower spike bears four to eight flowers. It occurs in Annam and flowers in the fall and winter.

C. giganteum. In spite of its large, fragrant flowers and early flowering habit, this species is not used as much now as it was at one time. It does not have the good keeping qualities that we now expect, and its hybrids are often dull in color. It is found in the ancestry of many hybrids, however, to some of which it has contributed its yellow-green color. It occurs in Nepal and flowers in fall and winter.

C. grandiflorum (preferably called *hookerianum*). These handsome plants are distinguished by having the base of each leaf expanded into a ribbed sheath, striped yellow and green. Their growth is tufted, the pseudobulbs scarcely thickened. The fragrant flowers reach five inches in diameter, and occur five to fifteen on a curving spray that originates from the base of the newly formed pseudobulbs. The petals and sepals are clear green, and the large lip is pale yellow spotted with red-purple. In using this species in breeding, growers have had to eliminate its only poor feature, that of frequently dropping its flower buds before they open. Sometimes the buds sit on the stem for weeks, apparently ready to open, only to turn pink and fall off. The hybrids we now have flower satisfactorily, and many of them trace their green color to C. grandiflorum. The species grows in Nepal, Sikkim, and Bhutan.

C. insigne. One of the most valuable of the species, it is prized for its vigor, its compact growth, and its tall, upright spikes of twelve to twenty flowers. The spikes grow three to four feet tall. The flowers range in color from white (var. album) and near white, to rose-lilac, with rosy dots at the base of the sepals and petals. They are three to four inches in diameter. The lip is rounded, dotted with rose, and has a yellow keel. Both the white and colored forms have been used in making many fine hybrids which have since been combined in various ways to give a wide variety of colors. Two of the important hybrids are the tetraploids C. Alexanderi 'Westonbirt' (Eburneolowianum × insigne), and C. Pauwelsii 'Compte d'Hemptinne' (lowianum × insigne). This species occurs in Annam and flowers in early spring.

C. lowianum. This is another handsome and much-used species. The plants are large, with pseudobulbs up to nine inches tall and leaves two to three feet long. The flower spike arches gracefully, and bears fifteen to thirty-five large flowers. It has many varieties that are almost as desirable as its hybrids. The flowers keep for two months or more, and this desirable quality, along with its floriferousness, has been handed down to its progeny. The flowers are greenish-yellow with faint red or brownish veins. The rather pale, yellow lip is downy and has a V-shaped red-brown blotch on the front lobe. One of its often-used varieties, var. concolor, has clear yellow-green petals and sepals, and its lip is marked with a light orange-buff patch. It occurs in Burma and flowers from late winter to early summer.

Var. iansonii has yellow sepals and petals, heavily lined with purple-brown, and the large, spotted lip is pale in contrast. Its most outstanding hybrid

is C. Ceres (l'ansoni × insigne) which ranges from pink to red and which, in turn, has been a most successful parent. Although it occurs in upper Burma, only a few plants have ever been found.

C. parishii. This rather rare species resembles eburneum, except that the pseudobulbs and leaves are larger, and the spike bears three to six flowers instead of one or two. The fragrant, white flowers are four inches in diameter, with the lip decorated with large purple spots. The parent of the many hybrids made from this species was the variety 'Sanderae', distinguished by much more color in the lip, and broader and more pointed petals and sepals. It has been combined with many of the other fine species. It grows natively in Annam and it flowers in the summer.

C. schroederi. This species is found in the ancestry of many hybrids but does not add much to them in quality. Therefore it has not continued in use. It has greenish-yellow flowers and a lip marked with dull red blotches. It occurs in Annam.

C. tracyanum. This species has contributed its early flowering season to its descendants. The yellow-green flowers are fragrant and occur five to twenty-five on a spray. The plants are vigorous and are grown with ease. It is said that, while the species is often grown outdoors, its flowers keep better in the damper conditions of a greenhouse. The flowers are yellow-green, marked with bright red, and have a yellow lip also marked with red. The plant occurs in Burma and Thailand. Flowers are produced in the fall.

The Species: Small-Flowered, Pendent Spikes, Warm-Growing

The plants in this group are smaller in general than in the previous group, and the flower spikes, instead of arching upward from the pseudobulb, travel across the potting medium and down over the edge of the pot. With one exception, they like intermediate or warm temperatures and may be grown in bark or loose cymbidium mix. They like plenty of sun. They are not common in cultivation as yet, but will probably be more readily available as time goes on. Some of them may be grown outdoors in such places as Florida and Hawaii. In a greenhouse be careful not to overwater them, and to pot them high to give their spikes a chance to grow out over the surface of the medium.

C. aloifolium. These straw-colored or tawny flowers have a yellow lip with brown markings.

They are borne on a pendent spike, and are about one and one-half to two inches across. The plant, from Burma, blooms in winter and spring.

C. atropurpureum. A dozen or more heavy little flowers are borne on a drooping spike about a foot long. They are fragrant of coconut. The sepals and petals are maroon-purple with a velvety sheen, and the lip is white. The plant, which is epiphytic, occurs at elevations of 500 to 3,000 feet in mountainous areas of Malaya and the Philippine Islands. It flowers in late spring and early summer.

C. devonianum. The flower spike of this odd plant will burrow down through the potting medium if not trained over the edge. It is said to have an unpleasant odor, which may not carry on to its hybrids. The dense flower spike carries more than twenty olive to tawny flowers that have a rosy lip decorated with a dark-purple spot on each side. A number of hybrids have been made with this species. The leaves are broad and fleshy and taper to a narrow base or petiole. It occurs in northern India, needs cool temperatures, and flowers in the spring (Fig. 14–6).

C. finlaysonianum. These large plants give many two-inch flowers that are borne on a pendent spike that reaches two to four feet in length. It grows natively along with *C. atropurpureum,* and is also epiphytic. The flowers are dull yellow with a cen-

tral stripe of reddish-brown and are fragrant in the morning. It flowers in the spring and summer. The plant grows easily in warm areas.

C. pendulum. The plant has stiff, upright leaves and a short, pendent flower spike. The pretty little flowers are light yellow trimmed with purple, and have a purple lip with yellow lines. This species is native to northern India. It flowers variably.

The Species: Miniatures

We are indebted to the orchid lovers of Japan for making us aware of the charms of the miniatures native to Japan and China, which the Japanese cherish for their beautiful foliage as well as for their flowers. The species *pumilum, devonianum,* and *tigrinum* were the first to become known and used in hybridization in England and subsequently in this country. Species from other countries are now making their way to our shores and offer a new array of possibilities in hybridization.

Fortunately for growers in this country, all of the miniature species and their hybrids (at least those made so far) can be grown along with cattleyas, although a few require a warm spot in a cattleya house. A few are epiphytic, identified by their velamen-covered roots. These do well in bark,

Figure 14–6 *LEFT:* Cymbidium devonianum. *RIGHT:* Cymbidium tigrinum.

(Courtesy of Fred A. Stewart, Inc.)

while the others will do well either in bark or in a cymbidium mix. Japanese growers apparently keep their plants somewhat cool during the winter, with night temperatures between 40° and 50°, growing them warmer in the summer and with "half-sun." Whether they would do better in our greenhouses if kept this cool during the winter we do not know, because they seem to do very well with cattleya temperatures all year 'round.

C. canaliculatum. This is an epiphytic plant that gives dense spikes of attractive little flowers in a wide range of colors, including brown, green, yellow, magenta, and maroon. The variety 'Sparkesii' is the favorite, with its deep maroon petals and sepals and its pink lip with red dots. The species occurs in Australia. It has fleshy, deeply channelled leaves from which it gets its name. It flowers in the spring.

C. ensifolium, meaning "sword cymbidium." The small flowers, many to the spike, are fragrant, yellow-green, and have a white lip blotched with dull red. The blossoms appear in the fall. It occurs in China and, rather rarely, in Japan.

C. faberi. The Japanese call this species *Ikkei-kyuka,* which means "many flowers on a scape." There are three color forms—reddish, greenish, and white. The plant needs plenty of water, especially during the growing season, and will do well with a bit less light than some other species. A native to China, it flowers in late spring and early summer.

C. forrestii. In Japan this species is known as *Shina-Shunran* or "Chinese spring orchid." The very fragrant flowers are green tinged with red and are borne singly on short stems. The plant occurs in China and flowers in the spring.

C. gyokuchin. The name is derived from *Gyochin,* meaning "young fish in the water." It was described in an ancient Chinese book on orchids and was imported into Japan over a century ago. The sepals and petals are pure yellow-green, and the lip is pure white. Less-fine varieties have touches of red. Some have the foliage striped or mottled with white or yellow. It occurs in China and Taiwan and flowers in the fall.

C. kanran. ("winter orchid.") The spikes of this species carry many fragrant little flowers which vary from green to red. The deep-green foliage is glossy, and in some varieties the margins of the leaves are white. A native of Japan and Taiwan, it flowers in late fall and winter and cannot take too-strong light.

C. hoosai. This species has up to fifteen fragrant flowers to a spike. Two forms occur. Those from China are called *Shina-hoosai,* and are such a dark purplish red that they are often called the "black cymbidium." Those from Taiwan are called *Taiwan-hoosai,* and are of a paler color. Both flower in the early spring.

C. madidum. Another of the delightful Australian species, this one is a huge plant but has miniature flowers one inch in diameter, as many as forty or more on a stem. They are very fragrant, chartreuse except for a dark spot in the lip, and have rounded parts. In spite of the fact that it is difficult to breed, Mary B. Ireland, who created many miniature hybrids, made many crosses between this and diploid and polyploid standard types. These were a disappointment, however, as the pseudobulbs of the hybrids were huge, spoiling their usefulness for almost any purpose. It blooms in spring.

C. pumilum. This very floriferous little plant bears thirty flowers to a spike. The blossoms are purplish red with a white lip dotted with red. Many of the plants have variegated foliage. They like a cool spot in the cattleya house, although the hybrids can be grown somewhat warmer. The species is native to China and flowers in early summer. The famous C. Minuet is *pumilum* × *insigne.*

C. suave. This is the third one of the Australian species, and a newcomer to this country, introduced by Emma Menninger. Except that it has a foot-tall stem rather than a pseudobulb, and produces grassy foliage, it is quite similar to *C. madidum.* Fragrant in nature (not always in cultivation), it has one-inch apple-green flowers with a brown spot on the lip. Its parts are rounded, the lip tongue-shaped. Emma Menninger, a leader in miniature breeding, was the first to make any headway in hybridizing it, and progress is being made.

C. tigrinum. A truly dwarf species, the pseudobulbs are about an inch tall and the leaves four inches long. The flowers are rather large, sometimes reaching three inches in diameter. Two or three blooms occur to a stem. The sepals and petals are green tinged or spotted with brown, and the large lip is white or cream colored, marked with red-purple. The plant, which occurs in Burma and Thailand and flowers in the fall, is frequently used in hybridization.

Cymbidium Hybrids

The destiny of the large-flowered cymbidium was determined by the discovery of *C. Alexanderi*

'Westonbirt' (C. Eburneolowianum × C. *insigne* 'Westonbirt') registered by H. G. Alexander in 1922. This lovely, large, white hybrid was so successful in transmitting its size, shape, and substance to its progeny that it became the most popular parent in cymbidium history, and its value in hybridization has become legendary. Many, many crosses were made with Alexanderi 'Westonbirt' before it was discovered to be a tetraploid (4 = 80 chromosomes).[*]

Many of the selected individuals from among its progeny have also proven to be tetraploid. Where crosses are made with both parents tetraploid, progeny that are almost entirely tetraploid are possible.

The dominance exhibited by Alexanderi 'Westonbirt' includes a strong influence on the color of the progeny. This influence causes a paling of the expected color, regardless of how brilliant the other parent may be, so that the offspring are almost entirely white, cream, or pale pink. This does not detract from the beauty of the hybrids themselves, for they are wonderful, large flowers. From this line of hybrids have come the best of the white cymbidiums, as well as many that are of delicately lovely coloring; but it has meant that other breeding lines have had to be developed in order to achieve more color.

The breeding of tetraploids should not overshadow the variety of diploid hybrids. Many of the diploids rival the tetrapoloids in quality, and many outshine tetraploids in brilliance and variety of colors, if not in size. In general, the diploids produce more flowers to the spike. The majority of good greens, yellows, and reds are diploids. Growers are constantly on the alert for the spontaneous appearance of tetraploid plants in these colors. These might arise from the accidental nonreduction of reproductive cells, allowing a 2n sperm cell to fertilize a 2n egg cell. If such plants should occur, and should be capable of transmitting their color to all of their progeny, they would be invaluable. (See Colchicine, Chapter 7, for work on creating tetraploids from diploids.)

In purchasing seedlings from such crosses, one should know in advance that they will not be uniform in coloring—for instance, a cross with a green diploid will give only a percentage of greens out of a variety of colors. With the swing to wider variety in sizes (as evidenced by hybridizing the smaller-flowered species) a diploid with brilliant color or a subtle combination of colors, also graced by nice form and heavy substance, should be admired for its own intrinsic qualities. With cymbidiums, as with cattleyas, we have passed the stage at which everything has to be big to be of value.

In conjunction with polyploid breeding of cymbidiums, there occasionally occur pentaploids (5n) and plants with odd numbers of chromosomes, aneuploids. The pentaploids are said not to be superior to tetraploids and triploids in quality of flowers and plant characters. The aneuploids may be abnormal in some way, either in plant growth or in the flowers themselves. It is possible that reluctance to flower or failure to flower may be caused in some cases, but not all, by the presence of extra chromosomes which may upset the physiological balance of the plant. A certain amount of sterility is encountered among the aneuploids as well as among hybrids between unlike species, for example, between miniature and large species.

An interesting observation has been made on the number of flowers produced to a spike in the primary hybrids of the Himalayan species. You might expect that if you crossed a species that usually produced one bloom with one that produced twenty-five, the resulting hybrid would give something close to the mean (average) between these two, or thirteen. But that is not the way it happens. Actually, a hybrid between a species that gives one and a species that gives twenty-five will itself produce about five or six flowers to a spike. Mathematically, five is the geometrical mean between one and twenty-five, arrived at by multiplying one by twenty-five and taking the square root of the product. Studies of various crosses have shown that cymbidiums follow this general rule, and the rule may be used to predict the number of flowers you will get in any primary hybrid. As inheritance becomes more complicated in advanced hybrids, it is not possible to trace this feature through the maze of habits represented in any one plant. This rule may not hold true in hybrids between the Himalayan species and the small-flowered ones. In C. Jean Brummit (*devonianum* × *eburneum*), the number of flowers per spike comes close to the number produced by *devonianum*.

Miniature hybrids have taken a great hold on the fancy, both of hybridizers who are excited by the challenge they present and growers who love them for their appealing qualities (Fig. 14–7).

The first crosses were made in England in 1944; McBean's C. Pumander (Lois Sander × *pumilum*), and Brummitt's C. Jean Brummitt (*devonianum* ×

---

[*] D. E. Wimber, G. A. L. Mehlquist, and E. W. Wells have made more than 300 chromosome counts in cymbidiums.

eburneum). The first American hybrid was Stewart's C. Flirtation *(pumilum × Zebra)* in 1955. These sparked a wave of hybridization in which Emma D. Menninger and Mary B. Ireland played large roles. Crosses were made almost entirely between the miniatures and diploid standard types, mostly from *pumilum* at first and then with *tigrinum, aloifolium, ensifolium,* and *devonianum* (see Fig. C33).

This type of hybrid is often called "miniature," although the size of the flowers is increased and the shape influenced by the larger parent. A better name is "novelty," for which, see figure C35. However, they are still delightfully small, and are more usable than the miniatures themselves for some purposes.

Crosses between miniatures and tetraploid standards followed. These are euphoniously called "polymins." Although the first was made by Bowers in 1955, Sweetheart *(pumilum × Alexanderi 'Hamilton Smith'),* it was a Menninger cross that started the wave of polymins. This was Fairy Wand *(pumilum × Princesse Maria)* in 1957.

These crosses, especially those made with *pumilum,* proved discouragingly sterile as parents, except for one, Bowers' C. Sweetheart, which he found to be fertile and with which he made hybrids with such famous parents as Blue Smoke *(C. Lynette),* Alexanderi 'Westonbirt' *(C. Showgirl),* and Nila *(C. King Arthur).* The results have so far been splendid. The chance appearance of tetraploids and the possibility of creating them by use of colchicine offer great promise for the future. It is to be hoped that in carrying on further hybridization the real meaning of "miniature" will be remembered, and small size kept as one of the sought-for attributes.

Culture of Miniature Cymbidiums

The general methods are the same as for the large types, except for a few things. Their temperature requirements are more those of intermediate orchids, cattleyas, for example, as well as their light requirements. They do well in fine bark or a more soillike mixture, bark probably being preferred. They should not be allowed to dry out, but care not to overwater is urged when the flower spikes appear.

CYRTOPODIUM

About 35 species make up this genus, from which the name of the subtribe is taken. While there are some rather small species in the genus, the two best-known ones are huge plants, the famous "cow-horn" orchids.

C. andersonii has spindle-shaped pseudobulbs up to four feet tall with leaves up to two-and-one-half feet long, that are deciduous and leave sharp spines when they fall. The six-foot spikes bear up to a hundred two-inch flowers. They are fragrant, waxy, long-lasting, and are yellow with green tinges. Colorful bracts, similar to a petal in shape, occur at the lower nodes on the stem. It is found from the West Indies to Brazil and flowers in the spring.

C. punctatum is the better-known of the two. Its pseudobulbs also grow to four feet in height, with deciduous leaves up to two-and-one-half feet long. The branching flower spike is up to five feet tall and holds a wealth of flowers one-and-one-half

Figure 14–7 *LEFT:* Cymbidium pumilum album, *a true miniature.* (COURTESY OF YOSHIO NAGANO.) *CENTER:* Cymbidium Devonianum, *with pendulous flower spike.* (COURTESY OF FRED A. STEWART, INC.) *RIGHT:* Cymbidium Flirtation 'Princess Royal', *a hybrid between* C. pumilum *and* C. Zebra. (COURTESY OF FRED A. STEWART, INC.)

inches across. They are yellow, richly spotted with red or purple, and quite wavy, especially the sepals. The large, petallike bracts situated at the nodes are also yellow and heavily spotted. This plant occurs from Mexico, where it grows in protected places on lava beds, through Central America, all the way to Argentina. It flowers in the spring.

GRAMMANGIS

A genus of about five species, one of which is well-known and very striking.

G. ellisii has four-angled, fluted, spindle-shaped pseudobulbs about eight inches tall, from the apex of which arise four or five rather leathery leaves up to two feet long. The flower spike comes along with the new growth. After the buds appear the spike elongates rapidly, becoming a long, arching inflorescence of forty or more flowers, spaced somewhat spirally around the stem. The waxy, long-lived flowers are two inches across, triangular in shape, with the somewhat wavy sepals displayed prominently. They are green-gold with two patches of brown etchings, one at the base and the other at the tip, leaving a plain band inward from the tip. The small, forward-held petals are white, tipped with rose. The small lip is white with clean red stripes inside and is like a little cymbidium lip in shape. It comes from Malagasy and flowers in the summer.

GRAMMATOPHYLLUM

This genus contains the largest orchid known as well as several species quite suitable for ordinary greenhouses. An odd characteristic is that the lower few blooms on the inflorescence are abnormal, lacking a lip and with the lateral sepals united so that they appear to have only four parts.

G. elegans has pseudobulbs six to eight inches tall with rather thin, broad leaves. The arching flower sprays are up to six feet in length and bear some fifty flowers with rounded oval sepals and petals that are dark green with chocolate blotches. This species comes from the Philippines and flowers in the spring.

G. fenzlianum. See *G. scriptum.*

G. measuresianum. See *G. scriptum.*

G. scriptum. Now considered to incorporate the above two species, it is a most interesting plant. Its flowers are variable in color, ranging from greenish-yellow to brownish-gold, and are marked with what look like letters of the alphabet in brown or purple, hence its name. They are some three inches across and occur a hundred or more on a forty-inch stem. The plant has thick pseudobulbs four to six inches tall, and four to six leaves that are fourteen to twenty inches long and three inches wide. From Luzon, and several other islands as well as Papua New Guinea, it flowers in summer.

G. speciosum is the giant of the orchid world, with plants that weigh up to 2000 pounds. Pseudobulbs and leaves together reach a height of fifteen feet or more, and plants have been found climbing fifty feet into trees. Flower stems of six to eight feet hold over fifty blossoms that are four or five inches across. They are dull-yellow with wine-colored blotches. The small lip is marked with carmine. From east and southeast Asia, Pacific Islands, and Papua New Guinea, it flowers in the summer.

CYPERORCHIS

The genus is much like *Cymbidium* in both plant and flower characters. The blossoms do not open as fully as those of *Cymbidium,* and are borne in dense clusters at the end of arching or drooping inflorescences.

C. cochlearis has small pseudobulbs and flowers and grassy foliage that can reach three feet in length. Its brownish-green flowers are shaped more like a typical cymbidium than those of the other species. From the Himalayas, it flowers in autumn.

C. elegans has dense clusters of nearly closed flowers of an ochre-yellow or bright-yellow color. It is said that this closed habit does not come through in its hybrids. The plants are about two feet tall, the flowers about one-and-one-half inches long. Also from the Himalayas and fall flowering.

C. mastersii has pretty, pale green flowers with narrow parts and a white lip ruffled at the outer end, centered with orange. It has an odd plant habit, a rather tall stem instead of a cymbidiumlike pseudobulb, from which two-foot leaves grow. The fragrant, two-inch flowers are spaced rather nicely at the end of the arching inflorescence. From the Himalayas, it flowers in autumn.

CYMBIDIELLA

There are three species of this genus, one of which is truly spectacular and much sought after. It needs a warm, humid atmosphere.

C. rhodochila has a three-and-one-half-foot inflorescence that bears twenty or more four-inch, long-lasting, beautifully colored flowers. Not all open at once. The narrow-triangular sepals are plain and straight. The broadly oval petals are shorter, spread flat and upright, green with dark olive-green spots and blotches. The lip, in complete contrast, is rich red and rather broadly ruffled. The plant grows natively on staghorn fern but can be grown in a basket in cultivation. The pseudobulbs are five inches tall, and the leaves more than three feet long, making a very large plant. From Malagasy, it flowers in late winter and spring.

ANSELLIA

Ansellia is a genus of continental Africa and has two established species. Their nickname "leopard orchids" is descriptive of their tawny flowers marked with red or purple-brown spots. They are handsome plants in every way. Some are fragrant, others apparently not, except that some become fragrant when raised in greenhouses. The plants are from eighteen inches to two feet tall, with spindle-shaped, jointed pseudobulbs that bear several pairs of tough, slender leaves at the top. The roots grow in a mass that conceals the rhizome. The branched inflorescences come from the upper leaf axils and bear many fleshy, long-lasting, two-inch flowers. All are winter-flowering.

Ansellia africana. This species, from the dense rain forests and bush of tropical western Africa, has erect racemes of yellow-green flowers boldly marked with dark red-brown bars and spots. Its petals are somewhat broader than the sepals. The midlobe of the bright yellow lip is rounded, broader than long, curved back at the tip, and has two keels on its crest. Its range is from Ghana to Uganda.

A. gigantea. Ranging farther south, out of the tropical area, this species has paler, more delicately marked flowers. The midlobe of the lip is longer than that of *africana,* with petals the same width as the sepals. It is native from Natal and Zambia to Mozambique.

A. gigantea var. *nilotica* has larger, brighter flowers than the others with lighter markings that in some are quite dense, borne on a downward-arching raceme. The golden lip is oblong and bluntly pointed, with three small, well-developed keels. The somewhat smaller plants and more numerous flowers make it horticulturally more desirable. It grows from Tanzania to Mozambique.

GALEANDRA

Galeandra is a genus of several species with sturdy pseudobulbs from six to twelve inches tall, bearing several narrow leaves. The flowers are showy, two to three inches across, with the sepals and petals spreading in a fan above the broad lip. The sides of the lip enfold the column, and it is spurred at its base. They like a warm spot in a cattleya house.

G. batemanii has short, round or ovoid pseudobulbs. The sepals and petals are light-green, while the large white lip has a broad rosy patch on the outer part. It has been mistakenly considered synonymous with *G. baueri.* It is from Mexico, and it flowers in the summer and autumn.

G. baueri has pseudobulbs ten inches tall, and a flower spike of twelve inches that produces flowers for more than one season. Blooms are three inches across, fragrant and long lasting, yellow-brown with a purple and white lip. It spreads from Mexico through Central America and into northern South America. It blooms fall and winter.

G. devoniana is a more compact species. Its three-inch flowers have sepals and petals of brownish-purple margined with green and a white lip striped with purple. The spur is green. This is native to Colombia, the Guianas, and Brazil. It blooms from winter to spring.

EULOPHIELLA

The warmth-loving species of this genus come from the island of Madagascar. Two species of the four are pretty and worth growing. They like warm conditions, shade, and plenty of water in a well-drained medium.

E. elizabethae has pseudobulbs six inches tall and several narrow, plicate leaves, with the flower stem from the base of the plant. The one-and-one-half inch blooms are waxy, fragrant, sweetly rounded, white with a touch of rose.

E. roempleriana has large flowers on a much heavier plant. They are four inches across, pink with a violet-rose lip. A hybrid between the two is *E. Rolfei.*

OECEOCLADES

There are some thirty species in this genus, most of them in tropical Africa and Malagasy, with one lone species in Brazil. The one chosen to be described here is a handsome one from central Africa.

O. saundersianum (syn. *Eulophidium saundersianum.*) This is a terrestrial plant, easy to grow and generous with flowers. The pseudobulbs are conical, entirely above ground, and bear two tough, wavy leaves from their extenuated tips, making a plant about fifteen inches tall. From the base of the pseudobulb arises a tall, straight, flower stem, a yard high, that bears up to fifty delightful one-and-one-half inch flowers. They are somewhat oblong in aspect, as the slender sepals are reflexed, allowing the broad earlike petals and three-lobed lip to be the prominent part of the flower. The lip has side lobes that stand out like wings, while the midlobe curves downward. The flower is colored in subtle shades of tan and brown. It is found from western Africa through to Tanzania, and flowers over a long period in spring and summer.

·15·

PAPHIOPEDILUM RELATIVES

The Cypripedioideae Subfamily

THE CYPRIPEDIOIDEAE SUB-family has not been divided into tribes and subtribes but consists simply of four genera, all terrestrial. One genus is native to the north temperate zone, one to southern Asia, and two to South America. The first two genera are well known, and both have been called *Cypripedium* in common usage. However, the name *Cypripedium* accurately belongs only to the ladyslippers of the north temperate zone, in the woods of North America, northern Asia, and Europe. The south-ern Asiatic genus is *Paphiopedilum*. The South American genera are *Phragmipedium* and *Selenipedium*.

Paphiopedilum is the genus usually cultivated by amateur and commercial growers, and was once nicknamed "Cyps." Included in this genus are some of the most striking of all orchids. In florist shops, they compete for admiration with cattleyas and cymbidiums and are becoming increasingly popular. They have been favorites of English growers for generations. Their marvelous range of colors—from yellow, green, brown, red, and purple, to white—is often subtly combined in single flowers. *Phragmipedium* is a genus of beautiful flowers and is becoming more popular every year. *Selenipedium* is seldom grown. Our native cypripediums are known by all who love and study wild flowers and may be grown with special care in gardens.

The flowers of the Cypripedium tribe are distinct, differing markedly from those of other tribes. The most appealing floral part is the lip, which is shaped like a pouch or slipper, and which suggested their name (*Cyprus,* sacred to Venus, and *pes, pedis,* Latin for foot). Conspicuous, too, is the dorsal sepal, often broad and brilliantly marked, standing guard above the lip. The petals extend laterally and are slender in proportion to the dorsal sepal. The other two sepals are fused together and lie behind the pouch. Usually they are hidden in a front view of the flower, but when they are enlarged, they add one more touch of beauty.

It would seem that these structures would be enough to distinguish these plants. But botanically speaking, the number of fertile anthers is more important. All members of the Cypripedium tribe have two fertile anthers, whereas other tribes have only one. A third anther, which is sterile, is modified to form the conspicuous shieldlike body called the staminode, which projects forward from the column and covers the reproductive parts.

The members of the Cypripedium tribe lack pseudobulbs and so are not equipped for storing water. There is a short stem from which grow the leaves. After the leaves have formed on a new growth, the flowering stem rises from the tip of the stem, between the leaves.

PAPHIOPEDILUM

This genus of handsome Asiatics has an almost lurid beauty. The flowers, of heavy substance and unexcelled keeping quality, may be enjoyed either on the plant or cut for a month or more. Some few remain fresh for as long as three months. The species vary in their flowering season so that blooms may be had at any time during the year. One of their chief attractions is their ease of culture. They are a good choice for amateurs who do not have a greenhouse, for a pot or two will grow beautifully on a window sill or in a Wardian case. The species, except the rare ones, are inexpensive, and a few dollars will buy many years of pleasure. The hybrids are more costly, particularly the more recent ones.

The fifty or so species are native to tropical Asia, Malaya, and the nearby islands. Some are found at relatively high altitudes in the mountain chains, where rainfall is abundant and temperatures are cool. Here they grow on accumulations of decaying vegetation, on ledges, or in crevices of limestone rocks, partially shaded by overhanging cliffs or trees. Other species occur at lower elevations where the temperatures are higher.

Culture

TEMPERATURE. Culturally, the cool- and warm-growing ones may be distinguished by their foliage. Those with plain-green leaves require a night temperature of between 50° and 55°. Actually, the

Figure 15–1 *Reproductive parts of* Paphiopedilum. *The petal has been removed and half of the lip cut away. The column has three parts. The structure at the top is the staminode, a shield that covers the other parts. The footlike structure that swings down into the lip is the stigma, the undersurface of which receives the pollen. There are two anthers, one on each side just above the stigma. The pollen grains are contained in a soft sticky wax, exposed on the lower surface of the anther.*

temperature need not be held as low at 50°, as long as it usually remains close to 55°. The day temperature should be kept between 65° and 72° in the winter, and it would be ideal if the summer day temperature could be kept not over 75°. However, the cool species, like most orchids, will accept and tolerate summer temperatures above this, but will do their best if they do not often exceed 85°. In order to protect the cool paphiopedilums where the heat of summer is prolonged, some growers put the plants outdoors in the shade of large trees. The pots may be set on cinder beds or on benches to assure drainage. They should be elevated to keep slugs and cutworms from reaching them.

The warm-growing species are those with mottled foliage, and hybrids between the plain and mottled foliage kinds come in this category. They prefer a night temperature that does not go below 60° but that may go above this in the summer. They may be grown comfortably with cattleyas, with day temperatures that suit cattleyas and companions.

Both the cool- and warm-growing kinds can be accommodated in a cattleya house, as a matter of fact, if the former can be given a spot that runs a bit on the cool side. Shade will have to be adjusted for them as described below.

The good keeping qualities of the paphiopedilums make it possible to have them for most holidays. Occasionally, however, it is desirable to slow down the opening of the blooms for a certain purpose. When the stem has reached its full length and the buds are almost fully developed, the temperature may be lowered a few degrees. Flowering is thereby slightly delayed. The temperature must not be lowered too soon or the stems will remain short and the plant will not be as handsome in bloom. Slightly lowered temperatures will allow the flowers to last longer, so that many growers, in order to keep a group of flowers as long as possible, keep the temperature a few degrees cooler after the plants have come into full bloom.

POTTING. The most popular medium is plain fir bark, preferably seedling grade, or one in which the largest size pieces are one-half inch. A mixture of 80 percent bark and 20 percent dried crushed oak leaves is also popular, as are bark mixed with tree fern, and plain tree fern. Perlite is a good additive for its water-holding capacity as well as its ability to keep the medium open. Charcoal may also be added. The chief essential in any compost is that it should have free drainage, because the roots, although never allowed to become dry, do not thrive in a sodden compost.

The plants are best repotted soon after flowering, at which time they may be divided into groups of not less than three growths. Remove all dead leaves and roots and all decayed compost. After adding crock for drainage, hold the plant at such a depth for potting that the base of the plant will be about one-half inch deep in the medium. If the plant is set too high the new roots will not thrive, and if too deep, the base of the plant may rot. The compost should be firmly tamped. After potting, water only enough to keep the compost damp until new root growth begins. In the meantime, give the plants a light mist spray once a day—just enough to dampen the outer portions of leaves and not so heavily as to allow water to collect in the leaf axils (Fig. 15–2). Water standing in the leaf axils encourages bacterial infection (Fig. 15–3). The plants will become reestablished in about three months.

WATER. Since growth is continuous in this genus, and because the plants have no pseudobulbs, the potting medium should not be allowed to dry out. The frequency of watering depends so much on environmental conditions and on the type of medium used that it is difficult to give any set schedule. During bright weather two waterings a week may be sufficient, with longer intervals between waterings in dull weather. Misting the plants is usually not necessary except in very hot weather. Always water thoroughly so that water runs out of the bottom to flush out excess salts, for accumulation of salts is injurious to the roots.

LIGHT. Paphiopedilums do best in diminished light. During the winter, when days are short and the light slants from the south they need between 1,000 and 1,500 foot-candles. When summer days become hot, shading should be applied to cut the amount of light gradually down to 800 or 900 foot-candles. In areas where summer heat is great, this

Figure 15–2 LEFT: *The new growth appears from within a leaf axil of the mature growth.* RIGHT: *The fuzzy root tips grow down among the pieces of crock in* *the bottom of the pot. These roots must not be allowed to become dry.*

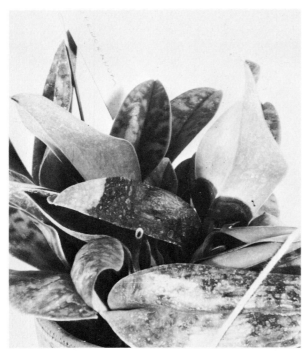

Figure 15–3 *Water standing in the heart of the growths encourages a bacterial rot that can spread quickly through the plant. Note the blackened areas of the leaves in the center.*

may even be reduced to 700 foot-candles. However, let the plants themselves be the guide. The foliage of the plain-leaved species should be a good green; yellow-green shows they have too much light. The mottled-leaved species can be an even richer green.

HUMIDITY. These plants require the same humidity as do cattleyas. Good air circulation is a must. Excessive moisture on the leaves encourages disease.

FERTILIZERS. Paphiopedilums are perhaps more resentful of over-feeding than any other kind of orchid. If the salt content of the growing medium is too high, root growth is reduced or, in extreme cases, eliminated. In osmunda fiber no extra nutrients are required. This is one thing that makes osmunda fiber such an excellent medium for this genus; all you have to do to get fine root and top growth is to water properly. In mixed composts an occasional feeding with a 10-10-10 fertilizer may be beneficial, perhaps no more than once a month, with the pots thoroughly watered with plain water in between times. In straight fir bark, a 30-10-10 fertilizer is essential, given every other watering. Again, flush the pots thoroughly in between times.

If root growth is lessened in any case where fertilizer is given, try reducing the frequency, perhaps giving an additional application of plain water between regular fertilizer applications.

PROPAGATION. Paphiopedilums are easily propagated by division, with three growths to a division. However, while this increases the number of plants of a kind, it does not usually increase the number of flowers from a group of plants. Plants may be allowed to become large specimens with many leads, which are extremely handsome. They actually need division only when the growths have extended out so far from the center of the plant that the center is empty of leaves. In such cases, the growing sections of the plant often separate themselves naturally, falling away from the old dead portion of the rhizome. When dividing a plant it is best to break the rhizome with your fingers rather than cut it. Just give the rhizome a quick twist to break it. Occasionally plantlets develop on the roots, at some distance from the root crown. These contribute to the formation of a plant with many growths, of course, but can be removed and potted separately when they are seen to be developing their own roots.

THE SPECIES

The genus is divided into three subgenera, according to certain features of the flowers.

Subgenus *Brachypetalum* has a pouch without ears whose edges are turned inward all around. The petals are broadly rounded and the foliage mottled. These are somewhat difficult to grow, so it would pay to consult someone who knows their culture.

Subgenus *Anotopedilum* has an earless pouch and very elongated, narrow petals. The leaves are plain green.

Subgenus *Paphiopedilum* has ears to the pouch and leaves mottled or plain. It is a large group that can be divided into sections, although here we shall put them in alphabetical order, including only the better-known ones.

Subgenus *Brachypetalum*

P. armeniacum is one of several stunning new species recently imported from China. Its large, golden yellow flower can reach a diameter of four inches, although most individuals are smaller. On a large flower, the pouch is some two inches wide, nearly round. Petals are about two-and-one-eighth inches by two-and-one-sixteenth inches long, while the dorsal sepal is somewhat smaller, pointed at the top. The stiff, dark green leaves are mottled, and up to one inch wide by four to six inches long. The plant sends out its new growths on long stolons, so it is best to grow it in a basket so it can spread. It is difficult to tell just what initiates flowering. Try it with intermediate temperatures, with perhaps cooler temperatures after flowering until new buds appear. It flowers from fall to spring and lasts a long time.

P. bellatulum. This species is attractive for its foliage as well as for it charming flowers. The leaves are up to ten inches long and are three-and-one-half inches wide. They are deep green, mottled with lighter green on the upper surface, purplish underneath. The three-inch flower is round, shaped like a deep saucer, with the almost egg-shaped lip backed by the broad petals. They are white to pale yellow and are marked with purple spots that run nearly into lines on the dorsal sepal and are smaller on the lip. The species occurs in China and flowers in the summer.

P. concolor. The plants are about the same size as *P. godefroyae,* with leaves mottled green on their upper surface and spotted with deep crimson below. The two- to three-inch flowers are yellow, spotted with purple. The dorsal sepal is concave and almost round, and the broad petals point downward. The paler lip is nearly cylindrical and somewhat flattened on the sides. The species grows in Moulmein. It blossoms in the fall.

P. delenatii. This beautiful little plant has oval leaves that are dark green mottled with light green above, light green mottled with red-violet underneath. The rounded flowers have an oval, pointed dorsal sepal that is velvety on the back and margins, white flushed with rose, and round white petals. The spherical lip is white and rose, lightly flushed with lavender. It occurs in Indochina and flowers in late winter and early spring.

P. emersonii is new from China, distinctive for its pale, near-white coloring. The petals and dorsal sepal are white, the lip pale yellow to ivory, with maroon spots inside that show through to the outside as brown dots. It is a heavy flower, about four inches wide, with velvety texture. The leaves are plain green, lighter on the underside, about six by two-and-one-half inches. It flowers in the spring.

P. godefroyae. This small species has leaves six inches long by one-and-one-half inches wide. They are mottled green on the upper surface, and green

spotted with brown-purple underneath. The short flower stem bears one or two white or pale-yellow two-and-one-half-inch flowers that are lightly spotted with magenta. The petals are oval and point downward. The species occurs in Viet Nam, and flowers in the summer.

P. leucochilum is very much like *P. godefroyae* except that it has a pure white lip. The petals and sepals may be white or pale yellow, spotted with red-purple. It comes from islands in the Indian Ocean off the west side of the Malay Peninsula, and it flowers in the spring and summer.

P. malipoense is another large-flowered species from China. It is colored in shades of green, with purple veins in the petals, fainter ones in the dorsal sepal, and fine purple spotting inside the pouch. The petals are longer than those of *armeniacum* and the dorsal sepal smaller. The staminode is white above and purple beneath, a striking feature. The blossoms come on very tall, straight stems and take a long time to open. The leaves are dark, tesselated green, close to two inches wide and rather wavy. This plant should be grown in a basket also. Intermediate temperatures suit it well, and it seems to flower easily, blooming in the spring.

P. micranthum was the first of this group of Chinese species to be imported. It is a spectacular flower of a beautiful pink color, but its large, over-long pouch makes it less well balanced than its sister species. The small, flat, round, dark pink- and green-striped petals and dorsal sepal overlap to form a circle of about the same breadth as the pouch. Its dark-green, very stiff, mottled leaves are only about two-and-one-half inches long by three-quarters to one inch wide, and are finely quilted in texture. It grows in intermediate to cool temperatures and flowers in late summer.

P. niveum. The plants have leaves four to six inches long, strikingly colored, green mottled with gray-green above and brilliant purple underneath. The two-and-one-half inch flowers are white with a scattering of purple dots, and the dorsal sepal is red on the back. The edges of the flowers are prettily waved. This species occurs in the Loncavi and Tambilan Islands. The flowers appear in the spring (Fig. 15–4).

Subgenus *Anotopedilum*

P. philippinense (Syn. *laevigatum*) has glossy, green leaves, and flowers that are bold and handsome. The dorsal sepal and synsepal are about the

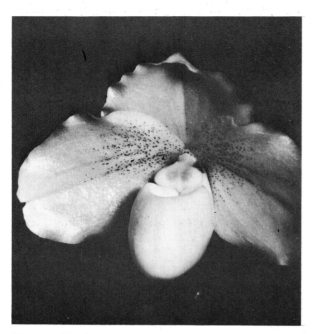

Figure 15–4 Paphiopedilum niveum. (COURTESY OF J.A. FOWLIE.)

same size—white, veined with green. The petals flare outward and are trimmed with hairs along their edges and also have a few warts along their basal edges. They are about six inches long, reddish-purple, with green tips. From the Philippines, it flowers spring and summer. Var. *Roebelenii* is a bit larger and has longer petals that are pendent.

P. praestans. The striking flowers are large and brightly colored. The two-inch tall dorsal sepal is whitish, decorated with sharp lines of purple. The spirally twisted petals are yellowish, veined with brown, and are about five inches long. They have hairbearing warts on their margins. The lip is rather long, somewhat flattened on the sides, and is shiny yellow, suffused with red. A native of New Guinea, it flowers in August.

P. rothschildianum. A handsome species, the plants have two-foot long, green leaves, and a spike that may bear several flowers. The flowers are stunningly colored. The dorsal and lateral sepals are yellow striped with black-purple. The fused lateral sepals in this species are larger than in many others and give the effect of a mirror image of the dorsal. The long, slender petals extend five inches and are pale green, spotted with purple, distinctly lined or nerved with dark green. The long lip is purple, veined with a darker shade and yellow toward the top. It stands sharply forward. A native of Borneo and Sumatra, it flowers in the winter.

P. sanderianum. This is a remarkable species. The petals are one and one-half feet long, twisted, pale yellow, barred and spotted with purple. The dorsal sepal is narrow and pointed, yellow-green with brown stripes. The long, projecting lip is brown-purple and yellow. It occurs in the Malay Archipelago, and flowers in early spring.

P. stonei. Three to five stunning flowers are borne on a stem. The dorsal sepal is white, trimmed with two or three crimson streaks, and the lateral sepals almost equal it in size. The twisted petals are five to six inches long, tawny, with crimson spots for two-thirds of their length and solid crimson at the end. The lip is rose, reticulated with crimson; the upper sides fold in and are white. This species is from Borneo and flowers in the fall.

Subgenus *Paphiopedilum*

P. appletonianum has a deeply eared, greenish brown pouch which is rather long and slender. The dorsal sepal is green, small, with its top edges turned forward. The petals are narrow and wavy on the green basal half, with wider pointed outer ends that are rose. The leaves are only faintly mottled. From the Himalayas, Assam, and Thailand, it flowers in the spring and sometimes the fall. A similar species, *wolterianum*, differs only slightly from this.

P. argus has distinctive, medium-size flowers. The dorsal sepal is oval and pointed, white striped with green, or sometimes with both green and purple. Occasionally it is spotted with blackish purple at its base. The wavy petals have a white ground with green veins for two-thirds of their length, and clear purple tips. Blackish warts decorate the inner surface of the petals. The lip is brownish purple, green underneath, and the narrow infolded lobes are light purple, spotted with a deeper shade. The foliage is mottled. Native to Luzon, it flowers in late winter and spring (Fig. 15–5).

P. barbatum is an attractive species whose deep purple tones often approach red. The nearly round dorsal sepal is folded at the midvein. It is white, green at the base, stained and striped with purple. The petals, which bear blackish warts on their upper edges, are brownish green at the base changing to purple at the tip. The lip is deep brownish purple. The foliage is mottled. It occurs in the Malay Peninsula and usually flowers in the summer.

Figure 15–5 Paphiopedilum argus. (Courtesy of J.A. Fowlie.)

P. barbigerum is astonishingly small, a real miniature. It looks like a little *P. insigne,* with its brown pouch, white-bordered dorsal sepal which has brown and green veins instead of the raised spots of *insigne,* and narrow brown petals. The flower looks fragile but actually lasts quite a long time. The plant, too, is tiny, its plain-green leaves barely one-half to three-quarters inch wide and two to three inches long. Intermediate temperatures seem to suit it well. It flowers in the spring. It is shown in Fig. C 41 with an average-size paphiopedilum, *P.* Rosy Dawn.

P. callosum. (P. callosum may be only a variety of *barbatum,* or possibly a subspecies.) This species contains beautiful, large flowers, noted for their huge dorsal sepal, which may be three inches across. It is folded at the midvein and somewhat wavy at the top, white with alternately long and short veins changing from purple at the base to green above. The petals are pale green with purple tips and have a sprinkling of blackish warts on the upper margin. The brownish purple lip is green beneath. The foliage is mottled. A native of Thailand, it flowers in the spring.

P. chamberlainianum is one of several closely related species often put into their own section, or subgenus, *Cochlopetalum.* These are *P. victoria-*

mariae, primulinum, liemianum, and *glaucophyllum,* which are described below. The foliage of *P. chamberlainianum* is finely stippled. The petals are white or greenish, spotted with rose, short and spirally twisted, bordered with tufts of hairs. The rounded dorsal is white or greenish, spotted with rose, while the jug-shaped pouch is pink. The flowers come one or two at a time on a zig-zag, ever-elongating stem most of the year.

P. charlesworthii. This is a charming species with mottled foliage and medium-sized flowers. The large and spreading dorsal sepal is white, suffused and spotted with rose-purple. The petals are yellow-green, reticulated with brown, and the lip is rosy purple. It occurs in Bengal. The blossoms appear in the fall.

P. curtisii. Distinctive flowers are borne on rather tall stems that rise above the leaves which are mottled on their upper surface. The flowers have a very long brownish purple lip whose infolded lobes are decorated with darker warts. The petals are long and slender, downward hanging, pale purple tending to white along the midvein, and covered with lines of small purple spots or warts from which arise blackish hairs. The small dorsal sepal is green with a white margin, marked with alternately short and long green veins. Its upper edges fold together to form a pointed peak. It occurs in Sumatra and flowers in May and June (Fig. 15–6).

P. dayanum. An attractive species with mottled foliage, it produces slender flowers on a long stem.

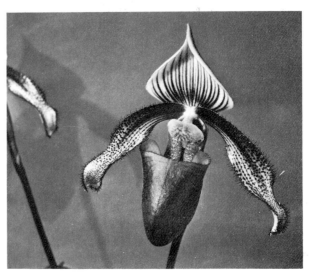

Figure 15–6 Paphiopedilum curtisii. (Courtesy of J. A. Fowlie.)

The dorsal sepal is prettily shaped, with the lower sides folded back and the upper edges folded forward to form a point at the top. It is white with green veins. The long, slender petals are greenish-brown changing to rose-purple. The slender lip is somewhat pointed at the tip, brownish purple, veined with green. The plants are native to Borneo. Flowers appear in May and June.

P. druryi is rather plain, its marks of distinction being a heavy, almost black stripe in the center of the green dorsal sepal and the brownish green petals. The top of the dorsal sepal and the tips of the petals are bent forward. The yellow pouch is rather long and slender. The back of the dorsal sepal and the lower edge of the petals bear fine, black hairs. The foliage is bright green. From southern India, it flowers in late winter and spring.

P. exul. The lightly marbled foliage is bordered with white. The yellow-green dorsal sepal has a white margin and brown spots. The petals and lip are yellow with faint brown markings. This species occurs in Thailand.

P. fairrieanum. Small plants with light green leaves have attractive, medium-size flowers. The tapering dorsal sepal is large in proportion to the size of the flower, with an undulating margin. It is greenish white, reticulated with violet. The petals hang down and then turn up at their tips. They are yellow to white, streaked with purple, bearing tufts of hairs on their wavy margins. The smallish lip is green and white. It occurs in Assam and flowers in the fall.

P. glaucophyllum is one of the group that resembles *P. victoria-mariae.* Its spirally twisted, hairy-edged petals are spotted with purple, while the dorsal sepal is veined with dotted lines of purple. The slender pink lip has a long narrow base. The foliage is glaucus, that is, bluish green with a "bloom" on the surface. From Java, it blooms all during the year.

P. haynaldianum has long, oar-shaped petals, very narrow at the base, broadening at the tip. They are yellowish on the inner half with large spots of purple, plain rose at the outer ends. The dorsal sepal is somewhat triangular, narrow at the base, spreading upward. The pouch spreads wide at the upper margin. It occurs in the Philippines and flowers at various times.

P. hirsutissimum. Large, iridescent hairy flowers make this a striking species. The roundish, wavy, dorsal sepal is marked with black-purple and bordered with green. The ruffled petals are slender near their base, wider toward the end, and some-

what twisted. They are mottled with deep purple on a green ground near the base, becoming bright purple at the tip. The deep-green lip is tinged with purple. The foliage is green. The plant is native to Assam. It flowers in the spring. It really needs to be kept cool in order to initiate flowers (Fig. 15–7).

P. hookerae has dull-green foliage, strikingly marbled with gray-green. The flowers are reminiscent of *venustum* in general shape. The rather small dorsal sepal is light green or green suffused with pale pink, and lightly veined. The bold sepals extend slightly downward, narrower at the base and broadening steadily toward the outer end. They are rosy, tinged with gold at the base, where they are wavy on the edge and lightly spotted. The pouch is rounded, pinched in just below the ears. From Borneo, it blooms in spring and early summer.

P. insigne. This is the easiest to grow and once one of the most popular of the genus. It still appears everywhere, in collections and in the florist's show window. Perhaps its most attractive feature is the shiny appearance of the flowers; they almost look as if they had been varnished. The broad, oval dorsal sepal has the top turned slightly forward. The central part is apple green, spotted with purple along the darker-green veins, and the upper part is white. The wavy petals are pale yellow-green, veined with brown. The lip is also yellow-green, suffused with brown. The species occurs in Nepal and Assam. It produces flowers in the winter. *P. insigne* has many named varieties, of which the variety 'Harefield Hall' has proved to be outstanding both in itself and as a parent of hybrids. This form is larger than the type, and recent stud-

Figure 15–7 Paphiopedilum hirsutissimum. (Courtesy of J. A. Fowlie.)

ies have shown it to be a natural triploid (having three times the usual haploid number of chromosomes). The standard chromosome number of *Paphiopedilum* is twenty-six in the vegetative cell, thirteen in the reproductive cells. 'Harefield Hall' has thirty-nine, or three times thirteen.

P. lawrenceanum. This handsome species has mottled, yellow-green foliage and large flowers. The beautiful dorsal sepal is nearly round, white, with deep purple, flame-shaped veins reaching nearly to the tip. The straight, veined petals are green with purple tips, and both margins carry black warts. The lip is dull purple, tinged with brown and green. It occurs in Borneo and flowers from April to July (Fig. 15–8).

P. liemianum is another rather recently discovered species and is a beautiful member of the *P. glaucophyllum* group. It is vividly colored, with a metallic-green dorsal sepal bordered in white, a bright-rose pouch also bordered in white, and hairy, wavy petals striped with cross rows of dark-red dots on a yellow background. The leaves are plain green on top, marked with fine red dots underneath. It comes from Sumatra and flowers are produced successively over a long period.

P. lowii. Quite an unusual species, it produces three to six dainty flowers on a long, nodding stem. The leaves are light green. The flower parts are slender. The oar-shaped petals are yellow with

Figure 15–8 Paphiopedilum lawrenceanum. (Courtesy of J. A. Fowlie.)

black spots toward the base and violet at the outer ends. The dorsal sepal is slender at its base, spreading at the top, yellow-green, veined with brownish-purple. The lip is brown. This native of Borneo blossoms in the summer. It tends to be epiphytic rather than terrestrial, and needs especially good aeration.

P. parishii. This is a most remarkable species. It bears a tall stem with five to seven flowers open at once. With their four- to five-inch, twisted, nearly black petals hanging down at an angle, they make a striking picture. The flowers are essentially brownish green or brownish yellow. The petals are sparsely spotted on the basal half and the outer half is tinged with red. Both the dorsal sepal and the pouch are dainty, rather slender. The flowering stem itself is downy. The foliage is bright, glossy green. This species tends to be epiphytic. It comes from Thailand and Burma, and flowers from spring to autumn.

P. primulinum. This is a delightful, small, green-and-yellow member of the *P. victoria-mariae* group. It has not been known very long, having been discovered in 1972 by Liem Khe Wie. The leaves are bright green, light gray-green on the underside, and young leaves are hairy on the margin. The flowers appear one after another on an elongating stem. The rounded dorsal sepal is yellow-green with a green stain along its midline and green veins. The petals are slender, slightly twisted, hairy on the edges, and the chunky pouch is yellow. It flowers continuously for most of the year.

P. spicerianum. These medium-size flowers are distinguished for the large dorsal sepal which is markedly wider than it is tall, yet is folded in a turretlike manner. The foliage is dark green. The dorsal sepal is white, with a simple crimson-purple band down the center. Its basal region is green, spotted with red. The petals have wavy margins and are pale green spotted and striped with purple. The lip is rather long, dull purple marked with green. One of the important ancestors of our modern hybrids, it occurs in Assam. The plants are in blossom from October to December.

P. sukhakulii burst upon the world in 1965. It was one of the first new species to come into cultivation for a long time and caused quite a sensation. It's an odd-looking flower, its small dorsal sepal quite out of proportion to the rest of the flower. The dorsal sepal is broad at the base and comes to a long point. It is white, veined with green. The petals, three-quarters inch wide and sharply pointed, stand straight out to the side.

They are green, spotted all over with brown, and edged with hairs. The pouch is downy, triangular in shape, brown, veined with darker tones. From Thailand, it blooms any month of the year.

P. urbanianum is another newcomer, discovered only in 1975. It has something of the look and coloring of a number of other species: If one be allowed to use some imagination, perhaps *P. hirsutissimum, barbatum,* and *purpuratum.* It makes a handsome, many-growth plant in a short time, with each flower stem bearing two blossoms, or one and a bud. The dorsal sepal is white with green stripes and the petals are narrow at the green-striped base and broaden toward the rich-rose-colored tip. The pouch is rather narrow, brownish in color. The leaves are beautifully tesselated on top, plain green underneath. It comes from the island of Mindoro and flowers in the spring.

P. venustum. This species has rather short leaves, marbled with gray-green on the upper surface and mottled with dull purple underneath. The flowers, which are produced singly on a tall stem, have a heart-shaped dorsal sepal that is white with dark green veins. The petals have the basal part green with dark warts and the outer portion dull brownish-purple. The pale-yellow lip is tinted with rose, veined and netted with brown. The plants are native to northeast India and blossom in late winter and spring.

P. victoria-mariae (syn. *victoria-regina*) and the similar species *Chamberlainianum, primulinum, liemianum,* and *glaucophyllum* are members of the section Cochlopetalum. Its rather long, green leaves have prominent veins and are lighter on the underside, sometimes pinkish at the base. The dorsal sepal is green to olive, bordered with cream, and hairy on the back. The pinkish petals are spirally twisted, becoming darker at the tip, hairy along the edges. The rather long, pointed pouch is somewhat compressed at the sides. Flowering is intermittent from an elongating stem.

P. villosum. Large, glossy, hairy flowers are produced on rather large plants whose leaves are green above, purple spotted beneath. The dorsal sepal is brownish purple with a green tip. The longish petals are wavy, yellowish brown with a prominent central band of purple. The lip is brownish yellow. It flowers in winter.

P. villosum var. *boxallii* is sometimes given as a separate species. In this, the dorsal sepal is marked in the center with numerous black spots. Var. *boxallii* has been a frequent parent of hybrids. It flowers in January and February. This species, which

occurs in Moulmein, has also been found growing as an epiphyte.

P. virens is somewhat like *venustum* but prettier. Its dorsal sepal is rounded, pointed at the top, cream with green veins. The quite straight petals are longer than in *venustum,* green basally, rosy-tipped, lightly spotted along the midvein and along the edges. The pouch is very pointed. It is from Mount Kinabalu and it blooms in late summer and fall.

P. wolterianum is so similar to *P. appletonianum* that some people feel it should be only a variety of the latter. The pouch is different, however, being narrower across the ears, and not so deeply notched, while the petals are more drooping and are more deeply colored at the apex. It comes from Cambodia and blooms in fall and winter.

GROWING PAPHIOPEDILUM FROM SEED

When a group of species as distinct and as beautiful as the paphiopedilums displays itself before you, you cannot down the urge to produce hybrids. Growers have long worked to blend the best features of several into new combinations, and there are today some stunning hybrids. But the casual observer cannot know the patient work and the many disappointments that lie behind the flowers he sees.

The first *Paphiopedilum* hybrid was made in 1869, a cross between *barbatum* and *villosum.* Since then, many successful hybrids have appeared, of which one of the most famous is *P. Maudiae,* the so-called green orchid. Its parentage is *callosum* 'Sanderae' × *lawrenceanum* 'Hyeanum'.

A number of difficulties exist in the breeding of *Paphiopedilum* hybrids. A great deal of effort has gone into the making of crosses in this genus, with less relative success than with other genera. Many of the beautiful hybrids shown today are almost the sole survivors of the matings that made them. In the first place, the hybrids are frequently partially or entirely sterile, according to their genetic makeup. This means that often only a small amount of viable seed is produced. In the second place, the seed is hard to germinate, so that much good seed never results in seedlings.

This does not mean that an amateur cannot breed *Paphiopedilum,* for he may hit on a combination that gives a fair amount of good seed. But even if he achieves only a few plants for his effort, he will be rewarded by a justifiable thrill at success under such challenging circumstances.

The pollen does not keep well, hence, it should be used shortly after it has been removed from the two anthers. A toothpick can be used to transfer the granular pollen directly to the stigma.

A seed capsule matures in approximately nine to eleven months, occasionally in a shorter or longer time. The technique used for sowing the flasks is essentially the same as that described for *Cattleya*. Calcium hypochlorite solution is usually used as the disinfecting agent. The seed coat is unusually hard and moreover is protected by hairs that make it more difficult to wet with a disinfecting agent. Some workers add a drop or two of a wetting agent, such as Santomerse, to the 140 cc of hypochlorite solution to aid its penetration. The exposure to the disinfecting solution is ten or twenty minutes.

A good growing medium is Knudson's "C" solution, with the addition of .05 gram of peptone to one liter of the agar nutrient mixture. The pH should be adjusted to 6 to give the more nearly neutral conditions suited to *Paphiopedilum*.

Often, out of a large number of seed sown, only a scant few ever germinate. Experts have germinated several hundred from a single capsule, and an occasional amateur has been as fortunate. Contrast this, however, with the many thousands obtainable from almost any cattleya cross. Sometimes seeds germinate after months or even years, but it is almost impossible to maintain the proper growing conditions over long periods. It is, therefore, suggested that a generous amount of seed be sown in each flask.

The reluctant germination suggests the possibility of the presence of an inhibitor in the seed. Burgeff used a soaking technique that improved the percentage of germination. He allowed the seed to stand in sterile water for two weeks to two months before sowing it in the flasks. His growing medium differed slightly from Knudson's "C," and he kept the flasks in the dark until the embryos began to lengthen. The "green-pod" method (see Chapter 8) often gives improved germination.

INHERITANCE IN PAPHIOPEDILUM

Crosses between certain species have produced hybrids that have proved fairly fertile, and these have been fruitful in the production of other hybrids. Crosses between certain other species have often given hybrids that are almost or entirely sterile. With great patience, breeders have obtained some offspring from the nearly sterile hybrids, as few as a dozen seedlings at times. Thus out of the tremendous numbers of hybrids given in Sanders' *Complete List of Orchid Hybrids*, a great many represent crosses from which but few plants were raised. A quick perusal of Sanders' listings gives a very striking introduction to the problems that have been involved in breeding. Under the names of some hybrids there appear long lists of other hybrids made with these parents. Under the names of others but one or two further crosses appear, indicating that these were not fruitful parents. Some of the hybrid names never again appear in the lists, indicating either that these were sterile or were not desirable enough to have been used. A few of the sterile hybrids have come down to us through vegetative propagation, or even by repetition of the crosses that produced them, because they were such lovely things. An example is *P*. Maudiae, an unsatisfactory parent but a very popular plant.

The problems in breeding stem partly from the range of chromosome numbers among the species, and partly from incompatibility even among some species with the same chromosome number. Among the chromosome numbers there are represented 26, 28, 30, 32, 34, 36, 40, 42, and the gametes from these species would contain 13, 14, 15, 16, 17, 18, 20, and 21. The natural triploid, *P. insigne* 'Harefield Hall', has 39 chromosomes and can produce gametes of 13 and 26 chromosomes.

Species with 26 chromosomes are: *bellatulum, charlesworthii, delenatii, druryi, exul, fairrieanum, hirsutissimum, insigne, niveum, stonei, villosum,* and *villosum* var. *boxalli*. Increasing in chromosome numbers we have *rothschildianum* with either 26 or 28; *praestans* with 28; *spicerianum* with 30, occasionally 28; *callosum* with 32 (and a number of other species not described in this chapter, with 32); *dayanum* with 34; *lawrenceanum* with 36 and occasionally 40; and *venustum* with 42.

The greatest number of older modern hybrids have come from the species *insigne, villosum, villosum* var. *boxallii*, and *spicerianum*, with *bellatulum* also entering into the line. Although *spicerianum* has 30 chromosomes, 4 more than those with 26, these species are quite compatible.

Aneuploidy naturally has resulted among the hybrids. Many polyploids also have appeared, having arisen from nonreduced gametes or by a doubling of the chromosome number in some other way during the process of seed formation (see Chapter 7). R. E. Duncan reported the following ranges of chromosome numbers among hybrids: diploid and near-diploid, 26, 27, 28, 29, and 30; triploid and near-triploid, 39, 40, 41, and 42; tetraploid and near-tetraploid, 52, 53, 54, 55, and 56; and one near-pentaploid with 70. The usual reduction of fertility that accompanies polyploidy, and which is further reduced by aneuploidy, is, in the case of the paphiopedilums, additionally reduced by low pollen fertility. Often pollen grains that appear to be normal fail to make tubes and thus cannot function. When we say, therefore, that hybrids from this group of species are fairly fertile, we mean that they are fertile by comparison with the far less fertile hybrids from other groups of species.

Analysis of the chromosome types (shape, size, etc.,) of the various species has enabled cytogeneticists to follow the behavior of these chromosomes in relation to each other when sets from different species are present in the hybrids and to see what happens to them during reduction division. Failure to pair, is of course, the chief reason for the production of many nonfunctional reproductive cells. However, it was found that in the primary hybrids among *insigne, villosum,* and *spicerianum,* the assortment of chromosomes frequently resulted in distribution of a basic set to the reproductive cells, which then could be functional. Chromosome counts on the progeny from these primary hybrids revealed that reproductive cells with thirteen and fourteen chromosomes had indeed functioned. Such analyses were made upon *P.* Leeanum *(insigne × spicerianum)* and *P.* Lathamianum *(villosum × spicerianum),* primary hybrids that were the start of the modern hybrids, and which appear many times in the breeding lines. The contribution of the extra chromosome by gametes bearing fourteen allows succeeding generations to build up their chromosome number by adding an extra chromosome here and there, accounting for the aneuploid numbers found among the hybrids. When nonreduced gametes function, these may also carry an extra chromosome or two to the polyploid offspring.

As is true in all species, there is a great amount of variation in color and form to be found among the members of the *Paphiopedilum* species. For instance, in a species that has characteristic spotting, there are forms that are heavily spotted, and forms that are spotted only lightly, and some not at all. In species that have characteristic red or purple coloring there are rare forms without the red or purple coloring; these are green, yellow, or pure white. Unfortunately, these are all called "albino," and in reading about these forms one must know whether reference is had to "green albinos" or "white albinos." A new term is badly needed here.

Inheritance of color in *Paphiopedilum* is not clearly worked out, but it is a very difficult field. C. C. Hurst, who worked out the white inheritance in *Cattleya* (see Chapter 7) found that the green and white types in *Paphiopedilum* both seem to follow a pattern similar to that of the white cattleyas. Apparently the red and purple pigments depend on the presence of the dominant C and R genes, and pure green or white can show up only when either or both pairs of these genes is recessive. Included in this group of so-called albinos is the yellow *P. insigne* 'Sanderae', which seems to behave similarly.

Certain features of the species, the color patterns in dorsal sepal and petals, the shape of the parts, etc., are perhaps incompletely dominant. Traces of a feature, from this species or that, are found in hybrid individuals, often combined with, or superimposed upon, other features. Such fine blendings occur in some of the modern hybrids that it would be difficult to say which feature came from which species. However, these features show up more strongly in some individuals in any cross, and in almost any group of *Paphiopedilum* hybrids one can at a glance pick out flowers that strongly exhibit the characteristics of one ancestor or another.

PHRAGMIPEDIUM AND SELENIPEDIUM

Phragmipedium, one of the South American genera of the Cypripedioideae subfamily, has about eleven species. It differs from *Paphiopedilum* in that the dorsal sepal is more or less like the petals, and the edges of the lip are infolded, giving it a more slipperlike appearance. It has smooth, rather leathery leaves, and can thus be distinguished from *Selenipedium,* the other South American genus, which has plicate (pleated) leaves. They may be grown with plenty of moisture from March to November, shaded from the direct rays of the sun. Osmunda fiber is a good medium, as is a mixture of fine bark and perlite. After potting, keep on the dry side until growth starts, and then water frequently and copiously.

PHRAGMIPEDIUM

P. caricinum. Three elegant little species form a group of similar types whose slight differences are very subtle. They are *P. caricinum, P. ecuadorense,* and *P. pearcei.* To distinguish them in words is difficult and reference is best made to a splendid article by Leslie A. Garay, in *The Orchid Digest,* July-August 1979, illustrated by helpful photographs and drawings. *P. caricinum* has stiff, grassy, foot-long leaves springing in tufts from a straggly rhizome. The several delicate three- to six-inch flowers appear successively on a two-foot stem and are green, faintly striped with rose and brown. The dorsal sepal is a tapering triangle, the narrow ribbonlike hairy petals are drooping and twisted, while the pouch is slender and egg shaped, with its basal lobes infolded and heavily blotched with brown. The staminode is broadly wedge shaped, with fine hairs along the upper edge. It is cool growing, native to Bolivia and Peru, and it flowers in the spring.

P. caudatum. This large species has rather stiff, upright leaves, and flower stems one to two feet tall. It is remarkable for its long, ribbonlike petals, which grow to a length of three feet. The petals are yellow shaded with brown and tinted with crimson toward the tips. The dorsal sepal is slender and wavy, about six inches long, pale yellow veined with green. The species occurs from Mexico to Peru and flowers spring and summer (Fig. 15–9).

P. ecuadorense is a delightful relative of *P. caricinum,* tending more to green and lavender in color, with less fully twisted petals, a rounder pouch, and a bit wavier dorsal sepal. The staminode is completely heart shaped and has a heavier fringe of dark hairs along the top edge. It comes from Ecuador and Peru and flowers in the spring.

P. pearcei. This is a third member of the *caricinum* group, a bit more dainty than the others. It has a smaller staminode that is wider in proportion to its height, and its edge is densely covered with thick hairs. Flower color tends toward green and dark brown in some forms, rose and brown in others. The degree of waviness along the petal edges

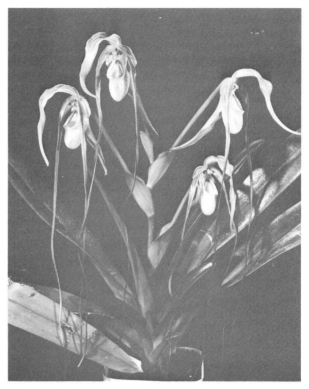

Figure 15–9 Phragmipedium caudatum *var.* wallisii. (COURTESY OF J. A. FOWLIE.)

also varies from quite dense to less so. The infolded parts of the lip are spotted with green. From Ecuador and Peru, it flowers in the fall.

P. sargentianum. The leaves are tufted, six to eight inches long, with golden margins. The flower stem bears two or three blooms. The oval dorsal sepal is pale yellow with red veins. The petals are slightly longer, twisted at the ends, yellow, with red margins and veins. The lip is rather long, also yellow marked with red. The plant occurs in Brazil.

P. schlimii. The narrow, foot-long leaves are bright grass-green above, purple underneath. The tall flower stem holds five to eight blooms which are about two inches in diameter and are covered with a velvety down. The flower parts are oval, rather short, and widespreading. The dorsal sepal is greenish white tinged with pink, the fused laterals white, veined with green. The petals are white, spotted and stained with rose near the base. The lip is globe shaped, rose, with the infolded lobes striped rose and white. It is native to Colombia (Fig. 15–10).

Figure 15–10 Phragmipedium schlimii. (Courtesy of J. A. Fowlie.)

SELENIPEDIUM

This is the other South American relative of *Cypripedium,* a very rare genus of tall, almost bamboolike plants not amenable to greenhouse culture. The reedlike stems bear large, plicate leaves, prominently veined, and at the tips clusters of rather small flowers. *S. chica* reaches more than twice the height of a man.

CYPRIPEDIUM

These are the moccasin flowers or ladyslippers of temperate zone woods and moist meadows. They may be transplanted to our gardens if the new locality is made to imitate their native spot. There are about thirty species. Like the other members of the subfamily, these are becoming less numerous with the passing years. Man probably has something to do with this, by using for himself the sunny areas where the plants would do best, so that they are forced to exist in the woods. They are sun-loving plants and do not grow so well in heavy shade. Lovers of these plants ask that instead of removing the wild clumps to your garden, plants be purchased from nurseries. The latter may even do better for you, for they will have been adapted to garden conditions.

These native cypripediums require plenty of moisture. A dam around their bed will help to retain water. They do best with some shade at noon.

C. acaule. Pink moccasin flower. The lovely single flower grows on a rather tall stem. The color is usually pale pink with deeper veining, but deep pink with light veins and pure white are also found. The lip is closed except for a slit in front. This species requires an acid soil and is the most difficult to grow. Often it lasts for a year or two and then dies out. It should be aided by the addition to the soil of such acid material as pine needles. It grows naturally from Newfoundland to North Carolina, and west to the Great Lakes region. The blossoms appear in May and June.

C. calceolus. The beautiful yellow ladyslipper is one of the most handsome and the easiest to grow. The whole flower is bright yellow, with narrow, somewhat wavy petals and a wider dorsal sepal. In culture it requires a porous, neutral soil, with plenty of moisture and some shade. It can be found throughout the United States, Canada, Europe, and Asia. The variety *pubescens* whose dorsal sepal and petals are brown is common to our western states. The variety *parviflorum,* common to the eastern states, is a real miniature, its flower only one and one-half inches long. The pouch is yellow spotted inside with crimson. The dorsal sepal and twisted petals are deep red-brown or wine color. They flower from April to August.

C. californicum. Tall plants produce leaves alternately on the stem. From six to twelve flowers occur on the upper part of the stem. They are small, with green sepals and petals and a white lip. The species is native to California and Oregon, and flowers from May to July.

C. candidum. The green flowers have a pretty lip that is white, striped inside with purple. The plant is found in the eastern and midwestern states.

C. montanum. This handsome, fragrant species grows rather tall. One to three flowers are produced on a stem. The petals are wavy, twisted, and dull brown, and the lip is whitish, veined with purple. It is found in western North America, and flowers from May to July.

C. reginae, or *spectabile,* is truly named the "Queen" ladyslipper. It is tall and robust and produces a wealth of large flowers. The white sepals and petals are set off by the rosy shades of the lip. It requires a sunny spot in the garden and moist, neutral soil. The species occurs from eastern Canada through our northern and midwestern states, and also occurs in western China. It flowers in early summer.

·16·

DENDROBIUM RELATIVES

The Dendrobiinae Subtribe

THE DENDROBIINAE INCLUDE six genera, of which we shall discuss the better-known four, one of them the marvelous genus *Dendrobium*. The name is derived from *dendro,* tree, and *bios,* life.

DENDROBIUM

Dendrobiums, which have been loved by amateurs for a hundred years, are enjoying perhaps their greatest degree of popularity right now. From their native lands, where they have always been appreciated, they were brought first to Europe, and more recently to Hawaii and to the mainland states. We are now benefiting from the loving care and interest bestowed upon them by the growers who have made them a specialty and who have not only nurtured the species but have created a fascinating succession of hybrids. The Hawaiian growers, especially in recent years, have done intriguing things with the dendrobiums, as they have with the vandas and their relatives.

The very size of the genus *Dendrobium,* with over 1,000 species, promises variety, both in size and character of the plants and of the flowers and the manner in which they are produced. There are species that give erect or arching sprays of five to twenty flowers, species that give drooping sprays of a dozen to a hundred blooms, and still others in which almost the entire length of the pseudobulb bears clusters of flowers at each node. Many have unique and appealing characteristics. The individual flowers are often small, but all are perky or dainty, often of a glistening crystalline texture or velvety softness. The colors are rich, ranging from rose and violet tones, occasionally almost to red, to the most brilliant yellow and gold. Some species are white.

The plants range in size from miniatures with little wiry or squat pseudobulbs to a large group of robust species with pseudobulbs from a foot to three feet in height, and on up to kinds that have stems six to eight feet long. Among these are some whose stems bear three to five leaves at the top nodes only, and others whose stems are leafy for almost their entire length. There are deciduous species that lose their leaves the first or second year, and evergreen species that keep their leaves for three or four years. Except for a few in which the stems are truly pesudobulbous, most of them have rather slender, jointed stems that resemble canes. All are epiphytic and all make new growths each year from a rhizome. The growths come close together so that a plant with many stems springs from a rather small basal area.

The flowers are characterized by a "chin" or mentum formed by the joining of the lateral sepals to the foot of the column. In some the base of the fused sepals forms a short spur covering the mentum. The dorsal sepal and the petals are free. The lip narrows at its base to a stalk attached to the base of the column foot. The side lobes of the lip usually enfold the short column, while the outer lobe is spreading, pointed or rounded, sometimes fringed. The flowers last for two to three weeks.

The genus is found in western Asia and the Pacific islands, from the Himalayas through Burma to the Malayan regions, Australia, New Zealand, New Guinea, China, Japan, the Philippines and Fiji. The variety of climatic conditions gives a variety of plant habits, and their cultural needs vary accordingly. Some grow where there is a warm season accompanied by heavy rains, followed by a season of cooler temperatures and little rain. Some come from regions that stay the same temperature all year, but where the rainfall is less heavy for part of the year. In some areas the rainfall stays about the same but the temperature cools off for part of the year. In other areas there is little change from "winter" to "summer." Because of such diversity of native habitat, the species have to be given somewhat individual treatment in a greenhouse. The reputation the dendrobiums have earned, of being somewhat tricky to flower, is perhaps justified, because they need to have everything just right for them. However, the reason one may not flower may be simply that it wants less water after its growths are mature, while another would flower if it were put in a cooler place in the fall.

We shall try to group the species according to sets of conditions that seem most generally suitable. All dendrobiums like good light, some requiring about the same amount as cattleyas, others even more. All thrive with good air circulation. If, from among the groups as we shall list them, some species do not flower for you, try changing the conditions a bit. Move them to a brighter spot, or to one that runs a bit warmer or cooler than the rest of the greenhouse. You can judge the right amount of light by watching the development of the stems and leaves. If they are weak and thin, put the plant in a brighter spot and watch it plump up and spread its leaves during the next few weeks. After the growth is mature, some species need what is loosely spoken of as a "rest," a time during which its active growth is checked to harden the new growth and prepare the plant for flower production. This involves for some a combination of cooler temperatures and less water, for others merely cooler temperatures without a reduction of water, and for still others merely reduction of water while the temperature remains the same.

GROUP 1. Grow plants in this group with cattleya temperatures, move to cool temperature and restrict watering after growths mature: *D. nobile, chrysanthum,* and *wardianum.* These are deciduous species. *D. nobile* does not lose its leaves until the second year, and it is these growths that produce flowers the second winter. *D. chrysanthum* and *D. wardianum* lose their leaves the first winter, before or during flowering. All three should be watered and fertilized generously while growing, have good light (*nobile* may not need quite as much as the other two), and temperatures 55° to 60° at night. In the fall, move them to a cool, bright greenhouse with a night temperature of 50° (as for cymbidiums). Cut down the frequency of watering, giving just enough to keep plants from shrivelling, and cease fertilizing through the winter. After flower buds are well formed, resume normal watering until flowering is finished, and then keep on the dry side until new growths are well started. At this time move back to cattleya temperatures and resume regular watering and fertilizing. If these species are not given "cool-dry" treatment in the fall, vegetative growths will form where flower buds should appear. These vegetative growths may be removed and potted separately when they start their own roots. Hybrids between *nobile* and species of Groups 1 and 2 require the "cool-dry" treatment also.

GROUP 2. Grow with cattleyas all year 'round, but keep on the dry side after growths are made up in the fall: *D. anosmum, findlayanum, heterocarpum, parishii,* and *pierardii.* These also are deciduous species. They require a night temperature of 55° to 60° all year 'round. While the growth is developing and until it is mature, water generously and give ample fertilizer, plenty of light, and good air movement. In the fall, as the last leaf appears, restrict the watering (no fertilizer) to just enough to keep the plants from shrivelling, until flower buds have formed. Then water moderately through flowering and until the new growth (which sometimes starts at flowering time) is well along. After the new growth sends out its own roots, resume more-generous watering and start fertilizing again. If *findlayanum* does not flower for you after the first attempt, try keeping it closer to 55° the next winter. If *D. anosmum* does not flower, try it in a spot where the temperature does not go below 60° during the winter. *D. aggregatum* is treated like this group although it is not deciduous.

GROUP 3. Grow at cattleya temperatures, move to cool greenhouse for the winter, but do not restrict watering: *D. chrysotoxum, densiflorum, farmeri, fimbriatum, moschatum,* and *thyrsiflorum.* These are evergreen and should not be allowed to dry out at any time of the year. From the time growth starts and until it is mature in the fall, keep them with cattleyas, with the usual good light, water frequently enough to keep the medium moist, and fertilize as for other species. *D. moschatum* may like just a little shade in a bright cattleya house, while the others may be able to take even more light than cattleyas. Syringe the foliage frequently to control red spiders (and spray with a miticide as well) for they find these plants very attractive. In the fall, move to a place where they can be given nights of 50° but continue to water often enough to prevent drying. After flowering and until new growth starts, the plants should be kept cool. After new growth starts, move them back to the cattleya temperature range.

GROUP 4. Grow moderately cool, with winter nights close to 55°, not over 60°, summer nights close to 60° and summer days not extremely hot. Handle like cattleyas as to water and light except give a short dry period after growth is made up: *D. dearei, formosum, lyonii, infundibulum, sanderae, schuetzei.* These are evergreen species. They grow well with cattleyas where cattleyas are grown under moderately cool circumstances, but may not do well in the warmest parts of the United States unless the grower has means for keeping down the temperature.

GROUP 5. While this group does not like excessive heat and humidity, it prefers a little more heat than Group 4. Thus this group can be grown with cattleyas almost anywhere, in a spot where the night temperature runs closer to 60°. If possible give them a bit more light than cattleyas, with free air movement: *D. gouldii, stratiotes, taurinum, undulatum, veratrifolium.* These are evergreen species. Some growers grow all of them without a rest period. Others give a short period of lessened water to *D. taurinum, undulatum,* and *veratrifolium* as growth matures. If any of these species seems not to be growing as vigorously as it should, or if the buds drop after they are well formed, put the plant in a spot where the night temperature does not go below 60°. The cultural conditions given here are suitable for hybrids between this group and *D. phalaenopsis, biggibum,* and *superbiens,* described below.

GROUP 6. Grow with night temperatures that run between 60° and 65°: *D. biggibum,* and *superbiens.* These are evergreen species (Fig. 16–1).

Figure 16–1 *UPPER:* Dendrobium Millie Sander (dearei X formosum) *is an example of the* dearei *type of hybrid. Note the long spur.* (COURTESY OF WM. KIRCH.) *LOWER:* Dendrobium bigibbum, *a cross between selected strains.*

Some growers feel that *D. superbiens* requires restricted watering after growth is made up and until the flower spikes start. They do require normal watering during flowering, and restricted watering from then until new growth is well along. New growth sometimes does not start until late summer. During the time of restricted watering, syringe the foliage frequently to keep the plant plump. *D. biggibum* does not require a drying-off period, or at best it needs only a very brief one. These species are frequently used in hybridization with those of Group 5. The hybrids in which *D. bigibbum* varieties figure are often referred to as dendrobium phalaenopsis hybrids. A curious thing about these hybrids is that some of them are much more tolerant of shade than the species and will do well under conditions suitable for phalaenopsis, that is, with about half the amount of light required by cattleyas. Plants have performed nicely for me in an orchid case in the living room, although they have not reached the large size they can achieve in a greenhouse. Note: A few delightful small-to-miniature species, not included in these groups, are described in other sections.)

General Culture

POTTING AND DIVIDING. Dendrobiums may be grown in osmunda, a good medium because it gives their fine, wiry roots a firm foothold and tends to hold the sometimes top-heavy plants in place very well. They may also be grown in bark if they are carefully staked. Some growers like to plant them on tree fern logs or slabs, from which they do not have to be removed for a number of years. Some of the deciduous species develop very long stems which cannot hold themselves upright and which therefore grow in a pendent manner. These are best grown in baskets of osmunda or tree fern fiber on tree fern logs, or on cork slabs, hung from the top of the greenhouse to give the stems room and light. A few, such as *D. chrysanthum*, which would drag the tips of its stems on the floor of the average small greenhouse, may be tied along one side of the greenhouse with a loop of string about every two feet of their length.

Dendrobiums may be divided like other sympodial plants. It is best to wait until the new growths have started. Repotting and dividing should be done just as new roots show or just before they make their appearance. They should be divided to retain three or four older stems along with the new lead. In some kinds the old stems flower for several successive years.

Small plantlets that develop along the older stems of both evergreen and deciduous species may be separated from the stem as soon as their roots start. When put in their own pots, these grow rapidly, sometimes flowering the first year. Old stems, after flowering, may be cut into sections between the nodes and placed on damp sphagnum moss (or a fine bark and sand mix) in order to encourage plantlets to develop (Fig. 16–2).

In general, dendrobiums do not need as large pots for their size as do many kinds. Their roots are fine and wiry, and they do not grow to any

Figure 16–2 *A young plant growing on the pseudobulb that produced the season's flowers. The plantlet may be removed and potted.*

great length. A four- or five-inch pot should accommodate a plant with four or five leads.

Water abundantly while growing. However, new growth on cane types is touchy and may rot if kept wet. Withhold water from the time it starts until new roots develop. In the meantime spray the foliage and the surface of the potting medium, using a fine mist.

DENDROBIUMS FROM SEED. Dendrobium seed germinates readily and the seedlings grow rapidly. The largest numbers of hybrids come from *nobile* and its relatives (Group 1 and 2), and *phalaenopsis* and its relatives with the ceratobium section, Groups 5 and 6. Another group of hybrids stems from intercrossing *dearei, formosum, infundibulum, sanderae,* and *schuetzii.* We should like to point out that the "cultural" groups as we set them up are not meant to follow the lines of botanical relationships, although for the most part they coincidentally do. The genus is divided botanically into sections and subsections too numerous to give here. Hybrids in general have been made within the botanical groups. In other words, it has been found that species that are structurally related breed together more readily than species from groups less alike. However, there are instances where crosses have been successfully made between species in different botanical sections and subsections. For example, *anosmum* has been crossed with several members of the group to which *phalaenopsis* belongs; *dearei* has been crossed with *farmeri*, from a different section.

The Species

D. aggregatum (syn. *lindleyi*). This charming dwarf species has little, chunky, four-jointed pseudobulbs bearing a single leaf. The flowers are very round, opening full and flat, with a squarish lip that is downy in the center. They are a delicate orange-yellow to pinkish-yellow, from ten to thirty on a drooping, rounded spray. The plants occur in northern India, Burma, and southern China. They flower in the spring.

D. anosmum. Richly colored, the three-inch flowers are of deep magenta with the heart-shaped lip shading into purple at its base. They are produced in pairs from the upper nodes of the three-foot stems. It is native to the warm regions in the Philippines. The flowers appear in the spring.

D. bigibbum has involved orchidologists in a sort of detective mystery. The problem was to determine exactly what constituted the species itself since it had so many well-known varieties, and just where these look-alikes fitted in. Finally, Australian scientists have reached a consensus. It's a bit complicated but it is good to record the decisions for the future.

D. bigibbum the type is called *D. bigibbum* var. *bigibbum*. It comes from the northern half of the Cape York Peninsula in Queensland, Australia. The neat, mauve flowers are one and three-fourth inches across, with reflexed petals. The lip has a crest that bears white hairs or calli, and often has a notch on the outer edge. It flowers in the fall.

var. *superbum* is actually what we have been calling *D. phalaenopsis* and is nicknamed the "Cooktown orchid" because Cooktown is in the area in which it occurs. var. *superbum* (the old *D. phalaenopsis*) is more familiar than var. *bigibbum*, having larger, flatter flowers without the white calli or hairs on the crest and no notch on the outer lip. It flowers from summer to winter (Fig. 16–3).

var. *compactum*. This is what has been known as *D. phalaenopsis* var. *compactum*. It is a dwarf plant, thick-stemmed, up to nine inches tall, with

fewer flowers. It is used in hybridization because it transmits its shortness to its offspring. It comes from the extreme southeastern part of the Cape York Peninsula and grows on rock faces. It flowers from late summer to winter.

Subspecies *laratensis* comes from outside of the continent of Australia, from the Tanimbar Islands off the northwest coast, 500 miles away from Australian relatives. It is the correct name for *D. schroederianum* and *D. phalaenopsis* var. *schroederianum*. It is called a subspecies rather than a variety because it has greater differences: narrower petals, more-pronounced, farther-apart lip veins, a more-robust habit, and a greater range of coloring. It flowers in late fall.

Hybrids in this group have been made by crossing varieties, and then crossing selected types among their offspring, creating a tremendous group of what we call "Dendrobium Phalaenopsis" hybrids. The term is not accurate for many reasons, but will probably continue in the trade. The range of colors, shapes and sizes is remarkable. The spread of their flowering season throughout the year reflects their mixed parentage. Other species have been introduced as well, to give more variety. All in all, they are among the most beautiful of orchids and the most satisfying to grow.

D. canaliculatum. This is a delightful small species whose stems are two to six inches tall. Its leaves are nearly terete, channeled on the upper surface, two to eight inches long. The inflorescence is upright, up to eighteen inches tall, and bears a wealth of dainty, feathery flowers. They are about two inches across, pale yellow-green with a purple edge to the lip. The sepals are narrow, the lateral ones spread sideways, and the petals are even narrower, a bit longer, and slightly twisted. It occurs in eastern Australia and Papua New Guinea and flowers in the spring.

D. chrysanthum. Golden-yellow flowers are produced in clusters of six or so from the nodes toward the end of a very long (six to eight feet) stem. The flowers are waxy, with two maroon spots on the lip. As the stems elongate, the lower leaves begin to fall, until finally all the leaves are shed at the time of flowering. This native of Nepal and Burma flowers from late fall to winter.

D. chrysotoxum. The ribbed, cylindrical or spindle-shaped stems are about fifteen inches tall and bear six or eight leaves. The golden-yellow flowers are borne in many-flowered erect or drooping sprays from the upper nodes of the stem. They are two inches in diameter and have a round,

Figure 16–3 Dendrobium bigibbum *var.* superbum *(was* D. Phalaenopsis) *flowers from both old and new growths, giving an array of flowers in rich, soft hues.*

Shown here is the selected strain 'Delicata'. (COURTESY OF JONES AND SCULLY, INC.)

fringed lip that has a deep orange-yellow spot and red lines in the throat. The species occurs from south China, the Himalayas, and Burma to Thailand and Laos.

D. cucumerinum. Nicknamed the "cucumber" or "gherkin" orchid because the fat one-inch leaves are covered with little tubercles, it grows from a branching, creeping stem. The tiny, greenish white flowers have a very ruffly lip marked with wine red. They are produced in short sprays, and are said to have a foetid odor. Flowering time is spring. The species is native to Australia.

D. dearei. Two-inch, pure-white flowers with a greenish throat are borne on sprays that come from the upper nodes of the stems. Each spray has seven to fifteen blooms. The flowers are characterized by a rather long spur and very round, flaring petals. The leafy stems grow from one foot to three feet tall. This species forms the starting point for a long line of white "dearei type" hybrids. It is native to the Philippines. The blossoms appear in the summer.

D. densiflorum. This species makes a stunning display with its drooping balloon- or lantern-shaped sprays of sunny yellow flowers, fifty to a hundred completely encircling the stem. The flowers are about an inch and a half across (sometimes a bit larger), golden yellow with an orange lip, of a sparkling crystalline texture, and with a finely toothed edge to the petals and lip. The lip, moreover, is covered with a deep-piled golden down. The plants are sturdy, with stems about fifteen inches tall, somewhat four-angled and a bit knobby at the nodes. The leaves are satiny, rather thick, becoming leathery with age. The plant is native to Nepal and Assam and it flowers in the spring.

D. falcorostrum. In its native New South Wales this is called the "beech orchid" because it prefers the giant beech trees of the rain forests. It is a cane type with a cluster of twenty or more two-inch flowers rising from its top. They are fragrant, waxy, and have a beautifully open, symmetrical shape. It grows best on a log or tree fern slab with intermediate temperatures.

D. farmeri. Similar to *chrysotoxum* but paler in color, this plant has stems that are four-angled and bear two to four leaves. The rounded flowers are about two inches across and have a downy lip. They are borne on loose sprays that droop from an upper node. The species occurs in Sikkim, Nepal, and Burma. It flowers in the spring and summer.

D. fimbriatum. Best known for its variety *oculatum,* this species is one of the most striking of the "drooping spray, yellow-flowered" types. The sprays are a little smaller than they are in *densiflorum,* carrying about a dozen to twenty flowers. The golden flowers are round, with a round, fringed lip that has a deep maroon spot or "eye" in its central portion. The crystalline texture makes them actually sparkle. The stems are about two feet tall, with closely spaced fairly thin leaves clothing almost their entire length. *D. fimbriatum* itself (not var. *oculatum*) is a taller plant whose flowers have an orange eye instead of the maroon spot. It occurs in Nepal and Burma. The flowers come from two- and three-year-old stems in late spring.

D. findlayanum. This is an odd-looking species whose stems consist of much-swollen nodes separated by constricted internodes. Daintily colored flowers are produced in pairs in the late summer from nodes near the very end of the stems. The petals and sepals are white, tinted with lilac, and the heart-shaped lip is white tipped with pink, yellow in the center. The species is a native to Burma.

D. formosum. One of the finest of the white dendrobiums, this species has flowers three to four inches across and a variety *giganteum* that has five-inch flowers. The long-lasting flowers, which appear in the fall, are deceptively delicate looking, pure white except for a yellow spot on the lip. They are produced in clusters of three to five from the upper nodes of rather stout, hairy pseudobulbs. The species occurs in Burma.

D. gouldii. These flowers, whose petals are slender and twisted, flaring upward like a pair of horns, are called "ceratobium" or, affectionately, the "antelope" orchids. A wealth of yellow blooms are borne on erect sprays from the upper nodes of three-foot leafy stems. The species occurs in New Guinea and flowers in the fall (Fig. 16–4).

D. heterocarpum. This is the correct name for the species also known as *aureum.* Fragrant, creamy-yellow flowers, whose brighter lip narrows to a pointed tongue and is streaked with purple, are borne in twins and triplets from the nodes of the previous year's growths (sometimes also from three-year-old growths). The flowers, which are about two inches across, appear in late winter.

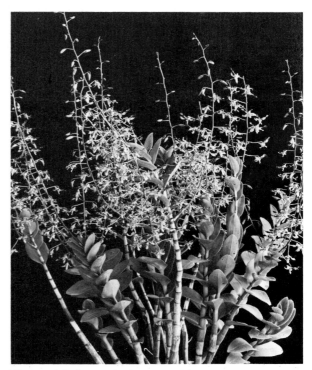

Figure 16–4 Dendrobium gouldei. *Vigor and generosity in flowering characterize this member of the ceratobium or "antelope-horn" group of species.* (Courtesy of Wm. Kirch.)

Stems are erect, yellow, and grow about eighteen inches tall. The species grows natively from the Himalayas to the Philippines.

D. infundibulum. The three-inch white flowers of this species have lip markings varying from red to yellow, quite similar to *D. formosum.* The plant occurs in Burma and flowers variably.

D. jenkinsii. This, once considered a variety of *D. aggregatum (lindleyi)* is now held to be a distinct species. It is a lovely miniature that spreads over a mount. Its one-and-one-half inch pseudobulbs are tapered, three jointed, and bear a single, hard, oval leaf. Flowers come in clusters of two or three. They are bright yellow, one inch across, and have a rounded, kidney-shaped, slightly fuzzy lip. The other flower parts are well hidden behind the lip. From Burma, it flowers in the spring.

D. kingianum. This is one of Australia's best-loved natives. It has slender, straight stems, slightly enlarged at the base, six to nine inches tall, which bear several leathery leaves on the upper part. The sweetly scented flowers are waxy, about one inch wide, borne on somewhat nodding stems four to eight inches long. The color range is marvelous—from white to pink, rose, and rich purple, and the lip is often spotted. It flowers in the spring and prefers cool temperatures.

D. lawesii is a most satisfactory plant. Its six- to fifteen-inch canes are fully leafy for the first year but lose their leaves during the second. They flower from the tip the first year, and thereafter from any and all nodes on the naked stem, continuing to produce buds for as long as ten years. The flowers last for several months. They are tubular, bright red or red-orange, with a long, wide spur or nectary, and rounded, out-turned tips to the sepals and petals. There is a veil or curtain formed by the tip of the lip which turns up, almost closing the opening of the lip. The flowers are about one and one-quarter inch long, in clusters of three to ten. From Papua New Guinea, flowers appear at almost any time of the year chiefly in late spring. They are bird-pollinated. The plant likes to be kept damp at the roots, and does well in osmunda fiber.

D. linguiforme. This is called the "tongue orchid" because of its tongue-shaped leaves, which are quite like those of *cucumerinum* without the tubercles, having instead a smooth skin and a few parallel depressed lines along the surface. The feathery flower spray is about six inches long and holds thirty or more little creamy or white flowers. It is a native of Australia, where it inhabits many different climatic areas, including those with a definite dry season, and benefits from restricted water after new leaves are formed. It is cool growing and flowers in the spring.

D. loddigesii. The slender, branching, creeping stems of this miniature species have something of the habit of a *Dichaea* plant. Tiny leaves clothe the stems and are deciduous eventually at which time the plant needs a dry rest. Aerial roots appear where the stem branches. The beautiful, delicately fragrant one-inch flowers come singly along the stem. They have slender rosy-lavender sepals and petals and a round, fringed lip which has an orange center surrounded by white and a lavender border (Fig. 16–5). Native to Hainan Island, it grows with cattleyas, and flowers in mid-winter.*

D. macrophyllum. As the name suggests, this species has unusually large leaves, borne at the top nodes of two-foot ridged stems. The sprays are erect and carry a dozen or fifteen attractive flowers. The oval, pointed sepals are hairy on the outside, pale yellow-green, and larger than the white petals. The large lip, its outer lobe long and recurved, is striped with purple. The species occurs in New Guinea and neighboring islands.

D. moorei. This is a dwarf plant with canes bearing a few slender leaves on the upper parts. The fragrant, half-inch flowers are white, marked with purple, and have slender sepals and petals and a round lip. Successive inflorescences come from the same stem, and appear several times a year, each bearing five to six blossoms. Native to Lord Howe Island, it grows with cattleya conditions.

Figure 16–5 Dendrobium loddigesii, *a lovely miniature, whose flowers are delicately fragrant and beautifully fringed.*

* For additional miniature dendrobiums, see *Miniature Orchids* by this author.

D. moschatum. These plants vary in size from those that reach three feet to some that grow to six feet tall. The lovely and unusual flowers are three inches across, with sepals and petals of pale yellow tipped with rose. The lip is slipper-shaped, downy, with five lines of fringe in the center, and is yellow except for two bright spots of maroon surrounded by orange. The flowers are produced in the winter, sometimes later, on sprays from the uppermost nodes of the previous year's growths. The plants are native to India and Burma.

D. nobile. This delightful species has over eighty named varieties. It was the most widely known of all dendrobiums, together with its hybrids, until the *phalaenopsis* hybrids came along to challenge but not replace them. The charming, brightly colored blossoms are produced in nodding groups of three or so from the nodes along the two-year-old stems. The flowers are three inches in diameter, with sepals and petals white tipped with rosy purple; the rounded lip is velvety, purple in the throat and bordered with white. The winter or spring flowers are long lasting and lend themselves, as do so many others, to dainty corsages. This species occurs at high elevations in India (Fig. 16–6).

D. parishii. Reminiscent of *nobile,* with its flowers borne at the nodes along the fifteen-inch stems,

these are amethyst-purple, with two maroon spots in the throat of the downy lip. The plants occur in Moulmein and flower in spring and summer.

D. pierardii (syn. *aphyllum*). Drooping stems that grow from three to five feet long produce an incredible wealth of flowers in pairs at the nodes. The blossoms are two inches in diameter, pale pink, with the yellow lip striped with purple. New growths appear in the early summer at about the same time as the flowers. The plant is native to India.

D. phalaenopsis. See *D. bigibbum* var. *superbum.*

D. sanderae. A very lovely species, similar in some ways to *dearei,* it has white, showy flowers, about three and one-half inches in diameter. The petals are broad and flaring, and the lip has a wide, spreading outer lobe. The throat is purple, with a few purple stripes extending from the center. There is a variety *parviflorum,* more generally seen in cultivation, which has the flowers a bit smaller but in which the throat is much darker. The flowers appear in the spring in clusters of six to twelve from the upper nodes of the two-foot stems. The species occurs in the mountains of northern Luzon.

D. schuetzii. Another of the *dearei* type, this is a smaller plant. The foot-tall stems are very slen-

Figure 16–6 LEFT: Dendrobium nobile, *flowering in midwinter close to the frosted glass of a cool house. Its velvety flowers come from the leafless canes of the pre-* vious years. RIGHT: Dendrobium fimbriatum *var.* oculatum *has bright yellow flowers set off by a deep-maroon center.* (COURTESY OF JACK SWEET.)

der at the base. The large white flowers appear in the fall and are borne in clusters of four or so. They last for many weeks. The plant is native to the Philippines.

D. sophronitis. A most delightful miniature, the plants have brilliant flowers larger than the plants themselves. The pseudobulbs are half an inch tall and the rough, dark green leaves are less than an inch long. The flowers are all shades of red and even range to orange, yellow and white. A native of cool, damp, high elevations of New Guinea, it flowers almost continually. Its flowers last several months.

D. speciosum is a cool-growing species that can be grown outdoors in climates with moderate summers and frost-free winters. It develops into a magnificent specimen, with stems that reach two feet in height and inflorescences up to two and one-half feet long, covered with fragrant, white flowers. The blossoms are a bit feathery looking, with slender sepals and petals and a wider lip marked with purple or red. It occurs in eastern Australia and flowers in the spring.

D. stratiotes. This is one of the attractive "antelope" dendrobiums. Both sepals and petals are twisted or wavy, the long petals standing up like a pair of horns. The sepals are creamy-white, the petals pale yellow-green. The lip is white, streaked with purple. It occurs in Indonesia and New Guinea and flowers in the fall.

D. superbiens. This is a natural hybrid between *D. discolor* and *D. bigibbum.* Its crimson-purple flowers have sepals and petals bordered with white. The broad lip is reflexed and wavy. The two-inch flowers are borne fifteen or more on arching-erect sprays from the top nodes of the three-foot stems. It occurs in Australia and flowers in late summer or fall.

D. taurinum. A strikingly colored member of the "antelope" group, the recurved sepals are pink, while the longer petals, which resemble the horns of a bull, are reddish-brown tinged with purple. The massive lip is rosy, marked with raised, reddish-brown lines, ruffled at its edge. The plant occurs in the Philippines and flowers in the fall. It needs more copious watering than other members of the group.

D. thyrsiflorum. Very close to *densiflorum,* and probably a variety of it, its flowers are identical in shape and size. They are borne in the same lantern-shaped spray and also have the sparkling, crystalline texture. The sepals and petals are white and the lip is deep orange. The plant occurs in Moul-mein, Burma, and Thailand, and flowers in the winter or spring.

D. undulatum. The flowers of this species are dull yellow, more or less spotted with purple, with extremely twisted sepals and petals. The lip is bright yellow dotted with purple and decorated with five white keels. This species and *taurinum* are about the same size, with three- to four-foot stems, and flower sprays two feet long. *D. undulatum* is native to Australia and New Guinea.

D. veratrifolium. A much larger plant than the other "antelope" species, this one has stems to five feet and flower sprays two and a one-half feet long bearing many more flowers. Its size and vigor are the characteristics it contributes to hybrids made with various of the other "antelope" species. Its flowers do not have the extreme twisting shown by some; in fact, the oar-shaped petals are not twisted at all but they do stand up tall between the sepals. The lip is broad and open. The flowers are variable in color, mostly white with the lip marked with branching veins of purple. The species occurs in New Guinea.

D. victoriae reginae. This is similar in habit to *D. lawesii* although with very different flowers. Its eighteen-inch canes lose their leaves and then continue to produce flowers for many years, the buds appearing from nodes near the top half of the stem. The blossoms are more or less star-shaped, with slender sepals that bend back at the tips, petals that stand forward, and an oval, pointed lip that juts forward. The flower parts are white for the basal half, bluish lavender at the outer end. As flowers age, the bluish color becomes more pink. From the Philippines, it is in flower most of the year.

D. wardianum. The flowers of this species are slightly larger than in *nobile.* They are waxy and white, with the sepals, petals, and lip all tipped with amethyst. The yellow throat is marked with two bright, clear-cut spots of purple. The three-foot stems are pendent and, in the spring, bear pairs of the three-inch flowers for almost their whole length. The plant occurs in Assam and Burma.

CADETIA

This is a genus of some 40 species, most of them miniatures and very delightful.

C. chamaephyton has inch-high, paddle-shaped

leaves and tiny, white, very fragrant flowers. From Papua New Guinea, it is cool-growing and is in bloom almost all year.

C. dischorensis is a little larger both in plant size and flowers. Its very wide lateral sepals and fiddle-shaped lip make it a fairly showy miniature. Also cool-growing and from Papua New Guinea, it is always in flower.

C. taylori is about four inches tall, with straight, fluted stems and oval leaves. The flowers have very slender, forward-bent petals that look like antennae and a fuzzy pink lip. It is from Australia and it also is in bloom all year.

EPIGENEIUM

About thirty-five species spread from China and India to the Philippines. Some of them have been included at one time or another in the genus *Dendrobium,* of which one is given herewith.

E. lyonii is a lovely species, with squat, four-angled pseudobulbs, a large, leathery leaf, and sprays of feathery flowers, blood-red on the inside. The blossoms are three inches across, star-shaped, with very slender sepals and petals, and a somewhat spade-shaped lip. It comes from the Philippines and flowers in spring or summer.

·17·

ONCIDIUM RELATIVES

The Oncidiinae Subtribe

A MONG THE NEARLY SIXTY genera in the Oncidiinae subtribe are found some of the most delightful orchids. So varied are they, so extraordinarily formed, that they readily conjure up visions of feathers and pixies, butterflies and pansies, filigree work and the classical ballet, sunbeams and frost crystals. As might be expected, where so many kinds are involved, numerous name changes have been made—sometimes back to original names, sometimes to new ones created for them. Members of the subtribe range from Mexico to Bolivia, and climb from the hot coastal regions to the cool, misty heights of the Andes. The species from lower elevations can be grown almost anywhere. Those from middle heights do well in a cattleya house, some in the cooler section. Those from highest altitudes, especially certain oncidiums and the "crispum" types of *Odontoglossum,* require a cool, damp climate such as is found in the San Francisco area and the Pacific Northwest, but can be accommodated where air conditioning alters the temperatures.

MILTONIOPSIS AND MILTONIA

The genus *Miltonia* has been divided between species from Colombia and Panama and those from Brazil and nearby countries. Not that the separation has been made on a geographical basis, but that the two groups differ taxonomically. We'll take up the "Colombian" ones first, *Miltoniopsis,* as they are probably more popular and at present more widely grown.

MILTONIOPSIS

These are the lovely pansy orchids, displaying fat, rounded flowers and a mask reminiscent of the face of a pansy. They are delicately fragrant, sweetly colored, and make beautiful show plants; unfortunately, they do not keep well when cut. Many wonderful hybrids with large flowers and marvelously rich colors have been and are being made.

These "Colombian" species were once thought to require quite cool conditions. It is now known that they can be grown at intermediate temperatures, with 60° nights, but they do not tolerate particularly hot days. Brisk air movement is a must and moderate humidity. They do well in fine bark, with perlite added if you wish, or in fine- to medium-grade tree fern, also with perlite. Do not let them dry out, but never let them become soggy at the roots. Some growers like to repot them every year, but others feel that plants should not be disturbed that often. If a plant is not doing well, it certainly should be repotted. Try always to repot just as new growth is starting.

Miltoniopsis endresii (syn. *warscewiczii*) was originally named *warscewiczii,* and should be changed to that. We give it here as "syn. *warscewiczii*" to avoid confusion. In the meantime a different species known as *Miltonia warscewiczii* has now been found to be actually *Oncidium fuscatum*. *Miltoniopsis endresii* (syn. *warscewiczii*) is a very lovely and dainty species, with a pale pink "bee" in the center of the flower. The flowers are about two inches across, sometimes larger, with broad sepals and petals and a much larger, rounded lip. They occur three to five to a stem and are delicately fragrant. The plant is small, with flattened pseudobulbs two inches tall and thin leaves eight to twelve inches long. It occurs in Costa Rica and Panama and flowers in late winter.

M. *phalaenopsis* is the ancestor of the beautiful "waterfall" or "teardrop" hybrids, which have a cascading series of pink or purple dots and bands marking the lip. This species has a less-round lip than the others, and it has rather definite side lobes. The sepals and petals are large in proportion to the lip, giving a somewhat rectangular-shaped flower, but the flower is small, barely two inches across. Flowers come on stems shorter than the foliage. The plant should be set so that the crown is level with or above the potting medium, and it should be kept well watered. It is susceptible to leaf spotting and needs an occasional application of fungicide. Keep it moderately cool with good light. It flowers in late summer and early fall.

M. *roezlii*. This lovely species is often found in the lineage of hybrids. The foliage is pale green and the pseudobulbs are tightly clustered. Two to four large, flat flowers are borne on each spike. The sepals and petals are white, the latter having a purple band at the base. The large lip is two-lobed, white with a tinge of purple. It becomes yellow at the base, where two little horns project backward on each side of the column. The species requires especially free ventilation, and plenty of moderated light. It occurs in Colombia and Panama and often flowers twice a year, winter and spring. The popular hybrid *Miltonia* Bleuana is a cross between M. *roezlii* and M. *vexillaria* (Figs. 17–1 and 17–2).

M. *santanaei* is a new species from Venezuela. It has a single, very slender, nine-inch leaf from its small, flat pseudobulb, and has smaller leaves from the side. The pretty, white, two-inch flowers have pointed sepals and petals and a somewhat triangular lip. The lip has a notch at the tip and a notch on either side. Its base has a yellow patch, fuzzy at the base, with short, bristly lines. It flowers in spring.

M. *schroederiana*. See with *Oncidium laeve*.

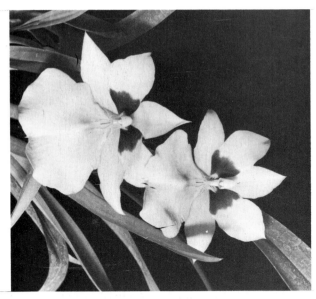

Figure 17–1 Miltoniopsis roezlii, *whose velvety texture and soft markings give it special appeal.*

M. *vexillaria*. This species has the largest flowers of the genus and is the most popular. It is also the most frequently used in hybridization. The plants are sturdy, easily grown, and generous in the numbers of blooms produced. The richly colored flowers are four inches or more in diameter, and occur two to seven on a spike. A single pseudobulb may give rise to several spikes. The small sepals and petals are bright rose in color, sometimes with a white margin. The huge lip is the striking feature of the flower and the character desired in its hybrids. It, too, is a rich shade of rose, shading to white at the base, and streaked with yellow and red. Two small horns project from the base of the lip on either side of the column. The plant has pale green foliage and flowers in spring and summer. It was native to Colombia but sadly is now extinct in nature. However, it is common in collections.

Miltonia warscewiczii. See *Oncidium fuscatum*.

MILTONIA

Only a few species remain in this genus, some having been transferred to *Oncidium*. The plants have a wandering rhizome and rather far-apart pseudobulbs, making them suitable for growing on a mount. They tolerate greater warmth than *Miltoniopsis* and the same amount of light as cattle-

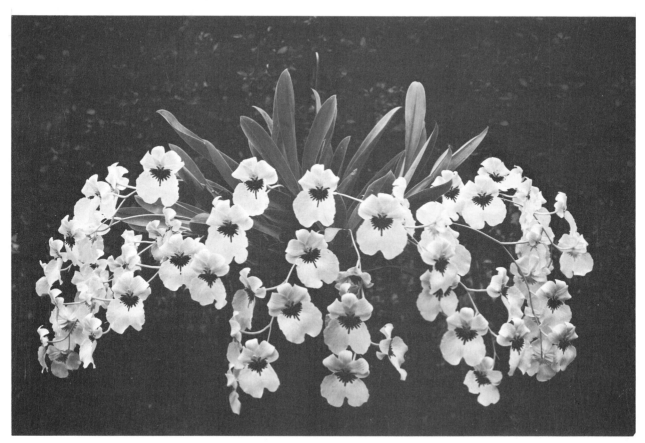

Figure 17–2 Miltoniopsis Charlesworthii, *a lovely hybrid that stems from the species* M. vexillaria *and* M. roezlii. *The butterfly marking in the center is typical of many* Miltonopsis *species and hybrids.* (COURTESY OF FREDERICK T. BONHAM.)

yas. Otherwise, water, fertilizer, and humidity should be regulated as for mounted plants in general.

M. candida. See *Oncidium candida.*

M. clowesii. See *Oncidium clowesii.*

M. cuneata. See *Oncidium speciosum.*

Miltonia flavescens. An interesting but less decorative species, this one has star-shaped flowers with narrow, dull yellow sepals and petals and a smaller, pointed, fiddle-shaped lip which is white with some purple streaks. It is native to Brazil and Paraguay and blooms in the summer.

M. regnellii. Three to five flat, subtly tinted flowers are borne on a short stem. The sepals and petals are white, suffused with rose toward the base. The heart-shaped lip is light rose, streaked with a deeper shade and having a white margin. The variety *purpurea* has darker coloring. The plant is native to Brazil and flowers in late summer and fall.

M. spectabilis. This was the first miltonia introduced into culture, and comes from Brazil. It is indeed a spectacle when in flower, for large, sturdy plants may bear as many as fifty flowers, each on a separate stem, and all opening at once. The flowers, which occur in the fall, are large, white or cream colored, with a large, wavy lip that is rose-purple veined with a darker shade. The pseudobulbs are an inch apart, and the foliage is yellow-green. It blooms in summer and fall. The variety *moreliana* is darker. Lovely hybrids have been made between *regnellii* and *spectabilis* and with other members of this subtribe.

Other species removed from *Miltonia* to *Oncidium* are: *kayasimae, russelliana,* and *velloziana.*

ODONTOGLOSSUM

Recent taxonomic events have removed many species from *Odontoglossum* to several smaller genera, all from the area extending from Mexico to Panama. In fact, with the approval of Leslie A.

Garay and others, Federico Halbinger has just published the most recent of these as *Lemboglossum*, making it the newest genus on the orchid scene. It seems now that true odontoglossums do not occur north of South America. Several characteristics differentiate the genera from the two areas: South American types have a channeled column and a lip without a claw; Mexican and Central American genera have a clawed lip, a column without a channel, and a boat or shield-shaped callus. It seems that the Greek *lembos*, after which the new genus was named, means, literally, "rowboat."

Species That Have Been Moved

To *Cuitlauzina: pendulum*.

To *Lemboglossum: apterum, bictoniense, candidulum, cervantesii, cordatum, ehrenbergii, galeottianum, hortensiae, maculatum, madrense, majale, rossii, stellatum*, and *uroskinneri*.

To *Mesoglossum: londesboroughianum*.

To *Oncidium: cariniferum, laeve, karwinskii, reichenheimii*, and *stenoglossum*.

To *Osmoglossum: anceps, convallarioides, egertoni*, and *pulchellum*.

To *Otoglossum: chiriquense*, which occurs in Costa Rica and Panama, while near relatives, *arminii, brevifolium*, and *coronarium* occur from Colombia and Venezuela south to Peru.

To *Rossioglossum: grande, insleayi, schlieperianum, splendens*, and *williamsianum*.

To *Ticoglossum: krameri* and *oerstedii*.

These and other taxonomic changes are used here to give the keen amateur up-to-date information. Not all of the new names will be recognized by the registrar of hybrids, so that in hybridization some old names must continue to be used.

South American Odontoglossums

These remarkably beautiful and decorative species are found at elevations from 5000 to 9000 feet and above. A few little-known ones are found at 12,000 feet. Those that live at the higher altitudes might require refrigeration if grown in the United States. The *crispum* group, from up to 9000 feet, should do well in our Pacific Northwest and in the San Francisco Bay area, where temperatures are cool and the air damp. From below that elevation, the species can be managed almost anywhere, with evaporative coolers for the more-sensitive ones.

All require abundant water and can be grown in bark or tree fern, possibly mixed with perlite. They like good light, some a little less than cattleyas, and do best with brisk air movement. Hybrids between the very cool- and the intermediate-growing ones are more tolerant of ordinary greenhouse temperatures.

O. cariniferum. See *Oncidium cariniferum*.

O. cirrhosum. A spray of these dainty flowers, white lightly spotted with rose, is sheer lace. Each part is slender and undulating, prolonged at its tip into a short tail. Even the outer lobe of the lip is but a pointed necktie hanging down. One of the most decorative parts is the basal section of the lip. Here the side lobes form a funnel under the column, bright yellow striped with red, flaring outward to form a portal to aid pollination by birds. Two prominent, upward curving projections are situated in the center. The plant is slender, with pseudobulbs to three inches tall and leaves a foot long. It is native to Ecuador and Colombia, flowers in late winter, and is cool-growing (Fig. 17–3).

O. confusum. See with *Oncidium laeve*.

O. crispum. Connoisseurs often call this species the most beautiful of all orchids. Its lacy two and one-half foot sprays are crowded with flowers, each two and one-half to three inches across. The sepals and petals are pointed, daintily ruffled, with their borders toothed or notched. They are white, sometimes tinged with rose, and may be spotted with crimson or brown. The flower is centered by a speckled lip that is fringed with teeth, and whose borders are even more finely notched than the petals. This species is extremely variable, and more than a hundred varieties have been named. It occurs in Colombia, at an elevation of 9,000 feet, and flowers at any time of the year. It is very cool-growing (Fig. 17–4).

O. harryanum. The variegated coloring of this species together with its striking shape make it the valued parent of many hybrids. Four or five three-inch flowers occur to a stem. The wavy sepals and petals are brown with irregular bands of yellow-green. The large, shield-shaped lip is flat and wavy, its lower half white, changing to yellow, and its basal part brown, veined with purple. Seven serrated crests decorate its base. This native of Colombia and Peru is cool-growing and flowers in the fall.

O. luteo-purpureum. This striking and varied species from Colombia produces flowers in horizontal sprays. The wavy, oblong sepals are brownish purple with a yellow margin. The petals are

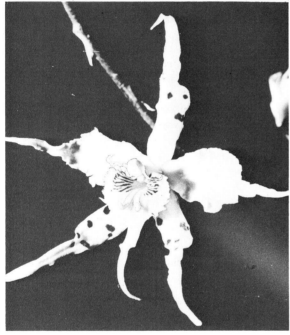

Figure 17–3 Odontoglossum cirrhosum, A: *A lacy flower, spray.* B: *A single flower.*

Figure 17–4 *A "crispum type" bigeneric hybrid,* Odontonia *Epha, which, through several generations, combines the species* Odontoglossum crispum *and O.* harryanum, *and* Miltoniopsis vexillaria *and* Miltoniopsis roezlii. *The flower is white with bright red markings.* (COURTESY OF GORDON M. HOYT.)

flowers of this species are quite eye-catching. They are borne on a slender stem, on which they open a few at a time over more than a year. The sepals and petals are similar, fairly broad, with pointed ends that curve forward. The lip, held out almost horizontally, is rather concave, with a sharp point at the tip and two fleshy protuberances at its base. It is one of the bird-pollinated species of the high elevations of Ecuador and is cool growing. Its flowering season is winter.

LEMBOGLOSSUM

Federico Halbinger has created a new genus named *Lemboglossum* for the species often called the stallata group, which he terms the O. *cervantesii* complex. The name refers to the boat-shaped callus. (*Lembos* means boat and *glossa* is Greek for tongue.) This is a beautiful and distinctive group, every one charming and dainty.

L. apterum (syn. *nebulosum*) has three to four rather fragile, white flowers, three inches across, papery looking, with a few brown spots at the base of the sepals and petals. The plant has two or three slender leaves six to twelve inches long from an oval, compressed pseudobulb. Widespread in Mexico, it flowers variously throughout the year.

L. bictoniense. This was the first of this genus to survive the voyage to England and has been

toothed, spotted with purple-brown. The deeply scalloped yellow lip is fringed and is spotted with purple or rose. The flowers appear in winter and spring.

O. odoratum. The flowers of this species are small, but produced in great numbers on branching sprays in winter and spring. They are golden yellow, marked with red-brown, and the wavy narrow lip is covered with down. It occurs in Colombia and Venezuela at 5,000 feet and blossoms erratically winter or fall.

O. retusum. Of solid orange wax, the one-inch

popular through the years. It bears three-foot sprays of small, yellow-green flowers with a white or rose-colored lip. It is found in El Salvador, Guatemala, and Mexico, and flowers in the fall.

L. cervantesii. The delightful round, flat flowers of this species have the basal half of the sepals and petals marked with concentric circles of brown lines. The flowers are white or pale pink, two to three inches in diameter, several to a more or less pendent stem. The rounded petals and oval sepals come to a sharp point at their tips. The lip has a round, heart-shaped, ruffled outer lobe, and very tiny side lobes. The plant has small pseudobulbs and leaves six inches long. It is a native of Mexico and Guatemala and blooms variably. It likes a damp, shady spot.

L. cordatum. A bold flower, its evenly spreading sepals and petals are broad toward the base and taper to a sharp point. The sepals are almost solid brown with a few yellow stripes at their base; their petals are yellow with brown spots that become smaller toward the base. The lip is heart-shaped with a long point at the end, white, with brown spots along the center and a brown tip. It is found in Mexico, Guatemala, Honduras, and Costa Rica, and blooms from summer to fall (Fig. 17–5).

L. ehrenbergii. This is a near-twin to *rossii*. The nearly two-inch flowers have a broad, pointed, dorsal sepal and narrower lateral sepals, all heavily barred with red-brown on a cream or white base. The petals are broad at the base, pointed at the tip, white with a tinge of rose. The arrow-shaped lip is ruffled, bordered with rose. The callus has two raised lines within the boat-shaped outer portion. The plant has small, flat, rounded pseudo-

bulbs and a single, slender leaf. It comes from Mexico and flowers in late summer.

L. maculatum. This species is distinguished by slender, pointed brown sepals and much broader yellow petals marked with brown spots on their basal half. The lip is a broad triangle, also yellow, marked with two rows of brown spots, much ruffled on its outer edge. On the crest of the lip two tall, stiff keels stand upright, tightly pressed together. A native of Mexico and Guatemala, it flowers in the summer.

L. rossii. One of the loveliest of the genus, this species has short flower stems that bear only two to five blooms, each three inches in diameter. The lack of numbers is compensated for by the beauty of the individual flowers and by their good keeping quality. The sepals are pointed, cream colored to greenish-yellow, spotted with dark brown. The blunt, somewhat curled petals are white with a few brown spots at their base. The large, round, wavy lip is pure white. It is found in Mexico, Guatemala, and Honduras, and it flowers in the winter.

L. stellatum. This is almost a miniature, with compressed, oval pseudobulbs two inches tall and a single, slender leaf up to six inches tall. A six-inch flower stem bears one or two delicate blossoms about two inches across. The sepals and petals are very slender, brownish with a few dark spots, while the arrow-shaped lip is white, often tinged with lilac, and its edges are lacerated. From Mexico, it flowers variously from winter to summer.

L. uroskinneri. Ten to thirty flowers of striking coloring are produced on long spikes in the spring. The sepals and petals are green, marked with chestnut-brown, and the large, heart-shaped lip is rose, mottled with white. This species occurs in Guatemala. It blooms in summer and fall.

ROSSIOGLOSSUM

The bold, brown and gold, or brown and bright-yellow flowers of this genus stand out in any collection. They are waxy and shiny, on strong arching or horizontal stems. All can be grown on the cool side of cattleya temperatures, that is, at 55° night temperature, sometimes a bit over that.

R. grande. Large, brilliantly marked flowers make this one of the most widely grown species. The flowers are from five to nine inches across; from four to seven occur on a spike from Septem-

Figure 17–5 Lemboglossum cordatum. (Courtesy of J. A. Fowlie.)

ber to December. The sepals are long and rather slender, yellow, barred with chestnut brown. The wider, wavy petals are brown at the base and yellow at the outer end. The generously rounded lip is white or cream colored, spotted with brown. The waxy flowers last for two weeks or so, and are very decorative (Fig. 17–6). The species occurs in Mexico and Guatemala, and has been nicknamed the "tiger orchid."

R. insleayi. This species has flowers that resemble those of *grande,* but they are smaller, reaching four inches in diameter. The sepals and petals are yellow, spotted with brown, and the lip is orange-yellow spotted with red-brown. It occurs in Mexico and flowers from October to December.

R. schlieperianum. Another species that resembles a small *grande.* This one has three-inch flowers whose yellow-green ground color is carried into the lip. The markings vary from brown in the type to gold in the variety *flavidum.* Its summer flowering season and the generous number of flowers (eight to fifteen to a spike), make it a worthwhile addition to a collection. This is a native of Costa Rica and Panama.

R. splendens is similar to *insleayi,* but the flowers are larger, bolder, more brightly colored. It is a distinctly handsome flower. It is from Mexico and it flowers in the fall.

R. williamsianum is similar to *grande,* but it tends to have more of the yellow background, that is, less of the heavy brown barring. The petals broaden suddenly from a narrow base and are shorter and wider than in *grande.* From Guatemala and Costa Rica, it flowers in early summer.

CUITLAUZINA

Taxonomists were never satisfied that *Odontoglossum pendulum* (or *citrosmum* as it was also called) belong in that genus at all. The species was originally named in 1825 after Cuitlahuatzin, governor of Ixtapalapa in Mexico, and so it has been returned to *Cuitlauzina,* undoubtedly a phonetic spelling of the governor's name. The flower spikes come from the new growth, poking out from among the still very short leaves and turning downward at once. The stem holds ten to twenty beautiful, flat flowers. The petals and sepals are earshaped, and are white to tan and green to pink, while the lip, which is kidney shaped, with a long

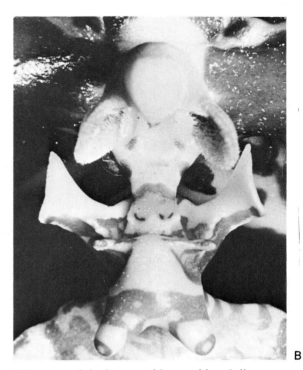

Figure 17–6 Rossioglossum grande. A: *The yellow and brown "tiger" orchid.* (COURTESY OF ROD McLELLAN CO.)

B: *The crest of the lip resembles a rubber doll.*

narrow isthmus, can be any of these colors, although more often white. The plant should be kept on the dry side through the winter and until new growth starts. From Mexico, it flowers in the spring.

OSMOGLOSSUM

Four lovely little species have been placed in this genus. The name *Osmoglossum* was used by Schlechter, so it is not new. The plants are all dainty, with slender, compressed, tapering pseudobulbs and slender leaves. The flowers are waxy, of heavy substance, and pure white except for a few dots on the lip crest.

O. anceps was recently thought to be a new species and briefly was called *O. dubium*. It is much like *O. pulchellum*, differing in that the lip hangs down at a ninety-degree angle, and the lateral sepals are not united. The column is decorated with three little wings that are tipped with pink. The two fat lobes of the lip crest are bright yellow, dotted with red. It is from Mexico and Costa Rica, and flowers in late summer. It is often self pollinating.

O. convallarioides has especially waxy, one-inch flowers on a somewhat drooping stem. The dorsal sepal and the petals form a hood over the column, while the partially united lateral sepals hug the sides of the lip. The lip is spade shaped, concave, with a yellow crest dotted with red. Found from Mexico south to Panama, it flowers in the spring.

O. egertoni has its lateral sepals united, and the lip has two low keels on the disc, which, like the others, is yellow, spotted with red. From Mexico and Central America, it flowers in spring and fall.

O. pulchellum, best known of the four, is sweetly fragrant. Its flowers are slightly larger than the others, reaching an inch and one-quarter or more in diameter. Its lip turns down at an angle and is quite small in proportion to the flaring sepals and petals. The lateral sepals are united for about a third of their length. Found from Mexico to Costa Rica, it flowers in winter.

OTOGLOSSUM

The species of this handsome genus are very much alike. There has been a lot of discussion as to just which were species and which varieties. A rather peculiar lip separates these orchids from other members of the Oncidiinae: It is folded back at its base and attached there to the column foot.

O. arminii. This has a creeping rhizome that grows along the surface of the ground without sending roots into the soil. The pseudobulbs are two to five inches apart, bearing a single, stiff, leathery leaf about five inches tall. The blossoms are borne on a stiff upright stem. They are two inches across, round, rich golden brown, with wide, wavy-edged petals and sepals and a "necktie" lip that has a knobby crest and a white tip. It is found from Venezuela and Colombia to Brazil and it is cool growing.

O. chiriquense (syn. *coronarium*). One of the most magnificent of orchids, it has a long, cylindrical head of glorious flowers atop a tall stem; the flowers are round, very ruffled in all parts, waxy, and long lasting. The sepals and petals are golden brown. Their edges are decorated with a yellow frill, and their bases with yellow spots. The lip is a little, flaring, yellow triangle. Two sharp projections on either side of the basal crest are formed by the fleshy side-lobes of the lip. The plant is straggly, unfortunately, with six to eight inches between pseudobulbs, and has to be grown on a tree fern slab or log. The leaves are short and broad. It is a native of Costa Rica, Panama, Colombia, and Peru and flowers in late summer. A close relative is *O. brevifolium*. They are cool to cool-intermediate growing.

MESOGLOSSUM

This genus was created for a single, rather strange, species.

M. londesboroughianum has a long rhizome on which the leafy pseudobulbs arise at intervals of several inches. They are flattened, about three inches tall. The long, soft leaves are deciduous at the end of the season. The flower spike is twenty to thirty inches long and bears fifteen to twenty two-inch blossoms that are yellow with concentric bars of brown on the bases of the petals and sepals. The lip has a long claw and a very large, flat, kidney-shaped midlobe, bright yellow with some red dots on the crest. The large petals are ruffled on the edge. From Mexico and Guatemala, it flowers in fall and winter. It is extremely difficult to use for hybridizing.

TICOGLOSSUM

The charming name of this genus is derived from the affectionate Costa Rican nickname, "Tico." It was created by the late Professor Rafael Lucas Rodriguez for two delightful dwarf species.

T. krameri has sweetly rounded, glistening, waxy, two-inch flowers. They are of soft rose color, shading at the edges to pale pink. The lip is a darker rose or purple and has a charming accent of yellow at its base, where a few dots of red and a dividing line of red-brown supply a colorful touch. In the fall, three or four flowers are produced in succession on a short stem. The plant has rounded pseudobulbs and a single leaf that can be nine inches tall. From Costa Rica, it flowers in the fall.

T. oerstedii has tiny pseudobulbs one inch tall, and a single, stalked leaf three to five inches tall. The little white flowers come singly on four-inch stems. They are shallow saucers, one and one-half inches across, with overlapping sepals and petals and a heart-shaped lip with upright side lobes. The saddle-shaped crest is spotted with orange. From Costa Rica and Panama, it flowers in spring.

ONCIDIUM

Whatever nature's mood may have been when she created the other orchids, surely it was fanciful when she designed the oncidiums. She seems to have caught dancing rays of light, flickering patterns of sun and shadow, little fairy forms not seen by man, and made them into friendly, whimsical, thoroughly delightful flowers. They are meant to be enjoyed with smiles and chuckles and many a held breath. Still generous after endowing so much beauty elsewhere, she seems to have poured out her warmth in this genus.

At least three hundred species of *Oncidium* have been discovered. The description of a mere handful is only a tantalizing glimpse of the whole genus. Favorites among the species are easy to find, and no two fanciers will list the same ones as deserving of attention.

The genus can be found throughout tropical America, from Florida and the West Indies, through Central America to the southern part of Brazil. As with odontoglossums, some are found in low, hot regions, others in the cool upper alti-

tudes. They are more amenable to changes in temperature, however, and most of them will adjust themselves to an intermediate greenhouse. This makes it easy for the average amateur to include a few oncidiums with almost anything else he grows. As cut flowers, the possibilities they offer are limited only by the imagination of the person working with them. Their filigreelike sprays are charmingly decorative when used alone or as a foil for other flowers. Dainty arrangements for the hair or stunning corsages can be made with groups or with single blossoms.

This genus of epiphytes encompasses great variety. The pseudobulbs are rounded and flattened at the edges, like those of *Odontoglossum,* but some species are without pseudobulbs. The foliage is usually clear green but is sometimes mottled. The leaves may be fleshy, oval, and pointed, with a single prominent midvein, or thinner, and many veined, or terete (cylindrical). The flower sprays are short or long, sometimes drooping, often erect. The blossoms may be large and showy, or small and dainty. All but a few have a lip crest decorated with many protuberances, which adds much to their charm. The column is short and winged.

Culture

Except for those from high elevations, which need really cool conditions, oncidiums do well with cattleya temperatures and humidity. Some may need a bit more light. They can be grown in pots, or mounted on bark or tree fern, or, if they have drooping flower sprays, in baskets. Fir bark is a good medium. Fertilize as for cattleyas. They respond easily to vegetative propagation: Divide them into groups of three or more pseudobulbs or single growths for equitant species. They are readily grown from seed.

The Species

O. ampliatum. Magnificent panicles, attractively branched and arched, reach a length of three feet. The attractive little dancing-doll flowers are clear yellow, spotted with red toward the base of the small sepals and petals. The round flat lip is cream colored on the underside. The round, flattened, ridged pseudobulbs look like turtles. The species occurs from Guatemala to Peru and flowers from March to June (Fig. 17–7).

O. ansiferum. Plants with tall, broad, flat, cardboard-thin pseudobulbs bear sprays of delicate-looking but long-lasting flowers in the summer. The flowers are in tones of yellow-green. The side lobes of the spreading lip are large and hold themselves horizontally, looking like an extra pair of petals. This species occurs in Guatemala, Nicaragua, Costa Rica, and Panama.

O. asparagoides. See *O. heteranthum.*

O. aureum. A lovely species from Ecuador, it produces a tall flower stem, slightly branched. The twenty to thirty one-inch flowers are solid yellow, without crests or markings, and are distinguished by the fact that the lip is attached by a slender claw. The sepals are slender, pointed ovals, the petals similar but broader, and the lip is rounded with an indentation at its tip. A plant that looks very much like this occurs in Peru and is tentatively called *O. dichromum* or *O. aureum* var. *bicolor.* It may be a distinct species. This has red sepals and petals and two teeth in front of the lip claw. Instead of opening its flowers more or less at the same time, as does *aureum,* the unbranched inflorescence gives rise to two or three flowers at a time over a period of a year or more.

O. aurisasinorum. This species is called *oreja de burro* in its native Honduras, and Standley and Williams used this nickname as the basis for its specific name in 1952. It is one of the many "burro-ear" species, actually one of the smaller ones. The stiff, light green leaves are attached to very short pseudobulbs. The milky white, waxy flowers are produced in a dense cluster at the end of an eighteen-inch stem. They are one and one-half inches long, with slender, spreading sepals and petals, the dorsal sepal cupped at the top. The lip is three-lobed and the sides of the lateral lobes fold

Figure 17–8 Oncidium aureum. *TOP: Tip of the flower spray. BOTTOM: A single flower. Note the slender claw by which the lip is attached.*

Figure 17–7 Oncidium ampliatum.

back to make them appear triangular, while the midlobe is anchor-shaped. It has a toothed callus. Flowering time is autumn.

O. batemannianum. Dense heads of small flowers are borne at the top of a four- to six-foot tall stem. They are unusually long lasting, an inch in diameter, and have green sepals, ruffled yellow-green petals barred with brown, and a flaring yellow lip decorated at its base with two crests, each consisting of two rows of teeth. It has spherical pseudobulbs that bear a pair of tall, slender leaves. The species is native to Brazil and Peru, where it is often found along rocky road cuts. It flowers in the fall.

O. baueri. The robust plants produce flower sprays that sometimes reach twelve feet but usually grow close to six feet in length. They are gracefully arched or drooping and bear many small blooms. The small sepals and petals are pale yellow spotted with olive-brown, and the larger lip is a brighter yellow with a brown band. This native of the West Indies, Brazil, and Peru flowers in August.

O. cabagrae. Almost a miniature, this species has leaves that barely exceed six inches. The dainty little yellow-and-brown flowers are produced on stems about two feet long. It occurs in Panama and Costa Rica and flowers in the summer.

O. candida. The lip of this species has more or less a cattleya shape, with the sides of the lip rolled up around the column. The oval-pointed sepals and petals are equal in size, and can be nearly all brown with yellow edges or yellow with varying amounts of brown markings. The lip is cream colored. The flowers are borne three to five to a stem and are about three inches across. Blooming season is autumn; native habitat is Brazil.

O. cariniferum. Greenish-red flowers, bordered with light green, have a white lip that makes the two-inch, perky flowers quite distinctive. The spring blossoms are borne on stems three or four feet tall, each of which has short branches with four or five flowers. The sepals and petals are narrow, pointed, not wavy, the edges infolded somewhat with a keel on the back. The lip is spreading at the outer edge, narrowing to a claw directly under the column. This species occurs in Costa Rica, Panama, and Venezuela at 5,000 feet.

O. carthagenense. This huge member of the "burro-ear" group produces a flowering stem five feet long. The one-inch, round, waxy flowers are much ruffled, with sepals and petals narrowed at the base, broadening suddenly, white with heavy markings of purple or brown-purple. The lip is kidney shaped, colored like the rest of the flower, and has a fleshy, complex crest. The pink column adds a decorative touch. It is very widespread, from Mexico through the West Indies to Venezuela, Brazil, and Colombia, and flowers in summer.

O. cavendishianum. Also a "burro-ear" type, this one is not so large as the preceding species, but is nevertheless a massive plant. It flowers on a three-foot stem. The sepals and petals are often clear yellow but usually marked with red. The bright yellow lip has very ruffled side lobes, and a ruffled, divided midlobe. The crest has protuberances in the form of a cross. Native to Mexico and Guatemala, it flowers in early spring.

O. cebolleta (syn. *longifolium*). Its name means "small onion" in Spanish, referring to the terete leaves that grow twelve to fifteen inches tall and taper toward the tip. The six-foot flower stem bears a loosely branched panicle at its tip holding many one- to one-and-one-half-inch flowers. The cupped sepals and petals are yellow-brown with dark markings, and the three-lobed lip is yellow with a few brown-red markings on the upper surface, pale yellow underneath. It is common to warm areas throughout the American tropics, and it is equipped to endure long dry seasons. It flowers mainly in winter.

O. cheirophorum. This delightful miniature has little rounded pseudobulbs that are one inch tall and bear two short leaves. They are bright green the first year and become speckled with purple as they age. The flowers, which grow in dense sprays about six inches long, are a bright, clear yellow and very waxy. The plant spreads rapidly to fill its pot and makes a charming show. It is a native of Colombia and southern Central America.

O. clowesii. This is a large, handsome species with pseudobulbs up to four inches tall and leaves to eighteen inches long. The flower is of the type with a fiddle-shaped lip. The sepals and petals are slender, pointed, yellow with brown bars. The lip is violet at the basal half, and the pointed outer part is white. The tall flower stem holds seven to ten of the three-inch flowers. Flowering season is fall. The species is native to Brazil.

O. crispum. This lovely species and its relatives *forbesii, gardneri,* and *marshallianum* add another variation to the oncidium theme, this time a type with huge petals and dorsal sepal, a large round lip, and lateral sepals partially united and hidden behind the lip. In contrast to the ballerina type such as *varicosum,* these might be feminine members of a folk dancing group, for which the vivacious and audacious *falcipetalum* and its relatives suggest themselves as male dancers. The broad petals of O. *crispum* remind one of the full sleeves of a peasant costume, and the spreading lip the skirt. It is a plant of modest size, with dark green pseudobulbs, compressed and somewhat channelled, each bearing two or three short, rather broadly oval, leathery leaves. The branched inflorescence reaches a height of about eighteen inches and bears ten to twenty two and one-half inch flowers. The blooms are greenish brown with a faint yellow border and a few yellow bars at the base of the parts. The broad petals are ruffled, as are the sepals and lip. The lip has a rectangular basal portion decorated with a fine-toothed crest, in front of which is a scalloped patch of clear yellow spreading down onto the ruffled, almost round midlobe. The large column has large, drooping, purple wings. A native of Brazil, it likes a cool spot in the intermediate house, and it flowers in the autumn (Fig. 17–9).

O. *crista-galli*. A lovely dwarf species that produces bright flowers, one to a short stem, but several from a growth. The pseudobulbs are less than an inch tall, and at their tip is an aborted leaf. Leaves come from the base of the pseudobulb, and are three inches tall. The flowers are huge for the plant though only one and one-half inches long. They are bright canary yellow, marked with a few red-brown spots at the base of the sepals and petals. The lip is three lobed, with the midlobe divided into four parts. The plants grow on the smallest branches in nature, exposed to the morning sun, and in constantly damp forests. They are cool growing, difficult to keep alive, and flower in the fall. The species is native from Mexico through Peru.

O. *cucullatum* is somewhat larger than *nubigenum* but very similar to it. It differs in that the flowers are larger; the lip is less divided at its end and has a sharp little point in the center; the side lobes of the lip are longer and more sharply set off from the midlobe; the crest is a long, single, vertical swelling, undivided and undecorated. The blooms open over an extended period and are less fragrant. It occurs in central Ecuador and flowers in late spring and summer.

O. *desertorum*. See O. *guianense*.

O. *excavatum*. A handsome species with large, ovoid pseudobulbs and usually a single leaf, it grows both as a complete epiphyte and as a near terrestrial on grassy slopes of Peru and Ecuador.

The tall flowering stem holds a branched panicle of long-lasting flowers. The one-and-one-half inch flowers have very large petals and dorsal sepal, a small lip, and a winged column. They are yellow except for the brown lip crest and a few brown bars on the other flower parts. The species flowers in the fall and is cool-growing.

O. *falcipetalum*. Whereas with some oncidiums one is reminded of the dainty grace of ballerinas, the group to which *falcipetalum* belongs brings to mind sheer masculine vigor and exuberance, flying banners and scarves, energetic folk dancers. This group of big brown-and-gold oncidiums is the ultimate for size and showiness. Their three-inch flowers are held on branched stems eight to ten feet long. It includes *macranthum, monachicum, lamelligerum, loxense, superbiens, gyriferum, chrysodipterum, serratum* and others. All have in common a short, tongue-shaped lip, and together they are referred to as the "cyrtochilum" group. They have huge sepals and petals, much ruffled and highly decorative, attached by stalks. In *falcipetalum,* the dorsal sepal is more rounded and wavy than the laterals, brown with a gold edge or gold marked with brown blotches. The lateral sepals widen out from their long stalks like solid-brown pantaloons. The petals are smaller, bright yellow with a few brown spots, and are highly ruffled, often curving forward to touch at their tips. The lip and crest are yellow. It is native to high elevations of Peru, Ecuador, and Venezuela, and flowers in the fall.

O. *flexuosum*. This species is a small member of the popular group of "dancing-doll" orchids. Because of the much-reduced sepals and petals and the voluminous lip, this group resembles a miniature ballet. The tiny, one-inch flowers of this species occur in dainty showers on a loose, airy panicle atop a tall stem. The sepals and petals are yellow, barred with brown, and the broad, full lip is yellow with a few red spots. It grows and flowers with great freedom and, because of its small size, is welcome in little greenhouses. This native of Brazil flowers at various seasons.

O. *forbesii*. This could be another feminine member of the folk dancing group. The full, round flowers are two and one-half inches across, shiny brown, with the edges of all parts wavy and marked with a splashed border of yellow. The yellow crest of the lip is dotted with brown and comes to a bodicelike point where the midlobe flares out. As a most delightful touch, the column wings, which surround the stigma as well as the

Figure 17–9 Oncidium crispum *var.* grandiflorum.   (Courtesy of J. A. Fowlie.)

anther, are white, dotted with red. The inflorescence reaches three feet in length and bears many blooms. Native to Brazil, it flowers in early fall and likes intermediate temperatures.

O. fuscatum. This is a completely charming species, very distinctive in shape and coloring, and quite fragrant. The narrow sepals and petals are ruffled along their edges, brown with a white border and white tips, curled back at their ends. The large lip is square with rounded corners, entirely rose-purple except for a white edge at its outer end. The plant has flattened pseudobulbs four to five inches tall and short, broad leaves. It is native to Panama, Colombia, Ecuador, and Peru, and flowers in the spring.

O. gardneri. Quite similar in shape to *O. crispum,* but daintier, perkier, and brighter colored, it is delightfully fragrant. The petals are brown, embroidered with a buttonhole stitch in yellow, and the parasol-shaped dorsal sepal is yellow, barred with brown. The lip is fan shaped, notched in the middle of the outer edge, clear yellow, rimmed, with a band of brown spots that leave a yellow border. The basal part is briefly narrowed and

gives rise to two earlike side lobes. The crest is decorated with red-brown protuberances. Also native to Brazil, it likes intermediate temperatures and flowers in late summer or fall.

O. globuliferum. This miniature has the peculiar habit of making long runners that twine around each other and any support they find, forming a spiderweb among their native trees. At each node of the runner is a small plant, which has a flattened round pseudobulb and one leaf. Each plant produces a single flower on a short stem, and then the following year can give rise to another runner. The flowers are large in comparison to the plant. They have abbreviated sepals and petals, yellow, barred with red-brown, and a large, round, undulate lip of bright yellow. It is very difficult to bloom in cultivation. It is native from Costa Rica to Peru and Venezuela and flowers in the summer.

O. guianense. This is one of the many equitant species with a fan of flat, curved leaves. Actually, each leaf has grown folded together, with only its edges separated, giving the appearance of a channel down one side. It is about two and one-half inches tall and produces a flowering stem a foot high, bearing many unique, bright yellow, inch-wide flowers, which appear to have three lips. The petals are broadened in an almost exact imitation of the lip but do not have the crest, and are attached by a brown claw. Native to the Dominican Republic and Haiti, it flowers in the fall.

O. gyriferum. This rare and lovely species from Colombia and Ecuador belongs to the *cyrtochilum* group. Its waxy, dark brown flowers are borne on an eight- to ten-foot stem with rather widely separated side branches holding several flowers each. The flowering stem has a fascinating vining habit: The tip of the stem makes circular motions as if groping for a support. When it contacts the stem of a neighboring plant (or a stake) it curls round and round it in an upward direction as it grows. The circular motion is called "circumnutation." Several other species of this group are also vining. The flowers of *O. gyriferum* are two inches long, with stalked, oval sepals that come to a graceful point. The petals are also stalked, broad in the middle, and slender pointed, with ruffled edges of bright yellow. The little strap of a lip curves under and is hidden from view, leaving the voluptuously carved crest as the center of attention. The species comes from high elevations in Ecuador and flowers in the fall, the flowers keeping for two months.

O. hastatum. This is a very pretty species. Its stylish one-and-one-half inch flowers are borne on a tall, branched spike. The slender, pointed petals and sepals vary from yellow to green, barred heavily or lightly with red-brown. The lip sets off the flower with its bow-tie white side lobes and narrow triangular red or rust-colored midlobe. Found in Mexico, it flowers in spring and summer.

O. henekenii. The lip of this species looks so much like a spider that the people of its native Hispaniola call it the "spider" or "tarantula." The lip even has a crest with six "legs" (the wrong number for a spider, better suiting a bee, and it is pollinated by a bee). The "spider" is a velvety purple-black with a pink "thorax." It grows in warm, dry areas where the air is humid, in the Dominican Republic and Haiti. The small, dark green leaves are arranged in tiny fans. This is one of the numerous species pollinated by pseudocopulation. It usually flowers in summer.

O. heteranthum. A startling difference marks this species and a few others, among them *abortivum,* undoubtedly caused by a mutation in the dim past. Instead of producing flowers along each branchlet of the inflorescence as is normal, flowers occur only at their tips. Where other flowers would be expected, there are only whorls of little green bracts, five in a group, that look like little green stars. These are aborted flowers. In *heteranthum,* the effect of many long, sinuous, branched stems with the groups of tiny bracts is reminiscent of asparagus fern. The plant itself is small. The little flowers have greenish-yellow sepals and petals barred with green-brown and a yellow lip. *O. heteranthum* comes from Costa Rica, Panama, Colombia, Ecuador, Peru, and Venezuela, and flowers in the fall. *O. abortivum* is endemic and quite rare in Venezuela and flowers in the spring.

O. incurvum. This species, which does best when grown a little cooler than the average, produces many dainty, gracefully branched panicles of lovely, one-inch flowers that are pale pink spotted with rosy purple. It comes from Mexico and flowers in late summer and fall.

O. ionesianum. From a plant very similar to *cebolieta* come striking and decorative three-inch flowers, ten to fifteen per stem. The dorsal sepal and the petals arch upward, while the lateral sepals are held behind the flower; all are cream-white, very ruffled, and marked with scattered red spots. The outer lobe of the startlingly white lip is broad and flaring, divided in the middle, attached by a claw from which two bright yellow ears spread sideways and which is decorated with a complicated crest. It likes bright light and not too much water. Native to Paraguay, Brazil, and Uruguay, it flowers in the fall.

O. kramerianum. See *Psychopsis kramerianum.*

Figure 17–10 Oncidium heteranthum. *All but the end flowers on each branch are aborted and have become mere bracts.*

O. laeve can be considered the type of a group of distinctive species, including *karwinskii, reichenheimii, schroederianum,* and *stenoglossum* (recent syn. *confusum*). Chief characteristics of *O. laeve,* which are reflected in the others, are narrow sepals and petals with reflexed edges, the petals curving upward beside the dorsal sepal like a pair of arms, and a long narrow lip whose basal edges turn down, allowing the crest to be rather humped out, and whose endlobe spreads out apronlike. The sepals and petals are greenish yellow, barred with brown, the center of the lip is rose color, and the midlobe is white. *O. stenoglossum* is the smallest; its flowers are about two inches long, with very slender parts, and it blooms in the fall. *O. karwinskii* is larger, with the lip edge somewhat ruffled, and very broad column wings. *O. reichenheimii* and *O. laeve* are very much alike: *reichenheimii* has a lip that extends almost straight out and *laeve* has a ninety-degree bend in the center of the lip. Neither of these has noticeable column wings. The lip of *O. schroederianum* spreads more gently from the isthmus and is square at the tip. It is from Brazil and blooms winter to spring. *O. reichenheimii* and *laeve* are from Mexico and Central America; *karwinskii* is from Mexico. All three flower in the spring. The plants are fairly large and have tall, stiff, many-flowered spikes.

O. lamelligerum. This is the most highly ruffled and most decorative member of the cyrtochilum group. It could be the chief dancer in the folk-dancing group to which *falcipetalum* and the others belong. The edges of the brown petals and sepals are decorated with a fine-toothed, yellow border that adds ruffles to the ruffles. The petals are tipped with yellow. The side lobes of the lip are violet, and the white crest is accented with a spot of purple. It is native to Ecuador at moderately high elevations, and was rediscovered a few years ago by the late José Strobel. It blooms in summer and fall.

O. lanceanum. An odd combination of colors makes this a very striking species. The showy flowers are two to three inches across. The sepals and petals are blunt and fleshy, yellow, spotted with chocolate brown or crimson. The spreading lip stands in contrast to the rest of the flower with its rose outer portion and violet base. The robust plants have no pseudobulbs. The wide, fleshy, burro-ear leaves are mottled with brown. The rather short, stout, erect flower stems bear a generous number of blooms in the summer. The species is native to Guyana (Fig. 17–11).

O. leucochilum. The beautifully colored flowers of this species are about one-and-one-half inches in diameter and are borne on a branched scape that reaches more than ten feet in length. The spatula-shaped sepals and petals are greenish brown barred with red-brown, and the lip has white side lobes and a spreading, wavy midlobe. Bright accents are given by the pink tooth of the crest and the pink anther cap and wings of the column. The flowering stem starts in January and takes eight or nine months to bloom. The flowers open in succession over a long period, producing blooms into the winter. It is native to Central America (Fig. 17–12).

O. luridum. These are big, mule-eared plants that give a tall, branched, flower stem. The flowers, though only an inch in diameter, are truly showy. They are waxy, with sepals and petals white, heavily barred with rose, and a rose lip edged in white. The sepals and petals are short and curving, very wavy on the edges. The side lobes of the lip are rounded but their edges fold back to give a square look. They are tinged with orange. The sides of the short midlobe also fold back in the center, pinching it in the middle, while the outer lobe flares abruptly. The yellow crest is marked with an orange linear design. This spring-flowering species spreads from Florida through the West Indies and Mexico to British Guiana and Peru.

O. macranthum. This superb flower is the most famous of the cyrtochilum group (described under *O. falcipetalum*). It is a lush and round flower, three to four inches across. The brown sepals and golden-yellow petals are about the same size and shape, oval, flat-spreading, gently undulating, attached by slender stalks. The petals are quite ruffled. The side lobes of the waxy lip are purple, the sharply pointed midlobe is yellow, and the crest is decorated with a burst of white spikes tipped with purple. It blooms in summer and fall on a long, vining, branched stem. It is native to high elevations in Ecuador and should be grown cool.

O. marshallianum. This is perhaps the most decorative of the feminine folk dancers. The plants are larger and lighter green, the inflorescence longer, and the flowers larger and brighter. The less conspicuous dorsal sepal bends forward over the column and is yellow with purple bands. The almost rectangular, ruffled petals are slightly fiddle shaped and bi-lobed at their tips, golden yellow, with large

Figure 17–11 UPPER: Oncidium lanceanum. *A stunning species with large, heavy flowers of chocolate and* *yellow with a pink lip.* (COURTESY OF JONES AND SCULLY, INC.) LOWER: Oncidium varicosum.

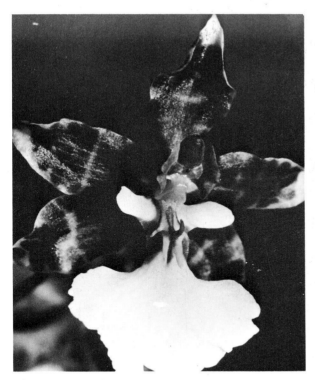

Figure 17–12 Oncidium leucochilum.

brown spots down the center. The large, wavy lip is deeply bi-lobed at its outer edge and spreads in a broad fan, all clear yellow except for the crest and small side lobes, which are spotted with orange-red. Native to Brazil, this one likes temperatures a bit cooler than its relatives, and it flowers in the spring.

O. *microchilum*. This is justly named, because the midlobe of the lip is reduced to a tiny protuberance. The sepals and petals are light or dark brown with yellow markings. The side lobes of the lip are rounded, convex; they are white marked with purple at the base. It grows natively through Mexico and Guatemala and flowers in the summer.

O. *monachicum*. This species is quite similar to *falcipetalum*. It, too, is brown except for a delicate border of yellow on its much-ruffled parts. The lateral sepals flare out sideways from their narrow stalks and their broadened outer parts are not quite as large as the dorsal sepal and petals. The tip of the lip curves under. It is native to the cool high elevations of Ecuador and blooms in late summer.

O. *nubigenum*. In addition to having attractive flowers, this small species is one of the most fragrant of orchids. The plants have oval, compressed pseudobulbs that bear one or two leaves eight to ten inches long. The flowering stem is about a foot tall and bears five to ten flowers, opening more or less at the same time. The green-brown sepals and petals are oval with a sharp little point at their tips and are somewhat cupped forward. The lip varies from pale to dark rose and is attractively spotted with a darker shade. It has rounded side lobes continuous with the midlobe. The midlobe is rounded but is bi-lobed at its outer end, often quite severely. The crest is composed of two fleshy, vertical lobes, each of which is subdivided into two lesser protuberances. The species occurs in northern Ecuador and Colombia and flowers in spring and summer.

O. *obryzatum*. An "almost miniature" oncidium, these plants are especially vigorous and may outgrow the miniature dimensions. This Central American species is a delightful addition to a collection. Its half-inch brownish flowers appear on dainty sprays in the fall.

O. *onustum*. This entirely lemon-yellow species has nearly round flowers. The sepals are hidden from the front view by the large and rounded petals and lip. The lip is three lobed, with the lateral lobes simulating a pair of petals, and the midlobe broad, divided slightly at its tip. The plants have small, mottled pseudobulbs, each bearing one or two fleshy leaves two to four inches tall. The flowers barely exceed an inch in diameter, but the erect or arching raceme holds a large number of them. The species occurs in Ecuador, Colombia, Peru, and Panama.

O *ornithorrhynchum*. The long specific name means "bird beak," and the drooping, tightly clustered sprays resemble flocks of birds. The rather small plants are easily grown and flower freely. The tiny, fragrant flowers occur in shades of soft rosy purple. The species, which likes to be grown a little on the cool side, occurs in Mexico and flowers in fall and winter.

O. *papilio*. See *Psychopsis papilio*.

O. *phalaenopsis*. A serenely beautiful species, it is quite similar to *nubigenum* except that the flower has a white ground color. The sepals and petals are barred with red-violet, and the lip and its large, scalloped side lobes are dotted with crimson, the dots merging into large areas near the center of the flower. The little flower spike holds five to seven flowers, and the plant itself is small. This native of warmer parts of Ecuador likes intermediate temperatures and blooms in the winter and spring.

O. pumilum. A very tiny burro-ear species, the rigid little leaves are two to four inches long, and the flowers but a quarter of an inch in diameter. The waxy, yellow blooms are held in clusters along a branched six-inch inflorescence. The sepals and petals are very small, the spreading lip the showy part of the bloom. Oddly, the lateral lobes are larger than the midlobe. This spring-flowering species is native to Brazil and Paraguay. A very similar one is *oncidium morenoi* from Brazil.

O. pusillum. See *Psygmorchis pusilla.*

O. sarcodes. Even though this species is not technically related to the *O. crispum* group (the lateral sepals are free, for one thing), it could well join them in general character and beauty. The large dorsal sepal is yellow with brown bars, as are the smaller lateral ones. The large, wavy petals are broader at their outer ends and are squared off, brown except for a yellow tip. The large lip is broad and wavy at its outer end, which is separated from two rather large side lobes, yellow with a few red spots. The crest has two large lobes with a small spike between them and is yellow dotted with brown. It comes from Brazil and flowers in the spring.

O. sphacelatum. This large, vigorous species gives huge panicles of brown-and-gold flowers. The panicles are particularly attractive because they are upright (and if not, should be tied up). The side branches are longest at the bottom, decreasing in length upward, giving a beautiful triangular shape to the spray—an espaliered appearance. The sepals and petals are brown and yellow, the lip pure yellow, brown at the base, the flowers about an inch in diameter. The species is spread through Mexico and Central America and flowers through winter and spring.

O. splendidum. This superb species has three-inch flowers that have a huge, pure-yellow, serenely simple lip. The brown- and yellow-barred petals and sepals curve back gracefully at their tips, all except the dorsal sepal, which stands straight. The great, long lip flares out wide from its narrower midsection and has a simple linear crest at its base. The inflorescence is more than two feet long, holding the flowers on short side branches of two to three each, widely spaced so that each shows off its charms separately. This is a large species in the burro-ear group. It is found in Mexico and Guatemala and flowers in late winter and spring.

O. stipitatum. This terete-leaved plant, native to Honduras, Nicaragua, and Panama, has a panicle of one-inch flowers. They have yellow, brown-barred sepals and petals and a spreading yellow lip. The side lobes of the lip are often raised to an angle paralleling the petals. The species can be grown warmer than some, in a pendent position, with care not to overwater. It blooms in the summer.

O. stramineum. This is called "Mexico's rarest orchid" by Stirling Dickinson; he found a restricted area where this orchid, seldom seen since its long-ago discovery, still grows. It is a small burro-eared plant with a panicle of half-inch flowers held in fairly dense clusters. The extremely waxy, cream flowers are delicately spotted with rose. They have rounded, somewhat cupped sepals and petals, and a small, complicated lip with side lobes more conspicuous than the midlobe and resembling a pair of up-curving horns. The column is a very pretty part of the flower, with its purple-striped auricles. Although native to a warm, low elevation, it can be grown with cattleyas. Flowering time is spring (Fig. 17–13).

O. superbiens. A little plainer than its fellow members in the cyrtochilum group, it is nevertheless a stunning flower. Its long-stalked sepals are moderately wavy on the edges, and the smaller pet-

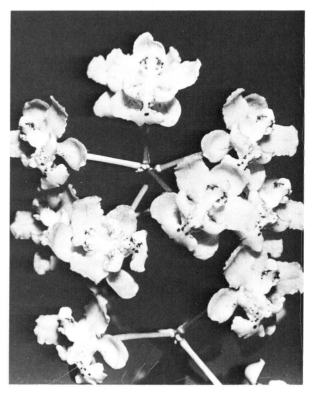

Figure 17–13 Oncidium stramineum, *a rare species.*

als, which are yellow, barred with brown from the middle to the base, are slightly more undulate. The small lip is blackish purple. This species grows natively in Colombia and Venezuela and flowers from winter to spring.

O. teres. Another terete-leaved species, this one has the distinctive characteristic of having a lip plain yellow on the surface but spotted with red-brown on the under side. The half-inch flowers are held on a dense panicle eighteen inches long. A native of Panama, it blooms in late winter and spring.

O. tigrinum. The startling flowers of this species are among the most showy of the genus. They have the appearance of being made of two flowers wired together. The rather large sepals and petals are rich brown, barred with slender lines of yellow. The large, bright-yellow lip is in complete contrast to this dark backing. The flowers are about two and one-half inches across, rather few to a stem. The species occurs in Mexico and flowers in the winter.

O. triquetrum. A veritable jewel among the equitant oncidiums, its one-inch flowers are unique. The nearly round lip is red or maroon in the center with lines spreading out into the white border. The broad, white petals are marked down the center with red dots. The slender sepals are greenish brown with a lighter border. The leaves are held in a fan of about five. Their edges spread apart a bit, giving a three-edged effect. Native to Jamaica, it flowers in the fall.

O. varicosum. One of the most beloved of the genus, the flower of this species is a "dancing doll" in a beautifully swirling skirt. Literally clouds of these sunny little flowers are borne in lacy, branching sprays. One to two hundred may occur on a single panicle. The sepals and petals are yellow-bronze, barred with brown. The lip is pure yellow, sometimes with a brown spot or band at its base, and a curiously toothed crest. The variety *rogersii* is considered by some to be the best of all. It is one that should be included in all collections. This native of Brazil flowers in winter and spring.

O. variegatum. A beautiful and varied species of the equitant group. Withner includes several other species as varieties of this. The flowers are dainty, very prettily marked. The sepals are greenish, the slightly upturned petals white with brown bars toward the base. The side lobes of the lip are almost as large as the petals and parallel them, giving the effect of a second pair of petals. The midlobe of the lip is broadly anchor shaped, and has at its base a "t" formed of yellow protuberances on the crest. The various forms come from several of the Caribbean Islands.

PSYGMORCHIS

Removed from *Oncidium,* these are little fan-shaped plants whose leaves are not channeled, as they are in other members of the equitant group.

Psygmorchis pusilla. Flowers the year around are produced by this delightful miniature, one of the equitant species (holding its flat, grown-together leaves in a fan) which is widespread natively through Mexico, Central America, much of South America, and the West Indies. The flowers are typical for the equitant group, with the split midlobe of the lip. They are borne on a stem that grows up between the folded edges of the leaf to emerge about half-way along. Each stem produces five or six flowers in succession. The plants require excellent drainage, drying between waterings, but a humid atmosphere. They are perhaps best grown on a tree fern slab which is soaked every other day or so. This one will do well in an orchid case (Fig. 17–14).

PSYCHOPSIS

The wonderfully evolved "butterfly" orchids have long deserved a genus of their own. The name is apt, Greek for butterflylike, and was given to these species in 1836. The genus was removed from *Oncidium.*

P. kramerianum. The "butterfly orchid," which

Figure 17–14 Psygmorchis pusillum, *an exquisite miniature.*

description it shares with its more famous relative, *papilio,* does not grow with the abandon usual to the genus, but it rewards careful attention with a succession of single, spectacular butterfly flowers. The petals and the dorsal sepal are drawn out to look like antennae. The lateral sepals are broad, golden yellow spotted with brown; and the large, round, ruffled lip is yellow with a fine-toothed border decorated by a band of brown spots. The flowers appear one after another at the tip of a tall, jointed stem. The foliage of the plant is green, mottled with brown. This Central American species has a variable flowering season.

P. papilio. This butterfly orchid is said to be responsible for the orchid craze that has swept the world. It is much like *kramerianum,* described above, but flowers more freely. It was shown at an exhibition of the Royal Horticultural Society soon after its introduction to England in 1823. Here its striking appearance so intrigued the Duke of Devonshire that he was inspired to start an orchid collection of his own. Thus was the fashion for private collections started among wealthy Englishmen. *P. papilio* has longer antennae than *kramerianum,* and the lateral sepals and lip are banded, rather than spotted, with brown. The upper sections of the jointed flower stem are flattened like the parts of a crab's leg. Flowers appear one at a time, in succession from both old and new stems, throughout most of the year. The species is a native of the West Indies (Fig. 17–15).

Figure 17–15 *A hand lens reveals fascinating detail in many flowers. Here is the column and lip crest of Psychopsis papilio.*

MEXICOA

This beautiful little species, endemic to Mexico, has been removed from *Oncidium* and given a genus of its own. Its new name was taken from that of its native country, and its old specific name retained.

M. giesbreghtiana has slender, conical, slightly fluted pseudobulbs two inches tall and a pair of narrow, five-inch leaves. Three to five dainty flowers come on a stem a bit taller than the leaves. They have oval sepals and petals of pinkish yellow striped with brick red, the former spread flat, the latter held forward. The flat, four-lobed lip has very broad side lobes and two smaller tip lobes, all pale yellow, with a prominent orange "Y"-shaped crest. It comes from south central Mexico, and blooms in spring, sometimes in fall.

ADA

Until recently the genus *Ada* was considered to have but one or two species. Now several erstwhile species of *Brassia,* from what was known as the glumacea group, have been added to *Ada.* Although they do look like little brassias, the structure of the pollinarium and the lip are more like true adas. The lip crest is particularly distinctive, with two pubescent, sausage-shaped keels at the base of the lip, each ending in a stumpy "tooth."

Ada aurantiaca. Bright little cinnabar-red, bell-shaped flowers are held seven to ten on an arching spray. The sepals and petals hold themselves in a tube for their basal half, with their slender, pointed outer ends spreading in starlike fashion, allowing the little point of the lip to protrude. Its slender, flattened pseudobulbs bear one or two leaves from the top and several from the base. Found in Venezuela and Colombia, it flowers in the spring.

A. allenii (from *Brassia*) appears to have no pseudobulb, but a very small one can be found hidden by the leaf bases. The leaves spread in a luxuriant fan more than one foot high. The flowers, with the fragrance of honey, are three inches long, reddish or yellowish, with short, pointed sepals and petals and a small, yellow, pointed lip that has a white disc outlined in red. It is from Panama, and it flowers in the fall.

A. glumacea (from *Brassia*) has slender, tapered pseudobulbs that bear a single leaf up to fifteen inches long. The inflorescence is about the same length and holds a few two-inch, greenish-yellow flowers whose sepals and petals are almost the same length. The shorter lip is rather shield shaped. All parts are spotted with chocolate brown. It is from Colombia and Venezuela, and it flowers in the winter.

A. keiliana (from *Brassia*) is similar to *A. allenii* except that it has a larger pseudobulb, which is also surrounded by several basal leaves. The inflorescence is more than one foot long but holds few blooms. Flowers are often six inches long, yellow-green, spotted with dark brown or dark maroon, with a creamy lip that grades to yellow at the edges. It is from Colombia and Venezuela, and it flowers in spring and summer.

BRASSIA

A very important member of this subtribe, *Brassia* is a genus of "spider orchids," whose long sepals and petals look like the legs of a spider and whose lip could be thought to resemble an elongated body. The species are much used in hybridization with *Oncidium, Odontoglossum,* and *Miltoniopsis.* There are about thirty species, all easy to grow with a mixed collection of orchids. They require abundant water during the growing season and must never be allowed to dry out.

B. antherotes. The extreme length of the sepals of this species make it a curiosity. The dorsal sepals are four to five inches long, and the laterals normally ten to twelve, a total of about fourteen to seventeen. It is interesting to watch the spiral buds open and the sepals unwind as they grow in length to their final mature size. The broad, flat pseudobulbs are about four inches tall and bear a single leaf. The species is widespread through Costa Rica, Panama, Colombia, Ecuador, and Peru, and is spring flowering. The variety *longissima* has flowers with even longer sepals and is a heavier plant. It is less common, however, and appears to occur only in Costa Rica, Panama and Ecuador. It flowers in the fall.

B. caudata. This species has flowers five to eight inches long. All parts are greenish-yellow with spots of dark brown toward the base. The slender, pointed lip has fuzzy calli which become toothlike in the front. It occurs from South Florida to Cuba, and from Mexico to northern South America. It can flower more than once a year.

B. gireoudiana. These ten- to twelve-inch flowers hold themselves stiffly erect with the very slender parts quite straight. The lip is creamy yellow, is not quite as sharply pointed as some, and has two sausage-shaped crests at its base. Native to Costa Rica and Panama, it blooms in late spring and summer.

B. verrucosa. The whole flower is seven or eight inches long, with the dorsal sepal and the shorter petals accounting for three inches of the length and the longer lateral sepals for the other four. They are pale yellow-green, spotted at the base. The lip is pinched in at the middle and is white with dark green warts. The phalanx of eight to ten flowers is borne in a neat row on a horizontal stem. It occurs from Mexico through Central America and flowers in spring and summer (Fig. 17–16).

COCHLIODA

Cochlioda is similar to *Odontoglossum* in appearance, habitat, and cultural requirements. Its long sprays of small flowers come in shades of rose, red, and red-orange. It is for the sake of the colors that its species are bred with those of other genera.

C. noezliana. This species has arching spikes of small, bright, red-orange flowers with a yellow disc on the lip. It occurs in the Andes of Peru and blooms in summer.

C. rosea. Flowers of rosy carmine have a pronounced white column. The blossoms are a little less than an inch in diameter but are numerous on the spikes. The plant occurs in Peru and Ecuador. It blooms late winter and spring.

Figure 17–16 Brassia verrucosa 'Horich'.

C. vulcanica. Larger, dark-rose flowers grow on erect spikes. The species is native to Ecuador and Peru. It can flower any time of the year.

SYMPHYGLOSSUM

This genus has six species, one of which, *S. sanguineum,* has long been known as *Cochlioda sanguinea,* and has been used in hybridization under that name with several members of this subtribe. *S. sanguineum* is a delightful plant, with slender, somewhat conical compressed pseudobulbs and thin leaves. It bears pendent sprays of small, bright-pink or rose-colored flowers, all on the upper side of the stem. They are waxy, somewhat globular in shape, and long lasting. The flower parts all hold themselves forward to conceal the lip and column except from a front view. This is a winter-blooming species.

ASPASIA

About ten species make up this genus, of which three are easily grown, quite popular, and used in hybridization. They can be grown on mounts or in pots with the same treatment as oncidiums.

A. epidendroides is a modest-looking one and one-half inch flower. Its oval sepals and petals are tan, faintly striped with red; the sepals spread wide and the petals curve down over the column. The rounded lip is broader at the base than the tip, white, striped with rose in the center. From Central America and Colombia, it flowers in the summer.

A. lunata is reminscent of the *Oncidium laeve* group in shape and coloring. Its blossoms are one and one-half inches across, and only one or two are borne on a very short stem well down among the leaves. It is from Brazil and flowers in summer.

A. principissa is a flat flower with green petals and sepals striped with cream, and a rectangular, four-lobed lip. Yellow, raised lines radiate from under the column. It is the largest of the group, about three inches across. Found in Costa Rica and Panama, it blooms in late winter and spring.

TRICHOPILIA

Several species in this genus have large, fragrant flowers, others have more modest and less-appealing ones. The plants are strong and dark green, with flattened pseudobulbs and single, leathery leaves. The flower stems come from the base of the pseudobulbs and extend horizontally in most so that the flowers droop over the edge of the pot.

T. fragrans has the plainest flowers, but they are heavily fragrant. The stems stand up from the pseudobulbs, bearing four or more four-inch flowers. The green sepals and petals are slender and wide-spreading, and the white, trumpet-shaped lip has a round, wide-open outer lobe. It is from Cuba, Jamaica, and Colombia, and it flowers from winter to fall (Fig. 17–17).

T. marginata (syn. *crispa*) has a more-slender flower, whose petals and sepals are creamy and tinged with red. The outer lobe of the lip is bright rose-red except for a narrow, white margin. This species continues to make buds over a long period, each on a single stem. From Guatemala, Costa Rica, Panama, and Colombia, it flowers in spring and summer.

T. suavis is probably the best-known of the genus. Its dainty, fragrant flowers come four or five to the stem. They are also the largest of the group, with a broadly flaring trumpet lip. The slender sepals and petals are white, dotted with red, and the white lip is also prettily dotted with red. From Costa Rica, Panama and Colombia, it flowers in late winter and spring.

T. tortillis has spirally twisted sepals and petals that are narrow and ribbonlike. They are greenish-purple with a lighter border. The white lip has a yellow throat spotted with brown. Found from Mexico to Central America, it blossoms in winter and spring.

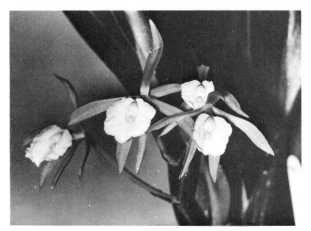

Figure 17–17 Trichopilia fragrans *has plain flowers compared to some of its sisters but perhaps the sweetest fragrance of all.*

HELCIA

Helcia sanguinolenta is a small plant with large flowers of reptilian coloring and markings. The two-inch, dull-green pseudobulbs are somewhat curved and compressed, and bear broad, thin leathery leaves about four inches long. The single flowers come on short stems. The slender, oval sepals and petals are greenish with bars and blotches of light brown neatly outlined in red. The large, ruffled lip is white with a few red lines. A native of Ecuador, it comes from high elevations, likes a cool greenhouse, and flowers mostly in fall and winter (Fig. 17–18).

Figure 17–18 Helcia sanguinolenta, *a flower with reptilian markings.*

RODRIGUEZIA

The plants are small, with delicate sprays of dainty flowers. The lateral sepals are united, and the lip is more or less spurred. Their culture is similar to that of *Laelia* and *Cattleya.*

R. secunda. The whole plant is dwarf in habit, and the six-inch-long spray carries twenty to thirty rose-colored flowers, all on one side of the stem. The plants, which occur in Trinidad and Guiana, flower in August.

R. venusta (syn. *bracteata).* The flowers are a little larger than they are in *secunda,* and the sprays more open. They are white, tinged with pink, and the lip is marked with yellow. It occurs in Brazil. Flowering time is variable.

COMPARETTIA

These are graceful little plants whose flowers are brightly colored and most eye-catching on their arching sprays. The flowers are curiously constructed. The lateral sepals are united and form a spur at their base. The lip has a double spur which fits into the sepals. The front lobe of the lip is somewhat heart-shaped, broad and spreading. The petals and upper sepal form sort of a hood behind the column. A single, rather broad leaf arises from the tiny pseudobulb. They may be grown in small pots or on driftwood or tree fern slabs. They grow natively on small branches in humid forests and must be kept damp in cultivation. A few crosses have been made between *Comparettia* and *Oncidium* and *Rodriguezia.*

C. coccinea. This has one-inch flowers in tones of yellow shaded with scarlet and a bright-scarlet lip. It is native to Brazil and is fall blooming.

C. falcata is similar to *coccinea* but its flowers are of bright cerise. It has a wider range, spreading from Mexico through Central America and northern South America. In Costa Rica it is found on the merest twigs on the lower parts of trees. Flowering takes place throughout the year.

C. macroplectron has a beautiful two-inch flower with an extremely large lip and a very long spur. It is light pink daintily spotted with rose. This is a native of Colombia and can flower at any time.

C. speciosa is bright orange with the dorsal sepal and petals veined with a darker shade. It, too, has a very long spur. This one is native to Ecuador and is fall blooming.

IONOPSIS

These are small plants, which have a many-branched flower stem with innumerable, delightful, small flowers.

I. satyrioides. This is a lovely small species, apparently without a pseudobulb. The one-third-inch flowers are white. The lip is slender and slightly divided and the sepals and petals are larger. Native to the West Indies, it flowers summer and fall.

I. utricularioides is a perfectly delightful little plant which gives lacy sprays of half-inch flowers ranging from pink to purple and even white. The prominent lip is broad and flat. The leaf, which should arise from the top of the pseudobulb, is aborted, and instead there is the merest little point of green in that place. The leaves therefore all come from the base of the pseudobulb. The species ranges from Florida and the West Indies, and from Mexico south to Peru. The species *I. paniculata* has now been combined with this one. They are mostly spring and summer flowering.

TRICHOCENTRUM

This genus is characterized by its odd trowel-shaped lip which is prolonged at its base into a prominent spur. The sepals and petals are free, sometimes longer than the lip and spreading, sometimes smaller and overlapping. The flowers are brightly colored, produced sometimes singly, sometimes several to a stem, and they are large in proportion to the size of the plant. The column is winged and usually covered with short fleshy tubercles.

T. albo-coccineum (syn. albo-purpureum). This species has stunning little flowers, greenish on the outside, maroon-brown within, with a white lip decorated with two purple spots. It occurs in Ecuador, Peru, and Brazil and flowers spring and fall.

T. panduratum. The sepals and petals of this species are extremely short and overlapping, and the lip is long and narrow with a long, taillike spur. The general appearance of the flower is that of an old-fashioned salt shovel. It occurs in Peru and blooms in spring.

T. pulchrum. This is an open flower, with broad sepals and petals that are green, spotted with reddish purple. The rectangular lip is ivory with purple spots. It is native to Venezuela, Colombia, Ecuador, and Peru. It flowers in summer and early fall.

LEOCHILUS AND MESOSPINIDIUM

Leochilus is a genus of miniatures, and *Mesospinidium* of almost equally small plants. Both are related to Oncidium although no hybrids have as yet been made. They have small, somewhat compressed pseudobulbs and short, thin, leathery leaves. The little flowering stems arch gracefully to about the height of the leaves, sometimes a bit more, and bear several half-inch flowers. In both, the flowers are greenish with a white or cream lip,

the sepals and petals spotted rather densely with brown, the lip only sparsely marked. In *Leochilus labiatus,* the lateral sepals are free-spreading except right at the base, and the lip is a rather long rectangle with a point at the tip, a fat basal callus, and hairs at the base of the column. It is a native of Guatemala, Honduras, Costa Rica, Venezuela, Trinidad, and the West Indies. It flowers summer and fall. In *Mesospinidium endresii,* the lateral sepals are united almost to their tips and are more conspicuous than the small, fleshy, bumpy lip that is held out horizontally. This one is native to Costa Rica and Panama and is winter blooming (Fig. 17–19).

LOCKHARTIA

Lockhartia is a genus of beautiful plants which need not bloom to be enjoyed but which do flower most generously and easily. The foot-tall stems are clothed by little clasping leaves (equitant), which give a braided effect. From the upper leaf axils come clusters of very small and dainty yellow flowers, mottled with red or brown. The little rounded sepals are held back to back above the rest of the flower; the petals, usually folded in half lengthwise, curve upward; and the complicated lip hangs down. The lip in most species has two long side lobes which curve together like arms, a very warty crest vividly marked with brown or red, and a flaring midlobe. They vary in size from one-half inch to one inch, according to the species.

L. acuta has stems more than one foot long with tightly clasping leaves that make it appear rather wide. The flowers are unusual for the genus, being white or whitish, more-or-less flat, on a branched stem three inches long. The sepals and petals are rounded, the lip four lobed, making the flower look more like an oncidium than the other species. Found in Panama, Colombia, Venezuela, and Trinidad, it flowers in summer.

L. amoena is one of the larger species, both as to breadth of leafy stem and size of flowers, the blooms reaching almost an inch in length. The rounded, heart-shaped bracts on the flower stems are especially large and very decorative. It is native to Costa Rica and Panama, and it blooms in the fall (Fig. 17–20).

L. micrantha has narrow stems about one-and-one-half feet long, and half-inch flowers of cream or pale yellow that do not open well. It occurs

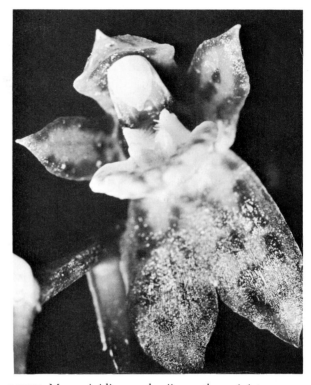

Figure 17–19 *LEFT.* Leochilus labiatus, *a curious little flower from a miniature plant.*

RIGHT. Mesospinidium endresii, *another miniature.*

from Nicaragua to Suriname and flowers in spring and summer.

L. oerstedii is most often seen in collections. Its stems stand up straight and are one foot or more tall. The flowers are an inch long, bright yellow with bright red spots. They come in clusters of three or so. Found from Mexico to Central America, it blooms almost constantly.

NOTYLIA

This genus has until recently covered two types of plants, those with an obvious pseudobulb topped by a single, leathery leaf with one or more leaves from its base, and those with a flat fan of knife-shaped leaves, the center one arising from a barely discernible pseudobulb. The latter have been transferred to the genus *Macroclinium* (see below).

Those which remain in *Notylia* give a straight, pendent spike closely covered with tiny greenish flowers. The pollinia sit on the back of the column tip and have an unusually long stipe. The sepals and petals are very slender, pointed, the lateral se-

pals joined for part of their length. The lip is sharply triangular and has a stalk.

N. barkeri can reach eight inches in height. Its flower spike is sometimes one foot long covered with greenish-white, half-inch blossoms spotted with yellow. From Mexico, it flowers more than once a year.

N. tridachne is smaller and has a shorter but more densely packed spray of greenish-yellow flowers spotted with orange. Found from Mexico to El Salvador, it flowers in the spring.

MACROCLINIUM

This genus contains the fan-shaped plants once included in *Notylia*. The flowers have a similar structure—feathery little blossoms with the pollinia lying on the back of the column tip.

M. bicolor has numerous spikes that hold twenty or thirty delicate lavender and green flowers toward the outer end of the stems. Found from Mexico to El Salvador, it flowers in summer.

M. manabinum is the correct name for a species

Figure 17–20 Lockhartia amoena.
A: Clusters of complicated little oncidiumlike flowers come from the tips of stems clothed with "braided" leaves.
B: Closeup of a single flower.

that has been mistakenly called *xiphorius* (and was so labeled in the third edition of this book). Its short flower spikes stick out in all directions, each holding a "dandelion puff" of rosy-violet blossoms with a dark purple lip. These stems make several bursts of flowers throughout the year. It occurs from Ecuador to Peru.

SIGMATOSTALIX

Sigmatostalix is a genus of dwarf plants of great charm. They have tiny pseudobulbs, each bearing two or more leaves. The whole plant is about four inches tall. The delicate flower spikes come from the base of the pseudobulbs and hold a score or so jaunty flowers less than one-quarter inch long. The most outstanding feature of the flower is the long column which is conspicuous in a flower so small and gives it somewhat the appearance of a miniature cycnoches. In some species the lip is attached by a long claw, giving it the shape of a broad trowel with a handle. In others the lip is "sessile," that is, it has no claw. Many of the species produce a second and third crop of flowers on the same stem (Fig. 17–21).

S. guatemalensis has a row of tiny brown-and-yellow birdlike flowers on its inflorescence. They are about three-quarters inch long, with a stalked, spade-shaped lip. The fan-shaped plant is about three inches tall, with the center leaf arising from a tiny pseudobulb. From Mexico to Panama, it produces successive flowers several times a year.

S. racemifera is a type with a clawless lip. Its plant has a pseudobulb with a single leaf from the top and two or three from the base, making a plant three to six inches tall. The quarter-inch flower is translucent, pinkish white, with a ruffled, orange-spotted lip decorated with a large cushion-shaped yellow callus. From Panama, it blooms in the fall.

OTHER GENERA

A few other genera that are attractive, although they by no means complete the list of Oncidiinae, are: *Capanemia, Cischweinfia, Gomesa, Ornithophora, Palumbina, Quekettia,* and *Warmingia.*

HYBRIDS

Hybrids between and among the various members of the Oncidiinae are increasing in number every year. There is as yet no end in sight to the possibilities.

A sampling of bigeneric hybrid names follows:

Figure 17–21 Sigmatosalix, *a genus of miniatures, reveals charming details under a hand lens.*
A: Sigmatostalix racemifera, *still perched on the twig on which it lived in the tropics.*
B: *Closeup of a single flower. The lip is sessile.*
C: Sigmatostalix guatemalensis *has bright little flowers. The lip is attached by a long claw.*

Adaglossum = Ada × Odontoglossum. Adioda = Ada × Cochlioda. Brassidium = Brassia × Oncidium. Miltonpasia = Miltonia × Aspasia. Miltonioda = Miltonia × Cochlioda. Miltonidium = Miltonia × Oncidium. Odontioda = Cochlioda × Odontoglossum. Odontocidium = Odontoglossum × Oncidium. Odontonia = Miltonia × Odontoglossum. Oncidioda = Cochlioda × Oncidium. Symphyglossonia = Symphyglossum × Miltonia. Symphodontoglossum = Symphyglossum × Odontoglossum.

Some of the tri- and quadrigeneric hybrid names are:

Burrageara = Cochlioda × Miltonia × Odontoglossum × Oncidium. Charlesworeheara = Cochlioda × Miltonia × Oncidium. Colmanara = Miltonia × Odontoglossum × Oncidium. Sanderara = Brassia × Cochlioda × Odontoglossum. Vuylstekeara = Cochlioda × Miltonia × Odontoglossum. Wilsonara = Cochlioda × Odontoglossum × Oncidium.

For other names, consult Garay and Sweet, 1966, and *Handbook on Orchid Nomenclature and Registration.* (Be sure to get the latest edition.)

Dendrobium bigibbum (phalaenopsis) type

Dendrobium thyrsiflorum

Miltoniopsis phalaenopsis

Miltonia spectabilis

Miltoniopsis vexillaria

Odontoglossum cirrhosum

Cuitlauzina pendulula

Odontoglossum crispum hybrid

Lemboglossum cervantesii

Ticoglossum krameri

Oncidium mimeticum (left), Oncidium cucullatum (right)

Oncidium forbesii

Oncidium fuscatum

Oncidium guianense

Oncidium hastatum

Oncidium macranthum

Oncidium onustum

Psychopsis kramerianum

Trichopilia suavia

Catasetum tenebrosum

Aspasia lunata

Mormodes igneum

Coryanthes speciosa

Stanhopea martiana

Bulbophyllum fletcherianum (plant)

Bulbophyllum phalaenopsis

Bulbophyllum fletcherianum (flowers)

Bulbophyllum barbigerum

Bifrenaria harrisoniae

Cirrhopetalum medusae (PHOTO BY FRED HOWSE)

Anoectochilus roxburghii

Maxillaria tenuifolia

Anguloa virginalis

Lycaste macrophylla

Masdevallia coccinea (group of plants)

Masdevallia tovarensis

Masdevallia veitchiana

Telipogon ampliflorus

Polystachya pubescens

Trichoceros parviflorus

Huntleya burtii

Bacterial infection on phalaenopsis leaf

False spider mite injury on phalaenopsis leaf.

Forest devastation in Mexico

Color break caused by TmVO (ORSV)

Necrotic streak and spot caused by CyMV

·18·

CATASETUM RELATIVES

The Catasetinae Subtribe

STANHOPEA RELATIVES

The Stanhopeinae Subtribe

CATASETINAE

NOT CONTENT WITH THE DE-vious methods used by other orchids to insure pollination, the members of the Catasetinae use a more direct approach—they shoot the pollinia directly at the visiting insect. Each kind has a trigger placed in such a way that the insect is bound to step on it or disturb it in some way. The instant this happens the pollinarium is shot

out, the viscid disc flips up, hits the insect, and adheres tightly to its anatomy. The creamy material on the disc is so copious that it actually splatters on contact, precluding any possibility of failure to stick to the hairy surface, and it sets instantly. To attract the proper insect, the flowers exude a potent fragrance, not always detectable by the human nose, although it is often quite enjoyable to us as well. The fragrance is not associated with nectar, but is bound in tissues upon which the bee scratches. The tissue is so placed in the flower, at some part of the lip, that the bee in its activity must touch the trigger. The anther is attached to a thin membrane that is stretched like a piece of rubber over a small dome. At the other end of the membrane is fastened the viscid disc. The trigger is inserted just under the edge of the taut membrane. When it is pressed, it acts as a lever to lift its edge and allow it to snap together, which causes it to fly off, taking the viscid disc and anther with it. When the pollinarium is examined, it is seen that this membrane substitutes for the stalk or stipe between the pollinia and disc. It can be unrolled and placed back on the dome, but you cannot recreate the same tension that held it in place originally.

Dr. Calaway H. Dodson has made a study of pollination in this group of orchids and in others. He has observed just how the bee is positioned to receive the pollinia and how the position of the pollinia is associated with placing them on the stigma of the female flower, or, where both sexes are contained in the flower, placing them on the next one visited. The pollinia may be placed "between the shoulders" or on the end of the abdomen. Furthermore, he analyzes the fragrances with which the flowers lure their pollinators.

So sensitive is the trigger apparatus that it makes it difficult to handle some of these flowers without causing the pollinarium to pop. You can cause it to do so by touching the trigger with your finger or a pencil, and you can feel the recoil of the flower as this happens.

In addition to being fascinating performers, the flowers are in most cases very beautiful, and those that cannot be called exactly pretty have a certain lurid appeal. Most of them bloom during fall and winter, but a few wait until spring. They are all deciduous, and with a few exceptions flower while the leaves are falling or after this has taken place.

Species having perfect flowers, those which have both male and female reproductive organs in the same individuals, have been removed from *Cata-*

setum to form the genera *Clowesia* and *Dressleria*. Those which have separate male and female flowers are retained in *Catasetum* and *Stanhopea*. *Mormodes* has a unique system: The flower functions as a female after the pollinia have been removed.

CATASETUM

Best known of the pollen shooters, there are several types of flowers in the genus. They have separate male and female flowers, and though the male flowers are quite distinct in each species, the females all look pretty much alike, with a fleshy, hooded lip and a short, blunt column. The same plant can produce both, but oddly enough female flowers rarely occur in cultivation, and even in nature are always fewer than the males. It seems that bright sun is necessary to develop them. Occasionally an hermaphroditic flower develops, one with female form but having a much-reduced anther. Among the types of male flowers, there are some with a large, hoodlike lip held uppermost, some with a saucer-shaped lip held ventrally, some that have a definite cup or sac at the base of the lip, and others whose lip is a bearded tongue. The cylindrical pseudobulbs are left with sharp spines after the leaves fall.

It is best to keep the plants quite dry from leaf-fall until new growth begins in the spring, giving water occasionally to keep the bulbs plump, once in a while in the pot but mostly by misting. They should be repotted when roots start from the new growth in the spring and then be watered regularly. They can be grown in any of the media with generous applications of fertilizer.

C. barbatum. This species has many variations that have been given separate specific names at one time or another, such as *appendiculatum* and *cristatum*. All have a narrow, tongue-shaped lip with many white, fingerlike projections standing up along its borders. These can be thick or thin, sparse or numerous, and it is on the basis of such differences that the separate names have been endowed. In some forms they are so profuse that they hide the whole lip surface. The flower parts are slender, the dorsal sepal and petals standing up together, the lateral sepals spreading down or sideways. The group is widespread through all of northern South America, Ecuador, Peru, and Bolivia.

C. macrocarpum. This is one of the most widespread species and is typical of the type with a hood

Figure 18–1 *The pollen-shooting mechanism of Catasetum macrocarpum.*
A: *The intact column with pointed anther showing swellings under which lie the pollinia. The sensitive trigger curves upward.*
B: *The column cut in half. Within the cavity near the trigger is the viscid disc, attached to a membrane stretched over a dome of tissue, the other end of which is fastened to the pollinia. Pressing the trigger releases the membrane and the viscid disc flies upward, bearing the pollinarium with it.*
C: *The trigger was pressed and the pollinarium flew up and attached itself to a piece of paper held above the column.*

lip (Fig. 18–1). The column and long, pointed anther project out from underneath. The pair of triggers extends back under the hood. One is nonfunctional and is curled back, the other, the functional one, stands upright. The lip is shiny green and spotted with dull red, heavily on the inside, lightly on the outside. The thin sepals and heavier petals overlap, surrounding and backing the column. This species is native to Venezuela, Brazil, Guyana, French Guiana, Trinidad, and Suriname. It blooms fall and winter. Some other species of this type are *viridiflavum*, whose lip is gold on top and whose petals and sepals are tinged with gold, native to Panama and fall flowering; *macroglossum*, pure lime-green except for a few spots of brown on the petals and sepals and inside the lip, from Ecuador; *oerstedii*, very similar to *macrocarpum* and native to Nicaragua, Costa Rica, Panama, and Colombia; and *collare*, native to Venezuela, with a light-yellow-green lip whose outer edge is rolled and dark-green sepals and petals.

C. pileatum. This is one of the most beautiful of orchids. It is sheer wax, butter-yellow, with a pure-white column. The lip is a broad, shallow saucer, held downward, and it has a slight coating of granular-looking papillae at its base, where there is also a small depression. The lateral sepals curve around the rim of the lip, while the dorsal sepal and petals stand up straight, overlapping behind the column. The column sits above the lip, with one trigger hanging down, the other curled under. It occurs in Venezuela, Trinidad, and the Amazon region and blooms variably (Fig. 18–2). *C. platyglossum*, is a similar and also very beautiful species. This one has a crest on the red-gold lip, and the other parts are yellow, tinged with green. It is native to Ecuador.

C. saccatum. Here is a species whose downhanging lip has a distinct cup or sac at the base, hence its name. Moreover, the lip is three-lobed, the side lobes spreading flat beside the sac, and the midlobe hanging down in front; all are greenish, spotted with brown, and fringed on their edges. The sepals spread at right angles and the petals stand up beside the dorsal sepal, and they are green spotted with brown. The species occurs in Brazil, Peru, and Ecuador and flowers any time of the year. A variety *christyanum* has at times been considered a separate species. There are several other species with saclike lips, among them *discolor*, which has a wide, gaping "mouth" with fringed jowls, a pale cream and cream-green flower with pink spots that become wine red inside the lip, na-

A

B

C

Figure 18–2 Catasetum platyglossum *visited by a bee.* A: *The bee depresses the trigger of the male flower.* B: *The viscid disc flips downward, fastening itself to the back of the bee. After the bee flies away the anther cap will fall off, leaving the pollinia ready to be deposited on a female flower.* C: *A bee with pollinia attached visits a female flower of* C. platyglossum, *and as it crawls into the lip the pollinia will be dragged into contact with the stigma.* (COURTESY OF CALAWAY H. DODSON.)

tive to Venezuela, Brazil, Guyana, the Amazon, Colombia, and Suriname; *fimbriatum,* another pink and pale green flower, whose turned-out lip edges are also fringed, from Venezuela, Guyana, Brazil, Paraguay, Argentina, and Bolivia; and *sanguineum,* a dark brownish green flower with a complicated lip that has a raised border around the sac, overhung by a comb of fleshy, pink projections on each side arising from the outer border of the lip. This last is from Costa Rica, Venezuela, Colombia, and Ecuador.

C. tenebrosum. This is another species with a flat, open lip and fantastic coloring. Its velvety black petals and sepals contrast sharply with its heavy, waxy, slightly brown-tinged creamy lip and column. The flower is stiff and flat, the petals and dorsal sepal standing upright, the lateral sepals extending sideways. The lip is shield shaped, toothed on the edges, with a swelling at its base and tip, and a dimple in the middle. The upright column has small brown triggers. It is from Peru, and it flowers in the spring.

DRESSLERIA

This genus was created to accomodate a few distinctive species with perfect flowers whose stigma is covered by the stipe of the pollinarium and not exposed until that structure is removed.

D. suavis will serve to introduce the members of this genus. There are several others that look very much like it, but they are difficult to tell apart. It has very waxy flowers of pure ivory color and delightful fragrance. The fleshy sepals and petals open flat at first but soon fold back sharply to lie along the ovary, leaving the fat, blunt column and scoop-shaped, saccate lip projecting forward. On first examining the column, it is impossible to see the stigma, but when the pollinarium is shot out by touching the sensitive protuberance on the anther cap, the stigma is revealed, having been concealed by the apparatus. This, of course, insures that the flower is not fertilized with its own pollen. The stipe (stalk) of the pollinarium is at first upright so that the pollinia cannot come in contact with the stigma. During the next few moments, it bends forward, by which time the bee would be visiting another flower (Fig. 18–3). Remarkably, according to Dodson, the pollinarium is fastened to the bee either just in front of the first pair of legs or on the basal section. It comes from Costa Rica. It

keeps its leaves for two or three years and does not require as drastic drying as others. It flowers in the summer. Other species are *D. dilecta* from Costa Rica, *eburnea* from Ecuador, and *helleri,* a new species from Nicaragua.

CLOWESIA

The members of this genus (which have both sexes in the same flower) were removed from *Catasetum* and returned to the genus created for them in 1843. They all have a more or less saclike lip with a sort of fringed apron or tongue that spreads from its outer edge. *C. rosea* was the first one described.

C. glaucoglossum is about two inches across, with a rounded, rather short sac that hangs straight down. The front lobe of the lip protrudes forward and is only one-half inch long. The greenish flower comes from Mexico and flowers July to August.

C. rosea is a small plant about ten inches in height, very much like warscewitzii in shape. The one-inch flowers are beautifully scented, bright rose, with rounded sepals and petals. The base of the lip is narrow, forming a shallow cup, and the tri-lobed outer portion bears a beard on each part. It is from Mexico and it flowers in the spring.

C. russelliana. This is a larger flower, some two and one-half inches across, with a long, deep sac that curves forward from under the fringed midlobe. The latter is quite long and voluptuous. The flower is gray-green or whitish with dark green veins. Found from Mexico to Panama, it flowers in late summer and fall.

C. thylaciochila has an unusual lip. Instead of a rounded sac, it has a pointed, almost chinlike lip that projects straight back under the column. It also is greenish white with green veins, and the front portion of the lip is fairly short. From Mexico, it flowers in late spring and summer.

C. warscewitzii (syn. *scurra*). The odd spelling of the name is due to an error in the original publication. This one is similar to *rosea* except that it is whitish green with pale green stripes. Its lip ends in a single beard. It is deliciously fragrant. Like *rosea,* it is a near miniature. It has an odd method of applying its pollinarium to a visiting bee. There are two cavities below the column, in a vertical line. The bee clings at an angle to the lip, puts its forelegs into the two cavities, and rubs them together, dislodging the pollinarium so that it be-

A

B

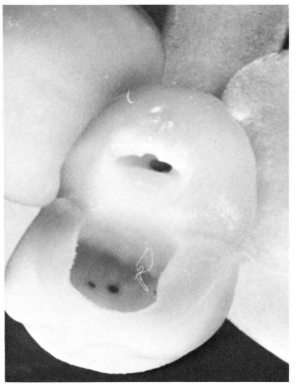

C

D

Figure 18–3 Dressleria suavis, *a type with both sexes in one flower.*

A: *The lowermost flower on the stem has had the pollinia removed.*

B: *Detail showing column and lip before the pollinia are removed; the stigma is completely covered by the viscid disc.*

C: *Touching the underside causes the viscid disc to fly out, bringing away the anther with the pollinarium and uncovering the stigma.*

D: *The stipe of the pollinarium straightens as the bee carries it around for a while so that it can be fitted into the very small cavity of the stigma.*

comes attached to the femur just above the knee joint. This is called "bee's-knees" pollination. The species occurs from Costa Rica to Venezuela at low elevations and flowers in fall and winter (Fig. 18–4).

CYCNOCHES

These are very lovely orchids, worth cultivating for their beauty as well as for their interesting habit. The name means "swan's neck," referring to the arching column. The lip in some species is shaped like the body of a swan, adding to the illusion that gives them their name "swan orchid." Plants can produce either male or female flowers, or both at the same time, and occasionally may produce a spray of bisexual or hermaphroditic flowers. The pseudobulbs are columnar, bearing five to eight broad, graceful leaves. The leaves are notoriously attractive to red spider and should be sprayed regularly for this pest. They prefer a hanging position in an airy spot and a daily misting with water. The flower spikes make their appearance from the axils of the leaves. During the de-

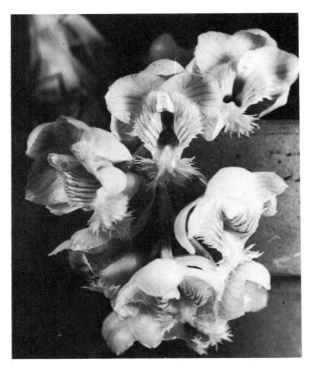

Figure 18–4 Clowesia warscewitzii (scurra), *a miniature species with fragrant, green flowers containing both sexes in each flower.*

velopment of the flowers the leaves will start to fall. After the leaves have fallen, the plants should be kept quite dry through the winter, with just an occasional syringing. Some growers divide them before carrying them through their rest period, separating the bulbs (without cutting back the roots) and standing them on the bench, sprinkling them with water occasionally. When new growth has begun its own roots, those left in pots through the winter should be put in fresh medium and the shrivelled pseudobulbs removed. Those separated in the fall should be potted. Regular watering is now resumed. Recently some growers have had exceptional success by adding manure to other media, such as any of the mixes, or bark mixed with tree fern and loamy soil. Cycnoches seems to thrive on a very rich medium. A cymbidium mix might also be used.

Pollination in *Cycnoches* is not as spectacular as in *Catasetum,* but is fascinating nevertheless, as described by Dodson and the late Paul Allen. In those with a rigid lip, such as *chlorochilon* and its relatives, there is a callus on the lip placed in such a way that the bee can hang on only by its front legs to get at the source of the attracting fragrance. This causes its rear end to hang down and "tickle" the sensitive viscid disc on the arching column. The pollinarium is thereby sprung, and the pollinia stick to the end of its abdomen. When it visits a female flower, this dangling pair of pollinia are caught by a hooklike notch in the end of the column and sink into the stigma (Fig. 18–5). In types with a fragile, stalked lip, such as *egertonianum,* the weight of the bee clinging to the underside of the lip causes the lip to swing down and bring the tail end of the bee in contact with the trigger. From then on the same sequence of events takes place.

C. aureum. This variety has larger flowers of a pale yellow-green, striped with green and toned with tan. They become more and more yellow with age. The sepals and petals are much broader than in *egertonianum;* the sepals spread wide without curling, the dorsal extending back and the laterals forward, while the petals curve backward a bit. The lip is somewhat boat-shaped, fringed, with slender upright processes. This variety occurs in both Costa Rica and Panama, and flowers in the fall (Fig. 18–6).

C. chlorochilon. The plant known by this name and widely grown as the "swan orchid" is actually *C. ventricosum* var. *warscewiczii,* described below. It is difficult to give up the association of the prettier name with the familiar plant. Paul Allen

Figure 18–5 *A bee with pollinia attached to its rear end scratching at the lip of a female flower of* Cycnoches ventricosum *var.* warscewiczii. *As it leaves the flower the pollinia will be caught by the hook at the tip of the column.* (COURTESY OF CALAWAY H. DODSON.)

Figure 18–6 Cycnoches aureum.
A: The delicate but long-lasting male flowers.
B: Hermaphroditic flowers on the same plant. These are identical in shape to female flowers but have both a receptive stigma and pollinia. In the flowers shown here, the pollinia soon aborted.

considered *chlorochilon* and *warscewiczii* both to be varieties of *ventricosum*. More recently Garay has returned *chlorochilon* to specific status. The flower is light yellow-green, lightly veined. The lip is pale ivory-green, shading to yellow at the base, and is not clawed. The callus at its base is raised, but there is no depression around it. As in all of this group, the flowers are upside down. The male and female flowers are much alike, the female having a shorter, stockier column. Occasionally, hermaphroditic flowers are produced; they look like the female but bear pollinia in addition to a stigma. The species occurs in northern South America and flowers summer to fall, sometimes into winter.

C. egertonianum and its variety *dianae*. The similarities between these are evident and it is clear that they are closely related. The delicate flowers are borne in a long pendent chain, sometimes with as many as thirty flowers open all at once. The male flowers have slender sepals and petals which are of rather thin substance (although the flowers are quite long lasting), a fleshy lip that stands on a stalk and has fingerlike processes around the edge, and a long, slender, arching column (Fig. 18–7). The female flowers are fleshy and are much like those of *chlorochilon*. They have greenish sepals and petals, a very thick waxy lip which is white and without processes, and a short, blunt

column. They are borne two or three on a short stem, and, as if to make up for their lack of numbers, they keep for two months. Sometimes hermaphroditic flowers occur, but the pollinia are so

Figure 18–7 *A bee clinging to the lip of* Cycnoches egertonianum. *Its weight causes the lip to bend downward, allowing the tip of its abdomen to touch the sensitive viscid disc and so obtain the pollinia. The one in this picture has already received pollinia from a previous flower.* (Courtesy of Calaway H. Dodson.)

quickly aborted that unless you spot them soon after the flowers open you may think the flowers are purely female. *C. egertonianum* occurs from Mexico through Central America to Colombia, Ecuador, Peru, and Brazil. There are slight differences among those from various areas, for instance, the flowers from Costa Rica are widely spaced on the stem and the lip processes are short, broad, arranged on a flat disc, and few in number, while plants from Ecuador have a more compact inflorescence and the lip processes are numerous, long, and almost filamentous. In general, the sepals and petals are green or greenish brown with veins of darker green or spots of purple. Sometimes the spots are quite dense, giving a very dark flower. The flowers are quite "curly"—the sepals tend to curl on the edges and the petals to curl entirely back on themselves, leaving the upward-

projecting lip on its stalk and the arching column as the conspicuous parts of the flower. When the flower is unfolded it is about two-and-one-half inches long. Flowering takes place in the autumn.

C. egertonianum var. *dianae.* This variety is native to Panama. It is pinkish tan with a green tinge, and has less-conspicuous markings than either of the others. The lip is more like that of var. *aureum* than like the various forms of *egertonianum* itself, but its edge processes are thicker and are held more rigidly upright and closer together. It, too, is fall flowering.

C. ventricosum. The distinguishing features of this member of the "swan" group are its long lip claw and the fact that the basal callus is only rounded, not particularly raised. Its flowers are waxy, fragrant, and long lasting. They are green at first, fading to yellow. The sepals and petals tend to bend downward. It occurs in Mexico, Guatemala, and Panama.

C. ventricosm var. *Warscewiczii.* This is the one long known as *chlorochilon.* Its heavy, waxy, chartreuse flowers are delightfully fragrant. The lip is white, and its basal callus is a projecting, fleshy triangle that arises from a severe depression; both callus and depression are dark green. The flower spike holds four to ten flowers that are four or five inches across. Flowers appear after the growth matures, sometimes before the leaves fall, sometimes afterward, usually in the fall. It is native to Panama and Costa Rica.

MORMODES

The name means "weird creature," from the fact that the column is twisted to lie with the back of the anther on the lip. They are also called "goblin" orchids. The position of the column is associated with pollination, and as Dodson recounts it, it is quite unusual. The tip of the anther has a pedallike trigger, and the column is positioned so that an insect crawling across the lip will step on it. The pollinarium flies out and fastens itself to the back of the thorax of the bee. Because the stalk is curled, the bee cannot leave the pollina on that flower (Fig. 18–8). Later on, the stalk straightens out to hold the pollinia upright and the bee leaves them on the stigma of a subsequent flower as it wanders around on the lip. In some flowers the column is not pressed to the lip but held up somewhat: These function only to receive pollen. Dodson has ob-

Figure 18–8 *In* Mormodes *the column is twisted and bent so that the back of the anther rests on the lip, exposing the sensitive trigger at its tip. A bee crawling on the lip will touch the trigger and the pollinia will be applied to its back. This is* Mormodes buccinator.

served the column in other flowers to raise up and untwist after the pollinia have been removed, making it more likely that it will receive pollen. Functionally, the latter flowers become female after the pollinia are removed. Apparently, a flower whose column remains in contact with the lip does not always become pollinated. A fascinating habit, is that in some flowers the flowers on the left side of the raceme twist the column to the left; those on the right side have their column turned to the right, while in other flowers, the columns all twist toward the stem.

The lip usually has its sides turned down, making it look something like a saddle. The pseudobulbs are fleshy, somewhat lumpy, and have no spines after leaf-fall. They usually flower sometime after the leaves fall, occasionally not until the following spring. Keep them on the dry side through this period of inactivity, resuming watering after the flower spikes start. If new growth has not started by the time flowering is finished, give them another short period of dryness until it does. They need not be repotted each year, though some growers prefer to do so, and can be grown like catasetums.

M. aromatica is a pretty and sweetly scented species. The flowers are so densely dotted with rose on a cream background that they appear to be of solid rose. They are rounded, the broad, pointed petals and sepals curling round the lip and column.

The lip is narrow, with three points at its tip, and it curves over the twisted column. It is from El Salvador, Mexico, and Honduras and it blooms in the fall.

M. buccinator. The colors of this species range from pure white through shades of yellow, green, and pink, to a dark red, according to the area from which the plants come. The sides of the lip are rectangular, giving a squared-off effect viewed from the side. The petals bend forward making an awning over the lip. The species is found throughout tropical America but is most common in Venezuela and Ecuador. Flowers winter into summer.

M. colossus. This can be a very large plant, but does not necessarily grow larger than other species. The flowers are nicely shaped, with the sepals and petals held back in a spreading star from the lip and the sides of the rather longish lip rolled under to meet at their edges. The sepals and petals are golden brown, or yellow, yellow-green, or cream, and the lip a darker shade. It is native to Costa Rica and Panama and flowers spring or fall.

M. hookeri. The most unusual but rather small flowers of this species are dark red with an almost black and very hairy lip. The dorsal sepal bends over the lip, the other sepals and the petals curve backward. It occurs in Costa Rica, Panama, and Colombia and is winter blooming.

M. igneum. This species ranges through the same colors as *colossus,* but its parts are more or less spotted with red. The sepals and petals are thin; the dorsal sepal stands up straight, the other parts are bent back. The more fleshy lip is round in outline when spread out, and in natural position has its sides sharply bent down. This one occurs in Costa Rica, Panama, and Colombia. Its flowering season is winter.

M. skinneri. This species has its yellow sepals and petals striped with dotted lines of purplish red and the lip marked with large blotches of the same color. The edges of the lip and its center portion are decorated with white hairs. This one is native to Guatemala and Costa Rica.

M. variabilis. A beautifully colored species, with dark rose sepals and petals and a downy, lighter rose lip. The dorsal sepal and petals arch over the column, the laterals are held back a bit. The rounded sides of the lip are turned down and tucked under both front and back, while the tip bears a projection that curves downward. The anther is unusually large with an exceptionally long point that rests on the lip. Found in Ecuador, its flowering season is spring and summer.

STANHOPEINAE

Within this subtribe are some of the most fantastic of orchids as well as some of the most serenely beautiful. All subject their pollinators to the most ignominious treatment, making them fall through the flower, or throwing them backwards against the pollinia, or dumping them in a bucket of water. The lip in every genus is constructed of three parts, marvelously carved with sacs, loops, knobs, and horns. The basal section is the hypochile, the midsection the mesochile, and the tip the epichile. The flowers lure their victims with potent and delightful fragrances but offer them nothing in the way of nectar. If they give them anything in return for their services it is merely a momentary pleasure in the fragrances for which they eagerly scratch, and which sometimes cause them to behave in a very silly manner and so distract them that they do not anticipate what is about to happen to them. Nor do the "accidents" they endure prevent their coming back for more.

The plants are for the most part epiphytic, with conical-to-globular pseudobulbs bearing broad, pleated leaves. Many have pendulous flower stems, and these should be grown in a hanging position or placed on stands. Some have flower stems that bore down through the medium; these are best grown in baskets or bottomless pots. They vary as to seasonal needs, but can be accommodated in an intermediate house.

CORYANTHES

This orchid has the notorious reputation of making its pollinators drunk, but like so many good myths, this may have to be toned down a bit. The series of experiences it forces on its pollinators is nonetheless excruciating, however. The flowers are very complex with the parts marvelously engineered. The very waxy lip is divided into three sections. The end part or epichile is formed into a bucket with a spout, shaped something like an old-fashioned coal bucket; this is attached to the basal part by a stalk, the mesochile; and the basal part is a fat globe which exudes a tantalizing fragrance. The column, instead of curving toward the lip as in most flowers, hangs down into the bucket and then bends up so that it forms the roof of the spout, with the anther and its viscid disc held just over

the end of the spout. The petals and sepals are bent and twisted in various ways to camouflage the opening of the spout and leave open the entrance to the bucket. Two protuberances at the base of the column exude a fluid that drips steadily into the bucket, keeping it full to the spout. With the plants in cultivation and no pollinators around to watch, this in itself is a fascinating procedure to observe. It seems to begin even before the bud opens, for as soon as you can look into the bucket you find it already half full. The strong and delightful fragrance is discernable as soon as the sepals begin to separate.

The late Paul Allen described the events that take place, and Dodson has not only observed the behavior of the bees but has analyzed the fragrances and experimented with their effects on bees in the field. Only male euglossine bees are attracted by the perfumes. Dodson discovered that while the fragrances of the flowers are made up of the same chemical components, they are in different proportions in the various species; thus they attract different species of bees.

The bees arrive at a flower, locate the source of the fragrance, and then, losing all caution, begin avidly to scratch or brush at the tissues with bristles on their forelegs. If nothing untoward happens, they fly off, transferring the substance they have acquired to organs on their hind legs. However, something untoward often does happen—frequently, a bee will lose its footing (because the waxy surface is slippery, not because the bee is drunk!), or come in contact with a drop of fluid dripping from the column glands and be felled into the bucket. There it flounders, unable to spread its wings. At last it finds the exit through the spout, helped by a "foot stool" or a "ladder" at its base. The necessity for a bee of the right size becomes apparent, because too small a one would slip through without removing the pollinia, and one that was too large would become stuck in the tunnel. One of the right size, and therefore of the right species, finds the tunnel sufficiently tight-fitting to necessitate a struggle to squeeze through, causing it to press against the anther and remove the pollinia. It then flies away to dry off. When the morning's activities are over, the flower's fragrance ceases. The events begin again the next day—the flowers are again fragrant, bringing back the bees with pollinia from the day before, and this time the ignominious treatment results in pollination.

The strange behavior of the bees gave rise to the legend that they were drugged or drunk. However, according to Dodson, a bee that falls to the ground instead of into the bucket recovers instantly and flies off, showing that it was probably neither. He believes that since only male bees are attracted, the fragrances must have some special appeal for them—whether sexual or as something they need in their physiological makeup is not known. What they do with the fragrant chemicals also remains a mystery—perhaps they mark their territory with it or attract females with some product they manufacture from it. At any rate, for flowers to have evolved such a complicated way to lure their pollinators and such a strange way to elicit their services is a remarkable feat of nature.

The roots of the plants in nature are inhabited by ants, who may defend them from natural enemies, and whose excretory material may be nutritive. The plants are difficult to keep in cultivation, but are most rewarding if they live and flower.

C. biflora. A remarkably colored flower in shades of tan and brown, it is marked with lines, dots, and circles of pink and maroon, with the hypochile covered with silky orange hairs. The mesochile is short, giving a squatty look to the flower, and the bucket is unusually broad and flaring, heavily spotted inside. It is native to Venezuela, Brazil, and Peru.

C. macrantha. Another brownish or yellowish flower, heavily spotted inside and out, its mesochile is decorated with toothed ridges. The bucket is small and less flaring than the preceding. It occurs in Venezuela, Guyana, Colombia, Peru, and Trinidad, and flowers in summer.

C. hunteriana. This species verges on pure yellow, with a green tinge to the sepals and petals, but some forms are spotted with maroon, lightly everywhere except in the bucket, where there may be large blotches. The flowers are three inches across, a bit more modest than the preceding two in size (Fig. 18–9). It is native to Costa Rica and flowers in summer. (Mistakenly called speciosa in third edition.)

GONGORA

The small flowers of this genus are borne in pendulous chains. They are pygmies compared to their large-flowered relatives but are fascinating nevertheless. They hang with the column underneath. In most species, the dorsal sepal swings down under the column, while the very much abbreviated petals are inserted on the column itself, extending from it like a pair of fins. The waxy, very complicated lip extends horizontally above the column. Dodson relates how the bee must hang to the under surface of the lip to get at the attracting substance. In order to leave the flower it has to drop from the lip, and in so doing it slides down the column, bumping into the viscid disc at its tip, and so removes the pollinia. The process is repeated on the next flower visited, this time with the pollinia left on the stigma. The petals attached to the column prevent the bee's falling off sideways.

The plants are very pretty, with sharply fluted, conical pseudobulbs and prominently veined leaves. They grow readily in an intermediate house, in most potting media, and flower willingly. They do not like to become dry at the roots, but must have good aeration.

G. cornuta. A cluster of these small golden flowers looks like a conference of bees, held as they are on the stem all facing inward and evenly spaced. The waxy lip is carved into a hollow at the base from which it swells out, only to be suddenly contracted into a sharp beak at the tip. It is native to Nicaragua, Costa Rica, and Panama and is summer blooming. (Mistakenly called *armeniaca* in the third edition.)

G. grossa. This species has some apparently distinct differences from *G. quinquenervis.* Most noticeable are the smaller general size of the lip and the fact that the basal horns are long and thick and curve straight downward. Also, the lip is open on its underside. The petals are narrowed abruptly in the middle to form a spikelike outer section (Fig. 18–10). This species occurs in Costa Rica and Ecuador. It blooms in summer.

G. horichiana. This was once named *G. armeniaca* var. *bicornuta* because of two projections that extend forward on the lip on either side of its beak. It has bright red petals, and the tip of the beak is also red. The beak is long and sharply hooked on the end. This is native to Costa Rica and Panama.

G. quinquenervis. There are so many variations of this species, some of which have formerly been considered separately, that it is difficult to give a description of one type to suit the lot. The flowers can be white, brown, red, or greenish, with or without spots or stripes. The lip is slender, with a tapering projection at the end and two downward pointing horns or whiskers at about the midpoint. At its base there may or may not be two more fleshy, down-pointing horns. Apparently the differences among the so-called separate species deal

A

B

C

D

Figure 18–9 Coryanthes hunteriana, *one of the* "*bucket*" *orchids.*

A: *The lip is the complicated structure at the right; attached by a narrow stalk, it is carved first into a globe that exudes a potent fragrance (the hypochile), then into a midsection (the mesochile), and from this it flares out into a bucket (the epichile). The column hangs down into the bucket. Lobes at the base of the column secrete fluid that fills the bucket to spout level. The ribbonlike petals drape the spout. A bee, scratching at the fragrant tissue and fascinated by it, comes in contact with a drop of the fluid that wets it and drops it into the bucket. Unable to fly, the bee must crawl out through the spout and removes the pollinia in the process.*

B: *Looking into the bucket you can see the opening into the spout with the column curving to form its roof. There is a mound of tissue that acts as a stepstool to assist the bee in finding the spout.*

C: *The flower is cut in half to reveal its structure, and the petals have been removed to show the spout and the tip of the column. Note the tiny beak of the anther.*

D: *Caught in the act of emerging from the spout, a bee has just tipped up the anther and will fly away with the pollinia on its back.* (D, PHOTO BY PAUL ALLEN.)

A

B

Figure 18–10 *A bee visits* Gongora grossa.
A: The bee clings to the underside of the lip, held in the proper position by its pairs of downward-projecting processes.
B: As the bee lets go in order to fly away, it bumps into

the column, slides off its tip, and removes the pollinia. It is prevented from falling off sideways by the petals that are attached to the column. (COURTESY OF CALAWAY H. DODSON.)

with variations in the lip. At any rate, this is a charming group, with long chains of flowers, thirty or forty at a time (Fig. 18–11). The native range spreads from Mexico south to Brazil and Peru, and to Trinidad. Flowering takes place spring through summer.

STANHOPEA

Stanhopeas are among the most dramatic-looking of orchids. The flowering stems bore down through the medium. The flowers, as they hang on their pendulous stems with long, horned lip and arching column, have the aspect of birds of prey about to swoop upon a victim. The waxy lip is carved into three sections: a saclike hypochile, a pinched-in mesochile with a pair of horns, and a

triangular, flattened epichile. The long column swings down in an arc almost to touch the tip of the lip. The broad sepals flare up like wings, while the smaller and somewhat wavy petals curl up between them. The secret of the weird shape is in the pollination system. A visiting bee, seeking the source of the alluring fragrance, enters the sac of the hypochile. Whether it loses its footing or bumps into the column as it attempts to fly out, it plunges downward between the column and the lip, exiting from the small space between them with the pollinia on its back. On falling through another flower it leaves the pollinia on the stigma. Dodson has found that stanhopeas lure specific bees in the same manner as coryanthes.

The plants have globular or slender, somewhat corrugated pseudobulbs and broad, pleated leaves. They grow in moist locations and suffer in too dry an atmosphere, and they thrive in moderate shade.

Figure 18–11 Gongora quinquenervis *is a species with many varieties. Shown here is a distinctive one, also known as* G. truncata *var.* alba.

They must be grown in an open container so that their flowering stems can grow downward through the medium. We once grew them in square "baskets" made of slats, but on removing some one year found that many flower stems had come up against the slats and failed to develop. Now we find that wire baskets with an inch and one-half or more between the wires are the answer. If you keep the roots damp they can be grown on a cork slab.

The species vary in the shape of the lip parts and in other ways, but it is very difficult to tell some of them apart without much study and careful charts to go by; even then the assistance of an expert is often necessary. All have a penetrating fragrance, usually quite pleasant. Sadly, the flowers last only three days, but true stanhopea lovers never turn them down because of that.

S. costaricensis. This species is one of the larger forms. It has tan or dull green sepals, and petals marked with large purple spots. The broad column does not arch markedly but instead quite parallels the lip. The base of the lip is marked with two large purple eyes. Native to Costa Rica, it flowers in September.

S. ecornuta. This is an odd form, without horns on the lip. It holds its petals closely appressed to the blunt lip and column. It does not depend on a fall-through by a bee, but instead on having the bee enter at the side under the petals and then crawl out past the viscid disc of the anther. It is white with a few orange spots on the petals. The base of the lip is orange with red spots. Occurring in Guatemala, Honduras, Nicaragua, and Costa Rica, it flowers in summer or fall.

S. florida. Almost a miniature plant, this species has dainty flowers about three inches long. They are faintly greenish white, with a light stippling of rose (Fig. 18–12). It is native to central Ecuador and flowers in the spring.

S. martiana. A rather lurid species, this one represents a group with a very pronounced sac at the base of the lip or hypochile, with the mesochile almost tucked under it. It is white or light yellow with the tips of the parts clear and a crescendo of spots converging toward the center, where they become huge reddish blotches. This is found in Mexico and flowers in the fall.

S. oculata. The very long and shallow hypochile marks this species, as well as the fact that the col-

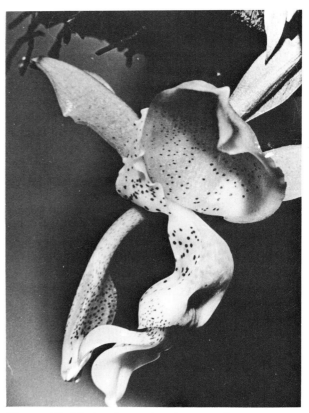

Figure 18–12 Stanhopea florida, *a small species native to Ecuador.*

umn and lip arch widely away from each other before they come close at their tips. The flowers are yellow with circular markings of reddish purple and have two eyes on the mesochile. From Mexico, it blooms in the summer.

S. saccata. A lovely small species, this takes its name from the deep, rounded cup at the base of the lip, the hypochile. This makes the lip itself rather short and chunky. The mesochile is almost nonexistent and the horns and epichile spring almost directly from the cup. The horns curve toward the broadly arrow-shaped tip of the lip. Sepals and petals are near white with a sprinkling of fine brown dots, the petals becoming yellow on the inner half. It ranges from Mexico to Nicaragua, and flowers in the spring.

S. wardii. A widespread and well-known species, this is also one of the most beautiful. Its sepals and petals are brilliant yellow, marked with dainty spots of reddish brown. The column is ivory or greenish white. The outer half of the lip is white, and the basal half bright orange with two large purple eyes (Fig. 18–13A and B). The species spreads from Mexico to Panama, and into South America. It blooms in the fall.

ACINETA

Acineta has pendent sprays of lovely, large, round flowers, delightfully fragrant, waxy, and richly colored. The broad, oval sepals are held forward somewhat, and the small petals lie close beside the column. The very waxy, chunky lip, carved into the three parts typical of this tribe, is almost concealed. The large plants have egg-shaped pseudobulbs and tall plicate leaves. They must be grown in baskets to allow the burrowing inflorescence to emerge from the bottom.

A. barkeri. This has yellow flowers striped with red-brown, twelve or more in a cluster, and is native to Mexico.

A. chrysantha is globe-shaped, bright yellow, spotted with red. The lip is tipped by a projecting horn. This one is native to Costa Rica and Panama and is fall flowering.

A. superba has flowers more open though still cupped. They have a cream ground color and are beautifully speckled with red or rose. The lip is complicated and has many projecting processes within. It grows from Panama to Peru and Venezuela and flowers from spring through summer.

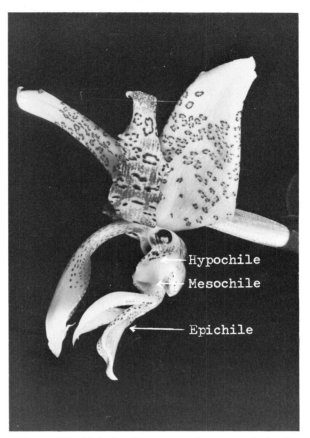

Figure 18–13A Stanhopea wardii, *one of the best-known species. Note the pointed tip of the viscid disc near the end of the column and the pair of horns on the lip guarding it.*

Figure 18–13B *A bee falling through the space between column and lip.* (COURTESY OF CALAWAY H. DODSON.)

AGANISIA

Aganisia cyanea. See *Acacallis cyanea.*

CIRRHAEA

Cirrhaea has about six species of peculiar structure. The plants have egg-shaped pseudobulbs about two inches tall, and a single, stalked leathery leaf some six or seven inches tall. The flowers hang in chains from pedicels that angle outward from the main stem. The lip is narrow, stalklike at its base, and it bears a waxy bi-lobed structure (callus) attached to its outer end, rising up from the lip to point backward or upward. The anther sits on the back of the tip of the column.

C. dependens holds its flowers facing upward, with the sepals and petals not spreading wide. They range in color from dark green with brown or purple spots to cream with almost no spots. The end of the lip is pointed, striped with red, and the callus is rounded flat, split into two pointed lobes. It is from Brazil, and it flowers in summer.

C. longiracemosa. This is very gongora-like in appearance. Its petals and sepals are oval and slightly spotted. The flowers hang upside down in a long chain, with the lip curved above the column. The crest holds its broad lobes just over the tip of the column as if to aid in positioning the pollinator. It is from Brazil, and it flowers in summer.

COELIOPSIS

C. hyancinthosma. This is the only species in the genus and it is native to Panama and Costa Rica. Its downward-boring inflorescence bears a dense head of one-inch, very waxy, globular flowers. Delightfully fragrant, they are white with an orange blotch on the lip. According to its native habitat, it requires intermediate conditions, but it is not easy to grow. It is spring flowering.

ERIOPSIS

Eriopsis has six species, all distinctive, showy, brightly colored, and waxy. More amenable to cultivation than some, they are becoming well known among amateurs.

E. biloba. An erect, two-foot-or-longer spike holds many one- to two-inch flowers which are sweetly fragrant. The flower has rather broad, somewhat cupped sepals, yellow-gold with edges shading to maroon, petals a bit slenderer, similarly colored, and a squarish lip whose sides bend up parallel to the column. The outer end of the lip extends in a short, bi-lobed tongue that is white, spotted with dark brown or reddish brown. The plant is variable and may have rather tall, slender pseudobulbs or short, much wrinkled, blackish ones. Three leaves are produced from their tip. From the rhizome grow great masses of roots, sometimes with upward-growing, very sharp spikes. The species is native to Costa Rica and Panama and northern South America. It flowers in late winter.

E. sceptrum. Light brownish gold flowers, whose edges shade to a darker tone, are borne many to a two- to three-foot spike. The sepals are broadly oval, the petals a bit narrower and curved down at their tips. The basal part of the lip is yellow, densely spotted with maroon. The projecting outer part of the lip is white with widely spaced maroon spots which gives a sharp accent to the flower. The column is creamy green. The plants have conical, wrinkled pseudobulbs, three leaves, and a mass of spiky roots. This species is native to Venezuela, Brazil, and Peru, at somewhat lower elevations than *biloba.*

HOULLETIA

Houlletia has large, bold, wide-open flowers. Some of the species send the inflorescence down through the medium while others have upright spikes. The sepals and petals of the flowers are slender and oval, and the lip is a very complex structure with various horns, crests, or other protuberances. The plants are similar to other members of the subtribe.

H. brocklehurstiana. Three-inch, fragrant, waxy flowers are borne on an erect stem up to one-and-one-half feet tall. The sepals and petals are red-brown streaked with yellow and spotted near the base with dark red. The lip is short, the basal part (hypochile) white with black warts and a pair of horns, the trowel-shaped epichile veined with yellow and covered with black warts. This native of Brazil is winter flowering.

H. ordoratissima. A terrestrial species with fragrant, somewhat nodding flowers on an upright stem, this is brown on the outside of the sepals and petals, dark maroon on the inner surface. The lip is white with several pairs of horns and a few red dots. This native of Venezuela, Colombia, Peru, Brazil, and Bolivia is spring flowering.

H. tigrina is also called *H. lansbergii.* It is a smaller plant with a burrowing stem that holds two-and-one-half-inch flowers in tones of red-orange with dark red-brown spots. The lip is purple at its base, barred with red, and white at the tip, and has a warty midsection. It occurs in Guatemala, Costa Rica, Panama, Venezuela, and Brazil. Flowering time is scattered from spring to fall (Fig. 18–14).

Figure 18–14 Houlletia tigrina. (Courtesy of J. A. Fowlie.)

KEGELIELLA

Kegeliella has dwarf plants with drooping (not burrowing) stems of tiny flowers.

K. houtteana. This is one of the two species. It has half-inch flowers whose pale green sepals and petals are covered with pinkish hairs. The sepals are fairly broad and pointed, the petals thin and ribbonlike. The column is broadly winged, making it the conspicuous part of the flower, while the tiny, three-lobed lip is quite inconspicuous. This is native to Panama, Venezuela, Suriname, Jamaica, and Trinidad and is fall flowering.

LACAENA

Lacaena is a genus of two rare species, one of which is very handsome.

L. bicolor. The arching or pendent inflorescence bears twenty to thirty two-inch flowers that have broad wavy sepals and petals, white striped with purple. The three-lobed lip has a triangular midlobe that is white with a densely velvety purple patch in its center. It is found from Mexico to Costa Rica. It flowers from May to July.

LYCOMORMIUM

Lycomormium is a rare genus of two species, having erect or arching spikes of large, globose flowers. The lateral sepals are joined to form a mentum (sac or chin) with the foot of the column. The species *elatum* and *squalidum* are native to Peru. Flowering time is summer.

PAPHINIA

Paphinia is best known for the very famous species, *P. cristata,* although there are a few other attractive ones. The plants are small, with pseudobulbs about two inches tall and plicate leaves six inches tall, but the flowers are large in proportion.

P. cristata. The three-inch, bold, red, star-shaped flowers hang upside down, each on its own stem, from the base of the pseudobulb. The long, slender dorsal sepal and petals are about the same size, while the lateral sepals are a bit shorter and curve outward. The very short lip, which has horns and protuberances on its inner sections, ends in a burst of white hairs that stand like a pompom over the tip of the column (Fig. 18–15). This species comes from quite hot and humid areas of the Guianas, Venezuela, Trinidad, and Colombia, and is difficult to keep in cultivation. If its secret could be learned, it would be welcome in all collections. It flowers in the fall.

P. grandiflora. This species has flowers up to five inches in diameter. The basal half of the sepals and petals is yellowish banded with chocolate-purple, the outer half entirely the latter color. The lip also ends with white hairs. This one is native to Brazil. It flowers in spring and summer.

P. rugosa. This species has smaller flowers that are yellow, dotted and red, and is native to Colombia. It flowers in summer and fall.

Figure 18–15 Paphinia cristata. (Courtesy of J. A. Fowlie.)

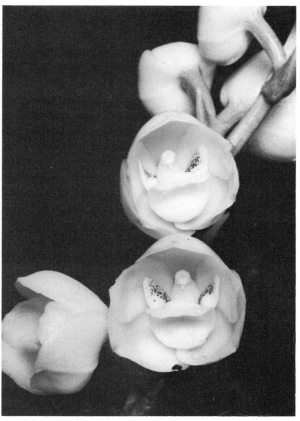

Figure 18–16 Peristeria elata, *the "Holy Ghost" or "dove" orchid, exemplifying purity and serenity. It is the national flower of Panama.* (Courtesy of H. Dunn and H. Griffin.)

PERISTERIA

Peristeria has several attractive species, one of which, *P. elata,* is the national flower of Panama and is now very rare. This is nicknamed the "Holy Ghost" or the "Dove" orchid. The plants have heavy, fleshy pseudobulbs topped by two or three very tall, pleated leaves. They require warm conditions and, while many people have difficulty flowering them, they have been grown successfully in this country. The leaves fall after the growth matures, and the plants should be kept dry from then until new growth starts. The inflorescence makes its appearance along with new growth. The plants like an open but quite rich medium.

P. elata. This stately plant is terrestrial. Its huge pseudobulbs require plenty of room and a rich, humusy soil. The erect flower spike bears many round, serenely lovely flowers, waxy white with a sprinkling of fine reddish dots on the outer surfaces. The round sepals and petals overlap to form a perfect cup. Within the cup sits the column between the wings of the hypochile, the "dove" that gives it one of its nicknames (Fig. 18–16). The fleshy, up-turned lip is jointed at the hypochile and is counter-balanced. When a bee enters the flower, its weight tips the lip inward, throwing it against the column so that the pollinia are applied to it. From Panama, Costa Rica, Venezuela, and Colombia, it flowers over a long period in the summer.

P. guttata. This species has a pendent spike of even more cuplike flowers, for the sepals are joined for part of their length. They are yellowish brown with heavy spotting of dark maroon. The wings of the hypochile are green, the outer portion of the lip white with a dark maroon stippling. This is native to Brazil, the Guianas, and Venezuela and blooms in the summer.

P. pendula. This is a smaller plant with dense heads of small flowers on pendent stems. They are cream colored with very heavy mottling of dark rosy red. This species flowers earlier than the others. It is a native of Venezuela, Guyana, Suriname, and Peru and flowers spring and summer.

POLYCYCNIS

Polycicnis has long chains of somewhat insect-like flowers, some species quite weird. The plants are similar to the rest of this group, and they can be grown like *Stanhopea.*

P. barbata. This is the most familiar species. The flowers are not too long lasting but are worthwhile nevertheless. Their parts are slender, the petals almost antennalike. The lip has erect side lobes and a somewhat trowel-shaped end lobe, all covered inside with hairs. The flowers are rather translucent, yellow spotted with red. The species is native to Costa Rica, Panama, Colombia, Venezuela, and Brazil and flowers in late summer.

P. lepida. A pretty species, it has long chains of twenty or more pale yellow flowers. Sepals and petals are dotted with dull purple, the lip with chocolate-brown. Two rows of tall, spiky hairs decorate the lip. It is a native of Colombia (Fig. 18–17).

P. muscifera. This one looks like a large mosquito. Its flowers are about an inch across, with their parts all dangling. The sepals are fairly broad, brown with spots of dull red, hairy on the back. The petals are long, thin antennae. The lip is a thick thread covered with bristles. The long, arching column is very thin except for the beaked tip. This is native to Venezuela, Colombia, and Ecuador. It flowers in summer.

P. vittata. Rather like *barbata* in general aspect, its sepals are dark red with deeper veins, the petals yellow with red veins, and the smooth, three-lobed lip pale green with reddish markings. The inflorescence is erect, with many flowers. The roots are a spiny mass inhabited by ants. This species is found through Brazil, Guyana, Suriname, Venezuela, Colombia, and Peru.

Figure 18–17 Polycycnis lepida. (COURTESY OF J. A. FOWLIE.)

SCHLIMIA

Schlimia would not compete with other members of this tribe for beauty, although its strange little flowers are interesting. The species *S. trifida* has tubular flowers with a deep, vase-shaped mentum formed by the lateral sepals, and within this is held the tiny lip. The petals barely protrude beyond the opening, and the dorsal sepal lies close over it. Four or five flowers are held on a pendent raceme. The species occurs in Venezuela, Colombia, and Ecuador, and flowers from May to July.

SIEVEKINGIA

Sievekingia has one species that seems to be well known and a few others that are very rare.

S. suavis. This has a pendent spray of four or five waxy flowers (Fig. 18–18). The rather broad, pointed sepals are lemon yellow, and the smaller

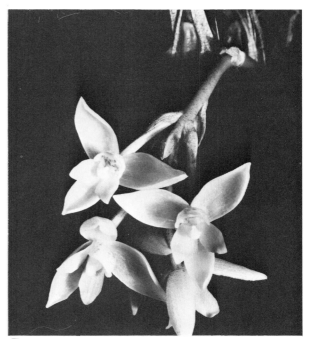

Figure 18–18 Sievekingia suavis. (COURTESY OF J. A. FOWLIE.)

petals orange. The outer lobe of the lip is cupped and is orange, spotted with reddish purple. The plant looks like a seedling *Stanhopea*. This species is native to Costa Rica and Panama. There is another, *S. peruviana,* which is not as attractive, its flowers being rather thinner and held more closed. *S. peruviana* is found in Peru, and it flowers in winter and spring.

·19·

COLLECTORS' ITEMS

Bifrenariinae to Ornithocephalinae

BIFRENARIINAE
Bifrenaria
Xylobium

BLETIINAE
*Acantho-
phippium*
Ancistrochilus
Arundina
Bletia
Bletilla
Chysis
Coelia
Phaius
Spathoglottis

BULBOPHYLLI-
NAE
Bulbophyllum
*Cirrhope-
talum*

COELOGYNI-
NAE
Coelogyne
Dendrochilum
Neogyne
Pholidota
Pleione

DICHAEINAE
Dichaea

DISINAE
Disa

GOODYERINAE
Anoectochilus
Dossinia
Erythrodes
Goodyera
Ludisia
Macodes

LYCASTINAE
Anguloa
Lycaste
Neomoorea

MAXILLARI-
INAE
Maxillaria
Mormolyca
Scuticaria
Trigonidium

MEIRACYLLI-
INAE
Meiracyllium

ORNITHOCE-
PHALINAE
*Ornithoce-
phalus*
Phymatidium
Zygostates

PLEUROTHAL-
LIDINAE
Barbosella
*Crypto-
phoranthus*
Dracula
Dryadella
Lepanthes
Lepanthopsis
Physosiphon
Platystele
Pleurothallis
Restrepia
Stelis

POLYSTACHYI-
NAE
*Neoben-
thamia*
Polystachya

SOBRALIINAE
Arpophyllum
Sobralia

TELIPOGONI-
NAE
Telipogon
Trichoceros

VANILLINAE
Vanilla

ZYGOPETALI-
NAE
Acacallis
Aganisia
Batemania
Bollea
*Chondror-
hyncha*
Cochleanthes
Colax. See
Pabstia.
Huntleya
Kefersteinia
Menadenium.
See *Zygose-
palum.*
Mendoncella
Pabstia
Pescatoria
Promenaea
Stenia
Zygopetalum
Zygosepalum

BIFRENARIINAE

BIFRENARIA

The handsome and showy flowers of this genus are round, waxy, and fragrant. They are all native to Brazil and will do well in an intermediate or warm greenhouse. The plants are similar to *Lycaste* and, as in that genus, the flowers are usually borne on single stems shorter than the leaves. The column has a basal extension called a foot, and the lateral sepals are attached to this in back, their

BECAUSE IT IS INTERESTING TO relate one kind to another, and to know that famous orchids have less-well-known relatives, we shall continue with the arrangement by subtribes. Do not be disturbed, however, if you find that one or another has been moved to another genus or subtribe or that separate genera have been combined into one genus. Sometimes it is difficult even for the experts to decide exactly how orchids are related.

sides folding around it to form a partially open spur.

B. atropurpurea. The two-inch flowers are fleshy, with their rounded sepals and petals wine red toning to yellow at the base. The lovely, full lip with its erect side lobes is white or rose. Flowering time is spring.

B. harrisoniae. This and the species below have all the qualities one could wish for in an orchid— rounded parts, an open aspect, and a full and decorative lip. The flowers are three inches in diameter, very fragrant, with sepals and petals varying from white to greenish yellow with red tones. The lip, covered with short hairs, varies from yellow to wine purple with dark red veins and has a hairy yellow crest. Blooms in the spring.

B. tetragona. A smaller flower, this also has a lovely shape. Its sepals and petals are greenish, faintly streaked with brown, and the lip is flushed with violet. It is summer blooming.

XYLOBIUM

This genus cannot compare in beauty to its showier cousins. Its little, pale yellow or straw-colored flowers do not open fully. They are borne on short, drooping or erect stems, a dozen to thirty at a time, in dense or loose clusters. Species are *elongatum, foveatum, palmifolium, powellii,* etc., and they are found from Mexico to Brazil and Peru.

BLETIINAE

ACANTHOPHIPPIUM

Acanthophippium comes from the hottest moist jungles of Java, where it grows in heavy shade. The odd flowers are borne on stems that grow from the base of the pseudobulbs. The broad, fleshy sepals enclose the petals and lip, giving the flower the shape of an urn. The species *A. javanicum* has yellow flowers flushed and striped with red.

ANCISTROCHILUS

Ancistrochilus has two, possibly three species that spread from Uganda to West Africa. They have conical pseudobulbs that taper at the top, and rather thin, stalked, deciduous leaves. They like warm to intermediate temperatures, and should be grown in pots. They need a dry rest after the leaves fall and generous watering during growth and flowering.

A. rothschildianus has a single leaf three inches tall atop a half-inch-tall pseudobulb. The three-inch flowering stem is pubescent, as is the ovary, and holds a fragrant rose-and-lavender flower, sometimes two, huge for the plant, more than two inches across, with oval, pointed sepals and petals, all pubescent on the back. The lip is creamy green, dotted with brown, with up-curving side lobes and a pointed midlobe on which there are five dark rose ridges. It is found from Sierra Leone to Uganda, and it flowers in the winter.

A. thompsonianus. This is a larger plant and has two or three leaves. The fragrant flowers are three inches across, with white sepals and petals, tinged with green at the base. The lip has greenish side lobes spotted with purple on the inside, and five purple lines on the outer lobe, which is hooked under. Found from Southern Nigeria to Uganda, it flowers in the summer.

ARUNDINA

This is a genus whose plants resemble sobralias and whose flowers are similar to *Cattleya.* Up to four feet tall, it needs plenty of room and can be grown outdoors in warm climates. The flower scape has few flowers, but the rosy lilac blossoms are attractive. The popularly known "bamboo orchid," *A. bambusaefolia,* should correctly be called *A. graminifolia.* It occurs in Indo-Malaysia and the Pacific islands. Flowers in summer.

BLETIA

This is a genus of twenty species native to tropical America. The plants have spherical pseudobulbs, from the apex of which the tall flower spikes are produced. They are terrestrial for the most part but occasionally grow on rocks or fallen logs.

B. purpurea has flowers with pink or rosy sepals and petals and a deep rose-purple lip; *verecunda* produces rose-colored flowers; the blooms of *shepherdii* are deep purple; and those of *sherrattiana* are bright rose. These plants all have leaves from three to four feet long. They are summer blooming.

BLETILLA

This is a genus from China and includes the species *B. striata*, popularly known as *B. hyacinthina*, often sold in grocery stores and by garden supply companies. It is terrestrial, with small corms underground, and can be grown out-of-doors in most parts of this country. The stem is a foot tall, with several pleated leaves, and bears a spike of small cattleya-like flowers that are amethyst-purple. They flower in summer.

CALANTHE

The name *Calanthe* means "beautiful flower," and each of the species known in cultivation lives up to this name. The genus contains some forty or fifty species, some of which are deciduous and some evergreen, but all are terrestrial. The deciduous species have tall, conical pseudobulbs that reach eight or nine inches in height, from which arise the handsome, heavily ribbed leaves. The leaves fall before or at the time of flowering. In the evergreen species the pseudobulbs are lacking and the leaves grow directly from the creeping rhizome.

Mr. Dominy, the original orchid hybridist, made his first cross with *Calanthe*. In 1856 *Calanthe* Dominyi *(C. masuca × C. furcata),* the first hybrid orchid, flowered.

Calanthe is potted in the same manner as *Phaius*. The bulbs may be separated once a year, when growth is just starting in the spring, or the plant may be repotted without being divided. New growths come from the base of the old bulbs. A method often used is to separate the bulbs and put several in one large pot, to be assured of a good display of flowers. Water sparingly until growth starts and give the new leaves extra shade for a while. After the leaves are well along, the plants need more light, but, as for cattleyas, the light must be properly moderated. *Calanthe* thrives in warm places in the greenhouse, with a temperature of 55° to 60° at night and with generous daytime humidity.

During their growing season, water the deciduous species generously. The frequency of watering is reduced when the foliage begins to turn yellow in the fall. When the flower spikes show, increase the watering and continue until the blooms are finished. After their winter flowering, the plants must have a decided rest. The pots may be laid on their sides in a cool place and given no water until the following spring. Some growers separate the bulbs, dust them with a fungicide such as Tersan or Arasan (or dip them in a solution), and store them in a dry place at 60°. As soon as root growth begins, the plants must be repotted. The evergreen species are watered all year round.

C. vestita. Once one of the most widely grown of all orchids, this species is still very popular. The lovely sprays of white flowers appear in winter, keep well, and lend themselves to decorations for holiday social affairs or to dainty corsages. The sepals and petals are more or less overlapping and hold themselves up and back from the long, beautiful lip. The front lobe of the lip is scalloped and flaring, with a touch of yellow or crimson in the throat. The pseudobulbs are silvery green and the deciduous leaves are nearly two feet long. The flower spike rises to a height of two or three feet. The plants are native to Malaya. It is winter blooming.

The hybrid *Calanthe* Veitchii *(rosea × vestita)* is one of the most popular and is as widely grown as *Calanthe vestita* itself. The flowers are rose colored, and the lip is decorated with a white spot near the base.

The parents of the first hybrid orchid were evergreen calanthes. *C. furcata* bears creamy white flowers generously distributed on a long spike. The plant has large fanlike leaves. *C. masuca* has deep violet flowers on spikes somewhat shorter than those of *C. furcata*. Both require warm, humid growing conditions.

CALOPOGON

Of the several species in this genus, the well-known *Calopogon pulchellus* grows from Newfoundland to Florida in bogs and moist meadows. It will do well in a shaded place in your garden in a porous soil, with ample water. The plants should not be disturbed very often, but offsets may be separated from the large clumps occasionally. The small offsets take several years to reach blooming size, whereas large clumps bought from collectors will flower immediately. *C. pulchellus* grows in clusters of corms, each producing a single, grassy leaf. The flower stem carries two to twelve attractive flowers that vary in color from magenta-crimson to white. The lip is uppermost in the flower and is bearded with white, yellow, or purple hairs.

CHYSIS

This is a genus of handsome plants with lovely flowers, native to tropical America. They have long, heavy, rather club-shaped pseudobulbs that grow in a pendent or horizontal manner. They bear lush, broad, pointed, plicate leaves, often twenty or more, which are deciduous. They require rather warm conditions and plenty of water while growing, and should be kept rather dry after leaf fall and until new growth starts in the spring. Flowering stems arise from the new growth. The inflorescence is usually shorter than the pseudobulbs and bears four to ten blooms. The flowers are lovely, waxy, wide open, with their sepals and petals broad in the middle, pointed at the tips. The lip is very fleshy, three-lobed, with the side lobes erect and the midlobe somewhat cup-shaped, partitioned from its base by a crest of teeth.

C. aurea has flowers of brownish yellow, shading to white in the center. The lip has five keels that look like teeth from the front. It occurs from Mexico to Peru and Venezuela and flowers in the summer.

C. bractescens has flowers of ivory white. Its lip is yellow, streaked with red. A native of Mexico, Belize, and Guatemala, it blooms in the summer (Fig. 19–1).

C. lemminghei is white, its parts tipped and marked with purple. Also summer flowering, it is found in Mexico.

C. tricostata (syn. C. laevis) has yellow sepals and petals tinted with lines of red-violet and a yellow lip marked with red and decorated with three vertical, fleshy keels. It is found from Mexico to Costa Rica and is summer flowering.

COELIA

The best known of this genus is *Coelia triptera* which produces a brushlike cluster of small, white, very fragrant flowers. The plants have a rounded pseudobulb which bears two or three tall, veined leaves. They like a cool spot in the cattleya house. It is native to Mexico, Guatemala, and the West Indies and flowers in summer.

PHAIUS

A genus of large, handsome plants, *Phaius* is composed of some twenty species that produce tall spikes of showy flowers. Some species are epiphytic, and there are better-known terrestrial ones. The former are seldom grown.

The terrestrial species are native to tropical Asia, Africa, Australia, Madagascar, China, and Japan. They have been cultivated since 1778, when *P. tankervilliae (grandifolius)* was imported from China. This is commonly known as the "nun's orchid" or the "veiled nun."

This genus likes an intermediate greenhouse with adequate shade and night temperatures that do not fall below 55°. The potting compost is a mixture of sandy loam, well-rotted cow manure, and shredded peat moss or osmunda, in equal parts. The pots must have plenty of drainage crock in the bottom. To insure adequate nutrition, the top surface of the soil is covered with a mulch of cow manure. A fertilizer solution may be added after the flower spikes have started. The plants grow vigorously and require plenty of water all year.

Plants of *Phaius* may be divided every two or three years, when the blooming season is over. Young plants may be grown from dormant buds on the flower scapes, in the manner described for dendrobium canes. After the flowers have withered, cut the stem, lay it on moist sand in a flat.

Figure 19–1 Chysis bractescens, *waxy flowers of ivory white, the lip toned with yellow and striped with red.* (COURTESY OF JONES AND SCULLY, INC.)

Cover with glass or muslin to keep in the moisture and provide shade. The little plants that grow from the dormant buds will be large enough in a few months to be potted up.

Dwellers in the southern states may grow members of this genus outdoors under the trees. In some regions they may be kept (in their pots) in the garden at least for the summer, being brought into the greenhouse before the nights turn cool.

P. flavus (syn. *maculatus*). Attractive yellow flowers, two to three inches in diameter, are borne in clusters of ten to fifteen on spikes two feet tall. The lip is erect with the front lobe recurved and streaked with orange. The base of the lip forms a prominent spur. The foliage of this plant is attractively variegated with yellow. It occurs in northern India and Japan and flowers in the spring.

P. tankervilliae or *tancarvilliae* (syn. *grandifolius*). These are majestic plants, familiarly known as the "nun's orchid." Three-foot spikes carry ten to fifteen flowers whose petals and sepals are white on the back, reddish brown inside. The lip is tubular, with a short spur, a yellow throat, and crimson sides. The species occurs in China and Australia. The flowers appear in winter and spring.

A number of bigeneric hybrids have been made between *Phaius* and *Calanthe;* these are named after both genera, *Phaiocalanthe.*

SPATHOGLOTTIS

This is a genus of terrestrial orchids native to India and China. They have small, cormlike pseudobulbs and grassy foliage. The small, bright flowers are usually produced in small numbers on rather tall spikes. Where they may be grown outdoors, for instance in our warm states where the climate is humid, they might be worth a try, for they are very attractive.

BULBOPHYLLINAE

There are several genera in this huge subtribe which spreads over all of the topical world, mainly in Asia and Africa and their offshore islands. Best known of the genera are *Bulbophyllum* and *Cirrhopetalum*. Some authors treat these two as one genus, others keep them separate. After you have seen a number of species, you will undoubtedly have a feeling for what makes a bulbophyllum and what a cirrhopetalum. They are certainly different in appearance, if not in botanical structure. They were treated as one genus in previous editions, but will be given separately here.*

BULBOPHYLLUM

There are among the species some of the most fantastic of orchids, some large, many small, and many with startling details best appreciated with a magnifying glass. Some are fragrant, some not so, and some produce the most foetid odors imaginable. (One to stay away from is *B. beccarii*: not only is it too large for a greenhouse, since it climbs a tree like a huge serpent, but its extremely tiny flowers give off an overpowering stench.) Most of them are delightful for their curious flowers. As there are more than two thousand species it is possible to describe but a few. However, almost any that come to your hand will prove oddities worth owning.

B. barbigerum. The tiny bearded flowers of this species give it its name. The plant is four inches tall, with a fat pseudobulb having a single leaf. The one-inch flowers would be most inconspicuous, with their slender, dull purple sepals and greatly reduced petals, were it not for the mass of reddish hair thrust out into the breeze by the fingerlike lip. These hairs are moved by the merest breath of air, and the lips respond by bouncing up and down like the keys of a musical instrument. The flowers are held on an upright spike, about fifteen or more opening in succession. The species is native to West Africa and flowers in summer.

B. fletcheranum. This is an absolute giant, with pseudobulbs the size of a man's fist, and leaves up to four and one-half inches wide, eighteen to thirty inches long, as thick as cowhide. The flowers come in a cluster of twenty-five or more, close to the base of the pseudobulb. They are fleshy, smooth and velvety, deep red with speckles on the dorsal sepal, and smell like cabbage cooking. The lateral sepals are four inches long, slender and held together; the dorsal sepal is wider, and the petals and lip are very tiny. From Papua New Guinea, it

---

* Bulbophyllum and Cirrhopetalum are also given as separate genera in my book *Miniature Orchids*, 1980.

blooms fall and winter. A close relative of equal size is *B. macrobulbum,* whose flowers are broader and worse smelling, and *B. phalaenopsis,* whose extremely heavy flowers are covered with shaggy papillae, also evil smelling. All of these attract carrion flies as pollinators. They like intermediate temperatures. Because of the long, heavy leaves, they are best grown in a hanging position. The pseudobulbs may be fastened to osmunda fiber packed into a wire basket, with cross-wires to hold them.

B. gravidum. A delightful species that produces more than a hundred tiny flowers, a few at a time, from a gradually lengthening spike. The flowers are one-third inch across, very waxy, their sepals and petals triangular, green in color. The tongue-shaped lip is red and is covered with hairs. It jiggles in the slightest breeze and is counterbalanced. The species is found in Malawi and in western Cameroon and Bioko—the whole continent in between the two locations! They flower over a long period, starting in the summer (Fig. 19–2). A similar little species from Africa is *B. cochleatum.*

B. lobbii. One of the largest-flowered of the genus, this orchid has spectacular flowers of yellow-gold with tones of purple or red, a sweet fragrance, and a unique shape. The two-inch, egg-shaped pseudobulbs bear a single leaf ten inches tall. Each flower is held on its own stem, which is either upright or arching. The tall, narrowly triangular dorsal sepals stand up straight, the lateral ones bend upward like knees. The petals curve out sideways, and the small, tonguelike tip curves forward. The lip is mobile, and like most of this type is counterbalanced so that a little weight, an insect, for example, causes it to tip inward. It comes from the warm tropics of Thailand, Sumatra, Java, Borneo, and the Malay Peninsula, and flowers from late spring to summer.

B. pachyrrhachis and *brachteolatum.* These might appeal to those who care for the unusual flowers without demanding that they be pretty. Both have tiny flowers inserted on a very fat, cylindrical rachis, almost hidden under their bracts. *B. pachyrrhachis* is from Mexico, Central America, and the West Indies; *brachteolatum,* from Venezuela, Suriname and Guyana.

B. purpureorhachis. A most peculiar habit characterizes this and a number of other species. The flowers are borne in a line down the center of a flat, fleshy rachis, inserted directly on its surface on both sides. The rachis is green, spotted with purple, and the half-inch flowers are brown, hairy

on the outside, with a tiny, yellow-brown, mobile lip. Other species with this type of rachis are *leucorhachis, lindleyi, maximum,* and *makakense,* a new species. All are African.

B. reticulatum. One of the larger species, it is a beautiful plant with broad leaves having a network of light green veins on dark green. The flowers are three inches in diameter and are fleshy and fragrant, produced two to a stem. They are quite similar in shape to *lobbii,* and are white, striped with purple. The species is found in Borneo.

CIRRHOPETALUM

Most cirrhopetalums have elongated lateral sepals that extend parallel to each other with their inner edges touching for part or all of their length. Their tips are often drawn out into filamentous tails. Their petals, as their name implies, are decorated with cirri (fringes of hairs) or even feathery or tassellike appendages. Bulbophyllums have a tremendous range of shapes and sizes that elude generalization, but both genera have tiny, hinged lips that bobble almost constantly.

C. guttulatum is one of the prettiest of the genus, with plants four or five inches tall whose small, angled pseudobulbs bear a single leaf. The flowers are held in an umbel (fan) on an upright stem. They are about an inch across, almost iridescent, with a gold background covered with lines of red dots on the sepals and petals, and with a bright rose-spotted lip. The sepals are only slightly lengthened, making this species one of the borderline types between the two genera. From the Sikkim Himalayas and Khasia Hills, it flowers in the fall.

C. medusae. Perhaps one of the most charming is this species, whose dense heads of straw-colored flowers have their lateral sepals elongated into five-inch threads, giving the effect of very delicate pompoms, often spotted with pink. The rest of the flower is less than one-half inch long. *C. longissimum* has flowers with even longer sepals, but fewer in a head. *C. medusae* comes from the Malay Peninsula, Sumatra, and Borneo; *longissimum* from Thailand. It blooms in fall and winter.

C. picturatum. Flowers of this species are arranged in a wheel. The lateral sepals are elongated and broadened and folded together to look something like a cloak. The tiny dorsal sepal resembles a Chinese hat and has a little waving knobbed hair

A

Figure 19–2 Bulbophyllum gravidum *from Malawi.*
A. *Up to ten flowers are open at a time on a stem that produces over a hundred through several months.*
B. *The flower is waxy, green except for the red lip, which is edged with golden hairs. The little counterbalanced lips jiggle in the slightest breeze. It was four-and-one-half months from the time this was collected until it reached Wyoming by surface freight.*

at its tip. The petals are very much reduced, and are red, as is the tiny, mobile lip. The other flower parts are light brown, somewhat spotted with red (Fig. 19–3). Similar to this species are *cumingii*, which has a fan of rose and white flowers with flatter, elongated lateral sepals and fringed dorsal sepal and petals, and *ornatissimum*, whose elongated sepals are much twisted and whose dorsal sepal and petals end in a burst of bristles. *C. picturatum* and *ornatissimum* are from the Himalayas, and *cumingii* from the Philippines.

C. rothschildianum. This is a bold, impertinent flower, one of the largest of the genus and a most spectacular species. The squat pseudobulbs bear single leaves and are widely separated on a wandering rhizome. This habit makes it difficult to contain the plant in a pot, so that it should be grown on a flat or a mount. Four to six "broad-shouldered" flowers are borne in a fan from an upright stem. They are densely spotted with red on a cream base, the tiny dorsal sepal and petals decorated with hairs along the edge, and topknots of red feathers. Long tails extend from the tips of the broad lateral sepals, making the flowers some eight

B

Figure 19–3 Cirrhopetalum picturatum *displays a wheel of little cloaked figures.*

to ten inches long. From Thailand, Sumatra, Malaya, New Guinea, and the Pacific Islands, it flowers in fall and winter. Other species similar to this but smaller are C. *longissimum, ornatissimum,* and *wendlandianum.*

COELOGYNINAE

This subtribe contains several genera, some quite well known, although *Coelogyne* is perhaps most widely grown. It ranges from China and the Himalayas through Southeast Asia to the Philippines and other Pacific Islands. All have somewhat rounded pseudobulbs topped by bright green, thin or rigid leaves. Their flowers are sometimes produced singly, but more often in attractive sprays or chains.

COELOGYNE

There are more than a hundred species of *Coelogyne.* Some are from high elevations and do best with cool treatment, although both these and those from warmer elevations can be grown in intermediate conditions with care as to their placement. They do well in almost any potting medium that offers good drainage and aeration and can be grown in pots, shallow pans, or hanging baskets. Some have rather a rambling habit and should be given plenty of room in the pot. Repotting and

dividing must be done while new roots are starting, else a plant may be badly set back. They are resentful of disturbance at the roots. With such care, however, they reward the amateur with a profusion of blooms. They require copious water during their growing period but are kept on the dry side during their period of lessened activity. They like moderate shade. In some regions they may be placed outdoors in a protected place during the hottest months.

C. *cristata.* Considered by some to be the most beautiful of East Indian orchids. The combination of sprays of snow white flowers, apple green pseudobulbs, and dark green leaves is most attractive. The blooms measure three to four inches, and occur many to the spray, which arises from the base of the pseudobulb. The petals and sepals are wavy, and project forward. The lip is three-lobed, the middle lobe decorated inside by five yellow, fringed keels. They keep beautifully and are highly decorative as sprays or for corsages. *Coelogyne cristata* likes fairly cool treatment and does not thrive in great heat. It is found in the Himalayas and flowers in the winter.

C. *dayana.* A large plant, with pseudobulbs five to ten inches long and leaves measuring two-and-one-half feet. The long chainlike sprays bear many flowers which are pale yellow except that the lip is decorated with brown fringed ridges and has brown lateral lobes. This spring- and summer-blooming plant comes from Borneo.

C. *lawrenceana.* If you looked only at the lip of this and the similar *speciosa,* you would be entranced. Otherwise, they are not very appealing flowers. C. *lawrenceana* is the handsomer of the two, with its huge lip decorated on the inside with rows of tall, brown protuberances that look like the tube feet of a starfish. The sepals are fairly broad, the petals very narrow and held back between the sepals. C. *speciosa* has quite droopy sepals and very threadlike petals. Its lip is lined with rows of brown, velvety protuberances. C. *lawrenceana* comes from Vietnam and flowers in the spring; C. *speciosa* occurs in Sumatra and Java and is fall blooming.

C. *massangeana.* This is one of the loveliest and most popular of the genus, with long sprays of two-inch flowers that are yellow with a very striking and decorative lip. The side lobes of the lip are dark brown inside, and this same color follows around the rows of yellow protuberances that decorate the central portion of the midlobe. The sepals and petals are pale yellow and the flowers are very fragrant. They are borne in long drooping chains. Native to peninsular Thailand, the Malay Peninsula, Sumatra, Java, and Borneo, it blooms from spring through fall.

C. mooreana. A dainty species, it is prettier in some ways than *cristata*, and much easier to grow. The white flowers are held on an erect, arching spray, five to ten at a time. The fairly broad sepals and less-wide petals spread in a star shape, and are wavy on the edges. The generous lip has long side lobes and a spreading midlobe decorated with yellow inside and two raised keels. It flowers in the winter and comes from Vietnam (Fig. 19–4).

C. ochracea. A perfectly delightful species, it is white with "painted" patches on the lip. The two circular yellow areas are outlined with a neat line of orange and punctuated in the center with an orange dot or two. The inside of the side lobes of the lip are also "painted" yellow, outlined in orange, and striped with brown. This is another easy-to-grow species, and rewarding with many-flowered sprays. It comes from the Himalayas, but does well in an intermediate house. Flowering time is fall.

C. pandurata. Sometimes called the "black orchid," although there are others that fit the name as well, the sepals and petals are emerald-green, and the fiddle-shaped lip is heavily veined and stained with black on a greenish ground. The middle lobe of the lip is ruffled and fringed and carries black warts and ridges. This species does well in the semitropical states. It is a native of Borneo. The blossoms appear in the summer.

C. tomentosa. Pendulous sprays of fifteen to twenty pale orange-red flowers are quite striking in appearance. It occurs in Borneo and Sumatra and flowers in the summer.

DENDROCHILUM

These are the "necklace orchids" whose minute flowers are produced in dainty chains. The single-leaved pseudobulbs are oval or conical, and the plants are generally quite compact.

D. cobbianum has very fragrant flowers, about three-fourths inch in diameter, produced on a twisted chain. They are white with a yellow or orange-yellow lip. From the Philippines, it flowers almost any time of the year (Fig. 19–5).

D. filiforme is a fountain of chains of fragrant, golden, quarter-inch flowers of crystalline texture. There are at least a hundred on each inflorescence. Many growths can be accommodated in a

Figure 19–4 Coelogyne mooreana, *white with lines of golden fringe in the lip.*

small pot. From the Philippines, it flowers in summer and fall.

D. glumaceum has fat sprays of feathery flowers whose slender sepals and petals are white and whose lip is yellow. They are lemon scented, very delightful. It is also from the Philippines and flowers in fall and winter.

D. magnum. This is a handsome plant, with stalked leaves sixteen inches tall and small, conical pseudobulbs. The beautiful flower spikes ascend for the height of the leaves and then turn down, trailing their chains of shiny, half-inch flowers almost to the base of the plant. The blossoms are rather tan, with a faint tinge of orange in the lip and a delicate scent. From the Philippines, it flowers in the fall.

D. uncatum is a more modest plant with shorter stems of flowers which are very pretty, a little larger than those of *D. filiforme*. They are yellowish with a brownish lip and are sweetly fragrant. It is also from the Philippines and flowers in summer and fall.

NEOGYNE

Neogyne is a genus of one species, *gardneriana*, which produces small white flowers that quickly wither. It occurs in the Himalayas.

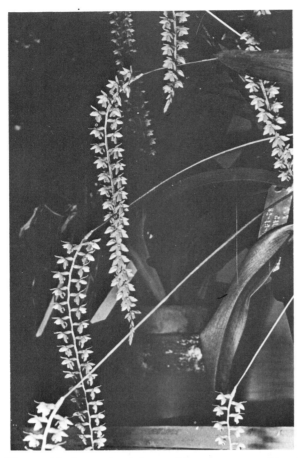

Figure 19–5 Dendrochilum cobbianum, *a "necklace" orchid.*

PHOLIDOTA

Pholidota has acquired the name "rattlesnake orchid" because the scales of the unopened flower raceme are reminiscent of the rattles of that snake. The flower stem grows from the top of the pseudobulb along with the developing leaf. Although the flowers are not colorful, being a yellowish white, a plant with many slender, trailing stems, each with over a hundred tiny flowers, is most attractive. Each flower peeks out from under a brownish bract. The best known species is *imbricata*, which is easy to grow along with cattleyas and flowers in summer (Fig. 1–3 and 19–6). *P. chinensis* is seen in old Chinese paintings and is native to India and China.

PLEIONE

Pleione, "mother of the Pleiades," has large, attractive flowers and peculiar plant habits. The

Figure 19–6 Pholidota imbricata. *Its nickname of "rattlesnake orchid" does not do justice to the dainty chains of flowers.* A. *The plant produces a chain from each new growth.* B. *Detail of the flowers.*

pseudobulbs, which last only a year, are persimmon-shaped, wrinkled, and sometimes warty. They bear one or more broad, plicate leaves which fall as the bulbs mature. At the end of the growing season, a new shoot develops from the base of the current pseudobulb, which withers as this takes place. The new shoot produces a flowering stem and roots and then, after flowering, stands still until the following spring. In the spring the resting shoot resumes its growth, forms leaves and pseudobulbs, and repeats the cycle. The plants should be watered only sparsely from November to April, and then regularly during the growing period.

P. humilis. This has flowers one to two inches in diameter, which range from white to pale purple. The sepals and petals are spreading, rather narrow. The large lip encloses the column at its base, and then spreads broadly. Its edges are marvelously fringed and the center is keeled and spotted. It comes from Nepal and Sikkim.

P. praecox. This has three-inch flowers, is fragrant, and of a rich rose-purple. The darker lip is fringed and decorated with fringed crests. This is native to southern China and Burma.

DICHAEINAE

The only genus in this subtribe is *Dichaea,* whose forty-odd species range throughout tropical America.

DICHAEA

Dichaea is unexcelled for sheer beauty of plant form. With few exceptions, the dainty stems continue to grow in length, branching from the sides, and rooting at the nodes. They are clothed with small, alternate leaves for their whole length, and the small globular flowers appear from leaf axils here and there along the stems. Plants can grow into handsome masses hanging from a mount or can cover a pot and extend over its edges. They thrive with shade and constant moisture.

D. glauca. This is a much larger plant, one that grows upright if potted. The leaves are covered with a silvery bloom, and the fragrant, heavy-textured, three-quarter-inch flowers are greyish white with light lavender or yellow spots. They appear on short pedicels from leaf axils along the back side of the stem. It is native to Mexico, Guatemala, El Salvador, Honduras and the West Indies, and blooms in spring and summer.

D. muricata. This has very neat, fleshy stems and leaves, and little one-half-inch, greenish,

purple-spotted flowers. It is found from Mexico to Brazil and the Lesser Antilles and flowers spring to fall (Fig. 19–7).

D. neglecta is much smaller but is considered by

A

B

Figure 19–7 Dichaea muricata.
A. *The plant is beautiful in itself, as it branches and clambers on a hanging mount.*
B. *Each flower is a jewel with crystalline texture, green with purple spots.*

some to be but a variety of *muricata*. It is distinguished, however, by dark spotting at the base of the leaves. Found from Mexico to Nicaragua, it flowers in the fall.

D. panamensis is more delicate, the stems more winding. Its leaves are ranked along the stem in alternating groups of unequal length. Its half-inch flowers are white with pink spotting. It is found from Mexico to Panama and flowers summer and fall.

DISINAE

Among the several genera in this subtribe, *Disa* is the best known, and some of its species are in cultivation. For details of the necessary methods, it is best to consult experts. For cultural directions see the *American Orchid Society Bulletin*, October 1981, "Cultivating Disas in Ohio," by Warren Stoutamire.

DISA

The "Pride of Table Mountain," *D. uniflora* is truly handsome. Its four-inch flowers are oddly constructed. The sepals are the conspicuous parts; the vivid red or red-orange dorsal sepal, veined with a darker shade, stands upright, while the broad laterals spread sideways, solid red in color. The lip is a mere strap between the laterals, and the tiny petals stand together in the center. A pointed spur extends from the back of the dorsal sepal. The plants are protected in their native South Africa, and exportation is prohibited. Seed can occasionally be obtained.

GOODYERINAE

These are the "jewel" orchids, loved for their beautifully variegated foliage. Their flowers are small, borne on little, upright spikes; in past decades people hardly looked at them. Now that the interest in tiny kinds has increased, people have discovered their fascination and are able to see that the flowers are just as interesting as those of many other "botanicals." However, this group has the added advantage of being showy for foliage alone.

They are reputedly difficult to grow, requiring a rich, humusy medium, shade, and high humidity. They are all terrestrial, with fleshy stems and succulent leaves. Some of the species in the various genera have been moved from one to another, and one genus, *Haemaria*, now goes under the name of *Ludisia*.

ANOECTOCHILUS

Anoectochilus regalis. This orchid has velvety leaves with a bright sheen, veined with gold. The flowers are white with the lip marvelously fringed. It comes from southern India and Ceylon.

A. roxburghii. From the Himalayas, it has green leaves with a gold zone in the center and a red suffusion toward the margin.

A. sikkimensis. From Sikkim, it has dark red leaves with gold veins on the upper surface. The flowers are olive green and white.

DOSSINIA

The single species, *D. marmorata*, has almost round leaves of deep green with a network of gold. The flowers are pale brown with white or pink tips. It is native to Sarawak.

ERYTHRODES

Erythrodes querceticola. This has yellowish or brownish green leaves with prominent veins. The flowers are yellow-green or white and have a spurred lip.

E. nobilis. Called the "silver" orchid for its beautiful gray-green leaves with a dense network of silver on the surface, and satiny silver undersurface. The small white flowers have a fringed lip.

GOODYERA

This genus has American representatives called "rattlesnake plantain" because of their mottled foliage. Some of the Asian species, however, deserve to be included in the group of "jewel" orchids.

Goodyera colorata has almost black leaves veined with red. It occurs in Java, Sumatra, and the Malay Peninsula.

G. hispida has leaves of green flushed with pink, with pink or white veins. It comes from a wide area, from the Himalayas to the Malay Peninsula.

LUDISIA

Ludisia discolor. This is found in two forms, one that has leaves plain green on the upper surface, red-purple underneath, with a glistening sheen, and as variety *dawsoniana,* whose leaves are dull red with veins of pale red or yellow on the surface, reddish on the underside (Fig. 19–8). The white flowers have a striking large yellow anther, which is twisted to one side, while the anchor-shaped lip is twisted in the opposite direction. This species is native to Burma and flowers in winter.

Figure 19–8 Ludisia discolor, *a jewel orchid whose leaves have a beautiful sheen and are veined with red-gold.*

MACODES

Macodes petola has heavy, lengthwise veins and dense, very fine cross-veins of gold. The undersurface of the leaves is purple. It is found from Sumatra to the Philippines. The variety *javanica* has a network of silver veins and is native to Java. Both have red-brown flowers in which the lip is twisted.

M. sanderiana has lengthwise veins of light green, and from these come cross-veins of gold. The flowers are brownish with a white lip. This is native to New Guinea.

LYCASTINAE

Most orchid collections contain a few members of this subtribe, particularly of the genus *Lycaste* itself. They are grown not only for their ease of culture but for their distinct individuality and charm. All members are natives of Central or South America or the West Indies. They are mostly high-altitude plants and therefore grow best under fairly cool conditions. The coolest spot in the cattleya house may suit them, with night temperatures of 50° to 55° in the winter. They like to be cool in the summer, too, and shaded from direct sunlight both winter and summer.

A mix such as is used for cymbidiums or fir bark makes a good potting medium. Watering must be handled judiciously so as not to let the medium become soggy. Propagation is by division, cutting through the rhizomes to separate the bulbs in groups of two. Repotting and division should be done just as new growth starts.

Bigeneric hybrids have been made between *Lycaste* and *Anguloa (Angulocaste)* and *Lycaste* and *Bifrenaria (Lycastenaria).*

ANGULOA

The genus *Anguloa* is native to the Andes. These orchids are noted for their fragrance and for their peculiar globular shape, which has given them a number of nicknames, such as "tulip orchid" or "boat orchid." Their hinged lip oscillates gently with the least movement and serves to tip a visiting bee against the column. In its struggle to free itself the bee removes the pollinia. The large, very waxy flowers are serenely beautiful.

The plants themselves are rather striking, with their long, broad, pleated leaves, and the tall, sheathed flower stem rising from the base of the conical pseudobulb, bearing a single flower. Although they are more or less terrestrial in habit, they will grow in osmunda fiber, to which may be added a third part soil, or possibly some well-dried cow manure, or in a fibrous mix or cymbidium mix. A night temperature of 50° is desirable in the winter, and a cool, shaded environment in the summer. They require ample moisture and water except for a brief rest after growth is completed to encourage flowering.

A. clowesii. These lemon yellow flowers are green inside with a white downy lip. A native of Colombia and Venezuela, it flowers in spring and summer (Fig. 19–9).

A. virginalis. Creamy white or pale pink blossoms are flushed or dotted inside with deep pink. Found from Colombia to Peru, it flowers in summer.

A. rueckeri. These flowers are greenish yellow, flushed with brown on the outside, spotted inside with red. From Colombia, it flowers in summer.

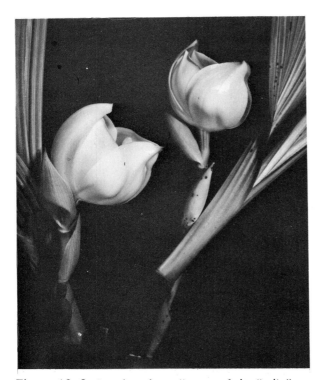

Figure 19–9 Anguloa clowesii, *one of the "tulip" orchids.* (COURTESY OF J. A. FOWLIE.)

LYCASTE

The oval, somewhat corrugated pseudobulbs bear broad, pleated leaves that last but a year or two. When the bulbs first start to grow, they are sheathed with smaller leaves that soon fall. The quaint flowers are borne singly on stems that arise from the base of the pseudobulbs, starting as the new leaves form. The broad sepals stand out gracefully, while the petals and lip give the impression of a sunbonnet in the center. The petals stand forward, each with its tip gracefully turned out, and surround the small lip that just protrudes from within. The lateral sepals are often united at the base to form a short spur or chin. The blooms last a long time, and a plant may flower for months. The plants are kept fairly dry through the winter and are watered generously during growth and flowering. The species from Mexico and Central America usually do well in a cool spot in the cattleya house; those from the Andes of northern South America in the cymbidium house, that is, with nights of 50° to 55°.

L. aromatica. This is an attractive species with flowers about three inches across, yellow, tinged with green. The lip is spotted with orange. It has a strong, pleasant fragrance. During its resting period it should have considerably less water but should not be allowed to remain dry for long periods. The plants are found in Mexico and flower in winter and spring.

L. ciliata. This large flower has downward-pointing lateral sepals that are quite broad and long, and petals that do not hold as close to the lip as some. The flower is green, with a white, fringed lip. It is native to Colombia and is cool growing, flowering in fall or winter.

L. cochleata. This has two-inch waxy, fragrant flowers that have green sepals and bright yellow-orange petals and lip. The basal parts of the sepals and lip are pubescent. Usually many flowers appear from the naked pseudobulbs just before new growth starts. Native to Guatemala and Honduras, it flowers in the spring.

L. cruenta produces four-inch flowers on rather tall stems. The plant is large, with broad, deciduous leaves. The handsome flowers are waxy and fragrant, with yellow-green sepals, bright yellow-orange petals, and a yellow lip spotted with maroon with a large maroon blotch at its base. From Mexico to Costa Rica, it blooms in the spring.

L. deppei. This interesting species has curiously

colored flowers. The sepals are dull green spotted with red, the petals white, and the lip is yellow spotted with red. The lateral sepals stand out horizontally. Occurring in Mexico and Guatemala, it is easy to grow, requiring intermediate conditions. It usually flowers in the spring but can also bloom in the fall.

L. dowiana. Prim, quietly colored flowers are produced in profusion. The sepals are olive-green on the back, brown in front, and the petals and little fringed lip are pale yellow or cream. It is native to Costa Rica, Nicaragua, and Panama. It flowers in early spring (Fig. 19–10).

L. leucantha. A very lovely, smallish flower, this has light green sepals and white petals and lip. The sepals stand at right angles to each other. The lip is sometimes fuzzy in the center. It occurs in Costa Rica, and it blooms in winter or fall (Fig. 19–11).

L. locusta. One of the most distinctive of all, this has big, heavy, dark green flowers, with a broad, fringed lip on which there is a ridged callus. The flower is quite open, the petals flaring sideways rather than over the column. It occurs in Peru and blooms in spring and summer.

L. macrophylla. A bright, rather bold flower, this has the typical shape. The sepals are green-brown, sometimes wavy; the petals are white with red markings on the inner surface, which may be dots or a solid patch leaving a white border; and the lip is white, also marked with red. This species is widespread from Nicaragua to Bolivia. Individual plants can flower at any time of the year.

L. skinneri. This is the preferred name for *L. virginalis,* one of the best of the genus. It can reach six inches in diameter. The flowers are waxy, white, tinged with rose. The midlobe of the lip is tongue shaped, marked with purple on the callus or variously dotted with purple. This is one of the easiest to grow. The flowers last well and can be enjoyed for a long time. There are many named varieties, which range from pure white to dark purple. This species requires a much less intense rest period than the more deciduous ones. It is the national flower of Guatemala and occurs in Guatemala, Mexico, and Honduras, blooming in fall and winter.

L. xytriophora. This species is similar to *dowiana,* though its sepals are reflexed and its leaves much larger and more luxuriant. A sure way to tell them apart is that *xytriophora* has no spines on the top of the pseudobulbs after the leaves have fallen, while *dowiana* does. *L. xytriophora* is native to Ecuador and flowers in the fall.

Figure 19–10 A. Lycaste dowiana. *Softly colored, appealing little flowers are each produced on a single stem.* (COURTESY OF H. A. DUNN.)
B. Lycaste xytriophora, *a stunning near twin to* L. dowiana.

NEOMOOREA

Neomoorea has but one species, *N. irrorata,* which is a magnificent thing. The plant is similar to others of the subtribe, but the roots form a dense mat about its base with many upstanding, spinous

Figure 19–11 Lycaste leucantha, *waxy green with white petals and lip.*

rootlets. Up to twelve large, bold flowers are held on an erect spike. The sepals and petals are broad, tapering to a sharp point, and are brownish gold, white at the base. The beautiful yellow lip is small but very decorative, having a pattern of dark lines and spots on the broad side lobes and tiny pointed midlobe. Two thin little horns stand up from its midsection. The species is native to Colombia and occasionally occurs in Panama, blooming in spring or summer (Fig. 19–12).

The best advice available on flowering this marvelous species is Dr. J. A. Fowlie's article in the *Orchid Digest* for December 1970. Tales of efforts to bloom it never agree in particulars, its blooming apparently being caused by one person's letting it dry down in the fall, another's accidentally killing the leaves with insecticide, another's letting it grow to huge proportions, and still another grower's putting it where the light was so bright as to burn the leaves. It is evidently an extremely sensitive plant, easily injured by insecticides or by cold.

MAXILLARIINAE

Four well-known genera are among the nine in this subtribe. They all have single-flowered inflorescences although they can have many blooms at a time. Many have a "chin" or "jaw," which gives the subtribe its name.

MAXILLARIA

Maxillaria is a genus of some 300 species, some of which are very charming and some that are (if you will pardon a species-lover for saying so) not

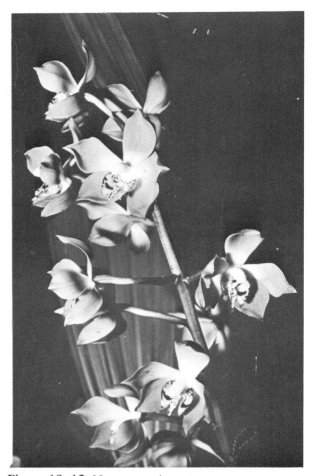

Figure 19–12 Neomoorea irrorata.

particularly attractive. The species are found from Florida through the West Indies, and from Mexico to Brazil. They vary tremendously in size, from miniature to those with stems several feet long. There are kinds with tiny pseudobulbs widely spaced on climbing stems that branch and rebranch; kinds with tiny pseudobulbs that do not have a climbing habit; kinds that look like a vanda and grow to quite some height; plants that have large pseudobulbs and leaves and look like a *Trichopilia*, and so on, and on. Most of them can be grown in an intermediate house, a few with cooler temperatures.

M. confusa. This little plant, barely three inches tall, rapidly spreads into a mass of tiny pseudobulbs and leaves and gives great numbers of small, nodding, pointed, white flowers. It is native to Costa Rica and flowers in summer.

M. juergensis. This beautiful miniature has pale green pseudobulbs three-quarters inch tall and paired, grass-thin leaves barely an inch long. The cup-shaped, half-inch flowers are green and wine-red. It is a native of Brazil and is winter blooming.

M. lepidota. The flowers are strange rather than pretty, with sepals and petals elongated somewhat after the manner of a brassia, yellow and brown, or all yellow. This one is native to Colombia and Ecuador and flowers variably.

M. neglecta. A pretty little plant that would climb if it had something to climb upon, it branches so fast that it will fill a pot like a bouquet. It has tight clusters of waxy, very tiny, white or white and yellow, round flowers at the base of each new growth. It occurs in Honduras, Nicaragua, Costa Rica, and Panama and is spring blooming.

M. picta. A very pretty and perky flower, tawny yellow marked with spots of red, about two-and-one-half inches in diameter, it is native to Brazil, blooming fall and winter.

M. sanderiana. This is the most magnificent of the genus. The flowers are quite like a lycaste in shape and size, borne on rather short stems. They are white, spotted with red, and the base of the sepals and lip are an incredibly rich, almost black-red, very velvety. It occurs at high elevations in Ecuador and must be grown cool, blooming in winter.

M. tenuifolia. This is somewhat climbing, with little pseudobulbs, each produced higher on the stem than the preceding ones. The leaves are grass-like. The pretty one-and-one-half- to two-inch flowers are dark red mottled with yellow and smell like coconut. It is found in Mexico and throughout Central America and blooms all year.

M. tigrina. To find when I got home from my first collecting experience in Costa Rica that this plant was a new species was a delightful surprise. I found it on a trip with Clarence Horich (Fig. 19–13). It almost covered a ten-foot stump of an old tree in a cleared area in upper Sarapiqui Canyon.

Figure 19–13 Maxillaria tigrina, *a new species discovered in Costa Rica, highlight of a collecting trip.*

Dr. Charles Schweinfurth described it and named it. The plant has small, oval pseudobulbs bearing a single, leathery leaf, spaced along a rambling rhizome that branches and rebranches, forming festoons that grow in all directions. The tawny, red-striped, one-and-one-half-inch flowers come in succession from the mature pseudobulbs, on short stems, and are rather long lasting although of thin substance. The oval, sharply pointed sepals stand quite flat, the lateral ones curve downward. The petals curve forward over the column. The hinged lip has a narrow, bluntly pointed midlobe, and short, pointed side lobes that are continuous with the folded crest. It stays in bloom from winter into the fall and grows extremely vigorously, which leads one to wonder why it should be so rare. It flowers in summer.

M. variabilis. As its name implies, it varies a good bit in coloring, from yellow to red with spots of one or the other color. The flowers are heavy, about three-quarters inch in diameter, and the little pseudobulbs can be quite round or elongated. It grows natively from Mexico to Venezuela and blooms all year.

M. valenzuelana. This is one to grow for the plant alone. The leaves form a beautiful fan, always growing downward. Actually, the leaves are "equitant," that is, they grow folded together, with their edges separated only at the base, where each overlaps the one next to it. They are bluish green and pointed, more than a foot long. The flowers are very tiny, white or yellow, and they barely protrude from the folded base of the leaves. It occurs from Honduras to Colombia, Venezuela, and Brazil, and also in Cuba. It flowers variably.

M. vitelliniflora. This is similar to *M. juergensis,* but the leaves are narrower and twice as long. The tiny flowers are yellow with a dark patch on the lip. It too, occurs in Brazil. It is winter flowering.

MORMOLYCA

Mormolyca is a genus of insect-imitators or insect-deceivers. The lip looks, even to our eyes, like some sort of insect poised on the lip of the flower, apparently partaking of its nectar. Actually, the lip is a decoy: It resembles the female of the insect species; the male is deceived into attempting to copulate with it. In so doing, the insect pollinates the orchid.

M. peruviana is not much more than two inches tall, with four-edged pseudobulbs and stiff, keeled leaves. Its flowers are also about an inch long but have broader parts and are more substantial, with a larger, furrier lip. They appear on single stems, once a year in the fall. It is a native of Peru.

M. ringens is about a foot tall with one-inch, round, sharp-edged pseudobulbs and slender leaves. Its many, one-inch flowers are produced singly on six-inch stems over a long period. The sepals and petals are slender, oval, yellow-green with reddish stripes, and the tiny reddish lip is shaped like the body of a small bee with its tail tucked under and its proboscis appressed to the base of the column. It is found from Mexico to Costa Rica and usually flowers in summer.

Figure 19–14 Mormolyca peruviana. *It doesn't take much imagination to see the lip as a bee with its head buried deep in the flower. This one actually deceives the male bee into thinking the flower is a female bee, and is pollinated by the act of pseudocopulation.*

SCUTICARIA

Scuticaria is a genus of three or four species with whiplike leaves and handsome flowers.

S. steelii is the best-known species. It is a remarkable plant, with pendent, terete, whiplike leaves that reach a length of six feet. They arise from pseudobulbs that are mere swellings but which remain when the old leaves fall. The flowers are three inches in diameter, with rather broad parts and an open aspect. They are fleshy, yellow-green or tan, with leopard spots of brown. The three-lobed lip has erect side lobes striped with brown, and a spreading midlobe with fewer spots and a downy crest. It is native to Brazil, Guyana, Suriname, and Venezuela, and flowers in the spring.

TRIGONIDIUM

Trigonidium is a lilylike flower, with a tube formed by the sepals, their tips turned out to give a three-part appearance. Two shiny, fleshy protuberances, which can just be seen between the sepals in most species, prove to be thickenings on the tips of the petals, and look rather like eyes. The column and lip are held within the tube. The plants have wrinkled, curved, conical pseudobulbs, and bear one or two slender leaves. The flowers are held singly on stems shorter than the leaves.

T. egertonianum. This flower is pinkish-green, striped with brown and suffused with rose. The thickenings on the petals are electric blue. It is native to Mexico, Central America, Venezuela, Colombia, and Ecuador and flowers in the spring.

T. lankesteri is greenish tan to cinnamon, veined with brown or purple, the petals spotted with purple. It is found in Costa Rica and Panama, and it blooms in spring and summer.

MEIRACYLIINAE

There is only one genus *Meiracyllium,* in this subtribe, and only two species, both delightful miniatures. Both are rambling little plants without pseudobulbs and with fleshy, rounded leaves not more than two inches tall. Close to the leaf comes a short spray of half-inch purplish flowers. They have spreading sepals and petals and a cup-shaped lip.

M. trinasutum. has the larger, more-open flowers, with a deep, upstanding cup to the lip. The color is reddish purple. From Mexico and Guatemala, it blossoms in the spring.

M. wendlandii has flowers a little smaller, rather nodding, and with a shallow cup. They are rosy purple. From Mexico, Guatemala and El Salvador, it flowers any time of the year.

ORNITHOCEPHALINAE

The fourteen-odd genera that belong to this subtribe are practically all miniatures, delightful plants with pretty flowers. Anyone would enjoy those we have singled out below.

DIPTERANTHUS

Dipteranthus seems to have eight species, all native to Brazil.

D. grandiflorus. This is larger than the rest. Its broad leaves reach six inches in height and form groups of five to six. The charming flowers are borne on six-inch inflorescences. They are rounded, cuplike, about three-quarters-inch across. The oval sepals are flat, the rounded petals swing forward like the blinders on a horse, and the column with its long, downhanging rostellum and the complicated, green lip callus form an eye-catching center. Flowering time is summer.

D. pustulatus is a tiny plant, a cushion of one-inch leaves with inflorescences that are twice that length, crowded with quarter-inch flowers. The sepals are hidden and the petals and tongue-shaped lip form a "T"-shaped flower. The column, with its long beak and the two prominent "eyes" of the anther, gives it an insectlike look. It blooms in summer.

ORNITHOCEPHALUS

Ornithocephalus is the very popular "bird head" orchid, named so because the long beaked column looks like the head of a bird. In fact, depending on

the species, you can almost say what kind of a bird it is, a hummingbird or a duck, for instance—that is, if you look with a magnifying glass. The dwarf plants have equitant leaves, arranged in a fan, and dense little sprays of white or greenish quarter-inch flowers. The sepals and petals are rounded; the lip is sometimes round, sometimes tongue- or strap-shaped, with a fleshy crest. There are subtle differences among the species as to shape of leaves, appearance of the fan, and details of the flowers.

O. bicornis. These flowers are fuzzy on the outside with a long, narrow lip with two horns from the crest at its base. It is found from Guatemala to Panama and flowers winter and spring.

O. cochleariformis, a native of Panama, has shell-shaped sepals and petals that are fuzzy on the back and are keeled and fringed. The lip is round, curved in on the sides and the end. Its beaked column looks like the head of a duck. It flowers in spring.

O. gladiatus has quite flat, open flowers with smooth parts, and a hummingbird beak. It is found from Mexico through Central and most of South America and many of the Caribbean Islands. It blooms in the fall.

O. inflexus and *iridifolius* are other species native to Mexico and parts of Central America.

ZYGOSTATES

Zygostates is distinguished by having little processes that stand up beside the columnlike arms or wings with thickened ends.

Z. alleniana. This has tufts of fleshy, sharply pointed, one-inch leaves and sprays of quarter-inch flowers. They are of crystalline texture, with oval sepals, rounded, somewhat sawtoothed petals, and a saucer-shaped lip. The green lip crest looks like a little bow tie under the column. The wings are green, tipped with yellow, and the long-beaked column is yellow. Flowering time is fall.

Z. lunata has two-inch leaves and a shower of drooping sprays of golden yellow flowers. They are one-third inch across, arranged all around the stem. The slender, oval sepals are greenish, the fan-shaped, sharply sawtooth-edged petals are gold, and the spade-shaped lip is greenish. The red-headed column has a long red beak. Beside it stand thick little arms tipped with red knobs. Flowering time is autumn.

·20·

COLLECTORS' ITEMS

Pleurothallidinae to Zygopetalinae

PLEUROTHALLIDINAE

THERE ARE ORCHIDS IN THIS subtribe whose flowers are large and spectacular. Others are so small that you have to use a hand lens, even a microscope, to see their parts; when some of these are studied, you find that they are even more fantastic than the large ones. A very large percentage of them, however, appeal only to true lovers of miniatures, for the chief attraction is their very minuteness. If you go hunting orchids in the wilds, you are bound to see many of them unless you shun them completely. And among those you find there may be some quite rare and unusual. They look very much alike when not in flower.

Some genera have so many species, and so many of them are superficially alike, that it is difficult for an amateur (even, I think, for the expert) to identify them. *Pleurothallis,* alone, is estimated to have a thousand species, *Stelis* five hundred, *Masdevallia* three hundred, some others close to a hundred, and the rest range on down to two. The plants have no pseudobulbs. The somewhat paddle-shaped leaves are carried on slender stems that are covered with bracts. In some, the stem is very short, so that it appears almost as if the flower stem came from the root area; actually, it does come from the juncture of leaf with stem.

They are found all over Mexico, Central America, and South America, living at elevations above 3,000 feet for the most part, many of them above 8,000 feet. They are epiphytic, inhabiting the damp forests, and like to be kept damp in cultivation. Except for those from extremely high elevations, they can be grown in an intermediate house.

BARBOSELLA

Barbosella is a rare genus of but few species. The plants have paddle-shaped leaves that arise almost without stems from the rhizome. The flowers have their long, slender lateral sepals joined completely, while the slender dorsal sepal stands up straight. The petals are tiny, held horizontally, and the lip barely equals the column in length.

B. caespitifica. The plant is barely two inches tall, with a rose-colored flower a half-inch long. It is native to Ecuador and blooms in the fall (Fig. 20–1).

B. cucullata. This one has flowers even more slender, with more-pointed parts, held on stems twice the height of the leaves. They are pale yellow-green. The species is native to Venezuela, Colombia, Ecuador, and Peru and blooms in winter.

Figure 20–1 Barbosella caespitifica, *a rare miniature.*

CRYPTOPHORANTHUS

Cryptophoranthus (syn. *Zootrophion*) is a genus called "window orchids." The sepals are joined both at their base and tip, allowing only a small opening, a little slit, or window, into the flower. The lateral sepals form a small chin with the column foot. The flowers look not unlike a bird's head.

C. *lepidotus* has dark-purple flowers, about three-quarters-inch long, produced in twos or threes at the base of the leaf. It is native to Panama.

C. *tribuloides* has leaves an inch and one-half or two inches tall and little, bright, orange-red flowers at their base. They are about a third of an inch long and form all year. This species is found from Mexico through Central America and to the West Indies.

DRACULA

Dracula, a genus separated from *Masdevallia,* was given this descriptive name because of its monster- or beastlike flowers. Almost all of them are covered with hairs that give a furry appearance, and their sepals, which are broad at the base, are drawn out into tails. The lip is a small, fleshy cup that is movable. Some of the species are so much alike that they are hard to tell apart. The plants have rather soft, folded leaves that do not have a basal petiole (distinct stem).

D. *bella.* This species has fragrant flowers whose extended tails give it a length of nine inches. The dorsal sepal is smaller than the laterals, whose joined bases are three inches across. The flowers are pale yellow, spotted with purplish brown. It is native to Colombia and is spring flowering.

D. *chimaera.* This set the pattern for the genus. The sepals are triangular at the base, which is about three inches long. The tips of the sepals are drawn out into slender tails, so that the flower is more than fifteen inches in length. The lip is a flesh-colored cup, and the petals are minute protuberances beside the column. Color is creamy with red or brown spots, and the "fur" or hair is gray. The flowers are so sensitive to moisture that they wilt as soon as they are removed from the greenhouse and must be sprayed with water at frequent intervals to keep them from collapsing. Native to Colombia, it flowers more than once a year. A number of species are similar to *chimaera,* varying in details, markings, and color, including D. *roezlii, senilis,* and *wallisii.*

D. *erythrochaete.* The basal part of this lovely miniature is a bit more than an inch across, cream colored, covered with rose-colored hairs. Its tails are two inches long, dark red-brown. The flowering stems stick straight out from the base of the plant, and there are two or three successive flowers. From Costa Rica and Guatemala, it blooms in spring. Other small species in this group are D. *astuta, houtteana,* and *velutina.*

DRYADELLA

Dryadella is another group of species removed from *Masdevallia.* The plants are miniatures, delightful little leafy cushions with tiny flowers peeping from between the leaves.

D. edwallii. This has fleshy, channeled leaves a little over an inch long. The fleshy flowers are the same length, barely protruding from among the leaves. The sepaline cup is open, showing tiny petals and a tongue-shaped lip. The sepals have a cream-colored base. The dorsal sepal is banded with red, the laterals are heavily spotted with red, and their tips are extended into tails. From Brazil, it flowers at various times.

D. lilliputiana is much like *edwallii.* The flowers show themselves a little better. They are cream colored, lightly spotted with red. The sepaline tails curve away from each other at the tips. From Brazil, it blooms in winter.

D. simula. This has wider sepals with shorter tails. The lateral sepals spread horizontally. The dorsal sepal is heavily banded with red, the laterals more lightly so. It blooms in the spring.

There are several similar species, *D. o'brieniana* and *zebrina* among them.

LEPANTHES

Lepanthes is a genus of true miniatures. Some are barely a half-inch tall while a few reach two or three inches. The flowers are extremely small and can best be appreciated with a hand lens. The stems are covered with funnel-shaped bracts that are hairy on the edge. The tiny flower stem comes from the base of the leaf and lies on the back or front surface or stands out sideways. Over many months it produces a series of flowers, and when flowering is finished the little "herring-bone" stem can be seen to have produced twenty or thirty flowers, sometimes in the space of only one inch. The flowers are one-sixteenth to three-sixteenths of an inch long, and are very complicated. The sepals are united for part of their length. The petals are bilobed and lie like wings on either side of the column. The column is bent downward and is surrounded by the fleshy side lobes of the lip that stand up around it like a collar. Underneath the tip of the column lies the midlobe of the lip, a tiny, bearded tongue. The flowers are mostly yellow and red, bright little spots of color. The species range from Mexico through Central and South America, and are particularly numerous in the West Indies. Some of the sixty-five species are *chiriquensis* from Panama and Costa Rica, *obtusa* from Jamaica, *papyrophylla* from Venezuela, Colombia, and Ecuador, *minutipetala* from Peru, and *selenipetala* from the Dominican Republic. New species are constantly turning up. Most are from cool rainforests and like a cool, damp greenhouse. They flower throughout the year (Fig. 20–2).

LEPANTHOPSIS

Lepanthopsis is related to *Lepanthes.* The plants are similar and equally small, and the flowers are minute. The flowers are produced in two ranks on tiny, wiry stems that exceed the leaves. The petals are very tiny, simple, and rounded. The lip is also simple, round or somewhat oval, and flat. There are fewer species than in *Lepanthes,* scattered through countries in Central and South America and the Caribbean. One of the most widespread is *L. floripecten.*

MASDEVALLIA

Masdevallia is the truly showy member of the subtribe, and some are among the most spectacular of orchids. The sepals form the conspicuous part of the flower. They are broadened at the base and are joined for part of their length to form a tube, with their tips often extended into tails. Within the tube are the very much reduced petals, lip, and column. A great many of them are from high elevations in the cloud forests and like a cool, gently humid atmosphere. Some come from lower down. If you do not have a cool house, try any that you may obtain in a cool spot in an intermediate house. They are quite susceptible to fungus rot at the point where the leaf joins the stem, and so should be watered with care and treated with a fungicide occasionally. Everyone will have favorites, so the list here will contain only a few distinctive kinds.

M. coccinea. This is a neat, velvety, dressy-looking flower, two inches across, in shades of red, red-orange, yellow, and cerise, with some paler forms. The dorsal sepal is narrow and has a stiff tail. The laterals are broadly oval, joined for half their length, and pointed at their tips. The tube is very small and narrow, scarcely revealing the other flower parts. The plant grows easily at cool temperatures, and gives a bouquet of flowers. Native to Colombia. The flowering time is summer.

Figure 20–2 LEFT. *The tiny flower of* Lepanthes selenipetala *lies on the back of its three-quarter-inch leaf, a minute symphony of gold sepals, yellow petals, with a touch of red in the center.* RIGHT. *The even smaller* flower of Lepanthes obtusa *(enlarged here to a greater extent) has wine-red sepals and bright red petals and lip. It has a sparkling, crystalline texture.*

M. erinacea (temporarily known as *M. horrida*). One of the miniatures, this is rare and very odd. The little, rounded, bell-shaped flowers are greenish, covered with hairs. The short, dangling tails have swollen, waxy, yellow tips that an insect could mistake for pollen or for nutritive particles. It is only one-and-one-half inches tall, with grasslike leaves, and is found in Costa Rica. It flowers variably.

M. infracta. A true gem, this one has a tall, slender, green, dorsal sepal and broader laterals whose flat, joined area is reddish, verging on purple-black, with a wonderful sheen. The shorter tails of the laterals are green. The tube is fairly open, allowing you to see the little white petals and orange lip. It is found in Peru and Brazil and blooms in summer.

M. minuta. This is another miniature, not as decorative as some, but interesting for its small stature (one-and-one-half inches). The tiny flowers are white, bell-shaped, with the tips of the sepals mere points and yellow in color. It is native to Venezuela, British Guiana, Peru, and Suriname and flowers fall and winter.

M. rolfeana and *M. reichenbachiana*. These are quite similar, both very fine, the former with a more open tube. They are fleshy, waxy, red shading to white inside, with short tails. Both are native to Costa Rica (Fig. 20–3).

M. tovarensis. With pure white flowers, several to a stem, this is one of the best known. The dorsal sepal is narrow and stands up straight, and the laterals are broad and joined almost to the tip, leaving short slender tails that cross over each other. It is found in Venezuela and flowers in winter.

M. triaristella. Another miniature one-and-one-half inches tall, with dark red, inch-long flowers. The joined area of the lateral sepals is rectangular, with little, hairlike tails that point out sideways. The base of the dorsal sepal forms a hood and its tail points upward. This is a native of Nicaragua, Costa Rica, and Colombia. It is summer blooming.

M. veitchiana is surely the giant of the genus, with flowers eight inches long. The basal part of the flower is a large, triangular, open cup, with the bases of the sepals narrowing gradually to points from which the tails extend. It is a brilliant orange-red with an iridescent sheen added by crimson-purple papillae that cover the sepals. It is from high elevations of Peru and flowers in early summer.

Figure 20–3 Masdevallia rolfeana *has a more open tube.*
A: *The petals, lip, and column.*
B: *The structure in (A), shown in greater detail.*

PHYSOSIPHON

Physosiphon has several attractive species. The basal section of the sepals forms a tube while the outer ends spread open.

P. tubatus. This is about six inches tall, with slender, rather tough, stalked leaves. Flowering stems are one foot long and bear 20 to 100 three-quarter-inch blossoms all on one side of the stem. They are yellow or yellow-green at the base, with bright orange tips. From Mexico and Guatemala, it flowers in summer.

PLATYSTELE

Platystele contains several miniatures, among them one of the smallest of flowers. Let G. C. K. Dunsterville* describe one of them, *P. ornata*, a newly discovered species named by Leslie Garay. "Of all miniature orchid treasures, none probably combines smallness of size with greatness of beauty in higher degree than *P. ornata*. A twenty-fifth of an inch in size, each flower is perfect in form and holds itself proudly open—each one-eighth-inch flower spray is a fit corsage for the tiniest of fairies." The plants are one-and-one-quarter inch tall and live in the tallest of forest trees. The flowers have round sepals, slender, fringed petals, and a broad, pointed lip, and are of deep purple with a tinge of green. This is a native of Venezuela. Not many growers are lucky enough to have even seen this species.

P. misera is about three inches tall, with almost filamentous flower stems holding delicate blossoms widely spaced. The quarter-inch flowers have slender pointed sepals, very small petals, and a purple velvet tongue of a lip. Flowers continue to form for a year or more on the same stems. It is native to Colombia.

P. stenostachya. A gem of a plant, this forms a cluster of two-inch-tall leaves. Bright little flowers form on stems at the base of the leaves, almost hidden by them. They are yellow with a velvety, orange lip (in the form from Mexico and adjacent countries), or green with a purple lip (from Panama, Colombia, and Venezuela). They often flower continuously, but summer is the peak season.

* Dunsterville, G. C. K. *Introduction to the World of Orchids.* 1964. Doubleday, Garden City, New York.

PLEUROTHALLIS

Pleurothallis The ten species mentioned here represent but one percent of the total number in the genus and can give only an inkling of the variety to be found. There are some that reach a height of two feet or more, but their flowers are no larger than those of smaller plants. Those chosen here are all moderate or miniature in size, and welcome to any collection.

P. alpina. The peculiar plant form of this and the similar species *sicaria* give them a special appeal. The leaf-bearing stems are fleshy and three-sided, becoming thicker toward the upper end, where they merge almost imperceptibly into the leaf. (There is a faint line indicating the joint.) The long, narrow leaf is fleshy and keeled. From the joint arises a cluster of tiny, waxy, green flowers that become orange with age. *P. alpina* is native to Costa Rica and Panama; *sicaria* to Venezuela, Trinidad, Colombia, and Ecuador.

P. calyptrostele. One of the smallest of orchids, a miniature miniature, this species spreads like moss on the lower parts of trees in damp forests. The leaves on their tiny stems are barely half an inch tall, and the threadlike flower stems not much more than an inch; in fact, the flowers on their stems are about the size of the fruiting bodies of mosses. The flowers are greenish white, quite transparent, bell-shaped, three or four to a stem. The species is native to Costa Rica and Panama (Fig. 20–4).

P. cardiochila. This is an example of the many species of orchids with beautiful, heart-shaped leaves, among them plants large and small, with leaves slender or rounded. They make attractive pot plants, capable of competing with many house plants grown for foliage alone. Some have their flowers nestled at the base of the leaf, appearing one or two at a time, while others produce several long stems with many blooms. *P. cardiochila* has moderately broad leaves which, including their stems, reach a height of ten inches. Two or three plump little clamshell-shaped flowers appear at a time, which are yellow with a tiny red lip. This one comes from Panama. Almost a twin is *P. palliolata* from Costa Rica.

P. gelida. Typical of scores of species that bear fairly tall stems of many small, bell-shaped flowers, this one has flowers of yellowish white, the sepals hairy on the inner surface. It is found in Florida, Mexico, Central and South America, and the West Indies (Fig. 20–5).

P. immersa. A strange habit characterizes this species. Its flowering stem appears to emerge from the middle of the leaf. On examination it is found to grow up through a tightly closed channel along the midvein, which can be split open to reveal the stem—hence the name *immersa.* The flowers droop from the underside of the stem, a row of purple bells. This is found from Mexico to Colombia and Venezuela (Fig. 20–6).

P. listerophora. The one-eighth-inch flowers of this miniature look like the open jaws of some ferocious animal. They are reddish purple and covered with hairs. The plant is two to three inches tall, and occurs in Costa Rica (Fig. 20–7).

P. raymondi. The little flowers of this rather tall species have petals ending in tiny brown boxing gloves, which protrude from the flower in a threatening manner. The flower itself is yellow with brown spots. It is native to Venezuela and Colombia.

Figure 20–4 Pleurothallis calyptrostele, *a mosslike plant with tiny, greenish white flowers.*

Figure 20–5 Pleurothallis gelida. *Use a hand lens to see the hairy surfaces of the quarter-inch flowers.*

P. testaefolia. This beautiful little plant forms festoons of overlapping leaves hanging from a few basal roots. The leaves are spotted with purple-brown, and the spots become raised with age. The

Figure 20–6 Pleurothallis immersa *has the curious habit of carrying the flower stem in a closed channel in the leaf.*

Figure 20–7 Pleurothallis listerophora. *The tiny flowers present a ferocious aspect when enlarged from their one-eighth-inch size.*

flower nestles close to the base of the leaf. It is purple-brown, also, and covered with hairs. This is native to Costa Rica, Venezuela, Colombia, and the West Indies.

RESTREPIA

This genus is included by some botanists in *Pleurothallis;* by others it is maintained separately. The flowers are quite insectlike, characterized by having the lateral sepals joined almost to their tips. The petals in some are threadlike, ending in little knobs. The plants have stems enclosed in quite large, papery bracts. The flowers appear singly, usually on stems that are shorter than the leaves, but each growth produces a succession of flowers. Most species grow vigorously, soon filling a good-sized pot.

R. elegans. This is a beautiful plant with flowers two inches long. They are so densely spotted with rich rose that they appear to be of a solid color. The rather straight-sided lip is forked at the tip and covered with tiny bumps. Native to Venezuela, it flowers fall and winter.

R. filamentosa. The little flowers of this species are slender, with red stripes on a cream base. They stand on wiry stems and jiggle in the breeze. The species is native to Costa Rica and Panama. It flowers continuously (Fig. 20–8).

Figure 20–8 Restrepia filamentosa *has an insectlike appearance.*

R. xanthophthalma (syn. muscifera). These little flowers grow on very short stems and are therefore held close to the leaf. They are cream or white, densely spotted with red. This one spreads from Mexico through Central America to Panama. It flowers spring and fall.

STELIS

In this genus more than in any other, admiration is gratefully extended to the taxonomists with the patience to identify and distinguish between the species! They have the tiniest of flowers in which it is usually impossible to distinguish the inner parts without a strong magnifying glass, even a microscope. The conspicuous part of the flower is the sepals, which are rounded and give an even, three-pointed star shape. The extremely tiny and very fleshy petals and lip are scarcely more than little swellings within the center. The plants are indistinguishable from *Pleurothallis* when not in bloom. Even though making a positive identification is frustrating, they make a delightful contribution to any orchid collection. Some of them have the habit of opening their flowers only during part of the day, or even at night, but the same flowers open and close over a long period.

S. argentata. This is a variable species which runs from reddish tones to silvery green, with the sepals plain on the edges or fringed with hairs. It is widespread from Mexico to Panama and all of northern South America.

S. bidentata. The little red flowers of this species are usually open only at night. It is native to Mexico, Guatemala, and Honduras, and it flowers in summer.

S. leucopogon. The largest of the genus, this has flowers of creamy white almost one-half inch across, held on stems that can reach one foot in height. The flowers open and close each day. It is native to Guatemala, Costa Rica, Nicaragua, and Panama. It flowers in spring (Fig. 20–9).

POLYSTACHYEAE

This is a tribe in itself, not a subtribe, but there are only four genera in it, of which we give two below.

NEOBENTHAMIA

This is a genus of one species.

N. gracilis has tall, leafy stems reaching six feet in height. They are topped by a beautiful head of small, tubular, white flowers that are sweetly fragrant. This species is not for all small greenhouses but can be a companion to reed-stem epidendrums and other tall plants. It is native to tropical and eastern Africa and flowers in spring and fall.

POLYSTACHYA

This genus has many charming little species and some in which the plants are quite large although the flowers are still small. Most of them are native to Africa, but some species are found in Southeast Asia and Indonesia and a few in this hemisphere.

P. affinis. This has flat, round, two-inch pseudobulbs and rather long leaves. The little, hooded, upside-down flowers are borne on a one-foot stem. They are one-half inch in diameter, bright yellow-orange, covered with hairs on the outside and striped with brown. This is native to Sierra Leone and Zaire. It needs warm conditions and flowers in summer.

P. pubescens. This is an ideal plant, in that the foliage is attractive and the bright three-quarter-inch flowers are eyecatching. Moreover, they are

Figure 20–9 Stelis leucopogon, *the largest of the genus, has flowers almost one-half-inch wide.*

long lived and there are always two or three open, for it takes a year for the twenty or so the plant produces to come and go. The flowers are wide open, yellow with brown stripes on the lateral sepals. There is a tuft of white hairs on the lip. It is native to southeast Africa.

P. virginea, the "snowdrop orchid" of Uganda, is a most delightful miniature with white flowers and a yellow lip. It is found in central Africa.

SOBRALIINAE

Of the five genera in this subtribe, two are attractive and often grown by amateurs. Most are tall and therefore need a good bit of space.

ARPOPHYLLUM

Arpophyllum is distinguished by a tall, thin pseudobulb that is little more than a slender stem, topped by a slender leaf, bearing a tall, dense inflorescence of small, bright flowers. The latter gives them the nickname of "hyacinth orchids." They resent being allowed to dry out.

A. alpinum. This is about three feet tall, and bears a densely packed cylinder of three-quarter-inch, pinkish-purple flowers. It is found from Mexico to Honduras, and it flowers in the spring.

A giganteum. More than a yard tall, this species is graced with an eighteen-inch, solidly packed cylinder of lavender flowers with pink lips. It is found from Mexico to Colombia and Jamaica, and it flowers in early spring.

A. spicatum. Tallest of all, reaching four feet in height, this species produces the usual densely packed cylinder of flowers that vary from rosy red to rosy pink. Native mainly to Mexico and other Central American countries and Jamaica, it flowers in the spring.

SOBRALIA

Sobralia is a genus of reedlike plants, whose pseudobulbless stems grow close together in thick, bushy clumps. They take up quite a bit of room in a greenhouse, but if space can be afforded they are worth growing for their handsome foliage and large, cattleyalike flowers. They vary in height from one to ten feet, and the flowers are from one-and-one-half to nine inches in diameter. The individual flowers do not last long, but the plants produce a succession of blooms that give a continuous show. The plants require a rich, porous compost, a mixture of loam, leaf mold, osmunda shreds, and cow manure. The pots should be large, with ample drainage to allow for the copious water supply they need during their growing period. During the winter they require somewhat less water, but they should never be allowed to become dry at the roots. They may be grown outdoors in our subtropical states, but they require cool greenhouse treatment farther north, and abundant light.

S. fragrans. One of the smallest of the genus, this species has flowers of sulfur yellow, one-and-one-half to two inches in diameter, borne two to a stem. One of their charms is the fringed lip, which is decorated with many fringed crests. It is native to Costa Rica, Panama, and neighboring countries.

S. leucoxantha. Plants three feet tall have a profusion of flowers. The sepals and petals are pure white. The gracefully waved lip is white, and its golden throat is striped with brown. The species is native to Costa Rica and Panama; it flowers in August.

S. macrantha. Tall, handsome plants reach a height of from four to seven feet, with rose-purple flowers often nine inches in diameter. The sepals are slender and twisted, the petals broader and wavy. The front lobe of the lip is almost round, deep purple, and beautifully ruffled. The throat is whitish with several yellow ridges. This native of Mexico and Guatemala flowers from May to July.

S. xantholeuca. A huge species, this may not be adaptable to greenhouse culture, but it can be grown in frost-free areas in full sun. Its tremendous, pure yellow flowers are extremely beautiful, with a waxy sheen, and reach nine inches in diameter. They are rather longer lasting than other blooms of the genus. This species is native to Mexico.

TELIPOGONINAE

Two of the four genera in this subtribe are rather well known and very intriguing. They are insect imitators, great curiosities in any greenhouse.

TELIPOGON

Telipogon plants are small, creeping epiphytes that are not easy to raise in cultivation. They need a cool, damp atmosphere with brisk air movement and fair shade. Most of the plants are found creeping on or in the mosses on tree branches or twigs, occasionally on the ground, the roots not penetrating the soil. They perhaps grow best on a mount, preferably cork. There are many spectacular species. All have large, triangular petals and a petallike lip, overlapping in some cases, hiding the small sepals behind them. The column is tipped by a bristly formation that resembles an insect, and which lures males to attempt copulation with what to them appears to be a female of their own species.

T. ampliflorus*. This grows somewhat like an oncidium, with three slender leaves arising from a short stem. They are about two-and-one-half inches tall. The four-inch flowering stem produces a number of flowers in succession; these are one-and-one-quarter inches across. They are tan, beautifully striped with red, and the "insect" in the center is also red. From Costa Rica, it flowers fall to winter.

T. nervosus. This is quite a different type of plant, having a slender stem with alternate leaves, rooting at the nodes, and sending out side branches. Flowering stems come from the tips of the branches and give three or four blossoms in succession, each one-and-one-half inches across. They are greenish ivory, striped with red, and the "insect" is also red. From Colombia, Ecuador and Venezuela, it flowers in the winter.

T. vargasii, hercules, klotzschianus, gnomus, and *radiatus* are among the large ones, but are by no means all the attractive species.

TRICHOCEROS

The incredible "fly orchids," *Trichoceros,* have flowers that look so much like the female of certain species of fly that the male flies attempt to mate with them, an activity called pseudocopulation. Even human beings are deceived, and many visitors to greenhouses where they are in flower will comment: "These flowers have bugs on them!"

* Called *costaricensis* in error in *Miniature Orchids.*

They make marvelous conversation pieces; and since they produce flowers through many months, they can be shown to all comers. The plants are small, with tiny pseudobulbs on top of which is an aborted leaf, a mere point. The shiny, rigid leaves come from the base of the pseudobulbs, as does the tall, willowy flower stem. To our eyes, the lip is the "fly"—the pointed midlobe is the abdomen, the very hairy crest the thorax, and the bristle-shaped side lobes the antennae. The column, which is covered with bristly hairs, is the head. It appears, however, that a fly sees it differently; to him, the shiny stigma resembles the genital opening of the female. The anther holds it viscid disc upright, and the merest touch causes it to stick to whatever surfaces comes in contact with it: In nature, this would be the tips of the abdomen of the fly attempting copulation. These plants grow natively on grassy slopes at high elevations, the plants hidden by the ground cover, and the "flies" hovering in the air. They need a cool greenhouse and are best grown in flats or on a mount over which they can ramble.

T. muralis. This has three-quarter-inch flowers of reddish purple, the side lobes of the lip are not so antennalike as those of *T. parviflorus,* as they are rounded and not striped. This evidently imitates another species of fly. From Peru and Ecuador, it blooms spring through fall (Fig. 20–10).

T. parviflorus. Native to Ecuador, Peru, Colombia, and Bolivia, it is greenish brown with dark brown spots. Its flowers are an inch across, and their "antennae" are long and slender, curved, and tipped with bristles. The flower stem often branches and produces several flowers at a time almost all year long.

VANILLINAE

There are five genera in this subtribe, of which only one will be described here.

VANILLA

Vanilla has tremendously long, vinelike plants, some with long, attractive leaves spaced evenly along the stem, others without true leaves. The species grow natively throughout tropical America, a few in Africa. Several species are grown for the seed pods, which are picked while still green and cured to produce the flavoring vanilla. The most widely grown commercially is *V. planifolia,* but *pompona* ranks a possible second, and other species may also be in use. Vanilla culture began in Mexico among the Aztecs, and was spread from there to Spain and thence to other countries, with the French developing the largest industry in their tropical possessions. Madagascar is the largest producer today, and Mexico, Tahiti, and other countries also have flourishing vanilla plantations.

The plants grow natively in warm, very humid climates, at relatively low elevations, where there is heavy rainfall. While they thrive with bright sun most of the day, they require some noon shade. The vines are grown from cuttings that include a piece of stem with its aerial roots. These are planted in humusy soil containing a lot of leaf mold, into which the lowermost roots will grow. The vine is trained to a support, preferably one to which the aerial roots can cling. One ingenious grower wrapped a length of hose with osmunda fiber and tied the vine along it. He could then hook this hose overhead in the greenhouse and move it at will.

Flowers are produced in clusters at the leaf axil. One or two open at a time over about a two-week period. They are fleshy, fragrant, greenish yellow to yellow, somewhat cattleyalike in shape with a trumpet lip, but are very short lived. Since they open and fade in a day, pollination must be done immediately on the plantations, with the workers going over each vine every day, pollinating from one to two thousand flowers per person. Women and children do most of this. Only those flowers that develop in such a position as to allow the beans to grow straight down are used, so that they can be packaged neatly for shipping.

The process of pollination is simple, but was frustrating until, according to the story, a Creole worker learned how to do it. The stigma is on the upper surface of a small "shelf" and is covered by a shield formed by the rostellum, which must be lifted in order to expose the stigmatic surface. Plantation workers do not go in for the niceties of sterile technique. Their method was described by Donovan S. Correll, who has made an intensive study of the vanilla industry. The only implements used are the fingers and a splinter of bamboo or a bit of wood whittled to a point. The worker pushes the lip down out of the way, then holds the column with the fingers of the left hand. With the splinter in the right hand, she lifts the rostellar flap that covers the stigma and folds it upward. With the left thumb, in one downward motion, she "mashes" the pollinia (actually the whole anther) down onto the stigma. It is not known what natural pollinator

A   B

Figure 20–10 Trichoceros muralis *imitates the female of a species of fly so cleverly that the male tries to mate*   *with it and thus carries out pollination.*

performs this function or how it is done, but so few flowers are ever pollinated in nature that commercial producers could not rely on insects to do the job. Moreover, the natural pollinators are of course absent in areas to which the species of *Vanilla* are imported.

ZYGOPETALINAE

This wonderfully varied subtribe has some twenty-six genera, most of them beautiful or spectacular. It is difficult to characterize them with a general description; structure of the column and anther brings them together taxonomically.

ACACALLIS

Acacallis is a monotypic genus, that is, it has only one species.

A. cyanea. This has delightful blue flowers, very prettily shaped, with wavy, oval-pointed sepals and petals and a lip that spreads broadly from its carved and somewhat horny basal part. The flowers are about two inches in diameter and are borne five to seven on an upward-arching stem. The species is native to Venezuela, Colombia, Brazil, and the Amazon regions. It blooms spring or summer.

AGANISIA

Aganisia is also a monotypic genus. The species is, although pretty, not as attractive as *Acacallis cyanea*.

A. pulchella. The plants are climbers and need to be put on tree fern slabs. The slender pseudobulbs bear a single, plicate leaf.

The flowers are small and few to the stem: It is nevertheless interesting to the collector. The blooms are white with transparent veins and a touch of pink in the lip. It is native to Guyana and northern Brazil and flowers in the spring.

BATEMANIA

Of the two species in this genus, the best known is *B. colleyi.* It is strangely shaped. The broad petals are angled upward like a pair of wings. The base of the lip with its broad side lobes is appressed to the column foot, almost forming a vase, while the midlobe curves outward. The lateral sepals do not seem to belong to this flower, for they are slender and trail down, their somewhat frail appearance out of character with the heavy flower. The sepals and petals are dark wine-red, tipped with green, and the lip is white with a reddish flush. The species is native to Guyana, Suriname, and Brazil, and flowers fall and winter.

BOLLEA

These are beautiful plants that have a fan of thin, somewhat keeled leaves and no pseudobulbs. The large, fragrant, waxy flowers are borne singly atop stems that are much shorter than the leaves. The fleshy, ribbed lip crest is prominently raised and covers a good portion of the lip.

B. coelestis. Supposedly blue, its color really tends toward blue-violet or even violet. The broad sepals and petals have white tips, then a broad band of intense violet; this fades to pale violet at the base. They are somewhat wavy, with the tips of the dorsal sepal and petals sharply pointed. The column is broad, the same color as the dark band on the other parts. From under it comes the neat, rather small lip which is violet in the center, white on the sides, sharply contrasted with the large yellow crest. This species is from the high, cool, damp forests of Colombia and requires cool treatment. It flowers in the summer.

B. hemixantha. The name means half-yellow. The dorsal sepal is white, tipped with yellow, the laterals are yellow at the tip and longitudinally half yellow and half white. The lip and callus are pure yellow. The huge column is almost as wide as the lip and has broad side wings, white tipped with purple. This is a warm-growing species from Venezuela and flowers in the summer.

B. lalindei. These fleshy, very fragrant flowers have sepals and petals of pale rose shading into rose-red and tipped with cream-yellow, and a large, bright yellow lip. The very broad column is rose colored. This is another cool-growing species from Colombia and is summer blooming.

CHONDRORHYNCHA

This genus has been undergoing revision, with many species removed to *Cochleanthes*. The plants of this genus and of those once included in *Warscewiczella* are quite similar. They have no pseudobulbs; the leaves grow in a fan.

C. aromatica. This species came to me marked *Zygopetalum wendlandii.* It was once named *Z. aromaticum,* and the specific name is most apt. Alex Hawkes now includes this in *Chondrorhyncha* as *C. aromatica.* The delightfully fragrant flowers have slender, waxy, green sepals and petals, quite long and a bit twisted at the tips. The essentially oval lip is much ruffled and undulated, rose with a white border, spreading from a basal semicircular crest that has vertical thickenings of purple. Native to Costa Rica and Panama, it blooms in the fall.

C. chestertoni has flowers three inches across, of a pale yellow-green. The sepals and petals are similar, but the lip is broad, yellow, spotted with red, and decorated with fringe. The plant should be kept damp throughout the year and likes a slightly shaded spot in the cattleya house. From Colombia, it is summer blooming.

C. rosea. The flowering stems are about half the length of the leaves, bearing one flower each. The three-inch flowers have green sepals with their edges rolled inward and broader white petals that hold themselves forward over the lip. The quite tubular lip is green on its undersurface, shading on the inside from pale yellow with pink spots at the base to yellow, then to dark pink, to white at the tip. A long, three-ridged crest is situated within the lip, and from it extend three lines. The species is native to Venezuela and requires intermediate greenhouse temperatures.

COCHLEANTHES

This genus has plants quite similar to those of *Chrondrorhyncha,* and the flowers are, to the amateur eye at least, also quite similar.

C. discolor. Long known as *Warscewiczella discolor,* this is one of the few orchids to approach blue in some of its color phases. The sepals are pale creamy green; the dorsal sepal stands more or less upright, the laterals extend back along the ovary. The rich, velvety lip is tubular, with the sides enfolding the column and the outer lobe spreading, sometimes a definite blue-violet, sometimes rich red-violet, but always more deeply colored within. The petals hold themselves forward parallel to the lip and are colored like it on their inner surfaces, paler on the outer. The crest is a

bright, yellow-toothed callus whose free edge spreads out over the base of the lip. The species flowers from spring to fall and is native to Cuba, Costa Rica, and Panama. It flowers during spring and summer (Fig. 20–11).

C. marginata. This beautiful pink flower has something of a cattleya shape since its petals spread wide and its sepals are not bent back. The sepals and petals are light pink, the ruffled outer margin of the lip a darker pink and the inner portion white with a dark pink center. The basal callus is white, as is the column. Native to Colombia, Venezuela, and Ecuador, it grows both in trees and in the fluffy humus on the ground. It flowers in winter.

COLAX

See *Pabstia.*

HUNTLEYA

Among the most striking of orchids, the large, handsome flowers are vivid in color and have a varnished appearance. The plants have a fan of broadly keeled leaves, up to a dozen to a growth, and are without pseudobulbs. One species is very well known, and several others are quite rare.

H. meleagris. It is now accepted that the species *burtii* is synonymous with *meleagris.* This flower is a wide-open star with the tapered points of the sepals and petals bent backward. The surface is

Figure 20–11 Cochleanthes discolor *has single flowers on short stems crowded at the base of the leaves. They are creamy green with the lip shading to deep blue.*

finely "quilted" and very shiny. The outer two thirds of the sepals and petals is golden brown and the inner third is white, with a narrow band of yellow in between. At the base of the petals is a splash of dark red with fine lines extending out, almost like a comb. The lip is small, of velvety texture, with a narrow white base and a rounded outer portion of dull red. The crest is a semicircle of short, white, taillike projections. The large, hooded column is white with a touch of red on its side wings. Native to Costa Rica, Panama, northern South America, and Trinidad, it flowers in the spring.

H. lucida. This is a rare species, a beautiful chestnut-brown-and-white flower. The dark inner portion of the sepals and petals is divided from the less intensely colored outer portion by a yellow-green line. It was discovered long ago but recently found in a restricted area of Venezuela by G. C. K. Dunsterville. It blooms in summer.

H. fasciata, a new species from Panama, was named by J. A. Fowlie. The outer portion of its yellow-green sepals and petals is barred with red-brown, the inner part is reddish tan. Flowering season is spring.

KEFERSTEINIA

This genus of small plants has delicate-looking flowers, some quite translucent in texture, but they are long lasting nevertheless.

K. graminea. The two-inch flowers are an almost transparent greenish-ivory, with slender, oval sepals and petals, widespreading, and of about equal size. They are decorated with dotted lines of red over their entire surface. The outer lobe of the lip spreads forward from the basal part that holds itself in an upturned crescent. Within the basal part lies a callus with its two sides sharply upturned. The lip is covered with dotted lines of dark maroon which coalesce in the center. This species is native to Venezuela, Colombia and Ecuador. It is summer flowering.

K. sanguinolenta. This species has pale green flowers dotted with purple. Its lip is quite stiff at the base and cupped, giving the typical crescent view from the front. The outer portion bends down abruptly and its margin is very wavy and toothed. The markings on the lip are of heavy purple blotches mixed with fine dots, and it has a fine

down on its surface. The crest consists of two forward-projecting teeth. The species is found in Ecuador and Venezuela.

K. tolimensis. Most dainty and transparent of all, the flowers are shaped like *sanguinolenta,* but the lip edge is very fringed or lacerated. The green sepals and petals are spotted with fine dots of purple that become blotches toward the base. The lip is very heavily dotted with purple, almost solid purple in the center. The callus is a square thickening divided into two parts in the front. The species is found in Venezuela, Colombia, and Ecuador. It is winter flowering.

MENADENIUM

See *Zygosepalum.*

MENDONCELLA

Mendoncella flowers superficially resemble those of *Huntleya* but have distinct differences. The large, shield-shaped lip is heavily ribbed and has a raised, ribbed crest; the column has long downward projecting wings; and the lateral sepals, which are inserted on the column foot, have a pocket at their base.

M. fimbriata is a striking species. Its six-inch flower has long sepals and petals that are broad at the base, tapering to a sharp point, and striped lengthwise with brownish purple. The lip is creamy white with dark purple lines on the crest, fainter ones toward the apex. Its edge is fringed, and its surface is hairy. The plant has rather small pseudobulbs that bear two leaves about eight inches tall. From Colombia and Venezuela, it flowers in summer.

M. jorisiana. This has five-inch pseudobulbs topped by a pair of rather broad leaves. The five-inch flower is boldly spotted with dark green on a light green background, each petal and sepal tipped with a solid patch of dark green. The outer lobe of the lip is white, unevenly toothed, and the crest is formed of seven bold pink ridges that end in raised points. The flowers are borne in pairs at the end of rather short stems. It is found in Venezuela and flowers in spring and fall.

PABSTIA

Pabstia has but two or three species, one of which is well known and widely grown.

P. jugosus. This is an unusual and pretty orchid. It has very round, fleshy, long-lasting flowers that are between two and three inches in diameter. The rounded sepals are pure white or ivory, broader than the petals. The petals are white, transversely striped with red or red-violet. The rounded lip and its small side lobes are also white, striped with a bluish violet, as is the column. This native of southern Brazil flowers in the spring.

PESCATORIA

The vegetative parts of plants in this genus are indistinguishable from those of many others of this tribe. The flowers are quite distinctive, very waxy and fragrant, with an unusually large, ridged callus forming a large portion of the lip. The sepals and petals are oval, rounded and somewhat wavy at the tip.

P. cerina. This pure white flower has such a large lip callus that it appears to have a tucked-in bib. The ridges of the yellow callus are carried on in lines down the front of the lip, which is also yellow. The corners of the basal part of the lip turn up around the column. This fall- and spring-flowering species is native to Costa Rica and Panama (Fig. 20–12).

P. dayana. This species has its sepals and petals tipped with green. The lip turns up and out at the

Figure 20–12 Pescatoria cerina *is white, with a tucked-in bib of yellow.*

end, rather than down as in *cerina.* It is flushed with violet and has rays of violet extending from the base of the very large, red-violet callus. It is native to Colombia and blooms in the winter and spring. In the variety *rhodacra,* the flower parts are tipped with rose; it blooms in the fall.

P. klaborchorum. The flower is shaped very much like that of the preceding species. The white sepals and petals are tipped with chocolate-purple. The lip is also white, but it is completely covered with rows of purple papillae. The callus is yellow, ridged with nineteen purple lines. From Colombia and Ecuador, it flowers in the summer.

PROMENAEA

The plants of this genus are miniatures, with pseudobulbs about an inch tall and leaves from two to four inches. They are all from Brazil and are tender and rather warm growing. They are rare in this country at present. The flowers are two inches in diameter, with broad, spreading sepals and petals, and a longish oval lip that has two tall side lobes.

P. paulensis. This has broader lateral sepals than *P. stapeliodes* and almost-round petals pointed at their tips. It is white, spotted with rose. Its blooming time is summer.

P. stapelioides. The flowers are greenish yellow, densely barred and spotted with purple, the lip almost solid purple. It blooms spring and summer.

P. xanthina (syn. *ovatilabia*). This has yellow-gold flowers which are fragrant and heavy in substance. The lip is long in proportion to the other flower parts. It blooms in summer and fall.

P. crawshayana. This is a hybrid between *stapelioides* and *xanthina.* The flowers are yellow-green, the sepals with but few spots, the petals lightly spotted with red. The spots on the lip become more dense toward the center and cover the side lobes and the tall, semicircular crest. It blooms in the spring and is completely delightful.

STENIA

Stenia is a rather rare genus of two, possibly three, species, but it makes a choice addition to a collection because of its large flowers produced by a small plant. The leafy plants have very tiny pseudobulbs, or none at all, and produce two-and-one-half-inch, round, almost translucent flowers on single stems. The petals and sepals are broadly oval, pointed at the tips, and spread evenly. The lip is saccate, pinched in the middle.

S. pallida. A serenely beautiful flower, this has greenish white sepals and petals and a small scoop-shaped lip that grades from white to yellow, with yellow-green side lobes and a many-toothed callus. It is found in Guyana, Venezuela, and Trinidad and flowers in the fall.

S. gutata is very speckled with purple on a straw-colored background. It is native to Peru and flowers in the fall.

ZYGOSEPALUM

Zygosepalum (old syn. *Menadenium*) has several species, but the one that is best known is indeed lovely.

Z. labiosum. This has sepals and petals softly shaded brown over green, or maroon over green, and their tapering points curve backward. The petals are held upright, sometimes with their tips crossed. The full, spreading lip is white with pink lines radiating from a semicircular, erect, pink crest at its base. The column is a most striking feature, with its long pointed beak and side wings that hang down like the sides of a bonnet. It is native to Venezuela, northern Brazil, Guyana, and Suriname and is summer flowering. The plant is of modest size, with oval pseudobulbs and two rather thin leaves.

ZYGOPETALUM

The large, pseudobulbous plants, with their broad, heavy, many-veined leaves and bold, strikingly marked flowers, well equip this species to be the "granddaddy" of the subtribe.

Z. crinitum (by some considered synonymous with *mackayi*). This species has pseudobulbs to four inches tall and leaves eighteen inches long. The flower spike holds five to ten three-inch flowers that are waxy, fragrant, and richly colored. The sepals and petals form a fan, the lateral sepals being held horizontally, and are of a green ground color heavily barred with greenish brown. Against this fan stands the lurid violet-striped lip and the

almost reptilian column. Flowering in the fall, it is native to Brazil.

Z. grandiflorum. A most unusual flower, this species has slender, tapering sepals and petals whose points curve backward, the lateral sepals actually flaring sideways. The lip is broad at the base, pointed at the outer end, with tall, finlike side lobes, all fringed at the edge. The whole flower is brightly striped with red, the sepals and petals on a green ground, the lip on white. This species is native to Guatemala.

Z. intermedium. Best known of the genus, although usually known by the wrong name, *Z. makayi,* for these two are very much alike. Both have green sepals and petals, blotched with brown, and a broad, white lip veined with branching lines of purple. The chief differences are that in *intermedium* the purple lip lines are actually rows of downy hairs, while the lip of *makayi* is smooth. Also, the petals of *intermedium* about equal the sepals in length, while those of *makayi* are shorter. Both are native to Brazil, and both are sweetly fragrant and winter flowering (Fig. 20–13).

Z. maxillare. In general, this is a smaller plant than the *intermedium,* and the flowers are also somewhat smaller, but they are very neat, colorful, and fragrant. The flowers are two-and-one-half inches across and the fleshy, rather plain lip is one-and-one-quarter inch in diameter. The petals and sepals are nearly equal, green, barred with large areas of brown. The cup-shaped crest is dark plum, with raised ridges on the inside. The outer lobe is rosy violet, shading off to pink. It easily makes a specimen plant with many spikes of four to five flowers each. Native to Brazil, it flowers in late summer and fall.

Figure 20–13 Zygopetalum intermedium, *a stunning and very fragrant species.* (COURTESY OF JACK SWEET.)

•21•

PROBLEMS, DISEASES, AND PESTS

ㅇ RCHID HEALTH DEPENDS ON three fundamentals—good inheritance, proper environment, and freedom from disease and injury. Enough has been said previously about inheritance to emphasize the importance of selecting strong, free-growing, promising plants, whether you acquire them as small seedlings or as mature plants. Environmental conditions that contribute to the health of the plant are the right amount of light, temperature within the proper day-night range, humidity coupled with good air circulation, water to suit the needs of the plants, and proper nutrition combined with root aeration. Deviations from the optimal in any of these conditions may cause variations from the normal thrifty condition of the plant. Diseases are caused by invading viruses, bacteria, or fungi. Prevention of insect injury is an absolute necessity.

AILMENTS ARISING FROM ENVIRONMENTAL CONDITIONS

LIGHT. When the light is too strong, chlorophyll (the green pigment) is destroyed faster than it is made, and leaves become yellow, or even white in young seedlings. Yellowed leaves cannot make as much food as leaves with the normal amount of chlorophyll. If the condition is not corrected, the older leaves may fall before they should. The general result is a retarded plant.

Sudden exposure to too-strong light may burn localized areas. Naturally, the efficiency of a leaf is decreased by the presence of a burned area. The sudden exposure may result from removing too much shading in the fall, from not applying it soon enough in the spring, or by allowing strong light to focus on a plant through a clear area on the glass or through an open ventilator. Flowers are sensitive to the excessive heat produced by too much light, and become dry and thin before their time from its effects.

Insufficient light causes the plants to become a darker green than normal. Even though the dark-green plants are handsome to the eye, they are not as healthy as when the foliage is a lighter shade. The plants are usually soft and succulent, susceptible to disease, and their new growths do not mature and harden as they should. Flower production is cut down or inhibited entirely.

TEMPERATURE. Each kind of orchid has its own temperature requirements. If night temperatures are too high for their kind, they will not flower. Growth is poor because food is used faster than it can be made. Often the leaves fall prematurely and death may result.

At temperatures below the specific requirement, water and minerals are absorbed but slowly, and formation of chlorophyll is hindered. Yellow foliage and poor development result, and poor flowering is the logical sequel.

There is also an optimal difference between day

and night temperatures. Too wide a gap, or not enough drop at night, retards growth.

Orchids can survive short spells of extremely hot weather if everything is done to aid them. The leaves absorb light with its associated heat, and their temperature is therefore usually warmer than the surrounding air. They have some protection from heat in their evaporation of water (transpiration), which acts as a cooling system. For cattleyas, it has been demonstrated that burning occurs if the temperature of the leaves remains at 110° for a few hours, or at 120°–125° for shorter periods. This means that during hot spells, when the greenhouse temperature soars above 100°, the temperature of the leaves may reach the danger point and sudden burning may occur. I know of a case where every plant in a small greenhouse was burned black when it was accidentally left unattended on a hot day. During hot weather everything must be done to lower the temperature of leaves. The plants should have cooling mists over the foliage and proper attention to ventilation, shade, and air circulation.

Burning due to strong light would actually seem to be a heat effect. Concentration of light on one area of a leaf raises the temperature of that area to the burning point.

Flowers are even more sensitive to heat than plants. Flowering plants should therefore be kept as cool as possible in hot weather to prevent premature fading.

In regions where hot summers are a rule, varieties should be chosen with care as to their particular temperature requirements.

Freezing kills plant tissues just as burning does. However, the frozen areas become soft and watery, dirty yellow-green in color, and then black. Frozen areas should be cut off and the surfaces treated with Tersan or other fungicide to prevent infection of the wounds. Do not syringe until the cuts have dried and healed. If severe freezing leaves only a small portion of the plant intact, it should be treated as a potted division until it is growing actively again. Dipping in a sugar solution (1 teaspoon to a gallon of water) can help a plant recover.

HUMIDITY. Insufficient humidity in the air makes it difficult to maintain an even water supply to the plants. The potting medium dries out quickly, and the plants lose water rapidly through their foliage. This is especially critical for newly potted plants, whose root systems are temporarily non-functioning, and for young seedlings.

Excessive humidity is dangerous for it brings about susceptibility to certain diseases. Flowers may become spotted, by simple engorgement of water or by fungus growths. *Botrytis* fungus causes pink or brown spots, and flowers may become spotted with a sooty black mold. Other plant parts may be attacked by bacteria and fungi.

The danger of infection during the high relative humidity maintained for the purpose of cooling the plants in the daytime is lessened by good air movement. However, very high relative humidity (above 70 percent) leads to succulent growth, which is more susceptible to infection than hard growth.

WATERING. Enough has been said about the effects of overwatering on plants and flowers, but we might repeat here that overwatering is one thing to suspect when a plant is not making vigorous growth or when its older leaves are turning soft and yellow. Examine the potting medium and the roots. If the medium is broken down and is wet and mushy it will contain few if any active roots. Repotting is then in order.

Underwatering will cause shrivelling of the leaves and pseudobulbs and new growths will be small. The roots may be thin and starved. If the medium is in good condition (and it probably is since it has been kept dry) simply step up the frequency of watering.

It may take more than a year to bring back the vigor of a plant that has been stunted by one of these conditions, but it is rewarding to see them improve.

NUTRITION. Chapter 4 gives the symptoms of various nutritional deficiencies. It is not likely that plants potted in good osmunda will suffer any nutritional lack, provided they are potted firmly. Plants potted loosely will suffer from lack of minerals and perhaps of water also. Some of the leaves will turn yellow and die. In bark, yellow leaves are a sign of lack of nitrogen (if it can be ascertained that the cause is not root loss). The fertilizers prepared for use with bark contain a higher nitrogen concentration because of the inherent lack of sufficient nitrogen in bark.

AIR RELATIONS. Industrial regions offer hazards to orchid growing, by the production of smoke and haze which reduce the light available to the plants and by the production of noxious fumes. The former is being reduced by modern methods of smoke control. The latter is not such a simple problem (see Sepal wilt, below).

If you live where soot and grime collect on the plants, wash them off with a forceful spray of water at frequent intervals. Dirt collecting on the leaves may plug up the stomata and cut down the working power of the leaf.

Artificial illuminating gas is disastrous to plant life. Even a small amount of the raw gas leaking into the greenhouse will quickly kill the plants. One grower lost a great many when the gas main in the street broke and the gas seeped through the earth into his orchid house. Artificial gas is not safe to use in the greenhouse, nor is gas that has the slightest amount of artificial gas mixed with it. On the other hand, absolutely pure natural gas is perfectly safe, as is bottled gas (butane), provided the heaters are vented to carry off all fumes from combustion.

SEPAL WILT AND PREMATURE AGING

When a flower fades normally, after having lasted its usual length of time, the sepals are the first parts to show signs of deterioration. Starting at the tips, they lose their waxy sheen, become thin and transparent, and finally become tissuelike. The rest of the flower follows suit soon afterward, sometimes remaining in good condition a few days longer than the sepals. Sometimes the aging process sets in prematurely, occasionally almost as soon as the flower opens. There are two types of premature aging, one caused by some failure in cultural, environmental, or inherited factors which prevent the flowers from attaining their normal vigor and substance, and another caused by actual poisoning by substances in the atmosphere. We shall take up the first under the heading "Short flower life" and the second under "Sepal wilt."

SHORT FLOWER LIFE. Anything that interferes with the health of a plant can result in flowers that are thin in substance and which do not last the normal length of time. Poor potting, improper watering, poor nutrition, excessive temperatures, lack of humidity, insufficient light, root loss—any or all can debilitate a plant. Flowers produced on such plants may be thin from the time they open, never

attaining the firm substance expected of them, or they may appear normal for a while but soon fade. Any kind of orchid may respond with poor flowers when the plants are not vigorous. Cattleyas seem to be the most sensitive to insufficient light, and this is most often the cause of their premature aging. They are also most sensitive to the causal agents of sepal wilt.

A plant brought into the house before the buds are open must be kept in a bright window until the flowers are fully mature, else they will be thin. Long spells of dull weather may cause cattleya flowers to be less firm than they are normally, with the sepals becoming limp and transparent soon after the bud opens and the rest of the flower lasting only a short time. This condition may be confused with "sepal wilt," but it differs in that the whole flower is thin or becomes thin soon after the sepals shrivel, while in true sepal wilt, the petals and lip are usually quite normal. Premature aging or short flower life, due to insufficient light, occurs in regions with prolonged spells of dull weather. It is also a common complaint where too-heavy shading is used at any season.

The sudden fading of a normal flower may result from pollination by a visiting insect. The petals usually fold together and turn papery. Notice whether there are pollinia on the stigma.

Removal or dislodgement of the anther causes premature fading of *Cymbidium, Catasetum, Cycnoches* and possibly some other kinds. A jostling of the buds or open flowers, even by a strong stream of water, may be enough to jar loose the anther in its socket. The fading of one or two flowers on a stem is often a clue to this.

Excessive heat may cause premature fading of flowers throughout the greenhouse, either extreme day temperatures or inordinately high night temperatures. This is particularly likely to happen when the air is too dry in the presence of high temperatures. Too low night temperatures, which do not allow the full development of the flowers, may also be a cause.

When all possible factors are checked, and a plant in apparent good health consistently gives poor flowers year after year, the cause is probably its genetic make-up. Within any species, or in any group of hybrids, there are a few individuals that just do not have the ability to give good flowers. It is not worthwhile to keep such plants. Also, some plants are not good growers, in spite of all the care that you can give them, and because of lack of vigor they flower poorly. These, too, should be discarded.

SEPAL WILT. Sepal wilt, also called dry sepals, is a peculiar condition whose mysteries have required much experimentation and detective work to unravel. Cattleyas are affected most severely. However, the factors that cause sepal wilt in cattleyas may also affect some other kinds in other ways, and may be doing damage not yet realized.

A typical sequence of events is this: In the midst of a period when flowers are opening in good condition, there comes an interval when some or all opening flowers have thin, dry sepals, brown at the tip. Then, just as suddenly, the interval is over, and newly opening flowers are again normal. In affected flowers the sepals wilt as soon as the bud opens. The rest of the flower usually gains its normal substance and lasts well, but the flower is, of course, ruined by the affected sepals. Often the sepals turn soft and leathery before the bud opens, and in many cases the bud is entirely prevented from opening. Observations during short periods of sepal wilt suggest that the causative factors act on the bud just as it is getting ready to open, because (1) flowers already open are not affected, and (2) buds that are still quite green subsequently open normally. The fact that not all flowers are affected, and that the degree of severity varies among affected plants, suggests that some are more resistant than others.

Experimental work has shown that ethylene gas will cause sepal wilt. Ethylene gas is used to ripen fruit that has been picked green for shipping. This is essentially an aging process. The gas is present in smog and in fumes from incomplete combustion of hydrocarbons (coal, oil, gas, gasoline, etc.). Sepal wilt is especially prevalent during periods of smog, frequently occurs in greenhouses heated by open-flame, nonvented gas heaters, and is more common in, or close to, industrial areas than in open country. It occurs when the wind brings fumes from factory areas, or areas of heavy traffic, and is absent when the wind blows the fumes in another direction. It occurs under certain atmospheric conditions when the air hugs the ground and smoke and fumes are layered within it. It is not necessarily connected to light conditions. Growers who have moved their collections away from cities and industrial areas have found that they are freer from sepal wilt. The new techniques for controlling air pollution have improved the situation in some areas.

The reason for the prevalence of sepal wilt among cattleyas is that they are far more sensitive to ethylene gas than other orchids and, indeed, than most other plants. According to O. Wesley Davidson, cattleyas just beginning to split their sepals are affected by one part of ethylene in 300,000,000 to 500,000,000 parts of air. Tomato plants, on the other hand, require as much as one part ethylene gas in 10,000,000 to 20,000,000 parts of air in order to cause their leaves to fold. Carnation flowers become "sleepy" in response to one part ethylene in 20,000,000 to 25,000,000 parts of air. Tomatoes and carnations are therefore not affected by the extremely minute amounts that cause sepal wilt in cattleyas. It would be desirable to have some indicator plant that is more sensitive than cattleyas, but so far we do not know of any.

Other orchids, which are not affected by the small concentration that injures cattleya flowers, may be injured by stronger concentrations. Plants themselves may also be injured. We have had two experiences that have alerted us to these possibilities. Both instances were caused by the rusting through or disconnection of the vent pipe from natural gas heaters in our own greenhouse. Cymbidium plants near the break showed premature aging of the flowers. The flowers turned pink and faded (just as they do when the anthers are removed). Flowers that opened after the break was repaired showed no symptoms. In the other case, the cattleya plants themselves were affected. On the plants near the break (where the fumes were strongest), the older leaves turned a bright orange and fell. For as long as a year afterward, leaves on these same plants continued to age prematurely, although the plants finally recovered. A report from Australia suggests that smog is the cause of a leaf-tip necrosis in cymbidiums. We have heard that cymbidium, paphiopedilum, and odontoglossum flowers were injured at the New York International Flower Show a few years ago when trucks were used to clean the building and the fumes were retained in the building.

Gases other than ethylene may produce the same type of injuries. Growers in smoggy areas have learned that activated charcoal will adsorb the poisonous gases. The greenhouse must be tight, and all incoming air must be filtered through containers of activated charcoal. The charcoal must be renewed from time to time. Repetition of sepal wilt signals the time to change the charcoal.

MECHANICAL AND CHEMICAL INJURIES TO PLANTS

Sharp bending of leaves, particularly the thick, brittle leaves of cattleyas and others, will cause injury to the tissues. The leaves may show a split down the midrib, or the end of the leaf beyond the point where it was bent may die. Young leaves are particularly tender and are sometimes unintentionally broken when a plant is handled. They are also susceptible to bacterial and fungus infections, so if a leaf turns black investigate to see whether its death has been caused primarily by a break or by infection.

Chemicals not specifically recommended for orchids should not be used on them. Those recommended should be used exactly as directed on the label. Injury can be caused by those not compatible with orchids or by too strong concentrations of those that are compatible. The injuries appear as burned or blistered spots on leaves. Flower buds may be killed or blossoms spotted.

FREAKS

Freak flowers or freak growths, called anomalies, occasionally occur; but for the most part they do not repeat themselves. Sometimes a flower has too few or too many parts, or the parts may be fused to each other. There have been reports of flowers having only two sepals, apparently a dorsal and a ventral sepal, of flowers having no lip or two lips, of flowers in which the lip has reverted to a petal in shape, of flowers in which petals have lip structure, of flowers in which the length of the lip is fused to the column or in which the sepals are fused for part of their length so that the bloom cannot open. Abnormal growths on plants have also been reported. For instance, a cattleya can have a growth with no leaf or a flower stem apparently arising from the base of the pseudobulb instead of from the apex. Sometimes a leaf may be tubular, not opening flat; and sometimes a sheath seems to be part true leaf and part sheath (Fig. 21–1).

Such anomalies are ordinarily accidents in development. They can occur on a plant that has till then given all normal flowers and which thereafter continues to give normal flowers. These are not caused by changes in the genetic make-up of the plant.

However, genetic changes can occur. They are very rare. If a plant gives deformed flowers from the start, the cause is in its genetic make-up. If one flowers normally at first and then starts giving, and continues to give, abnormal flowers, this indicates that some change has taken place in its genes.

One anomaly that is highly regarded is peloria, especially the situation where petals have the markings and/or shape of the lip. They can be quite handsome. Such are splash-petal cattleyas, or cymbidiums with feather stripes and spots in the petals. They do not often breed true but occasionally form charming hybrids.

Chromosomal aberrations, such as the loss of a chromosome or two, or acquisition of an extra one or two, may cause abnormal growth in a plant. Possession by the plant cells of an odd number of chromosomes (a number over or under an even multiple of the haploid number) is called aneuploidy. This condition may be the basis for some abnormalities.

PARASITIC DISEASES: BACTERIAL, FUNGAL, AND VIRAL

During recent years work on orchid diseases has been intensified. Much has been learned about the

Figure 21–1 *A freak flower that has three equal petals and three anthers. This is a particularly interesting anomaly because it shows an apparent reversion to some possible ancestral type, one in which the third petal had not been modified into a lip, nor the anthers reduced to a single one.*

diseases, their diagnosis, and the organisms which cause them; and many agents for their control have been developed. In this context, The American Orchid Society *Handbook on Orchid Pests and Diseases* is a must for all orchid growers. Orchid growers are indebted to research workers in many countries, and in the United States particularly to Peter A. Ark, D. D. Jensen, C. I. Kado, Harry C. Burnett, H. H. Murakishi, Irene Gleason, and Roger Lawson.

In even the best-managed greenhouse there is occasionally a diseased plant. Some diseases are mild, doing little damage and being easy to control, some are more serious and resist control quite stubbornly; however, with persistence, most can be cured. A few come on suddenly and run rampant through a plant, at the same time exposing other plants dangerously. A grower must always be on the alert, ready with an effective fungicide to treat any suspicious spots, and observant of any spread of disease in the plant in question or to its neighbors. If your experience with disease has been limited to an occasional incident it is a compliment to your management. Maintenance of healthy growing conditions is in itself a method of disease control and prevention. The presence of a few diseased plants in a greenhouse where bad conditions exist can set off an epidemic, particularly when the elements conspire to spread infection, with long spells of cold or warm, cloudy weather.

Bacteria, fungi, and viruses are ever-present. Many that attack common garden crops will also attack orchids. Some species of these organisms are parasites on plant tissue and digest the cells for their own food. They enter the plant through wounds, even through such a small injury as an insect puncture, or through the stomata. Bacteria reproduce in the plant tissue and come to the surface in minute, oozing droplets. They are spread from plant to plant by contact: contaminated hands or instruments, insects or splashing water. A fungus usually grows with its cobweblike body (mycelium) inside a leaf, pseudobulb, etc., destroying the tissues as it spreads. The only part that appears on the surface is that which bears the spores, the reproductive cells. The spores are carried from plant to plant by the same means as bacteria. Viruses (which have characteristics of both living and nonliving entities) reproduce only in living tissue and travel very rapidly throughout the entire plant. Once infected, the plant has the virus in all its parts. The infection can be spread to other plants by contaminated cutting tools and hands and by some aphids. Viruses can remain dormant on dead plant material or old dirty pots for years, ready to resume activity when introduced into living plants. As yet no cure has been found for virus diseases. Removal of a part that shows symptoms does not free the plant from the virus because it has traveled into every part (except possibly the minute tip of the growing stem). No chemical has been found that will kill the virus within the plant.

Bacterial and fungal diseases in their initial stages can be cured by the use of fungicides and, where necessary, by the removal of diseased parts plus treatment with fungicides. There are some bacterial and fungal diseases that typically advance so rapidly that they are rarely caught in time. Many of the latter flourish when temperatures are low and humidity high, conditions that often plague European growers. So readily do diseases occur at such times that the earlier growers thought improper environment itself was the cause of disease. This idea prevailed until the last half of the nineteenth century, when it was demonstrated that plant infections were caused by bacteria and fungi, thriving and multiplying under these very conditions. Other pathogenic organisms thrive under conditions of warmer temperatures coupled with high humidity. Soft, succulent growth is particularly liable to infection.

Moisture is of the greatest significance in the spread of disease. In order for fungus spores to germinate, or for bacteria to enter a plant, water must be present on rhizome, pseudobulb, leaf, flower, or sheath. Hence good orchid culture calls for watering and syringing early enough in the day to allow the plants to dry off before night. Then, when temperatures are lower and humidity runs up to the saturation point, the plants offer dry surfaces to the potential enemy. Avoid crowding the plants on the bench, as this cuts down air circulation and allows moisture to remain for long periods.

Fans to keep the air circulating are a necessity. A fan in connection with the heater is helpful. Some growers use turbulator fans or "Casablanca" type rotating arm fans like those used in homes placed toward the ridge. Another type is a small fan or muffin fan placed here and there to move the air over groups of plants. Others can be put underneath or over the bench to pull the air upward.

Sanitation is important. Pathogenic organisms may be perpetuated on plant debris accumulated on or under the benches and may be spread from these sources by splashing water or by insects. Weeds, plant trimmings, old flowers, and all other debris must be cleared away. When treating a diseased plant any parts that are cut off should be burned or should be wrapped and disposed of with trash that is to be burned. Insect control is related to sanitation, since insects play a dual role in plant infection. They inflict wounds through which pathogenic organisms can enter, and they sometimes place in the wound organisms they have picked up by contact with infected material. Aphids are particularly dangerous since certain species are known to be vectors of virus diseases.

When buying plants, choose those that appear to be disease-free. If you buy by mail, examine the plants carefully when they arrive before putting them with your other plants. A period of isolation is recommended for all new material. If any have soft, watery spots, or streaks or patterns of dead tissue in the leaves, reject the plants.

It is often difficult to know what disease we are dealing with from the appearance of spots on our plants, particularly at the onset of the disease. In fact, for a long time it was difficult even for pathologists to recognize the exact pathogen. In the past few years pathologists have developed methods for culturing bacteria and fungi from tissues of diseased plants, inoculating the pure strains into healthy plants, observing the symptoms, and then recovering the organisms from the inoculated plants. Thus they have been able to study the symptoms produced by specific organisms and follow the course of the disease each causes.

Similarly, viruses have been isolated, purified, and inoculated into healthy plants. The virologists are now employing serological methods adopted from the field of immunology for detecting the presence of specific viruses. Rabbits are injected with a pure strain of virus, to which they respond by forming antibodies. The antibodies, removed from the serum of the rabbit blood, will form a precipitate when added to plant sap that contains the specific virus. This is done in a number of ways, detailed farther on. The electron microscope has also been a marvelous instrument in virus research.

Laymen are for the most part not able to pin down each disease to its causative agent, but we can come a lot closer than we could a few years ago. Where a disease is quite specific to a certain kind of orchid, for example miltonia scorch or paphiopedilum crown rot, or when you have seen a certain type a number of times and have learned its course and how it responds to treatment, you become fairly confident of your diagnosis. The viruses are more elusive, although some are so characteristic that an amateur can recognize their patterns. Sometimes diseases may fool you, some little clue may escape you, or you may not notice the disease until it has gone beyond the beginning stages. As far as bacterial and fungal diseases are concerned, those you cannot treat you will recognize quickly, and for those that can be cured any of a number of fungicides can be used.

The first steps in control are to isolate the diseased plants, cut down the humidity, dispense with syringing, and increase ventilation. This will not only reduce the spread of disease to healthy plants but will help to check its spread in infected ones. Then treat the infected plants. If additional plants in the greenhouse become infected and it appears that the disease is spreading, the whole greenhouse may be sprayed with a fungicide.

CAUTION WITH CHEMICALS

Some of the products on the market today are deadly poisonous. We prefer not to recommend any of these. We see no use in risking injury to human life and health when products of lesser toxicity are available and perform satisfactorily. This does not mean that even those termed "moderately safe" are actually safe, for if used without caution or by persons sensitive to them they can cause serious illness. One should not be soothed by a moderate toxicity rating—*all should be handled with great care.* Any material that will kill a bug can affect a human being.

While many workers believe that they are unaffected by chemicals used as insecticides or fungicides (the "it can't happen to me" attitude), deaths have occurred from their use. (Some commercial growers have put all their spraying in the hands of professional contractors.) It is possible that a bad headache, a digestive upset, an unaccountable spell of fatigue or dizziness, or a feeling of sleepiness may be caused by them. These are all symptoms of poisoning.

Directions on the label should be followed exactly. Do not depend on memory for quantities as the danger includes injury to plants as well. Keep all chemicals locked up securely at all times. When a container is empty, dispose of it in such a way that it will not come into the hands of a child or a curious person for whom the few remaining drops could be deadly. Wear protective clothing. Take a bath immediately after spraying, and have the clothes worn during the job washed before using them again. Be careful not to inhale fumes, spray, or dust or get them on your skin. Face masks with felt or chemical cartridges are available from supply houses and are a good precaution, as are goggles.

A comprehensive list of chemicals and their toxicity is given at the right so that you may check a compound before deciding to use it and can check those you may have on hand. A confusing array of chemicals is manufactured today, and new ones come out frequently. If you do not find the name, perhaps you can find the active ingredient from the list. Before using any new product, find out whether it is safe for orchids as well as for yourself.

Poisons are rated on what is called an LD_{50} base; LD stands for Lethal Dose, and 50 means a 50 percent kill of test animals. The number of milligrams per kilogram of body weight necessary to produce the 50 percent kill becomes the LD_{50} number. For practical purposes *the lower the LD_{50} number, the more poisonous is the material,* which means that it takes less to do damage.

Substances with numbers 1–5 are deadly poisonous; those with numbers 5–50 are violently poisonous. All of these should be avoided. From 50–500 substances are poisonous; those with lower numbers should be avoided, those approaching 500 indicate great caution.

Over 500, substances become relatively less poisonous as the number increases, but even those with numbers up to 5,000 can cause illness in a child or a sensitive person.

Over 5,000, substances become relatively safe. However, all should be handled with caution.

SYMPTOMS OF POISONING. Symptoms include the following: unconsciousness, collapse, convulsions, tremor, nervousness, staggering, loss of coordination, dizziness, sedation (sleepiness), nausea, vomiting, diarrhea, cramps, excessive salivation, difficulty in breathing. If any of these occur, get emergency help at once. Take the container with the patient so that the doctor can know at once what the ingredients are and can contact the nearest poison control center if necessary.

SUBSTANCES DEADLY POISONOUS

Substance	LD_{50}	Notes
All arsenic compounds	10–50	Injurious to orchids as well as man.
All cyanide compounds	10–50	Injurious to orchids as well as man.
All organic mercury compounds	10–50	Injurious to orchids as well as man.
Acti-Dione (antibiotic)	5–50	See next list.
Aldrin	55	No longer produced in U.S.A.
BHC (benzene hexachloride) (in one form = Lindane)	125	No longer used in U.S.A.
Botran (Dimefox, BFPO)	50	Fungicide. Do not use on greenhouse ornamentals.
Ceresan	40	Used in commercial seed treatment. Not advised for home use.
Chlordane	250	Now banned.
Demeton (Systox)	2.5	Do not use on greenhouse crops.
Dieldrin	40	Banned in some states.
Dithio, Plantfume, Bladafume, Bladex, and other smoke fumigants	2.5	Never use in home greenhouse. Drift to home, neighbors, etc., extremely dangerous.
Endrin	7	Not for greenhouse crops.
Ethion	70	No recent information. Rarely used.
Guthion	11	Do not use on greenhouse crops.
Heptachlor	90	Now banned.
Lindane	88	Now banned.
Nicotine	50–60	Seldom used today because of toxicity to man.
Pano-drench, Panogen	5	No recent information.
Parathion	3	Organic phosphate. Never use in home greenhouse. Banned by law in some states.
Sulfatepp	5	No recent information.
Systox	2.5	Never use on greenhouse crops, especially not on orchids.

Substance	LD$_{50}$	Notes
Temik, Aldicarb	0–50	Highly toxic systemic miticide, insecticide. Federal registration required, to be used by trained personnel only.
TEPP	2	No recent information.
Thimet, Phorate	3	Limited to professional use only.
Vapona, DDVP	60	Organic phosphate. Not for greenhouse use.
Zectran	16	No longer available.

SUBSTANCES TO BE AVOIDED

Substance	LD$_{50}$	Notes
Chorobenzilate, Acaraben	960	Within USA only permitted use is on citrus.
Cygon	320–380	Do not use on greenhouse ornamentals.
Kelthane	684	Usage in U.S.A. is under investigation.
Metasystox R	70	Do not use on greenhouse crops.
Metasystox (i)		Analog of Metasystox R. Restricted. Permit required in California.

NEW SUBSTANCES

Substance	LD$_{50}$	Notes
Bayleton	363	Systemic fungicide. May cause skin irritation. Some stunting if used above recommended rate. Controls *Cercospora,* brown rot, *Fusarium* spp. and others.
Difolatan (Captifol)	6300	General fungicide for foliage problems. Avoid contact with skin and eyes.
Mavrik	261	Nonphytotoxic. May cause skin irritation. General insecticide and miticide. May be used

Substance	LD$_{50}$	Notes
		in greenhouse. Do not use in fogging apparatus.
Subdue	669	May cause skin irritation. Systemic fungicide. Controls *Pythium* spp., *Phytophthora* spp., and other leaf spots and rots. Soil drench and leaf spray. Long-lasting. Use only in extreme dilution, one-quarter teaspoon to five gallons of water. May lead to resistant fungi if repeated too often.

SUBSTANCES RECOMMENDED IN THESE CHAPTERS

Substance	Oral LD$_{50}$	Notes
Actidione (Germain's Mildew and Rust Control)	2	Control for stubborn fusarium wilt. Antibiotic. Extremely toxic. Use only in dire emergency and with great caution.
Banrot (Terrazole, which is the active ingredient in Truban, plus a systemic fungicide.)	2500	Soil drench for control of soil-borne diseases—damp-off, root rots, stem rots—caused by *Pythium, Phytophthora, Rhizoctonia, Fusarium.* Don't mix with other chemicals.
Benlate (Benomyl)	9590	General fungicide for foliage and flower treatment—leaf spots, black leaf tips, *Botrytis* on leaves and flowers. Still in general use although now under investigation as a possible carcinogen.
Bioquin 1	5000	Fungicide, fairly long residual action.
Diazinon	300	Cockroach and ant control. Use only

Substance	Oral LD$_{50}$	Notes
		granules sprinkled on the ground. Toxic to plants and man.
Ferbam	17,000	General fungicide.
8 Quinolinol benzoate or sulfate	49	Fungicide. Controls damp-off and other soil-borne diseases. Dip, drench, or spray. Especially useful for treating seedlings just out of the flask before potting.
Malathion	800	General insecticide. Not very effective for mites. Harms some ferns. Breaks down in the body rather quickly, making it safer than some other organic phosphates.
Metaldehyde	1000	Control for slugs and snails. Active ingredient in many baits. Mask advised if used as dust.
Mesurol	130	Slug and snail control. Caution for toxicity to man. At present available in the U.S.A. only as dry bait.
Natriphene	2000	Control for fungus and bacterial diseases.
Pentac	3160	Nonphytotoxic. Miticide. Slow-acting. Necessary to repeat. Long residual action.
Physan-20	3625	Fungicide, bacteriacide and algacide. Keeps water in trays and coolers clean. In weak dilutions can be sprayed on plants and flowers. Useful for cleaning walls and walks.
Resmethrin, Ortho Household Insect Killer.	2500	Ant and aphid control. Quick kill. Nonphytotoxic. Spray on plants, pots, benches, flowers and buds.
Shield	5000	Fungicide used in pots to control snow mold.
Simazine	500–5000	Herbicide for control of weeds on ground, under benches, etc.

Substance	Oral LD$_{50}$	Notes
		Scatter dry, water in. Lasts a year or more.
Tersan (Arasan, Thiram)	500	Excellent general fungicide. Can be used as drench, dip, or paste. Useful for preventing rot of stem tip in vandas, paphs, and others. Bad reaction with liquor.
Truban (Terrazole, see above under Banrot)	2000	Systemic fungicide.

REFERENCES

Thomson. W. T. *Agricultural Chemicals* Book I, 1989 edition; Book IV, 1988 edition. Thomson Publications, Fresno, California 93791.

U.S. Public Health Service. *Clinical Handbook on Economic Poisons.* Revised. U.S. Government Printing Office, Washington, D.C. 20402.

The American Orchid Society. *Handbook on Orchid Pests and Diseases* 1986 edition. West Palm Beach, Florida 33405.

BACTERIAL AND FUNGAL DISEASES

Bacterial and fungal diseases begin with water-soaked, semitransparent spots. As the disease spreads, a single spot may enlarge until it involves a whole leaf, sometimes spreading from there through the pseudobulb and into the rhizome, or a number of small spots may individually enlarge until they run together. Spots on leaves are easy to detect, but a diseased area on a pseudobulb may escape notice. If the side of a pseudobulb falls over, investigate to see whether there is an area softened by disease. Some diseases caused by soil-borne organisms may penetrate the plant by way of the roots, progressing to the rhizome and sometimes the pseudobulbs. These are less obvious at onset because their presence is not suspected until the leaves become soft and wrinkled, or the new lead turns black. In such cases you may have to cut through the rhizome, starting at the older end of the plant, to determine whether the root loss and leaf wilt are caused by disease. If the tissue of the rhizome is clean and white, or cream colored, it is healthy. If it has black or purple discoloration it is diseased. Before cutting into the rhizome, be sure that the root loss has not been caused by snails.

The list of effective fungicides is long, and new ones are being added to it rapidly. Among them are some with fairly long residual action: Bordeaux Mixture (copper sulfate and lime, an old remedy but still useful), Benomyl (Benlate 50), Tersan 75, Ferbam, Bioquin 1 (copper 8-quinolinolate) and Subdue 2E. These are all valuable both as curative sprays and as preventive sprays where large numbers of plants require treating, but they may also be used to spray or sponge individual plants. Some are insoluble in water and are used in suspension, some are combined with a sticker to make their application more permanent. Bordeaux Mixture may not be as effective as some of the newer fungicides, but if you are faced with the emergency treatment of a plant and cannot readily obtain one of the others, you can usually find Bordeaux Mixture at a local farm supply store. It can be made into a thick slurry, even as paste, and be applied to wounds or diseased spots. Tersan 75 may be used to treat infected plants. Use one tablespoon to one gallon of water and pour this over the plant and through the pot and medium. It may also be made into a slurry or a paste and applied to infected areas and wounds. If the tip of a new growth is becoming infected, pour some Tersan into the just-opening leaves.

With any spray, better spread and quicker drying are obtained by the addition of a wetting agent such as Triton B-1956 or Ortho spreader-sticker, used according to directions. A few drops of a mild household detergent may be used in an emergency, but repeated use is not advised as injury may result.

Fungicides which have a shorter residual action but which are very effective are: Natriphene, the sodium salt of o-hydroxydiphenyl, in a concentration of 1:2000, used as a spray or drench; 8-quinolinol sulfate, used in a concentration of 1:2000 as a spray or drench; Benlate or Truban powders, one teaspoon to one gallon of water, as a spray; Banrot powder, also one teaspoon to one gallon of water, as a soil drench. Those that can be used as drenches, in addition to being very effective, are nontoxic to plants; plants from community pot size on up can be soaked in the solution for several hours at a time.

Not much work has been done as yet with antibiotics on orchids, and we cannot recommend any without reservation at this time. Growers should follow developments in this field for it may be that some will prove safe and useful.

Since diseases can be spread from plant to plant by cutting tools, these should be disinfected after use on each plant. The best method is to flame them or soak for a few minutes in TSP (Trisodium phosphate.)

PYTHIUM BLACK ROT AND DAMP-OFF. A water mold, *Pythium ultimum,* causes this disease, which results in damp-off of community pot seedlings and which also attacks older plants. It requires free water in order to spread, and since community pots are kept damp and the plants are tender and close together, they are most vulnerable to this fungus. Prevention calls for watering the pots every month or so with Natriphene, 8-quinolinol sulfate, Banrot, or Subdue 2E. Subdue 2E must be greatly diluted, only one-quarter teaspoon to five gallons of water. Obey cautions on label. It is a systemic fungicide. If a seedling in a pot shows evidence of infection by turning brown and translucent, act quickly. Remove the infected seedling and drench the whole pot in one of the above. In older seedlings, black spots on the basal portion or on the leaves quickly spread to involve the whole plant. Cut out diseased areas and soak as for community pots. Older plants are usually infected through the roots, and the disease spreads into the rhizome and thence into the pseudobulbs. Occasionally the route is reversed, starting with a leaf and spreading to the pseudobulbs and thence from one pseudobulb to another. High humidity and cool temperatures favor infection. The streaked and blackened tissues sometimes become soft and limp, and exude water on pressure. As the leaves fall and the contents of the pseudobulbs become completely decayed, all that remains is dried and husklike remnants of the pseudobulbs. If the disease appears above the level of the rhizome of an adult plant, cut away the streaked and blackened tissue well down into healthy tissue, soak the whole plant, pot and all, for several hours in 8-quinolinol benzoate or sulfate, and then let it dry out completely. Treat it with Tersan or Ferbam or one of the systemic fungicides, and give water in the pot only (no syringing) for long enough to ascertain whether the disease is arrested. If the disease spreads upward through the rhizome, cut between the pseudobulbs until you find a healthy section of the plant (Fig. 21–2). Save only this section and treat as above. If the disease continues to spread the plant may have to be discarded.

Figure 21–2 *Pythium black rot on cattleya pseudobulbs.* LEFT. *The disease starting at the top.* RIGHT. *Disease spreading upward from the rhizome.* (COURTESY OF PETER A. ARK.)

COLLAR ROT OR ORCHID WILT. This disease, caused by the fungus *Sclerotium rolfsii,* affects many kinds of orchids, among them *Cymbidium* and *Paphiopedilum.* The base of the stem turns light yellow, later dark brown, and the infection spreads to the roots and up into the leaves. The white fungus growth can sometimes be seen on the stems. Later tiny, hard yellow bodies (sclerotia) are formed by the mycelium, which can live for a long time and serve to perpetuate the fungus (Fig. 21–3). The disease thrives with temperatures of about 85° and high humidity. Cut out the diseased portion and immerse the plant in Natriphene for an hour or more.

HEART ROT. *Phytophthora omnivora* causes a serious rot that starts in the heart of the plant where the leaves join the stem and spreads upward through the leaves. This fungus is related to the one that infects the potato, and which ruined the

potato crop in Ireland in 1845, causing the famine that killed some 250,000 people. The *Phytophthora omnivora* infection of orchids begins with the appearance of dark, sharply delimited lesions in the very heart of the plant. The infected area spreads rapidly, until within a few days the entire leaf is discolored and falls off. In severe cases the infection spreads from the heart to new leaves formed after the older ones have fallen. In milder instances, the infection may be confined to one of the older leaves, especially if the plant is kept dry. The disease spreads rapidly from plant to plant, injuring especially the highly susceptible *Vanda* and *Phalaenopsis,* but also infecting *Cattleya* and other genera. Young seedlings are very liable to infection. Moist, warm conditions favor its spread. Another species of fungus, *Phytophthora palmivora,* has been isolated from *Dendrobium* in Ceylon and *Vanda* and *Cattleya* in Java. Remove infected leaves or portions of leaves in hopes of saving the growing point of the plant. Treat with Truban/Benrot, or drench with Natriphene, or dip the plant (the section above the roots) in Tersan and sprinkle Tersan powder into the heart section. If the growing tip of a *Vanda* is killed, cut the stem well below the tip area and hope for a healthy side shoot. In *Dendrobium* or others, where the top or flowering section of the stem is killed, remove the stem to its healthy base. Repeat treatment with fungicide.

Figure 21–3 Sclerotium rolfsii *on the base of cymbidium leaves. Note the white fungus growth and the small, round sclerotia.* (COURTESY OF PETER A. ARK.)

ROOT ROT. Caused by the fungus *Rhizoctonia solani*, this is a brown rot that can rapidly kill small seedlings and bring about the death of older seedlings and mature plants. The brown mycelium infects the roots and progresses through the rhizome and the lower parts of pseudobulbs. Young seedlings are quickly girdled while older plants go into a slow decline as water and nutrient absorption is cut off. Their leaves and pseudobulbs become yellow, twisted, and shrivelled. Soak the plants in Natriphene 1:2000, or treat with Banrot, Benomyl, Tersan, Subdue, etc. Then repot in fresh medium.

FUSARIUM WILT. The organisms *Fusarium oxysporum* and *moniliforme* infect the plants through the roots or cut ends of the rhizome. A circle or band of purple discoloration appears in the outer layers of the rhizome, and a pink-purple color travels through the conducting tissue. The entire rhizome may turn purple, and this may extend into the pseudobulbs. Toxic substances produced by the fungus affect the plant, and plugging of the vessels causes failure of transportation of water. The edges of the leaves may turn grayish green and this may progress until the leaves die. To save a plant, all diseased tissue should be removed. This means cutting through the rhizome, sterilizing the knife each time, until perfectly clean tissue is reached. You may not have much plant left, but if it is a valuable one it will be worth the effort to save it. Spray the plant and those that surrounded it on the bench with Actidione, one tablespoon to one gallon of water. (This is also known as Germain's Mildew and Rust Control.) Use great caution as this is extremely toxic. Repeat three times every three days. It is possible that this disease is the one described for cymbidiums and illustrated in that chapter. Benomyl (Benlate 50WP) is also used.

CYMBIDIUM TIP BURN. *Botrytis* causes the tip of the leaves to become spotted; as the spots coalesce the whole tip dries. Powdery masses of spores may be seen on dead leaf parts (Fig. 21–4). Diseased tips should be cut off and the plant treated with Tersan or another fungicide.

ANTHRACNOSE OR LEAF SPOT. Many species of *Gleosporium* and *Colletotrichum* cause this disease in *Cattleya, Paphiopedilum, Epidendrum, Cymbidium, Vanda, Coelogyne, Laelia, Odontoglossum, Oncidium,* and *Phalaenopsis,* among others. The fungi are prevalent in most greenhouses and infection is favored by warm temperatures, excessive moisture, and insufficient light. Leaves develop circular or oval sunken spots that are reddish brown at first, becoming dark brown or gray with age. As the spots dry, black fruiting bodies of fungus form in the area; these can carry the disease to other plants. Infections are often quite mild and may be limited by reducing the humidity. However, the whole greenhouse cannot be kept dry in order to control anthracnose, so the plants are best treated. Copper compounds are especially effective swabbed on the spots, as are Tersan and other fungicides, especially Benlate. If the infection becomes more serious, and the spots enlarge and spread, entire leaves and occasionally a

Figure 21–4 *Cymbidium tip burn caused by botrytis fungus.* (COURTESY OF PETER A. ARK.)

whole plant may be killed. Cut off the badly affected leaves, and repeat treatments with a fungicide until the spread is ended.

One species, *Gleosporium affine*, spreads rather rapidly through leaves of *Oncidium, Odontoglossum* and *Dendrobium*. As the infection progresses toward the base of the leaf the outer portion dies, becoming thin, dry, and light brown. Fruiting bodies of the fungus develop in concentric rings which may be circular or diamond shaped. One's first thought on seeing these is that they may represent a virus infection, but close examination will reveal that the rings are formed by tiny black bodies (Fig. 21–5). If anthracnose is general throughout the greenhouse, spray with one of the long-acting fungicides described earlier.

LEAF SPOT. Several species of *Cercospora* cause leaf spot in a variety of orchids. These usually appear as yellow spots that become sunken and turn dark, or small brown spots that become darker and sunken, or as brown streaks. In all cases, the spots enlarge and the affected tissue dies, sometimes with the death of the whole leaf. Small seedlings may be killed. Remove affected leaves. Treat with Benlate.

LEAF BLIGHT. A water mold, *Pythium splendens,* causes leaf blight. The disease starts on a leaf, especially of *Cattleya,* as a round spot, often on the edge of the leaf. The spot is chestnut-brown. It enlarges rapidly and turns black. The area becomes thin. Cut out the diseased portion well below the infected area, and apply Tersan to the whole plant. Keep the plant parts dry and cut down on watering. Also try Subdue.

LEAF DIE-BACK. A fungus, *Glomerella cincta,* causes an infection that starts at the tip of the leaf and spreads toward the base, involving the whole width of the leaf. There is a marked line of distinction between the diseased and the healthy area. The infected area turns soft and brown; later it dries. Cut off the diseased area below the line of infection, and treat the cut edge and remaining part of the leaf with a fungicide such as Tersan or Benlate. Many kinds of orchids are affected.

FLOWER SPECK AND BLIGHT. *Botrytis cinerea, Sclerotinia fuckeliana,* and other fungi cause flower speck and blight. The disease appears at first as tiny water-soaked spots that become larger and turn pink, tan, or brown (Fig. 21–6). It is espe-

Figure 21–5 *Leaf spot caused by* Gleosporium, *on leaf of* Odontoglossum grande. (COURTESY OF PETER A. ARK.)

cially prevalent under damp cool conditions but can occur at other times. Infected flowers should be removed and destroyed at once as their presence allows for rapid spread of the disease. Old flowers can be a reservoir of infection. Reduce the humidity in the greenhouse and give good ventilation and air movement. If the nights are running too cool, raise the temperature a bit. Spray flowers and plants with Benlate or very dilute Physan, one teaspoon per gallon of water. Keep trash cleaned up as dead plant material can harbor disease-causing fungi.

Figure 21–6 *Flower speck caused by* Botrytis cinerea. (COURTESY OF PETER A. ARK.)

BLACK SHEATHS. Green sheaths are sometimes attacked by one or another of the fungi described, especially under humid conditions and when water is left standing in the pocket between leaf and sheath. If the sheaths are treated in time and are allowed to remain dry, the infection need not spread to the flower buds within. Cut off the sheath above the buds and spray the sheath and buds with Natriphene or Benlate.

RUSTS. Harry C. Burnett, in the AOS *Handbook on Orchid Pests and Diseases,* recommends destroying all plants infected with a rust disease.

SAPROPHYTIC FUNGI. These are not parasitic, that is, they do not attack living tissue. They live only on dead plant material, such as the dead sheathing leaves of stem, dead sheaths, or parts of leaves that have been killed by other organisms or have died naturally. They thrive under humid conditions where there is insufficient air movement. Oddly enough, a single plant may show saprophytic fungi on the tissues clothing the stems or rhizomes when others around it are free. Perhaps it is too crowded by surrounding plants to allow the air to move as freely as it should, or the plants may have been kept too wet for a period, allowing

the fungus to become established. Drying off the plant will stop the growth of the fungus, although the spots it caused will remain. While the saprophytic fungi are not a threat to the plant they indicate a condition that should be corrected. Perhaps spacing the plants farther apart is all that is necessary.

SNOW MOLD. A species of *Ptychogaster* produces a white powdery growth on the potting medium. This mold soon covers the roots and rhizome, causing suffocation and dehydration. It is quite impermeable to liquid and therefore prevents the roots from obtaining the water they need. Treat the pot with 10 percent Shield, one ounce to four gallons of water. If much mold is present, remove all potting medium and treat the plant, then repot it and water it with the Shield solution to prevent regrowth of the fungus. Other molds in the potting medium may be handled in the same way.

SOOTY MOLD. A sooty mold appears occasionally on plants, even on flowers. The organism does not attack the plant parts; it merely grows on the "honey" exuded by them or on the excrement of aphids or scale insects. It can be washed off with water and a cotton swab. It is fostered by high humidity. Spray with Physan.

BACTERIAL BROWN SPOT. This disease is caused by *Pseudomonas cattleyae,* which enters the plant through wounds or through the stomata. While it attacks *Cattleya* and other genera, it is particularly serious on *Phalaenopsis* and on community pot seedlings. It begins with a small water-soaked spot which is dirty green at first turning brown and sometimes black. The spot enlarges rapidly. On *Phalaenopsis* the spot is blisterlike and quickly spreads to the heart of the plant so that if it is not arrested it will kill the plant (Fig. 21–7). Seedlings are also killed quickly. The infected tissues are soft and watery, often breaking open and exuding masses of bacteria which can then quickly spread the infection. On cattleyas, older seedlings and mature plants, the disease does not travel so rapidly, except that a young lead can be quickly killed. Cut out all diseased areas as soon as the disease is detected. Soak community pots, young seedlings, and mature plants for several hours in Natriphene. As soon as the plant parts are dry, treat with Tersan, Difolatan, Truban, or Physan-20.

Figure 21–7 *Bacterial brown spot caused by* Pseudomonas cattleyae. *A, B, C: on phalaenopsis seedlings and full-grown plants; D and E: on* Cattleya trianaei. (COURTESY PETER A. ARK)

Figure 21–8 *Miltonia scorch. Also called bacterial tip burn and streak.* LEFT: *Infection originating in the pseudobulbs.* RIGHT: *Infection originating on the leaves.* (COURTESY OF PETER A. ARK.)

MILTONIA SCORCH. Also called bacterial tip burn and streak. This is found thus far only on *Miltonia* and the organism has not yet been identified. It is a cool-temperature disease and extremely infectious. It starts as water-soaked spots on the tip or margin of a leaf, often on newly developing leaves, and spreads to the pseudobulb. The pseudobulb becomes yellow to orange in color, and has areas that look eaten or burned away (Fig. 21–8). They become tough and leathery. The diseased parts should be cut away, and the plant should be immersed in Natriphene for several hours, or sprayed with Benlate.

BROWN ROT OF PAPHIOPEDILUM. This disease is caused by a bacillus, *Erwinia cypripedii,* which apparently enters through wounds. It starts as a small chestnut-brown spot on a leaf, usually spreading in both directions so that it soon reaches the crown of the plant. It spreads through successive leaves until a whole growth is affected. Sometimes the growth is killed before the outer ends of the leaves have turned brown. It spreads so rapidly that it can travel through a plant of many leads killing the whole plant. If it is caught soon enough, however, the plant may be saved by cutting off leaves below the infection or cutting out whole growths by severing the rhizome if they have been infected to the base. The plant is then soaked for several hours in Natriphene or 8 quinolinol sulfate, repeated two or three times at intervals of a few days, or the disease may start up again. After treatment try to keep the foliage dry, watering the pot carefully so as not to splash water on the

leaves. In a group of plants where this disease has occurred, it will help prevent further attacks if they are sprayed with Physan-20 or other fungicide every three months or so. Bayleton might be tried as a control.

BACTERIAL SOFT ROT. Incurable. This disease is called by a bacillus, *Erwinia carotovora.* Cattleyas are most seriously affected, although a large number of other kinds are also attacked. The disease is rare, but it is so destructive and infectious that it is suggested that plants be destroyed immediately rather than be treated. The disease starts with a water-soaked dark green spot on the upper end of a leaf. It feels watery and breaks open at a slight tough. The inner tissues of the leaf are destroyed rapidly and the leaf becomes flaccid and wrinkled. The epidermis is so soft that it often breaks open, exuding its watery content and thus contaminating the bench and in fact the whole area surrounding the plant. A foul smell often accompanies the disease. After destroying the plant, thoroughly disinfect the area by drenching bench, posts, and floor with mercuric chloride solution 1:1000, using caution and wearing rubber gloves. Treat neighboring plants with a fungicide (Fig. 21–9).

BACTERIAL LEAF ROT. The bacillus *Erwinia chrysanthemi* has recently been found to be the cause of leaf rot in a number of kinds of orchids in Hawaii. In *Grammatophyllum,* diseased areas are water-soaked and brownish. In *Dendrobium,* the leaves are water-soaked and yellow. In *Vanda* the disease begins with translucent areas on the leaves; the spots darken and finally become black and sunken. Prevention includes spraying with Na-triphene before and during wet weather, and control necessitates removal of the diseased areas and treatment with a fungicide.

VIRUS DISEASES

The study of virus diseases in orchids is a tremendous field; a great deal has been accomplished in the short time of work devoted to it. The study is complicated by many things. A certain virus may infect a number of different kinds of orchids, producing different symptoms in each. In order to separate the viruses and determine their action on just a few species, thousands upon thousands of purifications, inoculations into healthy plants, and reverse inoculations from these back to members of the original host species have had to be performed.

A virus can enter a plant through any kind of wound—a bruised root, a broken leaf, an insect puncture, injury by a snail—but most often the disease is spread by contaminated cutting tools or hands. Stakes and pots that have been used with diseased plants also carry the virus. The virus can remain infectious for a long time in a dry state and can thus be present on benches, etc. Stakes and pots can be disinfected by soaking in 10 percent Clorox or other bleach.

Figure 21–9 *Bacterial soft rot. Incurable. Caused by* Erwinia carotovora. *The affected leaf shows wrinkling due to collapse of internal tissues.* (COURTESY OF D. P. WIMBER AND B. A. FRIEDMAN.)

As described in Chapter 4, an effective and easy method is to keep them in a saturated solution of TSP, ready for use, and to dip them in it between each plant worked on. Keep the solution in a wide-mouthed jar. It takes only a few seconds in TSP to sterilize knives, shears, or stakes. To make the solution, put enough TSP in the jar so that when it is filled with water some undissolved material remains in the bottom. Rinse tools before replacing in TSP, and renew the solution when it becomes discolored. The same strength solution can be used to scrub benches that may be contaminated.

The role of pests in spreading virus should be explained. Most biting or puncturing organisms do not act as vectors; they merely inflict wounds. A vector is an insect that acts as an incubator for a virus by harboring it in its digestive tract or some other internal system, and then injecting it along with saliva into its "victim," much as a mosquito acts as a vector for the malaria organism. Cymbidium mosaic virus and odontoglossum ringspot virus are not transmitted by insect vectors, but cucumber mosaic virus and bean yellow mosaic virus are carried by the green peach aphid and perhaps also by nematodes.

Divisions of infected plants carry the virus with them. Plants known to be infected should be destroyed. This is a simple matter when the grower can recognize the symptoms, as in cattleyas with color break of the flowers, and when the plant does so poorly that the grower gets rid of it, probably without even knowing that it has had a virus infection. But when the symptoms are obscure or mild enough to pass unnoticed, it is not such an easy matter. One cannot always throw away plants on a mere suspicion. If you suspect a plant of having a virus infection and cannot be sure from descriptions or photographs, keep it separate from other plants and enlist the aid of some of the experienced growers you know or send specimens away for diagnosis.

Cymbidium Mosaic Virus and Odontoglossum Ringspot Virus

Two viruses are the cause of most infections in orchids today, and are far more widespread than we knew some years ago. They are cymbidium mosaic virus (CyMV) and odontoglossum ringspot virus (ORSV). The latter, first discovered in *Odontoglossum*, is now known to be identical to what we have been calling tomato mosaic virus—

Orchid-Type (TMV-O). A few other viruses, some rather rare, have been found in orchids here and there, and we hope they will not develop into real threats. Now that we know the dangers of virus infection and have learned to be careful to keep from spreading it, these virus newcomers may be stopped in their tracks.

There is no cure for a virus infection. Removal of a part with symptoms is of no use, for viruses move quickly from the point of infection throughout the plant. Even though a plant may show less spectacular symptoms as it becomes older, the virus is still there.

Symptoms in Flowers

COLOR BREAK. Severe forms of this infection are the easiest symptoms to detect. Caused by ORSV, the color is uneven, lighter and darker in an asymmetrical pattern, often with dark streaks bordering light areas. Occasionally the flowers are deformed. Mild forms of color break are caused by the same virus and can escape notice if one is not observant. This is especially true for pale flowers.

BLOSSOM BROWN NECROTIC STREAK. Caused by CyMV, the symptoms show up from a few days to a week or more after the flowers open, when brown streaks appear along the veins, sometimes showing up first along the midvein, although this is not always the case. The disease will not usually be mistaken for spotting by *Botrytis,* but if there is any question, watch the plant through its next flowering—if it shows up again you can know that it is the virus-caused disease. As the flowers age, the streaks become sunken and dead. The streaks and spots are more noticeable in white flowers than in colored ones at first, but become more evident in the latter as the blossoms deteriorate (Fig. 21–10). Symptoms may or may not show in the plant. In some cases yellow streaks along the leaf veins have accompanied the infection, but many plants are without symptoms.

Symptoms in Leaves

CYMBIDIUM MOSAIC VIRUS. It is this virus with which *Cymbidium Alexanderi* 'Westonbirt' is infected, and all of the divisions of that original plant carry the virus. The symptoms first appear as small elongated yellow (chlorotic) streaks on the younger leaves. As growth advances, the chlorotic streaks widen and elongate, and become more sharply defined, sometimes including in their width streaks of green tissue. Necrosis (death of tissues) does not usually occur on the young leaves, but older infected leaves frequently show black streaks and spots, often so severe as to cause the premature death of these leaves. This symptom gave rise to the original name of the disease "black streak." Sometimes the mottling that is present when the leaves are young becomes less conspicuous as the leaves grow old. Plants with mild infection are not greatly affected as to growth and production of flowers, but badly infected plants grow and flower poorly. Viruses extracted from *Laelia anceps, Angraecum eburneum, Epidendrum, Zygopetalum,* and *Oncidium* caused identical symptoms in *Cymbidium* and may be the cymbidium mosaic virus.

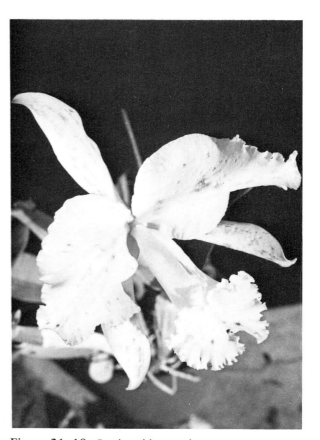

Figure 21–10 *Cattleya blossom brown necrotic streak. The lesions in general follow the veins of the flower parts, although when the disease has progressed to the point where spots have enlarged and coalesced this is sometimes difficult to ascertain.* (COURTESY OF HARRY C. BURNETT.)

323

PROBLEMS, DISEASES, AND PESTS

This virus causes leaf necrosis in *Catteleya* as well as necrotic streak of flowers. The initial infection may kill some of the leaves, and it produces various patterns of dead tissue in others. After the first shock to the plant, leaves formed subsequently may show only mild symptoms and be overlooked. Unless the disease is caught during the early stages, the plant may thus remain in the greenhouse as a reservoir of infection. Necrotic areas may appear as brown sunken pits on the underside of the leaves, as alternate black and chlorotic streaks, or occasionally as rings of dead tissue on the underside. Sometimes the leaves have lengthwise stripes of white or grey and are rough both in appearance and to the touch, and this symptom is easy to distinguish from fungus infections.

ODONTOGLOSSUM RINGSPOT VIRUS. This may also produce a variety of symptoms in leaves of various genera. Ringspots of dead tissue are often centered by a tiny red spot. This virus can also produce streaks of yellow or dead tissue (Figs. 21–11, 21–12, and 21–13).

CYMBIDIUM NECROTIC RINGSPOT VIRUS. Instead of causing merely yellowed areas, this produces dead areas—in a pattern of rings, spots, and streaks—on old as well as young leaves. It frequently kills new growths and sometimes the whole

Figure 21–12 *Odontoglossum ringspot virus.* Rossioglossum grande *with concentric rings of necrotic tissue enclosing normal or light green tissue.* (COURTESY OF D. D. JENSEN.)

plant. This is the virus that causes severe necrosis in *Cattelya* and a few others (Fig. 21–14).

Figure 21–11 *Severe flower break virus symptoms in* Cattleya *and* Cymbidium. *From* LEFT *to* RIGHT: *Flower showing severe color break and some malformation; young cattleya shoot showing rosy mottling; mature cat-*

tleya leaf with mosaic of dark-green raised areas; two cymbidium leaves with bar mottle caused by odontoglossum ringspot virus. (COURTESY OF D. D. JENSEN.)

Figure 21–13 *Cymbidium mosaic virus affecting* Cattleya *and* Cymbidium. *The three cattleya leaves at the* LEFT *show respectively light brown pits on the under surface; streaks of black and yellow tissue; and necrotic rings on the undersurface. The three cymbidium leaves at the* RIGHT *show various mosaic patterns of light and dark green tissue, with some black areas of dead tissue.* (COURTESY OF D. D. JENSEN.)

TESTING FOR VIRUS

The electron microscope is one of the most accurate tools for testing for virus. Special treatment of the plant tissue, and, of course, very expensive equipment and trained technicians are required. CyMV consists of fairly long, sinuous rods, while OSRV appears as short, straight rods.

Several kinds of tests employ serology. Rabbits are injected with a specific virus, to which they manufacture antibodies. Juice from an infected plant is added to a sample taken from the rabbit serum in specially prepared agar plates. If the juice contains the specific virus with which the rabbit was injected, the antibodies will react with it. One such test is called electrophoresis, another is agar double diffusion. Please see the American Orchid Society *Handbook on Orchid Pests and Diseases* for details of these and the plant assay test. For the plant assay test, be very gentle in dusting the leaf surface with the abrasive. It is best just to dust it on and shake it off or to mix it with the juice and simply spread that on the leaf.

Another system that uses antibodies (or antisera) is called enzyme-linked immunosorbent assay (ELISA), utilizing an array of very delicate equipment and requiring several stages of treatment. It is on a par with electron microscopy for accuracy.

A method using indicator plants can be employed by an amateur grower. It is fairly accurate and can weed out a good many infected plants. It is offered by commercial labs, and kits containing the necessary seeds, materials, and directions are sold. We refer the reader to the American Orchid Society *Handbook on Orchid Pests and Diseases* for best directions. The test depends on the localized reaction on surface cells of the leaves of certain nonorchidaceous plants. When abraded with carborundum and covered with sap from a plant under suspicion, the wounded cells respond to a virus present in the sap by developing brown spots. Lack of a reaction means no virus was present. It is necessary to make practice tests to learn to differentiate between lesions caused by too-strong abrasion and the true response to a virus.

OTHER VIRUSES

Until more is known about them, it is helpful to know that there are other viruses that can and do infect orchids. A bacilliform virus has been located in *Dendrobium phalaenopsis*. It causes white streaks and flecks in colored flowers. Cucumber mosaic virus has been found in *Dendrobium* species in Japan, causing color break in the flowers

Figure 21–14 *Necrotic ringspot virus of* Cymbidium, *the most severe disease of* Cymbidium, *which also causes severe leaf necrosis in* Cattleya. *The first two cymbidium leaves show necrotic rings and spots resulting from the original infection. The next two leaves, produced respectively several months and one year after infection, show necrotic and chlorotic mottling. At the right is a young cattleya leaf with severe necrosis caused by the cymbidium necrotic ringspot virus.* (COURTESY OF D. D. JENSEN.)

and faint chlorotic patches and rings in the leaves.

Bean yellow mosaic virus (BYMV), is now turning up, oddly enough, in *Masdevallia*, although it is surely infecting other kinds. Symptoms on *Masdevallia* include dark green spots, often in two parallel rows on the leaves, accompanied by twisting and size reduction of the new leaves. Plants deteriorate rather quickly.

Some of these viruses, notably BYMV and cucumber mosaic virus, are transmitted by aphids and/or other insects or nematodes. It would be well to watch for further reports.

REFERENCES

No one can explain the characteristics, symptoms of infection, and tests better than the experts, so, rather than devote many pages to these mat-

ters, let me refer you to the articles that will be most beneficial.

Ali, Shafqat, R. H. Lawson, and M. Ishii. A bacilliform virus in white-streaked *Dendrobium phalaenopsis* flowers. *American Orchid Society Bulletin,* Vol. 43, No. 6, 1970.

Allison, Arthur V. Virus diseases of orchids. *The Orchid Advocate,* Vol, IX, No. 5, Sept.–Oct., 1983.

————. Testing for the presence of virus. *The Orchid Advocate,* Vol. IX, No. 6, Nov.–Dec., 1983.

American Orchid Society. *Handbook on Orchid Pests and Diseases.* 1986 edition. West Palm Beach, Florida.

Bertsch, Walter. Virus research and accomplishments, Parts 1, 2, and 3. *American Orchid Society Bulletin,* Vol. 51, Nos. 10, 11, and 12, 1982.

Hadley, Geoffrey, Matsura Arditti, and Joseph Arditti. Orchid Diseases—a Compendium. *Orchid Biology. Reviews and Perspectives.* IV, 1987. Cornell University Press, Ithaca, New York.

Lawson, Roger. Virus-induced color-breaking in cattleya orchid flowers. *American Orchid Society Bulletin,* Vol. 39, No. 5, 1970.

————. and Ali, Shafqat. Orchid viruses and their detection by bioassay, serology, and electron microscopy. American Orchid Society *Handbook on Orchid Pests and Diseases.* 1975. West Palm Beach, Florida.

Van der Meer, F. W. Virus diseases in orchids. *South African Orchid Journal,* Vol. 15, No. 1, 1984.

Young, B. R. and W. L. Blundell. Orchid viruses in New Zealand. *New Zealand Orchid Society Review,* Vol. 23, No. 4, 1979.

Zettler, F. W., G. C. Wisler, T. J. Sheehan, N.-J. Ko, and A. E. Logan. Viruses—Some basics and a perspective for orchid growers. *American Orchid Society Bulletin,* Vol. 53, No. 5, 1984.

G. C. Wisler, M. S. Elliott and N.-J. Ko. Some new, potentially significant viruses of orchids and their probable means of transmission. *American Orchid Society Bulletin.* Vol. 56, No. 10, 1987.

PESTS

Many of the pests that attack orchids in their native habitats, and which used to come into this country with their hosts, are seldom seen in our greenhouses today. The U.S. Bureau of Entomology and Plant Quarantine bars them at our shores, and modern insecticides have pretty well eliminated those that had gained a foothold here. The pests that concern us now are those which live on garden plants and which invade our greenhouses.

A regular program for control of the various pests is easy to carry out and is better than waiting for populations to build up to high levels. It is difficult to get rid of a heavy infestation of any kind of pest, and a great deal of damage can be done by the pests in the meantime. A very small arsenal of weapons against pests will suffice. Malathion will take care of most insects and should be kept on hand. A metaldehyde preparation is a necessity for control of snails and slugs. A miticide, preferably one that kills both types of mites prevalent in orchids, should also be on hand. To control ants, cockroaches, etc., one might also have Diaznon. Where a regular program has not been practiced, and insects have built up to large populations, it is necessary to treat the greenhouse several times at short intervals, perhaps three times, ten days apart, with the specific chemical for the particular pests involved. Once the greenhouse has been cleaned up, a spraying every month or six weeks during warm weather and every two months during cold weather, should keep things under control. In the meantime, be alert for local infestations, and treat these as needed.

It is not yet possible to recommend a systemic insecticide without reservations.

SPIDER MITES. Called red spider or two-spotted mites, these are particularly troublesome on thin-leaved orchids, and seem to have a special affinity for *Cymbidium* and *Cycnoches*. They suck the plant juice and leave tiny white scars on the undersurface of the leaves, where they prefer to live. The result is a fine stippling or silvering of the leaf surface. They are also injurious to the flowers. Their favorite point of attack on flowers is along the seams where the sepals come together in the bud, where they leave small transparent spots surrounding the punctured areas. One such spot is a blemish, but many spots actually ruin the flower. Sometimes as the sepals split apart, the red spiders enter the bud and cause enough damage to distort the flower. Red spiders are very small, one-fiftieth of an inch long, and protect themselves and their eggs with a fine web. They thrive under warm, dry conditions, and their populations can be reduced somewhat by frequent syringing. They belong to the genus *Tetranychus*. The most common is *Tetranychus telarius*, of which one form is bright red and another yellowish or greenish. The best control is Pentac.

FALSE SPIDER MITES. These viciously destructive mites are so tiny they are impossible to detect without a twenty-power lens. They are different from the spider mites in that they do not spin webs, and they feed on both upper and lower surfaces of the leaves. They produce pits of dead tissue and often cause the death of leaves. The most common species are *Brevipalpus californicus,* the omnivorous mite; *Brevipalpus oncidii;* and *Tenuipalpus pacificus,* the phalaenopsis mite. All will do damage to a number of orchids. Pentac is the best control (Figs. 21–15 and 21–16).

FUNGUS MITES. There are many kinds, but two we have seen are a small, colorless mite, about the size of red spiders but covered with long hairs, and a round, dark brown mite which is hard and shiny with a little shield on each side over its legs. These may not do damage to plants, since they apparently feed on decaying organic matter or on fungi and algae. They are seen only occasionally, but appear in tremendous numbers when they occur. Like collembola, they are an eyesore, and if one is not forewarned about them they can be the cause of great concern. They may appear on an injured part of a plant, or on a new lead, to which they are attracted by the honey it exudes, or on algae covering roots or pots. They look like a sprinkling of fine sand. Malathion will get rid of them.

Figure 21–15 *Phalaenopsis mite,* Tenuipalpus pacificus, *one of the false spider mites.* (COURTESY OF DR. IRENE GLEASON.)

Figure 21–16 *False spider mite injury on oncidium leaf. The brown, irregular pits are typical. They first show as yellow flecks that can be mistaken for a virus disease, then enlarge, turn brown, and become necrotic.* (PHOTO BY TOM NORTHEN.)

THRIPS. These are small chewing insects with narrow, tapered bodies. They crawl about rapidly and hide at the slightest disturbance. They are about one-twenty-fifth of an inch long and can be yellow, gray, or black. Some species feed on leaves, on which they produce a fine silvery stippling. They can be particularly injurious to seedlings. Other species feed on flowers, and produce tiny, irregularly shaped scars scattered over the flower surface. Evidence of their presence, if the insects themselves are not seen, are the tiny black dots of their excrement. Species of *Anaphothrips, Taeniothrips,* and others are common on orchids. Malathion is effective against them.

SCALE INSECTS. There are two types of scales, the soft scaled and the armored ones. The young stages of both are free-moving, but as they mature

they select sites, stick their proboscises into the plant tissue, and remain there. The soft scales have a waxy or rubbery covering, while the armored scales secrete a hard shell. The soft scales excrete a sweet substance on which a sooty black mold grows. Eggs or living young are produced in large numbers by the females. As they emerge from under the bodies of the females, they crawl about for a few days. Colonies of scales may cluster under the sheathing leaf of a pseudobulb or rhizome, or at the juncture of leaf and stem, or on the undersides of leaves.

The most common species of soft scale are the soft brown scale, *Coccus hesperidum;* the orchid soft scale, *Coccus pseudohesperidum,* which is less often seen than the former; the hemispherical scale, *Saissetia hemisphaerica;* and the black scale, *Saissetia oleae.* They vary from one-quarter to one-third of an inch long, being in general larger than the armored scales. Repeated spraying with malathion will give eventual control. It will not kill all of the adults at first, but repetition will kill the crawling stages and eventually the adults.

Among the armored scales the most notorious is the Boisduval scale, *Diaspis boisduvalii.* The shells of the females are a grayish white, oval, somewhat like an oyster shell in appearance. They may occur so thickly as to form an encrustation on the plant. The males are found in cottony masses. They are about one-eighth of an inch long. Many other armored scales occur on orchids, and some of them inject a toxin into the plant in addition to injuring them by sucking the juice. Malathion will kill the young stages, but it will take several repetitions at weekly intervals to kill the adults and control successive hatches of young. Scrubbing badly infested plants with a malathion solution (using rubber gloves) is an effective way to handle scale on a few plants.

Unlike thrips, aphids, red spiders, etc.—which can enter the greenhouse from the garden—scale does not usually recur in greenhouses regularly treated with malathion. It can, however, be brought in on newly acquired plants, especially if these are from collections not properly cared for.

APHIDS. Soft-bodied, sucking insects of a number of species, some with wings and some without, can enter the greenhouse and are particularly attracted to flower buds and open flowers. The females produce living young which take about a week to reach adult size. They may enter the greenhouse by way of the ventilators, or they can be brought in by ants. Their punctures spoil the looks of the flowers. They are particularly troublesome on sprays of small flowers, such as those of *Oncidium* and *Epidendrum,* where their presence may not be noticed at first because of the denseness of the flowers and the minuteness of their parts. They are more easily seen on large flower buds and flower parts, such as those of *Cattleya* and *Cymbidium.* The work of ants can be suspected when isolated infestations are found. The pale green peach aphid *(Myzus persicae)* is commonly found in the greenhouse, and because of its color is not as readily detected as the black bean aphid *(Aphis fabae),* which is another kind commonly found. The latania aphid, *Cerataphis latania,* has been reported on orchids, but not as often. Malathion gives good general control. Soapy water is helpful.

MEALYBUGS. A number of species of mealybug generally infest greenhouse plants and are reported to be a particular pest on *Phalaenopsis.* They are flat, segmented, whiskery bugs that are coated with wax. Some produce live young and others lay eggs in cottony sacs. The wax they secrete makes their control somewhat difficult, but malathion used several times at three-week intervals will control them. Alcohol on a swab gets individual pests.

SLUGS AND SNAILS. Slugs are shell-less snails that slide along by means of a foot and lubricate their path with a trail of slime. Often the slime is the clue to their presence. They usually feed at night and hide in the daytime under the plant parts or the rim of the pot. Young slugs may be only a quarter of an inch long, while adults may reach several inches. The snails that are particularly bothersome are a small, flat-coiled, brown-shelled kind, that reaches about a quarter inch in diameter. Both snails and slugs are equipped with a radula, a series of rasps on a moving band, with which they rasp away plant tissue. They prefer succulent parts such as root tips, young leaves, and flower buds. One slug can literally mow down a pot of small seedlings in a night. Both slugs and snails lay eggs within the pot, usually near the bottom. Metaldehyde is the best control. It may be used in dust form, actually dusted on the plants and pots, and then watered into the pot, or it may be applied in liquid form. Repeated treatments are necessary to rid the greenhouse of slugs and snails. They are very stubborn pests and the grower must be equally stubborn. Mesurol, relatively new and highly toxic, is available in some baits.

ANTS. While they do not seem to damage plants, ants bring in aphids, mealybugs, and soft scale. The ants are attracted by the honey secreted by new leads and sheaths, and by the secretions of scales or mealybugs. They are killed by malathion. Ortho Household Insect Killer (resmethrin) gives quick control, sprayed on pots, plants, or ant trails.

COCKROACHES, SOWBUGS, MILLIPEDES. Sowbugs and millipedes are common in the soil and will invade the greenhouse. Cockroaches are prevalent in warm climates. All will feed on orchids. Diazinon granules sprinkled on the ground give good control. This may be absorbed through skin, therefore, do not handle without rubber gloves or inhale the dust. Do not get it on the plants.

COLLEMBOLA. These wingless insects are called springtails because they are equipped with a jumping apparatus on their tail. They are one-eighth inch long; may be gray, black, or banded; and live in soil all over the world. They do little damage to the plants, except possibly to root tips when they are present in great numbers, but pots swarming with collembola are an eyesore. A regular spray program that includes malathion will keep them under control.

BLACK FLY. Common in greenhouses, this little black fly thrives in over-wet soil or potting medium. Its tiny white grubs (larvae) dwell in the soil, and the adults flutter up from the soil surface when disturbed. Apparently they do no damage to orchids but, like collembola, they are a nuisance. Malathion will control them.

CATTLEYA FLY, DENDROBIUM WEEVIL, DENDROBIUM BEETLE. These are specific pests which used to plague orchid growers, and which still do where orchids are grown in the open in tropical areas. They are controlled by malathion and are now almost never seen in this country.

OTHER INSECTS. Various beetles, leaf hoppers, etc., occasionally enter the greenhouse, to say nothing of bees. Regular spraying will kill some of them, and hand capturing or swatting will get rid of the rest.

NEMATODES. There are many kinds of soil- and water-dwelling nematodes, called "eelworms," that are harmless to plants. Some are parasitic on plants, usually associated with certain hosts or groups of hosts. The parasitic kinds are almost microscopic, ranging from one sixty-fourth to one-quarter-inch long. Among the nematode species that infest plants are some that cause root knots, some that cause root lesions, some that invade leaf and stem tissue, and some that attack flower buds. As far as we know, only three kinds have been found on orchids: a species that feeds on and kills the flower buds of terete vandas in Hawaii; a root-lesion type recently found in cymbidiums of some California areas; and one that infests leaves of cymbidiums and other orchids in New Zealand. The vanda bud nematodes are controlled by picking off and burning all infested spikes. There is as

yet no safe control for root or leaf nematodes in orchids. The former live in the root tissue and feed upon it. Areas which they destroy are then subject to invasion by fungi and bacteria. Infested plants show rotted and discolored roots, the root system in general becoming much reduced. The leaf nematodes cause long black streaks. Soil intended for use in potting mixes can be sterilized to free it of nematodes, but chemicals that would kill the nematodes already in the plant pot are so toxic that they will also kill the plant. It is to be hoped that in the near future some safe control will be developed. It is also hoped that instances of nematode infestation remain as rare as they apparently are at present.

·22·

JUNGLE
ORCHIDS

ᕕ

HOW WONDERFUL IT WOULD be if the tropical forests were still in the glorious condition they were in even as recently as twenty years ago. But they have suffered dreadful destruction in the last two decades. Before we tell that sad story, let's see what life is like for the orchids in the intact areas. Fortunately, there still are some intact areas, large and small. The problem of saving them and the orchids in them is, however, of critical importance.

Most impressive are the cloud forests, which ex-

ist now mostly on the sides of steep valleys where timbering operations are too difficult to be economical. Viewing them from above, from an airplane or, better, from across an extensive valley, you will appreciate the name "cloud" forest. As warm air from below is moved upward, the moisture condenses into a steady succession of clouds flowing through the trees. The rounded heads of the tallest trees stand above a sea of shorter ones. This gives them another name—"storied" forests. At lower elevations there may be three or four distinct stories, or levels of tree height; at higher altitudes, only two. You can see the stories at close range when driving through a forest or approaching it from an area that has been thinned out. Step into it to see what it is like within. The ground is covered with a dense mass of ferns and other shade-tolerant plants. Aroids cling to the trunks and lower branches, vines disappear up into the foliage above, and rope-like roots hang down from epiphytes overhead. The huge buttressed bases of the largest trees are almost hidden in the vegetation, but if you were to try to walk among them, you would stumble and slip on their moss-covered surfaces. Everything glistens with moisture in the dim light. You will find but few, if any, orchids within these dense forests; most of them are up in the high tree tops, out of sight and out of reach. In clearings, where the light gets through to the ground, you will find orchids growing lower down (Fig. 22–1).

Then there are the scrub forests composed of small trees, often rich with orchids. Sunny banks and steep slopes bordering roads offer footholds for orchids. Oddly enough, these are mostly epiphytes whose roots travel through the litter on the ground without penetrating the soil. You may find the same species in nearby trees. In abandoned orchards or coffee fincas, orchids will have moved in from surrounding forests to inhabit the small trees.

Occasionally you come upon a treasure trove where some of the giants have been felled. As a great tree falls, many of the epiphytes are smashed from its branches, but some may still cling to them (Fig. 22–2). If you have a permit to collect (see below) you can reach plants that were two hundred feet in the air.

The people who dwell in remote areas in Latin America often live by what we call "slash and burn" farming. They clear a small patch, burn the trees, and plant a little garden. The thin soil soon becomes exhausted, and they have to move on. A tropical forest is one great recycling factory, with

A

B

Figure 22–1 A: *Clouds rise steadily from the valleys to bathe the forested mountains of Ecuador.* B: *The Sarapiqui Canyon in Costa Rica, a typical cloud forest. Note the two levels of trees in the foreground.*

c

Figure 22–2 *A fallen giant in an area cut over for farming. Orchid plants still cling to the branches and many could be found on the ground. Note the ropelike roots that extend to the ground from the epiphytes above.*

the nutrients mostly bound up in the trees and released when the leaves fall. Removing the tree cover removes the nutrients. This slash-and-burn farming has been slowly eating into the forests for hundreds of years, and might some day have been the cause of its destruction. Now timbering operations and developers have accelerated the devastation at an alarming rate.

The vegetation sometimes changes very quickly from place to place. A classic example can be seen as you travel from the mountains to the lowlands. Every few miles you can feel a perceptible change from the raw cold of the high country through a gradual warming until you reach the hot coastal region. The trees change on the way from short and weather-beaten to ever taller and increasingly magnificent specimens. Orchid plants are few at the highest elevations, become more frequent and varied at about 9,000 feet, are most numerous between 6,000 and 3,000 feet, and then taper off again toward sea level.

In the United States we are accustomed to seeing mountains more heavily forested on the north rather than the south-facing slope. Through much of Latin America the Atlantic side is more lush than the Pacific because of the moist Atlantic winds. Along a ridge you may find a damp, moss-festooned forest on the Atlantic side, and just a few feet away on the other side of the ridge, a dry forest. Quite different plants inhabit the two areas.

Land formations govern the air currents and drainage patterns, creating many kinds of microclimates. Swales and swamps, waterfalls and streams, rocky cliffs through which water seeps or which are dry and exposed to the sun—each has its own community of plants (Fig. 22–3). Fog patterns are controlled by the direction of air currents. In one place fog may fill a whole valley at precisely the same hour every day—at one-thirty it may still be sunny and clear; at two o'clock you will not be able to see the road ahead of you. In another spot the fog may come streaming through a gap on the Atlantic side to pour across the road and down the Pacific slope as if directed by a hose, wetting everything in its path and leaving areas on either side untouched.

A

B

C

Some regions have rather strict wet and dry seasons, some only seasons of more or less rain. In an area where little rain has fallen for months, you wonder how the epiphytes manage to survive until you realize that they are sustained by a humid atmosphere or heavy dew.

In the damp forests, trees are covered with mosses and colorful lichens—pink, yellow, and silver—which are interlaced with the roots of epiphytes (Fig. 22–4). In this soft padding the orchids extend their roots. After seeing this lovely medium and feeling the soft air, it seems miraculous that the plants can adapt to pots of strange media and the ups and downs of artificial conditions. In the dry forests the roots often cling to almost bare bark, offering a clue to their adaptability to pots and a greenhouse environment. An occasional little plant is found hanging by one root to the stem of a vine or the root of some other epiphyte. While it is clear that it must obtain nutrients washed from the branches above, you wonder how the seed that gave rise to it ever stayed in that spot long enough to germinate and grow! Tree trunks may be covered with young plants growing from seed drifted from those above. Oddly, one tree may have scores of plants of the same species, while neighboring trees have none of that kind but instead an assortment of others.

It might surprise and confound you to find that you can recognize very few. Perhaps at home you have a wide variety of species and feel quite competent. The chance of finding things you already have is rare, and even if they are present you may not know them. Plants have a way of changing their shape almost from tree to tree, and there will be genera you may never have seen. Plants that look alike may turn out to be different from each other; others that look different may prove to be the same species. You do not often find things in bloom, another fact that makes identification difficult in the forest.

For most of us, the benefit of orchid hunting is just to be in the places where they grow wild, to breathe the same air, to feel the soft atmosphere, watch the rains and fogs come and go, see how they grow and with what other plants, and per-

Figure 22–3 A: *Where roads have been built and the forest thinned, orchid seed filtering down from above can germinate on lower trees.*
B: *Orchids are often found on the rocky walls bordering streams.*
C: *Crossing an upper tributary of the Amazon in Peru by hand-cranked cable car.*

A

B

Figure 22–4 A: Lycaste macrophylla *growing on a rocky cliff in Peru.*
B: *Mosses and lichens cover the trees. Here a small* Masdevallia *is blooming on a tree trunk in Costa Rica.*

haps to photograph scenes and plants and people in the fascinating tropics.

PROCEDURE FOR IMPORTING ORCHIDS

Collecting and importing orchids are now practically forbidden by the Convention on International Trade in Endangered Species (CITES), a convention implemented in an effort to save wild species of plants and animals all over the world. This will be discussed below. The rules change almost from month to month however, so you must check in case there is any rare possibility of collecting, and you must find out what, if anything, you might be allowed to import. Just in case things become more lenient, you might as well obtain a standard import permit. It puts your name and address on record, and clues you into the files of the United States Department of Agriculture at the various ports of entry, as well as at their main office.

Write to U.S. Department of Agriculture, APHIS
Plant Protection and Quarantine Programs
Permit Unit
Federal Building
Hyattsville, Maryland 20782

State that you want a permit to import orchid plants. You will be issued a permit number that is good for three years, and which must be renewed every three years in order to be kept active. The permit number goes into their files and to files at each port of entry. You must obtain shipping labels from the same office, which must accompany each package of plants. The labels bear your permit number and are your tag of identification for the plants as well as your ticket for the services of the laboratory that will inspect and fumigate the plants. Labels are issued for specific ports of entry, so you must know before you order them to which one your shipment will come. The dealer from whom you buy the plants will tell you, if you ask him, to which port he will ship, and you can then ask the U.S.D.A. for labels for that port. You send the labels to him, and he will put one on the outside of each package. He must put your name and address inside the package, together with an invoice stating value, a phytosanitary certificate ob-

tained from the ministry of agriculture in his country, and the necessary CITES papers (see discussion on page 337).

The matter of how the plants will be shipped should be decided upon between you and the shipper. Those who make a regular business of shipping plants will know best how to send them. It has been our experience that air mail is most satisfactory. Not only is it speedy, but the Postal Service will collect the duty on the plants at your door, obviating the necessity of employing the services of a broker to handle this for you at the port of entry. The broker's fee often comes to more than the transportation costs, but a broker is necessary for both air cargo and air freight. We used to recommend air parcel post, only to learn that some countries don't use it.

If you wish to send home plants that you acquire from licensed dealers in your travels (if it is even then permitted), take the shipping labels with you on your trip. Have the dealer pack them with your name and address inside the box along with the necessary CITES papers and phytosanitary certificate, and an invoice showing the value of the plants. He will affix a shipping label to the outside. Have the postage paid all the way to your home. The box will go to the port of entry, be opened and inspected and the plants treated, and the original wrapping will be put back on for mailing to your home.

An invoice showing the value of the plants should accompany the package.

All kinds of plants arrive at the fumigation center, and the workers do not always know that orchids may be injured by too-extensive treatment. Put a note in the box, or ask the shipper to do so, requesting that they be treated gently to prevent injury. Sometimes they might dip them instead of treating them with gas, so you might request that gas not be used.

THE CONVENTION ON INTERNATIONAL TRADE IN ENDANGERED SPECIES (CITES)

The destruction of tropical forests is heartbreaking—currently estimated at 168,000 acres a day. As the trees are cut down, stripped, and sent to the mill, some 200 billion orchids and other plants are killed. The latter estimate was made by John Breckner, as quoted in the Ayensu-DePhilipps article referred to below. No amount of collecting can equal that. And yet it was on the supposition that collecting was the chief factor in the disappearance of species in the wild, ignoring the basic factor of habitat destruction for commercial purposes and expanding population needs, that the Convention on International Trade in Endangered Species, CITES, was set up. Its authors placed all orchids on their lists although one group is defined as "endangered" and the rest as "threatened." Special rules apply to each of these categories, as well as to plants grown in cultivation, plants grown from seed, and seeds alone. Representatives of scientific institutions who are authorized to collect orchids receive preferential treatment in the matter of permits, but they, as well as anyone else who desires to collect, must obtain the proper papers and must abide by the same rules. Permits are required from the U.S. Department of the Interior and also from the country in which orchids are to be collected. Collected plants must be inspected as to species before they can be shipped out, and they must be accompanied by a phytosanitary certificate. Export permits and the phytosanitary certificates are obtained by application to the ministry of interior or of agriculture, whatever authority is designated in the country from which you wish to import orchids. Plants arriving at our ports of entry without the proper papers will be confiscated.

For CITES applications and information as to current restrictions, etc., write to:

Federal Wildlife Permit Office
U.S. Fish and Wildlife Service
Box 3507, Arlington, Virginia 22203

In spite of its rules and regulations, its categories, its permits, and its good intentions, CITES is a very imperfect instrument for saving species. Supervising would-be collectors is difficult. Those who realize the importance of conservation do not take everything they see, rather, they take a few examples and leave some to propagate themselves. But there are greedy people whose destructive habits are legendary. And these are not always from outside the country; local people are often guilty.

Thus, among the faults of CITES are its uselessness in preventing people from over-collecting in their own country and its failure to protect habitats. The residents of tropical countries are accustomed to their own (once) rich flora, and they do not always appreciate the treasures they have. Education is necessary to show them how precious is all wildlife and how to protect it. Costa Rica is a leader in this, with intensive programs in schools, libraries, traveling displays, and young peoples' camps.

Habitats for orchids and other wildlife must be preserved. Tropical countries must be encouraged to develop forest preserves, even though it is too late to set aside more than a fraction of the great forests that once existed. As habitats diminish in size they become all the more precious. Costa Rica has some 22 reserves, both private and national, selected to represent different types of environments. When a species is lost it is gone forever. Any contribution its genes might have been able to make to science and medicine is forever irretrievable.

We must expand the seed banks now being organized. Mentioned earlier is the method of freezing seed and keeping it for many years (the cryogenic method). Over the years, some seeds can be withdrawn to replace examples lost along the way, or to make experimental hybrids, or for research of various kinds. Thus, we will be saving genetic material for future generations. It must be admitted that even seed banks are going to preserve mostly species considered important rather than the less beautiful or less desirable ones, which in the long run might have much to contribute to science. Ideally, we should all pollinate species in our collections, but unfortunately, attempts are not always successful. Many kinds are reluctant to set seed in cultivation. The late Goodale Moir remarked that he often had to try dozens of times to get a "take." Nevertheless, we should try.

Living plant collections are important. Various botanical gardens and universities are making an effort to maintain representative species, to propagate rare ones, and to collect rare, noteworthy hybrids, some of them very old, and with perhaps only one or two examples remaining in the world. Contributions of money and significant clones are sought.

Growers in tropical countries should be encouraged to cultivate their native species. Many are now doing so. In the matter of kinds in popular demand, it is better to export cultivated plants rather than to gather them fresh from the wilds, unless they are threatened with destruction.

The following two very fine articles set forth the

state of the problem at present and go much more into detail than we can here.

The International Regulation of Trade in Endangered Species of Wild Orchids, Edward S. Ayensu and Robert A. De Philipps, *American Orchid Society Bulletin,* Vol. 50, No. 5, August 1981.

CITES: Orchids as a Family Endangered by Legislation? Robert W. Read and Paul E. Desautels. *American Orchid Society Bulletin,* Vol. 52, No. 1, January 1983.

I hope that our generation will be intelligent enough to treasure the species. They are evidence of an evolutionary history, which, if allowed to disappear will never occur again. The following poem printed with permission of the author, speaks so well the tragedy of our lost forests, as does the photograph in Fig. 22–5.

Figure 22–5 *There was a flourishing tropical forest here. Now nothing remains. The soil will erode away, the land will soon be useless. So much has been lost that could have been preserved for future generations.* (PHOTO BY MICHAEL HILL)

THE SPOILERS

The picture's there
of a felled jungle on a hillside,
of a jungle ready for burning,
and I see desolation.

I see a quietus,
an aceldama where bulldozers
pushed live trees
to prone logs that shriek of destruction.
I see God looking down
through grey clouds,
causing sympathetic skies
to weep on shorn acres.

I see rare species lost
to impatient thoughtlessness.
And conscience, like a scared hare, races
over grounds of an overt act.

I see the dark curve of a crow
banked against the white clouds,
hawking his anger raucously
at such a waste of nature's bounty,

and I am sad.

CLARENCE S. LINDSTEN

CARE OF BARE ROOT PLANTS

For plants shipped out of pots (bare root), as soon as the box arrives, open it and remove the plants (Figs. 22–6 and 22–7). Examine them for any soft areas that show breakdown of plant tissues. It is always wise to dip the plants in a fungicide to prevent infection of any part that may have been damaged in handling or shipping. It is not likely that thick, hard leaves will show any injury, but the thin leaves of some kinds may be broken or bruised. Cut off any badly damaged parts and keep a watch over any that have slight damage. (If these later show evidence of infection, treat them again with fungicide.) Lay the plants on a shaded bench where they can have free air circulation.

Some plants will arrive with new growth started; others may be quite dormant (Fig. 22–8). Some may be plump, others shrivelled. For the most part, plants come through the shipping very well. Those that have growth started should be potted right away. The others can wait for a while. Syringe those lying on the bench once or twice a day to keep them from shrivelling, or to help plump them up.

We have found polyethylene bags of great help. They furnish a wonderfully damp atmosphere that encourages new roots to form and eyes to start growing. The jungle plants can be handled just like backbulbs. Put a little wet medium in the bag, set the plant upon it, close the bag and stand it upright on the bench so that the new growth will start in the proper direction. When new roots can be seen starting, remove the plant and pot it just as you would any other plant. Stake it carefully so that it will not wobble in the pot. Keep newly potted plants a bit shaded, and mist the foliage and just the surface of the potting medium once or twice a day until new roots are growing vigorously. Those which are potted right away are also kept shaded and are given mist sprays until growth is advancing nicely.

It is fun to have some hanging plants, and some lend themselves very well to growing on a slab. A piece of cork oak bark is ideal, with or without a pad of some fibrous material between the plant and the bark. A little pad of osmunda fiber or sphagnum moss may assist some plants to take root. The plant must be tied firmly to the slab, or the roots will move around and their tips be eroded. Nylon fishing line or narrow strips of nylon hose are good for tying the plant. The roots will soon wander around on the slab and attach themselves firmly. Usually only when the plant outgrows the slab is it necessary to move it to a new perch. Tree fern slabs, pieces of pressed bark panel, branches of almost any kind of tree, even pieces of styrofoam can also serve as mounts. They should be watered frequently, and they appreciate fertilizer every other watering. Kinds that have a rambling or pendent habit, such as some of the maxillarias, epidendrums, oncidiums, dichaeas, and so forth, lend themselves especially well to this treatment.

Baskets are decorative, especially those made of redwood slats. Better for such things as *Stanhopea*, and others whose flower stems bore down through the medium, are wire baskets, which allow more space between the barriers than do the slat type. The slat baskets are fine for plants whose flower spikes grow upward, although the wire ones can be used for these also. Osmunda fiber is a good medium for baskets. Lay a tough piece, cut to the right size, on the bottom, and then fill in around the plant with other pieces, packing it tightly enough to hold the plant firmly. If necessary, the plant can be held down by a hoop of wire until it forms a good root system. The basket can also be lined with sphagnum moss and filled with bark.

For plants which are to be grown in pots, the materials you use for your other orchids will be satisfactory. For terrestrials, a mix such as recommended for cymbidiums is good. If little plants, or those badly shrivelled, have a hard time getting started, put them pot and all into a polyethylene bag until they become well rooted.

Miniature gardens can be made in flats, with small plants of contrasting shapes and perhaps one or two a bit taller than the rest for accent. The pleurothallidinae lend themselves particularly well

Figure 22–6 *A whole flowering plant smaller than one cattleya flower. Here is a species of* Ornithocephalus, *whose little "bird-beak" flowers are individually the size of a single pollinium of the cattleya.*

Figure 22–7 *In the days when we were able to import wild orchids, the arrival of a shipment was most exciting.*

to this, as do small epidendrums, maxillarias, oncidiums, and many other little species. The greater ease of keeping a flat damp helps in growing miniature plants. Plastic trays are fine for the purpose. They can be purchased from many dealers, in different sizes. If they come without drainage holes, holes can be burned in with a soldering iron. Burn them from the outside. The plastic melts up around the iron, forming a dike that would impede the flow of water if it were on the inside. Lay a piece of hardware cloth over the holes, and on top of that a layer of gravel. Then fill the tray with your favorite potting mix (Fig. 22–9).

Figure 22–8 *New growth is fairly well along on some bare root plants when they arrive. The growth on this* Cycnoches *appears to be in good condition, but minute bruises on the tender leaves can become infected with fungi or bacteria if care is not taken. It is well to dip new plants in a fungicide solution on arrival.*

Such flats can be used to keep very tiny pots damp, if you prefer not to put the miniature plants in the flats directly. The little pots plunged in bark or gravel in the tray will not need to be watered so often. This method can be used to keep very small pots damp while you are away on vacation.

Decorative miniature trees may be made from pieces of driftwood or branches cut from trees in your yard. In damp climates you may not need to put pads of osmunda fiber on them, but in drier areas this is a necessity. Stuff the osmunda fiber in the crotches and holes or tie it along the limbs. Then wire the plants to the fiber. Sections of small logs with the bark intact are also attractive mounts (Fig. 22–10).

Various imaginative types of pottery can be used, such as strawberry pots or handcrafted containers. Shallow pottery "pans" sold for use with succulents or bonsais are pretty filled with miniature orchid plants (Fig. 22–11).

JUNGLE ORCHIDS

Figure 22–9 UPPER: *Left and right, "trees" made of driftwood support a large number of small orchids.*   LOWER: *Many small plants can be grown together in a flat.*

Figure 22–10 A: *Mounted on a small hardwood log, an* Aerangis *takes root.*
B: Pleurothallis grobyi *and a young resurrection fern grow on a moss-capped block of redwood.* (PHOTOS BY TED DULLYI; COURTESY OF H. PHILLIPS JESUP.)

A

Figure 22–11 *Imaginative hand-made ceramic containers offer decorative ways to display orchids. Here* Oncidium triquetrum *grows and blooms in a tier of pots with ample drainage holes.* (PHOTO BY TED DULLY; COURTESY OF H. PHILLIPS JESUP.)

·23·

HOUSING YOUR ORCHIDS

❧

T HE FIRST ADVICE TO PRO-
spective greenhouse owners is to build
a greenhouse large enough to hold an expanding
hobby. A small greenhouse will look tremendous
for a while, compared to the space ordinarily given
to house plants. But it is legendary that orchid
growers are never satisfied; they are always adding
to their collections. Perhaps you will be interested
in only one or two kinds of orchids at first, and
feel you would be satisfied with but a few plants
of each. Inevitably you will fall in love with an-

other kind, and then another. You will buy a few
seedlings of this and then a few of that. The seedlings will grow to maturity and the mature plants
will need dividing. Soon your benches will be over-
flowing, and you will join in the plaint common to
most amateurs, "Oh, for some more space!" We
suggest that you drive the old car for a few years
longer or take a less expensive vacation in order to
build a fairly generous greenhouse.

There are other reasons for not building too
small a greenhouse. A very small house is difficult
to manage, its small volume of air heats up quickly
and cools off quickly, creating a rapid fluctuation
of temperature. It is difficult to work in. Large
sprays of flowers become entangled with each
other. Plants become crowded, causing unhealthy
conditions and difficulties in handling.

At the very least (and this will not hold a large
number of plants) your greenhouse would be in the
neighborhood of eight by ten feet. This width
would allow two side benches and a center walk.
A twelve-foot width would give you two side
benches and a center bench. A greenhouse twelve
feet wide and fifteen or eighteen feet long is large
enough to give space for growing a truly satisfying
number of plants, and at the same time is not too
large for a busy person to care for in his spare
time. The cost of a greenhouse and its equipment
does not double when its size is doubled; instead,
the cost is about one and one-half or one and one-
third. In other words, you can get twice the space
for about a half or a third more in cost.

To obtain an idea of types and costs of greenhouses, send for catalogues from various greenhouse manufacturers. Visit some of the home
greenhouses in your town. Talk to the owners and
find out what faults lie in certain plans, and what
good features, so that you can avoid the former
and adopt the latter. Inquire about heater efficiency and notice whether certain installations
would be satisfactory for orchids. Examine
thoughtfully the relation between greenhouse
shapes and the amount of bench space allowed.

Perhaps the most economical, from the point of
view of space and efficient operation, are the types
that have been in use for many years. There are
some novelty styles that may appeal to some for
esthetic reasons, but before considering one of
these be sure that it will give you what you need
and want.

A greenhouse may be a free-standing unit, or it
may be attached to an existing building. In the latter case, it may be attached at one end, with its

length running out from the building, or it may be a lean-to, attached along one side, with the wall of the building substituting for one side wall of the greenhouse (Fig. 23–1). Less desirable for orchids, but still usable, is a breezeway, a glassed-in passageway between two buildings—the house and garage, for instance. A breezeway does not offer good light, but if the kinds of orchids are chosen for the location, they should do well and give much pleasure.

In locating a greenhouse, the aim is to give it a spot where it will receive as much light as possible throughout the day. If you are planning a greenhouse along with a new home you can assure it a good spot, but it is sometimes a challenge to find an ideal spot in an already established yard. A free-

Figure 23–1 *Two types of attached greenhouse.* UP-PER: *Attached at one end. In another situation this greenhouse could be extended to a greater length.* (COURTESY OF ALUMINUM GREENHOUSES, INC.) LOWER: *A lean-to. Note louvered section at end for ventilation in addition to roof ventilator.* (COURTESY OF LORD AND BURNHAM.)

standing type can be placed in any open spot, out of the shadow of the house or nearby buildings, and away from trees. If trees are present, pick a place that receives their shade for the fewest number of hours a day, and then plan to utilize the shade in place of artificial shade on the glass. A clear exposure from the south is important in the winter, because the sun swings to the south at that season. If the greenhouse is to be in a yard facing north, be sure that it stands where the house will not cast a shadow on it in the winter or where it will get morning sun if possible. It is generally thought that a greenhouse should run from north to south to allow the sun to travel across it from east to west. Home owners are not always able to achieve this, and should be comforted to know that a greenhouse that runs east and west or north-east and south-west will function very well (Fig. 23–2).

A lean-to should be located so that one side or one end receives light from the east and one side light from the south. A lean-to on the west side is difficult to manage in the summer, although an evaporative or refrigerative cooler may take care of the excessive heat that results from this location.

A place to do the potting and to store materials is a great convenience. The ideal situation (not achieved by all of us, by any means) is to have a potting shed attached to the north end of the greenhouse. If you have hot water heat for the greenhouse, the shed can also house the boiler. If the greenhouse is attached to the garage, or handy to it, perhaps part of the garage may be used for potting. Otherwise, a potting bench may be incorporated in the greenhouse, at the north end so as not to take the best growing space.

MATERIALS AND EQUIPMENT

Aluminum is at present the preferred material for the framework of the greenhouse. It does not rust and need not be painted. The sash bars are narrow and admit more light than does wood, which is still widely used for home greenhouses and is somewhat less expensive than aluminum. The upkeep of wood is more troublesome, both in labor and cost of paint. Cypress and redwood are chosen for greenhouse construction because they resist decay. Ordinary house paint tends to peel off the wood in a short time, actually seeming to be pushed off by moisture moving through the wood from within. Paint stays on the inside far longer

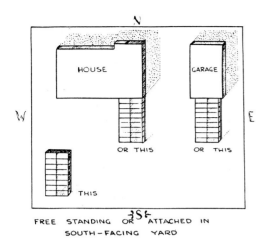

FREE STANDING OR ATTACHED IN
SOUTH-FACING YARD

FREE STANDING IN NORTH-FACING YARD

LOCATIONS FOR A LEAN-TO

Figure 23–2 *Suggestions for locating a greenhouse as to exposure and relationship to home.*

than on the outside. We hope that a paint will be developed to fill this need. In the meantime, it has been reported that two coats of aluminum paint on the inside provides a moisture barrier against exterior peeling.

In many home greenhouse styles, the manufacturers use large panes of double-thick glass instead of the older system of many small panes in each section. Construction is made easier by this means. The glass is held in place by patented clips or bar caps, and the owner can easily replace a broken pane.

Fiberglass is becoming popular to replace glass. Many growers like its diffuse light transmission. It is hail-proof and gives protection against falling tree limbs. Use only white or clear, or a yellow color, not blue or green. Some growers have installed fiberglass panels above glass for hail protection. Older types have had to be scraped and refinished rather frequently, but kinds that have a longer life are now available.

A masonry foundation is preferable to a wooden one, which will eventually rot out. The foundation walls should be set on a footing that goes below frost level, and may be of brick, stone, cinder block, or any similar materials.

Assembling a prefabricated greenhouse is simple. They come complete with all parts and hardware. The home owner and his family can put one up by following directions. Before building the foundation, however, obtain specific details from the greenhouse company for its dimensions and any fittings necessary to hold the sill of the greenhouse. There are definite advantages in buying a complete product designed by greenhouse experts (Fig. 23–3). If you do not want a package unit as offered, you can often buy what parts you wish from the manufacturer to fit a plan of your own. Many growers have built their own greenhouses, from new or used materials with great success, and have saved a good bit on the cost. A word of caution to the do-it-yourselfers—study standard greenhouse plans and construction first so that you can come as close to a professional model as possible.

Walks should be at least two feet wide, for plants have a way of hanging out into the aisle. We feel it is best to leave the ground under the benches bare. The damp earth helps keep the humidity up and serves as a method of draining off excess water. If you prefer a solid concrete floor, there should be a floor drain and adequate slope to it. Otherwise, you will be wading in water much of the time. Brick paving makes a decorative and useful

Figure 23–3 *A free-standing greenhouse with attached workroom. Note roller blinds for shading.* (Courtesy of Lord and Burnham.)

floor or walk. Brick or concrete can be kept clean with Physan-20 or Clorox.

Prefabricated benches are available. If you wish to build your own, you may make the frames either of wood (painted or treated with a preservative such as Cuprinol or Kopex, *never creosote)* or of pipe or concrete forms. Wooden bench legs should be set on bricks or concrete blocks to keep them from the wet floor. The bottom of the bench should allow free drainage, and free air movement up and through the pots. Such materials as hardware cloth (galvanized wire mesh), steel mesh, or perforated Transite are preferred, but wooden slats may also be used. Do not make the benches so high or so wide that you knock over plants in the front row in order to reach those in the back. Stepped benches can be used to give a little more room, provided that they do not cut off the light from plants on either side. A stepped bench is particularly useful on the wall side of a lean-to.

It is well to have both hot and cold water in the greenhouse. A mixing faucet, enables you to warm the water somewhat for use in the winter. An extra electrical outlet may come in handy for plugging in an emergency heater or some other piece of equipment.

THE HEATING SYSTEM. This is probably the item of greatest concern. In a very mild climate or where electricity is cheap, electrical heat may be feasible. An electric heater may be used to boost the temperature when a freak spell of cold weather hits your area. Otherwise, either warm air or hot water heat would be your choice. Hot water is perhaps ideal, but it is also the more expensive of the two. Before installing either, obtain information from a heating engineer as to the capacity of the heater or boiler, amount of pipe, etc., necessary for the size of your greenhouse and the temperature you wish to maintain (Fig. 23–4). If you obtain this information from an expert not in your locality, be sure to give him data on the weather in your region, especially how cold it can get and for how long.

The smaller the greenhouse, the larger the proportionate cost of a heating system for it. This is because certain items in the heating system cost the same whether they are for a large or small unit. Also, a heater or a boiler increases in price relatively little for each increase in capacity. However, the basic cost is still higher than we could wish, and it would be desirable to have some ingenious thought applied to the problem.

A hot water system keeps a relatively even temperature. The pipes continue to radiate some heat after the controls shut off the flow. Finned tubing is more efficient than plain pipe, and although it costs more per foot only about one fourth as much is required (Fig. 23–5).

Warm air heaters fired by gas or oil are used by

Figure 23–4 *A greenhouse partitioned to permit two temperature settings, in this case cool and intermediate.* (COURTESY OF ALUMINUM GREENHOUSES, INC.)

many orchid growers. Both types must be vented and be equipped with a thermostat and, for best performance, a blower. Gas heaters must have a safety shut-off valve. If gas is used, it must be 100 percent natural gas or bottled gas. Artificial gas must never be burned in a greenhouse, nor must gas that has any artificial gas mixed with it. There has been a definite improvement in the types of warm air heaters offered for small greenhouses. Some models are made especially for greenhouses, and some are intended to be used in the home as room heaters or space heaters but are equally satisfactory for greenhouses. Some require a flue or chimney to carry off the fumes from combustion. Others are self-venting, designed to be set in the wall, with a sealed-off firing chamber that operates outside the greenhouse. It is possible to use hot air from the home if a duct system can be installed conveniently.

Figure 23–5 *Zone-controlled, automatic, forced-hot-water heat, using finned tubing for circulation of water. The boiler can be fired by gas or oil. The flow to each of the two sections is controlled separately.* (COURTESY OF ALUMINUM GREENHOUSES, INC.)

An aid in heat conservation found useful by many growers is the installation of plastic sheeting inside the glass. This also keeps leaves from touching the freezing glass. Double glazing also conserves heat; the air space between the panes is a buffer between indoor and outdoor temperatures. One manufacturer uses bonded, double-wall fiberglass, while another encloses a rigid frame in a double balloon of plastic sheeting whose layers are kept apart by a small blower. Some years ago it was common to apply bubble-pack to the glass for insulation. Sometimes it stays on well, sometimes not, so it may or may not please you.

Emergency heating is a precaution where temperatures are likely to drop sharply below average readings. Electric heaters may be kept on hand in case of gas failure and portable butane salamander-type burners in case of power failure.

COOLING SYSTEMS. These may be evaporative or refrigerative; the former is most common. Both types come as self-contained units, in a number of sizes. It would be best to obtain the advice of a local expert in air conditioning as to the size required for your greenhouse. It takes a larger unit to cool a greenhouse than it takes for a room of the same size. For most efficient cooling, an evaporative unit should take in air from outdoors. It is therefore best set in an opening in the wall, with the cabinet projecting outside and the opening from the blower flush with the wall. A ventilator at the opposite end should be opened a few inches to allow the air to move through the greenhouse. A cooling thermostat should be installed to operate the unit. This type, which blows cooled air into the greenhouse, is called a "positive-pressure" system.

A pad and fan arrangement works on the same principal as an evaporative cooling unit, with the fan thermostatically controlled. An aspen pad is set in one wall. Above it is a perforated trough and below it a trough or pan. Water is conducted to the lower container by a small tube and its level is controlled by a float valve. A pump installed in the lower container moves the water through a tube to the upper trough, from which it trickles down through the pad, to be collected in the lower trough. A fan, placed either directly in front of the pad or in an opening at the opposite end of the greenhouse, pulls outside air through the moist pad. When the fan is directly in front of the pad, a ventilator should be open at the opposite end.

This is another example of the "positive-pressure" type. When the fan is in an opening at the opposite end, it pulls the air through the greenhouse and exhausts it, so that no ventilator need be open. This is called a "negative-pressure" type.

SHADING. Shading the greenhouse can be achieved in several ways. There are certain advantages to each system; this is to be expected when you are trying to adjust the light through various seasons. On glass, a white shading compound, sprayed or painted (with a paint roller on a long handle) is most widely used. Shading compounds may be obtained from greenhouse suppliers and are used according to directions. The advantages of a white shading compound are its low cost and the fact that it can be applied thin or thick according to the season.

Slat shading is made in sections that can be screwed to the sash bars or fastened on by brackets. It can be of wood or aluminum strips on frames of convenient size. The distance between the slats determines the percentage of outdoor light transmitted. During early spring and late fall a thin coat of white paint might be used, and the slat shading put up only for the warmer months. Diamond Mesh or Hi-Rib Lath can also be used. Louvered aluminum shading has very small louvers that break up the light, but this may give more shade than is needed except in particularly bright exposures. Roller blinds of wood or aluminum strips are often preferred and can be rolled up on dull days.

Various kinds of screening are available for shading. Plastic or fiberglass shade cloth comes in graded densities so you can choose the amount of shade you need. Another screen material, not promoted as yet for greenhouse shading, is a kind I have found good for adding shade where the fiberglass roofing is not sufficient—the fiberglass screening used for window and door screens. Its threads do not separate as do those on some other kinds so that it is always tight and neat. It gives about 20- to 25-percent shade.

VENTILATION. Using an automatic device is a great help to growers who must be away from home all day. Small motors, in series, are attached to the vent handles and are controlled by a thermostat. An ingenious self-powered vent control is made by Heat Motors, Inc. based on a patent developed by Lockheed Missiles and Space Company. It is a small, heat-sensitive motor housed in a cylinder. As the motor responds to changes in temperature, it pushes a shaft attached to the vent, opening and closing it with temperature changes from 50° to 90°. No electrical connection or thermostat is needed.

A new method of ventilation for cool weather uses perforated polyethylene tubing in association with an exhaust fan. The tubing is installed under the ridge, the length of the greenhouse. One end is fastened to a circular frame attached to a set of louvers. The other end is closed. The exhaust fan (this may be one used in connection with pad-and-fan cooling, or it may be installed for the purpose at any convenient spot) is set to turn on at a certain temperature. The louvers may be operated off the same thermostat or may be the free-swinging type that open and close with a slight change of air pressure. When the exhaust fan goes on, it creates a partial vacuum that pulls air in through the louvers and thence through the tubing. This air flows out through the perforations in gentle streams, mixing with the heated air in the upper level of the greenhouse, thus providing fresh, tempered air for the plants. If you prefer, a fan can be installed just inside the louvers to blow air through the tubing, in which case an exhaust fan is not necessary. Other uses for the tubing can be found. It could be used to conduct air from the heater, for instance, running under the center benches in this case (Fig. 23–6).

HUMIDIFIERS range from the simple spray nozzle placed in front of a fan (perhaps in front of the heater so that its blower distributes the moist air), to various kinds of mist-making apparatus. The latter are self-contained units which create a fine mist and blow it into the air. If the blower is strong enough, it will also help to circulate the air in the greenhouse. Sprayers that give a fine mist may be installed underneath the benches and be operated by a humidstat.

TEMPERATURE ALARMS are some of the most important pieces of equipment for any greenhouse. A standard high-low temperature alarm is wired to ring a bell in the house when the greenhouse temperature reaches a dangerous level. It has a temperature dial and a hand that moves with the temperature. On each side is a set-hand that you set for the minimum and maximum desired temperatures. When the moving hand comes in con-

tact with a set-hand it makes an electrical contact that rings the warning bell. The mechanism should be wired to batteries so as not to be affected by a power failure. The bell can be placed anywhere in the house where you can hear it easily.

SOLAR HEATING. This is a subject that is receiving a great deal of attention. Where some means of gaining additional heat from the sun is practical and economical it certainly is worthwhile. There are probably as many plans for solar heating as there are ingenious growers. Some installations are so fancy, or so poorly planned, or so expensive, that it would take years to make up for their cost in heat saved. Therefore, careful plans should be made. Because many manufacturers now sell solar greenhouses of one sort or another, and because ideas and methods are changing rapidly, we suggest that you send for catalogs, visit as many installations as you can, and above all send for the wealth of material offered by the government.

Making use of stored energy from the sun depends basically on having some material to absorb and store heat. Generally, people speak of a passive "heat mass" such as brick or stone walls, bins of rocks, stacks of black, water-filled jars or cans, or pads of some heat-retaining material. These simply sit there and get warm during the day and radiate the heat at night. In an active system the heat is drawn into the greenhouse by fans. Usually, the setup consists of a fan that blows through a duct leading from the heat mass (the bin of rocks, for example) into the greenhouse. In hot weather, the fan can be reversed to exhaust hot air. A solar greenhouse can help heat the home by means of ducts.

In New Mexico, the winter sun is bright but the nights are cold, and summers are bright, hot, and dry. Ingenious growers there have invented a system that is practical and esthetic, and suits their climate. They make intelligent and imaginative use of water as the heat-absorbing material. In several greenhouses, benches surround a large pool across whose surface fans blow, in winter distributing the warmth and humidity, and in summer adding needed humidity along with the cooling quality of evaporating water. One greenhouse has a solid rock wall at one side. Water flows over the wall and fans blow across it to distribute the humidity throughout the greenhouse.

Taking a cue from the old-type pit houses of

Figure 23–6 *Perforated plastic tubing for ventilation.* A: *Installation of tubing with motorized fan to pull in fresh air and force it through the tubing.* B: *Installation without fan. In this case an exhaust fan operating anywhere in the greenhouse causes a vacuum that pulls air in through louvers and through the tubing.* C: *Tubing in use in a greenhouse.* (A AND B COURTESY OF ACME ENGINEERING AND MANUFACTURING CORP.)

England and Europe, some growers in cold climates are building greenhouses partially into the earth—placing the lower sections or the whole north end below ground level. The special problem of drainage has to be met, of course, but they seem to work well.

A final suggestion is to use sun-heated water. The hot water can be piped through the greenhouse in the same type of finned tubing used with boiler installations.

ORCHIDS IN YOUR WINDOWS

For all of the pleasure and ease associated with a greenhouse, there is nothing quite like having orchids in your home. Those who would experience the thrill of growing orchids, but for whom a greenhouse is out of the question, should certainly try a few, on a windowsill or in a case made especially for them (Fig. 23–7). Growing orchids in the home is a somewhat different art from growing them in a greenhouse.* However, if you have a bright window, preferably east or south, with good light all day and direct light for part of each day, you can find kinds that will do well for you. In choosing a window for orchids, avoid one that becomes too hot as some west-facing bay windows or picture windows unfortunately do.

Where the night temperature cools off to 55° to 60° you can grow many of the intermediate kinds. Where the night temperature does not fall below 65° you had better try some of the warmth-loving kinds. The cool orchids are more difficult to grow in the home because, ordinarily, home temperatures do not go as low as the needed 50°, but if you have a glassed-in porch you might try some of these. Cattleyas, and some others which are quite light-demanding, have a fairly wide light range, and in the home during the brightest hours of the day they may receive enough light (perhaps in the neighborhood of 2,000 to 3,000 foot-candles when the sun is shining in the window) to enable them

Figure 23–7 *An orchid case in the living room.*

* For more information on window growing and growing with artificial light, see Northen, *Orchids as House Plants*. Revised 1976. Dover Publications, New York.

to grow and flower fairly well. They will probably not become the heavy, floriferous plants that they would be in a greenhouse, but will do well enough to give you great pleasure.

Some kinds will do better without the protection of a case—among them cattleyas, epidendrums, lycastes, some of the small oncidiums, and others—because they receive better light when directly in the window. If the leaves become too hot when the sun shines on them, pull a glass curtain or a piece of cheesecloth across the window and give them a mist spray over the foliage. The object is to give them all the light they can take because they do not have as many hours of it in the home as they would in a greenhouse. Water them when they need it, and give fertilizer a bit less frequently than you would for greenhouse plants. Do not let heat from a register blow on the plants. During warm summer nights the window can be left open to bring them the cooler, damper air. Watch for insects and control them as described earlier. Pests from other houseplants can attack orchids, and it is well to keep these free from insects also.

Among the kinds that need the extra humidity of a case are phalaenopsis, paphiopedilums, and miltoniopsis. In addition, these require less light than the cattleya group and hence do not suffer from having the light cut down by the extra pane of glass between them and the window. The case should be tall enough to have a good volume of air, and should be equipped with a top and bottom ventilator and a door that opens wide for ease in working with the plants. In the bottom there should be a pan to hold water and to catch the drip from watering. Above the pan is set a grille on which the pots stand. Depending on the temperature of the spot where the case is to be put, choose from the following types: Phalaenopsis and the mottle-leaved paphiopedilums if the temperature ranges between 60° and 65° or stays close to 65°; cooler-growing kinds if it ranges between 55° and 60°. An easy way to provide extra humidity is to place a small room humidifier inside the case or outside with the vent directed into it. This can be run manually or by a time switch.

Management of an orchid case follows pretty much the rules for managing a greenhouse. The sun shining in the window can heat up the case just as it does a greenhouse, and it may be necessary to draw a thickness of cheesecloth across the window during the hottest hours. At this time open the top and bottom ventilators and give the plants a mist spray. The case should be ventilated each day, even when the sun is not shining, and the plants may be given a mist spray once a day, allowing them to dry off by night. The air in the case should be kept fresh and buoyant, not stuffy or overdamp. Some of the troubles people have experienced with orchids in cases come from keeping the humidity too high; this causes black sheaths, spotted flowers, and rapid fading of flowers. Plants will dry out faster in the winter, with furnace heat, than in the summer, and this is true of those on the windowsill and in cases as well. Watering therefore has to be more frequent in the winter, though care against overwatering must always be exercised.

Flasks of seedlings or community pots will thrive in orchid cases. The young plants may be grown in their own case, with a shade across the window to subdue the light, or they may share a case with larger plants, being placed behind them so as to be shaded. When the seedlings grow larger and need more light, adjustments will have to be made for them.

GROWING WITH ARTIFICIAL LIGHT

The number of amateurs growing orchids indoors under artificial light is increasing every year. With their usual ingenuity they make use of almost any area in the home that can be adapted. A preferred place is the basement, which, with its concrete walls and floor, is not subject to damage. Since every home is different, and every amateur faces different problems, no two setups are identical. Chief considerations are temperature, air circulation, humidity, and watering, the kind of light to use, and the kinds of plants to grow. Some people keep their plants indoors all year, while others move them outdoors in the summer to benefit from a few months of sunlight.

Benches may be constructed of wood or other materials. Metal trays or benches lined with plastic and filled with gravel catch water and help keep up the humidity. Racks covered with steel mesh or wood slats should be placed over the gravel so that the pots do not stand in water. The surrounding walls and ceiling should be painted white to reflect light.

The lights must be close to the plants because intensity drops off rapidly as the distance from the plants increases. Fluorescent tubes will not ordi-

narily burn the leaves. The closer they are placed the better will be the growth and flowering—within six inches is ideal. They should be in white reflectors, hung by chains so that their height can be adjusted for differing needs, for instance, raised when bloom spikes develop or lowered if large plants are replaced by smaller ones. The ballasts for the fluorescent tubes become hot. If they can be relegated to a remote area, perhaps another room, it would be wise to do so.

To date, no one type of electric light has been developed which is capable of duplicating the spectrum of sunlight. Visible light ranges from violet through blue, blue-green, yellow, orange, and red. In photosynthesis plants make more use of the blue and red rays than of green or yellow, although the latter do play their roles. The red end of the spectrum is especially important for mature plants and for flowering. Incandescent bulbs, once widely used in combination with fluorescent tubes, are no longer necessary in view of the improvements to the latter. There are many types of tube on the market, and new ones appear frequently. For the latest information inquire of the major manufacturers, such as Sylvania, Westinghouse, and General Electric. All have departments to aid greenhouse and home growers.

To give just one example, many growers still like the combination of Wide Spectrum Gro-Lux with cool white tubes. At least four tubes side-by-side should be used to a bench twenty-four to thirty inches wide. These tubes can be two each of the Wide Spectrum and cool white. If a wider bench is used, additional tubes must be installed. The tubes should be continuous for the length of the benches; plants placed beyond the ends of the tubes will not get enough light. Four four-foot (40-watt tubes are sufficient for a bench four feet long. Four eight-foot, or two sets of four-foot ones, should be used for a bench eight feet long (Fig. 23–8).

For plants that need highest light intensity, or where the lamps must be farther above the growing area, higher-wattage lamps such as the High-Output (HO) or Very-High-Output (VHO) are available. There is also a High-Intensity-Discharge (HID), also called Maxi-Gro, a metal-arc, phosphor-coated lamp, for this purpose.

Why plants do well with the lower light intensity of artificial lights can perhaps be explained. In the first place, the light is constant—it is the same intensity from the moment it is turned on until it is turned off, no dawn, no dusk, no cloudy hours or

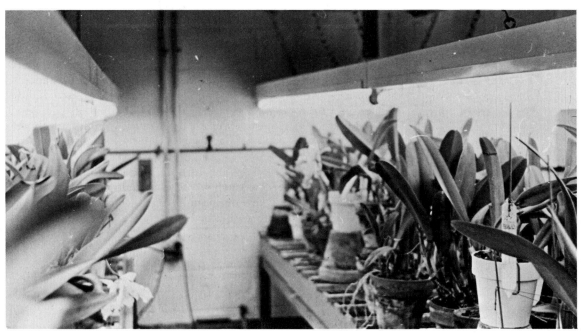

Figure 23–8 *A basement setup for orchids under lights. The plants stand on racks over galvanized trays that hold water. Each eight-by-two-foot light fixture holds six 40-* *watt cool white fluorescent tubes with sufficient incandescent bulbs spaced between them.* (COURTESY OF NORMAN MOORE.)

days. In the second place, except when plants that are sensitive to daylength are concerned, the lights can be kept on for sixteen hours a day all through the year.

Temperatures should be managed to suit the needs of the plants, as described in previous chapters. If it is necessary to have a heater, be sure that it is equipped with a fan to distribute the heat evenly and that it does not blow directly on the plants. It is best if the heat is directed against a wall or under the benches so that it is diffused.

Fans for air circulation are a must in any setup. These, also, may be directed against a wall to create a circular current over and around the plants. In hot weather, they may be placed so as to bring air from a nearby window.

Fresh air may be a problem in a room without a window, but perhaps can be solved by circulating air from an adjoining room. Basement growers often find that a window can be opened a crack somewhere near the plants without harm. A baffle may be used to direct the flow of air to the floor, so that it will pick up heat before it reaches the plants. Windows may be left open all during the summer, particularly at night, to bring about a drop of 10° or more from day temperatures.

A nicely balanced atmosphere includes a relative humidity somewhere between 50 and 70 percent. Small humidifiers can be purchased. For a very small group of plants a kind intended for use in a sick room may be adequate. Misting the floors and walls may be sufficient. To combat the growth of algae on these areas and in the trays under the plants, Physan-20 may be used as directed for greenhouses.

As to what kinds to grow, one's own ingenuity is the only limiting factor, together with the size of plants and their natural demands. In one small basement collection miltonias, epidendrums, oncidiums, cattleyas, catasetums, maxillarias, lycastes, odontoglossums, and even vandas all flower together. In this same collection, however, there are others that are not doing well, but this is true of any collection even under the most ideal conditions. Plants may receive a shock when first put under lights and it may take them a while to become acclimated. As with all plants, patience and experimentation are required. General methods are the same as for greenhouse care—potting, potting materials, watering, and so forth. A word of caution must be given about the use of insecticides in the home. Only those most safe for human beings should be used. If it becomes necessary to use the more toxic ones, take the plants outdoors to treat them.

ORCHIDS IN YOUR GARDEN

Growers in such a fortunate climate as that of Hawaii, Florida, and parts of California can grow orchids in their gardens all year round, using them as an integral part of the landscaping (Fig. 23–9). Those of us not so blessed in the matter of climate can at least have a few plants outdoors in the summer. In fact, in areas with quite hot summers, many kinds benefit from being moved outside; these include cymbidiums, especially, but also cattleyas, dendrobiums, oncidiums, and others.

In regions where orchids can be put outdoors for only part of the year, it is best to hang the pots or baskets on the lower limbs of tall trees, or to place them on a bench and build a lath or screen roof over them. Pots can sometimes be set in places where they will add to the decoration of a patio if the light conditions are right. Plants will dry out faster outside than in a greenhouse, so careful attention to watering is in order. Rain may do the job at times, but it cannot be depended upon. (Sometimes the rain overdoes it!) Guard the plants from the usual array of garden insects by spraying when needed. When moving greenhouse-tender plants outside, do not let them have too much sun at first. Some kinds can be hardened to take clear early morning and late evening sun, with some shade during the hot noon and afternoon hours.

A screen house is a useful adjunct to backyard orchid growing and can be decorative, too. It can be used for "summering out" during the hot season, for all-year growing in frost-free areas and, with a cover and a small heater, where winters do not go below the high twenties. The latter conditions hold where I live. My screen house is shown in Fig. 23–10. The first photo (A) shows it newly built, before I realized that it would have to be covered. It is of redwood, eight by fourteen feet, eight feet high on one side, seven on the other. (Another foot in height would be welcome.) It is entirely of redwood, with lattice on the northeast side, 25 percent saran on the opposite side and one end, and the other end open. Since then it has been enclosed with fiberglass at the bottom and a removable winter door furnished. The roof is of

Figure 23–9 *Orchids in a Florida garden. The plants are naturalized on the tree or hung from the branches. In this group are cattleyas, phalaenopsis, dendrobiums, oncidiums,* Renanthera coccinea, *and* Vanda coerulea. (COURTESY OF H. F. LOOMIS.)

Reichold fiberglass, with 75 percent light transmission. The cover (Fig. 23–10B) is of Grifolyn, plastic sheeting bonded over a strengthening network of threads. It transmits 95 percent of sunlight. It is made in panels edged with velcro and fastened to the uprights with snappers (Fig. 23–10C). They can be rolled up during changeable weather and removed to be put away. The small heater shown in Fig. 23-10D, is sufficient to keep the temperature around 40° in winter, and a fan helps to cool it in the summer. Mist sprayers on a timer help with humidity and cooling. In my area, with cool summer nights, the screen house enables me to grow orchids from the cool, high elevations, such as masdevallias, sophronitis, some oncidiums, laelias, and many others.

Figure 23–10A *Newly built screen house. The four corner posts are fastened to steel straps imbedded in concrete pylons sunken in the ground.*

Figure 23–10B *The winter cover is of Grifolyn, made in panels that can be rolled up if desisred, and taken off for storage.*

Figure 23–10C *Detail showing how the velcro is put on with snappers, over which the velcro on the adjacent panel fastens.*

Figure 23–10D *Interior of the screen house. Note welded wire on benches, electric heater, concrete slab walk.*

Almost all of the greenhouse epiphytes can be naturalized on trees (Fig. 23–9), where they will take root and grow just as they do in the wild. Plants that are potted in osmunda can be removed from the pot, and the ball of fiber and roots can be wired firmly to a branch or to the trunk. For plants taken from bark, a chunk of fiber should be wired to the branch and the plant then wired in place upon it. The new growth should be next to the bark. As the roots grow, they extend out of the fiber and attach themselves to the tree. Another method is to fasten a half-pot or half a coconut husk to the branch and then settle the plant in the container with enough fiber to keep it firm. Plants naturalized in these ways must be watered regularly when there is not sufficient rain and should be given frequent applications of fertilizer since they will not have so rich a source of nutrients as they would on jungle trees.

Some orchids can be grown in beds especially prepared for them. Terrestrials such as *Phaius, Bletia,* and *Calanthe* need a well-drained bed in which the soil has been replaced with the loose, fluffy type of compost you would use for them in pots. A mixture of sand, gravel or bark, leaf mold, and fibrous loam should be satisfactory. The bed must be located in a spot where the light will be right for the specific plants you intend to grow.

Epiphytic or semiepiphytic kinds can also be grown in beds, but the bed should be raised eighteen to twenty-four inches to allow especially free drainage, somewhat after the manner of a rock garden. The bottom twelve inches of the bed is filled with very coarse gravel and the upper eight to twelve inches with a mixture suitable for epiphytes, perhaps bark mixed with shredded tree fern or leaf mold. Vandas, reed-type epidendrums, some dendrobiums, *Cyrtopodium,* and some of the warmth-tolerant miniature cymbidiums can then be planted in the bed. Tall plants should always have some support, perhaps that furnished by a wall to which they can be trained or tied. Plants grouped in the same bed should, of course, have the same light requirements, and the bed itself should be located to receive the proper amount of sun and shade.

·APPENDIX·

ORCHID LITERATURE

M ANY KINDS OF BOOKS ON orchids are listed below. Some are descriptive of the orchids of particular areas, and are of special interest to those who have a wide variety of kinds in their collections. Others are on culture. Some are old, some are new. Those written before our time, and especially those on culture in other countries, employ terms and describe methods that are strange to us. Nevertheless, we can learn much from them. Any grower who is seriously interested in orchids will be well re-

warded by reading a few of the old books. Not only will he come to know more about his plants through learning something of their history and their handling in other eras, but he will come to feel a kinship with the growers who nurtured the plants and learned their ways and who handed on this rich heritage to us. Books that are out of print can often be obtained in used condition through dealers in old books. And some, of course, are rare and quite expensive. They may also be obtained for short periods through the Inter-Library Loan Service for a fee that covers handling, postage, and insurance. Reprints of some of the old ones are currently being made, and are available from book dealers.

BOOKS

Ames, Blanche. *Drawings of Florida Orchids,* with explanatory notes by Oakes Ames. 1959. 2nd edition. Botanical Museum of Harvard Univ., Cambridge, Massachusetts 02138

Ames, Oakes. *Orchidaceae.* Seven fascicles, several out of print. Those available may be obtained from the American Orchid Society, Inc. Botanical Museum of Harvard University, Cambridge, Massachusetts 02138.

_____ . *Orchidaceae of Costa Rica.* Included as part of *Flora of Costa Rica,* Paul Standley. 1937. Field Museum of Natural History, Botanical Series, Vol. XVIII, pp. 197–306. Chicago, Illinois.

_____ . *Orchids in Retrospect.* 1948. 172 pages. Botanical Museum of Harvard Univ., Cambridge.

_____ . *An Enumeration of the Orchids of the U.S. and Canada.* 1924. Boston, Massachusetts.

_____ , and Donovan S. Correll. *Orchids of Guatemala.* 1951–1953. Two vols, 726 pages. Fieldiana: Botany, Vol. 26, Nos. 1 and 2. Field Museum of Natural History, Chicago. Supplement, 1966, by Correll. Reprinted simultaneously by Dover Publications and Twin Oaks Books, 1985.

_____ , F. T. Hubbard and C. Schweinfurth. *The Genus Epidendrum in the U. S. and Middle America.* 1936. Available from the American Orchid Society. Cambridge, Massachusetts.

Arditti, Joseph. *Orchid Biology.* Cornell University Press, New York. Vol. I, 1977; Vol. II, 1982; Vol. III, 1984. Vol. IV, 1987.

Atwood, John. *Orchids of La Selva Botanical Station,* Costa Rica. Reprint from Selbyana, Vol. 10, No. 1. 1988.

Australia National Herbarium. *Australian Native Orchids*. 1965. Available from the American Orchid Society, Cambridge, Massachusetts.

Bailey, Liberty Hyde. *Standard Cyclopedia of Horticulture*. Popular edition. 1935. 3 vols., 3,639 pages. The Macmillan Co., New York.

Ball, J. S. *Southern African Epiphytic Orchids*. 1978. Republic of South Africa.

Banerji, M. L., and P. Pradhan. *The Orchids of Nepal Himalayas*.

Bateman, James. *A Second Century of Orchidaceous Plants*. 1867. A small-size reprint with title *Hundert Orchideen, 1979*. Germany.

Bechtel, Helmut, Phillip Cribb, and Edmund Launert. *The Manual of Cultivated Orchid Species*. 1981. Dorset, U. K.

Bedford, Roger. *A Guide to Native Australian Orchids*. 1969. Angue and Robertson. Sydney, Australia.

Bennett, Keith S. *The Tropical Asiatic Slipper Orchids*. 1984. *Genus Paphiopedilum*. Australia.

Birk, Lance A. *The Paphiopedilum Grower's Manual*. 1983. Pisang Press, Santa Barbara, California.

Black, Peter M. *Beautiful Orchids*. 1973. London, England.

————. *Complete Book of Orchid Growing*. Great Britain and U.S.A. 1980.

Blowers, John W. *Pictorial Orchid Growing*. 1966. 128 pages. Published by the author, 96 Marion Crescent, Maidstone, Kent, England.

————. *Orchids*. 1962. 130 pages. Agent for U.S., St. Martin's Press, 175 Fifth Ave., New York.

Bose, T. K., and S. K. Bhattacharjee. *Orchids of India*. 1980. Calcutta, India.

Boyle, Frederick. *The Culture of Greenhouse Orchids, Old System and New*. 1902. London.

————. *About Orchids, A Chat*. 1893, reprint 1983.

————. *Woodland Orchids*.

Braem, Guido J. *Paphiopedilum*. 1988 Brucke-Verlag Kurt Schmersow. Hildesheim, Germany.

Brooklyn Botanic Garden. *Handbook on Orchids*. 1967. 81 pages. Brooklyn, N.Y. 11225.

Bruhl, Paul. *A Guide to the Orchids of Sikkim*. 1926. Thaker, Spink and Co., Calcutta and Simla, India.

Burberry, H. A. *The Amateur Orchid Cultivator's Guide Book*. 1899. 3d edition. Liverpool, England.

Burgeff, Hans. *Die Samenkeimung die Orchideen*. 1936. Jena.

Burnett, Harry C. *Orchid Diseases*. 1974. Booklet pub. by University of Florida, Winter Haven, Florida 32882.

Cady, Leo and T. Rotherham. *Australian Orchids in Color*. 1970. 50 text pages, 107 color plates. A. H. and A. W. Reed, Sydney, Australia.

Capps, Anne L. *Source Handbook of Orchid Species*. 1965. 106 mimeographed pages. Available from the author, Rte. 4, Box 376, Vienna, Virginia 22180.

Case, Frederick W., Jr. *Orchids of the Western Great Lakes Region*. 1964. 148 pages. Cranbrook Institute of Sciences, Bloomfield Hills, Michigan. Revised 1988.

Cheng, Chow. *Taiwan Native Orchids*. 1967. Chow Cheng Orchids, 194 Litoh St., Taichung, Taiwan.

Cherry, Elaine C. *Fluorescent Light Gardening*. 1965. 256 pages. Information for plants in general. Van Nostrand Reinhold Co., New York, N. Y. 10001.

Cogniaux, A. *Orchidaceae Florae Brasiliensis*. 1893–1906. Reprinted 1966.

Cooper, Dorothy. *New Zealand Native Orchids*. A Field Guide. 1981. Wellington, New Zealand.

Costantin, Julien. *Atlas en Couleur des Orchidées Cultivées*. 1000 orchids in color. Circa 1915. Paris.

————. *La Vie des Orchidées*. 1917. 185 pages. Paris.

Correll, Donovan S. *Native Orchids of North America, North of Mexico*. 1950. 400 pages. Chronica Botanica. Now published by The Ronald Press Co., 15 East 26th St., New York.

————. *Supplement to Orchids of Guatemala and British Honduras*. 1965. Fieldiana: Botany, Vol. 31, no. 7. Field Museum of Natural History, Chicago, Illinois.

Cox, J. M. *Cultural Table of Orchidaceous Plants*. 1946. Sydney, Australia.

Craighead, Frank S. *Orchids and Other Air Plants of the Everglades National Park*. 1963. 125 pages. University of Miami Press, Coral Gables, Florida.

Cribb, Phillip J. *The Genus Paphiopedilum*. 1987. Royal Botanic Garden, London and Timber Press. Portland, Oregon, U.S.A.

————. *Revision of Dendrobium*, Sect. Latourea. Reprint from Kew Bulletin. 1983. London

————. the Antelope Dendrobiums. Reprint from Kew Bulletin 1986. London

————. and Christopher Bailes. *Hardy Orchids*. 1989. Timber Press. Portland, Oregon, U.S.A.

————, C. Z. Tang and Ian Butterfield. *The Genus Pleione* 1983 Vo. CLXXXIV, Part III Curtis Botanical Magazine, London.

Curtis, Charles H. *Orchids for Everyone*. 1910. London.

————. *Orchids*. 1950. 274 pages. Putnam and Co., Ltd., 42 Great Russell St., London.

Darwin, Charles. *On the Fertilization of Orchids by Insects*. 1899. New York.

Dassanayake, M. D. and F. R. Forsberg, Editors. *A Revised Handbook to the Flora of Ceylon*, Vol. II. 1981. New Delhi, Bombay, Calcutta.

Davis, Reg. S., and Mona Lisa Steiner. *Philippine Orchids*. 1952. 270 pages. The William Frederick Press, New York.

de Oca, Rafael Montes. *Hummingbirds and Orchids of Mexico*. 1963. 158 pages. Reproductions of water color paintings. Editorial Fournier, S.A., Apartado Postal 31413, Mexico 20, D. F., Mexico.

de la Bathie. H. Perrier. *Flore de Madagascar, 49th family: Orchidées*. Tananarive. 1941. Reprinted 1977 by Margaret Ilgenfritz, English translation bv Steve Beckman, 1982.

Dienum, Dick. *Orchideen van Nederland*. 1944. 174 pages. Text in Dutch.

Dietrich, Helga. *Orchid Bibliography*. 3 vols; 1900–1978, 1900–1981, 1982–1986. Jena.

Dockrill, A. W. *Australian Indigenous Orchids*. 1969. 825 pages. Sydney, Australia.

Dodson, Calaway H. and Robert J. Gillespie. *The Biology of the Orchids*. 1967. 158 pages. Mid-American Orchid Congress, Inc., Nashville, Tennessee.

_____ and Piedad Marmol de Dodson. *Orchids of Ecuador*. 1980–1982. *Icones Plantarum Tropicarum*. Marie Selby Botanical Gardens, Sarasota, Florida.

Dressler, Robert L. *The Orchids, Natural History and Classification*. 1981. Harvard University Press. Massachusetts.

_____ and Glenn E. Pollard. *The Genus Encyclia in Mexico*. Associacion Mexicana de Orquideologia, A. C., Mexico.

Dunsterville, G. C. K. *Introduction to the World of Orchids*. 1964. 104 pages. Doubleday and Co., Inc., Garden City, New York.

_____, and Leslie A. Garay. *Venezuelan Orchids Illustrated*. Vols. I, II, III, IV, V, VI, 1959–1976. Andre Deutch, Ltd. London, England.

_____. *Orchids of Venezuela*. 3 vols. 1980. Museum Books.

_____ and E. Dunsterville. *Orchid Hunting in the Lost World, and Elsewhere in Venezuela*. 1988. American Orchid Society, West Palm Beach, Florida.

Duperres, A. *Orchidées d'Europe*. 1955. 239 pages. Native orchids of Europe. Text in French.

du Petit-Thouars, A. A. *Histoire Particuliere des Plantes Orchidées Receuillées sur les Trois Isles Australes d'Afrique*. 1822. Reprint 1979. Stanfordville, New York.

Du Puy, David and Phillip Cribb. *The Genus Cymbidium*. 1988. Timber Press.

Duthie, J. F. *The Orchids of Northwestern Himalaya*. 1906. Calcutta. A supplement to King and Pantling. German reprint 1967.

Duval, L. *Les Cattleya: Traité de culture practique*. 1907. Paris.

_____. *Les Odontoglossum*. 1900. Paris.

_____. *Les Orchidées*. 1905. Paris.

Eigeldinger, O. *Orchids for Everyone*. 1957. 144 pages. John Gifford Ltd., 125 Charing Rd., London, WC2.

Erickson, Rica. *Orchids of the West*. 2nd ed. 1966. 107 pages. Terrestrial orchids of Western Australia. Paterson Brokensha Pty. Ltd., 65 Murray St., Perth, Western Australia.

Fawcett W., and A. B. Rendle. *Flora of Jamaica: Vol. 1, Orchids*. British Museum, London.

Fennell. T. A., Jr. *Orchids for Home and Garden*. 1956. Revised 1959. 160 pages. Rinehart and Co., Inc., New York.

Firth, M. J. *Native Orchids of Tasmania*. 1965. 90 pages. C. L. Richmond, Tasmania.

Fitch, Charles Marden. *All About Orchids*. 1981. Doubleday and Co., Garden City, New York.

Foldats, Ernesto. *Orchidaceae*, Vol. 15 of *Flora de Venezuela*, 5 parts and Field Guide. 1969–1970. Edicion Especial of the Instituto Botanico, Caracas, Venezuela.

Fowlie, J. A. *The Genus Lycaste*. 1970. La Cañada, California.

_____. *The Brazilian Bifoliate Cattleyas and Their Color Varieties*. 1977. La Cañada, California.

Freed, Hugo. *Orchids and Serendipity*. 1970. Prentice-Hall, Inc., New York.

_____. *New Horizons in Orchid Breeding*. Malibu, 1979.

Garay, Leslie A. and Herman R. Sweet. *Natural and Artificial Hybrid Generic Names of Orchids*. 1966. 212 pages. Botanical Museum Leaflets, Vol. 21, no. 6, Harvard University, Cambridge, Mass. 02138

_____. *Orchids of the Southern Ryuku Islands*. 1974. Harvard Botanical Museum, Massachusetts.

_____. *Orchidaceae*, Vol. 1 of Richard A. Howard's *Flora of the Lesser Antilles*. 1974. Arnold Arboretum, Harvard University, Massachusetts.

Garrard, Jeanne. *Growing Orchids for Pleasure*. 1966. 302 pages. A. S. Barnes and Co., Inc., South Brunswick, New Jersey.

George, A. S. and Herb Foote. *Orchids of Western Australia*. Westviews Pty. Ltd., Perth, Australia.

Ghose, B. N. *Beautiful Indian Orchids*. 1959. 155 pages. G. Ghose and Co., Town-End, Darjeeling, Indian Union. Second edition 1969.

Gilbert, P. A. *The Charm of Growing Orchids*. 1952. 2nd edition. Shepherd Press, Sydney, Australia.

_____. *Orchids: Their Culture and Classification*. 1951. 252 pages. Shepherd Press, Sydney, Australia.

Graf, Alfred Byrd. *Exotica 4. Pictorial Cyclopedia of Exotic Plants*. 1,828 pages. Includes 1439 illustrations and descriptions of orchids. Roehrs Co., Rutherford, New Jersey 1982.

————. *Tropica* II, 1980.

Halbinger, Federico. *Odontoglossum and Related Genera in Mexico and Central America*. 1985. Vol. XIII of Orquidea, Bulletin of the Mexican Orchid Society.

Hamer, Fritz. *Orchids of El Salvador*. Vols I and II, 1974. Ministerio de Education, El Salvador. Vol. III, 1981. Marie Selby Botanical Gardens, Sarasota, Florida.

————. *Orchids of Nicaragua*. 1982–1984. *Icones Plantarum Tropicarum*. Marie Selby Botanical Gardens, Sarasota, Florida.

Hamilton, Robert M. *Orchid Flower Index*. A World List of Reproductions in Color in Books and Periodicals. Vol. 1, 1736–1966, 1967. Vol. 2, 1966–1979. 1979.

————. *Index to Plant Illustrations in The American Orchid Society Bulletin*, Vols. 1–40, 1972; Vols. 41–46, 1978; Vols. 41–49, 1981; Vols. 41–54, 1986;

————. *When Does It Flower?* The Blooming Months of 3500 Species Orchids in the USA. 1977. Second edition, 1986.

————. *The Orchid Doctor*. Remedies, Recipes, Recommendations, and Referrals. 1980. All Robert M. Hamilton books published by the author, 9211 Beckwith Road, Richmond, B. C., Canada V6X 1V7.

————. *The New Orchid Doctor*, 1988.

Harrison C. Alwyn. *Commercial Orchid Growing*. 1914. London, England.

————. *Orchids for Amateurs*. 1911. London, England.

Harrison, E. R. *Epiphytic Orchids of Southern Africa*. 1972. Natal Branch of Wildlife Protection and Conservation Society of South Africa.

Harvard Univ., Botanical Museum Leaflets. By subscription, or separately from Amer. Orchid Soc., Inc.

Hawkes, Alex D. *Orchids: Their Botany and Culture*. 1961. 297 pages. Harper and Bros., New York.

————. *Encyclopaedia of Cultivated Orchids*. 1965. 602 pages. Faber and Faber Ltd., London, England.

Hennessy, Esmé F. and Tessa A. Hedge. *The Slipper Orchids*. 1989. Acorn Books, Randburg, RSA.

Hillerman, Fred. *A Cultural Manual for Angraecoid Orchid Growers*.

————. and Arthur W. Holst. An Introduction To The Cultivated Angraecoid Orchids of Madagascar. 1986. Timber Press.

Hoehne, F. C. *Orchidaceae*: Fascicles 1, 5, 8, and 10 of *Flora Brasilica*. 1940–1953. Secretario da Agricultura. Sao Paolo, Brazil.

————. *Iconografia de Orchidaceas do Brazil*. 1949. Secratario da Agricultura. Sao Paolo, Brazil.

Holttum, R. E. *A Revised Flora of Malaya*. Vol. 1, *Orchids of Malaya*. 1953. Government Printing Office, Singapore, Malaya.

Hooker, Sir Joseph Dalton. *Century of Orchidaceous Plants*. 1851.

————. *Himalayan Journals*. 1854.

————. *Flora of India*. 1855.

————. *Century of Indian Plants*. 1895. Reprint 1967.

————. *Icones Plantarum*. 1892–1894. Reprint, 1972.

————, and George Bentham. *Genera Plantarum*. An important contribution to plant classification. 1862–83.

Hrong-Jye Su. *Native Orchids of Taiwan*. 1st ed. 1974, 2nd ed. 1975. Taipei, Taiwan.

Hunt, P. F. and Mary A. Grierson. *Orchidaceae*. 1973.

————, and Mary Grierson. *Country Life Book of Orchids*. 1978, Burton Press, Ltd., London, England.

————and T. Kijima. *The Orchid*. 1979. Octopus Books, London, England.

Hurst, Charles C. *Experiments in Genetics*. 1925. Cambridge University Press, Cambridge, England.

————. *Mechanism of Creative Evolution*. 1932. Cambridge University Press, Cambridge, England.

Icones Plantarum Tropicarum. A continuing series being published by the Marie Selby Botanical Gardens. Participating authors include H. Calaway and P. M. Dodson, Fritz Hamer, Roberto Vasquez, and others. Countries being covered are Ecuador, Bolivia, Nicaragua (completed), Chile, with a start on some others. Published in sets of 100 sheets at a time, with text and line drawings back-to-back on the same sheet.

Jackson, B. D. *A Glossary of Botanical Terms*. 1928. 4th edition. Reprinted, 1948. Duckworth and Co., London, England.

Japan Orchid Growers Association. *Quality Stream Cattleyas*. 1981

Jayaweera, D. M. A. *Orchidaceae*, in *Revised Handbook to Flora of Ceylon*. Vol. II, 1981. Netherlands.

Kamemoto, H., R. Tanaka, and K. Kosaki. *Chromosome Numbers of Orchids in Hawaii*. 1962. 28 pages. Hawaii Ag. Exp. Sta. Bulletin 127. University of Hawaii, Honolulu.

Kano, Kunio. *Studies on the Media for Orchid Seed Germination*. 1965. 80 pages. Memoirs No. 20, Faculty of Agriculture, Kagawa University, Mikityo, Kagawa-ken, Japan.

Karasawa, K. *Orchid Atlas. Paphiopedilum* and *Terrestrials*. 1987. Japan.

————. *Dendrobium and Bulbophyllum*.

King. C., and R. Pantling. *Orchids of The Sikkim-Himalaya*. 1895–1906. Calcutta. Reprint 1967.

(SPECIAL NOTE: The above and Duthie, *The Orchids*

of the North-Western Himalaya and Hooker, *A Century of Indian Orchids* are now available in a single-volume reprint.)

Koopowitz, Harold, and Hillary Kaye. *Plant Extinction, A Global Crisis.* 1983. Stonewall Press, Washington, D.C.

Kramer, Jack. *Growing Orchids at Your Windows.* 1963. 151 pages. D. Van Nostrand Co., Inc., New York.

Kupper, Walter. *Orchidées.* Translated from German to French. Circa 1955. 100 color plates. Service d'Images Silva, Zurich, Switzerland. English translation also available.

Kränzlin, F. *Beiträge zu Orchideenflora Sudamerikas.* 1911. Uppsala and Stockholm, Sweden.

Lawrence, W. J. C. *Practical Plant Breeding.* 1951. Revised 3d edition. 166 pages. George Allen and Unwin, Ltd., London, England.

Lecoufle, Marcel, and Henri Rose. *Orchids.* 1957. 112 pages. English edition. Crosby and Lockwood and Son, Ltd., 26 Old Bromptom Road, S. W. 7, London, England.

Lemmon, Kenneth. *The Covered Garden.* 1962. 284 pages. Historical Museum Press Ltd., London

Leon, H. and Herman Alain. *Flora of Cuba: Orchids.* 2 vols. 1948. Lubrecht and Cramer. Reprint of orchid section by Twin Oaks Books, Michigan. 1979.

Lindley. *Folia Orchidacea.* 1852. Reprinted by A. Asher and Co., Amsterdam, The Netherlands. 1964.

———. *Genera and Species of Orchidaceous Plants.* 1840.

Logan, Harry B., and Lloyd C. Cosper. *Orchids Are Easy to Grow.* 1949. 312 pages. Ziff-Davis Publishing Co., Chicago.

Long, John C., *Native Orchids of Colorado.* 1965. 34 pages. Museum Pictorial No. 16. Denver Museum of Natural History, Denver, Colorado.

Luer, Carlyle. *Native Orchids of Florida.* 1972. New York Botanical Garden.

———. *Native Orchids of the United States and Canada.* 1975. New York Botanical Garden.

———. *Systematics of Masdevallia,* Missouri Botanical Gardens.

———. *Thesaurus Masdevalliarum.* 1983. Watercolora by A. M. Trechslin. Munich, Germany.

——— and Rodrigo Escobar R. *Thesaura Dracularum.* Illustrated by Stig Dalström. German translation by Fritz Hamer. A continuing series beginning with Vol. 1, 1988. Missouri Botanical Garden.

Lyons, John. Remarks on the Management of Orchidaceous Plants, 1843. Ireland. Reprinted 1983, The Boethius Press, Ireland.

Marston, Margaret E., and Pisit Voraurai. *Multiplication of Orchid Clones by Shoot Meristem Culture.* A review of the literature. Misc. Publication No. 17. University of Nottingham, Dept. of Horticulture, Sutton Bonington, Loughborough, England.

McLeish, John, and Brian Snoad. *Looking at Chromosomes.* 1957. 87 pages. Macmillan and Co., Ltd., London, England.

McVaugh, R. *Orchids of Western Mexico.* Vol. 16 of *Flora Novo Galiciano.* 1985. University of Michigan Press.

Mee, Margaret. In search of *Flowers of The Amazon Forests.* 1988. Nonesuch Expeditions, Suffolk, England.

Mikulska and Madalski. *The Orchids of Poland.* Reprint of 1971 edition, in reduced size.

Michigan Orchid Society. *North American Terrestrial Orchids.* Symposium II. 1981. Southfield, Michigan.

Millican, Albert. *Travels and Adventures of an Orchid Hunter.* 1891. London, England

Missouri Botanical Garden. *Index to Plant Chromosome Numbers.* 1979–1981. Reprint by Twin Oaks Books, Michigan.

Moir, W. W. G. and May Moir. *Variegata Oncidiums.* 1970. Honolulu, Hawaii.

———. *Breeding Variegata Oncidiums.* 1980. Lyon Arboretum, Hawaii.

———. *Creating Oncidium Intergenerics.* 1982. Hawaii.

———. *Creating Laeliinae Intergenerics.* 1982. Hawaii.

Morris, Brian. *Epiphytic Orchids of Malawi.* The Society of Malawi.

Morris, F., and E. Eames. *Our Wild Orchids.* 1929. New York.

Moulen, Fred. *Orchids in Australia.* 1958. 148 pages, 100 colored figures. Australia Edita Pty. Ltd, Sydney, Australia.

Nicholls, W. H. *Orchids of Australia.* 1969. 129 pages of text, 476 pages of color. Thomas Nelson (Aust.) Ltd. Sydney.

Nicolai, W. *Orchideen.* 1939. Frankfurt (Oder).

Noble, Mary. *You Can Grow Cattleya Orchids.* 1968. 148 pages. Published by author, 5700 W. Salerno Rd., Jacksonville, Florida 32244.

———. *You Can Grow Orchids.* 1954. Revised. 152 pages. Published by author. 1964.

———. *Florida Orchids.* 1952. 88 pages. State Dept. of Agriculture, Tallahassee, Florida.

Northen, Rebecca T. *Orchids as House Plants.* 1955. Van Nostrand Reinhold Co., New York. Revised 1976. Dover Publications, New York.

———. *Miniature Orchids.* 1980. Van Nostrand Reinhold, New York.

O'Brian, James. *Orchids.* 1890. London.

Ortiz V., Pedro. *Orquídeas de Colombia.* 1976. Bogotá, Colombia.

———, Alfonso Martinez, M., and Guillermo Misas U. *Orquídeas Ornamentales de Colombia.* Bogotá, Colombia.

Osorio, L. F. *Colombian Orchids.* 1941. Medellín, Colombia.

Ospina, Mariano. *Orquideas Colombianas.* 1958. 305 pages. Publicaciones Technicas Ltda., Bogotá, Colombia.

——— and Robert L. Dressler. *Orquideas de las Americas.* 1974. Bogotá, Colombia.

Pabst, G. F. J., and F. Dungs. *Orchidacea Brasilienses.* 1975–1977. Hildesheim, Germany.

Piers, Frank. *Orchids of East Africa.* 1968. 2nd fully revised and enlarged edition. 300 pages. Wheldon and Wesley Ltd., Codicote nr. Hitchin, Herts, England.

Poddubnaya-Arnoldi, V. A., and V. A. Selenzneva. *Orchids and Their Culture.* 1957. 175 pages. Text in Russian. Academy of Sciences of the USSR, Moscow.

Pradhan, Udai C. *Indian Orchids.* Vol. 1, 1976. Vol. 2 1979. Kalimpong, India.

Quisumbing, Eduardo A. *Philippine Orchids, Complete Writings, in two volumes.* 1981. Manila.

Rentoul, J. N. *Growing Orchids:* Book 1, *Cymbidiums and Slippers.* 1981. Timber Press.

——— Book 2, *Cattleyas and Other Epiphytes.* 1982. Timber Press.

——— Book 3. *Vandas, Dendrobiums and others.* 1982. Timber Press.

——— Book 4. *The Australian Families.* 1985.

——— *The Special Orchid Grower.* 1987.

Reusch, Glad. *Orchid Corsages and Leis.* 1963. 33 pages. Earl J. Small, Orchids, Inc., P. O. Box 11207, St. Petersburg, Florida.

——— and Mary Noble. *Corsage Craft.* 1951. 148 pages. Van Nostrand Reinhold Co., New York, N. Y. 10001.

Richter, Walter. *Die Shönsten aber Sind Orchideen.* 1958. 280 pages. 64 color plates. Neumann Verlag, Dr. Schmincke-Allee 19, Radebeul 1 Germany. English translation and revision under new title *The Orchid World,* 1965. E. P. Dutton and Co., Inc., New York

——— *Orchid Care.* 1965. U.S.A. 1972.

Riehl, Matthias, *Grosse Liebe zu Orchideen.* 1958. 112 pages. Falken-Verlag Erich Sicher, Schellendorffstrasse 29, Berlin-Dahlem, Germany.

Ritterhausen, Brian and Wilma Rittershausen. *Orchids in Color.* 1980. England.

———. *Popular Orchids,* 1982. England

———. *Orchids as Indoor Plants.* 1983. England.

———. *Orchid Growing Illustrated.* 1985. England.

Rittershausen, R. R. C. *Successful Orchid Culture.* 1953. 136 pages. London. Printed in New York by Transatlantic Arts., Inc.

Rittershausen, Wilma, Editor. *Growing Your Own Orchids.* 1982. London, England.

Rodriguez, Rafael Lucas C. *The Genera of Orchids of Costa Rica.* A memorial publication of his paintings. 1986. Editorial de la Universidad de Costa Rica.

Rolfe, R. A., and C. C. Hurst. *The Orchid Stud Book.* 1909. List and discussion of hybrids to that date. Kew Herbarium, London, England.

Rotor, Gavino B. *Daylength and Temperature in Relation to Growth and Flowering of Orchids.* 1952. Cornell Experiment Station Bulletin #885, Cornell University, Ithaca, New York.

Rupp, H. M. R. *Orchids of New South Wales.* 1943. National Herbarium, Sydney, Australia. Reprint 1969.

Sagarik, Rapee and Haruyuki Kamemoto. *Beautiful Thai Orchid Species.* 1975. Orchid Society of Thailand. Bangkok.

Sander, David. *Orchids and Their Cultivation.* 1962. Revised edition of earlier book by the Sanders of St. Albans. Blandford Press, London, England.

Sander, (C. R., F. K., and L. L.). *Sander's Orchid Guide.* 1927. Revised edition. Reprinted.

Sander, Fred. *Reichenbachia.* 1888–1894. 4 vols. Plates are now collectors' items.

Sanders. *Complete List of Orchid Hybrids.* Compilation of hybrids to 1946, in first volume. Addenda: three volumes, 1946–48, 1949–51, 1952–54. *One Table List of Orchid Hybrids,* 1946–1960. Addenda, 1963, 1966, 1961–1979, 1971–1975, 1976–1980, 1981–1985, England. Available from American Orchid Society, Inc., 600 S. Olive Ave., West Palm Beach, FL 33405. Addenda published from time to time, will also be available from American Orchid Society.

Schelpe, E. A. C. L. E. *An Introduction to the South African Orchids.* 1966. 109 pages. MacDonald and Co., Ltd., Gulf House, 2 Portman St., London W1 England.

Schlecter, Rudolph. *Die Orchideen.* 1927. 2nd edition. Berlin. Being revised and edited by F. G. Breiger. Thirteen parts of twenty finished as of 1984. Published by Verlag Paul Parey, Lindenstrasse, 1 Berlin B1, Germany.

———. *Beitrage Zur Orchideenkunde von Zentral Amerika.* 1922–1923. Germany. Reprinted 1980.

_____. *Beitrage zur Orchideenkunde von Rio Grande do Sul,* Rprt. of 1925 Edition.

_____. *Orchidacea Perrierianne Zur Insel Madagascar.* Rprt. of 1925 edition.

_____. *Flower Analysis of New Species.* Rprt. 1980.

_____. *Beitrage Zur Orchideenkunde Von Colombia.* Reprinted 1980.

_____. *Orchidaceae of German New Guinea, 1911–1914.* Reprinted 1974. English translation by Australian Orchid Foundation, 1983, 107 Roberts St., Essendon, Victoria 3040, Australia.

Schultes, Richard Evans. *Native Orchids of Trinidad and Tobago.* 1960. 257 pages. Pergamon Press, New York.

_____ and Arthur Stanley Pease. *Generic Names of Orchids.* 1963. New York and London.

Schweinfurth, Charles. *Orchids of Peru.* 1958–1961. Fieldiana: Botany, Vol. 30, Nos. 1, 2, 3, 4. 1,005 pages. Field Museum of Natural History, Chicago, Illinois. Reprint 1983.

_____ and Alvaro Fernandez Berez. *Flora de la Real Expedicion Botanica del Nuevo Reine de Granada: Orchidaceae,* I. 1963. Reproduction of plates made in 1760–1817. Several volumes to follow. Ediciones Cultura Hispanica, Madrid.

Segerback. B. *Orchids of Nigeria.* Handbook. Includes checklist by C. Z. Tang and P. Cribb. 1982. Netherlands.

Seidenfaden, Gunnar. *Notes on Cirrhopetalum.* 1973. Dansk Botanisk Arkiv., Copenhagen, Denmark.

_____. *Orchid Genera in Thailand.* 1959–1983. Dansk Botanisk Arkiv. Copenhagen, Denmark.

_____ and Tem Smitinand. *The Orchids of Thailand.* Parts I–IV. 1969–1988. The Siam Society, Bangkok.

Sessler, Gloria Jean. *Orchids and How To Grow Them.* 1978. Prentice-Hall, Inc., Englewood Cliffs, New Jersey.

Sheehan, Tom and Marion Sheehan. *Orchid Genera Illustrated.* 1979. New York.

Sprunge, S. Editor. *Orchids from Curtis Botanical Magazine 1878–1948.* 1986. Cambridge University Press, England.

Stewart, Joyce and Bob Campbell. *Orchids of Tropical Africa.* 1970. South Brunswick and New York.

_____ and E. F. Hennesy. *Orchids of Africa.* 1981. South Africa.

_____, H. P. Linder, E. A. Schelpe, and A. V. Hall. *Wild Orchids of Southern Africa.* 1982. South Africa.

Summerhays, V. S. *Wild Orchids of Britain.* 1951. London, England.

Sweet, Herman R. *The Genus Phalaenopsis.* 1980. The Orchid Digest Inc., Pomona, California.

Skelsey, Alice, and editors of Time-Life Books. *Orchids.* 1978. Alexandria, Virginia.

Thomale, Hans. *Die Orchideen.* 1954. Eugen Ulmer, Ludwigsburg, Germany.

University of California. *The U. C. System for Producing Healthy Container-Grown Plants.* 1957. Manual #23. Agricultural Publications, Grinnell Hall, University of California, Berkeley 4, Calif.

Vacherot, Maurice. *Charme et Diversité des Orchidées.* 1957. 68 pages. Paris, France.

_____. *Les Orchidées.* 1954. 270 pages. Librairie J. B. Bailliére et Fils, 19 rue Hautefeuille, Paris, France.

Valmayer, Helen. *Orchidiana Philippiniana.* 1984. 2 vols. Eugenio Lopez Foundation, Inc., Publisher. Philippines.

van der Pijl, L., and Calaway H. Dodson. *Orchid Flowers: Their Pollination and Evolution.* 1967. University of Miami Press, Coral Gables, Florida.

Van Royen, P. *The Orchids of the High Mountains of New Guinea.* 1980. Reprint of the orchid part of Van Royen's *The Alpine Flora of New Guinea.* Germany.

Vasquez Ch. Robert, and Calaway H. Dodson. *Orchids of Bolivia: Icones Plantarum Tropicarum.* 1982. Marie Selby Botanical Gardens, Sarasota, Florida.

Veitch and Sons, *Manual of Orchidaceous Plants.* 1887. 2 vols. London, England. Reprinted 1962.

Veitch, James. *Hortus Veitchii.* 1906. London, England.

Warner, Robert, and B. S. Williams. Orchid Album. 11 vols. 1881–1896. England.

Waters, V. H., and C. C. Waters. *A Survey of the Slipper Orchids.* Shelby, North Carolina.

Watkins, John V. *ABC of Orchid Growing.* 1948. 3d edition, 1956. 190 pages. Prentice-Hall, Inc., Englewood Cliffs, New Jersey.

Watson, W., and W. Bean. *Orchids: Their Culture and Management.* 1890. London. Reprint, 1979. Princeton, New Jersey.

Webster, Aimée and Ancile Gloudon. *Caribbean Orchid Growing.* 1977. Gordon Town, Jamaica.

White, E. A. *American Orchid Culture.* 1927. Revised 1942. A. P. DelaMare Co., Inc., New York.

Williams, B. S. *The Orchid Grower's Manual.* 7th edition revised by Henry Williams. 1894. Reprinted, 1960. Wheldon and Wesley, Ltd., Codicote, Hitchin, England.

Williams, John E., and Andrew E. Williams, paintings by Norman Arlott. *Orchids of North America, Field Guide.* 1983. New York.

Williams, B. et al. *Orchids for Everyone.* 1980. New York.

Williams, Louis O. *The Orchidaceae of Mexico*. 1952. Four parts, as Vol. 2 of "Cieba." Escuela Agricola Panamericana, Tegucigalpa, Honduras.

———, and Paul H. Allen. *Flora of Panama*, Part III, Fascicles 2, 3, and 4: *Orchidaceae*. 1946–49. Annals of the Missouri Botanical Garden. St. Louis, Missouri. Reprint 1980, with chapter and checklist by Robert Dressler, Missouri Botanical Garden.

Withner, Carl L. Editor. *The Orchids: A Scientific Survey*. 1959. New York.

——— *The Orchids: Scientific Studies*. 1974. New York.

——— . *Cattleyas and Their Relatives*. Ongoing set of six volumes. Vol. 1. *Cattleyas*, 1988. Vol. 2, *Laelia*. in progress.

Woolward, F. H. *The Genus Masdevallia*. 1890–1896. England. Reprint in 8″ × 10″ size. 1978.

Wright, N. Pelham. *Orquideas de Mexico*. 1958. 120 pages. Bi-lingual text. La Prensa Médica Mexicana, Copilco-Universidad, Mexico 20, D. F.

PERIODICALS AND HANDBOOKS PUBLISHED BY ORCHID SOCIETIES

It is of benefit to an amateur to belong to an orchid society, a group of growers with whom he can exchange information and share mutual interests, either on a person-to-person basis or through the pages of a publication. Most of the larger societies publish a periodical which is included with membership fees. In addition to news about orchids and growers, methods and problems, the periodicals offer the advertisements of dealers from whom the amateur can obtain plants and supplies.

American Orchid Society. *Bulletin*. 12 issues a year. American Orchid Society, Inc., 6000 S. Olive Ave., West Palm Beach, Florida 33405.

———*Lindleyana*, Scientific Journal. Alec M, Pridgeon, Editor. Quarterly.

——— *Handbook On Judging and Exhibition*. 7th Edition, 1982.

——— *Handbook on Orchid Pests and Diseases*. 1986 Revised Edition.

——— *An Orchidist's Glossary*. 1974

——— *Handbook on Orchid Nomenclature and Registration*. 3rd Edition, 1985.

The Orchid Digest Corporation. *The Orchid Digest*, Editor, J. A. Fowlie. Quarterly. P. O. Box 916, Carmichael, California.

——— *The Genus Phalaenopsis,* Herman R. Sweet. 1980. (See in Books Appendix).

The South Florida Orchid Society. The *Florida Orchidist*. Quarterly. 6940 SW 111th Place., Miami, Florida.

Oregon Orchid Society. *Bulletin*. 11 issues a year. 12591 S. New Era Rd. Oregon City, Oregon 97045.

——— *Your First Orchids and How To Grow Them,* Frequently Revised.

Pacific Orchid Society of Hawaii. *Bulletin*. Quarterly. P. O. Box 1091, Honolulu, Hawaii 96808.

Honolulu Orchid Society. *Na Okika o Hawaii*. Quarterly. 3860 Manoa Road, Honolulu, Hawaii 96822.

The Orchid Review. Ltd. *The Orchid Review*. 12 issues a year. John Blower, Editor, Katukele House, Victoria Village, Jersey, Channel Islands.

Colombia Orchid Society. *Oquideologia,* Issued irregularly. Apartado Aéreo 4725, Medellín, Colombia.

Australian Affiliated Societies. *The Australian Orchid Review,* Quarterly. Graphic World Ltd., 14 McGill St., N.S.W. 2049. Australia.

New Zealand Orchid Society. *Orchids in New Zealand*. Quarterly. P. O. Box 36–297, Northcote. Aukland 9, New Zealand.

Marie Selby Botanical Gardens, *Selbyana,* Eric Christenson, Editor. Journal of the Marie Selby Botanical Gardens. Annual. 811 South Palm Ave., Sarasota, Florida 34236.

Philippine National Museum. *Philippine Orchid Review*. 3 issues a year. Herron and Taft Aves., Manila, R. P.

The Canadian Orchid Society. *The Canadian Orchid Journal*. Quarterly. 128 Adelaide St., Winnipeg, Manitoba, Canada R3A OW5

The Cymbidium Society of America. *The Orchid Advocate*. 6 issues a year. Edited by Bob Burkey, 931 Hermes Ave., Leucadia, California 92024.

Indian Orchid Journal. Indian Orchid Journal, Kalimpong, India. 734301.

Royal Horticultural Society. *The Orchid Review*. The orchid journal of the Royal Horticultural Society, P. O. Box 2, Torrington, Dewn EX38 8AP, England.

PROCEEDINGS OF WORLD ORCHID CONFERENCES

These contain all of the papers presented. (Not all are available new at present. To find any, both old and new, inquire of dealers in orchid books.) World Orchid Conferences were held as follows:

ORCHID LITERATURE

First, St. Louis, 1954 (No proceedings, reported in AOS Bulletin, Dec., 1954)
Second, Honolulu 1957
Third, London 1960
Fourth, Singapore 1963
Fifth, Long Beach, Calif. 1966
Sixth, Sydney 1969
Seventh, Medellín 1972
Eighth, Frankfurt 1975

Ninth, Bangkok 1978
Tenth, Durban 1981
Eleventh, Miami 1984
Twelfth, Tokyo 1987
Thirteenth, Aukland 1990
Fourteenth, Glasgow 1993
(Future World Orchid Conferences will be held every three years.)

INDEX

Acacallis, 269
  cyanea, 300
Acanthophippium, 269
  javanicum, 270
Acaraben, 313
Acineta
  barkeri, 263
  chrysantha, 263
  superba, 263
Acti-Dione, 312, 313
Ada, 240–241
  allenii, 240
  aurantiaca, 240
  glumacea, 240–241
  keiliana, 241
Adaglossum, 248
Adenine, 82
Adioda, 248
Aerangidinae, 142–144
Aerangis, **342**
  brachycarpa, 143
  citrata, 143
  friesiorum, 143
  luteo-alba var. *rhodosticta*,
    143
  rhodosticta, 143
  somalensis, 143
Aeranthes
  arachnites, 142
  ramosus, 142
Aerides, 12, 61, 119–138
  embryo culture of, 103
  species
    fieldingii, **134**
    odoratum, 134
      var. *lawrencea*, 134
      var. *quinquevulnerum*,
        134, **135**
Aganisia, 269
  cyanea, 300 (see also
    Acacallis cyanea)
  pulchella, 300
Air relations, 306
Alarm, temperature, 351
Aldicarb, 313
Aldrin, 312
Alexander, H. G., 189
Allen, Paul, 259
American Orchid Society, 62
Ancistrochilus, 269
  rothschildianus, 270
  tompsonianus, 270

Aneuploid, 78–79
Angraecum, 139–142
  dasycarpum, 139
  distichum, **139**
  eburneum, 139, **140**
  eichlerianum, 139–140
  giryamae, 140
  indundibulare, **140**–141
  leonis, 141
  magdalenae, 141
  scottianum, 141
  sesquipedale, **141**, 142
  superbum, 142
Anguloa, 269
  clowesii, **282**
  rueckeri, 282
  virginalis, 282
Anoectochilus, 269
  roxburghii, 280
  sikkimensis, 280
Ansellia, 192
  embryo culture of, 103
  species
    africana, 192
    gigantea, 192
      var. *nilotica*, 192
Anthracnose, 317,–318
Aphids, 327
Arachnis
  flos-aeris, 136
  moschifera, 136
Arasan, 314
Arpophyllum, 269
  alpinum, 297
  giganteum, 297
  spicatum, 297
Arsenic compounds, 312
Artificial light
  Gro-lux lights, 354
  growing with, 354, **355**,
    356
  Maxi-Gro, 354
Arundina, 269
  bambusaefolia, 270
  graminifolia, 270
Ascocentrum, 136
  embryo culture of, 103
  species
    curvifolium, 136
    hendersonianum (see
      Dyakia)
    miniatum, 136

Aspasia
  epidendroides, 242
  lunata, 242
  principissa, 242

Bacterial diseases, 309–311,
  319–320
Banrot, 313
Barbosella, 269
  caspitifica, 289, **290**
  cucullata, 289
Bare root plants, care of,
  338–340
Bark, 20
  fertilizer for, 33
Barkeria
  cyclotella, 165
  elegans, 165
  lindleyana, 165
  scandens, 165
  spectabilis, 165
Baskets, for potting, 339
Batemania, 269
  colleyi, 300
Bayleton, 313
Beds, orchid, 358
Bees, pollination and, **13**,
  14–15, 87, **251**,
  255, **258**–259, **260**,
  261, **263**
Benlate, 313
Benomyl, 313
Benzene hexacloride, 312
BFPA, 312
BHC, 312
Bifoliate cattleyas, 151–155
Bifrenaria, 269–270
  atropurpurea, 270
  harrisoniae, 270
  tetragona, 270
Biofoliate cattleyas, 19
Bioquin, 1, 313
Black fly, 328
Black sheaths, 319
Bladafume, 312
Bladex, 312
Bletia, 269
  purpurea, 270
  shepherdii, 270
  sherrattiana, 270
  verecunda, 270

Bletilla, 269
  hyacinthina, 271
  striata, 271
Blight, 318
Blossom brown necrotic
  streak, **322**
Bollea, 269
  coelestis, 300
  hemixantha, 300
  lalindei, 300
Boron in plant nutrition, 37
Bortan, 312
Botrytis, **317**, 318, **319**
Bowers, 190
Brassavola
  hybridization with
    Cattleya, 65
  species
    cordata, 170
    cucullata, 170
    digbyana, 72–73
    fragrans, 170
    glauca, 72–73
    nodosa, 170
      Orchidglade, **171**
    subulifolia, 170
Brassia
  antherotes, 241
  caudata, 241
  gireoudiana, 241
  verrucosa, 241
    'Horich', **241**
Brassidium, 248
Brassocattleya, 72, **73**
Brassolaeliocattleya, 72
  embryo culture of, 103
Broughtonia
  negrilensis, 171
  sanguinea, 171
Brown rot, 320
Brown spot, 319, **320**
Brummitt, Jean, 190
Bulbophyllum, 269
  barbigerum, 273
  beccarii, 273
  brachteolatum, 274
  fletcheranum, 273
  gravidum, 274, **275**
  leucorhachis, 274
  lindleyi, 274
  lobbii, 274
  macrobulbum, 274

makakense, 274
  maximum, 274
  pachyrrhachis, 274
  phalaenopsis, 274
  purpureorhachis, 274
  reticulatum, 274
Burrageara, 248

Cadetia
  chamaephyton, 218–219
  dischorensis, 219
  taylori, 219
Calanthe, 61
  hybrids
    Dominyi, 61, 271
    Veitchii, 271
  meristem culture of, 101
  species
    furcata, 271
    masuca, 271
    vestita, 271
Calcium in plant nutrition, 36
Calopogon, species, *pulchellus*, 271
Calypso, 3
Calyptrochilum christyanum, 143
Capanemia, 247
Captifol, 313
Case for indoor growing, 353–354
Catasetum, 15, 249–257
  barbatum, 250
  collare, 251
  discolor, 251
  fimbriatum, 252
  macrocarpum, **16**, 250–**251**
  oerstedii, 251
  pileatum, 251
  platyglossum, **251**
  saccatum, 251
    var. *christyanum*, 251
  sanguineum, 252
  tenebrosum, 252
  viridiflavum, 251
Cattleya, 3, 7
  bifoliate group, 151–155
  blossom brown necrotic streak, **322**
  buying plants, 19
  embryo culture of, 99
  flower bud initiation and development, 10
  flowering, 38
  flower parts, **12, 13**
  flower quality, 20
  flower storage, 38
  history of, 145
  hybrids
    Beverly Boswell, 7
    Bow Bells, 3, 79
    Brabantiae, 151
    Fabia, 62
    Hardyana, 62, 69
    Iris, **63**
    Princess Royal, 62
  labiata (unifoliate) group, 147–151
  light for, 25–27
  meristem culture of, 101, **103**
  natural hybrids, 155
    deckeri, 155
    guatemalensis, 155
    hardyana, 155
    pachecoi, 155
    victoria-reginae, 155

pH of water for, 32
pollination of, 87, **88**, 89
potting, 43–53
reproductive parts, **87**
semi-alba, 75–77
sepal wilt, 308–309
species
  aclandiae, 151
  amethystoglossa, 152
  aurantiaca, 152
  bicolor, **63**, 146, 152
  bowringiana, 152
  citrina (see *Encyclia citrina*)
  claesiana, 7
  deckeri (see *Cattleya*, natural hybrids)
  dolosa, 152
  dormaniana, 152
  dowiana, 62, **63**, 67, 69, 73, 146, 147
    var. *aurea*, 62, 69, 147
  eldorado, 146, 147
    'Alba', 83
  elongata, 152
  forbesii, 152, 153
  gaskelliana, 56, 146, 147
    var. *alba*, 83
  gigas, 3, 67, 69, 146, 147–148
    var.'Firmin Lambeau', **149**
  granulosa, 152, **153**
    var. *schofeldiana*, 152
  guatemalensis (see natural hybrids)
  guttata, 153
  harrisoniana, **153**
    var. *alba*, 83
  intermedia, 153, **154**
    'Alba', 83
    var. *acquinii*, 154
  iricolor, 148
  jenmanii, 148
  labiata, 56, 57, 59, 60, 62, 69, 145–**146**, 148
    'Alba', 77, 83
    'Harefield Hall', 83
  lawrenceana, 146, 148
  leopoldii, 154
    'Alba', 154
  loddigesii, 151, 154
    'Stanley', 83
  lueddemanniana, 146, 148
  luteola, 146, 148
  maxima, 146, 148
  mendelii, 146, 150
    'Alba', 83
  mossiae, 56, 69, 146, 150, 167
    'Mrs. Butterworth', 77
    var. *wageneri*, 83
  nobilior, 154
  obrieniana, 'Alba', 83
  pachecoi (see natural hybrids)
  percivaliana, 56, 146, 150
    'Alba', 83
  rex, 146, 150
  schillerana, 154
  schroederae, 146, 150
    'Alba', 83
  skinneri, 154
    'Alba', 83
  speciosissima, 'Alba', 83
  superba, 155
  trianaei, 56, 65, 146, 150–**151**

  'Alba', 83
  'Broomhills', 83
  'Llewellyn', 77
  'Verdonck', 83
  uddemanniana, 'Alba', 83
  velutina, 154
  violacea, 154–155
  warneri, 146, 151
    'Alba', 83
  warscewiczii
    'Firmin Lambeau', 83
    (see also *gigas*)
  structure of, 9
  temperature for, 18
Cattleya fly, 328
Cattleyopsis
  lindenii, 173
  ortgiesiana, 173
Cattley, William, 145
Caudicle, **13, 14, 15**
Caularthron
  bicornutum, 172
  bilamellatum, 173
Ceresan, 312
Charlesworthea, 248
Chelates, 37
Chlordane, 312
Chondrorhyncha, 269
  aromatica, 301
  chestertoni, 301
  rosea, 301
Chorobenzilate, 313
Chromosomes, 64, 65, **66**, **67**, 77–82
Chysis, 269
  embryo culture of, 103
  species
    aurea, 272
    bractescens, **272**
    laevis, 272
    lemminghei, 272
    tricostata, 272
Cirrhaea
  dependens, 264
  longiracemosa, 264
Cirrhopetalum, 269
  embryo culture of, 103
  species
    cumingii, 275
    guttulatum, 274
    longissimum, 274
    medusae, 274
    ornatissimum, 275
    picturatum, 274, 275, **276**
    rothschildianum, 275
Cischweinfia, 247
CITES, 337
Clone, 63
Cloud forests, 331
Clowesia, 252, 254
  glaucoglossum, 252
  rosea, 252
  russilliana, 252
  scurra, 252
  thylaciochila, 252
  warscewitzii, 252
  warscewitzii (scurra), **254**
Cochleanthes, 269
  discolor, **301**
  marginata, 301
Cochlioda
  noezliana, 241
  rosea, 241
  sanguinea, 242
  vulcanica, 242
Cockroaches, 328
Coelia, 269
  triptera, 272

Coeliopsis hyancinthosma, 264
Coelogyne, 269
  crisata, 276
  dayana, 276
  lawrenceana, 276
  massangeana, 276
  mooreana, **277**
  ochracea, 277
  pandurata, 277
  speciosa, 276
  tomentosa, 277
Colax (see *Pabstia*)
Colchicine, 80, **81**, 82
Collar rot, 316
Collembola, 328
Colmanara, 248
Column, **12, 13, 15**
  structure of in *Cattleya*, **13**
Comparettia
  coccinea, 243
  falcata, 243
  macroplectron, 243
  speciosa, 243
Convention on International Trade in Endangered Species, 337
Cool-dry treatment, 210
Cooling systems, evaporative, **23**
Copper in plant nutrition, 37
Coryanthes
  biflora, 259
  description and culture, 258–259
  hunteriana, 259, **260**
  macrantha, 259
Cryptanthemis slateri, 16
Cryptophoranthus, 269
  lepidotus, 290
  tribuloides, 290
Crytopdium
  andersonii, 190
  punctatum, 190–191
Cuitlauzina, 227–228
  pendulum, 224
Cut flowers, 38
Cyanide compounds, 312
Cycnoches
  aureum, **4**, 254, 255
  chlorochilon, 254
  egertonianum, 255, **256**
    var. *dianae*, 255, 256
  vetricosum, 256
    var. *warscewiczii*, 254–**255**, 256
Cygon, 313
Cymbidiella rhodochila, 192
Cymbidium, 3, 5, 61, 177–190
  colchicine treatment of, 81–82
  cool growing, 185–186
  description and culture, 177–185
  dividing and potting, **181**–182
  embryo culture of, 100
  fertilizing, 183–184
  flower spike, **178**
  garden culture, 184
  greenhouse culture, 179–184
  humidity, 182–184
  light, 180
  potting, 180–182
  ventilation, 182–184

hybrids
  Alexanderi 'Westonbirt',
    77, 186, 188–189,
    190
  Blue Smoke, 190
  Ceres, 186
  Eburneolowianum, 185,
    189
  Fairy Wand, 190
  Flirtation, 190
  Flirtation 'Princess
    Royal', **190**
  Jean Brummitt, 189, 190
  King Arthur, 190
  Lynette, 190
  Nila, 190
  Pauwelsii 'Compte
    d'Hemptinne', 77,
    186
  Peri 'Beefeater', **178**
  Pumander, 189
  Showgirl, 190
  Sweetheart, 190
meristem culture of, 101
miniatures, 187–188
  culture, 190
seedlings, 184
  flower spike, **185**
species
  aloifolium, 186–187,
    190
  atropurpureum, 187
  canaliculatum, 188
  devonianum, **187, 190**
  eburneum, 185
  ensifolium, 188, 190
  erythrostylum, 185
  faberi, 188
  finlaysonianum, 187
  forrestii, 188
  giganteum, 185
  grandiflorum, 185–186
  gyokuchin, 188
  hookerianum, 185–186
  insigne, 186
    var. *album*, 186
    'Westonbirt', 189
  kanran, 188
  lowianum, 185, 186
    var. *iansonii*, 186
  madidum, 188
  parishii, 186
  pendulum, 187
  pumilum, 188, **190**
  schroederi, 186
  suave, 188
  tigrinum, **187**, 188, 190
  tracyanum, 186
temperature for, 17
warm growing, 186–187
Cymbidium mosaic virus,
  321, 322–323, **324**
Cymbidium necrotic ringspot
  virus, 323, **325**
Cymbidium pseudobulb rot,
  182, **183**
Cymbidium tip burn, 317
Cyperorchis
  coclearis, 191
  elegans, 191
  mastersii, 191
Cypripedioideae, 195–208
Cypripedium
  acaule, 208
  calceolus, 208
    var. *parviflorum*, 208
    var. *pubescens*, 208
  californicum, 208
  candidum, 208

montanum, 208
reginae, 208
spectabile, 208
Cyrtorchis
  arcuata, 143
    var. *variabilis*, 143
    var. *whytei*, 143
  praetermissa, 143
Cytosine, 82

Damp-off, 315
Daylength, control of
  flowering, 55–60
Day neutral plants, 55, 57
DDVP, 313
Demeton, 312
Dendrobium, 5, 12, 61, 209–
  219, 269
description and culture,
  209–213
embryo culture of, 103
growing from seed, 212
hybrid, Millie Sander, 211
meristem culture of, 101
species
  aggregatum, 210, 213
    var. *jenkensii*, 216
  anosmum, 210, 213
  aphyllum, 217
  bigibbum, 211, 213, 218
    var. *bigibbum*, 213
    var. *compactum*, 213
    var. *superbum*, 213,
      214
  canaliculatum, 213
  chrysanthum, 210, 212,
    213
  chrysotoxum, 210, 213
  cucumerinum, 214
  dearei, 211, 212, 214
  densiflorum, 210, 214–
    215
  discolor, 218
  falcorostrum, 215
  farmeri, 210, 215
  fimbriatum, 210, 215
    var. *oculatum*, 215,
      217
  findlayanum, 210, 215
  formosum, 211, 212,
    215
    var. *giganteum*, 215
  gouldii, 211, **215**
  heterocarpum, 210,
    215–216
  infundibulum, 211, 212,
    216
  jenkinsii, 216
  kingianum, 216
  lawesii, 216
  lindleyi, 213
  linguiforme, 216
  loddigesii, **216**
  lyonii, 211
  macrophyllum, 216
  moorei, 216
  moschatum, 210, 211,
    217
  nobile, 210, 212, **217**
  parishii, 210
  phalaenopsis, 211, 212,
    213, **214**
    var. *compactum*, 213
    var. *schroederianum*,
      213
  phalaenopsis (see also
    *Dendrobium
    bigibbum*, var.
    superbum)

pierardii, 210, 217
sanderae, 211, 212, 217
  var. *parviflorum*, 217
schroederianum, 213
schuetzii, 211, 212,
  217–218
sophroniis, 218
speciosum, 218
stratiotes, 211, 218
superbiens, 211, 218
taurinum, 218
thyrsiflorum, 210, 218
undulatum, 211, 218
veratrifolium, 211, 218
victoriae-reginae, 218
wardianum, 210, 218
subspecies, *laratensis*, 213
temperature for, 18
Dendrobium beetle, 328
Dendrobium weevil, 328
Dendrochilum
  cobbianum, 277, **278**
  filiforme, 277
  glumaceum, 277
  magnum, 277
  uncatum, 277
Dendrophylax
  fawcettii, 142
  funalis, 142
Deoxyribonucleic acid, 82
Deoxyribose, 82
Diacattleya, 174
Dialaelia, 174
Diazinon, 313, 314
Dichaea, 269
  glauca, 279
  muricata, **279**
  neglecta, 279
  panamensis, 280
Dieldrin, 312
Diforlatan, 313
Dimefox, 312
Dimorphorchis
  lowii, 137
  rohaniana, 137
Dinima polybulbon, 162–163
Diploids, 66, 77–82
Dipteranthus
  grandiflorus, 287
  pustulatus, 287
Disa, 269
  uniflora, 280
Diseases
  bacterial, 319–320
  fungal, 309–311, 315–319
  viral, 309–311, 321–325
Dithio, 312
Division of plants, 46, **47, 48**
DNA, 92–93
Dodson, Calaway, H., 68,
  249, 252, 257, 258
Dominy, J., 61
Doritaenopsis, embryo
  culture of, 103
Doritis
  embryo culture of, 103
  pulcherrima, var.
    buyssoniana, 127
Dossinia, 269
  mamorata, 280
Dove orchid, 266
Dracula, 269
  astuta, 290
  bella, 290
  chimaera, 290
  erythrochaete, 290
  houtteana, 290
  roezlii, 290
  senilis, 290

velutina, 290
wallisii, 290
Dressleria
  dilecta, 252
  eburnea, 252
  helleri, 252
  suavis, 252, **253**
Dryadella, 269
  edwallii, 291
  lilliputiana, 291
  obrieniana, 291
  simula, 291
  zebrina, 291
Dyakia hendersonianum, 136

EDTA versene compound, 37
Encyclia, 155–159
  embryo culture of, 103
  species
    alata, 156
    aromatica, 156
    atropurpurea, 156
    boothiana, 156
    boothii (see *Nidema
      boothii*)
    brassavolae, 156
    ceratistes, 156–157, **158**
    chaconensis, 157
    citrina, **156**
    cochleata, 155, 157, **166**
      var. *triandrum*, 157,
        166
    cordigera, 156, **157**
      var. *radnianum*, 156
      var. *randii*, 156
      var. *roseum*, 156
    fragrans, 157
    ghiesbregtiana, 157
    gravidum, 158
    hanburii, 157
    inonophlebium, 157
    mariae, 157
    mooreana, 157–**158**
    nemorale, 158
    oncidionides, 158
      var. *gravidum*, 158
    prismatocarpa, 158
    radiata, 158, **159**
    tampense, 158
    vespa, 158–159
    vitellina, 159
Endrin, 312
Epicattleya, 175
Epidendrum, 5, 12, 61, 159–
  162
  embryo culture of, 99
  hybrid, Obrienianum, 160
  species
    anceps, 159
    boothii (see *Nidema
      boothii*)
    ciliare, 159
    coriifolium, 159
    difforme, 159–160
    endresii, 160, **164**
    exasperatum, 160, **166**
    ibaguense, 160
    ilense, 102, 160
    latilobium, 160–161,
      164
    laucheanum, 161, **166**
    lockhartoides, 161
    mirabile, 161, **164**
    (Nanodes) medusae (see
      *Neolehmannia
      medusae*)
    nocturnum, 161
    obesum, 161
    paniculatum, 161

parkinsonianum, 161–162
var. *falcatum,* 162
pfavii, 162
porpax (see *Neolehmannia porpax*)
pseudo-schumannianum, 162
radicans (see *Epidendrum ibaguense*)
schlechterianum, 163
sophronitis (see *Kalopternix sophronitis*)
stamfordianum, 162
umbellatum, 159–160
temperature for, 18
Epidiacrium, 175
Epigeneium lyonii, 219
Epilaelia, 175
Epiphronitis, 175
Veitchii, **160**
Epiphytes, definition of, 5
Eriopsis
biloba, 264
sceptrum, 264
Erythodes, 269
nobilis, 280
querceticola, 280
Ethion, 312
Ethylene
damage to plants, 308
sepal wilt caused by, 308
Euanthe sanderiana, 131
Eulophidium saundersianum, 193
Eulophiella
elizabethae, 192–193
roempleriana, 193
Euphalaenopsis, 123–124
Euploid, 78

False spider mites, **326, 327**
Ferbam, 314
Fertilization process, 66
Fertilizer
essential minerals and, 33
kinds and application, 33–36
plant activity and, 33–34
Flask seedlings, 5
Flowering, 55–60 (see also Flowers)
care of plants in flower, 38–40
control of flowering time, 55–60
encouragement of, 39
flower bud initiation and development, 55–57
Flowers
initiation of, 10, 55
premature aging of, 307
Flower speck, 318
Foliar feeding, 53
Freaks, **309**
Fungal diseases, 315–319
Fungus mites, 326
Fusarium moiliforme, 317
Fusarium osysporum, 317
Fusarium wilt, 317

Galeandra
batemanii, 192
baueri, 192
devoniana, 192
Gametes, 66

Garden orchids, 358–359
screen house, 358, **359,** 359
Gastrochilus, 137–138
bellinus, 138
bigibbus, 138
dasypogon, 138
Genes, 65–69
dominant, **67**
incomplete dominance, 68
recessive, **67, 68, 70**
Genetics, 65–83 (see also under Hybrids)
mechanics of, 65–72
Germain's Mildew and Rust Control, 313
Gillespie, Robert, 68
Gleosporium affine, **318**
Gomesa, 247
Gongora
armeniaca, var. *bicornuta,* 259
cornuta, 259
grossa, 259, **261**
horichiana, 259
quinquenervis, 259, **262**
Goodyera, 269
colorata, 281
hispida, 281
Grammangis ellisii, 191
Grammatophyllum
elegans, 191
fenzlianum (see *Grammatophyllum scriptum*)
measuresianum (see *Grammatophyllum scriptum*)
scriptum, 191
speciosum, 191
Gravel culture, 34–35
Greenhouse, 345–352
construction of, 346–348
cooling systems, 350
heating systems, 348, **349,** 350
humidifiers, 351
locating, 346, **347**
materials and equipment, 346–352
perforated polyethylene tubing, 351, **352**
prefabricated, 347
shading, 350
solar heating, 351–352
temperature alarm, 351
types, 345, **348**
ventilation, 350–351
Greenhouse conditions, 21
Grifolyn, 356–**357**
Guanine, 82
Guthion, 312

Habenaria obtusata, pollination by mosquitoes, 16, **17**
Haemaria (see *Ludisia*)
Haploid, 66
Hapuu, 20, 44
Haraëlla odorata, 138
Harris, Dr., 61
Heart rot, 316
Helcia sanguinolenta, **243**
Heptachlor, 312
Heterozygous plants, 69
Hexaploid, 77–82
Hexisea
bidentata, 174
imbriacata, 174

Holcoglossum kimballiana, 131
Holy Ghost orchid, 266
Homozygous plants, 69
Houlletia
brocklehurstiana, 264
ordoratissima, 265
tigrina, **265**
Hozon attachment, 35
Humidity
diseases and, 25
effects of temperature on, 23
plant health and, 23–25, 306
plant response to, 25
relative, 23
Huntleya, 269
burtii, 301
fasciata, 302
lucida, 302
meleagris, 301
Hurst, C. C., 206
Hurst, Charles C., 74
Hybrids
blue, 74
crosses between hybrids, 62
first bigeneric hybrid, 61
first hybrid, 61
flower characteristics in, 68
history of, 61–62
inheritance, 61–83
mechanics of inheritance
back cross, 69, **70,** 71
generation F$_1$, **70, 71**
generation F$_2$, 69, **70**
primary crosses, 62
purple and yellow inheritance, **67, 68, 69, 70–72**
reduction division, **66**
self-pollination, 69
size inheritance, 67, **68, 69, 71, 72**
white inheritance, 74–77
naming hybrids, 62–64
red, 73–74
registration of, 62
remake of cross, 63–64
Hyponex, 35

Importing orchids, 336
Injury to plants
chemical, 309
mechanical, 309
Instant Vigoro, 35
Ionopsis
paniculata, 244
satyrioides, 243
utricularioides, **243,** 244
Ireland, Mary B., 188, 190
Iron chelate, 37
Iron in plant nutrition, 36
Isochilus
aurantiacus, 174
linearis, 174
major, 174

Jungle orchids, 331–340, **341, 342, 343**
care of, 338–340
conservation, need for, 336–338
importing, 336
miniature gardens, 339–340, **341, 342, 343**
occurrence in nature, 335–336

Kalopternix sophronitis, 163, **164**
Kamemoto, H., 75, 80
Kefersteinia, 269
graminea, 302
sanguimolenta, 302
tolimensis, 302
Kegeliella houtteana, 265
Kelthane, 313
Kingidium decumbens, 127

Lacaena bicolor, 265
Laelia, 61, 165, 167–169
embryo culture of, 103
hybridization with *Cattleya,* 65, 69
influence in yellow inheritance, 70–72
species
anceps, 167
var. *oaxaquenla,* 167
autumnalis, 167
cinnabarina, 67
crispa, 167, **168**
flava, 67, 167, **168**
furfuracea, 167
harpophylla, 67, 167
jongheana, 167
lundii, 167–**168**
milleri, 74, 168
perrinii, 168–169
pumila, 169
purpurata, 70, 169
rubescens, 169
sincorana, 169
speciosa, 169
tenebrosa, 67, **169**
xanthina, 67, 169
temperature for, 18
Laeliocattleya, 70–73
embryo culture of, 103
Exoniensis, 61, 167
Luminosa, 73
Rosa Kirsch, 79
Laeliopsis domingensis, 173
LD-50, definition of, 312
Lead, development of, 10
Leaf blight, 318
Leaf die-back, 318
Leaf rot, 320–321
Leaf spot, 318
Lemboglossum, 224, 225–226
apterum, 224, 225
bictoniense, 224, 225–226
candidulum, 224
cervantesii, 224, 226
cordatum, 224, 226
ehrenbergii, 224, 226
galeottianum, 224
hortensiae, 224
maculatum, 224, 226
madrense, 224
majale, 224
nebulosum, 225
rossii, 224, 226
stellatum, 224, 226
uroskinneri, 224, 226
Leochilus labiatus, 244, **245**
Lepanthes, 269
chiriquensis, 291
minutipetala, 291
obtusa, 291, **292**
papyrophylla, 291
selenipetala, 291, **292**
Lepanthopsis, 269
floripecten, 291
Leptolaelia, 175

Leptotes, 173–174
  bicolor, 174
  unicolor, 174
Liaopsis, 175
Light
  burning by, 25, **26**
  control of, 22
  foot candle measurement
    of, 26
  plant activity and, 21
  seasonal control of, 26–27
Lindane, 312
Lip, definition of, **12**
Literature, orchid, 359–367
Lockhartia
  acuta, 244
  amoena, 244, **246**
  micrantha, 244–245
  oestedii, 245
Long day, control of
    flowering by, 55,
    57, **58,** 59–60
Ludisia, 269
  discolor var. *dawsoniana,*
    281
Lycaste, 61, 269
  aromatica, **4,** 282
  ciliata, 282
  cochleata, 282
  cruenta, 282
  deppei, 282
  dowiana, **283**
  leucantha, 283, **284**
  locusta, 283
  macrophylla, 283, **335**
  skinneri, 283
  virginalis, 283
  xytriophora, 283
Lycastinea, 281–284
Lycomormium
  elatum, 265
  squalidum, 265

McBean, 189
McLeod, R. A., 80
Macodes, 269
  petola, 281
    var. *javanica,* 281
    var. *sanderiana,* 281
Macroclinium
  bicolor, 245
  manabinum, 245–246
Magnesium
  in fertilizer, 37
  in plant nutrition, 36
Major elements in plant
    nutrition, 36
Malathion, 314, 326
Manganese
  in fertilizer, 37
  in plant nutrition, 37
Masdevallia, 12, **335**
  coccinea, 291
  erinacea, 292
  horrida, 292
  infracta, 292
  minuta, 292
  reichenbachiana, 292
  reitchiana, 292–293
  rolfeana, 292, **293**
  tovarensis, 292
  triaristella, 292
Mavrik, 313
Maxillaria, 269
  embryo culture of, 103
  species
    confusa, 284
    juergensis, 284
    lepidota, 285

    neglecta, 285
    picta, 285
    sanderiana, 285
    tenuifolia, 285
    tigrina, **285**
    valenzuelana, 285
    variabilis, 285
    vitelliniflora, 285
Maxillariinae, 284
Mealybugs, 328
Mehlquist, G. A. L., 75, 189
Meiracyllium, 269
  trinasutum, 287
  wendlandii, 287
Menadenium (see
    Zygosepalum)
Mendoncella
  fimbriata, 302
  jorisiana, 302
Menninger, Emma, 80, 188,
    190
Mercury compounds, 312
Mesoglossum
    londesboroughianum,
    224, 228
Mesospinidium endresii, 244,
    245
Mesurol, 314
Metaldehyde, 314
Metasystox, 313
Metasystox R, 313
Mexicoa giesbreghtiana, 240
Millipedes, 328
Miltonia, **7,** 61
  description and culture,
    222–223
  embryo culture of, 103
  meristem culture of, 101
  species
    candida (see *Oncidium*
      candida)
    clowesii (see *Oncidium*
      clowesii)
    cuneata (see *Oncidium*
      cuneata)
    flavescens, 223
    kayasimae, 223
    regnellii, 223
    russelliana, 223
    spectabilis, 223
    velloziana, 223
  temperature for, 18
Miltonia scorch, **320**
Miltonidium, 248
Miltoniopsis, 221–222
  hybrids
    Bleuana, 222
    Charlesworthii, **223**
  species
    endresii, 221–222
    phalaenopsis, 222
    roezlii, **222**
    santanaei, 222
    schroederiana (see
      Oncidium laeve)
    vexillaria, 222
    warscewiczii, 221–222
    (see also *Oncidium*
      fuscatum)
Miltonpasia, 248
Mineral nutrition, 36
  major elements, 36
  minor elements, 36
Miniature orchids, 339–**340,**
    341, 342, 343
Minor elements in plant
    nutrition, 37
Mites, **326, 327**
Mitosis, **80**

Molybdenum in plant
    nutrition, 37
Monopodial, definition of, 9,
    11
Mormodes, 256–257
  aromatica, 257
  buccinator, **257**
  colossus, 257
  hookeri, 257
  igneum, 257
  skinneri, 257
  variabilis, 257
Mormolyca, 269
  peruviana, **286**
  ringens, 286
Mystacidium, 143
  capense, 144

Nakasone, H. Y., 80
Nanodes discolor, 163
Natriphene, 314
Nematodes, 328–329
Neobenthamia, 269
  gracilis, 296
Neofinetia falcata, 137
Neogyne, 269
  gardneriana, 277
Neolehmannia
  medusae, 163
  porpax, 163
Neomoorea, 269
  irrorata, 283, **284**
Nicotine, 312
Nidema
  boothii, 165
  ottonis, 165
Nitrogen
  in fertilizer, 37
  in plant nutrition, 36
Notylia
  barkeri, 245
  tridachne, 245
Nucleotides, 82
Nutrition, 306

Odontioda, 61, 248
Odontocidium, 248
Odontoglossum, 5, **7, 12,**
    61, 223–225
  hybrid, Epha, **225**
  meristem culture of, 101
  species
    cariniferum (see
      Oncidium
      cariniferum)
    cirrhosum, 224, **225**
    confusum (see *Oncidium*
      laeve)
    crispum, 224
    harryanum, 224
    luteo-purpureum, 224–
      225
    odoratum, 225
    retusum, 225
  temperature for, 18
Odontoglossum ringspot
    virus, 321–322, **323**
Odontonia, 61, 248
  meristem culture of, 101
Oeceoclades saundersianum,
    193
Oestedella
  exasperata, 160
  pseudo-schumanniana, 162
Ohio W. P. Solution, 35
Oncidioda, 248
Oncidium, 5, 12, 229–239
  description and culture,
    229

  embryo culture of, 103
  meristem culture of, 101
  species
    abortivum, 234
    ampliatum, **4,** 229
    ansiferum, **230**
    asparagoides (see
      Oncidium
      heteranthum)
    aureum, **230**
      var. *bicolor,* 230
    aurisasinorum, 230–231
    batemannianum, 231
    baueri, 231
    cabagrae, 231
    candida, 231
    cariniferum, 224, 231
    carthagenense, 231
    cavendishianum, 231
    cebolleta, 231
    cheirophorum, 231
    chrysodipterum, 232
    clowesii, 231
    confusum, 235
    crispum, 231–232
      var. *grandiflorum,* **233**
    crista-galli, 232
    cucullatum, 232
    desertorum (see
      Oncidium guianense)
    dichromum, 230
    excavatum, 232
    falcipetalum, 232
    flexuosum, 232
    forbesii, 231, 232–233
    fuscatum, 222, 233
    gardneri, 231, 233
    globuliferum, 233
    guianense, 233–234
    gyriferum, 232, 234
    hastatum, 234
    henekenii, 234
    heteranthum, **234**
    ionesianum, 234
    karwinskii, 224, 235
    kayasimae, 223
    kramerianum (see
      Psychopsis
      kramerianum)
    laeve, 224, 235
    lamelligerum, 232, 235
    lanceanum, 235, **236**
    leucochilum, 235, **237**
    longifolium, 231
    loxense, 232
    luridum, 235
    macranthum, 232, 235
    marshallianum, 231, 235
    microchilum, 232, 237
    monachicum, 237
    nubigenum, 237
    obryzatum, 237
    onustum, 237
    ornithorhynchum, 237
    papilio (see *Psychopsis*
      papilio)
    phaloenopsis, 237
    pumilum, 238
    pusillum (see
      Psygmorchis pusilla)
    reichenheimii, 224, 235
    russelliana, 223
    sarcodes, 238
    schriederianum, 235
    serratum, 232
    sphacelatum, 238
    splendidum, 238
    stenoglossum, 224, 235
    stipitatum, 238

stramineum, **238**
superbiens, 232, 238–239
teres, 239
tigrinum, 239
triquetrum, 239, **343**
varicosum, 231–232, **236**, 239
variegatum, 239
velloziana, 223
temperature for, 18
Opsisanthe, hybrid, Juliet, **131**
Orchid beds, 358
Orchids
 buying of plants, 5, 8
 history of, 1–3
 hybrids of, 2–5
 literature, 359–367
 number of species, 1
Orchid wilt, 316
Ornithocephalinae, 287
Ornithocephalus, 269, **339**
 bicornis, 287
 cochleariformis, 287
 gladiatus, 287
 inflexus, 287
 iridifolius, 287
Ornithosphora, 247
Ortho Household Insect
 Killer, 314
Osmoglossum
 anceps, 224, 228
 convallarioides, 224, 228
 dubium, 228
 egertoni, 224, 228
 pulchellum, 224, 228
Osmunda fiber, 20
 fertilizer for, 33
Otoglossum
 arminii, 224, 228
 brevifolium, 224, 228
 chiriquinse, 224, 228
 coronarium, 224, 228
Ovary, **16**
Overwatering, effects of, 31
Oxalis, 40

Pabstia, 269
 jugosus, 303
Palumbina, 247
Pano-drench, 312
Panogen, 312
Paphinia
 cristata, 265, **266**
 grandiflora, 265
 rugosa, 265
Paphiopedilum, 5, 12, 61
 brown rot of, 320
 description and culture, 195–198
 embryo culture of, 100, 103
 growing from seed, 204–205
 hybrids
  Grace Palm, **4**
  Lathamianum, 206
  Leeanum, 206
  Rosy Dawn, 201
 inheritance, 205–206
 ovary of, **16**
 reproductive parts, **196**
 species
  appletonianum, 200
  argus, 200, **201**
  armeniacum, 198–199
  barbatum, 200
  barbigerum, 201

bellautlum, 199, 205
callosum, 201, 205
chamberlainianum, 201
charlesworthii, 201, 205
concolor, 199
curtisii, **201**
dayanum, 201–202, 205
delenatii, 199, 205
druryi, 202, 205
emersonii, 199
exul, 202, 205
fairrieanum, 202, 205
glaucophyllum, 201, 202
godefroyae, 199
haynaldianum, 202
hirsutissimum, **202**, 205
hookerae, 202
insigne, 202, 205
 var.'Harefield Hall', 77, 202–203
 var.'Sanderae', 206
laevigatum, 199–200
 var. *Roebelenii*, 200
lawrenceanum, **203**, 205
leucochilum, 199
liemianum, 201, 203
lowii, 203
malipoense, 199
micranthum, 199
niveum, 199, **200**, 205
parishii, 203
philippinense, 199
praestans, 200, 205
primulinum, 201, 203
rothschildianum, 200, 205
sanderianum, 200
spicerianum, 203, 205
stonei, 200, 205
sukhakulii, 203–204
urbanianum, 204
venustum, 204, 205
victoria-mariae, 201, 204
victoria-regia, 204
villosum, 204, 205
 var. *boxallii*, 204, 205
virens, 204
woltrianum, 204
 subgenus
  Anotopedilum, 198, 199–200
  Brachypetalum, 198–199
  Paphiopedilum, 198, 200–204
 temperature for, 17, 18
Paphiopedilum bacterial rot, **198**
Papilionanthe
 hybrid, Miss Joaquim, 133
 species
  hookeriana, 133
  teres, 133, **134**
Paraphalaenopsis
 denevei, 126
 esmeralda, 127
 laycockii, 126
 serpentilingua, 126
Parasitic diseases, 309–311
 (see also kind in question)
Parathion, 312
Pentac, 314
Pentaploids, 66, 77–82
Peristeria
 elata, **266**
 guttata, 266
 pendula, 266

Pescatoria, 269
 cerina, **303**
 dayana, 303
 klaborchorum, 303
Pests, 325–329
Petal, definition of, **12**
pH, 32
 adjustment of, 32–33
Phaiocalanthe, 273
Phaius, 61, 269
 embryo culture of, 103
 meristem culture of, 101
 species
  flavus, 273
  grandifolius, 273
  maculatus, 273
  tancarvilliae, 273
  tankervilliae, 272, 273
Phalaenopsis, 4, 5, 12, **120**, **122**
 description and culture, 119–123
 embryo culture of, 100
 hybrids
  Chieftain, 123
  Doris, 123
  Dos Pueblos, 124
  Gilles Gratiot, 123
  Grace Palm, 124
  Juanita, 124
  Vallemar, 124
  Winged Victory, 123
 species
  amabilis, 123
   'Elizabethae', 77, 123
   var. *rimestadiana*, 123
   var. *sanderiana*, 123
  amboionensis, 124
  amethystina, 127
  aphrodite, 124
  cochlearis, 124
  cornu-cervi, 124, **125**
  decumbens (see
   *Kingidium
   decumbens*)
  equestris, 124
  fimbriata, 124
  gigantea, 124
  hieroglyphica, 125
  intermedia, 124
  lindenii, 124
  lowii, 124
  lueddemanniana, 124
  maculata, 124
  mannii, 124–125
  mariae, 125
  micholitzii, **125**
  pulcherrima, 127
  pulchra, 125
  rosea, 124
  schilleriana, 124
  stuartiana, 124
  sumatrana, 125
  violacea, 125
 temperature for, 18
Phalaenopsis mite, **326**
Pholidota, 269
 chinensis, 278
 imbricata, **4**, **278**
Phorate, 313
Phosphate, 82
Phosphorus
 in fertilizer, 37
 in plant nutrition, 36
Phragmipedium
 caricinum, 207
 caudatum, 207
  var. *wallisii*, **207**
 ecuadorense, 207

pearcei, 207
sargentianum, 207
schlimii, 207, **208**
Physan-20, 40, 314, 355
Physosiphon, 269
 tubatus, 293
Phythium ultimum, 315
Phytophthora omnivora, 316
Phytophthora palmivora, 316
Plantfume, 312
Platystele, 269
 misera, 293
 stenostachya, 293
Pleione, 269
 humilis, 279
 praecox, 279
Pleurothallidinae, 289–293
Pleurothallis, 269
 alpina, 294
 calyptrostele, **294**
 cardiochila, 294
 gelida, **294**
 grobyi, **342**
 immersa, 294, **295**
 listerophora, 294, **295**
 raymondi, 294
 sicaria, 294
 testaefolia, 295
Pod parent, 70
Poisons, 311–314
 caution with, 311–312
 symptoms of poisoning, 312
 toxicity tables, 312–314
Pollen shooting mechanism, 249–**250**
Pollinarium, 14
 ejection of, in *Catasetum*, 15
Pollination, 14
 agents of, **13**–16, **251**, **255**, 258–259, **260**, **263**
 first done by hand, 61
Pollinia, 13, 14, **15**
 in *Vanda* 'Miss Joaquim', 14
Polycycnis
 barbata, 266–267
 lepida, **267**
 muscifera, 267
 vittata, 267
Polyploids, 66, 77–82
Polyradicion, species, *lindenii*, 142
Polystachya, 269
 affinis, 296
 pubescens, 296
 virginea, 297
Polystachyeae, 296–297
Potassium
 in fertilizer, 37
 in plant nutrition, 36
Potinara, 73
Potting, 43–53 (see also plant in question)
 care after, 53
 materials for, 43–44
 method for barks and mixes, 49, **51**
 method for osmunda fiber, 50, **52**
 tools and potting area, 46
 when to repot, 45–46
Premature aging of flowers, 307
Pride of Table Mountain orchid, 280
Problem plants, 46

Problems, diseases, and pests, 305–329
    environmental conditions, 305–308
Promenaea, 269, 303
    crawshayna, paulensis, 303
    ovatilabia, 303
    stapelioides, 303
    xanthina, 303
Pseudobulb, 9
Pseudocopulation in Trichoceros, 15
Psychopsis
    kramerianum, 239–240
    papilio, **4,** 240
Psygmorchis, 239
    pusilla, **239**
Pythium black rot, 315, **316**

Quekettia, 247
8 quinolinal benzoate, 314
8 quinolinal sulfate, 314

Red spiders, **41**
Renanthera
    embryo culture of, 103
    species
        coccinea, 135
        imschootiana, 135
        lowii (see Dimorphorchis lowii)
        matutina, 135
        monachica, 135
        storiei, 135
Resmethrin, 314
Restrepia, 269
    elegans, 295
    filamentosa, **295**
    muscifera, 296
    xanthophthalma, 296
Rhizanthella gardneri, 16, **17**
Rhizome, 9, **10**
Rhyncholaelia, 73, 169–170
    embryo culture of, 103
    species
        digbyana, 73, 170
        glauca, 73, 170
Rhynchostylis
    coelestis, 136
    gigantea, 136
    retusa, 136–137
Ribonucleic acid, 82
Ribose, 82
RNA, 92–93
Rodriguezia
    embryo culture of, 103
    species
        bracteata, 243
        secunda, 243
        venusta, 243
Root rot, 317
Rossioglossum, 226–227
    grande, 224, 226–227
    insleayi, 224, 227
    schlieperianum, 224, 227
    splendens, 224, 227
    williamsianum, 224, 227
Rostellum, **13,** 14
Rotor, Gavino, 80
Royal Horticultural Society, 62
Rusts, 319

Sanderara, 248
Sander, David F., 62
Sander, Fred. K., 62
Saprophytic fungi, 319
Sarcanthinae, intergeneric hybrids in, 138

Sarcochilus
    ceciliae, 137
    falcatus, 137
    fitzgeraldii, 137
    hartmannii, 137
Scale insects, 49, 327
Scaphyglottis
    cuneata, 174
    livida, 174
    prolifera, 174
Schlimia trifida, 267
Schombocattleya, 80
Schomburgkia, 171–172
    lueddemannii, 172
    lyonsii, 172
    superbiens, 172
    thomasoniana, 172
    tibicinis, 172
    undulata, 172
Sclerotinia fuckliana, 318
Sclerotium rolfsii, **316**
Scrub forests, 331, **332**
Scuticaria, 269
    steelii, 286
Seed banks, 337
Selenipedium chica, 208
Sepals, definition of, **12**
Sepal wilt, 22, 39, 307–308
Severe flower break virus, **323**
Shield, 314
Shipping of purchased plants, 20
Short day, 55–57, **59**
    control of flowering by, 55–57, **59**
Short flower life, 307–308
Sievekingia
    peruviana, 268
    suavis, **267**
Sigmatostalix, 246, **247**
    guatemalensis, **247**
    racemifera, **247**
Simazine, 314
Slugs, 40, **41,** 328
Smoke fumigants, 312
Snails, 40, 41, 328
Snow mold, 319
Sobralia, 269
    fragrans, 297
    leucoxantha, 297
    macrantha, 297
    xantholeuca, 297
Sobraliinae, 297
Soft rot of paphiopedilum, 320
Sooty mold, 319
Sophrocattleya, embryo culture of, 103
Sophronitella violacea, 171
Sophronitis
    embryo culture of, 103
    hybridization with Cattleya, 65
    species
        brevipedunculata, 170
        cernua, 170
        coccinea, 73, 170, **172**
        wittigiana, 170–171
Sowbugs, 328
Spathoglottis, 269, 273
Sphagnum moss, 44
Spider mites, 326
Sporothrix schenkii, 44
Sporotrichosis, 44
Stakes, 40
Stanhopea, 61
    description and culture, 261–262

species
    costaricensis, 262
    ecornuta, 262
    florida, **262**
    martiana, 262
    oculata, 262–263
    saccata, 263
    wardii, **263**
Staurogloslttis, 124–126
Stelis, 269
    argentata, 296
    bidentata, 296
    leucopogon, **296**
Stenia, 269
    guttata, 304
    pallida, 304
Sterilizing of tools, 39
Stewart, 190
Stigma, **13,** 14, **15**
Stipe, **13**
Stomata, 23, **24**
    detection of polyploidy by size of, 81
Storey, W. B., 75
Stud plant, 69
Subdue, 313
Sulfatepp, 312
Sulfur in plant nutrition, 36
Symphodontoglossum, 248
Symphyglossonia, 248
Symphyglossum sanguineum, 242
Sympodial, definition of, 9–**10**
Syringing, 25
Systox, 312

Telipogon, 269
    ampliflorus, 298
    gnomus, 298
    hercules, 298
    klotzschianus, 298
    nervosus, 298
    radiatus, 298
    vargasii, 298
Temik, 313
Temperature, 21–23, 305–306
    control of, 21–23
    cool, intermediate and warm groups, 17–18
    plant activity and, 21
Tenuipalpus facificus, **326**
TEPP, 313
Terrazole, 313
Tersan, 314
Tetranychus telarius, 326
Tetraploids, 64, 66, 77–82
    colchicine and, 80, **81,** 82
Thimet, 313
Thiram, 314
Thrips, 327
Thymine, 82
Ticoglossum
    krameri, 224
    oerstedii, 224
Trichocentrum
    albo-coccineum, 244
    albo-purpureum, 244
    panduratum, 244
    pulchrum, 244
Trichoceros, 269
    insect imitation, 15
    pseudocopulation in, 15
    species
        muralis, 298, **299**
        parviflorus, 298
Trichoglottis, 135–136
    brachiata, 136

    philippinensis, 136
Trichopilia
    crispa, 242
    fragans, **242**
    marginata, 242
    suavis, **13,** 242
    tortillis, 242
Tridactyle tridactylites, **144**
Trigonidium, 269
    egertonianum, 286
    lankesteri, 286
Triploids, 66, 77–82
Trisodium phosphate, 39
Truban, 313, 314
TSP, 39

Underground orchids, 16, **17**
Unifoliate cattleyas, 147–151
Uracil, 82

Van Cott, Ann, 81–82
Vanda, 5, 7, 61
    amphidiploids, 133
    chromosome number variation in reproductive cells of, 132
    description and culture, 11, 12, 127–129
    embryo culture of, 100
    hybridization in, 131–133
    hybrids
        Emma van Deventer, 132
        Miss Joaquim, **15**
        Rothschildiana, 129
        Waipuna 'Hodama', 128
    semiterete hybrids, 80
    species
        amesiana, 129
        coerulea, 127, 129, 132
        concolor, 130
        cristata, 130
        dearei, 130
        hookeriana (see Papilionanthe hookeriana)
        kimballiana (see Holcoglossum kimballiana)
        lamellata, 130
        merrillii, 130
        roxburghii, 130
        rupestris, 131
        sanderiana, 130
        spathulata, 130
        sumatrana, 130
        teres (see Papilionanthe teres)
        tessellata, 130
        tricolor, 130
    temperature for, 18
Vandanthe
    hybrids
        Ellen Noa, 130
        Mevr. L. Velthuis, 132, **133**
        Nora Potter, 132

Vandopsis
    species
        batemannii, 130
        gigantea, 131
        lissochiloides, 131
Vanilla, 269, 298–300
    planifolia, 299
    pompona, 299
Vanillinae, 298–300
Vapona, 313

Varietal name, 63
Velamen, 11
Versene compound, 37
Virus, sterilizing of tools, 39
Virus diseases, 321–325
  symptoms in flowers, 322
    blossom brown necrotic
      streak, **322**
    color break, 322
  tests for, 324
Viscid disc, **13**, 14, 15
Vuylsterkeara, 248

Warmingia, 247
Warscewiczella discolor, 301
Water, acidity and alkalinity,
  32–33
Water breaker, **30**
Watering, 29–32, 306
  frequency of, 30–31
Weeds, 40
Wells, E. W., 189
Wilsonara, 248
Wimber, D. E., 81–82, 189
Window growing, 352–354

Xylobium, 269
  elongatum, 270
  foveatum, 270
  palmifolium, 270
  powellii, 270

Zectran, 313
Zinc in plant nutrition, 37
Zygopetalinae, 300–304
Zygopetalum, 61, 269
  meristem culture of, 101
  species

  aromaticum, 301
  crinitum, 304
  grandiflorum, 304
  intermedium, **304**
  mackayi, 304
  maxillare, 304
Zygosepalum, 269
  labiosum, 304
Zygostates, 269
  alleniana, 287
  lunata, 287